W9-BWV-180

ALSO BY JOHN FEINSTEIN

A Season on the Brink
A Season Inside
Forever's Team

HARD
COURTS

HARD COURTS

JOHN FEINSTEIN

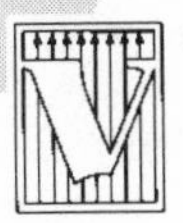

VILLARD BOOKS ○ NEW YORK ○ 1991

 Published in the United States by Villard Books, a division of Random House, Inc., New York, and simultaneously in Canada by Random House of Canada Limited, Toronto.

Villard Books is a registered trademark of Random House, Inc.

Library of Congress Cataloging-in-Publication Data

Feinstein, John.
Hard courts / by John Feinstein.
p. cm.
ISBN 0-394-58333-7
1. Tennis—History. 2. Tennis—Tournaments—History. I. Title.
GV992.F45 1991
796.342—dc20 91-50060

Design by Robert Bull Design

9 8 7 6 5 4 3 2

First Edition

This is for Bud Collins . . .

who taught me how to love tennis as a kid
and how to cover it as an adult. . . .

And it is for Ted Tinling . . .

who always had the answers and always made it fun.

ACKNOWLEDGMENTS

A few months ago I read a magazine story on book acknowledgments. It was frighteningly accurate, full of anecdotes about authors who go to great lengths to thank virtually everyone they have ever met when they reach the end of a book. No one is more guilty of this than I am, but I can't help it. The fact is, I would never get any book written without considerable outside help.

Never has this been truer than during the past fifteen months. The two tennis tours consist of 142 major tournaments (78 men's, 64 women's) played across the world, with more than $63 million in prize money ($40 million for men, $23 million for women) available. Those don't even include the exhibitions, the one-nighters, the Satellite and Challenger (minor league) tournaments and the gone-berserk guarantees. Trying to make sense of just some of this morass and the people who live it was, at times, an overwhelming task. As a result, this has been, without question, the most difficult book I have ever done in terms of logistics, and the list of people I must thank is extremely long.

No endeavor like this one can get off the ground without sources. In delving into the tennis world I was often confronted by people who had no idea what the hell I was doing or what I meant when I said I was writing a book. One player kept saying to me, "An hour isn't enough time [for an interview]? What in the world could take more than an hour?"

Most of the people I interviewed gave me more than an hour, some of them considerably more than that. The list of those who were giving of their time is a lengthy one. It includes: Ivan Lendl, Stefan Edberg, Andres Gomez, Aaron Krickstein, Jay Berger, Goran Ivanisevic, Andrei Chesnokov, Alberto Mancini, Henri Leconte, Yannick Noah, Karel Novacek, Brad Pearce, Richey Reneberg, Jim Grabb, Rick Leach, Jim Pugh, Luke Jensen, Aki Rahunen, Pat Cash, Michael Chang, Mark Kratzmann, Bryan Shelton, Leif Shiras, Grant Connell, Paul Chamberlin, Derrick Rostagno, Paul Annacone, Tim Mayotte, Malivai Washington, Christo van Rensburg, Wayne Ferreira, Paul Haarhuis, Amos Mansdorf, Vijay

Amritraj, and Steffi Graf, Martina Navratilova, Arantxa Sanchez, Mary Joe Fernandez, Pam Shriver, Natalia Zvereva, Jennifer Capriati, Laura Gildemeister, Carrie Cunningham, Patty Fendick, Andrea Leand, Carling Bassett, Katrina Adams, Louise Allen, Stephanie Rehe, Amy Frazier, Kathy Rinaldi, Gretchen Magers, and Angelica Gavaldon.

It will be more than apparent that a number of players were patient enough to sit down with me on several occasions throughout the year, sometimes for sessions that became marathons. That list includes Zina Garrison, Monica Seles, Elise Burgin, Shaun Stafford, Boris Becker, John McEnroe, Patrick McEnroe, Pete Sampras, Jim Courier, David Wheaton, Glenn Layendecker, and Jimmy and Gina Arias. I owe each of them an extra debt of gratitude—at the very least.

I would also like to thank for their time rookie TV commentators Chris Evert and Jimmy Connors, as well as a number of their television colleagues, including Arthur Ashe, Cliff Drysdale, Fred Stolle, Sara Harrison, David Stern, Brian Williams, and Peter Englehardt.

Clearly, a number of nonplayers were major players in this book and contributed time and information and guidance that was invaluable. People like the coaches: Bob Brett, Tom Gorman, Sergio Cruz, Joe Brandi, Bill Drake, Tom Gullikson, Craig Kardon, Tony Pickard, and Tony Roche. The agents: Ion Tiriac, Heather McLachlan, Stuart Wilson, John Evert, John Wheaton, Cino Marchese, Bob Kain, Gavin Forbes, Virginia Ruzici, Jerry Solomon, Ivan Blumberg, Dick Dell, Sara Fornaciari, Dewey Blanton, Peter Lawler, Micky den Tuinder, Tom Ross, Kelly Wolf, Jeff Austin, Slade Meade, and Phil dePicciotto. The officials: Gerry Armstrong, Richard Ings, Richard Kaufman, Dana (Cheeseburger) Loconto, Gayle Bradshaw, Chris O'Brien, Ken Farrar, and Steve Winyard. The tournament directors: Paul Flory, Butch Buchholz (and his able assistants Temple Pouncey and George Pharr), Barbara Perry, Marilyn and Ed Fernberger, Josh Ripple, Franco Bartoni (who got me medical help when I broke a bone in my foot in Rome), Gene Scott and Suzy Rothstein, Patrice Clerc, Steve DeVoe, and Bill Hoffman.

There were many others: at the ITF, Philippe Chatrier, Brian Tobin, Bill Babcock, Barbara Travers, and Camille Guthrie. At Wimbledon, John Curry, R.E.H. (Buzzer) Hadingham—who I hope someday gets to see a Mets game—Christopher Gorringe, and Richard Berens. At the USTA, Marshall Happer, Ed Fabricus, Bruce Levy, Art Newcombe, Art Campbell, and Andy Deitel. At the ATP Tour, Hamilton Jordan, Mark Miles, Greg Sharko, Jay Beck, Benji Robins, Bill Norris, Todd Snyder, J. Wayne Richmond, Bob Green, George Rubenstein, Lauren Goldenberg, Craig

(Mats) Gabriel, and Caroline Hutton. At the WTA, Gerry Smith, Giselle Marrou (the world's most patient human being), Ana Leaird, Lee Jackson, and Robin Reynolds. At Virginia Slims and Kraft General Foods, Jim Fuhse, Lesley Allen, Suzette Betteridge, Bettina Petterson, Annalee Thurston, Janine Bell, Leo McCullagh, Ina Broeman, Anne Person, and last but far from least, Nancy Bolger-King, whose patience and persistence were my saviors on the women's tour.

I had a number of key advisers on this book, people whose knowledge of the tour I kept going back to: Bud Collins's, Mary Carillo's and Ted Tinling's input will be obvious as you read the book; Peter Bodo's will be less so, but his was just about as important. All four of them kept pointing me forward when I was about to fall backward. I miss Ted and I miss Mary Lou Collins every single day. Both of them defined the words *courageous* and *caring*.

Two others without whom I doubt I could have gotten anything finished are my indefatigable agent, Esther (Sally UConn) Newberg, and my editor at Villard, Peter Gethers. Their coworkers—Kathy Pohl and Britt Hansen at ICM, and Janis Donnaud, Stephanie Long, Janet Bolen, and Corinne Lewkowicz at Villard—are almost as invaluable to me as they are to Esther and Peter. An extra thanks to Brad Snyder, who spent countless hours helping me wade through the tapes and notes that eventually became this book.

At *The National,* I have worked with terrific people, most notably my ever-patient boss, Frank Deford, who has given me more time and independence than any writer could possibly hope for. Others at the newspaper I have to thank are Pete Alfano, Rob Fleder, Steve Clow, Mike Bevans, Mark Godich, Lisa Dillman, Mike Lupica, and Ellen Thornley.

Traveling the world, you make a lot of friends, especially if you are a part of the tennis media. I have been bolstered, advised, and counseled by a group of colleagues I value greatly. They include Richard McKinnon, Mark Fogarty, Tim Prentice, Philippe Bouin, Judith Elian, John Roberts, John Barrett, John Parsons, David Irvine, Neil Harman, Malcolm Folley, Andrew Longmore, Chris Martin, Barry Wood, Gerald Williams, Mike Dickson, the remarkable Rex Bellamy, Bjorn Hellberg, George Homsie, and the irrepressible Italians Gianni Clerici, Rino Tomassi, and Ubaldo Scanagatta.

Then there are the Americans: Tommy Bonk, Sally (Girl) Jenkins, Robin Finn, Richard Finn (who *is* Finn), Steve Flink, Pat Calabria, Cindy Shmerler, Donna Doherty, Alex McNab, Cindy Hahn, David Higdon, Marty Lader, Bob Greene, Barry Lorge, Curry Kirkpatrick, Alex

Wolff, Sandy Harwitt, Russ Adams, and Carol Newsom. An extra thanks to the boys of the European AP: Larry Siddons, Steve Wilson, and Sal Zanca, each of whom at various times fed me, clothed me (who knew I would need cuff links and studs for the Wimbledon champions dinner?), and bolstered me throughout my time in Europe.

All of my travels were made far more comfortable than I ever could have imagined, because of the help I had from Dan Fisher and his staff at Travel Management, most notably the saintlike Michelle Virgolino, who will, no doubt, write her own book about how this book could not have been written without her. And then, of course, there were my friends, who keep me going through all of my projects: Keith and Barbie Drum, Bill Brill, Doug Doughty, Luiz and Claire Simmons, Steve and Lexie Barr, Terry Hanson, John Hewig, Bob Basche, Dave Kindred, Len Shapiro, Tony Kornheiser, Juan and Delise Williams (and Antonio Williams, my godson), David Maraniss, Ken Denlinger, Tom Kenworthy, the political activist and tennis buff Norbert Doyle, Bob and Anne DeStefano, Tom and Linda Mickle, Sandy "Flailin'" Genelius, Carol Harvey, Chip Campbell, Jennifer "Wailin'" Proud-Mearns, Charlie Brotman, Mark Schramm, Tom Goldman and Bob "the Colonel" Edwards, Joe Valerio, Neil Amdur, Bill Brink, Dick "Hoops" Weiss, Ray Ratto, Lesley Visser, Jill Mixon, Jeff Neuman, Rick Brewer, Stan Schuck, and, of course, Jacquese Moss and little Jacquese.

Last, though certainly not least, is my family. I have said it before, and I will say it again: my mom and dad, my brother, Bobby, my sister, Margaret, and all my in-laws: Arlene, Jim, Kathleen, Annie, Gregg, Jimmy, Brendan, and David are all remarkable people if only for their patience in putting up with me. Mary Gibbons Feinstein has specifically ordered me not to write anything sentimental about her. I won't. I follow orders well, and she knows how I feel, anyway.

Okay, there it is: the textbook example of how to go overboard in your acknowledgments. I plead guilty—with an explanation: All of the above doesn't begin to express how strongly I feel about the people mentioned.

—John Feinstein
Bethesda, Md.
January 15, 1991

o

CONTENTS

Acknowledgments ix
Introduction xv

PART ONE: AUSTRALIA

1. "You *Cannot* Be Serious" 3
2. Happy New Year 15
3. Down Under 30
4. The Flinders Park Jinx 46
5. Ted 82

PART TWO: INDOORS AND OUT

6. Guarantees, Defaults, and Tanks 95
7. The Virginia Slims of Capriati 120
8. The Agents 130
9. Lipton 144
10. Carillo 156

PART THREE: THE CLAY

11. The Queen, The Lege, and The Kid 167
12. Paradise 174
13. Rome Is Rome 192
14. Roland Garros 217
15. Tiriac 259

CONTENTS

o

PART FOUR: THE GRASS

16. Queen's 267
17. The Umpires 285
18. Eastbourne 297
19. Wimbledon 306

PART FIVE: THE YANKS COME HOME

20. Newport 353
21. Summer Heat 361
22. Craziness Rules 380
23. Davis Cup 419

Epilogue 433

o

INTRODUCTION

On the night of December 26, 1989, I was standing in line at the Qantas Airlines counter at Los Angeles International Airport to check in for a flight to Hawaii. Qantas flight 4 stopped in Honolulu en route to Sydney, Australia. My wife and I were getting off the plane in Honolulu for four days before boarding another version of flight 4 to go on to Australia. There, on New Year's Day, I would begin researching this book.

As I stood in line I heard a familiar voice next to me, talking to the agent. I looked up and saw Samantha Frankel Lendl. Standing behind her was Christo van Rensburg, the South African who was ranked twenty-seventh in the world.

"How are you feeling?" I said to Samantha, knowing she was about four months pregnant.

"Oh, fine," she said. "So far, so good."

"Where's Ivan?" I asked.

"In the lounge."

Of course. Ivan Lendl is nothing if not completely organized. He had known for almost a year that he would leave for Australia on this day, on this flight. He had planned to travel with Van Rensburg so he would have a practice partner when he arrived in Australia. And he knew that Samantha didn't mind checking them in for the flight if it meant he could avoid autograph hounds.

When we boarded the flight a little later, Ivan and Samantha were already in their seats. "I take one sleeping pill after we take off from here, then another after we leave Hawaii," Lendl said. "When we land, Tony Roche has a helicopter waiting for us. We fly to his ranch, land in time for lunch. Then we practice for an hour, play golf, and sleep like hell that night."

Even an earthquake couldn't mess up Lendl's schedule. In fact, an earthquake would occur just as his helicopter was landing at Roche's, and it *didn't* affect his schedule. "I've been in earthquakes before," he said later. "Once, I had to jump out of a window into the snow during an earthquake in Romania," he said. "Now *that* was scary."

Lendl sat back with a smile on his face. He had come a long way since he was a twelve-year-old in Ostrava, dreaming of becoming a rich tennis player with a home somewhere in the West. He had come a long way since the time he couldn't look the Russian players who came on tour in the eye because his memories of 1968 were so vivid that he hated all Russians. He had come a long way since the time he and John McEnroe almost started swinging at each other during an exhibition.

"By the way," he said, "you know McEnroe is on this flight, too?"

This surprised me. The doors were getting ready to shut and there was no sign of McEnroe. "Are you sure?" I said. "I don't see him."

Lendl laughed. "He may have gone home. I heard him on the phone. He didn't know the flight stopped in Hawaii. He was screaming at somebody about it."

This fit perfectly: Lendl knew when he was going to take his sleeping pills; McEnroe didn't know where the plane stopped. A flight attendant came up. "Mr. Lendl, there are going to be two young children coming on board. Would you like to go upstairs? It's empty up there."

"Absolutely," Lendl said, and he, Samantha, and Van Rensburg went up the winding staircase.

A couple of minutes later there was a commotion in the doorway. "There won't be anyone smoking, will there?" John McEnroe was saying. "I really don't want my kids inhaling smoke all over the place." He looked up and saw me. "You don't smoke, do you, John?"

I didn't smoke. Once he had determined the plane was safe, McEnroe led his wife, Tatum O'Neal, his sons, Kevin, three and a half, and Sean, two, and their baby-sitter onto the plane. McEnroe stood in the aisle, looking as if he had lost something.

"I thought Lendl was on this flight," he said.

They always want to know where the other guy is. "He's upstairs," I said. Satisfied, McEnroe sat down. Once the plane had taken off and the kids were settled, he stopped by to talk.

"Jeez, I didn't think the flight stopped twice before we got to Perth," he said. "I'm going down there to play that Hopman Cup thing. I don't know why I got talked into that. At least I've got the family with me. Last year I went down without them, and I was really miserable. This way is harder, but it's much better."

He talked, almost without pause, for several minutes. By now Lendl had, no doubt, taken his sleeping pill, but McEnroe was wide awake. He talked for a few more minutes, as always, without commas. "Well," he said finally, "I have to go read Kevin and Sean a bedtime story."

I sat back and tried to sleep, but couldn't get Lendl and McEnroe out of my head. "This is going to be a wild ride," I kept thinking.

I didn't mean Qantas flight 4.

When I first decided to write a book on tennis, many of my friends in journalism questioned my sanity. After all, they correctly pointed out, tennis is the least accessible major sport in the world. It is the only sport covered regularly by the American media in which there is virtually no locker-room access. In fact, the media usually can't even get into the players' lounge.

Developing the kind of casual relationships with the athletes that lead to the best stories is extremely difficult without that sort of day-in, day-out contact. Tennis players, even more so than athletes in other sports, see the media as a nuisance that is best flicked away by holding a postmatch press conference and being done with it. The only reason players come to those is because they can be fined if they don't.

"It will be a challenge," I told my friends.

It was. When I think back on my year traveling the two tours, I think of something Gerry Smith, the executive director of the Women's Tennis Association, told me: "Working in this sport is like being in the army," he said. "You spend a lot of time standing around waiting."

Certainly true. But twelve months after flight 4 landed, I can honestly say I enjoyed the ride. I made many new friends—and a few new enemies—and enjoyed getting to know a lot of the people who live this sport. I tried to get to know a real cross section of the people: from the rock-star millionaires to the qualifiers; from the deal-making agents to the overworked tour staffers; from the umpires who help bring sanity to the sport to the coaches who try to bring some perspective to it. No doubt there are people and subjects not in this book who should be. I did my best, though, to capture the flavor of a very big, very wide, very chaotic world.

I did find a couple of surprises. One was that the women's tour is a far more insular world than the men's. This may have had something to do with my being a man, but I don't think so. I think it has more to do with the men, in general, being older. They are likely to be in their twenties, rather than, like many of the women, in their teens, and they are less shy about sharing what they have learned with an outsider.

o

Mike Estep, who played on the men's tour for ten years and has now coached on the women's tour for seven, described the difference between the two this way: "When I first started coaching Martina [Navratilova], Betty Stove, who was coaching Hana [Mandlikova], came to me one day and said, 'Mike, you have to understand one thing about the women's tour. Everyone stays in their own houses.'

"What she meant was that the camaraderie I had taken for granted on the men's tour doesn't exist on the women's side. When I played, we all tried like hell to beat one another but then went to dinner or out for a beer at night. That doesn't happen on the women's tour. They're all friendly to one another in the locker room, but once they leave the locker room, they almost always stick to themselves."

The men's tour has gone in that direction in recent years with the coming of the Entourage Era, but it still remains a more likely place to find people hanging out and swapping stories than the women's tour is. Again, I think age is a factor. The women, as a whole, were very nice, but shy. The men weren't always nice, but they were, more often than not, very open.

My other surprise came as I began to understand the life these players lead. I never questioned the work or the time that went into tennis. I always knew that the players who make millions today made sacrifices in the past to make all that money. And I also knew that for every player whose sacrifices paid off, there were ten thousand who made the sacrifices without a payback.

But until I did this book and interviewed approximately one hundred players at length and several dozen others during shorter sessions, I never realized the lack of normalcy in their lives. Most tennis players never went to the prom or to graduation. A lot of them never had a date in high school. Almost none of the Americans ever went to a football homecoming. Few of the Europeans have friends from school.

"All I ever did in high school was play tennis," Jim Pugh, the American Davis Cup doubles player said. "Every day at lunch, I played. After school, I played. On weekends, I went to tournaments. I never had a date in high school. I didn't have very many friends."

Pugh told me this after we had sat next to each other at a baseball game in Cincinnati. Knowing he had grown up in Los Angeles, I casually asked him if he had been a Dodgers fan or an Angels fan growing up. Pugh shrugged. "To tell you the truth, neither," he said. "This is the first time I've ever been to a baseball game."

A twenty-six-year-old from Los Angeles who had never been to a baseball game? There are exceptions, of course. Pugh's doubles partner, Rick Leach, is an Angels fan. Brad Gilbert is a fanatic sports fan. Jim Courier wears his Cincinnati Reds cap everywhere he goes.

But Courier went to Nick Bollettieri's Tennis Academy, in Bradenton, Florida, when he was fourteen and cried every Sunday night when his parents dropped him off after a weekend at home. Andre Agassi went there when he was thirteen and didn't get to go home on weekends. Las Vegas, Agassi's hometown, is a long way from Bradenton. Boris Becker feels old at twenty-three. Steffi Graf predicts that Chris Evert and Martina Navratilova will be the last superstars to play past the age of thirty.

"It takes too much out of you," she says. "I hope I last until I'm twenty-five. I wonder if Jennifer [Capriati] and Monica [Seles] will. So much is being asked of them."

So very much. These kids don't choose tennis; it chooses them. Because as soon as they show any kind of skill, their parents and coaches and—soon thereafter—agents tell them to forget school, forget their friends, forget all responsibility, and hit the tennis ball. At fourteen, Jennifer Capriati has already hopped from Fort Lauderdale, Saddlebrook, and Broken Sound, Florida (for one day), and then back again to Saddlebrook.

She does a large chunk of her schoolwork on the road and faxes it to teachers. She spent her summer vacation, which started long before school ended, in Milan, Rome, Marbella (Spain), Paris, Eastbourne (England), and London. She came home for five days and went to Mount Cranmore, New Hampshire. Just after school began in September, she went to Tokyo, then to Singapore for two days, back to Tokyo, and—ten days later—home.

She is very rich. Her parents, like all tennis parents, say, "She loves to play." She loves to *win.* Who doesn't? But for Jennifer Capriati there is no normalcy. She will grow up with no idea what high school or weekend dances or a crush on the kid in math class is like.

And she is the lucky one. Most who make the same sacrifices don't get rich like Capriati has.

And so, I come away from this ride feeling differently about tennis and the people in it. I certainly don't condone a lot of what goes on in the sport—especially the business of the sport—and I feel little sympathy for the hangers-on who surround many of the top players or for the parents who push and push and push and then say they are doing it because they care so much about their son or daughter.

For many of the players, though, and for many of the people who work in the game because they love it, I come away with respect and, in many cases, great affection. I come away remembering something Dana Loconto, the outstanding and very funny ATP Tour umpire, said to me during a long rain delay at Wimbledon.

"You know something?" Dana said in his Gadsden, Alabama, drawl. "You really gotta love this game to love this game."

A year ago, I would have had no idea what the hell that meant. Now, I understand it completely. Which worries me, just a little bit.

PART ONE

AUSTRALIA

1

"YOU *CANNOT* BE SERIOUS"

It was Sunday in Melbourne. Hot, breezy, humid. A typical late-January, Australian summer day. Day seven of the Australian Open was winding down to an uneventful conclusion. There had been some minor upsets but nothing that was going to knock the Melbourne trolley-car strike off the front page.

In the pressroom, the Australian tabloid writers glanced nervously at the clock again and again, hoping that John McEnroe would make short work of Mikael Pernfors. An easy McEnroe victory would get Rachel McQuillan, the country's latest female hope, on court to play her match in time to make first edition deadlines. Rachel McQuillan was nineteen, blond, and ranked fortieth in the world. Headline stuff for the tabloid boys.

There was no reason for any of them to believe that McEnroe and Pernfors wouldn't cooperate. McEnroe had been the talk of the tournament for three rounds, dropping just fifteen games in nine sets. He had looked very much like the old untouchable McEnroe, losing as many as three games in a set only once.

It wasn't only the numbers that were impressive. McEnroe looked relaxed on court, happy with himself, his game, and the Australian public. Everyone was reveling in seeing him produce a brand of tennis that many, McEnroe included, had wondered if they would ever see again.

One of the people who had marveled at McEnroe during his second-round victory over Austrian Alex Antonitsch was Gerry Armstrong. He had umpired a match early that afternoon and, with the rest of the day off, had done something he almost never did: gone to watch a tennis match on his own time. "If there's one player I'll go out of my way to watch play tennis when I'm not working, it's McEnroe," Armstrong said. "The guy is an artist. There's no one in the game quite like him."

On this Sunday afternoon it was not McEnroe's artistry that was on Armstrong's mind as he walked to the umpire's chair to work the match between the artiste and Pernfors. Armstrong had been a full-time professional umpire for a little more than three years. He had worked the men's final at Wimbledon in 1988 and the women's final in 1989. By any account, he was one of the top two or three umpires in the game—which is why he was in the chair for this match. In making the umpiring schedule, Ken Farrar, the supervisor of officiating at all Grand Slam tournaments, was keenly aware of which matches might be troublesome and, no matter how well he had been playing or how smoothly his previous matches had gone, any McEnroe match was worrisome. Armstrong, a thirty-four-year-old Englishman who had spent most of his adult life as a soccer goalie before a chronically separated shoulder had forced him to retire, had assumed he would get McEnroe in the fourth round or the quarterfinals, and that was fine with him. He had worked McEnroe matches often in the past, not without problems, but he'd never encountered a situation he couldn't handle. As he walked onto court that afternoon, Armstrong had no reason to suspect this match would be any different.

"What you learn about the job, though, is that you can never predict what will happen," he had said earlier that week. "The most innocuous, innocent match can blow up anytime, anywhere. You always have to concentrate totally because you never know where a problem is going to come from."

Certainly, no McEnroe match was ever considered innocuous or innocent. In his ten years as a supervisor, Farrar had always made certain to be nearby whenever McEnroe was playing. He had assigned himself to center court that Sunday and, as the match began, he was seated across the court from the umpire's chair, hoping he wouldn't be needed. "To be honest," he would say later, "the way things had been going, there was no reason to expect a problem."

What Armstrong and Farrar couldn't know was that McEnroe had awakened that morning feeling uneasy. He knew how well he was playing. He also knew that Ivan Lendl was not at the top of his game. He had spent enough time with Boris Becker during the week to know that Becker was still emotionally wiped out from the Davis Cup final and wanted to go home more than he wanted to play tennis. He respected Stefan Edberg, but he certainly didn't fear him. And he knew beyond a shadow of a doubt that if he stayed at this level, those were the only players in the field who had any chance of beating him.

Once, McEnroe would have been so focused on winning the tournament that his mind's eye could have seen only Pernfors that morning. He would have seen a combative, pesky ground-stroker, talented enough to have been a French Open finalist in 1986 but who, after various injuries and setbacks, had come into this tournament ranked sixty-third in the world. But McEnroe had let his thoughts wander into the future. "I got myself messed up," he said later. "I knew how well I was hitting the ball. I wasn't serving as well as I can, but I was hitting the ball as well as I ever have. But instead of thinking about winning the Australian, I started thinking about my schedule.

"I had already been on the road for almost four weeks. It hadn't been so bad, because I had my family with me. But if I made the semifinals, which I was almost sure I would, it meant I would barely have a week at home before I had to leave for Milan. And then there was Toronto and Philadelphia right after that.

"That should have been the last thing in the world I was thinking about, especially in the middle of a Grand Slam tournament. But it was almost like I wasn't prepared to play as well as I was playing. I had always had trouble getting ready that soon after Christmas. All of a sudden, there I was. I couldn't handle it."

Almost from the start of the match, it was apparent that this was a different McEnroe. He won the first set 6–1, but that was deceptive. Every game was close. Pernfors had all sorts of chances, starting with three break points in the first game of the match. McEnroe, however, kept coming up with the important shots, and there was every reason to believe that even this less-sharp McEnroe could wear his opponent down.

Pernfors's reputation on tour was not exactly that of a blood-and-guts battler. He was Swedish born and American educated, having played tennis at the University of Georgia. Unlike most of the other top-rated Swedes, it had been in college, not as a junior in Sweden, that he had come of age as a player. He fit none of the Swedish stereotypes. He wasn't blond or bland. He spoke perfect English—with a Southern accent—and was known as someone who enjoyed a good party at least as much as he might enjoy rolling in the dirt to win a five-setter.

He had come to Melbourne, however, with new resolve. He would turn twenty-seven in 1990, and he knew time was running out. He had been ranked as high as tenth in the world, in 1986, but had done little since then. So he had made the long trip to Australia ten weeks early to work and play himself back into top shape. This work had paid off for three rounds. Pernfors had lost just one set and came into the match with McEnroe convinced he was capable of winning.

The first set did little to change his mind. It had been closer than 6–1. Pernfors is the kind of player who chases down so many balls that no point is easy, and that made McEnroe uptight and nervous. He had complained about a couple of calls and had whined about photographers moving during points. To Armstrong, in the chair, and Farrar, sitting across the court, those weren't good signs.

Early in the second set, Pernfors finally converted a break opportunity, aided by a close call on the baseline. When Pernfors then held serve to go up 4–1, McEnroe came out of his chair after the changeover and walked directly over to the lineswoman who had made the close call against him two games earlier. Standing a few feet from her, he repeatedly bounced a ball on his racquet strings and stared at her. The crowd began to hoot, but McEnroe never said a word, just stared balefully.

In the chair, Armstrong made a decision. He thought McEnroe might be headed for an explosion. "A lot of times when John is edgy early in a match, a warning will calm him down," Armstrong said afterward. "It's as if you're saying to him, 'Okay, John, you've had your say, now let's just play tennis.' I was hoping that would happen here. What he was doing was intimidation, there was no questioning that. So I gave him a warning."

A warning is step one in tennis's code of conduct. Prior to 1990, the code had four steps: a warning, a point penalty, a game penalty, and a default. But in the Byzantine world of tennis politics, the men's sport had been split at the start of the year into two separate governing bodies. One of the ramifications of the split was a tighter code of conduct. Step three—the game penalty—had been eliminated. Now tennis players were like baseball batters: Three strikes and they were out.

Still, the warning was hardly cause for concern. McEnroe had been only one step from default many times in the past and had always kept himself under control from that point on. Now, he was still two strikes away. A long way from serious trouble.

"The strange thing about it," he said later, "is that I've been *so* much worse in the past. There was no reason for him to give me that warning. No reason at all. I never said a word to the lady."

But Armstrong had made a judgment call, guided by his instincts. "Something just tells you that the right thing to do is to warn a player," he said. "I was hoping John would understand what I was doing and that would be the end of the trouble."

Farrar was hoping the same thing. When Armstrong warned McEnroe, he sat impassive as always, arms folded, his eyes hidden behind his ever-present sunglasses. Farrar never lets anyone see him sweat—but he does plenty of sweating. "The last thing in the world I wanted was to have to go out there on court," he said. "But once Gerry warned him, I had to be ready in case John started to argue."

Farrar is a latecomer to tennis, a New Englander who grew up playing hockey. Later, while working in the Midwest, he became a hockey referee, but when he moved back to Boston in the 1960s, he found it tough to break into the establishment world of hockey officiating.

When a friend told him he could get into the annual tennis tournament at Longwood for free if he was willing to work as a linesman, he jumped at the chance. "They gave you two tickets and a hot dog in those days," he said. "I thought it was a great deal."

Farrar quickly fell in love with his new avocation. He began working at any junior tournament he could find, driving around with a stepladder in his trunk that he would set up as his umpire's chair. In the 1970s, he went to work for World Team Tennis and, in 1981, was offered the chance to become one of the first professional supervisors for the Men's Tennis Council (MTC). He was in the construction business at the time and a little bit bored, so he took a shot.

At age fifty-five he had been named head supervisor for the Grand Slams. This was his first tournament in that capacity, although his role was the same as it had been when he had been an MTC supervisor. Seeing McEnroe in a snit was nothing new for Farrar but, as had always been the case in the past, he could feel his palms beginning to sweat when he heard Armstrong call the warning.

McEnroe's argument was brief, though. The danger passed. Pernfors went on to win the second set and, as Armstrong had hoped, McEnroe dug in to play tennis. There were distractions: a baby crying in the stands, a few stray fans trying to bait McEnroe by yelling when he threw the ball up to serve, a few others telling him loudly to "just shut up and play" whenever he argued a call. The match kept evolving from a curiosity into one filled with excellent tennis. Pernfors looked a little like the Pernfors of 1986, slugging his ground strokes, chasing McEnroe's volleys, passing him at key moments. McEnroe seemed equal to the task. When he won a taut third set 7–5, it looked as if everything was going to work out. Rachel McQuillan would be on court in time for the Aussies to make their deadlines.

And then, all hell broke loose.

Serving at 2–3, deuce in the fourth set, McEnroe pushed a forehand approach wide. Frustrated with himself, he hurled his racquet to the ground. The crack could be heard throughout the stadium. Farrar heard it and stiffened. "That's an automatic," he explained later. "If a player throws his racquet, it's up to the umpire to decide whether to penalize him—*unless* it cracks. Then he has no choice. He *has* to call it."

Armstrong did just that. "Racquet abuse, Mr. McEnroe," he announced. "Point penalty."

The timing could hardly have been worse for McEnroe, because the point penalty gave Pernfors the game and a 4–2 lead. If Pernfors could now hold serve twice, the match would come down to one set. McEnroe certainly didn't want that. So he tried to talk his way free, saying he really hadn't thrown the racquet that violently.

"You broke the racquet," Armstrong told him. "That's automatic, John."

"All I did was crack it," McEnroe said. "I have every intention of continuing to play with it. Look, it isn't broken, it's just a crack."

McEnroe wasn't going to win the argument, but he continued anyway. Armstrong let him go for a while before saying, "Let's play."

Those two words are a code. They mean "I've heard enough." Players know it as well as umpires do. McEnroe couldn't let go, though. As he had often done in the past, he demanded to see the referee.

The referee for the Australian Open was Peter Bellenger, a tall, quiet, balding man. His job was more directly connected to making court assignments each day than to officiating disputes. So, even though Bellenger did come trotting onto the court, it was actually Farrar who Armstrong signaled for. He was the man in charge. He was the one who had the authority to reverse Armstrong's decision.

He didn't.

"In this case," he said later, "I had one goal: to get John back on the court and playing again. He wasn't going to win the argument, because it wasn't a judgment call. The racquet had cracked. I've dealt with him enough times to know that this wasn't going to be an easy one."

McEnroe repeated his argument to Farrar, claiming again that he could still play with the racquet. Farrar kept shaking his head and telling McEnroe that the crack made the call automatic. Sitting in the chair, Armstrong listened impassively. Bellenger stood a few feet away, watching silently. Throughout the argument Pernfors stood on the baseline, holding the tennis balls, preparing to serve whenever McEnroe came back to play. By now, the crowd was whistling loudly, wanting the match to continue. McEnroe kept insisting that he could play with the racquet and it should still be 2–3, advantage Pernfors.

Farrar shook his head one more time and finally told Armstrong, "Let's play." With that he turned to walk back across the court to his seat.

Bellenger headed back to the tunnel. McEnroe hadn't moved. By now, he was furious and a little bit scared. He was looking at a five-setter and, in his current mood, he didn't want that. Yet there went Farrar, walking off, confirming his sentence. In his mind at that moment, McEnroe was still *two* strikes from default. He had forgotten the new rule, had forgotten he had only one strike left. And so he decided to get in one last parting shot.

"Just go fuck your mother!" he shouted.

It wasn't whispered. It wasn't even spoken in a normal tone of voice. Five rows back in the stands, the profanity was audible. John Alexander, the ex-Australian Davis Cup player who was doing courtside commentary for Australian television, heard it clearly. "John McEnroe has just used a terribly abusive profanity," Alexander told his audience, adding, "and I don't think Ken Farrar is going to let him get away with it."

Farrar took two more steps before what he had heard sunk in. "My first thought was, 'Did he really say that?' Then I said, 'Yeah, he *said* that.' I turned around and went back to Gerry right away."

Seeing Farrar turn around and walk back to Armstrong, McEnroe was disgusted—at least in part with himself. "I thought, Oh God, the guys's going to give me a game penalty," he said. "I was upset with myself because I shouldn't have said what I said. I've gotten into the habit the last few years of using that kind of language, and when you do that, sooner or later it's going to come out when you don't want it to."

Farrar had no intention of giving McEnroe a game penalty—especially since it no longer existed in the rules. But even under the *old* rules, Farrar would have responded the exact same way. "No player has ever spoken to me that way," he said. "Not John, not anyone. Not ever.

"Right there, that was gross misconduct under the rules. If he hadn't had a single strike against him at that point, the same thing would have happened."

What happened was swift and shocking. Farrar called Bellenger back to the chair. "Gerry," he asked, "did you hear that?"

Armstrong nodded that he had. "If Ken hadn't heard it and hadn't come back, I would have called him back," Armstrong said. "My reaction was exactly the same as his."

Having confirmed that his ears weren't playing tricks on him, Farrar turned to Bellenger. "Peter," he said, "I think we're looking at a default here."

Bellenger nodded. Farrar looked up at Armstrong one more time. "Default him," he said. And then he turned and walked quickly back across the court. He was halfway there when Armstrong made the announcement. "Verbal abuse, audible obscenity, Mr. McEnroe. Default. Game, set, and match, Pernfors."

The whole thing—from McEnroe's profane outburst to Armstrong's announcement—took no more than twenty seconds. For a split second, no one in the place moved. It was as if they knew they had heard wrong. Few of the fans had any idea what the rules were. McEnroe had cursed, but so what? He had done that for years and had never been defaulted. Why was this different? How could a fourth-round match in the Australian Open be over *just like that*? There had to be a mixup here; there had to be someone McEnroe could appeal to.

But there wasn't. Armstrong climbed down from the chair. Neither player had moved. Pernfors was still on the baseline, waiting to serve. McEnroe stood in the same spot where he had unleashed the fatal phrase. His hands were on his hips, a stunned smile on his face.

It was what his friends call his "you cannot be serious" look, a combination of amazement, anger, and disbelief. They had all seen it before but never quite like this. Watching the incident on tape over and over several hours later at her home in Florida, Mary Carillo, McEnroe's onetime mixed-doubles partner and lifelong friend, would think to herself, He's standing there, thinking, "I haven't even cleared my throat yet and I'm defaulted? You *cannot* be serious!"

In fact, they could not have been more serious.

The chaotic scene that unfolded in those first moments after McEnroe's default was a perfect metaphor for what professional tennis had become as the 1990s began. Tennis was in a period of turmoil and transition—again. The men were split politically, while the women had sponsor problems and were counting on a thirteen-year-old to replace the irreplaceable Chris Evert as both icon and girl next door.

The great irony of McEnroe's default was that the two men responsible, Armstrong and Farrar, were on opposite sides of the civil war being waged for control of the men's game. In 1989, both had been employed by the Men's Tennis Council, then the governing body for all of men's tennis. By 1990, the MTC no longer existed. Farrar was an employee of the International Tennis Federation, the group that ran the four Grand Slams—Wimbledon and the Australian, the French and U.S. Opens. Armstrong was one of ten full-time umpires who worked for the new ATP (Association of Tennis Professionals) Tour.

The ATP Tour had replaced the MTC because the players were unhappy with many of the rules they were forced to follow. As a result, they now had control over all the non–Grand Slam tournaments, the week-in, week-out events that snaked endlessly around the world. The game's umpires were as divided as the bureaucrats and the players. Farrar, who had once hired Armstrong and all of his fellow full-time umpires, was now considered the enemy.

"There were a lot of hurt feelings," Farrar said. "I know they all felt I had let them down."

On this Sunday, though, Armstrong and Farrar had found common ground: John Patrick McEnroe, Jr. For each of them and for the sport, his banishment from Australia was a crisis. It was the first time a top-ranked player had *ever* been evicted from a major tournament. And even though he had not won a Grand Slam title since 1984, McEnroe was still the game's most visible figure. It was bad enough that the angry crowd was shouting and gesturing furiously, demanding that the match begin again. The next day, the front page of virtually every newspaper in the world would carry the story. Every television station would be repeating images of McEnroe's ejection. This Australian Open, which for better or worse was the beginning of a new era in tennis, would now be remembered for one thing and one moment: 5:30 P.M. on January 21, 1990.

As soon as he had announced the default, Armstrong walked up the players' tunnel and found that he was completely lost in the maze of halls that run underneath the Flinders Park Stadium, since, in his haste to depart, he had come offcourt on the wrong side. He had to ask for directions several times before he finally found his way back to the umpires' lounge.

"When I walked in, one of the Australian supervisors was talking to everyone in kind of a hushed tone," he said. "He was saying things like, 'Everyone remain calm; don't answer questions and just go about your business.' That was when it really hit me that something very drastic had taken place."

The weight of it all hit Farrar more quickly. By the time he got off the court he was sweating profusely and he could hear his heart pounding. He walked back to his office and found his boss, Bill Babcock, sitting there staring at the television set. The cameras were still showing the stadium where the crowd had now broken into a chant of "We want McEnroe!"

Babcock looked up when Farrar walked in and saw the pained look on his face. "Ken, you had no choice," he said. "You did the right thing."

Farrar sank into a chair. "What a hell of a way to start a new job," he said.

Babcock didn't even crack a smile.

Armstrong knew he had to call home. It was 7 A.M. in Eastbourne and his longtime girlfriend, Julie, and their four-month-old son would just be waking up. Soon, he knew, their phone would start ringing off the hook. What's more, Richard Kaufman, the most experienced of the full-time umpires and the man looked to as a mentor by almost all of his colleagues, was visiting Julie for the weekend. Kaufman was in a Ph.D. program at the London School of Economics, two hours away by train.

When Julie answered the phone, Armstrong briefly explained to her what had happened and then asked to speak to Kaufman. When Kaufman picked up the phone, Armstrong cheerily asked, "How are you, Rich?"

"Asleep," Kaufman answered.

"Well," Armstrong said, "I've just had to default McEnroe."

"*Now,*" Kaufman said, "I'm awake."

Since the tournament's junior competition would begin the next morning, the men's locker room was aswarm with teenage players, many of whom had stood watching as the wild scene unfolded on television. Just as McEnroe began walking down the long hallway that led from the court to the locker room, one of the Australian junior coaches raced inside.

"Everyone out!" he screamed. "I want every junior player out of this locker room right now!"

As McEnroe approached, a stream of juniors began piling into the hallway, all of them wishing, no doubt, that they had been allowed to stay and witness what was to come.

But the fury had passed for McEnroe. Seconds after Armstrong had left the court, he had walked to his chair to begin gathering his racquets and clothing. Pernfors, who was at least as stunned as McEnroe, walked up, put his arm on his back, and said, "John, I'm really sorry."

McEnroe didn't respond. He didn't even hear Pernfors. If someone had fired a cannon behind his back at that moment, he wouldn't have flinched. He was in the kind of shock people go into when they have been shot. McEnroe would not feel the pain until much later. By the time he reached the locker room, he was resigned to his fate. He tossed a few racquets—perhaps as a matter of principle—but that was it. His agent, Sergio Palmieri, who had been sitting in the stands with his client's wife, Tatum O'Neal, greeted him at the door. Palmieri knew his job right then was to listen to everything McEnroe said—whether it made sense or not—nod his head, and say, "You're right, John, you're right."

Twenty minutes after his default, McEnroe, escorted by a coterie of security guards, came into the pressroom. Photographers were literally climbing over one another, trying to take his picture. They kept snapping and flashing and yapping until McEnroe finally said, "If they don't stop, I'm leaving." The reporters screamed at the photographers to stop. Grudgingly, they did.

If John McEnroe has been consistent in anything throughout his career, it is his remorse in the aftermath of his worst on-court incidents. McEnroe has come into post-disaster press conferences and said "Bless me, father, for I have sinned" so many times that reporters who have been around him through the years have begun to feel a bit like priests in the Catholic confessional.

This confession was no different. McEnroe rambled—as always—and ruminated. At one point he said, "It was just one little four-letter word. The guy could have let me off." But in the end, he knew that wasn't true.

"In a way, this was inevitable," he said. "This is like the icing on the cake. This is a long story and now it culminates in me getting defaulted in a big tournament."

He paused for a minute and shrugged. "I can't say I'm surprised."

There was more. McEnroe has never in his life cut a press conference short. He admitted to forgetting the rule change from four steps to three and very rationally conceded, "In that sense, it was my fault."

But not everything was so rational. All the rules in tennis, he said, had been made for him. This was proof, he added, that the players have no power. (Actually, it was the players who had created the new stricter rules because of concerns about their image.) He could have played, McEnroe insisted, with the cracked racquet.

"You know, it's really not fair," he said. "Everyone understands English. Pernfors could be cursing in Swedish and the guy would never know it."

Also not true. Several years earlier, the umpires had put together a profanity cheat sheet that contained the key profanities in just about every language spoken on the tennis tour. Some knew the words by heart; others carried a copy of the cheat sheet with them so if they heard something that sounded familiar, they could check it out. If Pernfors had cursed at Armstrong in Swedish, Armstrong would have known.

McEnroe was flailing, knowing he had messed up and messed up badly. When he left the interview room, it was as if the entire tournament had stopped dead in its tracks. After a lengthy delay (brought on by the unruliness of the crowd), Rachel McQuillan was at last on court. If she had won 6–0, 6–0 (she didn't), she *might* have gotten a sentence in the next day's newspapers.

With his arm around Tatum, McEnroe walked through the tunnel to the underground garage, where a car waited to take him away from the carnage he had left behind. Tatum looked neither right nor left as the photographers continued to snap away from every possible angle. McEnroe looked as if he had just come back from an afternoon practice session. His face was completely blank. He even paused to give the photographers an extra few seconds while he loaded his racquets into the trunk. Then he got into the backseat of the car and was gone.

McEnroe had left the building. The Australian Open was in tatters. Tennis's new era had begun.

2

HAPPY NEW YEAR

Ted Tinling's life ended one month shy of eighty years. He spent the last sixty-five of those years in tennis, as a player, an umpire, a dress designer, a confidant to many of the great players, and as the game's leading historian. Without question, he was as bright as anyone who has ever given tennis any thought. It was Tinling's theory that the beginning of the end for the sport of professional tennis came in Bournemouth, England, on April 23, 1968. On that afternoon, what is now known as the "Open Era" began in tennis. For the first time, pros and amateurs were allowed to mix, competing in the same tournament.

In truth, the difference between the so-called pros and the so-called amateurs was minimal. The pros took their money openly and publicly. This act was considered so crass by the tennis pooh-bahs of the time that the pros were banned from the tournaments that really mattered: the four Grand Slams.

The so-called amateurs got their money under the table in various forms, although cash was generally considered preferable. The pros barnstormed from one small town to another; the amateurs, funded by their national tennis associations, played the glamour stops of the game. The pros spent a lot of time in Kansas City, Bologna, Memphis, Liverpool, and Louisville. The amateurs hung out in London, Paris, and Rome.

Slowly, though, the pros were making inroads. The money was getting better and public interest was growing. The pooh-bahs were concerned. So, in one of the most shocking moves of the twentieth century, they *entered* the twentieth century, led by the All England Club—Wimbledon. When Wimbledon voted to open its tournament to professionals in 1968, the other Grand Slams had no choice but to go along and do the same thing.

Most people consider the men who run Wimbledon to be crotchety old snobs with their feet planted firmly in the past. In truth, these men are usually a step ahead of their tennis brethren. Their decision certainly propelled tennis into the future, changing the game forever. Since that week in Bournemouth, the hot-breathed pursuit of the dollar (pound, franc, Deutche mark, yen, take your pick) has continued nonstop.

By the time Ted Tinling died, on May 23, 1990, he had come to believe that his sport was destined to parallel the characters of Wagner's *Ring* cycle. In the fourth and final opera of the *Ring—Götterdämmerung* (Twilight of the Gods)—all the gods perish, destroyed by their own greed and selfishness.

"There is no doubt in my mind that tennis is the *Ring,*" Tinling said. "As soon as they discovered the gold [Bournemouth, in tennis; Siegfried, in the *Ring*] the end was inevitable. Great and godlike as all these players are, the sport will have to be destroyed—and then completely rebuilt again—before it will ever be sane. Ever since the game's been professional, there's been nothing but chaos. Now, they all smack their lips and count their money. It won't last, though. It can't."

On January 1, 1990, there was good reason to believe that Tinling's *Götterdämmerung* was not all that far away. Once again, tennis was entering a new era. Men's tennis changes eras the way George Steinbrenner changed managers when he ran the New York Yankees. Rarely, however, does anything *really* change other than the names of the people in power. Lamar Hunt becomes Bill Riordan who becomes Jack Kramer who becomes Donald Dell who becomes Mark McCormack who becomes Marshall Happer who becomes Hamilton Jordan. The one thing they have in common is that they're all chasing their own piece of the gold.

Marshall Happer was the administrator of the Men's Tennis Council, the organization that governed men's tennis throughout the 1980s. Jordan, the onetime White House chief of staff under Jimmy Carter, took over the Association of Tennis Professionals (ATP) in 1987. After twelve months of planning, he launched a palace coup, convincing the players that if they dumped Happer and the MTC they could have more money, more power, and less discipline.

Happer crawled out of the wreckage of the MTC to become the executive director of the U.S. Tennis Association. The USTA runs the U.S. Open, one of the four Grand Slams, and is part of the International Tennis Federation (ITF). The ITF still retained control of the Grand Slams. Confused? Buried in names and initials? There's more. Before Jordan's new ATP Tour was a year old, he would be out of tennis, replaced by yet another name, Mark Miles.

As the nineties dawned, women's tennis had yet to have these sorts of troubles. Only four names had really mattered in the women's game since Bournemouth: Billie Jean King, Chris Evert, Martina Navratilova, and Virginia Slims. King gave the women's game credibility, not by winning twelve Grand Slam singles titles but by beating Bobby Riggs in the infamous "Battle of the Sexes" match, in September 1973. If Riggs, who was then sixty-three, had beaten King, it would have been years before anyone would have taken the women's game seriously.

But King won—easily—and, with the financial backing of Virginia Slims, the women's tour became a reality. But it wouldn't have survived and flourished if not for Evert and Navratilova. Evert put sex appeal into the game. She was pretty and feminine and she could play. She won matches and dated Jimmy Connors, Burt Reynolds, and President Gerald Ford's son Jack—among many others.

When Tracy Austin and Andrea Jaeger burned out, it was left to Navratilova to first compete with and then surpass Evert. Navratilova took the game to another level with her athletic ability, her conditioning, and her strength. Many resented her because she wasn't American, she didn't date Burt Reynolds, and because she eventually dominated Evert. But when Evert, spurred by Navratilova, remade herself as a player in the mid-eighties, they became linked in tennis lore—Chrissie and Martina—and gave the women's game an enduring and endearing rivalry.

Evert, Navratilova, and Slims gave the game glamour, exposure, and financial stability. But as the eighties ended, Evert had just retired, Navratilova was looking down the barrel of birthday number thirty-four, and Slims was fighting to hang on to its place in the game.

The new women's champion was Steffi Graf, already, at age twenty, considered by some—including Tinling, who had seen them all—the best player of all time. In 1987, when Graf first moved past Navratilova into the No. 1 spot on the computer, Navratilova disputed the legitimacy of that ranking, noting that although Graf had won that year's French Open, she had lost both the Wimbledon and the U.S. Open finals—to Navratilova.

"If you win Wimbledon and the Open you've won the two biggest tournaments of the year," Navratilova reasoned. "I think that makes you No. 1, no matter what the computer says."

Graf certainly didn't agree with that assessment. Rather than get into a drawn-out argument with Navratilova over the issue, she responded in 1988 by having one of the greatest years in the history of tennis, becoming only the third woman and fifth player ever to win all four Grand Slams in one year.

Graf's ascendancy was not greeted with overwhelming enthusiasm by either the Women's Tennis Association or Virginia Slims. Evert and

Navratilova had become superb spokeswomen for the sport. Both were excellent on television, good public speakers, and willing to do their part in promoting women's tennis. Navratilova, who had defected from Czechoslovakia in 1975, could talk about football or basketball as comfortably as any American and had certainly earned the respect of the public (if not the dewey-eyed affection reserved for Chris America).

Graf was nineteen when she won the Grand Slam. It was easy—and convenient—to forget that when Evert and Navratilova were that age, they had not been nearly as comfortable with the public as they were now.

Graf radiated intensity on and off the court. She made no pretense of being "one of the girls," not the way Evert and Navratilova had been—and still were. She was in and out of the locker room in lightning-fast bursts and she rarely attended any WTA or Virginia Slims functions.

And then, there was her father. Peter Graf had guided his daughter's tennis career almost from birth, and he remained a dominant and domineering presence in her life. He was a tough, calculating businessman given to screaming outbursts when he did not get his way. The impression was that he controlled his daughter's every move, on the court—where he was often accused of illegal coaching from the stands—and off. Steffi often came off as aloof, arrogant. The truth is, she was painfully shy. Giving even the simplest television interview or the briefest acceptance speeches made her sick to her stomach. She was as nervous and as scared of performing off the court as she was nerveless and fearless on it. She followed up her matchless performance of 1988 by winning three more Slams in 1989, her second straight sweep stopped only by her loss in the French Open final to Arantxa Sanchez on a day when she was beset by menstrual cramps. Even so, the Sanchez victory was hailed as extraordinary and was a much-needed boost for a game that was rapidly becoming a one-woman show.

Graf's two-year death grip on the major championships, combined with the inevitable fade-out of Evert and Navratilova, made the impending debut of Jennifer Capriati that much more important. Capriati would not be fourteen until March 29, but she had first been talked about as a future star when she was nine years old—yes, *nine years old.* At the age of eleven, she had been labeled a can't-miss star.

By the time the players began boarding planes for the long flight across the Pacific to start the new year in Australia, Capriati had already signed a five-year, $3 million deal with Diadora, the Italian clothing and shoe company, and a three-year, $1 million racquet deal with Prince. Those were guaranteed numbers that didn't include potential bonuses.

She would not play her first professional match until March 6, but she was already a millionaire and the talk of the women's tour. For Capriati and her father, Stefano, every bit as calculating a businessman as Peter Graf, the timing was perfect. Evert had retired in September at the U.S. Open in a soap-opera scene that would have embarrassed any daytime-TV scriptwriter. The climax was the sight of the USA cable network's Diana Nyad crying during the postmatch interview.

Capriati was the next Evert—at least, that was the plan. She was from Florida (like Evert), she had been coached briefly by Evert's father, she was managed by Evert's brother (what a coincidence!), and she was adorable—dark, pretty, and bubbly. The big money and buildup had as much to do with all of that as with her backhand.

But Capriati was, at best, the near future. The present was the continued dominance of Graf.

The men had no such problem. Though Ivan Lendl had controlled the No. 1 ranking almost without interruption for more than four years, he couldn't win Wimbledon, the most important title in the sport. That chink and the steady rise of Boris Becker kept the men's game afloat.

This is not to imply that all was sanguine. The top men had become fat—not literally, but in the wallets—so fat that it was virtually impossible to get a male tennis player to cross the street without giving him a large chunk of change. The top players were making so much money that someone like Andre Agassi, who had never even reached the final of a Grand Slam tournament much less won one, was as rich and as arrogant as any superstar who'd ever played the game. Agassi made mealymouthed excuses about skipping the Australian Open and Wimbledon, and not only got away with it but became more popular and more wealthy almost by the day.

Lendl had succeeded McEnroe as the No. 1 player in the world when he had beaten him in the 1985 U.S. Open final. That loss began a tailspin for McEnroe, who spent most of the next four years fading in and out of the game, unsure about whether he wanted to make the effort necessary to get back near the top. McEnroe's fall and the inevitable—although remarkably slow—slide of Jimmy Connors as he pushed deep into his thirties left tennis searching desperately for an American star. Lendl lived in Greenwich, Connecticut, and, like Navratilova, had become completely Americanized. But with his mechanical-looking game, his humorless, dour appearance, and his machinelike approach to tennis, he was never going to be someone who charged people's emotions. As many people hated McEnroe and Connors as loved them—but the important thing was that all those people *cared.*

Lendl stirred no emotions at all. Neither did Stefan Edberg, the fluid Swede who won back-to-back Australian Opens and then won Wimbledon in 1988. Edberg *was* the Swedish stereotype personified: totally blond and totally bland, a person who went out of his way to be more boring than he actually was, because he craved his privacy. Mats Wilander, the other brilliant Swede of the post–Bjorn Borg era, was a bright, interesting man, one of the few players whose intellect McEnroe respected. But his game was deadly, especially on clay, where his strategy most often was to bore his opponents to death. Everyone in tennis respected Wilander, but no crowd outside of Sweden was ever moved by his play.

Boris Becker *did* stir emotions. He played the game with a brash freshness that people could relate to, and he was bright and outspoken. He was as comfortable doing interviews or giving speeches as Graf was uncomfortable, and, almost from the moment he won Wimbledon in 1985, at age seventeen, he became the game's top attraction. But after winning Wimbledon in 1985 and 1986, he began to struggle. Most of his problems were predictable: troubles with girls, lack of practice discipline, a breakup with his coach. It is difficult to conceive the magnitude of Becker's post-Wimbledon stardom. Consider this, though: In 1986, 98 percent of the German people knew who he was. At the same time, less than 50 percent of them knew of Chancellor Helmut Kohl. Becker was rich beyond his wildest dreams, but he found little joy in his money or in the demands made on him by his adoring public.

His game was not nearly the same in 1987 and 1988 as it had been the previous two years, and suddenly the three players dominating the major tournaments were Lendl, Wilander, and Edberg. In 1987, Lendl and Wilander met in both the French and the U.S. Open finals in matches that, if seen in the right places, could have ended insomnia forever.

The following year, Wilander won three of the four Grand Slams, his only loss coming at Wimbledon, where Edberg beat Becker in the final. But just when it began to look as if men's tennis might become a forgotten sport, especially in the U.S., where TV ratings dropped almost completely out of sight, a savior appeared.

His name was Andre Agassi, and his personality seemed as irresistible as his alliterative name. He was a teenybopper's dream, with long, streaked blond hair and funny-looking clothes that enhanced his young-rebel image. To top it off, he was from Las Vegas.

Agassi was another in a long line of backcourt players produced by Nick Bollettieri, the maven of the live-away-from-home teen tennis academy, but he had a flair for the game, a love of The Show, that made him an immediate star. Agassi first attracted attention in 1986, at age sixteen, when he reached the quarterfinals at a tournament in Stratton Mountain, Vermont. The national media was there that week because McEnroe was making the first of his comebacks; Agassi made a name for himself with his play and his multihued hair.

After an up-and-down 1987, it all seemed to come together for Agassi in 1988. He reached the semifinals at the French Open and lost a thrilling five-setter to Wilander. He then reached the semis at the U.S. Open, losing there to Lendl. By then, Agassi had become the game's cover boy and he was already starting to run into trouble. His showmanship on the court made some players unhappy, some because they were jealous, some because they felt Agassi carried the "Let me entertain you" routine too far.

That sentiment peaked during the summer when Agassi, in the process of routing Argentina's Martin Jaite in a Davis Cup match, caught a ball that Jaite served, giving Jaite a game in the third set. Agassi had shown Jaite up, saying, in affect, "I feel sorry for you, so I'll give you a game." By the U.S. Open he had earned the rancor of many of his fellow pros but the fans couldn't have cared less. Agassi was fun to watch, he was an American, and he was winning. He signed endorsement contracts that made him a millionaire, and he began traveling with an entourage that included his older brother, Philip; his coach, Bollettieri; his agent, Bill Shelton; a religious guru who advised Agassi on his born-again Christianity; and a hitting partner.

By the end of 1988, Agassi was ranked No. 4 in the world. But 1989 was a disaster. Agassi had traveled so much in 1988, pushed by his entourage to chase every available dollar, that he was burned out. He came to tournaments unprepared and often made no pretense of even trying. After losing to Carl Uwe-Steeb of Germany in the first round of the Lipton Championships, in March, Agassi actually bragged about the fact that he had never even heard of Steeb and had no idea he was left-handed until the match started. At the French Open, he lost in the third round, then he skipped Wimbledon for a second straight year. He did manage to repeat his semifinal performance at the Open, which was a tribute to his pure talent more than anything else.

Agassi's most embarrassing performance of that year came in July, in Munich, during the United States Davis Cup semifinal against West

Germany. On the first day, with the U.S. up 1–0, Agassi played unconscious tennis for almost three sets against Becker, leading by two sets, 5–4. But, serving for the match, he began to fade. Becker broke back and won the set before a midnight curfew caused the match to be suspended until the following morning. Becker came back the next day and won in five sets.

There was no shame in that. Beating Becker indoors is almost impossible. However, the next day, with the U.S. down 2–1 in the best-of-five series, Agassi had a chance to tie things up. All he had to do was beat Steeb, his old left-handed friend. Agassi lost. Worse than that, when he fell behind, he blatantly gave up. At each change of sides, U.S. captain Tom Gorman pleaded with him to try to fight back.

"It's too tough," Agassi kept saying. "Just too tough."

Tanking—giving up, quitting, just going through the motions—when playing in a tournament is a rotten thing to do. At least when Agassi did it in tournaments, he was representing only himself. In the Davis Cup, he was representing his country. To tank was unthinkable.

And yet, Agassi had done it. In one short year he had gone from being the delight of the tennis tour to its mystery player. He had become the most blatant tank artist in the game and didn't seem the least bit bothered by it. When the media began to criticize Agassi for his half-hearted efforts, he responded by turning down virtually all interview requests, saying that he had been treated unfairly. Shelton, his agent, became known in tennis circles as "Dr. No."

"Bill, do you think Andre could . . ."

"No."

"Well, maybe tomorrow he might . . ."

"No."

"Okay, then, when the tournament's over, perhaps he'll . . ."

"No!"

While Agassi was struggling, a brand-new crop of young American talent began quietly sneaking up on him. The best of them, in 1989, was Michael Chang, who was as serious-minded and as colorless as Agassi was goofy and colorful. Chang had little of Agassi's natural gift for the game, but he had a heart as big as Las Vegas. He proved that in spades when, in one of the most remarkable performances in tennis history, he won the French Open just three months past his seventeenth birthday, coming from two sets down to shock Lendl in the fourth round. Chang then came from behind again to beat Edberg in a five-set final. He became the first

American male since Tony Trabert, in 1955, to survive two weeks on the red clay of Roland Garros and win the French title.

It was an extraordinary performance and it made Chang a star—and, of course, a millionaire—almost overnight. Chang hated all the attention. The son of immigrant Chinese-Americans, he rarely cracked a smile, and his explanation for what he had done to win the French Open—and all his other matches—was "I won because of the Lord Jesus Christ."

Unlike Agassi, who seemingly invoked being born-again as a publicity tool (he fired his traveling chaplain after losing a match in the summer of 1989, shouting to Bollettieri as he walked off the court, "Fire Fritz!"), Chang was very, very serious about his religion. He honestly believed that his victory over Edberg was the result of his having a closer personal relationship with Jesus than Edberg did. How he knew anything about Edberg's relationship with Jesus didn't really matter. What did matter was that Chang believed it—and told everyone that he believed it ad nauseum.

Deservedly, Chang got most of the attention during 1989, but three other young Americans were drawing some hard looks: Jim Courier, another Bollettieri kid who stepped out of Agassi's shadow at the French by beating him; David Wheaton, a tall, big-serving Minnesotan who had also spent some time at Bollettieri's; and Pete Sampras, a gangly Californian who some people thought had the most potential of them all.

By the end of 1989, American tennis had made an amazing comeback. McEnroe had managed to stay interested enough to finish the year ranked No. 4 in the world; Brad Gilbert, a career journeyman, had had the year of his life to finish No. 5; Agassi, tank jobs and all, was still No. 6; Chang was No. 7, and Aaron Krickstein, only twenty-two years old although it seemed he had been around forever, was No. 8. And looming in the distance were Courier, Wheaton, and Sampras.

Nonetheless, Chang's miracle was the only American Grand Slam victory since 1984. Becker—who had found himself again in 1989 winning Wimbledon and the U.S. Open—Lendl, and Edberg were still the elite three of the men's game. Wilander, who had finished 1988 ranked No. 1 after his three Grand Slam victories, had gone through a disastrous 1989 and had slid completely out of the Top Ten. Becker, by virtue of his two Grand Slam titles, had been declared the world champion for 1989 but had not yet passed Lendl on the computer.

That appeared to be only a matter of time, though. Having just turned twenty-two, the German was coming into his prime as a player.

Lendl, who was turning thirty in March, was starting to have some thoughts about retirement a few years down the road. What few people knew was that there was potential disaster looming for the world of men's tennis: the twenty-two-year-old, the player in his prime, had spent far more time thinking about retirement than the thirty-year-old.

The trouble had started, strangely enough, on the morning after Becker's happiest moment in tennis. The Monday after he had beaten Ivan Lendl to win the U.S. Open, he awoke feeling monumentally depressed. The previous evening, when he had blasted his final serve past Lendl to win the grueling three-hour-and-fifty-one-minute final, Becker had felt as elated as he had ever felt. Dana Loconto, the chair umpire for the match, vividly remembers Becker grasping his hand and saying over and over again, "Thank you, thank you, thank you."

"It was as if," Loconto noted, "he thought I had won him the match."

Becker had won his own match, capping a remarkable ten months in which he had turned himself around as a tennis player. He had bottomed out at the U.S. Open the previous year, losing in three quick sets in the second round to Darren Cahill, a solid workmanlike player who had no right to think he could beat Becker, much less whip him in straight sets. Becker had had a foot problem in that match and really hadn't wanted to play. "I didn't think I belonged on the court," he said later. "As it turned out, I wasn't there long."

After that ordeal, Bob Brett sat Becker down for a long talk. Becker had hired Brett to coach him at the end of 1987, a year in which he advanced past the fourth round of only one Grand Slam tournament—the French. Brett had just turned thirty-four when Becker hired him, but he was already a veteran coach who had worked with twenty-two different players. None of them had been at Becker's level, though, and for Brett this was a completely new challenge.

It was one he relished. Brett had grown up outside of Melbourne, fighting to make up for what he lacked in size with grit and intensity. He never grew past five feet seven and never made it to the top one hundred as a player, so he turned to coaching. Here, he found success. Knowing he was never going to overwhelm anyone with his physical talent, Brett had carefully studied the game and its various training techniques. He was a great believer in weight training, being a disciple of Stan Nickles, one of tennis's first weight-training gurus.

Brett had a good deal of success helping a number of middle-of-the-pack players, often working with them in groups so he could make living on the road forty weeks a year financially worthwhile. He met Becker while coaching John Lloyd, Scott Davis, and Robert Seguso; Becker worked out with that group from time to time. When Becker, against the advice of his agent and mentor, Ion Tiriac, asked Brett to coach him in November of 1987, Brett said yes.

After the Cahill loss, Brett felt it was time to put things on the line with Becker. He had worked his way into the job cautiously that first year, but the time for caution had passed. "You need two months away from the game," he told Becker. "You need to heal, you need to rest, and you need to get in shape. You're too heavy. You lack quickness. If you don't take a different approach, you'll be out of the game in eighteen months."

Following Brett's plan meant dropping out of several tournaments and giving up lucrative exhibitions. Becker did exactly that. He weighed 205 pounds at the 1988 Open. A year later, when he walked on court to play Lendl in the final, he weighed 185. He followed Brett's plan: resting completely for three weeks, then working strictly on conditioning for three more. It wasn't two months, but it was close enough. He came back to the indoor circuit in late October and finished the year by beating Lendl in the Masters final in an extraordinary five-set match that lasted well over four hours.

"The last point of that match, he was running me from side to side and I kept chasing the ball down," Becker remembered. "I couldn't have done that in the past. When I won the point with a net cord, I thought I deserved it, that all the hard work had paid off."

It paid off in spades in 1989. At Wimbledon, he destroyed Edberg in the final. But the key match in that tournament for Becker was his semifinal against Lendl.

Rain had postponed the match from Friday to Saturday. Lendl's quest to finally win Wimbledon was well documented by this time, and he seemed to be playing well enough to finally pull it off. When he went up two sets to one on Becker and broke serve early in the fourth, it looked as though he would be playing Edberg in the final.

But then, as happens so often at the great English tournament, the weather intervened. A rain shower sent both players to the locker room. Brett found Becker sitting at his locker, looking despondent, beaten. "I can live with losing," Brett told his player. "Anyone can lose a tennis match. But you've quit. You've given up. How can you do that? Are you really such a loser that you can walk out in a Wimbledon semifinal and *quit?*"

Becker never said a word. He simply came back on court, broke Lendl back, and went on to win the match in five sets. "It hurt me when Bob said those things," he said. "But he was right. This was a Wimbledon semifinal. I was mad at him for what he said, but I knew why he had to say it."

The pep talk that won the U.S. Open that year came not from Brett but from Becker. On the first Thursday of the tournament, Becker found himself locked in a second-round match with Derrick Rostagno, a talented American with a reputation for flakiness and the ability to get up to play the best players. Rostagno was way up on this day. The weather was brutally hot and humid, the kind of day when Becker, with his fair complexion, suffers greatly. Rostagno won the first two sets.

As Becker walked to the chair after losing the second set, he decided he was never returning to the U.S. Open again. "I just decided this was it. I was going to lose and get out and never come back. I never wanted to hear another of those bloody airplanes flying overhead, I never wanted to deal with the heat or the crowds or any of it. I was through. And then, as I sat there, I looked around again and remembered that this was a Grand Slam. This was what I played tennis for. If I couldn't make myself at least try in a Grand Slam, what kind of player did that make me? I decided to go back out and try to win one set. Just win one set and see what happened. If I lose, I lose, but at least I'd lose trying as hard as I can."

In ninety seconds Becker talked himself back into the Open—although not without some help from above. He won the third set, then he and Rostagno played a superb fourth set, going to a tiebreak. Rostagno led 6–4—two match points. Becker saved one with a serve. Serving at 6–5 to win, Rostagno came in behind a deep approach shot. Becker ran it down and hit a forehand crosscourt. Rostagno read it perfectly and sat at the net, racquet poised ready to make the easy volley that would give him the victory. But an instant before Rostagno could hit that volley, the ball clipped the net cord. It skidded up and over Rostagno's poised racquet.

Both players still remember that shot clearly. "I am a believer in destiny," Becker said. "When I saw that shot, I honestly believed I was destined to win the match and, for that matter, maybe the tournament."

"It was the shot of my life," Rostagno said. "To beat the Wimbledon champion in my home country, to have a chance to really make a dent in the tournament was something that may not happen for me again. Or it might. But who knows? I still see that ball hitting the net cord in my dreams. Every day."

Becker went on to win the tiebreak and the fifth set easily. From that point on he played brilliant tennis, culminating in the final with an ace and a clean winner that a nervous Lendl barely touched, giving Becker another Grand Slam title and a rush of pure joy he had never felt before. But the joy didn't last. After a celebration dinner that night, Becker woke up the next day with a serious case of Peggy Lee Syndrome—Is That All There Is? He had worked so hard and so long for this, and what was his reward? The money, by now, could just as easily have been Monopoly money. It meant nothing. The satisfaction of winning didn't seem to last. He already had an exhibition to play in Stuttgart the next week. Then he had a tournament. Then another exhibition. The treadmill seemed endless. Maybe, Becker thought, it was time to get off. That night he sat up until dawn, writing in the journal he had started at the end of 1987. Whenever he felt frustrated or confused, Becker wrote. It helped him deal with his emotions and his ideas more clearly. It also became a companion for him when he was unhappy. "The better I feel, the less I write," he said. "That night I wrote for five hours."

In the next few weeks, Becker wrote a good deal more. Finally he told Brett and Tiriac and his parents what he was thinking and writing about: retirement. Tiriac and his father were stunned, frustrated, confused. Brett and Becker's mother understood.

"If a player, any player, feels he doesn't want to play, there is nothing a coach can do," Brett said. "If I had said to him, 'You must play' or 'You can't quit,' that probably would have given him another reason to walk away. That's just the way he is. Decisions have to be *his* for him to want to make them work. I believed he was just beginning to scratch the surface of his potential, but if he didn't respect the game enough to want to work at it, there wasn't any point in his continuing to do it."

Becker's mother felt the same way. Becker says he is more like his mother than his father, that his independence and his stubbornness come from her. His father is a "typical German," Becker says with a smile. "He likes to go along with what everyone else is doing."

Tiriac, who had known Becker since he was fifteen, knew that Brett's logic was exactly right. If you told Becker that only a fool could quit tennis at twenty-two as the No. 1 player in the world, Becker would almost certainly quit.

"Boris is the kid who, if you tell him not to put his hand in the fire because it's hot, he'll stick his hand right in the fire," Tiriac once said.

"And if you say to him, 'You see, I told you so,' after he burns the hand, he'll stick it right back in. Maybe—*maybe*—after he has lost two or three fingers he will look at you and say, 'You know, that fire is very hot.' "

Instincts aside, Tiriac felt he had to tell Becker how he felt. Like Becker, Tiriac was a very rich man, an entrepreneur who had his hand in many, many ventures. Although Becker was certainly the best player he had ever managed or coached, and Becker was clearly a redheaded money machine, Tiriac's affection for him was quite genuine.

Becker returns that affection. Even when rumors crop up in the tennis world that Becker and Tiriac are fighting, other agents rarely even think to make a move on Becker. They know his relationship with Tiriac goes beyond that of the normal player and his agent.

When he disagrees with Becker, Tiriac tells him what he thinks. Most agents see their big-name clients as indispensable meal tickets. They are afraid to ever speak up, no matter how wrong their client may be. Would Bill Shelton—Dr. No—think for even a second of telling Andre Agassi that not playing Wimbledon is ludicrous? No, no, a thousand times no. Becker has made Tiriac a lot of money, but his retirement from tennis certainly wouldn't send Tiriac to the poorhouse. Tiriac's distress at Becker's plans had less to do with his bank account than with his personal feelings for Becker and what he could become.

"First of all, the very fact that he would *think* of retiring is not good," Tiriac said. "I said to him, 'You are what you are. You are twenty-two years old and a great tennis player. Because of your talent, you have responsibilities. There are things you can do beyond tennis because you play tennis. That is one thing to think about. The other thing is this: What can be more satisfying in the world than to find out how good you can be? You win Wimbledon three times, you win one U.S. Open. But who gives a shit about that when you can do so much more?' "

As often happens when Tiriac and Becker talk, Becker came away convinced that Tiriac simply didn't understand him. But, as happens just as often, Tiriac's words stuck in the back of Becker's brain. As he went through the fall trying to decide what to do, he decided at one point that he would play the Davis Cup final against Sweden, in December, and then retire.

"No one will believe how close I was to doing that," he said months later. "I was *this* close [he held two fingers an inch apart] to it. I thought to win the Davis Cup at home and then walk away was the right way. It would be a clean break. I wouldn't be letting anyone down or not fulfilling any commitments.

"But the more I thought about it, the less clear I was on it. What did I want to do? Someday I would like to work with kids in tennis. Maybe be the captain of the German Davis Cup team. But not now, not when I'm so young. Maybe work in films, do production work. I'm not sure though, really. I'm still only twenty-two. I didn't go to university, so I'm not sure where all my interests may lie.

"What I finally realized was that I needed time. I wasn't ready to make those decisions. I decided to give myself six more months and see how I felt about playing during that time, see if there was something else I really wanted to do or see if I just really hated being out there."

That was not exactly the ideal attitude to begin a new year with. Becker played superbly in the Davis Cup final, easily beating both Stefan Edberg and Mats Wilander to lead the Germans to a second straight title. Then he took ten days off to go skiing—and found no snow in Switzerland—before he and Brett left for Australia on New Year's Day, 1990. Like Becker, Brett had decidedly mixed emotions about the trip. He was excited, as always, to be going home. He was hoping that the atmosphere of a Grand Slam tournament would inspire his player. But deep down he knew Becker was still exhausted—mentally and physically—from the previous year.

"This is all too soon," he said, finishing breakfast one morning in Sydney, waiting to see what would happen when Becker stepped back on a tennis court. "He hasn't had a break, a real rest. He's sitting in his room right now, frustrated because he doesn't know what he's doing here."

Brett shook his head. "With that attitude," he said, "we won't be here for very long."

3

DOWN UNDER

The tournament that brought Becker to Sydney was the Holden New South Wales Open, one of two tour stops in the world—other than the Grand Slams—where men and women shared a tournament site simultaneously.

Like most of the Australian circuit, the New South Wales tournament had undergone many changes over the years, including the addition of a title sponsor—the Holden Car Company. The title sponsor is now as much a part of tennis as is the net. Every tournament in the world, with the exceptions of Wimbledon, the U.S. Open, and the French Open, has a title sponsor. The Australian Open was forced to bring in a title sponsor in the 1970s. First Marlboro and then Ford had placed their names in front of the words *Australian Open,* much to the dismay of tennis traditionalists. It was okay for the weekly tournaments to have names like Holden New South Wales Open or Virginia Slims of Everywhere or the Lipton Championships. But for a Grand Slam to give up its name was quite another thing.

"Every time I look up and see *Ford Australian Open,* it kills me," said Philippe Chatrier, the president of the ITF and the French Tennis Federation. "We had to go to a title sponsor for two years [1971 and 1972] when our tournament was struggling, and I hated every minute of it. As soon as we were strong enough, we got rid of it. I hope the Australians will be able to do that when this contract is up."

Whether the Australians would be willing to do so and give up the considerable amount of money—about $2 million a year—Ford paid for the right to plaster its name on everything that did or did not move was another question. "Could happen," said Brian Tobin, the outgoing president of Tennis Australia. "We'll have to wait and see."

New South Wales was the second stop on the Down Under circuit for both the men and the women. The women had opened their year in Brisbane (the title sponsor was Dannon Yogurt), while the men had opened with tournaments in Adelaide and Wellington, New Zealand (BP

Oil). The men also had a tournament in New Zealand this second week—in Auckland (Benson & Hedges). Putting the men and women together is a recent change, having come about when the Australian Open was moved from the end of the year to the beginning in 1987.

The Sydney tournament—one of the oldest and most traditional in the world—is played at White City Tennis Club, one of the most venerable tennis grounds in Australia, a place that has hosted innumerable Davis Cup ties over the years and was once one of several rotating sites of the Australian Open. White City is a mix of the old and the new in tennis, a mix immediately apparent when one walks onto center court and finds two courts there: one grass and one Rebound Ace. (Rebound Ace is the synthetic hard-court surface on which the Australian Open is played; all the clubs that host Australian summer-circuit tournaments have put Rebound Ace down on their courts, replacing the traditional grass.)

The grass/Rebound Ace stadium is not the only anomaly at White City. The musty old hallways of the clubhouse are filled with plaques that list tournament champions and club champions dating to the nineteenth century. Out back, grass courts still abound with junior players. From the stadium, one can see soaring trees and the rooftops of Sydney peeking over the grandstand. The scoreboards on court are hand-operated by ball boys and girls, and when players on courts 1, 3, and 5 walk to or from their courts, they must cross courts 2, 4, or 6—and must often wait until a changeover, rather than interrupt an ongoing match. Most of the line judges are teenagers, part of a long-standing White City tradition of training future line judges and umpires on the job. Richard Ings, one of the top umpires in the world, got his start at White City.

But if you walk out and sit on the players' balcony, the twentieth century crashes in on you. Across the street from the six resurfaced outside courts that are used for the tournament, sit the Oakford Luxury Service Apartments. These buildings would be considered the ultimate eyesore were it not for the Chevrolet service-and-parts building down the street. That building makes the Oakford look like the Sydney Opera House. The doors in and out of the clubhouse are electronically operated, and from the Garden Enclosure, the fifteen-hundred-seat auxiliary court, one can see the subway rattling past beyond the trees.

The players notice very little of this. Few of them take note of aesthetics anywhere in the world unless they create some kind of inconvenience for them. To players, the key elements of a tournament are amenities, not aesthetics. How efficient is transportation to and from the airport and the hotels? How large is the players' lounge, and is the food good there? Are there enough practice courts and practice balls? How nice are the player gifts?

In 1989, the most popular tournament on the men's tour, as voted by the players, was not played in Paris, Rome, Monte Carlo, or Sydney. It was played in Indianapolis. Why? The player gifts are the most generous in the world—Gucci bags, Rolex watches; the players' lounge is the size of a football field, and the tournament conducts competitions throughout the week in Ping-Pong, golf, darts and pop-a-shot for prizes such as Jet Skis, golf clubs and bags.

The men's field in Sydney was remarkable considering there was a Grand Slam beginning the next week. Both Becker and Ivan Lendl were playing; in all, eight of the top twenty players in the world were there. The prize money for the tournament is only $150,000—*total.* So the question must be asked: Why was the field so strong?

The answer is easy: the new ATP Tour.

In putting together the tour, Hamilton Jordan and company made two major changes, designed to get the top players to play more often. First, they changed the ranking system to what is known as Best of 14.

Under Best of 14, a player may play as many tournaments as he wishes, and *only* his best fourteen results count in the rankings. Under the old system, a player's ranking was based on his average results—if you played twenty tournaments, the points you received were added up and divided by twenty. Now if you play twenty tournaments, you take your best fourteen results and add *them* up. No averaging.

It is a little bit like telling Major League baseball players that only their best 120 games will be counted for their batting averages. All those nasty oh-for-fours just drop right out, as if they never happened.

The other step taken to get players to play more often is even more appealing: the legalization of guarantees at fifty-four of the seventy-eight stops on the tour. A guarantee is an appearance fee. If a tournament wants a big-name player, more often than not it will have to pay him to appear. By the nineties, guarantees in the Far East were running as high as $300,000 for players such as Lendl, Edberg, Becker, Agassi, and McEnroe. Everywhere else in the world, top players were commanding six figures—just to show up.

Every one of those guarantees was a violation of Men's Tennis Council rules. But no one cared. Name players mean successful tournaments. Successful tournaments mean television contracts. It was Ted Tinling's *Ring* theory at its most obvious.

The public has no understanding of this. When told that Ivan Lendl wins a first prize of $70,000, it's assumed that Lendl has made that much for the week. In reality, Lendl probably has received somewhere between $100,000 and $300,000—*before he even stepped on court to play his first match.*

When he was running the MTC, Marshall Happer occasionally tried to stop guarantees. Happer even went so far as to suspend Guillermo Vilas for one year when he was caught dead to rights accepting a $60,000 guarantee for playing in Rotterdam in 1983. But when Vilas appealed the suspension, a hearing board threw out Happer's suspension. Instead, Vilas was fined $20,000.

"He got sixty thousand dollars for taking the guarantee and they fined him twenty thousand dollars after finding him guilty," Happer said. "Where is the deterrent in that?"

There was very little deterrent. After Vilas got caught, all that happened was that players and tournament directors became a little less blatant. Players were paid to do a clinic or to attend a cocktail party or for holding a pretournament press conference. In many cases transactions were still just payoffs. In 1989, rather than take cash from the tournament in Bordeaux, Lendl asked for several cases of French wine to stock the wine cellar he was building. "*Pas de problème, Monsieur Lendl,*" the tournament replied, only too glad to comply.

The guarantee situation had gotten so outrageous by 1989 that some players were demanding—successfully—that they receive part of their guarantee even if they pulled out of a tournament at the last minute. Their logic for this was that the tournament had sold tickets—and made money—by using their names in advertising. During 1990 the ultimate guarantee would take place: Alberto Mancini, whose ranking had dropped from No. 9 to No. 81, would be paid by the tournament in Stuttgart for agreeing *not* to play, since he was no longer a gate attraction.

Jordan had arrived on the scene swearing to clean up this messy situation. But he was quickly informed by the players that if he wanted their support for his coup, he'd better not try to wipe out guarantees. Thus, Jordan came up with a "compromise." Tournaments on the new tour would be divided into two categories: Championship Series and World Series. The twenty Championship Series tournaments would have prize money ranging from $420,000 to $2 million, most of it falling into the $1 million range. No guarantees were allowed. The fifty-four World Series tournaments would be, in most cases, for much smaller prize money—but would be allowed to pay guarantees.

o

Initially, Jordan and company decreed that players designated as Top Ten—which could include name players who were not actually ranked in the Top Ten at the time—would be allowed to play in a limited number of World Series tournaments. Becker and Lendl put a crimp in that idea when they announced plans to begin play in 1990 in Adelaide and Sydney, respectively. Neither tournament was about to tell Becker or Lendl *not* to come, so the ATP Tour was forced to make one of many rules "adjustments" it would make during the year.

Under the adjusted rule, the Top Ten *could* play as many World Series events as they wanted, and accept guarantees, but they were required to play at least eleven Championship Series events or be fined 10 percent of their prize money at the end of the year. In the case of the top money winners, this could be a substantial figure. But, in the case of those same top-money winners, almost *no* figure was really substantial enough to stop them from doing what they wanted to do.

The combination of Best of 14 and legal guarantees *did* improve the quality of the fields. In 1989, the lowest-ranked player among those who submitted entries to get into the Sydney field without having to qualify was No. 93. In 1990, the cutoff came at No. 63. Lendl, Aaron Krickstein, Tim Mayotte, Mats Wilander, and Yannick Noah all received legal guarantees for playing—ranging from about $10,000 to about $50,000—and everyone was happy.

Becker would have received a guarantee in Adelaide but had given it up when he withdrew the week beforehand. He came to Sydney without a guarantee because he felt he needed to play somewhere in Australia and get used to the heat before the Australian Open began.

The only ones left out in the cold were the fans, who knew nothing about the new ranking system or the legalized guarantees. The top players certainly didn't come to Sydney for the prize money, and none of them had to worry about their ranking if they had a bad tournament—they could always drop the results from their rankings just by playing in more than fourteen tournaments. The only incentive left them was pride. In most cases, that was enough. But what about the day when a top player woke up feeling a little sore? Or if he had a minor injury and didn't really want to go all out? Or if he had just been on the road a long time and felt like going home for a rest? What was there to deter him from either defaulting, retiring during the match, or not giving his best effort? By the end of the week in Sydney, these questions would come up for the first time in 1990—but certainly not for the last.

HARD COURTS

O

. . .

The weather in Sydney was less than ideal the first three days of the tournament. While the players dreaded the tropical heat that was so often a part of playing in Australia, they were not at all thrilled when that heat was replaced by cool, on-and-off rain showers. The rain was playing havoc with the schedule—and no one wanted to play two matches a day the week before a Grand Slam.

The women—with a fifty-six-player draw—managed to get nineteen of twenty-four first-round matches in on Monday before the rain began. The men—with a thirty-two-player draw—finished only three of sixteen.

Two players not the least bit disappointed to see the rain on Monday and Tuesday were Pete Sampras and David Wheaton. Thanks to the new tighter cutoffs, Sampras and Wheaton had both been forced to play in the qualifying tournament—thirty-two players competing for four spots in the main draw.

Most players hate qualifying. The pressure is brutal; you must win three matches just to get into the tournament. Once you have won those three matches, the odds are you'll draw a seeded player in the first round, and boom!—a few hours after you've survived qualifying, you're out of the tournament.

Wheaton and Sampras didn't really mind playing qualifying—or "qualies," as the players call it—because neither had played a tournament match since November. Both were eager to find out how the conditioning work they had done in December was going to pay off back on the court.

While Chang had been winning the French Open the previous year and Agassi had been making millions, Wheaton, Sampras, and Jim Courier had been quietly sneaking their way up the tennis ladder. By the end of 1989, Courier had made the most noise, beating his longtime rival Agassi at the French, then winning the Swiss Indoor Tournament with a victory over Edberg.

That tournament had vaulted him to No. 24 in the rankings and, at nineteen, began to make him a marketable commercial entity. He was skipping Sydney to plan an exhibition—the "Rio Challenge" (Rio being an underwear company)—that included Edberg, McEnroe, Henri Leconte, Australian Darren Cahill, and Thomas Muster. He'd been paid up front for playing, a sure sign he was arriving as a tennis player.

Like Agassi and Chang, Courier, who would not turn twenty until August, was a baseliner, a blond bull on the court who hit his forehand as hard as almost anyone in the game. But he was still a one-note player. With his huge forehand, he was the equivalent of a young pitcher with a great fastball who hadn't yet learned how to throw a curve or a slider. His serve was decent but inconsistent at the big moments, and he rarely volleyed.

Sampras and Wheaton were both serve-and-volleyers. Tennis history indicates that baseliners mature faster than attacking players—one reason why women become stars so young—and since Wheaton would not be twenty-one until June and Sampras would not be nineteen until August, they were just beginning to tap their potential.

Wheaton had been a phenom growing up in Minnesota. He was the baby in a family of four, but was the star of the family. By the time he was eight, he was winning 12-and-under tournaments in Minnesota; by fifteen, he had run out of people to compete with at home. It was then that he and his parents made the difficult decision to send David down to Bollettieri's.

"I was stagnating as a player because there just wasn't anyone for me to really play with, especially in the wintertime," Wheaton said. "But my parents were very concerned about the way the kids lived down at Bollettieri's. They didn't want me in one of those bunk rooms with eight people or whatever; they just didn't think that was a good atmosphere."

Bollettieri, who knows talent when he sees it, didn't want to lose Wheaton over housing assignments. He agreed to let Wheaton stay in an extra room in the condo Aaron Krickstein was living in. At the time, Krickstein was seventeen, ranked in the world Top Ten, and still a Bollettieri pupil.

"The first two weeks I was there," Wheaton said, "Aaron never said a word to me. I really thought he didn't like me being there or just plain didn't like me. It wasn't until later that I found out he didn't talk to *anyone.*"

Krickstein, who is quiet today, was almost catatonic at seventeen, a shy teenager forced into the spotlight because he could crush a forehand. He and Wheaton eventually got along just fine, but Wheaton found that the long silences in the condo made him rather lonely. His parents solved the problem by renting out their house in Minnesota and moving to Bradenton.

Once his parents moved down, Wheaton was quite happy at Bollettieri's. He became friendly with both Courier and Agassi, even though those two barely spoke to each other. He also grew steadily, eventually reaching six feet four. If he had grown up at Bollettieri's, Wheaton might never have developed his huge serve. Since he was there only two years, he came away with solid ground strokes to go with his own attacking game.

When a talented tennis player graduates from high school, especially one who has made the commitment of going to a tennis academy, the temptation to turn pro can be overwhelming. In the spring of 1987, Wheaton had already seen Agassi turn pro, win some matches, and sign several lucrative contracts. Courier, a year younger, wasn't sure what he wanted to do. Neither was Wheaton.

"Part of me felt like I was ready to be a pro," he said. "I wanted to go out and see how I would do. But I had a chance to go to Stanford. My family is very education-oriented, and the thought of not going to college at all kind of went against my background. I decided to go to Stanford and just see how things went."

Before he could get to Stanford, though, Wheaton played the summer circuit in the U.S. in 1987. In Washington, he won a match and found himself playing Ivan Lendl. It was one of those awful Washington summer days, the humidity suffocating, the conditions miserable. All Wheaton knew was he had a chance to play the No. 1 player in the world. He came out blazing, firing serves past Lendl, and before anyone could say "shocking upset," he was up a set and a service break.

Lendl came back, figuring out Wheaton's serve, while Wheaton, realizing he could win, tensed up. Lendl finally won it in three sets, then collapsed in the locker room, overcome by heat exhaustion. Later, he told Wheaton that if the match had lasted one more game he would have had to default; he was starting to see spots in front of his eyes.

If Wheaton had won that match he probably would never have made it to Stanford. The three major management groups that dominate the game—IMG (International Management Group), ProServ, and Advantage International—would have been shoving potential deals at him in waves. Already, all three had expressed great interest in him.

The Lendl match stayed with Wheaton during that fall at Stanford. If he was good enough to have the No. 1 player in the world in deep trouble, why wasn't he on the tour? Wheaton brooded about that for weeks. Then he began to look around and realized he was brooding his way through what should be a great time in his life. By the end of the semester, he was in love with college life.

"It was the best year of my life," he said. "Part of me wishes I had stayed four years. But as good a time as I had, I felt like I was losing time as a tennis player. I knew by the end of my freshman year that it was time to go."

By this time, the management groups were after him hot and heavy. The recruiting that agents do in tennis is not that different from what college basketball coaches do. Players are wined, dined, and flattered. The difference is that the riches agents can offer are far more immediate than any offered by a basketball coach.

When Wheaton turned pro he signed with IMG. He also signed a long-term contract with FILA, guaranteeing him $60,000 a year to wear their clothes and shoes, and a racquet contract with Head worth about $40,000 annually. Shortly after he signed with IMG, his brother John went to work for the company, setting up an office in Minneapolis. His main job, though, was to represent David Wheaton.

This is hardly uncommon in tennis. Tracy Austin, Chris Evert, and Tim Mayotte all have brothers who work for the management company that represents them. Many other players employ relatives as coaches, advisers, and racquet carriers. Often, part of their deal with the management company includes having the relative's salary paid by the company.

Wheaton turned pro on July 4, 1988, and promptly forgot how to play tennis. The summer was a total loss. "I wanted everything to happen too fast," he said. "I would space out in matches and lose to guys I never should have lost to. By the end of the summer my ranking was down to eight hundred forty-four and I was just about ready to quit. I was totally frustrated."

That fall Wheaton decided to play on the Hawaiian satellite circuit. Satellites are the lowest minor league of pro tennis. They are run around the world, each lasting four weeks—three week-long tournaments, and then a "Masters" for the players who have the best record during the first three weeks. They are the starting point for young players looking to acquire the computer points needed to get into bigger tournaments. They are also the last stop for older players trying to hang on. Almost everyone who has played the game has a story about the satellite that launched him or the one that left him so depressed he seriously thought about going home for good.

Wheaton went to Hawaii mostly because he had always enjoyed himself there. He spent the month surfing and having a good time. He forgot about all the pressure he had been inflicting on himself, and played well enough to finish third on the satellite. That performance got him back in the top five hundred and turned him around in terms of confidence.

By the next summer, Wheaton was starting to serve players off the court. At Stratton Mountain, the tournament that had launched Agassi, he upset Agassi in the third round (it was his victory over Agassi that prompted Agassi to order Bollettieri to fire his religious guru), then beat his friend Courier in the quarterfinals. In the semifinals, Wheaton served for the match against Brad Gilbert but couldn't finish him, once again letting his mind get ahead of his body.

Still, he was quite happy when he finished the year ranked sixty-sixth in the world—a jump of 375 places from the end of 1988. But he knew he had to get himself into better physical shape if he wanted to take the next step up in 1990.

During most of 1989, Mark Wheaton, a doctor, had taken time off from his residency to travel with his little brother. The family decided that in 1990, brother John would travel with David, coaching him and managing him at the same time. To David, this was an ideal setup. He enjoyed the company of both his brothers. The Wheatons are a close-knit, religious family. They don't talk about their religion very much, although John and David, if you press them, will tell you that they sometimes read the Bible together on the road.

"I just think that's something that should be private," David said. "If Michael [Chang] and Andre [Agassi] want to tell everyone about it, that's their business, but I'm not that way. To tell the truth, when Michael talks about having a better personal relationship with Jesus than another player, I just can't understand that. If I play Michael and we're both Christians, does God sit up there and choose between us? I don't think so."

Wheaton is as open and as honest as any player on the tour. In the "personal" section of Wheaton's biography in the 1990 ATP Tour player guide, John McEnroe is described as Wheaton's "idol." When Wheaton was asked about that in Australia, he shook his head emphatically.

"I admired the way McEnroe played when I was a kid, and I still do," he said. "But idolize him? No way. If I idolized him, I'd go around acting like him, and if I did that my parents wouldn't ever let me out of the house."

Wheaton was a long way from his parents' house at the tournament in Sydney. He swept through three qualifying matches in two days, then saw that he had been placed in the main draw opposite Andres Gomez—

the No. 6 seed. That was fine with him. "The guy hasn't played a match in two months," he said. "I've played three matches. I'm match tough. He's not. I should have the advantage."

Pete Sampras had also drawn a seed after winning his three matches in qualifying and, like Wheaton, felt pretty good about it. The seed was No. 4 Tim Mayotte. Sampras's first important victory as a pro had been in Detroit, in November 1988. The victim had been Tim Mayotte. Since then, they had played in a big-money exhibition in Japan the previous summer, and Sampras had won again.

In less than two years as a pro, Sampras had proved that he could beat good players. The previous September, at the U.S. Open, he had upset Wilander—the defending champion—in the second round and had reached the round of 16. But instead of building on that victory, Sampras had gone through a horrendous fall, losing in the first round of three tournaments and in the qualies of the Paris Indoor Tournament.

He was frustrated by those losses, but not discouraged. That just wasn't in his nature.

Sampras is the son of Soterios and Georgia Sampras. His father, who works for NASA as a mechanical engineer, was born in Chicago. His mother emigrated from Greece as a young adult. Neither played tennis. Pete, the third of their four children, had been born in Potomac, Maryland, and first displayed his tennis skills by hitting balls in the family's laundromat with a little racquet he had found.

When the family moved to Los Angeles in 1977, Pete, then seven, and his sister Stella, who was nine, were sent to the Jack Kramer Club. Two years later, they began taking lessons from Robert Landsdorp, whose most famous pupil had been Tracy Austin. At ten, Pete played in his first tournament and lost his first match, 6–0, 6–0. "I cried and cried and said I never wanted to play again," he remembered.

He did play again, though, and the results got better. At thirteen, Sampras left Lansdorp and began working with Dr. Pete Fischer, a family friend, who made his living as a pediatrician. Fischer thought that Rod Laver was the greatest player of all time and, even though Sampras was right-handed, tried to model his game and his demeanor after Laver's. When Pete was fifteen, after he had played horribly in the prestigious Orange Bowl Tournament, Fischer convinced him that it was time to switch to a one-handed backhand. For six months, Sampras was miserable.

"I couldn't hit a ball, or at least it felt that way," he said. "But Pete Fischer knew what he was doing. He told me this was a move that might make it tougher in the present but would pay off in the future. He showed me films he had of Laver. I stopped being whiny on the court and started to play more aggressively. By 1987, I was a different player—and a much better one."

He was good enough to beat Michael Chang at the U.S. Open juniors that year. Chang had won the 18-and-under championship that August, in Kalamazoo, Michigan (beating Courier in the final), and had received a wild card into the main draw at the U.S. Open. When Chang, who was only fifteen, beat Australian veteran Paul McNamee in the first round of the tournament, then carried another solid player, Nduka Odizor, to five sets in the second round, he became the rage of the Open. Agents lined up twenty-four hours a day to talk to his family. Shoe, clothing, and racquet companies lined up right behind them, each panting a little harder than the other.

After he lost to Odizor, Chang played in the junior tournament the following week. On the day of his match with Sampras, Bud Collins, the man who invented tennis on television in the U.S., sought out his closest friend, Gianni Clerici, an Italian journalist.

"Gianni," Collins said, "you must go to court sixteen this afternoon and see the future of American tennis. This kid is sensational."

Clerici, who prides himself on spotting young talent, made his way to the far corner of the grounds at the U.S. Tennis Center that afternoon, to court 16. He knew immediately that Collins was right. "I looked out on the court," he said, "and I saw Manuel Santana. He was so graceful, his strokes flowed, *he* flowed. I saw a Wimbledon champion."

Clerici was so excited that he ran back to the press box and called his friend Sergio Tacchini, president of the Italian clothing company that bears his name. Before Clerici had left for the Open, Tacchini had asked him to keep an eye out for any young players who looked as if they had talent. Tacchini was looking for a future star to invest in. Clerici called Tacchini and said, "I've found your young star."

He quickly filled Tacchini in on what he had seen. "Santana," he told Tacchini, remembering the elegant Spaniard who had won Wimbledon, the U.S. Open, and the French Open in the 1960s. "He is Santana."

Several months later, based largely on Clerici's recommendation, Tacchini won a bidding war for Pete Sampras and signed him to a three-year deal worth close to $500,000.

That night, when Clerici saw Collins, he hugged him and gushed, "Collini, I love you for sending me to see this kid play today. I have already told Tacchini about him. I told him this kid is another Santana!"

Collins was delighted that Clerici agreed that this was the next great

American player, but a bit baffled by his description. "I'm glad you like him," he said, "but he's really not Santana."

"What do you mean not Santana!" Clerici roared. "He is tall and dark and elegant. The strokes are so smooth . . ."

"Tall and dark, what do you mean?" Collins said. "He's short and Chinese!"

Clerici stopped. "Chinese? What do you mean Chinese? Sampras can't be Chinese! The little kid he was beating up on was Chinese."

Clerici and Collins looked at each other.

"You sent me to see the little Chinese kid?"

Collins nodded. Both men laughed. "I didn't even notice the other kid!" Clerici said. "I had eyes only for Sampras."

Twenty months later, the little Chinese kid, wearing Reebok clothing, won the French Open. Sampras wasn't ranked in the top one hundred. But he did look terrific in his Tacchini clothes.

Although Clerici might have thought then that he had fallen in love with the wrong player, there was still plenty of hope for Sampras. In a sense, his game was still only two years old; that was how long he had been playing the one-handed backhand.

Sampras turned pro early in 1988. The Tacchini contract gave him financial security, so he dropped out of school at the end of his junior year. By the end of the year, buoyed by the victory over Mayotte in Detroit, he had signed with IMG and cracked the top hundred—at No. 97.

Because of the easy fluidity of his strokes, Sampras tends to look effortless on the court. Some observers, watching him on a bad day, tended to mistake that effortlessness for lack of effort. They wondered if he had the mental toughness to live up to his obvious physical potential. And, because of the success of Agassi and Chang, many forgot the old rule about baseliners growing up faster.

Sampras worked that year on and off with coaches provided by the USTA, which employs several coaches to work with young players who show potential. Often as not, though, Sampras spent his time on the road with Courier, who had started working full-time that year with Sergio Cruz, a coach who had worked at Bollettieri's.

Late that fall, during a rare trip to a tournament, Soterios Sampras asked Cruz if he could recommend a coach for his son. Cruz mentioned Joe Brandi, who was then also working at Bollettieri's. He and Courier suggested that Sampras come to Florida during the December break in the tennis schedule and work out with them and with Brandi.

Sampras liked the idea. He flew to Florida in early December and shared a condo with Courier. Every morning the two players and the two coaches were up by 6:45, working in the Florida heat. For Sampras this was not easy. "Pete is always on California time, no matter where he is in the world," Courier said, laughing. "Getting him out of bed before noon is a very big deal."

Sampras did it, though. He liked Brandi, a short, funny-off-the-court but dead-serious-on-the-court man. Brandi had seen it all in tennis; Sampras had seen almost nothing. They were the perfect Odd Couple. By the time he left Florida for Australia, Sampras knew two things: He was in the best shape of his life, and he wanted Brandi as his full-time traveling coach. He flew to Australia with his older brother Gus, while his agent at IMG, Gavin Forbes, went to work on hiring Brandi away from Bollettieri's.

On the third day of the tournament in Sydney, the rain finally stopped and Sampras and Mayotte were assigned to court 4, which sits right under the PA system used to make court announcements. Between the constant noise from the PA—"Aaron Krickstein and Paul Annacone, please report to the Garden Enclosure; Aaron Krickstein and Paul Annacone, the Garden Enclosure please"—and a defective umpire's microphone that kept crackling in the whipping wind, both players found themselves distracted. Mayotte lost serve and asked if there weren't some way to turn the PA down. Sampras lost serve and said to the umpire, "Why don't you just turn that stupid microphone off?"

It was that kind of uptight first set. They went to a tiebreak at 6–6, and Sampras promptly jumped ahead 5–0, aided by a Mayotte double fault. As good a player as Mayotte has been, spending the better part of the last five years ranked in the Top Ten, he has always had a tendency to double-fault under pressure. Other players know this and will move around on big points to try to distract him.

Two points from losing the set, Mayotte suddenly righted himself and hit six straight winners. When he blasted a backhand return past Sampras, he shook his fist and yelled, "Yeah!" Down 5–6, facing set point, Sampras twisted in a service winner. He slammed down the ball he was holding and yelled, "Come on, now, come on!"

Suddenly, on an outside court in the first round of a warm-up tournament, with perhaps one hundred spectators in the bleachers, Sampras and Mayotte found themselves in a match that meant much more than just a spot in the second round of the Holden New South Wales Open. At twenty-nine, still ranked twelfth in the world, Mayotte could look across the net into Sampras's face and see thirty and beyond. He didn't want to lose to Sampras again, didn't want to give Sampras another push up the ladder. "Not yet, kid," he was trying to say. "Not yet." Eleven years younger, Sampras's answer was "Why not yet? I'm ready. I've worked hard. Get out of my way."

And so there they were, two of the calmer players on the tour, stoking and yelling in the first set of a first-round match. Youth would prevail on this day. Sampras hit another good serve to go up 7–6. Facing set point Mayotte double-faulted . . . again. That was all Sampras really needed. Mayotte double-faulted twice more in the first game of the second set, and Sampras raced through it, winning the match 7–6, 6–2. He walked off the court with a satisfied smile on his face, feeling fairly certain that this would be the last tournament for which he would have to qualify.

Later that day, the sun actually put in an appearance and the players got their first taste of the Australian heat. David Wheaton didn't mind a bit. He could see, as he and Andres Gomez walked out to the Garden Enclosure for their first-round match, that Gomez was overweight. Gomez, who was six weeks shy of thirty, was playing in Australia for the first time in his career. He had always skipped Australia because it meant leaving home during the holidays. This year, though, he had decided to come down and play his way into shape instead of waiting until spring.

That was fine with Wheaton, who drilled Gomez in straight sets, then beat another good player, Guy Forget, the next day to reach the quarterfinals. Sampras also made it to the quarterfinals. Both young Americans exited there, though, Wheaton losing to the steadiness of Aaron Krickstein, while Sampras lost to his old friend Wilander in an extraordinarily frustrating match. "I had him, I had him, I had him," Sampras said. "And then I let him get away."

Sampras won the first set and had no fewer than twelve break points in the second set. He failed to convert any of them, and Wilander pulled out the set and the match. It was an experience Sampras wouldn't forget. "He served-and-volleyed on every break point. I didn't react, didn't change what I was doing. That was his experience beating me."

Sampras walked into the locker room, looked at his brother, and said, "Screw it. This is just Sydney. I came down here for the Australian Open. Let's go to Melbourne."

Nothing wrong with that attitude or that plan. The departure of

Sampras to Melbourne that Friday afternoon was no big deal to anyone. What was a big deal, though, were the departures that same day of Ivan Lendl and Boris Becker. Becker went down first, losing to his friend and countryman Carl Uwe-Steeb in straight sets. Lendl followed him on to the court and won exactly five games against Yannick Noah.

In the locker room, everybody giggled as Noah made beating Lendl look so easy. The consensus was simple: No way was Lendl letting Becker fly off to Melbourne without him. The Australian Open started in two days, and Lendl had seen enough of Sydney.

Had Lendl and Becker tanked? No, not really. But were they fired up for the match, intense, diving for balls, doing everything they could to win? Not likely. This was an example of the dangers of Best of 14 and legal guarantees. Becker and Lendl had almost nothing to lose by losing. They certainly didn't need the money, and they didn't need the extra computer points they would have gotten for winning the tournament. They had played three warm-up matches, and now it was time to get to Melbourne. The fans at White City didn't really grasp this. They cheered Steeb and Noah wildly.

"It's always nice to beat the number one player in the world, no matter where or how," Noah said months later. "But you know when Ivan is into it and when he isn't. I think he tried, but we all know there is trying and *trying.*"

Two days later, with Becker and Lendl practicing comfortably in Melbourne, Noah would beat Steeb in a taut three-set final filled with wonderful tennis. Eighteen hours after Noah accepted the trophy, the Australian Open began.

4

THE FLINDERS PARK JINX

Until you have been to Australia during summer, it is almost impossible to comprehend how important tennis is to most Australians.

For the better part of six weeks tennis is ubiquitous. You cannot turn on a television set without finding a live tennis match on the screen. The three major Australian TV networks are identified by numbers, rather than the letter system used in the U.S., and it is Channel 7 that holds the rights to televise the entire Australian circuit.

"Seven's Summer of Tennis" begins in Perth three days after Christmas, with the Hopman Cup, a hokey but very popular exhibition named after the legendary Australian Davis Cup captain Harry Hopman. The Hopman Cup is a team competition. Sixteen countries enter teams consisting of one man and one woman. Each round consists of a men's singles match, a woman's singles match, and a mixed-doubles match. The big-name players receive up-front guarantees to show up. It is a lucrative, relatively laid-back, pre–New Year's way to work your way into shape for the Australian season.

The American team at the Hopman Cup consisted of John McEnroe and Pam Shriver, about as unlikely a combination as you could find. McEnroe has never made any secret of his disdain for the women's game. He thinks it outrageous that the women receive the same prize money as the men at the Australian and U.S. Open and cannot understand how Shriver, who never won a Grand Slam singles title, has become wealthy. Shriver, naturally, believes that women deserve everything they've gotten, having had to work hard to get it. She feels she's put in a lot of time and a lot of work to achieve her financial status.

McEnroe's feelings about Shriver were best summed up by his description of the waffling he went through while trying to decide who to vote for in the 1988 presidential election:

"I was going to vote for Dukakis," he said. "I never liked Reagan, and I agreed with Dukakis on most of the issues. But then when I watched the guy during the campaign, I thought, No way can this guy handle being president. So, I thought I'd vote for Bush. I figured at the least he had some experience, even if I wasn't crazy about him. But then I said, 'Wait a minute! *Pam Shriver* is his biggest supporter.' No way could I vote for him. So I went to Europe that week, played a tournament, and didn't vote."

Shriver could laugh at that story and she could play doubles with McEnroe because she understood, as did most everyone else in tennis, that as sincere as McEnroe was in his opinions, there was almost never genuine meanness attached to what he said. It was personal, but it wasn't *that* personal. So McEnroe and Shriver played together and lost the Hopman Cup final to the Spanish brother and sister team of Emilio and Arantxa Sanchez. Even after the loss, McEnroe was in a good mood and ended up ringing in the New Year singing loudly with Yannick Noah and Mikael Pernfors at the post-tournament party.

New Year's Day brought the start of the 1990 circuit for both the men and the women. That meant seven hours a day and four hours a night of coverage on Seven. Starting at 11 A.M. each day, eleven of the next thirteen hours on Seven were devoted to tennis.

And the Australian people were watching. No country has a greater tennis tradition than Australia. The list of great champions—from Frank Sedgman to Lew Hoad to Ken Rosewall to Rod Laver to Roy Emerson to Fred Stolle to John Newcombe to Tony Roche to Pat Cash—is remarkable for a country with a population of 16 million. Australia has won the Davis Cup twenty-seven times. Only the U.S.—with fifteen times the population—can top that, with twenty-nine.

But when Newcombe and Roche began to wind down their careers in the late 1970s, there was no one waiting to step in, as they had stepped in for Emerson and Stolle, who had, in turn, stepped in for Laver and Rosewall. John Alexander and Phil Dent, the next generation, were talented players but not Grand Slam champions. Australia was a country that *demanded* Grand Slam titles from its players.

At the same time that Australia's top players were beginning to fade, the Australian Open was running into serious problems. Because of the travel involved, the Australian had always been number four on the Grand Slam ladder. But it had been a solid number four. In 1974 Jimmy Connors won his first Grand Slam title there. That same year, Evonne Goolagong beat Chris Evert in the women's final. A year later, the finals were Newcombe over Connors, and Goolagong over Martina Navratilova.

But it was getting tougher and tougher to get the players to make the trip to Australia around the Christmas holidays, which was when the tournament was held. Guarantees were beginning to push player income so high that the top players saw no reason to make the long trip. Bjorn Borg never played the Australian after 1974. Connors hasn't been back since 1975. Evert didn't go for six straight years after her loss to Goolagong, and Navratilova skipped four years after *her* loss to Goolagong.

The tournament deteriorated quickly. Kooyong, the venerable Melbourne tennis club where the tournament was held, was a badly outdated facility. It was overcrowded and the grass was not in good shape. In fact, many players complained that on one side of center court you were actually running uphill to get to the net.

In 1978 Chris O'Neil beat Betsy Nagelsen in the women's final. The next year Barbara Jordan beat Sharon Walsh. None of those four players ever came close to a Grand Slam final again. The men faded more slowly, but by 1980, when the less-than-immortal Brian Teacher beat the equally mortal Kim Warwick in the final, it was apparent that the Australian was in serious trouble.

Philippe Chatrier, the ITF president, was extremely concerned about what he saw in Australia. He had fallen in love with the country on his first trip there as a young sportswriter in 1956. Chatrier knew that the Australian had become a Grand Slam in name only. Brian Tobin, the president of Tennis Australia, knew that, too.

"I honestly thought Australia was in danger of losing Grand Slam status completely in the early eighties," Chatrier said. "The Christmas dates were killing them. The guarantees the players were able to get for exhibitions were killing them too. And I knew that Butch Buchholz wanted to start a two-week tournament in Florida. I was afraid that might end up becoming the fourth Grand Slam, and I didn't think that would be good for tennis."

Chatrier's concern was shared by Tennis Australia. The women had upgraded their half of the tournament in the early eighties by splitting from the men. Chatrier and Tobin together convinced the Men's Tennis Council to move the tournament to the last week in November. That helped a little. Then came the matter of talking the women into going back to the old two-week format.

"The women weren't too keen on that," Tobin said. "By 1980 the top women like Chrissie and Martina were coming here again and they were doing quite well on their own. But we knew to be a true Grand Slam again, we had to be a two-week tournament."

There were still major problems. Not only was Kooyong an awful facility for a major championship, it was costing Tennis Australia $1 million a year to rent. A new facility was desperately needed, but that would cost, according to estimates, $40 million. Tennis Australia just didn't have that kind of money.

Just when it seemed as if the tournament was destined to be second class—or worse—forever, fate and luck intervened. Sitting at his desk one morning, Tobin saw a small story in the paper, which noted that the government of Victoria—the state in which Melbourne is located—was looking for a site to build a new entertainment center. Tobin called John Cain, the premier of Victoria, and asked for a meeting. Perhaps there was some way for the government and Tennis Australia to build a facility together.

Cain was interested but there was an obvious problem: Grand Slam tennis tournaments were played outdoors; most entertainment events were staged indoors. It was Cain who came up with the solution. "Why not build it with a roof that opens?" he suggested.

The rest, as they say, is history.

The site chosen to build the National Tennis Center was Flinders Park. The land was owned by the government and was little used, even though it was only five minutes from the heart of Melbourne. The environmentalists put up a brief, futile fight and ground was broken early in 1986. (The projected cost to build a tennis facility/entertainment center with an opening roof was about $70 million. Before it was done, the cost was more than $100 million. But the government took responsibility for the financing and, even with horrendous inflation pushing the interest payments up by almost $5 million a year, the facility opened and, with luck, will be paid off in twenty-five years.)

During this time, the Australians did two things: They studied the other three Grand Slam facilities to try to figure out how to build the best possible venue for players, fans, sponsors, and the media. "We studied the U.S. Open site in order to see what *not* to do," Tobin said, laughing. They also proposed another date change to the MTC, asking that the tournament be moved to mid-January. That way the MTC could move its season-ending Masters to the end of November, and Australia could be postholiday and come at the start of the year, when players were fresh and eager, rather than at the end, when they were tired, sore, and uninterested.

The MTC approved the calendar change. The last Australian Open at Kooyong was played in January 1987, and when the tennis world arrived in Melbourne the following January, it was clear that the Australian had arrived as a Grand Slam. The stadium seated fifteen thousand, with excellent sight lines everywhere. Most of the seats were in the shade, which helped even on the days when the heat was most unbearable. The women's final that year was completed with the roof closed, when it started to rain after the match had begun. The locker rooms were the roomiest in the world. The walkways were wide, and there were two ministadiums that served as courts 1 and 2. Chatrier called it "the tennis stadium of the twenty-first century."

With the new dates, everyone came to play. Steffi Graf started her Grand Slam by beating Chris Evert in the women's final, and Mats Wilander beat Pat Cash in an epic five-set men's final. The Australian Open had survived and, in the end, flourished. In 1990, Channel 7 would be on the air for about 120 hours during the two-week tournament.

Most of the country would be watching most of the time.

Day one of the 1990 Australian Open was, like any opening day, full of hope for everyone. Fans stared at the program and tried to figure out how to find the outside courts where the players they were interested in were playing. Players, coaches, agents, tournament directors, ex-players, and media mingled as if it were the first day of summer camp.

The two tennis tours are like traveling carnivals that circle the world's stages every twelve months. Five times a year—at the four Grand Slams and the Lipton International—the two carnivals become one. The two tours are rivalrous and jealous of each other, but they also share the same hopes, fears, dreams, and frustrations.

Relationships between players often spring up during Grand Slams. Some last, most don't. More often than not, the combination of separate travel schedules and the clash of major egos makes it almost impossible for a short-term fling to become a long-term love affair. Chris Evert did marry—and later divorce—John Lloyd; Carling Bassett and Robert Seguso married and had their second child early in 1991; Laura Arraya and Heinz Gildemeister married and have a three-year-old son.

More often, though, player-player flings go the way of Jimmy Connors–Evert; Boris Becker–Susan Mascarin; Eliot Teltscher–Kathy Jordan; Steffi Graf–Alexander Mronz; Tracy Austin–Matt Anger, just to name a few of the more publicized on-again, off-again tennis couples.

Several years ago, Anne White and John McEnroe began dating at the U.S. Open. This was shortly before McEnroe would meet his future wife, Tatum O'Neal, and a year before White would make her biggest splash in tennis by showing up to play her first-round match at Wimbledon in a sheer white bodysuit.

Several weeks after the Open, White was in Los Angeles to play a tournament and called McEnroe, figuring they would pick right up where they had left off in New York. McEnroe fumbled through several excuses about being busy or having to practice. White was stunned. She called Mary Carillo, a good friend of hers and of McEnroe's, and reported the conversation. At White's request, Carillo called McEnroe, demanding to know why he was snubbing White after they had spent so much time together at the Open.

"What does she expect me to do?" McEnroe asked. "Go sit in the stands and watch her *play*?"

White, who quit tennis in 1989 to try modeling and acting (then came back as a doubles specialist in 1990) was used to men lining up for the honor of watching her play tennis. McEnroe had little interest in watching her—or anyone else for that matter—play tennis. In short, White could not have been serious.

The first day of a Grand Slam, then, is a renewal: friendships and flings may begin or spring up again; someone new to the tour may turn some heads. At the very least, gossip will crop up in locker rooms and in every corner of the players' lounge.

There is tension, but there is also anticipation. Everyone feels the pressure, but there is also a sense of opportunity, not just for the players who are likely to be playing on the last weekend, but for those who would love to make it to the *first* weekend.

Each Grand Slam has a singles draw of 128 players. To win a championship, a player has to win seven matches. Perhaps no other major sports event in the world is as grueling mentally. Two weeks of playing, then waiting, more playing, then more waiting. The players hate the days off between matches, they hate having to answer the same questions again and again, they hate the tension that inevitably builds during such a lengthy event.

The first week of a Grand Slam is really two separate events. On the show courts there is glitz, a parade of millionaires marching through the early rounds, usually without much difficulty. Occasionally a high seed will find trouble and word will spread around the grounds; the stadium or grandstand court where that match is being played will fill up quickly.

More often, though, the big names whip through their early matches, then meet the media to give the same answers to the same questions that crop up during every single tournament:

Q: Would you rather have an easy match or a tough match at this stage of the tournament?
A: I always prefer an easy match.
Q: Are you happy with your game right now?
A: Well, I'm happy I won. I can do some things better, but it's still early.
Q: What did you think about the story in today's paper in which [fill in a name] was quoting as saying [he/she] thinks [he/she] is ready to win this tournament?
A: Well, I think [he/she] has every reason to be confident. [He/She] has been playing very well. But I feel confident too.
Q: Was it [hot/cold] out there?
A: Yes, very [hot/cold].

The first week, the *real* tennis tournament takes place on the outside courts, far from the millionaires and Minicams. Here, the players who are trying to make a living at tennis are sent to scratch their way through a couple of rounds, to make the extra three or four or five thousand dollars that may mean they can make the fourteen-hour flight home in business class instead of coach, without worrying about the extra expense.

There are many different levels of survival in tennis. Roughly speaking, the financial caste system breaks down this way: the top five or six players on both tours are so rich that money has become practically meaningless to them. This group—Lendl, Becker, Agassi, McEnroe, Connors, Edberg, Graf, Navratilova, Evert (still), Sabatini, Seles, Capriati—will make anywhere from $3 million to $10 million in a given year.

The next fifteen or twenty are extremely comfortable but more dependent on on-court results. A second-echelon male can make close to $1 million during a good year; a female perhaps half that. The next forty to fifty are making a very good living—usually well into six figures. The next fifty are making a living—perhaps $100,000, although half of that can be eaten up by expenses. After that, it is a question of how much longer your money will hold out if you don't start winning.

There are also players on both tours with virtually no ranking in singles who are making passable to solid to, in a couple of cases, excellent livings playing doubles.

The numbers are different on the two tours. The men make about 40 percent more prize money and, because of major differences in the rules, they make far more money in guarantees. The top ten female players can keep up in prize money and endorsements, but the drop-off is fairly steep after that.

Shaun Stafford and Elise Burgin both fell into the making-a-solid-living category. Stafford had just turned twenty-one, and in 1989, her first full year as a pro, had earned $60,852 in prize money. Add another $24,170 from Team Tennis, a couple of exhibitions, and a little money from endorsements, and she was comfortable, though, given the enormous expenses that are part of being a tennis player—a midlevel player will probably spend close to $50,000 a year on travel and coaching—certainly a long way from being wealthy.

Burgin, who would turn twenty-eight in March, had been on tour for six years. She had a viciously funny sense of humor—with most of her barbs directed at herself—and was the producer/director/writer of the annual talent show the players put on at the Eastbourne pre-Wimbledon warm-up tournament.

In 1989 Burgin made $99,537, a decent chunk of that coming from doubles (she had been among the top ten or fifteen doubles players in the world for her entire career). Everyone in tennis liked Elise Burgin and, during 1989, most of tennis had ached for her.

On the night of March 4, Burgin had gone to dinner in Oklahoma City with her doubles partner Liz Smylie and Smylie's husband, Peter, to celebrate their semifinal victory that afternoon and Elise's birthday, which was the next day. Elise had returned to her room and found an urgent message to call her father.

"As soon as I heard his voice, I knew something was terribly, terribly wrong," she said.

It was worse than that. Her mother, a teacher, driving to a weekend retreat in Pennsylvania, had been killed in an accident. Burgin couldn't get out of Oklahoma City until the next morning. Smylie, Carling Bassett, and Lori McNeil sat up with her all night.

Many of the people involved with women's tennis came to the funeral. Pam Shriver, who had grown up with Burgin in Baltimore, kept in constant touch with her during the next few weeks, from home and from the road. Burgin was touched by the outpouring of genuine affection, but nothing could change what had happened. She had worshipped her mother, who'd been tall and beautiful, smart and self-reliant. Disbelief became shock, which became terrible, terrible pain.

"I never knew until then how good my life was for twenty-seven years," Burgin said, her usually strident voice soft as she looked back. "The two worst things that had ever happened to me had been the year before, when I had to have my knee operated on and then got bounced from the Olympic team at the last minute when the USTA convinced Chris (Evert) to play.

"But that was nothing. It's funny; you hear people who have been through tragedy talk about gaining perspective from it, but you don't understand what they mean until you go through it. After what happened there was no way I could look at losing a tennis match as tragic. I had done that before at times, brooded over losing. The last six months of last year, I don't think I was ever nervous on a court. I was just glad to be playing. I still wanted to win—don't get me wrong—of course I wanted to win. But it couldn't possibly be as important as it had been before."

Helped by her friends, Burgin came back to the tour and played the best tennis she had played in several years. Her singles ranking had dropped out of the top one hundred in 1988. By the end of 1989, she was back up to No. 62—well short of the career-high No. 22 she had reached in 1985, but nonetheless respectable. What's more, she and her regular doubles partner, Roslyn Fairbank, closed the year with a rush and qualified for the eight-team Virginia Slims finals in New York, where they almost upset Navratilova and Shriver.

After the Slims finals, Burgin went home and came down with the flu. It was then that her mother's absence began to hit her all over again. "I had never in my life been sick without my mother there to take care of me," she said. "I would wake up and expect her to be there and she wasn't. That really hit me hard."

Burgin was one of a handful of players on either tour with a college degree, having graduated from Stanford. She knew she didn't want to hang on to tennis when the time came for her to leave, but she also knew that whenever that time came, it would be very difficult for her.

"I have a niche here, a place," she said. "I joke all the time about having had my name mispronounced all over the world—you know, Elsie Bugin or Eileen Virgin or maybe Elsie Bugin-Virgin—you name it, I've been called it. But the tour has, in many ways, been home for me for a long time. I know the time when I have to leave is coming, but I hope it won't be for at least a couple more years."

Which was why a first-round match in the Australian Open with Shaun Stafford was important for Bugin-Virgin. Stafford was ranked eleven spots higher; the match was tough, but winnable. Stafford's view of the match was almost identical. She knew Burgin was a tough competitor, but drawing her was a lot different than drawing Graf.

"It's the kind of match you have to win if you think you are capable of being in the top twenty," Stafford said. "I think with my size, my ability, and my game, I can be in the top twenty *if* I have the confidence and the discipline."

Stafford was one of the more striking players on the women's tour, almost six feet tall with, as Ted Tinling put it, "elegant legs" and a sparkling smile. She had grown up in Florida as the second daughter in a tennis-playing family. Her older sister, Nicole, had been an All-American at Clemson. Shaun opted for the University of Florida, where for two years she had led an idyllic life—dating a football player, being voted college tennis player of the year as a sophomore. The next step was to turn pro, and she had made steady improvement in just fifteen months on the tour.

The only setback had come near the end of 1989, when a bad ankle sprain had kept her off the court for a couple of months. Now, though, she felt healthy and eager as she and Burgin walked through the crowds in the midday heat to court 6. Both were fairly satisfied with the way they had played in Sydney: Stafford had saved five match points and come from 5–1 down in the third set to beat Etsuko Inoue in her first match, before losing later that same day in three sets to Raffaela Reggi. Burgin had beaten Claudia Kohde-Kilsch, a former top-five player, in her first match, then lost to another German, Claudia Porwick.

To those watching, Stafford and Burgin looked very much like Mutt and Jeff. Stafford was a good eight inches taller, with classic long, flowing ground strokes and a hard, flat first serve. Burgin was a lefty, her game all flying elbows and topspin, as awkward looking as Stafford was fluid.

While Stafford might let out an occasional sigh or soft cry of frustration over a missed shot, Burgin kept up a running monologue throughout the match: "Oh come on, Elise, hit the ball. . . . Oh, nice shot there, very intelligent . . . What in the world was that supposed to be, Elise?" Occasionally the chair umpire was included in the conversation: "You saw that ball *in*? How could you see that ball in? Did you see that ball at all? Why am I even asking these questions? You aren't going to do anything; you're just going to sit up there and do nothing."

There wasn't much anybody could do to help Burgin for the first set and a half. Stafford was controlling every big point, using her strength to run Burgin around the court. When Burgin did have chances—such as five break points in the second game of the match—she couldn't convert. In less than an hour it was 6–2, 4–2; Stafford and the top twenty looked a small step closer.

"God, I'm so goddamn stupid!" Burgin yelled as another Stafford winner screeched past her. She didn't quit, though. Serving at 40–30, trying to go up 5–3, Stafford missed an easy forehand. It was the first nervous shot she had made in a long time. Burgin sensed a tiny opening. She attacked on the next two points, sneaking up to the net and hitting solid volleys. All of a sudden it was 4–4. One missed shot had changed the mind-set of both players.

"I started thinking, Come on, Shaun, don't blow this, close this out now," Stafford said later. "Of course, the minute I started thinking I was going to blow it, instead of just thinking about winning, I was in trouble."

Burgin sensed that trouble. "For once in my life I just kept fighting when I was down," she said. "I mean, part of me thought it was over, I was done, but another part of me kept pushing. I didn't want to give up, even if it turned out she was just too good."

They went from 4–all to 6–all, but now Burgin was the one putting the pressure on. In the tiebreak, Burgin quickly jumped ahead 6–3. Three set points. Stafford got angry and began blasting the ball—four straight winners—and just like that had match point at 7–6. "I was dead," Burgin said. "Gone. Three set points blown was all I could think about."

She floated a short backhand on match point, and Stafford closed for the kill—an easy forehand, with Burgin out of position and helpless. But instead of whaling the ball as she had done when she was behind and angry, Stafford got careful. The ball floated wide as Stafford shrieked in horror.

"Oh, what a choke that was," she said with a sad shake of her head the next day.

Burgin knew a choke when she saw one. "It was like she just couldn't close it out," she said. "It was all right there for me."

One careful forehand. One blown point. One moment on an outside court with perhaps two hundred spectators watching. Stafford was deflated. Burgin closed out the tiebreak, 9–7. She flailed her way through the last set—blowing three match points herself before she could finish it off—but won 6–3.

Stafford was devastated. "The hardest thing about playing tennis is knowing you're going to lose just about every week of your life," she said. "It's not a matter of *if,* but *when.* You hope it won't come too early and that when it does come, it won't be the kind of match where you sit up all night and know you should have won. This was one of those matches. It really, really hurt."

For Burgin, the thrill of coming from so far behind, of saving match point, of hitting big shots at big moments, was almost indescribable. "You play tennis for those matches," she said. "You want to make money, but the reason you play is for matches like that; the feeling, coming off the court, knowing you won because you didn't give up."

For most tennis players, glory is short-lived. Defeat lingers. That night, Burgin looked at her draw and saw that her next match was against Anke Huber. She had never heard of Anke Huber, so she began calling friends, looking for a scouting report. The answer she received was short but not very sweet. "She's fifteen, German, and slugs the ball. They're calling her the next Steffi Graf."

Two days after the Stafford match, Burgin lost to Huber 6–2, 6–0. She walked off the court and saw at least thirty German reporters waiting for "the next Steffi." "Nothing like launching a career," she cracked, a wry, defeated smile on her face.

Burgin's joy had lasted forty-eight hours. Stafford's pain lingered for much longer. She would not win another singles match until May.

Later on that first afternoon, after the weather had changed again from hot and windy to cold and overcast, Tim Mayotte and Pete Sampras found themselves reunited on court just five days after their match in Sydney. The draw was an absolute fluke.

Sampras was not quite as happy to see Mayotte's name next to his on the draw sheet as he had been in Sydney. He knew that Mayotte would be aching to get even, and that he would have to play much better than he had in Sydney, where, in a best-of-three format, winning a first-set tiebreak had, for all intents and purposes, given him the match.

This was best-of-five against an angry, wounded player who knew all about Grand Slams, having been to the quarterfinals at Wimbledon six times (the semifinals once) and the quarterfinals at the U.S. Open four months earlier.

Mayotte had mixed emotions about playing Sampras again. Part of him was delighted with the chance to get even, but part of him wished it were in the third round, after a couple of quick and easy early matches.

As soon as the match began, Sampras knew he had a chance to win. Mayotte was intense, no doubt about that, but he was clearly nervous, wound tight as a spring. They split sets, each winning a tiebreak, then Mayotte won the third set, appearing to take control. But Sampras steadied in the fourth, and nerves again hurt Mayotte when he threw in a double fault in the last game of the set.

Two more double faults put Mayotte behind early in the fifth, before a rain shower intervened. The twenty-minute break killed the rhythm Sampras had built, and Mayotte was able to break him back when he served for the match. From there, it was a grinding battle of nerves and fatigue.

If this had been one of the weekly tournaments or the U.S. Open, they would have played a tiebreak at 6–6. But at the Australian Open, Wimbledon, and the French Open, the final set—third for the women, fifth for the men—is played out. Someone has to break serve to win. The feeling is that when the stakes are so high and the players have played so long, it should take more than one good return or one mistake to decide a winner. And so, at 6–6, with the conditions growing more arctic and eerie by the moment, they slogged on.

Mayotte broke to lead 7–6 and had a chance to serve the match out. But once again he tossed in a key double fault, and Sampras broke back to 7–7. With Mayotte down 7–8, he faced a match point but saved it with a big serve. On they went, each holding serve to reach 8–8, 9–9, and 10–10. Sampras held for 11–10, and Mayotte jumped ahead 40–15, trying to pull back to 11–11. Up popped another double fault. Sampras hit a winner to get to deuce. Mayotte double-faulted again.

Match point for the second time. Mayotte missed his first serve. Sampras began moving around, hoping for one more double fault. He finally jumped into the doubles alley, daring Mayotte to go down the middle for a winner. Mayotte took the dare—and served an ace.

"Everyone knows his second serve is his weakness," Sampras said. "That's why I was moving around, hoping he would go down the middle and miss. When he came up with that ace I thought, This guy has balls as big as walnuts." Sampras was undeterred, however. He crushed a return at deuce to reach match point again. But Mayotte served another winner. Sampras rolled his eyes as if to say, "Will this never end?" Mayotte just wanted to get through the game and catch his breath. It wasn't that simple, though. He served another double fault—his eighteenth of the match.

Match point four. Mayotte went for the big serve and missed. Sampras began his routine once more, creeping in as if he were going to take the ball early and pound it. Mayotte went for a little too much. The serve smacked the net tape, hung there for a second, and fell back. Sampras collapsed in a heap of joy and relief. Mayotte hung his head. Six weeks of preparing for Australia had produced two first-round losses.

The match had taken four hours and forty-five minutes—not counting the rain delay—the longest match in Australian Open history. It would prove to be a turning point for both players. For Sampras, it was a springboard—he would go on to reach the round of 16 before a groin pull and Yannick Noah combined to send him home.

Mayotte found the loss tough to take. He played fairly well in his next three indoor tournaments but was unhappy with his play and his attitude. He took a long break from the tour, split up with Bill Drake, his coach of six years, and arrived at Queen's Club in England in early June, hoping for a new beginning at age thirty. By then, Sampras, the qualifier in Sydney, was the sixth seed—one spot behind Mayotte—and still gaining.

If there was one thing that seemed a certainty at the Australian Open, it was Steffi Graf's third straight title. After all, Graf had won seven of the last eight Grand Slam tournaments. What's more, the players most likely to have any chance of beating her weren't even *in* Australia: Martina Navratilova was home resting, opting not to make the long trip for what she knew was a long-shot chance to win; Monica Seles had a sore shoulder because she had played one exhibition too many in Europe and had developed tendinitis; and Arantxa Sanchez, the only player to beat Graf in a Grand Slam in the past two years, had played the money-up-front Hopman Cup and then gone home, proving that Agassi wasn't the only teenager in the sport who hadn't yet figured out what mattered and what didn't.

That left Gabriela Sabatini, Zina Garrison, and Helena Sukova as Graf's most likely challengers. None of the three had ever won a Grand Slam, and their combined record against Graf was 4–40.

If all of that made Graf happy, it certainly didn't show. An hour before her first-round match against American teenager Carrie Cunningham, she went out to hit with her coach, Pavel Slozil, and found Boris Becker finishing a practice session on center court. Becker asked Graf if she would like him to warm her up. Graf said fine.

Graf and Becker are friends, having grown up in small towns just fifteen miles apart in southern Germany and, more important, having faced the same pressures of stardom in a small, newly tennis-mad country. When word spread among the German media that Graf and Becker were hitting together, a mad stampede to witness the event ensued. Becker was having fun. Graf was wound up, intense, slugging the ball as if trying to prove something.

Actually, Graf was taking out her frustrations. She had already been in Melbourne for two weeks and was bored stiff. "Melbourne is a nice city," she would say later, "but it isn't New York or London. There just isn't that much to do after a few days. All I did was practice, go to the hotel, practice, go to the hotel. I was losing my mind."

There was more than just boredom involved. Peter Graf had told his daughter earlier that month that he was being harassed by Nicole Meissner, a nude model in Germany, and that there might be some ugly publicity ahead. Steffi Graf wasn't exactly sure what was involved, but she was concerned. Even though as she got older she was becoming more and more independent, her father was still the most important person in her life.

People tend to think that Graf worships her father, that she is incapable of seeing fault in him. There is no questioning her devotion to him, but Graf knew long before Nicole Meissner came along that her father wasn't perfect. She knew that he could be overbearing and she also knew that there were times when he drank too much. Peter Graf's drinking was an open secret on the women's tour, something everyone knew but rarely talked about. More than once, Steffi had been seen quietly but firmly taking a drink out of her father's hand. The previous summer, in San Diego, Peter Graf had said to Ted Tinling one morning, "I've been bad again, I've let Steffi down. I must stop doing this."

In fact, when Peter Graf's alleged affair with Nicole Meissner became public later in the year, the real surprise among tennis people was that a woman and not alcohol was the source of the scandal (although some people speculated that the two were connected).

All of this was preying on Graf's mind in Australia. She was a long way—mentally—from being the player who had been virtually unbeatable for two years.

This was evident in her match against Carrie Cunningham, a seventeen-year-old lefty who had won the U.S. Open junior title in 1988. If Cunningham had a problem as a tennis player, it was her normalcy. As talented as she was, she had been unable to reconcile herself to the notion that tennis was a be-all and end-all. She had become something of a minor legend among the other teenagers on tour when she stayed up almost all night before playing the junior Open final in 1988 and then breezed through the match the next day in straight sets. She was pretty and popular and sounded more like twenty-five than seventeen when she talked.

"Actually, I was out just about every night that week," she said, laughing. "I like to go out. I like to spend time with my friends. I like having a boyfriend. In junior tennis I've been able to live that way and get by on talent. I know I can't do that and be a successful pro. That's why I have to decide if being a pro is what I want to do."

Cunningham was a high school senior who, if she couldn't hit a tennis ball, would have gladly gone to Stanford to study to be an architect, something she had wanted to do since the age of eleven. But tennis clouded an otherwise clear decision. The Graf match would make things even murkier.

Because on a cool, breezy evening, Carrie Cunningham came very close to winning the second set against Graf. She led 5–2, partly because she was blasting the ball off both wings and partly because Graf's forehand was still somewhere on the other side of the world. "When I got up 5–2, I started to think, I'm going to win a set from Steffi, this is incredible," Cunningham said later. "That's when it all fell apart."

Graf, already unhappy at having spent more than an hour on court, finally focused on what she was doing long enough to win the last five games of the match. "As soon as I started thinking about how astonishing the whole thing was, I got nervous," Cunningham admitted. "I went out there just hoping I could give her a match. I feel very good that I did."

Graf would move on, lurching her way through the tournament, looking vulnerable in almost every match. Cunningham would go home to finish high school and decide what to do next: school or tennis. In that sense, Graf and Cunningham were very similar when their paths crossed that night in Melbourne. Neither knew exactly what she wanted next from her life.

As the tournament hummed through its first five days, the major surprise was in the lack of fireworks coming from the bureaucrats running the men's game.

For six months leading up to the Australian, the rhetoric had flown back and forth between the ITF and the ATP Tour almost nonstop. Each saw the other as the root of most of the evil in world history.

It had taken the ITF a little while to understand what Hamilton Jordan had done when he put together his rebellion in 1988. Jordan was the classic Southern politician, a drawling Georgian who could charm you out of one side of his mouth and then nail you out of the other—all in one sentence.

He was, if nothing else, a proven fighter, having beaten Gerald Ford first and cancer second, with a loss to Ronald Reagan in between. He had taken over the ATP, in 1987, at the urging of an old White House crony, Tim Smith, who had gone to work for the Professional Golfers Association Tour after the Republicans had taken back the White House.

Within a year of Jordan's move to the ATP, he had moved the association's headquarters from suburban Dallas to Ponte Vedra—just down the road from PGA headquarters—and, with Smith's help, had come up with a plan to completely make over—and take over—men's tennis.

What Jordan wanted to do was recreate the PGA Tour. The logo he chose for his tour was almost identical to the PGA logo, and that symbolized the effort from the beginning. Jordan believed he could do what Deane Beman had done in golf: subvert the star system; build the game around the events themselves, subsidized by huge corporate sponsorships; and funnel the power in the game to the top—his office.

Pulling off his coup wasn't all that difficult, since men's tennis has always existed in a state of near anarchy. All Jordan had to do was convince the players that the ITF under Philippe Chatrier and the MTC under Marshall Happer were dictatorships that were making them work harder than they needed to for less money than they deserved. From there he went to the tournament directors with a simple message: Become part of our tour now or you won't have a tournament next year. We have the players. You can't have a tournament without them.

The tournament directors, who in Homer's time would have been cast as Penelope's suitors, fell quickly into line, scared to death that their idyllic life-styles might be threatened by a rival tour.

With the players and tournament directors in line, Jordan had the votes he needed to kill the MTC. The MTC had nine voting members—three player representatives, three tournament directors, and three ITF representatives. Jordan had six votes, one more than he needed.

The U.S. Tennis Association made things even easier for Jordan when it refused to allow the ATP to use any space on the grounds of the National Tennis Center to stage a press conference during the 1988 U.S. Open. The USTA might just as well have funded Jordan's public relations budget for the next six months. Barred from the grounds, the ATP announced it would hold its press conference in the parking lot outside the main gate. Too late, the USTA realized its gaffe and offered up the main interview room on the morning of the press conference. "Sorry," the ATP said, "we've already told everyone to be in the parking lot at noon."

In the interview room, the press conference would have been nothing more than a propaganda session, the ATP announcing how unified the players were behind Jordan's plan to change tennis. In the parking lot, symbolism was everywhere, with the players on the outside looking in at the arrogant martinets who controlled the game they all loved so much. To this day, every single ATP program or publication contains references to and pictures of "The Parking Lot Press Conference."

When the MTC was voted out of existence by the six player/tournament director reps—with the new ATP Tour scheduled to begin on January 1, 1990—the ITF finally began to understand that it had a problem. For the first time ever, the four Grand Slam tournaments united, forming the Grand Slam Committee, a fancy name for a war council that would take on the players.

The Grand Slam Committee's first act was to hire Bill Babcock, who had been the MTC's legal counsel, as administrator and point man. Babcock was a tall, lean Minnesota-bred, Harvard-educated lawyer who had played the tour briefly, mostly at the Satellite and Challenger levels, before going to law school. He was very bright, very eager, and very willing to knock heads with Jordan and his band of merry men.

Babcock started work in the London office of the ITF on July 1, 1989. It didn't take long for him to get the attention of the ATP—which had now incorporated as the ATP Tour, ceasing to be a players' union, a fact that went almost unnoticed at the time.

First, Babcock hired Ken Farrar, the most respected and experienced of the MTC's officiating supervisors. The ATP Tour had already hired most of Farrar's top umpires, so Farrar set to work finding umpires the ITF could hire on a full-time basis to work the Grand Slams. Message one to the ATP Tour: We aren't going to need your umpires at our tournaments.

The ATP Tour had decided to move its season-ending championships out of New York to Germany, a country that hungered for tennis and to spend money on tennis. The Grand Slam Committee decided that if the ATP Tour would hold a $2 million tournament in Germany, *it* would hold a $6 million tournament in Germany four weeks later. The Grand Slam Cup was born. Players would qualify based on their records in the four Grand Slams. If the ATP Tour had any plans to try to take control of the Grand Slams by threatening a boycott, it might have a little trouble selling the concept to players who not only would be missing a Grand Slam but would be missing the chance to qualify for the most lucrative tournament in history.

Message two to the ATP Tour: Tennis needs the Grand Slams more than it needs Sydney, Stuttgart, Monte Carlo, and Toronto.

The announcement of the Grand Slam Cup, which came during the week of the Paris Indoor Tournament, in early November 1989, sent ATP Tour officials into a frenzy. After each match in Paris, players were called in and briefed on what to say about the new tournament. Most got their lines so exactly right that it was apparent they were being fed them from behind the curtain. It was left to McEnroe to sum it up in his own inimitable style: "If we take that kind of money," he said, "it will make us look like a bunch of money whores."

Lendl, blunt as ever, announced immediately that he *would* play the Grand Slam Cup. "When someone offers you two million dollars [the top prize], you don't spit in their face," he said.

Already, chinks were showing in the ATP Tour's armor. The rule book, unveiled in a lavish ceremony *inside* the gates of the National Tennis Center, was already being rewritten because Top Ten players and their agents had categorically refused to accept it.

The top players were whining loudly because they had been told they would be asked to play less and were now finding they would be required to play *more.* The old MTC tour had insisted they play fourteen tournaments total—including the four Grand Slams. That meant they had to play ten non-Slam events. The ATP Tour wanted a commitment to eleven non-Slam events, although older players such as Jimmy Connors, McEnroe, and Lendl had to play only eight, nine, or ten events under a formula worked out based on tournaments played over the years. Connors would no doubt be *owed* tournaments by the time he got around to retiring.

There was more. Lower-ranked players were upset about the dissolution of the union. Did they have a voice anymore? The Top Ten felt it didn't have enough representation on the ATP Tour board and council. Bob Green was their representative. Green, a former player, had once reached the round of 16 at the U.S. Open and played McEnroe. After losing in three sets, Green, who majored in Russian literature at Boston University, had been asked how it felt to play McEnroe.

"Now I know how Gary Gilmore felt," Green said. Gilmore had just been shot to death by a firing squad in Utah.

Green and the Top Ten quickly became heartily sick of one another, so Green was reassigned to put together the weekly ATP Tour's syndicated TV show, which Jordan kept telling people was being seen in twelve zillion homes. If one could believe television ratings, many of those homes had to be in China. With Green gone, someone decided Eliot Teltscher would be a good Top Ten representative. The ATP Tour would pay him a $20,000 salary, and he would tell the board and the council what the hopes, fears, and dreams of the top players were. Teltscher lasted three months in the job. The last thing he was heard saying before he disappeared—going off to make a comeback as a player, at thirty-two—was, "None of them will return my phone calls."

The Top Ten then decided that Vijay Amritraj, an elegant Indian and one of the few people in tennis who seemed to have no enemies, should represent them. Amritraj was already president of the player council and the tour board, but what the heck, what's a little conflict of interest among friends, especially in tennis, where those without conflicts of interest rarely survive very long?

The Grand Slam Committee watched all the squabbling within the ATP Tour with a good deal of amusement. It was further amused when, amid the cries of "United we stand, divided we fall," several players posted a petition on the locker-room wall, in Paris. Dated November 1, 1989, it read:

> The undersigned ATP members are disgusted and outraged at the recent developments and decisions undertaken by the ATP Players Council. An explanation is demanded by all as to how certain "paychecks" have been distributed.
>
> We all know the potential of the ATP Tour is boundless if ALL people concerned contribute in an unselfish way with the good of the pro-game being the BOTTOM LINE—It seems to the undersigned there is [sic] some serious EGO MANIACS making decisions on our behalf. If the ATP fails it will be because of problems "within"—An explanation please. AND QUICKLY.

There was an addendum on page two:

> Apparently, "the tour board," after recently being voted into their positions by the ATP Members, have decided to pay themselves US$20,000, plus 1ST CLASS AIRFARES on top of ALL EXPENSES.
>
> Is the tour no longer the voice of the players? We feel there is no longer an ATP but a tour run as a company. Do we as players still have a voice?
>
> ALSO. Hamilton Jordan has had a pay increase of US$300,000 from US$200,000 to $500,000. AND Hamilton is also involved in attempting to purchase an NFL franchise. Is this a conflict of interest? We need an explanation for all of the above! And Fucking FAST!

The undersigned included Robert Seguso, the longtime American Davis Cup doubles star, and several journeyman players: Kelly Evernden, John Fitzgerald, David Pate, Laurie Warder, and Mansour Bahrami. Brad Gilbert's signature was not on the petition, but there was a note at the bottom for "all interested parties to meet Wednesday night in Brad Gilbert's room."

The paychecks, the expenses, and the first-class airfare were a reference to Teltscher, Amritraj, and to Larry Scott, the vice president of the council. Scott was a Harvard graduate who had had a brief fling on the tour before getting involved in tennis politics. He was bright, engaging, and hardworking, but to many of his fellow players he was still a guy who had never really made it out of qualies. So, they reasoned, why should he be flying first class?

While not a major insurrection, the petition was certainly a sign that the unity of the "parking lot press conference" was not likely to last. Jordan's dream of a PGA-style ATP Tour was fading before the first ball had been hit. This was no surprise, really, because even though tennis and golf are individual sports played by very rich men, the similarity ends there.

Glenn Layendecker, a Yale graduate and one of the more thoughtful players in the game, sees tennis as being more akin to boxing than golf. "In golf, you don't lose to another guy," he said. "You lose to the golf course or to yourself. There isn't someone else who you go one-on-one with, except in a playoff. I doubt if you have the tensions between golfers that you have between tennis players because of that."

Layendecker's boxing reference was especially interesting in light of a survey that the ATP Tour had done early in 1989: It showed that in the United States, only boxers had a worse image than male tennis players.

By the time he received the results of the survey, Jordan wasn't the least bit surprised. He had quickly soured on the players he had led into revolution. He began making references to the Top Ten as "those selfish assholes" and made it clear that his only real disagreement with the ATP survey was that it had probably been unfair to boxers. After having dinner with Stefan Edberg, he told several friends, "That was the longest night of my life."

More than anything, Jordan was frustrated by his inability to bring the Top Ten into line. Lendl and Connors had made it clear from the start that they wanted no active part in the new tour and didn't want anybody trying to change their life-styles. That was okay with Jordan as long as he could get players such as Becker, McEnroe, Edberg, Wilander, and Agassi to go along with him.

All were initially supportive, but when it came down to serious talk, Jordan couldn't get anywhere. On the afternoon of September 11, 1989, the day after Becker had beaten Lendl in the U.S. Open final, Jordan and his staff met with most of the Top Ten and their agents. The reason for the meeting was to figure out exactly what rules the Top Ten would and wouldn't follow.

Things deteriorated quickly. The tour wanted a player who withdrew from a tournament with an injury to be required to make an appearance at the tournament site or face a possible suspension. "Forget it," said the agents and the players.

"Okay," Jordan responded, "but we've got to do something about the bad publicity we're going to get for legalizing guarantees at the World Series tournaments. I want you guys to stop taking guarantees from the Championship Series tournaments." He even went so far as to say that he might try to force the players to open their books if he suspected them of taking guarantees. "Fine," said Lendl. "All you'll find are fees for clinics and press conferences and cocktail parties. Second, if you try to open our books, I doubt if many of us will sign our player commitments. You're already asking us to play more often than last year, so don't try to stop us from getting our guarantees." Lendl called for an immediate vote. How many players, he asked, wanted to continue getting guarantees—in one form or another—from Championship Series events? Every player in the room raised his hand.

That ended the no-guarantee discussion. Edberg, who made about $500,000 annually for playing the two Japanese tournaments, was certainly relieved. So were the others, who *all* had six-figure offers from Japan. Lendl, who would play in Sydney in early October, for six figures, certainly had no intention of giving up his guarantees to help Jordan out on the public relations front. Lendl was the most straightforward bargainer in the group: For every ten hours he had to fly to and from a tournament, his price went up $50,000. Usually, he got it.

By the time the Grand Slam Cup was unveiled and the petition went up in the locker room in Paris, Jordan realized what he had suspected a year earlier: that he didn't have the stomach to live this life anymore. The same headhunter that had recommended Jordan in 1987 was brought back in to search for a replacement.

In the meantime, the rhetoric kept flying. The ATP Tour claimed that the Grand Slam Committee was trying to ban it from the Australian Open. The Tour representatives, the trainers, the publicity people, and the umpires were all being barred.

Not true, said the Grand Slam Committee. *It* claimed that the ATP Tour had demanded a $1 million fee for the services of those people at the Grand Slams, and it would not pay the fee.

There was more. On December 6, David Markin, the president of the USTA, had sent a memo to his executive-committee members, updating them on the ongoing battle. The memo asked the question, "What is the best policy for the ITF and the Grand Slams?" Nine answers were listed, including "Absolute independence from the ATP Tour"; "Make no further concessions to the ATP as to their official position vis-à-vis the Grand Slams"; "Promotion of the Grand Slam Cup, which forces the ATP to do the one thing they fear more than anything else—compete with another tennis force."

Provocative stuff. This wasn't surprising. Of all the Grand Slam Committee members, Markin was the most antagonistic toward the ATP Tour. A wealthy man born into his money (his father founded Checker Cab), Markin had no patience with underlings who questioned his authority, and to him, that's what the ATP Tour was.

His counterpart in the fan-the-flames department on the ATP side was Weller Evans, the longtime player representative who had been promoted to director of operations in the new hierarchy.

Evans was a Princeton graduate who had been a good college tennis player but never good enough to succeed on the tour. He had stayed in tennis as a player rep—running qualies each week, helping players with scheduling, and being a troubleshooter for the tour. He was good at his job and earned the trust of most of the players.

But Evans still tended to think of himself as a player. Few people could remember seeing him in long pants, and he took everything dealing with the new tour personally. This was "our" tour (the players') and no one else's, in Evans's mind—and anyone who attacked it or criticized it was the enemy.

When a copy of Markin's memo reached Evans in Melbourne, he copied it, put it up on the wall in his office and in the locker room, and wrote in bright-blue felt tip at the bottom "HOW ABOUT THIS?" When Babcock arrived in Melbourne on the Friday before the tournament, he went to see Evans for what he hoped would be a soothing talk. The two men had been friendly adversaries throughout most of the years he had worked in tennis. At each Grand Slam tournament, they found one morning or one evening to play a semigrudge match with each other. But when Babcock walked in and saw the "HOW ABOUT THIS?" tacked to Evans's bulletin board, the friendly adversary routine quickly went out the window and the first shouting match of the new era took place.

When the dust and rhetoric finally cleared, everyone from the ATP Tour who wanted to be at the Australian Open *was* at the Australian Open. Jordan didn't make the trip, Amritraj and Scott stayed for one day, and Jay Beck, Jordan's college roommate, who had been hired as the tour's communications director, also stayed only a day before going scuba diving off the Barrier Reef.

Seven ATP Tour umpires were invited to work at the tournament, along with their new ITF brethren. This brought on the only real dispute of the tournament: The ATP umpires refused to wear the ITF-certified badges that were handed out at the start of the tournament. Okay, the ITF said, don't wear the badges. But in return you have to promise not to wear your ATP Tour caps while working matches. Done, said the umpires.

Peace and harmony reigned again in men's tennis.

The first week of a Grand Slam tennis tournament is filled with one-day-wonder stories. An Anke Huber becomes a budding legend one day, then loses to Raffaela Reggi the next. Then, someone like Angelica Gavaldon comes along and becomes Star for a Day. Gavaldon, a sixteen-year-old Californian, the daughter of Mexican parents, was still an amateur. She was impossible not to notice, with her dark hair, ruby-red lipstick, and giant hoop earrings. "I collect earrings," she said. "I still remember when I was a little girl, my grandmother told me, 'Girl, whatever you do, don't ever leave the house without your earrings on.' I have about fifty pairs now."

Gavaldon was tiny—barely five feet two—and her earrings were so striking that even other players who notice almost nothing if it's not about them, noticed. Peanut Louie-Harper took one look at the earrings before a match one day and said, "How do you stand up with those things on? You must have really strong ears."

A classic Chris Evert clone who stayed in the backcourt and blasted away, Gavaldon also had really strong ground strokes. In the third round, she blasted Hana Mandlikova out of the tournament, a feat that was becoming less and less impressive as time went by, but was nonetheless a major story in Australia—since Mandlikova had become an Australian citizen.

Her citizenship was considered one of the better running jokes in the sport. In a very bizarre scene, Mandlikova had married an Australian restaurant owner in 1986, during the Federation Cup in Prague. Amid all the hype and hoopla attached to Martina Navratilova's first trip home since her 1975 defection, Mandlikova had called a press conference to announce that she had been married that morning at the Prague city hall.

"How could you have done that?" asked a Czech journalist. "It takes months for someone to reserve time for a wedding at the city hall."

"It doesn't take months," Mandlikova replied, "if your name is Hana Mandlikova."

Mandlikova's husband didn't appear at the wedding reception that evening. Instead, Mandlikova and a few friends played croquet at her parents' house. She then spent the night there—alone. When someone asked her how she felt about not spending her wedding night with her husband, she shrugged and said, "It won't be every week of my life that the Federation Cup is played in Prague."

Of course.

Within a year Mandlikova applied for Australian citizenship. She got it, established a residence in Queensland, and a year later announced that she and her husband were divorcing. It was the perfect backdoor defection. She insisted on being introduced as "Hana Mandlikova of Queensland." According to people who lived in Queensland, she had spent all of one day there, in 1989. The Australian media took to mockingly referring to her as "Aussie-Hana."

Mandlikova's temperament was baffling. She could be charming when in the right mood, infuriating when not. In 1987, while losing a fourth-round match at the U.S. Open to Claudia Kohde-Kilsch, Mandlikova destroyed a scoreboard on court and reamed out an umpire with a tirade worthy of McEnroe at his worst.

She then refused to come to the mandatory postmatch press conference. When reporters trooped to the locker room—the U.S. Open is the only Grand Slam tournament that allows reporters into the locker rooms—Mandlikova hid in a back room while her doubles partner, Wendy Turnbull, told reporters she wasn't there. A WTA official found her, and she promised she would speak to the media after her doubles match. When she came off court after that match, she announced that she had changed her mind. Seeing reporters trailing her and knowing that the locker room wasn't off-limits to them, Mandlikova ducked into a public bathroom and locked herself in a stall. The bathroom involved will be known forevermore as "Hana's loo-loo."

Once, Mandlikova had been a wonder to watch, good enough to break the Evert–Navratilova Grand Slam death grip four times—with two Australian Opens, one French Open, and one U.S. Open. But now, at twenty-eight, her brittle body was wearing down and, facing such a steady ground stroker as Gavaldon, she tired badly, losing the third set 6–1.

One person who was thrilled was Ted Tinling. Mandlikova's inconsistent play and equally inconsistent temperament drove him crazy. What's more, he loved Gavaldon, whom he immediately nicknamed "Lolita" in honor of her lipstick and earrings.

"Lolita" turned out to be a sweet and funny kid who sounded like a Mexican Valley Girl. Her eyes lit up when discussing the good-looking guys on the men's tour. "That guy Steffi was going out with [Alexander Mronz] is *real* good-looking," she said. "I heard he was really mean, but if it was me, I wouldn't care. I wouldn't give him up, no way. I *swear* he's good-looking." "I *swear*" immediately became the new buzz-phrase of the tournament.

Lolita followed up her victory over Mandlikova by upsetting Gigi Fernandez in the round of 16 before losing in the quarterfinals to Claudia Porwick. She said she wasn't sure if she wanted to turn pro, because she had always wanted to play college tennis. Now that she would be ranked in the top one hundred, she might consider it. Her parents were very comfortable financially, so it wasn't as if she had to have the money.

A month later, after the management firms had all told her there were contracts out there waiting for her, Gavaldon turned pro. I *swear* those agents could sell swampland in Manhattan.

The most disappointed losers of the first week were two players whose careers appeared to be heading in different directions.

One was Jim Courier, the nineteen-year-old American who had finished 1989 knocking on the door of the top twenty. Courier had come to Australia smack in the middle of the hoopla over the Young American Five. He was still well behind Chang and Agassi in the rankings, in attention, and in endorsement deals. But his yearlong performance had moved him well ahead of Sampras and Wheaton in ranking and attention as well as guarantees and exhibitions, if not in endorsement deals.

Courier first learned tennis from his great-aunt, Emma Spencer. She had been the women's tennis coach at UCLA, in the 1960s, and began working with Jim when he was five. Jim excelled both as a pitcher and as a tennis player. His true love was baseball (he travels nowhere without his Cincinnati Reds cap), but when he was thirteen he felt he had to make a decision between the two sports. "I had been No. 2 in Florida in 12-and-unders as a tennis player," he said. "Realistically, I knew I wasn't close to being the second-best baseball player. So I decided to stick with tennis."

A year later, after reaching the Orange Bowl final in the 14-and-unders, he got a call from Nick Bollettieri, asking him if he wanted to come to the academy full-time. Bollettieri's, in Bradenton, was a ninety-minute drive from the Couriers' house in Dade City. Courier could go home every weekend. He and his parents decided to make the move.

"It was very, very hard," Courier said, shaking his head at the memory. "There's no question I gave up my childhood to become a tennis player. Personally, I think it was worth it. I mean, you can't have everything in life. I wanted to play tennis. That doesn't mean there weren't times I hated it. The first year, every Sunday night when my parents dropped me off, I would go off by myself and cry. But I got through it."

That first year Courier shared a room with seven other teenagers, including Andre Agassi. "He was a different guy then, he's a different guy now," Courier said. "We were all very competitive. There were never any real fights, but a lot of scuffles and a lot of bickering."

Early on, Courier didn't see a lot of Bollettieri, who was on the road much of the time with Aaron Krickstein and Jimmy Arias. But as he and Agassi improved, they began spending more and more time on Nick's court. Among the players at the academy, Bollettieri is known as "the world's best five-minute coach." He will throw out an idea, watch a player hit the ball a few times, tell him he's the best there's ever been, and then go off to make an important business deal.

Courier smiles when asked about Bollettieri. "Nick is a great motivator," he says. Next subject.

Courier starred as a junior, in many ways a classic Bollettieri player: huge forehand, inconsistent backhand, decent serve, no volley to speak of. His real strength was his competitiveness.

After graduating from high school, Courier wasn't sure whether to go to college or to turn pro. He had done well in juniors, traveling with Chang, Sampras, and Wheaton as a member of the American Junior Davis Cup team. He, Sampras, and Wheaton became friends. They all liked Chang but never could get close to him because of the omnipresence of his parents, especially his mother. Sampras still vividly remembers Betty

Chang reaching inside her son's shorts, with his teammates standing right there, to see if his underwear was wet.

After playing well in the summer of 1987, Courier decided to play the circuit for a few months before deciding whether to turn pro or to go to college. He played miserably. "Point me to SMU," he told a friend that November. But the following month he won the Orange Bowl, beating the then highly touted Nicholas Pereira in the final. From there, he went to Chile for a $25,000 Challenger. Just hoping to qualify, he won the tournament. That was it. Courier told his parents he wanted to turn pro.

In the fall of 1988, he hooked up with Sergio Cruz, a onetime Portuguese Davis Cup player who'd been coaching at Bollettieri's for about a year. Cruz had a hard-ass reputation among the players, but Courier needed help in Europe and no one else from Bollettieri's could go.

"Serge was a [Harry] Hopman guy, and he believed in hard work all the time," Courier said, laughing. "If you were put on his court the joke was that you better bring your track shoes. But when I needed someone to go to Stockholm, I asked him, and we hit it off right away." Courier made it to the semifinals in Stockholm, then reached the quarterfinals in both London and Detroit. That put him in the top fifty, and he asked Cruz to travel with him full-time. By this time, Agassi was in the top five in the world and Bollettieri, still technically Courier's coach, was traveling with Agassi full-time. Cruz wasn't certain about full-time travel. He was thirty-five years old and had a wife and three children.

In February 1989, with Bollettieri still his official coach, Courier played Agassi in Philadelphia. Bollettieri sat with the Agassi entourage throughout and cheered his most successful student on as he beat Courier in three tight sets. The scene was replayed two months later at Forest Hills. Same seating arrangement, same result, same frustrations for Courier. He asked Cruz to become his coach full-time. This time, Cruz agreed.

A month later, in the third round of the French Open, Courier got another shot at Agassi and this time beat him in four long, grinding sets. It was a sweet victory—to say the least—but Courier had no chance to savor it. The next day, he blew a two-set lead and lost to Andrei Chesnokov. "I didn't sleep through the night again until Wimbledon," he said. "That one was a killer."

Even with the loss to Chesnokov, Courier had stamped himself as a comer. He moved steadily up the rankings the rest of the year and, after his victory over Edberg in Switzerland, appeared ready to make 1990 a very big year.

"My goal for 1990 is to make an impact at the Grand Slams," he said. "They're what tennis is about, I know that. I think I'm at the point where I'm ready to make a mark there. I think I've got the experience now to play with the best players."

Courier was seeded fourteenth at the Australian, but being seeded didn't protect him from a tough draw. He beat Jimmy Arias easily in the first round, then had to play Jonas Svensson in round two. Svensson, one of the best-liked players on the tour, was a talented Swede with a good sense of humor who had been in the French semifinals in 1988. He was usually ranked in the top twenty but had played poorly in the latter part of 1989 and dropped to forty-first on the computer. That left him unseeded—what is known among the players as "a dangerous floater" in the draw.

He floated right through Courier in the second round, keeping him under pressure the entire day. In the third set, Courier lost his cool when he could least afford to.

One of Courier's strengths as a player is his tenacity. He is an in-your-face banger, someone who struts and shouts and yells at himself to play better. Off the court, Courier is bright, witty, and fun—well liked by most of the other players. But on court, that image changes.

"He can be a real jerk," said Arias, who likes Courier. "He gets the red ass real quick, and when he starts pointing and stuff you kind of want to go, 'Come on, grow up.' "

Intellectually, Courier understands all this. He knows it hurts his tennis when he goes off, and he knows it isn't attractive. "I have to work at it," he said. "But sometimes I just get so intense I sort of snap."

He did just that against Svensson, screaming, pouting, pointing, foot-faulting, swearing.

Cruz, sitting fifteen feet away in the bleachers, kept turning his palms down, trying to signal Courier to calm down. It was hopeless, though. At one point, a self-destructing Courier missed two forehands, the second one a mishit that brought giggles from the crowd. "Stop laughing, goddammit!" he screamed.

Naturally, that brought more giggles. Courier lost it completely. Svensson won the next five games and the match, and Courier stormed off the court. By the next morning he had calmed down, but it was too late. One Grand Slam had slipped away from him. On the flight home, Cruz told him in no uncertain terms that his behavior had been awful.

"He told me I had to grow up," Courier said. "I didn't like it, but I knew he was right. That was a real long way to go to play like that."

While Courier was self-destructing on court 5, Pam Shriver was trying to survive on the stadium court.

Shriver knew her tennis career was in serious jeopardy. She would be twenty-eight in July and had gone through a disastrous 1989, dropping out of the Top Ten (to No. 17) for the first time since she had come on the tour as a full-time player, in 1980.

Shriver was going through a tennis version of midlife crisis. For years she had been behind only Evert, Navratilova, and Mandlikova, all of them older than she. Now, younger players—Graf, Sabatini, Sanchez, and Seles—were passing her. For the first time, Shriver was forced to come to grips with the notion that her trip to the U.S. Open final as a sixteen-year-old high school kid, in 1978, might be her only appearance in a Grand Slam singles final. She had won twenty-one Grand Slam doubles titles (twenty with Navratilova) but had never come that close again to winning a major in singles.

She had, however, become quite rich, earning more than $4 million in prize money. With her breezy, articulate manner, she had also made a lot of money in endorsements. But in 1989, Shriver began to retreat from tennis. "I'm more than just a tennis player," she told anyone who would listen. She repeated the line so often that friends began calling her Pam "Not a Tennis Player" Shriver.

As if to back up that claim, Shriver played *awful* tennis. She lost in the third round at Wimbledon and in the first round at the U.S. Open. Navratilova told her to take six months off from the game. Shriver didn't like that advice and kept on playing. Navratilova responded by ending their eight-year doubles partnership in what became an ugly, public spat.

Shriver arrived in Australia still uncertain about what she wanted from tennis. She had gone to a USTA camp for "young" players, in December, and found it invigorating and fun. But just when she thought the old feeling was coming back, three days before she was supposed to leave for Australia her elbow blew out. For the first time in her life, Shriver took a cortisone shot.

"I feel like I came down here as much to get out of the cold weather and to see my friends as anything else," Shriver said. "Let's face it, that's not a great attitude to start the year with.

"I keep trying to convince myself that it's okay to just be a tennis player at this stage of my life. All the other stuff will come when the time is right. The thing I have to do this year is focus just on tennis. I'm at a point in my career where if I can't do that, I'm not going to be able to win anymore. People aren't scared of me. Last year, I went out there hoping players would freeze in the clutch and I'd slide through. It worked for a while but eventually it wears out. You can't go out there and fake it forever."

That had been evident in her opening match in Sydney against Jana Pospisilova, a one-dimensional Czech ground stroker Shriver would have gobbled up in her pre–I'm-more-than-just-a-tennis-player days. Instead, Shriver, after coming from a set down to lead 5–4 in the third set, collapsed completely, losing eleven of the last twelve points and the match, 7–5.

Watching her play that day, Ted Tinling had commented, "Rarely do you get something if you want it too much. She's playing scared and there isn't a tennis player in the world who can't tell when her opponent is frightened."

It wasn't much different in Melbourne. Shriver managed to make it past the first round, against another less-than-overwhelming Czech, Eva Sviglerova. But in the second round, she found herself on the stadium court against Nicole Provis, another of the onetime Australian wonder girls.

A lot of people thought Provis, now twenty, all but washed up. In 1988 she had been one point away from reaching the French Open final but choked the match away to Natalia Zvereva. Since then she had struggled, losing one close match after another. Tall, blond, and elegant, Provis had star quality. But when a match got tight, Provis always seemed to hit the wrong shot at the wrong time.

"Talent and looks, ten; brain, three" was the assessment of one agent who had seen her play for years.

Talent and looks had Shriver in trouble most of the afternoon. Serving for the match, after a two-hour uphill climb; Shriver choked, just as she had against Pospisilova. She went from up 6–5 to down 6–7. Furious, Shriver hurled her racquet a good twenty feet. It brought a gasp from the crowd, which was unused to such outbursts from her.

"I was just *so* angry and frustrated," she said. "It was as if I simply couldn't serve out a match. I sat there during the changeover and said, 'Okay, this is it. If you can't win this match, you should just go home and forget about it. Just quit, period. I was that upset with myself."

The combination of Shriver's sheer fury and Provis's sheer terror combined to get Shriver through the match. She finally won it 9–7, but still walked off court shaking her head. "Neither one of us handled the pressure," she admitted. "I'm not really sure what happened to her because, right now, it's not as if beating me is a big deal. I know I was lucky today, because she easily could have won the match. It's not as if I'm a big victory for someone, though. I'm not really a scalp anymore."

Two days later, Shriver lost to Kimiko Date, a nineteen-year-old Japanese, 6–4, 6–3. In player terminology, Date "routined" her, beating her easily—routinely. Shriver's first instinct after losing was to catch the next plane home. But ESPN asked if she wanted to hang around and do some commentary. Shriver thought about it overnight before saying yes.

"I guess the time has come to stop thinking about what comes next and start acting on it," she said. "It's hard to look in the mirror and say it, but at twenty-eight I'm a lot closer to the end than I am to the beginning."

During the first weekend, the tournament began to fall apart.

First, Gabriela Sabatini got her foot stuck on the sticky center court and tumbled head over heels, badly spraining her ankle. She went out of the tournament in a wheelchair.

Less than two hours later, on the same court, Australian Mark Woodforde did exactly the same thing in his match against David Wheaton. The foot caught, Woodforde tumbled, and the same wheelchair took him off. He had torn ligaments that would require surgery.

That night, again on center court, Zina Garrison took a dive. Garrison, though, had the benefit of having watched both Sabatini and Woodforde, so instead of trying to stop her fall, she just allowed herself to roll right over. She came up bruised and shaken, but she came up.

It was getting scary, though. There had been much talk among the players about the rubberized hard court called Rebound Ace that Tennis Australia had selected for Flinders Park, in 1988. In ideal weather conditions Rebound Ace was a superb playing surface. The bounce was true, it was not too slick, not too slow, and the traction was excellent. But when it got hot and humid, like any rubber it quickly absorbed the heat. That not only made for miserable conditions, it was becoming apparent it could make the court dangerous.

Becker, who had been slogging through his matches in spite of his malaise, was blunt in his criticism of the surface. "It's too sticky," he said. "When you're tired, it's very easy to get caught and take a fall. It was a mistake for Australian tennis to go away from the grass. On grass, the heat matters less and it isn't as sticky."

He stopped and grinned for almost the first time since he had been in Australia. "Also, if they left the grass in I would have a better chance to win the tournament."

By Sunday evening, he certainly had a better chance of winning the tournament than John McEnroe, who made everyone forget the Rebound Ace controversy, the injuries, *and* the heat with his extraordinary outburst. His default cast a pall over the entire tournament. His play in those first three rounds had been so electrifying that his stunning departure left even his competitors saddened.

Months later, Becker would shake his head like the father of a wayward child when the subject came up. "John should have won the tournament," he said. "He was playing better than anyone." He paused for a moment and began asking questions:

"How much would that have meant to tennis to have McEnroe win there? How much would it have meant to *John* to win there? It could only have been good, so very good, and all of a sudden it was bad, so very bad."

There were repercussions in the wake of the default—a death threat to Gerry Armstrong, the umpire who'd ejected McEnroe, the most serious among them.

It would take McEnroe several weeks to understand what had happened. He flew home to Los Angeles with his family and called his brother Patrick in Florida. Patrick had been down there training with his coach, Carlos Goffi. He and Goffi had come off the court on that fateful Sunday morning and been greeted by an ashen-faced friend.

"Patrick," he said, "I'm so sorry about your brother."

For a moment, Patrick's heart stopped. "I thought, 'My God, is he dead, did one of the kids get kidnapped, what in the world happened?' When the guy said, 'He got defaulted in Australia,' I was almost relieved."

Relief quickly turned to disappointment, though not shock. Like anyone who knew John—including John—this sort of thing had always been a possibility. Nonetheless, Patrick was surprised two days later when the phone rang and an almost cheerful voice said, "Hey, Pat, did you hear what happened in Australia? I got defaulted."

In the meantime, the tournament slogged on.

The men's quarterfinals broke down this way: Pernfors–Noah, Lendl–Cherkasov, Edberg–Wheaton, and Wilander–Becker. The two surprises in the group were Wheaton and Cherkasov. Both had been a bit lucky: Wheaton had been ahead of Woodforde when the Australian took his tumble but had been saved considerable work by it. His fourth-round victory over his old roommate, Aaron Krickstein, was impressive but tarnished slightly by Krickstein's pulled groin muscle. Even so, Wheaton was less than pleased when Krickstein laid his loss at the feet of the injury and flatly predicted, "He won't go any farther."

The two seeds in Cherkasov's path to the quarterfinals were Thomas Muster, who lost to Jean Fleurian, and the out-of-shape Andres Gomez, who was delighted just to scratch his way through to the round of 16 and not at all bothered when Cherkasov beat him.

Cherkasov lost quickly to Lendl, but Wheaton almost made a liar out of Krickstein. He lost to Edberg in four tough sets, forcing the Swede to save set points in the second set before he finally went down 7–6 in the fourth. Wheaton was hardly discouraged by the loss.

"My goal at the start of the year was to make the quarterfinals of a Grand Slam," he said. "Now I've done that, so I'll reset my goals. I learned something here. I know now I can get to four-all with these guys. But that isn't what tennis is all about. It's going that next step and winning the set point, making the big shot. That's what I have to learn to do next."

Lendl's semifinal opponent was Noah, who had made short work of Pernfors, who was still in shock from his experience as the winning bystander against McEnroe. Edberg no doubt expected to play Becker in the semifinals. He got Wilander instead. Seemingly rejuvenated after his wandering 1989, Wilander whipped Becker in three sets. Becker had come back from two sets and 3–1 down to beat Miloslav Mecir in the fourth round and clearly had nothing left emotionally after that.

"He got to bed at four A.M. after the Mecir match," Brett said. "And I never even got a chance to talk to him about what had happened. There are too many people around. The masseuse, the handlers [agents], the stringer. A coach and a player need to be alone after a match like that, and it just isn't happening. I feel like we've done nothing but go backward since he won the Open. If I don't figure out how to get through to him soon, this will be a lost year."

Becker didn't feel much different. After the Wilander match, he was tired, uptight, and confused. He went home to write in his journal for hours, trying to sort out his life.

Edberg–Wilander and Lendl–Noah figured to be good semifinal matchups, especially given Noah's defeat of Lendl in Sydney. But this was the real thing now, not a little warm-up tournament. Lendl lost seven games, needing just an hour and forty-six minutes to bludgeon Noah.

"I liked the way he played much better in Sydney," Noah said. "He was much nicer there. He missed and missed. Today, he didn't miss."

Lendl's performance was nothing compared to what Edberg did to Wilander. He needed even less time—an hour and twenty-two minutes—and gave up only four games in one of the most dominant performances anyone could ever remember seeing.

"Oh, that was *wonderful,*" Ted Tinling cried, coming off court. "I don't think I've ever seen anything more brilliant. It was beautiful to watch."

The women's semifinals had provided no such exhilaration. Graf, still bored, still worried about her father, still vulnerable, beat Helena Sukova for the fifteenth straight time, 6–4 in the third set. Sukova was in tears after the match, knowing she would never have a better chance to beat Graf. "Someone was going to choke at the end," she said. "It turned out to be me."

No one choked in the other semifinal except perhaps the fans. Claudia Porwick, who had been down 6–1, 1–0 to Sabatini when Sabatini had rolled her ankle, lasted just sixty-seven minutes against Mary Joe Fernandez, winning three games.

Fernandez, playing her first Grand Slam final, had Graf down 4–1 in the second set after losing the first, but Graf turned on her tired engine one last time to win the last five games and her third straight Australian Open. As she accepted the trophy, she managed a smile—but it was a weak one.

Watching her, Shriver shook her head. "Something's going to happen before this year is over," she said. "She isn't all there. There's a hiccup in there somewhere. I don't know if it's because she's been so dominant or what it is, but she isn't the same player. You can see it in her face."

Edberg wasn't the same player in the final that he had been in the semifinals by any means, but there was a good reason: Late in the Wilander match, he had pulled a stomach muscle.

Even injured, Edberg managed to win the first set and go up a break at 6–5 in the second. But Lendl, who had seen the trainer come out to treat Edberg and knew something was amiss, hung in. Despite a bad case of nerves, he broke back and won the tiebreak. He was up 5–2 in the third when Edberg, shaking his head, dejectedly walked up to the chair.

"I can't play," he said simply. "I have to stop."

It was not a complete surprise when Edberg retired from the match, but it was a flat, damp ending to a tournament that had seemed jinxed from the beginning.

Edberg, almost doubled over in pain, hobbled off, leaving Lendl alone to accept his award. Lendl is a pragmatist, and winning his eighth Grand Slam title was no small thing. He had been in Australia for a month, working toward this goal. But even he knew this was no way to win a championship.

"I'm sorry the match ended the way it did," he told the crowd. "I feel badly for Stefan. I hope next year we get a chance to slug it out until the end."

They handed Lendl the trophy at 5:30 P.M. It was exactly one week—to the minute—since McEnroe had been defaulted on the same court.

5

TED

On the morning of January 8, Gerard F. Smith began his second week as executive director of the Women's International Tennis Association. Gerry Smith had been chosen in November for his new job by a WITA search committee. He left a very comfortable—though often frustrating—job as publisher of *Newsweek* magazine to take over an organization that was entering a critical and potentially difficult period in its history.

On this Monday morning, Smith had approximately ten thousand things he wanted to get done before he left for Australia on Thursday. This would be his first Australian Open and his first appearance in the new job. Waiting for him when he arrived at his office was a fax.

It had come in from Sydney, and the handwriting was barely legible. But the words jumped off the page. "You *must* come down here earlier than planned," it read. "The Australian circuit is in serious jeopardy. Sydney has been turned over to the men—*totally.* Brisbane is threatened by Hopman Cup. I will tell you more when you arrive but you *must* come to Sydney ASAP."

Smith shook his head as he read the fax. The last thing in the world he needed was to move up his travel plans. How serious could the problems be? He hadn't heard anything from any of his staff there about difficulties. But staring at the scrawled signature at the bottom of the fax, Smith knew he needed to heed the warning.

The fax was signed by Ted Tinling—and when Ted Tinling spoke, only fools refused to listen. Gerry Smith was no fool.

When Smith arrived in Sydney, Ted was waiting anxiously. He had been in Australia since Christmas, and he didn't like what he had seen. The people who ran the Hopman Cup exhibition in Perth were asking Tennis Australia to allow them to move their final to Monday night. It was a move made because of the demands of television.

"That could be disastrous for Brisbane," Tinling explained to Smith. "The tournament there begins on Monday. If a top player makes the

Hopman final, they might decide to skip Brisbane to get a rest. What's more, who knows how far into the week they might choose to push once they've been allowed to overlap? You might lose TV exposure. It must be stopped *now.*"

As for Sydney, Tinling simply handed Smith the week's schedule of play. The women were being used as a warm-up act for the men. Their center-court matches were starting in the morning or the early evening, while the men's were in the prime—read "TV"—times. The WITA had complained about the scheduling to no avail. Muscle was needed. To Tinling, Smith was that muscle.

Smith knew Tinling was right. He also knew that neither situation was at a crisis stage—yet. Allowed to continue unchecked, it could become a crisis. That's why Tinling had faxed Smith.

"These bloody people *need* me," Ted said, sipping a cup of tea after he had finished his meeting with Smith. "The problem is, I'm not going to be around much longer. That's why I have to push them so hard *right now.* There just isn't that much time left."

Ted Tinling was dying. He knew it and, deep down, everyone who spent time with him knew it, too. His problem was simple: He couldn't breathe. There was a certain cruel irony in this because it had been respiratory problems that first exposed him to the game of tennis.

He was born on June 23, 1910, in Eastbourne, England, the third and last child of James Alexander and Florence Elizabeth Tinling. Almost from the beginning of his life, Ted had breathing problems. He suffered from bronchial asthma and, in 1923, his parents decided to take him to the French Riviera for the winter because the doctors had told them that cold weather aggravated their son's condition.

The warm weather helped, and Ted began to play tennis at the Nice Tennis Club, taking lessons twice a week. He quickly became enamored of the sport and of the game's stars. Bill Tilden was then the top male player in the world; Suzanne Lenglen was the dominant female player.

Lenglen and her family spent winters on the Riviera, and she often played exhibitions at the Nice club. Her father, known to everyone in tennis as "Papa Lenglen," controlled her career and her life completely. "Suzanne was his creation and he lived his life through her," Ted said years later. "The similarities between Suzanne and Steffi and their fathers are remarkable. Both fathers built their lives around the daughter. Both daughters adored the father no matter what his flaws."

Ted began making a habit of hanging around the Nice club on Thursday afternoons, knowing that was the day Lenglen usually showed up to play an exhibition. It was on a Thursday, January 10, 1924, that he was hiding in the bushes leading to the court, hoping for a close-up glance of Lenglen, when he overhead the woman in charge of arranging the match, one Mrs. Wollaston Richards, explaining to Papa Lenglen that she had somehow forgotten to arrange for an umpire for Suzanne's match that day.

Papa Lenglen was becoming quite distraught when the now-panicked Richards spotted Tinling, who was already well over six feet tall, trying to hide in the bushes. "You, boy," she said, pointing her finger at him, "do you know how to umpire?"

Sixty-six years later to the day, Ted remembered his answer. "I just nodded my head," he said. "I was too petrified to speak. Suzanne was standing no more than five feet away, staring at me."

It was, in all likelihood, the first and last time in his life that Ted was rendered speechless. His mute nod did the trick, though. Richards turned to Lenglen and asked, "Would you mind if this young man umpired your match?"

Lenglen smiled up at Tinling and said, *"Mais, avec plaisir,"* and a lifelong obsession began. In spite of a bad case of nerves, Ted made it through the match, and for the next two years was Lenglen's personal umpire. It was his relationship with her that led to his first Wimbledon, in 1927.

The rest of his career is the stuff of tennis legend: player liaison at Wimbledon twice—from 1927 to 1949, and then from 1982 on; decent player; dress designer to almost every great woman player of the twentieth century; Wimbledon pariah for thirty-three years after he designed the lace panties made famous by Gussie Moran in 1949 (thus the break in his Wimbledon employment); historian and spokesman for the game. If you needed someone to put anything in perspective or cut through the rhetoric of an occasion, it was Ted you went looking for.

His résumé hardly begins to describe the man. He was almost six feet six, completely bald throughout the latter half of his life, and wore a diamond stud in his left ear—eons before that sort of thing became fashionable. Ted was gay, something he didn't talk about much but never tried to hide from his friends. That's how you knew Ted really trusted you—he began to tell jokes and stories that related to his sexuality.

One of his favorites was about a day at Eastbourne, in the 1970s, during a time when women's tennis was just beginning to establish itself as an independent entity. Female players were still fighting all the stories and rumors about homosexuality in the locker room (some true, others exaggerated). Ted was watching a match one afternoon between two women known to virtually everyone in tennis as being homosexual. Ted always loved watching the tournament at Devonshire Park, in Eastbourne, because he had seen his very first tennis matches there with his mother when he was a little boy.

On this afternoon, though, his reverie was interrupted by a very loud spectator—"I think he must have been quite drunk," Ted said in telling the story—who stood up during a changeover and announced he was leaving in this way:

"That's it, that's *it*, I'm not watching these bloody dykes play for one more second! I've had it!" He then spun around, pointed his finger at Ted, and said, "And you, Tinling, you fucking homosexual you, you shouldn't be watching them play either!"

Ted's response? "You know, if I had been a *practicing* fucking homosexual and getting something out of it, I wouldn't have minded. But as I wasn't, I was rather offended!"

That sort of story was typical Ted. There was almost nothing he wouldn't say. He insisted that his bluntness was a product of age, but peers who had known him for years insisted that wasn't true. "Teddy was born telling people exactly what he thought," Dan Maskell, the voice of the BBC at Wimbledon—seemingly forever—once said. "I doubt if there's ever been an opinion that he failed to express." Three years older than Ted, Maskell liked to say that in spite of it all, "Teddy's a nice boy."

The nice boy was a spy for British Intelligence in World War II, went through a fashion war with Fred Perry in the fifties and sixties, and then became one of the first key people in women's tennis when he went to work for Virginia Slims as their "player-media liaison," in the 1970s.

Although he continued to design dresses during that period, Ted's role as the game's spokesman became more and more important from that point on. He was one of the few people—if not the only person—who had the ear of *everyone* in the game, including, most important, the players. He cared about all of them because they were all part of *his* game, but he made no bones about his favorites.

He loved Chris Evert; she defined the sort of grace and femininity that was his ideal. He was close to Billie Jean King and designed the dress she wore in the Bobby Riggs match. He was one of the few people who could talk to Peter Graf, and he adored Steffi.

On the morning of the Australian semifinals, Graf's coach, Pavel Slozil, came to Ted, begging him to talk to Steffi before her match with Helena Sukova. She was so sluggish, so bored, so out of it, Slozil actually believed she could lose to Sukova. By this time, Ted was having so much trouble breathing that he had to carry oxygen with him everywhere he went. Walking down the hall to the bathroom exhausted him. His doctors had told him not to speak unless he had to.

"I'm to behave like a great actor," he said. "Not a word unless I'm paid." He laughed at the thought. He wasn't going to shut up now. He had too much to say.

And so he hobbled from the pressroom on that Thursday morning in Australia, wheezing and gasping for air, and dragged himself out in search of Graf. When he found her, he spoke briefly. "She was in an awful mood," he said. "All I said to her was 'please try to remember that you are the best player in the world.'

"She looked at me and said, 'Maybe not today.' "

She scraped through that day and won the tournament, but Ted wasn't happy. "She's bored, unmotivated, unhappy, and upset," he said. "She comes all this way to play seven ridiculous matches. She needs a talking to—maybe from me—although they might be my last words. Something is up with Papa, there's no doubt of it. Nothing else would put her into this sort of funk."

He was right, of course, as events later in the year would prove. Ted Tinling was usually right.

Even as his body betrayed him, Ted remained the smartest, funniest person in the sport.

In Sydney, the press was fed in a rather raunchy tent set up on the far end of the grounds, on the edge of a drainage ditch. To get into it, one had to step across the ditch. One afternoon, Eleanor Pollard, wife of the newly anointed president of Tennis Australia, Geoff Pollard, made a swing through the pressroom to make sure everyone was happy. It was a tour more for taking bows than taking notes, but that didn't really concern Ted.

"Aah, Mrs. Pollard, how *lovely* it is to see you," he said formally, the very picture of English charm.

"Oh, Ted, wonderful to have you here. Everything is all right, then?"

"Lovely. Except for all of us having to sit with our feet in a *bloody moat* during lunch."

"A what?"

"A moat! It's extraordinary. How can you allow this to go on! What do you intend to do about it?"

Eleanor Pollard knew nothing about the media's eating arrangements and no doubt couldn't have cared less about them. But she sure as hell didn't want Ted Tinling screaming at her in front of a roomful of people.

"I will see about it today, Ted, I promise," she squeaked, retreating toward the door as quickly as possible.

"I should hope so!" Ted roared. "A moat! Whoever heard of sitting in a moat? The food is bad enough as is!"

Later that same week, a young woman from one of the Sydney papers showed up wearing a low-cut orange halter top. "Who is *that*?" someone asked as she sat down at her desk.

"You mean Miss Orange Tits?" Ted asked, his voice booming around the room.

"Ted, she's sitting right there," someone hissed.

"So what? She knows she has orange tits. She *designed* them that way."

No one was immune. During the Australian Open, one of Channel 7's commentators was Wendy Turnbull, the top Australian woman player of the 1980s once Evonne Goolagong retired for good. Turnbull was a classic ex-jock commentator—she spent most of her time shamelessly hyping the women's tour and its sponsors.

One night, after a rain delay, Turnbull's partner asked her which player would benefit most from the play stoppage. "Oh, I think *both* players will benefit," Turnbull said.

Each night, Ted left the tennis at about six o'clock, went back to his room, ordered a bowl of soup, and turned on the night matches. By the end of the first week he had seen quite enough of Turnbull. "Commentary for the *blind,*" he said. "I know a crosscourt backhand when I see it, without being told 'that was a crosscourt backhand' by Miss Turnbull!"

Naturally, since Ted told anyone who would listen what he thought of Turnbull's work, word of his opinions eventually reached her. Never one to back away from a confrontation, she marched into the pressroom one morning, looking for Ted.

"I understand," she said stiffly, "that you've been quite critical of my TV commentary."

"Absolutely!" Ted screamed. "It's *awful*! Don't tell everyone what they can see or what they already know, tell them what they *don't* know. You are on the telecast because you have *been* there. You've played these players, been on this court. You know what it feels like to try to return Steffi's forehand. I don't. Tell me what that's like. Tell me what it *feels* like to be out there."

Turnbull didn't say another word. She just turned and walked out.

Every day in Australia was difficult for Ted. In the mornings, as the crowd was filing in, he would go on court and talk about the day's matches. He had always enjoyed introducing players, and this was Tennis Australia's way of letting him continue, in some small way, to do that.

When he was finished, Ted would come shuffling back to the pressroom, exhausted. "It won't be long now," he would say.

"Stop it," someone would always answer. "You aren't going anywhere."

"Oh yes I am. I just hope I can make it through Wimbledon."

Talking about death didn't bother Ted. For one thing, he was a believer in both the afterlife and reincarnation. "I do hope I come back as something that walks upright," he said one day. "I think I've at least earned that."

On January 10, Ted celebrated the sixty-sixth anniversary of the day he had become Lenglen's umpire.

"When I die, I'm going to heaven," he said. "And I know Suzanne is going to be waiting for me. She's going to greet me at the gate, look me right in the eye, and say, 'How can you *possibly* say that Steffi covers the court better than I did? How dare you say such a thing?' "

He laughed. "I'm far more terrified of that than of dying."

He had made explicit and detailed plans for his death. If he died overseas, his diamond stud was to be removed and used to pay the cost to fly him to Philadelphia, where he had lived for the last fifteen years. Since he was concerned with the future of the planet—after all, he was coming back—he willed his body to the University of Pennsylvania for medical research.

Shortly after he had added this provision to his will, Ted got a call from the medical school at Penn. "Mr. Tinling," the caller said, "we really appreciate what you've done, but there's one problem: There's no provision for getting you from the airport to the school."

Ted was nonplussed—at least for a minute or two. "I finally told the man to send the will back," he said. "Then I added a provision for taxi fare from the airport to the school. After all, I didn't want them putting me on the bloody *bus*!"

By January, Ted had a doomsday line for almost anything you could say to him.

"See you tomorrow, Ted."

"God willing."

"How are you, Ted?"

"I shall never feel good again in *this* incarnation."

"Great match, wasn't it, Ted?"

"Absolutely. Glad I lived to see it."

Ted joked about his impending death so often that everyone on the circuit began to think that somehow, someway, he would hang on at least until Wimbledon. His eightieth birthday was June 23, and the International Club of Great Britain was planning to honor him at its annual dinner, held the Saturday night before Wimbledon began. Ted, being Ted, had agreed to take part in the occasion but only if members of the non-English media were invited. This had never been done before, which was exactly why it was important to Ted.

Ted was an old Englishman who cherished tradition—as long as the tradition made sense. He did not believe in tradition for its own sake. It was Ted who first convinced the Wimbledon Committee to invite foreign reporters to their morning meetings during the tournament. It was Ted who convinced the committee to give reporters access to the hallowed tearoom at Wimbledon, pointing out that if agents were to be allowed to sit up there making their deals, the media should at least be allowed up there to give the public some idea of what the place looked and sounded like.

In 1985, when Anne White showed up at Wimbledon in her sheer white bodysuit, Ted raved. "It's marvelous," he said. "It's the next step in fashion, no doubt. The only thing left after this will be body paint. I can't wait for that to happen."

A member of the English tabloid media overheard Ted's comments and splashed them all over the front page of his newspaper the next morning. The committee, which banned the bodysuit the next day, was not at all pleased with Ted and told him so. "I've been a bad boy," Ted said. Then he grinned. "Bloody English will never join the twentieth century, will they?"

Ted was always trying to make people think. He had no patience with stupidity or political rhetoric. When Larry Scott, the vice president of the ATP Tour board, began spouting off one day about what he claimed was an ITF injustice, Ted looked at him and said, "Young man, you have no idea what you're talking about. Have you even bothered to read the ITF rule book?

"Well, no," Scott said. "I don't have a copy and . . ."

"Here," Ted said, reaching into his briefcase, "take mine. They aren't hard to find. Read it, learn the rules, and *then* come back and talk to me."

Scott walked away with the rule book and a sheepish look on his face. "Tough guy to argue with," he said.

"Tough guy to try and bullshit," he was told.

On the last day of the Australian Open, Ted showed up in one of his most flamboyant outfits; every color of the rainbow seemed to be represented. "I'm an old freak," he liked to say, "so why shouldn't I dress like one?"

When Lendl finished his acceptance speech, Ted stood up from the courtside chair he had been seated in—complete with fly swatter to protect him from Melbourne's omnipresent insects—and looked around the stadium.

"One last look," he said. "I won't be here again."

He was right.

Ted's last grand moment was in Boca Raton, when Jennifer Capriati made her debut. By then he was in a wheelchair, but he still made it to the tournament and held court with one reporter after another, talking about Lenglen and Helen Wills Moody and Maureen Connolly and Billie Jean King and Margaret Court and Chris and Martina and on and on.

"There were thirteen photographers on court for Maureen's debut," he remembered. Not ten to fifteen or a dozen—*thirteen,* exactly thirteen.

Capriati thrilled him. He loved her exuberance, her ability to deal with the pressure and the hype, her joy at playing the game. After Capriati's first match, a 7–6, 6–1 victory over Mary Lou Daniels, he was exultant. "That wasn't a debut, it was a *performance*!" he said. "It was opening night at the theater."

That night, he was still buoyant. "I think now I've seen all the great ones of the century," he said. "That was the beginning for Jennifer, the end for me. I am so glad I lived to see it, so very glad."

One week later, in Miami, he was taken to the hospital in the middle of the night. He probably would have died there if Nancy Bolger of Virginia Slims had not disobeyed his orders and called an ambulance. He lived through the night—to the surprise of the doctors—and was sitting up in bed barking orders a week later. On March 29, Capriati's fourteenth birthday, Ted wrapped fourteen chocolates for her. He went home to Philadelphia the next week and then to his hospital in London a week later. The plan was for his doctors there to get him healthy enough to make it to the French Open and to Wimbledon.

He didn't make it, though.

Three days before he died, I received a fax from Ted, with detailed instructions about his International Club dinner and equally detailed comments about the ongoing Italian Open. He also said this: "I'm beginning to think I won't see Wimbledon this year. Martina will win; Steffi is too distraught over her father to beat her. I only wish I could be in Paris. I truly believe Monica [Seles] is ready to win there. I would love seeing that."

For Ted, Seles was Lenglen all over again. He loved everything about her. "She's Doris Day," he insisted. "My God, she's a normal person, the first one we've had in years. We've had the awkwardness of [Margaret] Court, the bitchiness of Billie Jean, the brown sugar of Chrissie, the butchness of Martina, and the manic shyness of Graf. Now we shall have Seles, and she will be wonderful. Completely wonderful."

Three days after Ted sent that fax, the doctors allowed him to leave the hospital briefly to attend a reunion of his old bowling team (Ted had been an excellent bowler in his day). He came back from the reunion quite happy, went to bed, and died in his sleep.

When I learned of his death, my first instinct was to cry. But if you knew Ted, you started thinking about the will and the cab fare and the bus in Philadelphia. The proper response to Ted Tinling's death was laughter, not tears.

Four weeks later, on the day before Wimbledon began, most of the tennis world gathered in St. James Church in downtown London for a memorial service in Ted's honor. He had planned the whole thing, including the recessional—the theme song from an English soap opera. The key words were "even neighbors need good friends." Ted was sending a final message.

Tommy Bonk of the *Los Angeles Times* and I were ushers that day. We were told to leave four rows empty near the front of the church, so there would be seats for the players. Chris Evert, who was one of the speakers, arrived. Pam Shriver, out injured, also showed up. Virginia Wade, the 1977 Wimbledon champion, now a member of the Wimbledon Committee, was there. Three longtime tour players, Kathy Rinaldi, Jill Hetherington, and Candy Reynolds, showed up.

But at 3 P.M., when the service was scheduled to start, that was it. Disgusted, Bonk and I filled in most of the four rows with nonplayers. I was angry. Sure, Wimbledon was starting the next day, but most of the women wouldn't play before Tuesday. And even so, they could have given up an hour for Ted. Where was Capriati, for whom he had made a birthday present while practically on his deathbed? Where was Graf? Where the hell was Billie Jean King? They had all found excuses not to show up.

And then, as I was about to sit down, I looked up and there was Monica Seles. Two weeks after she had fulfilled Ted's prediction by beating Graf in the French final, she had fought her way through the tabloid press that was congregated outside and made it into the church. As much as any of them—perhaps more—she could have found an excuse not to come. But she was there.

I looked up to wherever you look in those situations and I said, "Ted, you always knew how to pick 'em."

And then I cried.

PART TWO

INDOORS AND OUT

6

GUARANTEES, DEFAULTS, AND TANKS

When Australia is over, after every Grand Slam is over, tennis scatters. The men head for Europe and the United States, while the women go first to Japan and then to the U.S. From the heat and humidity of Melbourne, the players and their entourages dive right into snow and wind and ice and indoor tennis. Many players enjoy playing indoors. The conditions for every match are the same: no wind, no rain, no heat. No rain delays.

John McEnroe has always said the fairest test of tennis is indoors because most of the variables are eliminated. When Steffi Graf arrived in Tokyo—she had to play in the tournament there as part of her deal with two Japanese companies—it was snowing. She was thrilled. "After a month in Melbourne, I was so happy to see snow, I can't tell you," she said. "Right away, I felt better than I had in Australia."

For most players, though, the indoor circuit is a tough, grinding time of year. Cities such as Tokyo, Toronto, Philadelphia, Washington, Chicago, Memphis, Milan, Brussels, and Stuttgart certainly do not lack for charm. But in February they are all almost uniformly gray, cold, and snowy. Not everyone revels in snow the way Graf does.

Most indoor facilities have only one or two courts. That means to get the tournament played in a week, matches must begin as early as 9 A.M. Often, they last until well after midnight. One long match can throw off an entire tournament schedule. Unlike an outdoor tournament delayed by rain, there are no extra courts that can be used to make up for lost time.

An indoor tournament can become an endurance test, not so much on the court, but off it. Every day starts to seem the same as every other day; the facility begins to feel like a prison. When a player finally gets on court, if he isn't one of the big names, he'll often find himself playing in a near-empty arena. Outdoors, on a side court with seating for only one thousand, a crowd of eight hundred people is sufficient. In an indoor arena with fifteen thousand seats, the place can feel awfully empty with only eight hundred people watching.

O

For the men, the start of this indoor season was particularly important. While the two warm-up tournaments in Adelaide and Sydney had been something of a prologue for Hamilton Jordan's new ATP Tour, the European/American indoor circuit would really be its debut.

Almost from the beginning there were problems. They began in San Francisco. With guarantees now legal in the World Series tournaments, tournament director Barry McKay, one of the more honest people in the game, willingly announced that he had offered three players guarantees: Andre Agassi ($175,000), Michael Chang ($125,000), and Brad Gilbert ($30,000).

Chang had been forced to drop out because of a hip injury. Gilbert, who was furious when he learned how much Agassi was getting, promptly lost his first-round match. (Gilbert really didn't have much to complain about, though. Even though San Francisco was his hometown, it wasn't likely that his presence would sell any tickets. Friends and family, sure—but they would want freebies, anyway.) People couldn't help but note that Gilbert had received $30,000 to play and lose one match, while Todd Witsken, after battling his way through to the final, collected $19,000.

Agassi won the tournament. But how excited could the crowd get when they knew Agassi's check for winning was $30,000, but he had made nearly six times that amount just for showing up?

Things were even dicier in Europe. In Milan, Jimmy Connors, receiving $100,000 for his appearance, not only lost in the first round to that giant of the game, Marcus Zoecke, but broke his wrist during the third-set tiebreak. That meant he couldn't play the following week in Brussels. Edberg had already been forced to withdraw because of the stomach injury he'd suffered in Australia.

This left the ATP Tour in a bind. There were *two* Championship Series tournaments being held in one week (Brussels and Toronto). Hoping to keep these tournaments from paying guarantees, the ATP Tour had promised tournament directors at least three Top Ten–type players.

The three for Brussels were Becker, Edberg, and Connors. Even though Connors was no longer in the Top Ten, promoters and tournament directors still considered him a Top Ten "type." Even though guarantees were supposed to be against the rules for a Championship Series event, each of the three was receiving one. But now Edberg and Connors couldn't play. In the very first week of Championship Series play, it was beginning to look as if the ATP Tour would blow its commitment right off the bat.

Phone calls were made. ATP Tour officials talked to agents, who talked to their players. Presto, Emilio Sanchez and Carl Uwe-Steeb were on their way to Brussels. Hamilton Jordan sent out a press release declaring that the last-minute entries of Sanchez and Uwe-Steeb in Brussels in the wake of the injuries to Edberg and Connors were "an example of the new spirit of cooperation on the ATP Tour."

Jordan neglected to mention one thing: Both Steeb and Sanchez were *paid* to go to Brussels. Sanchez received $20,000. Steeb had the option to receive $20,000 or back out of a nonpaying commitment in April. Who paid them? The ATP Tour. In other words, the group that was supposed to be enforcing the rule *against* guarantees was now *paying* guarantees.

By May, the ATP Tour had paid Andrei Chesnokov $25,000 to play in Barcelona, Jay Berger $25,000 to play in that same tournament, and Steeb $25,000 to enter the Italian Open. Steeb hurt his thumb the day before the tournament began—counting the money, perhaps?—and had to withdraw. Graciously, he returned his payoff.

These figures were hardly staggering when compared to the six-figure-plus guarantees the big names were receiving. Certainly, everyone involved with the ATP Tour acted as if they were no big deal. Tour officials claimed that the "extra designation fees" had been part of the plan all along. Yet *many* players, including members of the ATP Council, knew nothing about them until May, when the payments were made public. What's more, Weller Evans and Vittorio Selmi, the two operations directors who made the deals with the players and their agents, told those involved not to submit written invoices.

Steeb earned his fee in Brussels, reaching the final. Sanchez lost his first-round match, collected his money, and went home.

That same week in Toronto, a different problem cropped up: defaults—six in all. Five players retired with injuries during matches, and one player defaulted just before he was to go on court. Four of the retirements happened on the same day, during the first round.

Weller Evans called an informal locker-room meeting of about twenty players that day to talk about the quickly growing image problem. Patrick McEnroe, John's brother and a member of the ATP Player Council, was one of the players who had quit during his match. He had been bothered by a stomach problem similar to Edberg's, which had grown worse and worse in his match against Paul Haarhuis. Finally, afraid that he might hurt himself seriously if he continued, McEnroe defaulted.

"It was a tough situation for all of us," McEnroe said. "Weller was concerned because it just didn't look good. Here we were getting more prize money than ever, getting free hotel rooms for the entire week, and guys were quitting. Could I have gone on? Maybe. But I had to think about what it would mean long-term if I kept playing. It was just bad luck more than anything."

Certainly there was truth in this—Robert Seguso, one of the players who had to quit, underwent knee surgery the next week—but the new tour was being watched closely, and its first big week in both Brussels and Toronto did not hold up well when scrutinized.

There was one more problem that week: After Ivan Lendl was publicly critical of the officiating in his match with Kevin Curren, he was fined $1,000. Lendl promptly turned around and ripped the ATP Tour, comparing it to the oppressive government he had escaped from in Czechoslovakia. A bit melodramatic, perhaps, but the point was well taken. Despite Jordan's belief that if his minions pretended everything was wonderful then the world would believe that everything was wonderful, gagging players wasn't going to make things any better for the ATP.

While the men were dealing with the inevitable growing pains of the new tour, the women were having difficulties of their own. On February 6, Graf tore ligaments in her thumb in a skiing accident in St. Moritz. She had gone there to film a cameo spot in a movie, arrived to find the place swarming with paparazzi, and freaked out. That afternoon, when she went out to ski, the photographers were everywhere.

"I tried to turn on my skis and I slipped," she said. "I put my hand down to stop the fall and felt it jam. We went inside, and a doctor looked at it and said it didn't look so bad. But it kept swelling more and more. Finally, we decided we better go home and have a specialist look at it."

Three specialists ended up looking at it. Graf was given two options: operate and be out at least eight weeks but with guaranteed full recovery, or wait and see if the injury would heal itself. If it didn't and the surgery had to be done in March, it could jeopardize her French Open chances. "I hate operations," Graf said. "I decided to take a chance."

If all went well, Graf would be back in April, in plenty of time for the Grand Slams, although her movie career was shot. Her absence, along with Sabatini's absence because of her ankle injury, left the indoor circuit shy two key players. The WITA had to put into action a new bonus pool, not all that different from the ATP Tour's "extra designation fee."

The WITA guarantees a certain number of ranked players to its tournaments; the guarantees are dependent on the prize money involved.

Players are designated in four categories: 1–2, 3–4, 5–8, and 9–16. These designations do not always follow the computer. A player designated as a 3–4 in the U.S. might be only a 5–8 in Europe, or vice versa. In 1991, Jennifer Capriati, who finished 1990 ranked tenth in the world, is designated as a 3–4 in both Europe and the U.S. Obviously, box-office appeal counts as much, if not more, than on-court ability.

If the WITA fails to meet its designation requirements at a tournament, it has to pay a fee to that tournament. This had already occurred in Sydney, where no player ranked in the top four participated. It had also happened several times during 1988 and 1989. As a result, the WITA had set up a new bonus pool for such occasions. If a player from a ranking group was injured or dropped out of a tournament, the WITA could pay another player from that ranking group to step in.

In other words, when the tournament in Chicago came up shy of its commitment for players designated 5–8, the WITA was able to offer Arantxa Sanchez $25,000 to play. The rules were a little tougher than the ATP's. Sanchez could only collect the money if, at the end of the year, she had met all her other commitments. There was a total of $325,000 in the fund. If a player designated 1–2 (Graf or Navratilova) stepped into a tournament at the last minute, she would receive $75,000; a 3–4 player would get $50,000; a 5–8, $25,000, and a 9–16, $10,000. Many players turned down the money—especially early in the season—knowing that if they missed one tournament later in the year, they wouldn't collect.

Chicago proved to be a 1990 coming-out party for Martina Navratilova, who, having skipped Australia, started her year there with an easy win. Monica Seles also started her year in Chicago but not nearly as impressively: She lost in the first round to Roslyn Fairbank. Seles had been the darling of the tour in 1989. At fifteen she had gone from eighty-sixth on the computer to sixth, beating Chris Evert in Houston for her first title in April, then reaching the French Open semifinals in June.

Seles was like no one else who had ever come on tour. Born in Yugoslavia, she moved with her family to Nick Bollettieri's academy at the age of twelve. She was a lefty, hit the ball with two hands off both sides, and grunted like no one had ever grunted before. She let out a two-syllable cry that sounded something like *aaah-eeee!* each time she hit the ball, the grunt growing louder and more dramatic as the point accelerated. Some players were already claiming the grunting was a tactic, not an instinct.

Off the court, Seles spoke in rapid-fire English with an accent that sounded a little bit midwestern and a little bit Eastern European all at once, punctuating everything with a Woody Woodpeckerish giggle. She was delightfully accommodating, so much so that she not only produced answers, she helped with the questions too. A conversation with her might go something like this:

Q: Monica, in the third set you started . . .

A: To look nervous, I know, I was feeling nervous, you know, just in my stomach a little bit, but it's something you have to try to forget about out there, and you have to realize that the other opponent is nervous out there, too, and if you do know this then you can forget how nervous you are and hit your shots, and if you hit your shots then you're going to have a good chance to win, but of course if you stay nervous and don't hit your shots then you are probably going to lose, which isn't necesarily that bad, because it's just a tennis match, but you're certainly out there trying to win. Hee-hee, hee-hee, hee . . .

Q: Could you look ahead a little and talk . . .

A: About playing Martina? Sure, perfect, perfect, you know, I've always really looked up to Martina and Chris, and Steffi a little bit, too, even though she's younger, because they're such great players, and I've always been watching them play since I was little or at least since I was, like, eleven, twelve, but to get to play on the same court with them, well, it's just an unbelievable feeling, because, you know, when I played Chris in Houston I don't even think I was thinking about what I was doing because if I had I never would have beaten her, which is what I think happened at the U.S. Open, where I know a lot of people were thinking I would beat her, but she just played great and the crowd was so for her, which was good because she's done so much for the game, if I had been in the crowd I would have been for her, too, although of course I wasn't so I wasn't but I still felt good about her playing like that even though it meant that I lost, of course, but that was okay too because I'll definitely have more chances, I think, at least I would think I would. Hee-hee, hee-hee, hee-hee.

Seles was a lot like other phenoms, in that her entire childhood had been built around becoming a tennis player. Her father had managed to make it fun for her, though. A cartoonist, he had drawn little bunnies holding a tennis racquet to teach his daughter how to serve. He had tried to keep tennis from becoming drudge work.

"He always made it seem like fun," Seles said. "Without that, I think it would have become boring in a hurry. I still feel now like I'm just a kid. When I'm on the court with Martina or Chris or Steffi, I want to say, 'Wait a minute, what are you doing here? I watch you only on television. I didn't really understand how good I had become until I watched myself on tape, when I was hurt. Maybe that's why I'm feeling more pressure right now, because I know I am a good player. But I also know I have to play better to beat the really top players."

Seles was about as American as a teenager could be. She wanted a car but her father didn't think she was ready. She had learned most of her English by watching TV, and now found herself thinking in English most of the time. "My mom says I talk in my sleep," she said. "And now when I do she says I talk in English."

Beneath the joyful demeanor, though, Seles was ice on the court, a resolute competitor who tried to beat the brains out of everyone she played. More often than not she succeeded. Which was why her loss in Chicago was so galling.

"I don't think I had ever lost in the first round of *anything* my entire life," she said. "I was so embarrassed. All I wanted to do was go somewhere and play another match and get that one out of my mind."

It wasn't that simple, though. The next stop for Seles was Washington. She arrived Sunday and didn't get to play a match until Friday. As the No. 3 seed, she had a bye in the first round. This was because of what Ted Tinling called "the Martina–Chrissie rule."

The rule allowed tournaments to have a draw of either fifty-six or twenty-eight players rather than sixty-four or thirty-two. A draw of sixty-four or thirty-two means that *every* player has to play a first-round match. The fifty-six draw gave byes to the top eight seeds. Washington, with a twenty-eight draw, gave the top four seeds byes. The rule meant that a top player could show up for an indoor tournament as late as Wednesday and not play until Thursday. During the Washington week, Navratilova was able to play an exhibition against Evert in Milwaukee, on Monday, as part of their never-ending farewell tour (each player pocketing $50,000 for the night's work) and then arrive in Washington in plenty of time to play her first match on Wednesday. The rule was there, according to Tinling, to make sure that Evert and Navratilova didn't have to spend an entire week in a city. (The men had stayed away from byes in most tournaments in the past, but the new ATP Tour was now copying the women. This made the Top Ten happy: less play, more money.)

Seles wasn't sophisticated enough yet to take advantage of her bye.

She was in town Sunday, hoping to play her second-round match on Tuesday. It was scheduled that way, but then Stacey Martin, her opponent, got hurt and had to default. That gave Seles a walkover into the quarterfinals, which weren't until Friday.

Seles is not, by her own admission, a good tourist. She is too focused on her tennis to enjoy wandering through museums or seeing the sights of a city. So for five days in Washington, Seles practiced, sat in the hotel, did a little shopping, and sat around the players' lounge, doing an occasional interview.

When she finally did get to play, she clearly wasn't sharp. She managed to beat Pam Shriver, but in the semifinals Navratilova rolled her 6–3, 6–0. This was disappointing; even though she had lost twice to Navratilova in 1989, both had been close, three-set matches. Yet Seles, even with a 1–2 match record after two weeks in 1990, wasn't panicked.

"I've studied the records of a lot of players who did really well their first year, and almost all of them had tough times the second year," she said. "I had a shoulder problem the end of last year and missed some time practicing, and I've grown almost five inches in the last year. Right now, the court looks different to me because I'm taller. I never even had to bend my knees to get down to the ball before, but now I do. It's all different. That and the pressure. People expect a lot more out of you when you're number six than when you're number eighty-six. I know it won't be as easy for me this year, but I think I can handle it."

If anyone could handle it—the height, the pressure, *and* the stardom—it would be Seles. She had been labeled a phenom by the age of twelve, which was why Bollettieri had been willing to move her entire family—mother, Esther; father, Karolj; and brother, Zoltan—to Florida. But in 1989, when Seles was emerging as a star, Bollettieri was spending a lot of time with Agassi (largely because Agassi insisted on it). The Seles family wasn't thrilled by this; by the end of the year they were looking to break with Bollettieri. This didn't please Bollettieri, who had put both time and money into Seles's development.

The break would not really become a public issue until the Lipton tournament, in Key Biscayne, in March. From that point on it would become increasingly bitter. The Seles family began insisting that Karolj had been Monica's only real coach all along. Bollettieri kept saying that that wasn't true, that if the Seleses had any complaint with him at all it was that he had not been able to give Monica all the time they felt she needed.

By the French Open, the situation had become embarrassing

enough that IMG, which had won a battle with Ion Tiriac for the right to represent Seles, stepped into the fray. Seles agreed to an interview with NBC, specifically with Chris Evert, the network's new tennis analyst. An interview with Evert was a lot safer than an interview with Bud Collins or ESPN's Mary Carillo. The latter two might pose tough questions and follow up if Seles said anything that didn't make sense. Evert, on the other hand, may have been retired but was still a player at heart. In fact, she was still president of the WITA. She threw a couple of easy questions about Bollettieri; Seles, following instructions from IMG, said that of course Bollettieri had been helpful to her and to her family in their early days in the U.S., but she just felt more comfortable working now with her father because "he does know me best."

Everyone was happy after that—although the Seleses thought Evert had been a bit too tough. Never had there been a better example of managing the news. IMG client Evert had interviewed IMG client Seles about IMG client Bollettieri, and all the viewers could see that all those nasty stories about Seles and Bollettieri saying nasty things about each other just couldn't be true.

One person who was happy with Seles's image and was now just hoping she wouldn't keep losing was Gerry Smith. He was in Washington, on what amounted to an ongoing goodwill tour. "The more the players see me and get to know me, the more they're going to have a chance to feel comfortable with me," he said. "I don't think I can get anything accomplished if they don't have confidence in me."

Smith had succeeded Merrett Stierheim as the CEO of the women's tour, and it was apparent from the start that his approach would be different than Stierheim's. One of the first things he did after taking the job was arrange a meeting with Stefano Capriati, knowing just how important Capriati's daughter was going to be in 1990 and beyond. Capriati was already upset with Stierheim and the other bigwigs of the game for making rules that prevented Jennifer from turning pro until she was fourteen. Smith felt the gaps that had developed between them had to be filled as soon as possible.

At the same time, he tried to arrange a similar meeting with Peter and Steffi Graf. The Grafs had long been estranged from the WITA hierarchy. They felt that most of the top people in the organization were Chris/Martina people and therefore anti-Graf. There was some justification for this feeling—most of the WITA staff *was* at the beck and call of the two superstars. That didn't mean they disliked Graf, though. Peter, perhaps, but not Steffi.

In 1987, after Graf had won her first French Open title, beating Navratilova in the final, Ana Leaird, public relations director of the WITA and a close Evert friend since childhood, walked up to Peter Graf at Wimbledon to congratulate him.

"Don't bother with that," Peter Graf said. "I know you are against Steffi all the time."

Smith thought it was important to at least attempt to change Peter Graf's feelings about the WITA. He requested meetings with father and daughter. He got them—in July—eight months after the initial request. Welcome to tennis, Mr. Smith.

"I feel a little bit like I'm back in the military," Smith said later in the year. "You spend a lot of time in this job standing around, waiting for someone to have time to talk to you."

Smith had been a good enough basketball player in college to make the team at Belmont Abbey (North Carolina) as a walk-on. The coach at the time was Al McGuire, who would go on to fame and fortune at Marquette. McGuire, who later became legendary for his flaky ways, was a little bit off even then. "I went through tryouts for the team, and no one ever told me I made it," Smith said. "I just kept on showing up for practice."

Smith, who later transferred to Seton Hall, never played much in his two years at Belmont Abbey. McGuire occasionally sent him out to get him an ice cream cone during games, but he didn't neglect Smith entirely. "He used to say to the players, 'Come on, we have to get up forty so I can put Smith in the game,' " Smith said. "It didn't happen that often."

Smith went into the air force after college and spent time in Vietnam. After leaving the service, he got into advertising. In 1985 he landed the job as publisher of *Newsweek.* While he was there, he convinced Katherine Graham, the chairman of *Newsweek*'s parent company, *The Washington Post,* to invest considerable money in tennis. *Newsweek* became the title sponsor of a men's tournament in California (at a cost of nearly $1 million) and also paid about $250,000 annually for a sponsor's tent at Wimbledon. Smith made contacts in the tennis world, became a director of the International Tennis Hall of Fame, in Newport, and became an avid player.

When Stierheim was not-so-subtly pushed out the door by the WITA, Smith was intrigued by the job. He had grown tired of the Byzantine politics of the Washington Post Company and was willing to believe that tennis, while certainly as Byzantine as the *Post,* would at least provide him with *new* headaches. When he met with the WITA board during the final round of interviews in New York, in November, Smith, having done some homework, told the board members he saw four major problems that the WITA had to deal with:

1. Lack of clout in the tennis world. "The ITF set up the Grand Slam Cup without talking to us at all," Smith said. "They just ignored us. Granted, our championships are part of their tour, so there seems to be no need for a women's Grand Slam Cup. But if they're going to put six million dollars into a men's tennis event, shouldn't the women get something? Shouldn't we at least be told or consulted? They seem to think because the men have tried to exclude *them* that they can exclude *us.* It shouldn't work that way."
2. A lack of visibility in the eyes of the general public. "To most people, women's tennis is Virginia Slims tennis," he said. "That has to change. Their contribution to the sport has been enormous, but if we're going to be a strong player association we need visibility: a trademark people recognize, endorsements, and more revenues. We should be able to reduce the amount of money the association receives from each tournament (seven percent as opposed to the ATP Tour's twenty-five percent), so all the money can go to the players."
3. Better benefits for the players. An improved retirement fund, better health services and trainers. A permanent home.
4. Clearer direction for the staff. "I didn't think the staff was getting the leadership it needed," Smith said. "Morale was very low, and so was the pay for the hours they were putting in."

Smith's first two problems were going to bring him into direct conflict with two of the more important entities of the game: the International Tennis Federation and Virginia Slims.

Smith came into the job feeling that the ITF treated the women as second-class citizens. As the year progressed, that feeling grew. In Australia, he requested a meeting with the Grand Slam Committee and was granted it—with two hours' notice. When he told the committee that he felt the ITF had overlooked the women in their announcement of the Grand Slam Cup, he was greeted with polite smiles and assurances that that just wasn't true.

"We should be given some compensation," Smith told the committee.

More polite smiles. "This will come up again," Smith said, not smiling politely.

Virginia Slims was a far more important issue and one that was not going to go away. Smith was acutely aware of the role Virginia Slims had played in making the women's tour a reality. He was just as aware, however, that their presence as the title sponsor at most major women's events in the U.S. made getting more women's tennis on television almost impossible.

At the beginning of 1990, Kraft General Foods (KGF) had succeeded Virginia Slims as the primary sponsor of the women's tour worldwide. Kraft General Foods was, like Virginia Slims, a subsidiary of the Philip Morris Tobacco Company. At the same time, Virginia Slims had retained control of thirteen events in the U.S., of the computer rankings, and, perhaps most important, of the season-ending tournament, the Virginia Slims finals.

That set up a cumbersome, confusing situation. The women now played on the Kraft General Foods World Tour. In each tournament they earned Kraft General Foods points. *But,* the eight top finishers on the Kraft General Foods World Tour earned the right to play in the Virginia Slims finals. *And* the computer rankings for the players were determined by the Virginia Slims computer.

Confused? Smith was. "The whole thing just doesn't hang together as a marketing concept," he said. "The public doesn't understand what's going on and probably never will. They think of women's tennis as Virginia Slims tennis, and as long as we have the current setup, that isn't going to change."

All of this confusion had come about in 1988, when the WITA had hired one of the management groups, Advantage International, to find a new tour sponsor. With more and more pressure being brought to bear by antismoking groups, they felt it was time for a change. Advantage came back with an offer from Proctor and Gamble, which was willing to pay $6 million a year to take complete control of the tour, the computer, and the championships.

But Slims wasn't ready to bow out. The company had almost twenty years invested in women's tennis and, as Smith pointed out, through hard work, excellent marketing, and one of the best public relations staffs in the sports world, had made itself synonymous with the women's game.

The WITA was adamant about not having a cigarette company be the title sponsor of the tour. Philip Morris came back with a compromise: It would find another company to take over title sponsorship, but Virginia Slims would retain the computer, the U.S. tournaments, and the championships.

For a solid month leading up to the WITA board and player meetings at Wimbledon that year, the women's locker room was a war zone. The Advantage people would grab people, take them in a corner, and tell them why the P&G deal made sense; the Slims people would take up residence in another corner, reminding people about all they had done for the game.

In the end, loyalty won out over logic. The older players such as Evert, Navratilova, and Shriver, who had grown up with Slims as the major backer of the game, decided to throw their support to Slims. The P&G offer was turned down. In many ways, it was an admirable choice. But it was one that left Gerry Smith with some serious headaches.

"It isn't just the marketing problem with all the confusing names," he said. "That's part of it. More important is the TV problem. Since I've been on the job, I've discovered a fifth problem, and that's lack of exposure. We've got only three or four recognizable names in the sport right now, and that's not enough. We need to get more of these young players into the public eye. I'm not just talking about Capriati. She'll get exposure. I'm talking about the other young players we have coming along.

"We can't do that without more TV. Right now we have thirteen U.S. tournaments with the Virginia Slims name on them. Television has banned cigarette advertising. That means that at all those tournaments, no Philip Morris company can buy TV advertising—their lawyers have told them that if they did they would probably get in trouble with the government, because it would be seen as a backdoor way of advertising for Virginia Slims on television.

"In other words, Kraft, our tour sponsor, can't buy advertising time on a Virginia Slims tournament. Right now, our championships are on national TV [ESPN] for only the last day, and that's on tape. The rest of the week we're on MSG cable, which gets into three million homes. That's a crime. We have to do something about that. But the sponsor situation makes it very tough for us to do that."

Every time Smith finished a sentence he would carefully add, "But don't misunderstand, I appreciate everything Slims has done for tennis." Disclaimers aside, Slims knew that Smith was not happy with their presence. And that made everyone just a little bit uncomfortable—to say the least.

○

Smith arrived in Washington on the third day of the Virginia Slims of Washington. That afternoon, he watched Pam Shriver and Patty Fendick play a superb three-set match. Afterward, Smith was glowing. "That's the kind of match we have to get out to the public," he said. "That was great tennis, but only fifteen hundred people saw it. That's where more TV exposure comes in."

The next morning, Smith arrived at the matches and found pickets outside the entrance to the building. Antismoking pickets. At the same time, Dr. Louis Sullivan, the newly appointed U.S. Secretary of Health and Human Services, was saying that he thought it was wrong for athletes to be used to promote cigarettes.

Inside George Washington University's Smith (no relation) Center, Virginia Slims officials, who had been through this drill before, were carefully briefing each player before they went into their press conferences, telling them to point out that no one at Virginia Slims had ever asked them to smoke or to promote smoking. One by one the players marched in, faced the question about smoking, gave their little speech, and marched out.

It was well orchestrated, but it wasn't what Smith was looking for. "This is not the way to promote the game," he said. "That's something we all have to face up to. These questions are not going to go away any time soon."

One player whose postmatch press conference that day made the Slims people extremely nervous was Natalia Zvereva. Everyone in women's tennis knew there was no way to predict how Zvereva would react in a situation like this one. For all they knew, she might say something like "you know, in the Soviet Union, cigarettes are hard to come by, so I pocket as many as I can whenever I play in a Virginia Slims event."

Zvereva did just the opposite. She talked about the fact that even the Soviet players, as new as they were to the tour, knew how much Virginia Slims had done for the game. And never—not once—had anyone from Slims asked her to say anything positive about cigarettes. "They care only," she said, "about helping us with our tennis."

In the back of the converted handball court being used as the interview room for the week, all the Slims officials breathed a deep sigh of relief. "She's such a moody little thing," one of them said. "She's apt to go up there and say anything."

Zvereva made no bones about the fact that she was moody. In a sense, she felt she was entitled. "The American players, most of the players, just don't understand how hard it is to be Russian," she explained. "Everything is so different for them. They can't understand what it is like for me."

Zvereva was part of the second wave of Soviet players to arrive on tour after the Soviet Union allowed tennis players to travel internationally again. She won the French, Wimbledon, and U.S. Open junior titles in 1987, at age sixteen, and got rave reviews as a future champion that same year, when she reached the fourth round at Wimbledon before losing a tough three-setter to Gabriela Sabatini.

Her rise continued steadily in 1988, peaking when she upset Martina Navratilova in the French Open fourth round and went on to the final. But she was humiliated by Graf 6–0, 6–0, and left the court in tears.

Players noticed a change in Zvereva after that. She had always been shy, but most people assumed that was because she was still learning English. After the French, she became almost a recluse, spending almost all of her time with her father, Marat, who had been her coach since she started playing at the age of seven. She finished that year ranked No. 7 in the world.

Then, early in 1989, she announced that she no longer wanted to turn the bulk of her prize money over to the Soviet Tennis Federation. Andrei Chesnokov would take the same step shortly thereafter, but for Zvereva, still only eighteen, this was a very difficult thing to do.

"Every time I went home after that I wondered if they would give me my passport back," she said. "There were times when I was sure I would not travel anymore. I was very distracted the whole year, and I didn't play good tennis."

By the end of 1989 she had dropped to No. 27 in the rankings. Her play was spotty and so was her behavior. She grew tired of being asked questions about her battle with the federation and began turning down even the most routine requests from tournament officials. She refused to show up at sponsor parties or photo shoots. The only good news was that by the end of the year, she was playing so poorly that no one really wanted to talk to her.

"I actually enjoyed that," she said, laughing. "I was old news. No one cared about me and I had more time for myself. The only thing I didn't like about it was the losing."

Zvereva went home to mull over her future. The Soviet federation, in the grip of *perestroika,* agreed to allow her and her father to make her schedule and to let her keep her prize money, as long as she promised to represent the country in Federation Cup play and in the Olympics. Zvereva decided the best way to start fresh was to make the trip to Australia for the first time.

That trip proved successful. Zvereva won both warm-up tournaments in Brisbane and Sydney, and although she lost in the second round of singles at the Australian Open, she and Jim Pugh won the mixed doubles.

This was a milestone. No American–Soviet team had ever won a Grand Slam title. "Playing with a Russian isn't so bad after all," Pugh joked during the awards ceremony.

"I can't tell you why," Zvereva said after the victory," "but I was as happy and excited as I've ever been in tennis. Maybe it was because Jim is an American, maybe it was because we had so much fun, maybe it was because I played so poorly last year. But I was very, very happy."

That was not a state many people had seen Zvereva in during the previous eighteen months. By the time she arrived in Washington, though, things were back to normal. She was tired, having been away from home for eight weeks, and cranky. She had to come from behind to beat Halle Cioffi in three sets in her first match and should have lost to Nicole Provis in her second. Just as she had done against Shriver, in Australia, Provis led the whole match, seemed to have it under control, but couldn't finish it. She blew an easy overhead that would have put her ahead 5–3 in the last set. Zvereva was hardly overjoyed with the victory.

"Lucky is all it is," she said. "If she makes that overhead, I lose. The one good thing this year is that I can win three-set matches. Last year I was so out of shape that if I went into a third set, I knew I was going to lose. Every time. Now, I think I can win. That's improvement. But my tennis still isn't as good as it was in 1988. In Australia, in the two tournaments I won, I fought hard but I didn't play that well. I don't know if I will play again as well as I did in 1988."

Why not?

She paused for a long time. "You cannot understand how hard it is for me," she said. "I don't think I am a money monster, but last year it was impossible for me to play, knowing I am giving all the money I make for winning to someone else. It just was not fair. This year, at least right now, it is better. My father can travel with me, we make our own schedule. But will that change? I don't know. It could tomorrow. I could go home from this trip and not be allowed to come back. If I play very poorly, I might not be allowed to come back.

"I know Gorbachev is huge in the States. But to me, he is just a politician. Things are better now, but not so much better that everything is okay. I want to be a good player. I still enjoy my tennis. But I do not know if I will be as good as I want to be. I just don't know."

The next day, Zvereva lost her semifinal match to Zina Garrison and went home for a rest. She came back to play a month later in Hilton Head but not before she and her father were scared out of their minds by a Soviet customs official who told them that if they didn't agree right then and there to turn 40 percent of their prize money over to the federation, they would never travel again.

"I was convinced this was the end for me as a tennis player," Zvereva said later. "We told him, 'No, we won't do this.' He just looked at us and said, 'Okay.' I still don't understand it but I'm very happy."

As happy as a Soviet teenager living on the tennis tour can hope to be.

While the women toiled away in Washington, the men were two hundred miles and a lifetime away, up highway I-95 in Philadelphia. The U.S. Pro Indoor has been a part of the men's circuit since the dawn of Open tennis, the personal creation and stepchild of Marilyn and Edward Fernberger.

Marilyn Fernberger belongs on the *Reader's Digest* list of unforgettable characters. Her nickname in tennis is "The Dragon Lady," partly because of her toughness, partly because of her aggressiveness, and partly because her nails are always long and lacquered blood-red. What Marilyn Fernberger is, more than anything else, is a survivor.

She and her husband have kept the Philadelphia tournament alive and kicking through all the management changes in tennis, through the ups and the downs in the game's image, and through snow and ice. Other tournament directors joke that Marilyn always gets a good field because no one in tennis wants to listen to her scream the rest of the year if she doesn't. Tennis writers show up in Philadelphia because they don't want to spend the rest of the year explaining to Marilyn why they weren't there. One way or another, Marilyn gets her way. Her husband, Ed, is, almost literally, her silent partner. Marilyn is the star and that's just fine with Ed.

The Fernbergers have always tried to set Philadelphia up as the winter version of Wimbledon. Like Wimbledon, the draw sheet makes reference to "the Gentleman's Singles" and "the Gentleman's Doubles." All of this is kind of silly since there are *only* gentleman's singles and doubles.

There's more, though: Every year, the Fernbergers hire Alan Mills, the Wimbledon referee, as their tournament referee. They hire Richard Berens, Wimbledon's media director, as their media director. They even hire the Wimbledon transportation people to run their transportation. (This last is ironic, since players complain constantly about the quality of transportation at Wimbledon. They seem to have no such problems in Philadelphia, though. Must be the London traffic.)

In 1989, Marilyn's field had not been as strong as in the past. It is not nice to fool with Mother Marilyn, and those running the ATP Tour heard more than once over the rest of the year that a much stronger field was expected in 1990.

She got just that. Ivan Lendl and Boris Becker, the No. 1 and No. 2 players in the world, were in Stuttgart (this was one of the ATP's five "Championship Series double-up weeks"), but Marilyn had John McEnroe and Andre Agassi and that was fine with her. In Philadelphia, the two Americans were a much stronger draw than the two Europeans, no matter how much land Lendl owned in Connecticut.

The Philadelphia Spectrum, the site of the U.S. Pro Indoor since it first opened in 1968, has a basic griminess to it that is both inescapable and, in a strange way, charming. It feels like a hockey arena and is at its best for hockey.

For tennis, the Spectrum floor is large enough to hold two courts, which enables Marilyn to have a forty-eight-player draw for the men's—whoops—*gentleman's* singles. Most indoor tournaments can handle only thirty-two players. The adjoining courts make for some strange scenes—balls bouncing from one court to the other and players, chasing down shots, sprinting onto the other courts. One year Jimmy Connors flew onto the adjacent court in pursuit of a ball. He hit the ball from his match crosscourt for a winner, then looked up just in time to see a ball from the other match coming right at him. He snapped off a winner there, too, threw his arms up in triumph, and walked back to his own court while the crowd went wild.

The two-court setup can be disconcerting for players and spectators but it is the only way to get the tournament finished in one week. Even at that, it is a difficult task. One long match can throw off the entire day's schedule and two long ones ensures chaos.

On the third day of the tournament, Wednesday, chaos reigned in the Spectrum. It started when a lethargic McEnroe lost to Richey Reneberg in three sets. McEnroe had arrived in Philadelphia in a foul mood.

The shock of his default in Australia had worn off, replaced by anger and frustration.

McEnroe thought that the new tour was forcing him to play too much. He had played Milan and Toronto before Philadelphia and was scheduled to play Memphis the following week. Part of this was his own fault. He had played Milan for a six-figure guarantee, which he was also getting for Memphis. He could have played in the two Championship Week tournaments—in Toronto and Philadelphia—and met his commitment to the tour, but he opted for the easy money and the smaller tournaments.

McEnroe, of course, didn't see it that way. Like the other top players, his feeling was that the new tour was costing him money. Since the ATP guaranteed at least three and often six Top Ten players to each of the tournaments designated as part of its Championship Series events, tournaments were able to cut back considerably on their guarantees to players. The top players could still pick up guarantees at the non–Championship Series tournaments (such as Milan and Memphis), but since they were required to play in eleven Championship Series tournaments, it meant they had to play more often than in the past if they were to make as much money.

One agent, Jerry Solomon of ProServ, put together a chart proving that if a player like Lendl or Becker or McEnroe played the same number of tournaments in 1990 and won the same number of matches as he had won in 1989, his income would go down about 10 percent.

That didn't sit well with any of the players. And so by the time he reached Philadelphia, McEnroe was a mess. He was still upset and confused about what had happened in Australia; he was tired because he had been away from home for eight of the previous ten weeks; he was sore, feeling pain in both his groin and his shoulder; and he was feeling the kind of malaise that hits an athlete when his birthdays begin with the number three. McEnroe had reached thirty-one the previous Friday and was in no mood to celebrate.

"I shouldn't even be here," he kept telling people. Then he went out and played that way.

For Reneberg, his second-round opponent (McEnroe had a first-round bye), this was an awkward situation. Reneberg had grown up in the juniors with Patrick McEnroe and, for years, had stayed with the McEnroes during the U.S. Open. He had become friends with John and, for a couple of years, had played some warm-up matches during McEnroe's exhibition tours.

"I got the chance to see the side of John most people don't see," Reneberg said. "He's always gone out of his way to help me and be nice to me. The guy was my idol before I got to know him. Knowing him and liking him, I sort of hate seeing him this way."

Sitting in the locker room before the match, listening to John complain about how tired he felt, about how bad his tennis was, about how much he hated the new tour, Reneberg couldn't help but feel a little bit sad. He wanted to win the match but he also wanted to see John snap out of it.

John didn't. He played well in spurts, but not well enough. After winning the third set and the biggest victory of his life, Reneberg walked off the court feeling guilty. "To beat one of the greatest players ever was a thrill, I was really happy about that," he said, looking back. "But on the other hand, I couldn't help but feel bad for John."

Later, when he tried to describe the match to Patrick McEnroe, Reneberg just said, "It was almost as if it wasn't John out there. It was like I beat somebody else."

Marilyn Fernberger could only wish that it had been somebody else. It was McEnroe, though, who announced he was withdrawing from Memphis the next week, guarantee or no guarantee, and going home to figure out what the hell was going on with his life. Officially, he was withdrawing from Memphis with a groin injury. Everyone in tennis knew the problem was much higher up than the groin area.

On the same night that Reneberg beat McEnroe, he got a taste of how bizarre indoor tennis could become. Because his match and several others had run long, the scheduled doubles matches pushed farther and farther back into the night—and then into the morning. Shortly after 2 A.M. the last two matches on the schedule began. Reneberg and his partner, Glenn Layendecker, faced Grant Connell and Glenn Michibata; Jim Courier and Pete Sampras played Paul Chamberlin and Tim Wilkison.

The building was virtually empty. The ball boys and ball girls had all been sent home at 1 A.M.; volunteers were working in their place. One of the volunteers was Richard Kaufman, the ATP Tour's senior umpire. Kaufman had finished his last match, then been dragged out to work as a ball boy by desperate tournament officials.

Reneberg–Layendecker and Courier–Sampras were not at all

pleased with the situation. All had to play singles matches later that day. All had asked for the matches to be postponed a day. Their opponents, though, all of them out of the singles, wanted to play. So they did.

Reneberg and Layendecker had done well in doubles the previous year, reaching the quarterfinals of the U.S. Open. Neither was a glamour player, neither had a lot of endorsements, neither was ranked in the top fifty. Layendecker, a Yale graduate, was twenty-eight and had bad knees. He also had enough smarts to know that a twenty-eight-year-old with bad knees wasn't going to be playing tennis for too much longer. There was good money to be made in doubles and that meant you didn't tank, even at 3 A.M., with a singles match later that day.

Connell and Michibata, one of the better doubles teams in the world, won in three tough sets, just before 4 A.M. Both players lost in singles later that day—Reneberg to Mark Kratzmann, Layendecker to his close friend Tim Mayotte. Layendecker lost his match 7–6 in the third set. Another hour of sleep could have meant the difference.

"I thought about that, believe me I did," he said. "It's not as if guys don't tank. But we just thought we could win the match, so we gave it our best shot. Maybe that was a mistake."

During the Australian Open, Layendecker had been involved in one of the stranger tanking stories of the year. Sitting in the locker room before his first-round mixed-doubles match, Layendecker was approached by Alex Antonitsch. Layendecker and his partner, Elise Burgin, were supposed to play Antonitsch and Barbara Paulus.

"Listen, Glenn, I've got Davis Cup at home in Vienna next week and I've got to get out of here tomorrow," Antonitsch told Layendecker. "I've got a flight booked, so I'm tanking and getting out of here."

That was fine with Layendecker; a win was a win. But in the first game of the match, Layendecker felt something snap in his stomach as he went up to hit a serve. He had pulled a muscle. Antonitsch had not bothered to clue Paulus in on his travel plans, so every time Layendecker threw in a patty-cake serve, Paulus rammed it down his throat. Burgin wasn't playing a whole lot better than the injured Layendecker or the tanking Antonitsch, thus Paulus became the dominant player on the court. "God knows, Antonitsch tried," Layendecker said. "But we were so bad, he couldn't lose to us single-handed."

Antonitsch and Paulus won the match, much to Layendecker's dismay—and embarrassment. Antonitsch then had to come up with an "injury" early the next morning so he could default in the second round and fly home. In all, there were three prematch defaults on that same day in the mixed doubles, which should reveal something about how seriously mixed doubles is taken by many of the players.

Tanking comes in many different forms, of course. Antonitsch's tank was the most blatant—he actually told his opponent he was tanking and why. There are also tanks carried out with an ulterior motive. For example, at the U.S. Open in 1989, Agassi had told a number of players in the locker room that there was no way he was going to play a tournament in Los Angeles two weeks later, even though he had been designated to play there by the Men's Tennis Council (top-fifty players can be designated to tournaments two times a year). Agassi was still angry with the organizers in L.A. for not giving him a wild card three years earlier when he was an up-and-coming player.

The week after the Open, Agassi was supposed to play in an exhibition sponsored by the DuPont Corporation, in Florida, an eight-man event—Americans only—called the DuPont All-American. Agassi didn't want to play. He claimed he had pulled a groin muscle in his Open semifinal loss to Lendl. DuPont is one of Agassi's sponsors. Phone calls were exchanged. Threats were made. Agassi showed up on Thursday to play his first match against Tim Wilkison—and did everything in his power to lose.

The reason? Each week, the deadline for pulling out of the next week's tournament without incurring a major fine is Friday at noon. If Agassi beat Wilkison he would be scheduled to play again Friday night. He couldn't very well withdraw from the Los Angeles tournament at noon, claiming an injury, and then play that night in Florida.

So the easiest thing to do was to lose to Wilkison, tell the DuPont people you did the best you could but that darned groin was just too sore, then withdraw from L.A.

There was a problem, however. Wilkison had the flu. His skin was green and he kept throwing up during changeovers. Wilkison is known on tour as "Dr. Dirt," because he will do *anything* to win. No way was Dr. Dirt going to quit. But he couldn't play. Try as he might to lose, Agassi was up a set and a service break. Dr. Dirt couldn't put a ball into play.

Agassi had to do something. At 3–1 in the second set, he suddenly broke into a hobble, walked to the net, and took the umpire's microphone. He then explained to the crowd in great detail how awful he felt to do this, but he had to default. His groin was killing him and he was afraid if he continued he might seriously injure himself. The crowd gave him a standing ovation as he hobbled off.

The next day Agassi withdrew from Los Angeles, keeping the promise he had made at the Open. In the meantime, Dr. Dirt was so sick that his doctor ordered him to stay in bed. He had to default his next match to Jay Berger without hitting a ball.

In Philadelphia, Courier and Sampras were not as calculating as Agassi or Antonitsch, but both were a lot more concerned about their singles matches the next day than a middle-of-the-night doubles match. They decided to play the first set hard and see what happened. They did, and lost 6–4. "We weren't going to stay out there for three sets," Sampras said. "In the second set, all we tried to do was hit the other guys. Not hurt them or anything. Just have some fun and get to bed as fast as we could."

Even with the tanked second set, Sampras was still working on short sleep when he played Agassi the next evening in the round of 16.

After skipping Australia and the first round of Davis Cup, Agassi had started his year by winning in San Francisco. His new obsession was weight-training, which he had decided was the key to tennis success. Over and over he told people how much stronger he was, how much stronger he was going to become. His new best friend was Gilbert Reyes, the former strength coach at the University of Nevada–Las Vegas.

Reyes had a chest that Dolly Parton would envy. He looked as if he was better suited to *lift* the Spectrum than fit inside it. Everywhere Andre went, Gil went, acting as his bodyguard. At matches, Gil would constantly shout from his seat at Agassi, "You're too strong for him, Andre, no one is as strong as you."

On this night, though, almost anyone was stronger than Agassi. He had eaten some bad pasta at a restaurant and it began to kick in midway through the second set. Agassi asked permission to go to the bathroom—in tennis you must ask permission to leave the court at any time—and when he departed, Sampras decided to do the same thing.

"I walked in and Andre was throwing up all over the place," he said. "I didn't know if it was bad food or if he was dehydrated."

Whatever he was, it was enough for Sampras to win the second set. At that point, Agassi quit. This wasn't a tank—there was no doubt the guy was sick—but Sampras was disappointed because he felt he was capable of beating Agassi.

Agassi's departure left Marilyn without her two biggest draws. She was brave about it, though. "Pete Sampras is my discovery, remember that," she told anyone and everyone. Sampras had played his first pro tournament in Philadelphia in 1988, when Marilyn had given him a wild card into the qualifying.

Now Sampras was in the quarterfinals. And who should be waiting there for him? His old friend Tim Mayotte. "God, the guy must hate me by now," Sampras said after beating him *again.* Mayotte wasn't a hater—but he was no doubt heartily sick of Sampras by this point.

Sampras expected to play his pal Courier in the semifinals, but in what was to become a distressing pattern, Courier lost his quarterfinal to Kratzmann. The point that killed him came at 7–7 in the last set tiebreak. Kratzmann floated a forehand and Courier had an easy forehand volley put-away—except he put it into the fourth row. Stunned, he lost the next point and the match, then did his very best to destroy the locker room. Failing that, Courier did what any healthy nineteen-year-old would do: He went back to the hotel and got bombed.

"All I wanted to do was get so numb I couldn't even remember that volley," he said. It didn't work. He woke up the next afternoon with a headache and a too clear memory of that volley, if not the rest of the evening.

By the time Courier made it to the Spectrum that day, Sampras had already beaten Kratzmann to reach his first pro final. His opponent there would be Andres Gomez, who had surprisingly come through the lower half of the draw. Gomez didn't usually get his wake-up call for the season until clay-court time but, having shed fifteen pounds since Australia, he was playing well.

Not well enough to beat Sampras, though. Still six months shy of his nineteenth birthday, Sampras won his first pro tournament, whipping Gomez 7–6, 7–5, 6–2 on a snowy Sunday afternoon. His play in Australia had been noticed in the tennis world, but the victory in Philadelphia really turned heads. In less than eight weeks Sampras had gone from prospect to rising star. His ranking had shot from sixty-first going into Sydney to seventeenth coming out of Philadelphia. He was now ahead of his friend and big-brother figure, Courier, for the first time.

"It was all kind of a shock to me," he said months later. "It was as if the schedule had been pushed ahead. I always expected to win a tournament but not that soon. And yet, the way it happened, I didn't feel as if I had done anything I shouldn't be doing. I beat players I thought I was better than."

Bob Brett, Becker's coach, likes to say that when a player is called a prospect, "it means he hasn't done anything yet." After Philadelphia, Pete Sampras's days as a prospect were over. For him, the timing could not have been better. His contract with IMG was up on April 1. All three management groups would now line up (again) for the chance to represent him. He was about to become a very wealthy young man.

As for Marilyn, she went home happy. Her Agassi–McEnroe dream final had never materialized. But her discovery had won the tournament. She would use that—and Sampras's return in 1991—as a selling point in her search for a new title sponsor. Ebel, the watch company that had sponsored the tournament for five years, was letting its contract lapse. That left Marilyn, like many other tournament directors, searching for a sponsor in an economy in which corporations were pulling out of sports faster than you could say the words *red ink.* In 1989, the U.S. Pro Indoor had one hundred sponsors who paid at least $4,000 each to be part of the tournament. In 1990, sixteen of those companies dropped out. Money was that tight. Four thousand dollars was suddenly a lot of money.

But Marilyn would survive. Philadelphia would survive. And when the early flyers went out for the 1991 tournament, the name Pete Sampras would be played over Ivan Lendl's.

Things change very quickly in tennis.

7

THE VIRGINIA SLIMS OF CAPRIATI

Elise Burgin stood in the middle of the pressroom, taking a poll on the last day of the Virginia Slims of Washington. Every time a reporter or photographer she knew came into view, she asked the same question:

"Are you coming to Boca?"

Every time, the answer was the same: "Of course."

Finally, Burgin shook her head. "Well, that's it. Every single person in tennis is going to show up down there, and there is no doubt in my mind that I'll have to play her. Absolutely no doubt. They'll make the draw and there I'll be, with the whole world watching and no tennis game at all, playing *her*!"

Burgin was *almost* right. The whole tennis world was about to descend on Boca Raton for the Virginia Slims of Florida. Normally, Boca was a nice little tournament, a welcome respite from cold cities and indoor arenas. It was played on the grounds of the Polo Club, the exclusive development where Chris Evert and Steffi Graf owned homes, and it drew several thousand vacationers or retirees each day.

This year would be different, though. This year Jennifer Capriati—*her* to Burgin and all the other players—would be playing Boca. That was why the entire tennis world was en route to the Florida resort town.

Long before she played her first match as a professional, Jennifer Capriati was the hottest thing going in women's tennis. Labeled a prodigy at the age of nine and, without having hit a ball yet as a pro, a thriving corporation at the age of thirteen, she had already been the subject of lengthy stories in *Sports Illustrated, The New York Times,* the *Los Angeles Times,* and *USA Today. Time, Newsweek, The Washington Post, The National,* and the rest of the world would follow shortly. Each would tell essentially the same story:

Capriati was the oldest of Stefano and Denise Capriati's two children. Stefano was Italian; Denise, American. They had met in Spain; Denise had been lounging by the pool when Stefano had popped his head out of the water and asked her to dinner. He was fifty-four, she was thirty-nine. He was dark and stocky, she was blond, petite, and very pretty. He had played soccer, worked in real estate, and, for the past ten years, focused much of his life on Jennifer. Denise was a flight attendant. They had moved from Fort Lauderdale, where Jennifer had taken lessons from Chris Evert's father, at age five, to Saddlebrook, a tennis resort. There, the people who ran the resort, the USTA, and anyone else who could get in the door, fought to take credit for Jennifer's prowess.

Jennifer Capriati wasn't just another teenager who could stand at the back of the court and bang ground strokes all day. First and perhaps foremost, she was American. Born on Long Island, raised in Florida (after a brief interlude in Spain), she was an all-American girl who happened to be very pretty. She had her father's dark skin and broad shoulders and her mother's attractive features.

Women's tennis was desperately in need of an American star with sex appeal. Even at thirteen it was apparent that Capriati was the answer. Ever since Chris Evert had first flashed across the tennis horizon in 1971 en route to icon status, tennis had been in search of the next Chrissie. Tracy Austin and Andrea Jaeger had burned out. Pam Shriver never won Grand Slam singles titles. Steffi Graf and Gabriela Sabatini weren't American. Neither was Monica Seles, even if she had lived in Florida for four years, even if she did speak English with a midwestern accent.

Everyone in tennis has always agreed on the need for American stars. When no American-born male reached the semifinals of a Grand Slam tournament in 1986, near panic set in. That was why Andre Agassi became so rich so fast when he began to win in 1988. He was the American that sponsors, television people, bureaucrats, and fans were starving for.

The situation had never gotten quite that desperate on the women's side. Evert was still a top-five player right up until the day she retired, at the 1989 U.S. Open, and Martina Navratilova was accepted as an American by some, if not by all. Starting out 1990, though, the only American-born player in the Top Ten was Zina Garrison, who was black. The people who control the money in tennis—corporations—don't think there is much market for a black player in their sport. As a result, Garrison, the fourth-ranked player in the world, didn't even have a shoe or clothing contract.

That was where Capriati came in. By age nine, agents and manufacturers were already negotiating with her father. She was wearing Ellesse clothing by the time she was ten. Cino Marchese, the IMG agent who is the majordomo of the Italian Open, remembers having a handshake agreement with Stefano to bring his daughter to the Italian Open when she turned pro. Jennifer was nine when the two men shook hands.

In 1989 Capriati won both the French and U.S. Opens junior titles, confirming her status as The Next One. Already, the Women's Professional Tennis Council was passing what would become known as "Capriati Rules." The first (Capriati I) stated that a player could not participate in professional events before turning fourteen. The second (Capriati II) amended that to say that a player *could* play a pro event in the same month that she turned fourteen. Capriati turned fourteen on March 29; Boca began on March 5. What a coincidence! The press release announcing the amendment specifically said that these rule changes were not aimed at Jennifer Capriati. (And Zina Garrison's lack of a clothing contract had nothing to do with her being black. . . .)

The shoe and clothing manufacturers, along with what seemed like half of corporate America, were at Capriati's door throughout 1989. She was still wearing Ellesse clothes then, a "gift" from the company that had dressed Evert for years. Naturally, Ellesse wanted to continue the tradition. Stefano was also seen in Ellesse almost everywhere he went, and if you were a bettor you could give pretty good odds that he hadn't bought the stuff at retail.

The Capriati bidders came not to Saddlebrook but to Cleveland. There they were greeted by John Evert, who just happened to be Chris's younger brother and just happened to work for IMG, Chris's management company.

Jennifer Capriati was the biggest thing that had ever happened in John Evert's twenty-nine-year life. Almost since the day he was born, he had been Chrissie's little brother, a role he had accepted for the most part with good humor. John Evert would never be as smooth or as polished as his sister, but as 1990 wore on he surprised people with his humor and his ability to deal with criticism. John Evert made a lot of money in 1990 for the Capriatis, for IMG, and for himself. Whether it was all worth it was a question only he could answer. By the time the year was over, he looked ten years older. His eyes seemed perpetually bloodshot, his cheeks were hollow, his skin pale.

The main reason for this was Stefano Capriati, although John Evert was too good an agent to ever be heard even mumbling a disparaging word about his star client. And make no mistake about it—Stefano, not Jennifer, was the client. He was heard referring to "my deals" and talked about the book he intended to write that would tell the real story about how he had made Jennifer a champion. At one point, in November, Stefano announced to IMG that there would be no further interviews with him or his family "until my deals are done."

By December, the two major deals were done: Capriati signed a five-year shoe-and-clothing deal with the Italian company Diadora, for a guaranteed $3.5 million over five years. She would make much more on the deal if she came anywhere close to the expectations of her as a player. She also signed a three-year deal with Prince racquets for a guaranteed $1 million.

For John Evert and Bob Kain, Evert's supervisor at IMG, the Capriati negotiations were like nothing they had ever been through. Kain, who had been in the agent business for sixteen years, shook his head when he thought about it. "I've never had so many guys angry at me over a deal," he said. "Not with Chrissie, Martina, Borg, any of them. This was wild."

John Evert was even more blunt. The week he finally closed the Diadora deal—to the dismay of Ellesse, Nike, and L.A. Gear—he said, "I've been called a motherfucker more in the last week than in my whole life combined. And that's saying a lot."

The announcement of the racquet and clothing contracts built the Capriati hype even further. In Australia, when someone walked up to Zina Garrison in the locker room and started to tell her the Diadora numbers, Garrison waved them away. "Don't even tell me," she said. "It will just make me crazy."

By the time Boca began, the Capriati hype was off the charts. Sally Jenkins, then of *The Washington Post,* was the first person to dub the tournament "The Virginia Slims of Capriati" and the name stuck. Other players understood. When Pam Shriver beat Sarah Loosemore on the morning of the Capriati debut, she looked at the half-dozen reporters who came to talk to her after her match and said, "It's really nice of you guys to come all the way down here just to see me play."

Capriati was entered in the tournament as a wild card since she didn't have any points on the computer yet. Every tennis tournament reserves several places in its draw for wild cards—Boca Raton had two spots saved—in case a big star decides to enter at the last minute or an injured player comes back from an injury or an up-and-coming young player comes along. Wild cards are frequently abused by tournament directors (more on that later), but in Boca they had been used perfectly. The two wild cards were Capriati and Anke Huber, the fifteen-year-old German who, in Australia, had been dubbed the next Graf.

Huber wasn't about to get noticed this week, though. It was as if the rest of the tennis world had become invisible. This would turn out to be a wild and fascinating tournament, but almost no one would pay attention. Jen-Jen mania was completely out of control. Laura Gildemeister's shocking upset of Monica Seles in the third round was virtually ignored. In that same round, Shriver became so aggravated after losing the first set of her match to Dinky van Rensburg (yes, her real name) that she kicked a chair so hard she broke a bone in her foot and had to default. Pam *who*? Gabriela Sabatini made her return at Boca from her Australian ankle injury. She would win the tournament. That did get her some attention—but only because she beat Capriati in the final. Angelica Gavaldon, Ted Tinling's Lolita, was playing her second tournament as a pro. She upset Huber in the first round and ended up reaching the round of 16. Exactly two reporters asked to speak with her after her second-round victory.

Tuesday, March 6, was the day the hype finally became reality. By this time Capriati had been forced to sneak off to faraway courts in order to practice in private. Evert had gone off to Aspen for the week to leave the stage clear for her protégéé. The day was hot and sunny. Capriati–Mary Lou Daniels was the fifth match on the schedule. By noon there was chaos in the press tent because there weren't enough seats to go round. There was no press section, so seats in the stands had to be found, and there were not very many of them available.

"Where did you seat the press in the past?" someone asked Peter Land of Virginia Slims.

"We never had to seat them *anywhere* in the past," Land answered. In the past, there were enough empty seats around that they could just walk in and sit where they wanted to. But not at the Slims of Capriati.

By 3:40 the stands were packed and the crowd was restless. The previous match had been over for twenty minutes but there was no sign of Capriati. Rhythmic applause broke out. There were a few whistles too. Finally, at 3:43, Capriati and Mary Lou Daniels appeared. They walked exactly three feet onto the court and were besieged by photographers. They stopped and posed. And posed. And posed.

"Let's play!" people began shouting from the stands. Capriati walked toward her chair; the photographers followed, snapping away. She sat down. More snaps. Stood up. *Snap-snap.* Daniels stood waiting, a bemused smile on her face. "It was all kind of mind-boggling," she said afterward.

Daniels was almost a perfect opening-day opponent for Capriati. She was twenty-eight, married, and had been featured in commercials for

Coast soap at one point. She had once been ranked as high as No. 15 on the computer, but that was eight years ago, when she was still fresh-faced Mary Lou Piatek. Now she was winding down her career; playing the foil didn't bother her—except when the photographers asked her to shake hands with Capriati before the match began.

"You shake hands *after* the match, not *before,*" Daniels said firmly, walking out to begin the warm-up.

Getting the photographers to leave the court was not easy. By the time the last one was escorted off, the crowd was booing heartily. Then the umpire's microphone didn't work. Through it all, Capriati bounced around, slamming balls back and forth with Daniels, seemingly unbothered.

Seeing her up close for the first time, many in the crowd—the temporary stadium at the Polo Club seats about six thousand—were surprised by her size. Still three weeks away from fourteen, Capriati was almost five feet seven and weighed at least 130, perhaps more. None of it was fat, though; she was simply big boned and extremely mature.

"She doesn't hit the ball like a thirteen-year-old," Daniels said. "She hits it more like Steffi Graf."

Capriati's nerves and Daniels's competence kept the first set close. Capriati lost the first point of her career—history will record that it came at 3:57 P.M., when she netted a backhand—but quickly won the first three games. Daniels came back to lead 6–5, but Capriati won the tiebreak 7–1, then won the second set easily, 6–1. It had taken seventy minutes.

Everyone was happy. The crowd knew it had seen the real thing and responded with a standing ovation. Daniels was impressed. "She's worth all the hype," she said. Other players who had wandered out to watch were equally impressed. "Gee, I wish I had brought my camera," Pam Shriver said, watching all the commotion. Stefano was happy, too, accepting congratulations from all sides. John Evert, who from that day forth would be known in the media as "Colonel Parker" (remember Elvis's manager?) was thrilled to see that the kid could handle it all.

Even the ravenous media was happy. When Capriati came in to a jammed press conference, someone asked her about what she thought of the whole experience. "Well," she said with her brown eyes wide, "I think playing my first match was great. But the media is really sort of out of control."

From the mouths of babes.

The rest of the week was all Jen-Jen. In the second round, she recovered from losing the second set 6–0 to Claudia Porwick to win her first three-setter. She upset eighth-seeded Nathalie Tuaziat and crushed No. 4 Helena Sukova 6–1, 6–4 in the quarterfinals. Then she beat Gildemeister in the semis. In five days she had won five matches, beating three top-twenty players along the way. She also played doubles with Billie Jean King, even winning a first-round match.

"It was fun playing with her," King said. "I think I've actually found someone who talks more on the court than I do." More seriously, King said, "I told her, if she needs me, I'm there for her. But I won't hang around. Right now the whole world wants to hang around with her. I won't do that."

Capriati's joyride ended—at last—in the final, when Sabatini beat her 6–4, 7–5. But it didn't matter. The match was close, the crowd loved the whole thing, and it proved that as good as the kid was, she was human. People were beginning to wonder.

What made it all so appealing was Jen-Jen herself. She was completely thirteen, full of giggles and "I means" and "you knows."

John Evert had advised the Capriatis not to hire a media trainer, at least for the moment. Evert figured—correctly—that a wide-eyed thirteen-year-old who sounded like a wide-eyed thirteen-year-old would be much more appealing than someone who sounded trained.

Virginia Slims, image conscious to a fault, had kept a media trainer on staff for years. More often than not, this training was beneficial to the players although one could tell from a hundred miles away when a player had just been through the sessions. Seles, for example, never referred to a tournament as just "Washington" or "Houston"; it was always "Virginia Slims of Washington" or "Virginia Slims of Houston."

For now, Capriati would be allowed to be herself. She mouthed all the appropriate clichés and charmed everyone right out of their socks. When the week was over, there was no doubt that a star had been born and that Jen-Jen mania would continue unabated for quite a while.

Bud Collins summed it up best when the tournament was over. "What was that old broad's name?" he asked. "Everet? Evette? Played twenty years ago, right?"

In 1990 at the Virginia Slims of Capriati in the year of Jen-Jen I, Chris Evert might as well have played twenty years ago.

While most of the tennis world spent March 5 counting the hours until the Capriati debut, Elise Burgin spent it trying to keep her mind on tennis. Letting her mind wander, she knew, would be a disaster.

It was her twenty-eighth birthday. It was also the first anniversary of her mother's death. The pain was still palpable.

She had gone home the week before the tournament in Washington and realized again, after six weeks away from her father, how deep his pain still was. Then, in a cruel twist, she had drawn Pam Shriver as her first-round opponent.

"It was all timing," she said softly. "There I was at home, seeing how tough things were on my dad, knowing that it was just a couple of weeks away from my birthday and I have to play Pam in the first round. Pam, who got me through the year. If it had been in Australia, in January, fine, I could handle it. But not here and not now."

The whole scenario was too much for Burgin. She crumbled, losing to Shriver 6–0, 6–2 in less than an hour. After the match, Burgin walked into her press conference and said, "Can you believe I got paid $3,000 for that?"

That was typical, funny, wise-guy Burgin, but the hurt was deep. Without going into any great detail, she tried to explain to the press why it was so hard to play Shriver forty-five minutes from her house, two weeks before March 5. When Burgin was finished with the press, she walked down the hall to the players' lounge, collapsed on a couch, and purged herself for a few minutes.

"That was the worst press conference of my life," she said. "They probably think Pam and I are lovers or something. What was I supposed to do, just tell them that my mother got killed and Pam was there for me more than any person in the world? That I couldn't have lived through the last year without her?

"My tennis is terrible. I just went out there and choked, completely choked. Before the match I told [longtime coach] Lenny [Scheuermann] that there was a good chance I was going to go out and humiliate myself. That's a great attitude, huh? Oh God, that's exactly what I did. I humiliated myself. I did everything wrong. I should have served hard and flat and I didn't. Damn, I played so *stupid.*

"That may have been my worst match ever. Why put myself through this any longer? There's nothing worse than to be humiliated in public. That's it. I don't want to see anyone for a week. I'm going home and lock myself in my house. Of course I won't sleep, not for a minute. Jesus! Why here? Why did we have to play here?!

"You know, intellectually I understand all of this. All of it. Emotionally, though, I'm a wreck. Oh God, I hate myself. You know, I could have *won* that match. It was tough for her, too. She could have collapsed. But *she* didn't. I did. I hate this sport, you know, I hate it."

She stood up. "I have to go find out when I play doubles tomorrow."

After Washington, Burgin knew she had to take a break from the tour. She had to spend some time at home with her family and she had to clean up her thoughts. She had passed from the shock stage to the reality stage. "For a long time everything was a whirlwind after the accident," she said. "I didn't have a chance to sit down and think about my loss and my family's loss and that was probably good. I spent six months on autopilot. But that wears off and you realize your life has changed forever. You have different responsibilities, people depending on you for different things. I'm exhausted right now, totally drained. I have to get away for a while."

Burgin had committed to playing in Boca and at the Lipton tournament and she decided to fulfill her commitments before going home. At Boca, on the morning after her birthday, she played Claudia Porwick in a 9 A.M. match. Players dread the nine A.M.ers—it means getting up at six in order to eat and warm up properly.

Burgin–Porwick at 9 A.M. with one hundred spectators watching provided a stark contrast to the scene surrounding Capriati's debut seven hours later on the same court. For most tennis players, this kind of setting and this kind of match is what the tour is about: grinding it out in the morning heat, knowing that only you and a few friends really care about the outcome.

Burgin began as if this were to be a replay of the Shriver debacle. She won one game and twelve points in the first set. It was over in twenty-three minutes. But rather than roll over, Burgin dug in and worked her way into the match. She broke Porwick in the opening game of the second set and made it stand up, saving six break points during the set, serving it out at 6–4.

By now, both players were pouring sweat in the humidity. Burgin's eyes were slits as she tried to focus. On the surface, even with the traumas of the past year, Elise Burgin was as funny and as logical as any player on the tour. She could joke about the sport, the people in it, and herself. But inside beat the heart of a competitor who had devoted herself to one thing since the age of eight and wouldn't let go of that thing until it was ripped out of her hands. Now, having split sets with an Australian Open semifinalist, she had a shot at a significant win.

Ironically, a victory would put Burgin exactly where she had predicted she would be two weeks earlier in Washington: across the net from Capriati. The winner of Burgin–Porwick would be Capriati's second-round opponent.

That winner turned out to be Porwick. Two foot faults unnerved Burgin and it went quickly after that. When it was over, Burgin turned and slammed a ball off the red concrete wall behind the court before walking up to shake hands. She had toiled in the heat for a little less than two hours and felt as if she had nothing to show for it.

Ten days later, at Lipton, she won three games in her first-round match against Wiltrud Probst. Clearly, the last place she wanted to be was on a tennis court. "When I'm ready to play, there's nothing I enjoy more than a tough match," she said. "It's what I've done for twenty years. It's been my life, but I'm not there right now. It's just pointless."

She shrugged her shoulders. "I have to go home right now, spend some time with my family, and try to get my life in order." She smiled grimly. "And I have to start thinking about what I'm going to do when I grow up."

8

THE AGENTS

On the night of February 22, Tom Ross, Tom George, Phil Sloan, and Jeff Austin of Advantage International pulled up to the terminal at Atlanta's Hartsfield Airport in a crowded taxi. As they piled out the door, each dressed elegantly, you might have guessed that these were four highly successful agents in the cutthroat world of tennis management.

And you would have been right.

Except that Ross, George, Sloan, and Austin were not feeling successful as they made their way into the terminal. It was almost midnight. The four men were exhausted. And they were on what could only be described as a desperate mission.

They were there to meet a Delta flight arriving from Los Angeles. On board, if their information was accurate, were Betty and Joe Chang and their son Michael. The son, as it happened, was the reigning French Open champion, the first American to win that title in thirty-four years. He had turned eighteen that day, was already a millionaire several times over, and, most important, was a client of Advantage International.

At least, as of that moment he was a client.

Chang's contract with Advantage had lapsed at the end of 1989. For most of that year, the company had been trying to convince him to sign a new one. As recently as 1988, Advantage had been the hot management company in tennis, but these were not the best of times for its tennis division.

Back in 1988, it represented Steffi Graf, who that year had won the Grand Slam and an Olympic gold medal. It represented Stefan Edberg, the Wimbledon champion. It corepresented (along with his father) John McEnroe. And it had Chang, who along with Andre Agassi was considered the future of American tennis. Once, Advantage had even represented Agassi, but in 1987 when Advantage was still hot, Agassi and his agent, Bill Shelton, had left Advantage for IMG. No one, not Advantage, not IMG, dreamed at the time that Agassi would turn into a gold mine.

There are three major management companies in tennis. The International Management Group (IMG) is by far the largest and most powerful. Run by Mark McCormack, it represents everyone from the pope to movie stars to athletes to most of the major names in sports television. It is a colossus, running tournaments all over the world in both golf and tennis, even controlling the computer that assigns worldwide rankings to golfers.

ProServ, run by Donald Dell, isn't nearly as large as IMG but it, too, has its tentacles into almost every corner of tennis. ProServ manages players, runs tournaments, produces TV for tournaments, and sells sponsorships for others. At times Dell, one of the great control freaks in all of sports, has found himself doing the TV commentary on matches in which he manages the two players, manages the tournament, and has sold the television time and the sponsorships. It is at those moments, no doubt, that he is happiest.

Advantage is, literally, ProServ's cousin, even though it hates that label. It was born in 1983 when Dell and his partners had an irreconcilable falling out over anything and everything. Three partners, Frank Craighill, Lee Fentress, and Dean Smith, left to form Advantage. Legally, two brand-new companies were formed out of one, with clients and employees split up between them. Much bitterness still lingers between the partners, although the men who work for them at the two companies tend to get along in their business dealings most of the time.

Note the word *men.* It is used advisedly. Even in the 1990s, tennis management is very much a man's world. At the beginning of 1990 only three women, Sara Fornaciari of ProServ, Micky den Tuinder of Advantage, and Stephanie Tolleson of IMG, were major client managers. By the end of the year, Fornaciari, deserted by two of her most important clients (Pam Shriver and Zina Garrison) and frustrated by changes at ProServ that often left her on the outside looking in, left to form her own sports marketing company.

She acted very much like a woman freed from bondage after seventeen long years. "I do not want tennis players as clients," she said. "I'm out of that business forever. I will never ever beg a player to do anything again. I've been the doormat, now I'll be the doorman."

While many of her colleagues in the business might snicker at Fornaciari's declaration of independence, they all no doubt would snicker with a tad of wistfulness. There isn't an agent alive who hasn't had to beg a tennis player to do something, usually something he or she has already promised to do and then decided at the last minute not to.

In fact, players not meeting their commitments had become so prevalent that in 1989, ProServ had added a sentence to its basic client contract that all but demanded that players meet their commitments and spend at least part of their time doing charity work.

Written by Jerry Solomon, who succeeded Dell as the company's CEO (Dell is still the chairman) in 1987, the so-called "goodwill" paragraph reads: "As a highly visible athlete you have a responsibility to set an example, to be involved in various causes, and to give your time to charity at different times throughout each year."

Prior to that, Solomon had sent a letter to ProServ's tennis clients pointing out to them that the marketplace in their sport was down, that TV ratings and attendance were down, and that not fulfilling commitments was just bad business. When that plea didn't work, Solomon and Ivan Blumberg, the company's legal counsel, came up with their goodwill clause.

Getting players to sign the clause and getting them to act on it were, of course, two different things. But it came about, according to Blumberg, "because we got sick and tired of being put in the position of constantly having to call people and make excuses for our clients, which, often as not, we knew weren't true and they knew weren't true."

Agents had to make excuses when players decided they didn't feel like playing in a tournament or when they decided to skip an exhibition or a corporate appearance. Often, these were paid appearances. The players were often willing to pass up the money, though, if they didn't feel like doing something. Passing up a $50,000 payday was no big deal anymore, not to the top names.

Agassi and Chang had become notorious for not showing up as promised. In April, Agassi would decide at the last minute that he didn't feel like playing in Monte Carlo, so he withdrew from the tournament with one of the mysterious injuries that often afflict tennis players. He also canceled a clinic he was scheduled to do for one of his sponsors in Vienna.

The Changs often canceled interviews with the simple explanation that Michael just didn't feel like it at the moment. They pulled this routine in September, when a conference call was scheduled with five reporters from Hong Kong. The interview had been arranged by the sponsors of an exhibition that is paying Chang approximately $1 million over the next three years. ProServ needed the goodwill clause that week.

Even Boris Becker, generally considered one of the class acts in the sport, would duck commitments. In March, during the Lipton tournament, he told people that his next tournament was Monte Carlo. He was designated to play in Barcelona two weeks prior to that. Guess what? Becker was hurt that week.

Solomon and Blumberg are no different in their feeling about tennis players and their willingness to live up to responsibility than are any of their colleagues. Every agent has horror stories to tell about players and their families lying, cheating, and stealing.

The players feel the exact same way about the agents. Jimmy Arias once described walking into the Wimbledon tearoom as "walking into a shark tank. Everywhere you turn there are agents making deals. You feel like you have to get out of there before you get eaten alive."

To the players, the three management groups are not IMG, ProServ, and Advantage, but IMGreedy, ProSwindle and DisAdvantage. Almost to a man or woman, the players will tell you they don't trust agents. Just as quickly, the agents will tell you not to trust players. In truth, both are, for the most part, right.

While the agents often work with one another, putting together tournaments and exhibitions and fighting such groups as the ITF, the ATP, and the WTA for power, they will fight like rabid cats over a player, especially one who is a proven big-money maker. On this rainy night in Atlanta, as the Advantage Four made their way toward the gate where the Changs' flight was expected, they were locked in one of those cat fights—and had already been cut up badly.

They knew they weren't in danger of losing Chang to IMG, because IMG had Agassi. Players don't like to share the spotlight in a management company with someone whose age and ranking are similar. Different as Chang and Agassi were as people, they were now peers as players.

But ProServ had no such problem. It needed a young player of Chang's status. Three years earlier, in one of the sport's more publicized falling-outs, it had lost Ivan Lendl. It was an ugly split filled with lawsuits and counter suits. For Solomon, Lendl's departure had been particularly painful—he had worked with Lendl for seven years, baby-sitting him all over the world, often for twenty-four hours a day. The saying in tennis for a long time was that when Lendl sweated, Solomon changed shirts; when Lendl got tired, Solomon took a nap.

Solomon had gradually pulled away from that relationship and Lendl resented it, finally leaving the company. Lendl eventually landed at IMG after trying unsuccessfully to start his own management company. ProServ needed a top young player, and it went after Chang hard, to the point where Solomon, who had stayed away from managing clients himself since Lendl's departure, had pledged to the Changs that he would manage Chang himself if Chang made the switch.

The previous day, Joe Chang had called Advantage to say that Solomon's pitch had worked. They were on their way to Atlanta for the Super Show, a four-day marketing expo where sports-industry manufacturers show off their products and the stars who wear them. Chang was scheduled to make an appearance at the Reebok booth the next day. He was also supposed to meet with ProServ to finalize the new deal.

Players switching management companies has always been common practice in tennis, especially in recent years. Whenever a player made a switch, the group that lost the player claimed that the player's new group cut fees or offered guarantees. Sometimes this was true, other times it wasn't.

Players looked for the best deal, plain and simple; loyalty means almost nothing. Among the Advantage Four, Ross knew this best of all. Ross had represented Stefan Edberg for more than six years, working with him from the time ProServ (later Advantage) first signed him as a promising sixteen-year-old Swedish junior right through his victory at Wimbledon.

Ross, thirty-two years old, was a Californian who played tennis at the University of California. He had gone straight from law school to ProServ and then to Advantage when the companies split. Ross looked like a slightly overweight Ken doll, with blond hair, blue eyes, and California boy-next-door good looks. Beyond that, he fit none of the stereotypes attached to such an appearance.

A workaholic, he was famous at Advantage for sending secretaries scurrying out the door, screaming for mercy after putting in five straight twenty-hour days. When Peter Lawler, Ross's boss, and Micky den Tuinder, a colleague, got married, Ross showed up at the wedding with a couple of files he needed to discuss with Lawler. "It was just five minutes," he explained later.

There was no questioning Ross's loyalty, though. If anything, he was perhaps too loyal, unable to see faults in his clients that were obvious to others. For more than six years, Ross told people over and over that Edberg was really a funny, interesting guy if you just got to know him. As far as anyone can tell, no one has *ever* gotten to know Edberg well enough to discover that side of him.

Six months after Edberg won Wimbledon, he left Advantage in a dispute over the taxes he had to pay as a result of living in London. As with Lendl at ProServ, there were lawsuits, counter suits, and, eventually, an out of court settlement. Edberg went out of his way to tell Ross that none of this was personal, and the two men still talk cordially. When Edberg won Wimbledon for a second time, in 1990, one of the congratulatory telegrams he received was from Ross.

Personal or not, Ross was crushed by Edberg's departure. It was like losing a first love, one in whom he had invested over six years. Ironically, Ivan Blumberg of ProServ, who succeeded Ross as Edberg's agent, was now going through the same thing, having lost Jimmy Connors to Advantage the previous month after he had put six years of *his* life into managing Connors. The main reason for Connors's departure? He felt that Blumberg couldn't devote enough time to him because he was now working with Edberg.

That's the way the business works: Advantage loses Edberg to ProServ but ProServ loses Connors to Advantage because Edberg is at ProServ. The circle never stops. Tennis agents as a whole are cutthroat, slick, and sleazy, but there are also times when they become very close—perhaps too close—to their clients: Solomon with Lendl, Ross with Edberg, Blumberg with Connors.

Advantage did not want to lose Chang to ProServ. In the last year, in addition to losing Edberg, it had also lost its half of McEnroe. Advantage couldn't afford to lose another high-profile, high-revenue player.

Jeff Austin was Chang's agent. When a company signs a client it is usually with the understanding that a specific agent will coordinate all his work. Austin, thirty-nine, Tracy Austin's older brother and a onetime top-fifty player himself, had known Chang for years, often hitting with him when they were neighbors in California. His presence had played a major role in Chang's signing with Advantage in 1988.

Ross was there that night because he had always gotten along well with the family. Tom George scheduled Chang's exhibitions and he, too, had a good rapport with the family. Phil Sloan had worked at ProServ before coming to Advantage. His job was to explain—in a totally unbiased way, of course—why Advantage was better suited for the Changs.

As they waited at the gate, the four men spotted a limousine driver. They knew that Reebok was sending a limo to meet the Changs. Was he there for them? He was. Perhaps, if they could get a limo of their own, the four men could divide the Changs up and talk to them in separate cars en route to the city. Could the driver get a second limo out there? He could.

When the plane landed, Ross was to talk to Betty; Austin would talk to Michael about all they had been through in the past thirty months; and George and Sloan would take Joe and talk hard business.

All of them were fully aware of how desperate this effort was. Five Advantage people had flown to California just before Christmas to make a lavish presentation to the Changs. The family hadn't bought it then; there wasn't very much hope now. But they had to try.

When the plane landed, the agents went into their routine, greeting their targets and talking as they made their way, first to baggage claim and then to the terminal entrance. They were all so wired that instead of splitting the Changs, they let them all climb into the same limo. For a moment, Ross and Austin almost got into the second limo, with Sloan and George riding with the Changs. That seemed senseless, though. Austin tossed $10 at the second driver and he and Ross piled into the first limo. There were now seven people—and the driver—squeezed into the car, with everyone, it seemed, talking at once.

At the hotel, the conversation continued in the Changs' suite. The agents kept switching off, talking to different family members, hoping to find an opening somewhere. Finally, just before 3 A.M., Betty Chang said, "We'll talk about this again in the morning. Some of what you say makes sense."

Drained, the agents walked down the hallway together. "I think maybe we've got a chance," Ross said. "I think Betty, at least, has some doubts." Austin said nothing. He, after all, knew the Changs best. He wasn't nearly as confident.

The next day Ross and Austin found Michael Chang signing autographs at the Reebok booth. "We signed with ProServ this morning," Chang said softly. "I'm sorry." The two agents, each feeling a little bit sick—though not surprised—wished him well and left. Like doctors who have worked on a patient for hours to no avail, they called their office. "We lost him," was the message. Chang had signed for only eighteen months with ProServ, a clear sign that the family was not *completely* sure about the switch.

Jerry Solomon would be the client manager for the Changs, that was part of the deal. For Solomon this represented, in some ways, a step back. He was thirty-five, also a Californian, but he came across more like a street-smart New Yorker. Even though he was more of a pragmatist than Ross, there was still some lingering pain from the Lendl split. Intellectually, Solomon knew it was inevitable: Lendl needed attention twenty-four hours a day and Solomon had grown out of that. When he got married, divorce from Lendl was bound to follow.

"There was a time, when Ivan was younger, when we used to talk about him playing tennis until he was thirty-three or thirty-four, then becoming a professional golfer with me representing him on the golf tour," Solomon said, laughing at the memory. "There's no question we were close. For a long time, we did everything together."

Solomon had started working with Lendl full-time in 1981. He was twenty-six, Lendl twenty-one. Wojtek Fibak, Lendl's mentor when he first moved to Connecticut, was part of the mix then, but he and Lendl drifted apart. That left Solomon and Lendl. In 1985, Lendl took over the No. 1 spot on the computer from McEnroe. Shortly after that, he and Solomon began to argue frequently.

It was a clash of two strong wills. Solomon believes an agent is worthless to a client if the client doesn't listen to him. More and more, Lendl was making his own decisions. More and more, Solomon was spending time on other things. In 1987, when Solomon was made CEO, there was little doubt that Lendl would bolt.

"I think we all hoped that we could work things out so that Ivan and I would remain friends," Solomon said. "But it was impossible. We should have been able to sit down and work out what fees he was going to pay us in five minutes. We couldn't do it. That pissed me off. We had been through too much together to sit there and fight about stuff like that. I held the guy's hand for seven years. It shouldn't have ended that way."

Lendl and Solomon have barely spoken since Lendl left ProServ. Bitterness lingers on both sides. Why, then, would Solomon want to get back into the client-management game?

"Couple of reasons. One, I see Michael as the kind of person who can have an impact on the world that goes beyond tennis. I never felt that Ivan used the platform he had as the number one player to make an impact on *anything.* I didn't care what it was, but he needed to put his time into something other than playing tennis and making money. He never felt that way.

"I think Michael does. I think he understands that athletes are in a different stratosphere than most people. They can have a tremendous influence—good or bad—on kids. For me, it's sort of a challenge to see if Michael is that kind of person, if he can transcend tennis.

"My relationship with Michael won't be like it was with Lendl. It can't be. I'm seventeen years older than he is, not five years. I'm into other things now. The Changs know that. I don't have to be at every match and baby-sit him around the world. The Changs know I don't want to just be a conduit for making more money for them. As long as they understand that and I get the work done for them, we'll be fine."

Other agents shook their heads when Solomon took on the Changs. They all agreed that if a big-ticket item like Michael Chang was willing to come on board, you did what you had to in order to get him. But everyone in the business knew how tough the Chang family was to deal with. When a reporter complained to one of Solomon's colleagues at ProServ about Betty Chang's disdain for the media, he shook his head and laughed.

"You've got it all wrong," he said. "Betty Chang isn't disdainful of the media. She's disdainful of *everyone.*"

By the time the fall rolled around, Jerry Solomon was talking less and less about Michael Chang's ability to transcend tennis. He had enough on his hands trying to get him to do the conference call in Hong Kong.

"In another year, Jerry Solomon may pay the Changs' cab fare to send them back to Advantage," one agent joked.

And would Advantage take the pain-in-the-neck, disdainful, demanding, already-betrayed-them-once Changs back?

In a New York minute.

While Michael Chang was making the decision to change management companies, Pete Sampras was telling people he had no intention of making a switch, even though his contract with IMG was up on April 1.

Sampras had signed with IMG in 1988, after deciding during his junior year of high school to turn pro. All three management groups had come to Los Angeles to make presentations. His decision had come down to IMG or Advantage; he chose IMG at least in part because Advantage already had Chang.

"We were the same age and he was ahead of me as a player," Sampras said. "It was Jeff Austin who was going to be doing my stuff, and even though I liked him, I felt like I would be number two with him behind Michael."

At IMG, Sampras was assigned to Gavin Forbes, a young South African, the son of Gordon Forbes the onetime tour player who had written a book called *A Handful of Summers* that had become a cult hit in the tennis world because of its colorful descriptions of the players and personalities of the 1950s and '60s.

Sampras had no complaints with IMG. They had signed him to a three-year $500,000 clothing and shoe contract with Sergio Tacchini (aided, of course, by Gianni Clerici's recommendation to Tacchini) and had made good on the various promises that had been made during the recruiting period. Sampras had become best friends with his doubles partner Jim Courier, who, in 1989, was also being managed by Forbes. Courier had been placed with Forbes when it became apparent that Bill Shelton wasn't going to have time to do anything but manage—and baby-sit—Andre Agassi.

The first group to make a play for Sampras was Advantage. On the night Sampras lost his fourth-round match in Australia to Yannick Noah, he met with Tom Ross, who knew at the time that his company might be losing Chang. He couldn't say that to Sampras, but he did remind him that IMG had *three* young American players who were ranked ahead of him at that moment: Agassi, Courier, and David Wheaton. Sampras thanked Ross for his time, said he would talk to his family, and didn't give the meeting much more thought. He was happy with IMG.

But Philadelphia changed things. All of a sudden Sampras was no longer a player who *might* become a star. He was clearly on the verge. Big money loomed for him and any company that managed him.

Advantage, having finally lost Chang, stepped up its sales pitch. It could honestly say now that Sampras would be *the* young American in the company. The standard fee players pay agents when they first turn pro is 10 percent of their prize money and 20 to 25 percent for all other revenue. Advantage was willing to cut their fees in a way usually reserved only for superstars.

Superstars usually get their prize-money fee waived and their off-court fees cut to as low as 10 percent, occasionally even lower. Advantage was willing to go as low as 10 percent with Sampras. It was also willing to guarantee in writing that it would not sign another young American player without the approval of the family. All of this got the Samprases' attention. A meeting was set up for March 28—three days before Sampras's IMG contract would lapse.

While all of this was going on, Pete had gone to Scottsdale to play an exhibition after winning Philadelphia. He was quickly learning how life changed when you began to make a name for yourself. Every day he had to do several interviews—a couple on site and a couple more on the phone. Gavin Forbes called to tell him that Marilyn Fernberger was extremely upset because Pete had said in his postmatch press conference after the final that he was happy to win the tournament, but "the Grand Slams are what people remember. No one remembers who wins Philadelphia."

"I shouldn't have said it," he laughed. "I understand where Marilyn's coming from, especially right after I won the tournament. Not great timing. But I'm a kid, I'm learning."

He was learning a lot of things. In Scottsdale he met a girl while signing autographs at a corporate booth and asked her out. She accepted. This too was new for Sampras. "I never went to a dance, to my prom, to my formal, to anything when I was in high school," he said. "I was always away playing tennis. All my friends tell me how much I've given up for tennis. In a lot of ways, they're right."

Courier helped him dress for the date. A tournament victory and a date in less than seven days. Things were moving quickly for Pete Sampras.

From Scottsdale he went to Key Biscayne to play Lipton. In the fourth round he played Jean Fleurian on a cold, windy night. Fleurian had just beaten Becker and was playing well. Sampras won a tough first set. Then, in the first game of the second, he chased down a Fleurian backhand. As he reached for the ball, he felt something tug in his leg. For a second he thought it was the groin injury that had bothered him in Australia. This was different, though. The pain got worse as the match went on. Sampras finally won it in three sets, but by the time he got back to the hotel, he could barely walk.

"I had a feeling I wasn't going to be able to get out of bed the next day," he said. "I was right. It really hurt."

Sampras went to the site and was examined by a doctor, who told him he had pulled a hip flexor. He would be out two to three weeks. Sampras defaulted his quarterfinal to Jay Berger and flew home, frustrated and a little scared. "Here I am eighteen years old, and I have two bad injuries in three months," he said. "It didn't make sense."

Ten days after he got home, Ross and Peter Lawler came to the house for dinner. By now, word was out on the tennis grapevine that the Samprases were asking for substantial fee cuts and that IMG was balking. ProServ had called and also asked for a meeting.

Ross and Lawler made their pitch, trying to convince the Samprases that because Advantage was smaller than IMG, Pete would be more of a priority. With Edberg gone, Ross could devote a large portion of his time to Sampras. Forbes was already splitting his time between Sampras and Courier. That wouldn't be the case at Advantage.

Ross and Lawler flew home the next day. Their offer was an excellent one. "It was almost too good," Sampras said. "I couldn't understand why they had lost Chang and Edberg, though. I couldn't get that out of my head. It didn't make sense."

It didn't make sense to Ross and Lawler, either, but there was no way to explain that to the Samprases. The family was now convinced that it was also worth hearing what ProServ had to say. On Sunday, April 8, Solomon and Blumberg flew to Los Angeles. Solomon had already explained that since he was working with Chang, he could not handle Pete. But Blumberg could.

Solomon and Blumberg met with Pete, his brother Gus, and with their father at the hospital where Pete Fischer worked. Fischer was the pediatrician who had been Sampras's coach and had convinced him to switch to the one-handed backhand. He was now advising the family on this decision, since it had gone from being a simple re-signing with IMG to a complicated IMG-Advantage-ProServ triangle. ProServ had the last shot—and, as it turned out, the last word.

The six men—Sampras, his brother, and his dad, Fischer, Blumberg, and Solomon—sat around an examining-room table for two hours and talked. Sampras remembered the room well. It was the same one in which he had met with the IMG people two years earlier.

Blumberg and Solomon explained that Blumberg would handle Pete at ProServ. Although he also had Edberg, they didn't think that would be a problem. The two were at different stages of their careers and, since one was European, the other American, had appeal in different markets. That seemed to make sense. What about fees?

"What do you want?" Solomon said. He picked up a paper plate sitting nearby and handed it to Soterios Sampras. "Write down what you want here."

Soterios Sampras did that. The Advantage offer had a fee structure based on earnings: the more Pete earned, the higher Advantage's fee would be, peaking at 12 percent when his earnings off court went over $1 million a year. The Samprases asked ProServ to base their fees on ranking: The higher Pete was ranked, the lower the fee. It went to 10 percent if he made the top five and bottomed at 8 percent if he reached number one.

When Soterios Sampras was finished, he handed the paper plate to Solomon. Solomon nodded his head. "I can handle that," he said. He put the plate down on the examining-room table and signed his name. "This is a contract if you sign it," he said, offering the pen to Pete and his father. Father and son looked at each other, then at Fischer. Everyone nodded.

They signed. The deal was done. In two hours ProServ had wiped out months of work on the part of Advantage and two years of work by IMG.

"It wasn't an easy decision but it wasn't really a hard one, either," Sampras said. "I felt comfortable with Ivan right away. I liked his experience with Connors and with Edberg. The Advantage offer was actually a little better, but I just felt like they were too small for me. The only hard part, really, was getting up the next morning and calling Gavin to tell him."

A lot of tennis players wouldn't have called Gavin Forbes. Most would have had someone else do the dirty work. Sampras made the call himself. Gavin Forbes was stunned, shocked, hurt, panicked. Pick a phrase.

"Hang on, hang on a minute, Pete," he said. He dashed down the hall to Bob Kain's office and Kain put Sampras on the speakerphone.

"Pete, why are you doing this?" Kain said. "Tell me one thing we haven't done for you that we should have."

Sampras told Kain there was nothing. ProServ had just offered a better deal and he felt a little uncomfortable with Gavin also handling Courier at such a similar stage in their careers. "I'll get you Peter Johnson," Kain said, tossing out the name of IMG's top client representative, a man whose client list included Martina Navratilova, Ivan Lendl, and Joe Montana.

It was too late, though. "Bob, I signed with them last night," Sampras said.

Three months later, Kain still winced at the memory. "It was like a kick in the stomach," he said. "It always is, but especially with this kid. We all knew how good he was, that he was a guy who could win Wimbledon and the U.S. Open. And we did a hell of a job for him. ProServ will do a good job, but there was no reason for him to move. It wasn't fair to Gavin or to us."

Sampras's name from that day forward was mud at IMG. When he returned to the tour from his hip-flexor injury, a number of IMG operatives wouldn't even say hello to him. "Business is business," Sampras said. "God knows, IMG of all people should know that. The only one who had any right to take it at all personally was Gavin, and he was the one person from IMG who called to see how I was doing when I was hurt. He showed a lot of class."

The only person who might have taken Sampras's decision half as hard as Forbes was Tom Ross. He had followed up his meeting with letters and phone calls. He had talked to Fischer a couple of times to stay updated on the situation. On the day that Solomon and Blumberg went to meet with the family, Ross flew to Japan. He knew the meeting was taking place that night and he wondered all the way across the Pacific about what might happen.

"I figured the *best* thing that would happen was that after ProServ came in, Pete would call us and say our offer was the best, where do we sign," Ross said. "I thought the most likely thing that would happen was they would tell us that it was now a three-way race, let's talk some more. I thought the worst that would happen was they would tell us, Look, your offer was very good but there's no reason for us to leave IMG. I never for a second figured we would lose him to ProServ that day that way."

Ross arrived in Tokyo on Monday night with his chronic back problem flaring up again after the long flight. He tried to call his office for news. No one was in yet. He dropped into a brief, fitful sleep until the phone rang. It was Jeff Austin.

"Pete signed with ProServ last night," Austin announced from Washington.

Ross thought the connection was bad. "Say that again," he said. "I thought you said he signed with ProServ."

"He did. I think for three years."

Ross was in shock. He put in a call to the Samprases and Pete Fischer. No answer. He stumbled out of bed and began writing notes to himself—Ross leads the world in note-taking and memos—trying to figure out what he could say to turn things around. He called Fischer again. This time he got him.

There wasn't very much Fischer could say—even though the call lasted an hour. The contract went through 1993—almost four years. Advantage had wedged the door open; ProServ had walked through it. "This won't make you feel any better," Fischer said, "but it's kind of ironic. Two years ago, you lost Pete because you *had* Michael Chang. This time you lost him because he couldn't get over the fact that you *didn't* have Michael Chang."

Ross hung up the phone and stood up. His back was killing him.

9

LIPTON

The second meeting of the tennis world takes place each year on the site of a former garbage dump. The formal title of the tournament held where Floridians once dumped their trash is the Lipton International Players Championship. To everyone in tennis it is just the Lipton.

The Lipton is the creation of Butch Buchholz, a former pro who, after his playing days, became executive director of the ATP. Buchholz had always dreamed of starting a tournament—modeled after the Grand Slams—that would be the players' favorite tournament of the year.

"I felt, having been a player myself, that I could put together an event that the players would enjoy, want to take part in, and look forward to," said Buchholz, a friendly, outgoing man of fifty, whose younger brother Cliff also played professionally. "Back in 1961, a year after I had turned pro, open tennis missed being passed in the ITF by five votes. That meant, as it turned out, that we had to wait seven more years before we could play in the Grand Slams again.

"We used to sit on the buses, back in the sixties, and talk about the day we would run our own tournament. I never forgot that."

While he was with the ATP, Buchholz got the Men's Tennis Council to agree to clear two weeks on the calendar if he could put together the sponsorship for his tournament. In all, it took him three years to put the pieces together. In order to hold the tournament in 1985, Buchholz had to have his site and sponsorship in place by March 1, 1984. He signed the final two contracts on February 29, 1984. "Thank God for leap year," he said, laughing.

From the beginning, the tournament had excellent fields. It was sort of a mini–Grand Slam, with 128 player draws in singles, the men playing best-of-five sets. But in spite of Philippe Chatrier's fears that Buchholz might attempt to usurp Australia's role as the traditional fourth Grand Slam, Buchholz never saw it that way.

"I'd like us to be right below the Grand Slams," he said. "We aren't going to be a Grand Slam, and that's not what we're trying to do. The problem we have, the problem we've always had, is establishing a place to play this tournament, one that we'll be in for the next fifty years. You can't build tradition without that."

In three years, the Lipton was played in three different Florida cities. Buchholz agreed to move it to Key Biscayne in 1987, because he decided that going to a place where there was nothing was better than trying to be part of a resort. At the resorts where the tournament had been played—Delray Beach, Boca West—the residents had complained that the influx of players, fans, and tourists for two weeks a year was a hassle and a nuisance. Why not go, Buchholz reasoned, someplace where there were no residents to be hassled?

"I can remember driving across the bridge from Miami to Key Biscayne and looking at the dump that was there," he said. "I thought, This is the place."

Only it wasn't that simple. While Buchholz was putting up a temporary stadium in 1987, environmentalists were objecting to his plans to build a permanent one. Where Buchholz saw a garbage dump, they saw park land. Where Buchholz saw the opportunity to build his tournament, they saw more unneeded development. And so, the battle was on.

Three years later, it was still on. On the first morning of the 1990 tournament, Buchholz sat at breakfast with an exasperated look on his face. "It just won't go away," he said. "Right now, if I were a betting man I would say we won't be here in two years, perhaps not even next year. We're talking to other people very aggressively now about moving."

Specifically, Buchholz was talking to Scottsdale, Arizona, about taking the tournament there. He really didn't want to move, but felt he might have to. "Until we get established somewhere and build a permanent stadium, we're nothing more than just another tour stop with a lot of prize money. That isn't what I want."

The tournament had already undergone several changes amid all the site problems. The men had been complaining about playing seven best-of-five matches in the Florida heat. As a result, the draw for both men and women had been cut to ninety-six, meaning the top thirty-two players drew first-round byes. The only match in the tournament that would be best of five would be the final. All of that meant a lot less work for the men. Of course, as the work went down, the prize money had gone *up*.

The tournament had lost $726,000 in 1989, not bad considering all the site problems and growing pains any new event must experience. But with the economic recession becoming more and more of a factor in tennis, Buchholz was looking at more and more headaches. Fortunately, his title sponsor, Lipton, was locked into a thirty-year deal through the year 2018. It was at the other levels that trouble loomed.

"The corporations are all taking a different approach now," Buchholz said. "They've gone from chateaubriand to ham sandwiches. A lot of CEOs are worried about what their stockholders are thinking. They aren't just handing out money the way they used to."

Buchholz was late that first morning for a meeting in the press tent. When he arrived, huffing and puffing, he was stopped by a guard. "Press only," he told Buchholz.

"I know, pal, and you're doing a fine job," Buchholz replied. "But I'm the tournament director."

The guard looked at him suspiciously. "Whatever you are," he said, pointing at Buchholz's badge, "you aren't press. That means you can't go in there."

And so, on the first day of the sixth Lipton Players Championship, the man who had created the tournament had to rely on a reporter to get into his own press tent.

"Okay, you can go in," the guard said after the reporter intervened. "But don't stay long."

Buchholz laughed. A good thing. A man in his position needs a sense of humor.

The Lipton has always had strong fields—even though it does not pay guarantees. "I told the Lipton people right from the start that guarantees are a cancer," Buchholz said. "We're all getting to be like the baseball owners. We push salaries higher and higher and the players have less and less reason to perform. If we failed, we failed, but we weren't going to pay guarantees."

The players came anyway because of the unique nature of the tournament, because the prize money was high, and because of corporate tie-ins. The women got their big names through to the final: Chris Evert, for years a Lipton spokesman, played in the first five finals; Steffi Graf, an Adidas client just as the Lipton was, won the tournament twice.

But strange things always seemed to happen to the men. Tim Mayotte was the first winner of the tournament, in 1985, his first tournament victory *ever.* His victim in the final? McEnroe? Connors? Lendl? Wilander? Edberg? Try Scott Davis.

In 1986, Connors and Lendl met in one semifinal, but the match ended when Connors walked off the court after a raging argument with chair umpire Jeremy Shales. He was suspended from the tour for ten weeks. Lendl then lost the final to Miloslav Mecir in straight sets.

In 1989, Thomas Muster, a rising star, reached the final with a dramatic five-set victory over Yannick Noah. En route back to the hotel on the Key Biscayne causeway, Muster's car was struck by a drunk driver. His knee was shattered. He needed major surgery and didn't play tennis for almost six months. Needless to say, there was no men's final.

Maybe the garbage dump was haunted. There *were* stories that it once was an Indian burial ground.

Patty Fendick knew none of those stories. What she did know when she walked on court on the third day of the tournament to play Jennifer Capriati was that she was tired of all the Capriati hype, which had quadrupled since Capriati's stunning debut at Boca.

"I had heard it and heard it and heard it," she said. "I watched her play. There's no doubt she's good. But my attitude was, she's just a player. I'm going to go out and hit the ball and not be afraid of her. It seemed like the other girls were playing afraid of her. I wasn't going to do that."

Fendick likes to describe herself as being "twenty-five going on fifteen." She is a Stanford graduate who makes up for what she lacks in size (five feet five, 117 pounds) with a lot of intensity. She is a talker on the court, constantly urging herself on, scolding herself, or commenting on her play. In March of 1989, she cracked the top twenty for the first time, at No. 19. But a shoulder injury bothered her the rest of the year and she finished at No. 31. After making the quarterfinals of the Australian to start 1990, she arrived at the Lipton convinced she was ready to make a serious run at the Top Ten.

"I have Top Ten talent," she said. "It's a matter of staying healthy and keeping the right attitude. I know I can play with the best players, because I've done it before. I need to do it more consistently."

On this warm Sunday afternoon, Fendick was doing more than competing with Capriati: She was beating her. "Everyone said, 'Don't play her backhand, it's too strong,' " Fendick said. "I just figured I'd surprise her and play her backhand."

Fendick was trying to do that when she sliced an approach backhand of her own and felt her knee lock up. In the Florida humidity the court had gotten sticky—much like in Australia—and instead of being able to slide forward, Fendick's foot caught on the court. Fendick had felt her right knee lock up before, but it usually would pop back into place when she hit her next shot. So she hobbled to the net and tried to hit a volley.

The knee locked completely. She sat down on the court, straightened her leg out, and then tried to bend it. No chance. "I said, 'This is not good.' "

It wasn't. Fendick had to be helped into the locker room. She would never find out if Capriati was as beatable as she believed. No one really knew how seriously Fendick was hurt—including Fendick. That night at the hotel, she was hobbling through the lobby on crutches when she ran into Carrie Cunningham, who expressed condolences about the injury and the default. Fendick was still hoping the injury might not be that serious and that she could play doubles.

"Well, if you don't, let me know," Cunningham said. "I'm the first one in if someone drops out."

The comment wasn't as insensitive as it sounded. Players will often try to minimize concern over injuries by acting as if they aren't that big a deal. The next day, Fendick found out it *was* a big deal. She needed knee surgery. If she was lucky, she would be back in six weeks. Rather than have the operation done in Florida, she insisted on flying home to California. That turned out to be a mistake. On the airplane, a blood clot developed in her knee. The doctors discovered it after the surgery. Fendick had to go back to the hospital. She was there for eight more days. On the fourth day, the clot somehow moved. A few particles got into Fendick's lung. She woke up at 4 A.M., unable to breathe. The doctors managed to clear the lung out, but Fendick had come very close to dying.

"I could have checked out right there, easy," she said, months later. "It made me think. I'm always thinking that God is testing me when I lose matches or when I get injured. But what the heck, here I've got another chance I might not have had. I feel a lot different about tennis now than I ever did. I still want to win as much as ever, but if I lose, so what? I'm here, aren't I?

"It's always bugged me that my ranking isn't higher than it is. The top players never ask the question, 'Why?' They just go out and do it. That's what I'm trying to do from now on."

No one at the Lipton knew what Fendick would go through during the week following her injury. In fact, within twenty-four hours, Fendick, her early lead over Capriati, and her injury were all but forgotten. Because on a hot Monday morning, Capriati suffered the first bad loss of her extremely brief career.

Her conqueror was Nathalie Herreman, a twenty-four-year-old Frenchwoman who had beaten Hana Mandlikova in 1987 at the French Open but had done little to distinguish herself since then. Herreman's ranking was so low—130—that she had been forced to play qualifying to get into the tournament. This was her seventh match in seven days. "If it had gone three sets, I lose," she said. "I only had energy for two sets."

That was all the energy she needed. Herreman kept feeding short, low slices across the net, and Capriati kept spraying. She needed to adjust to what Herreman was doing, but she couldn't. She really *was* only thirteen—at least, for ten more days—and she didn't know how to change tactics during a match.

Capriati hardly seemed shaken by the loss. "I'm learning," she pointed out. "I've played two tournaments and I'm happy with them. Next time, I think I'll know what to do better."

Even as Capriati spoke, the question of where she would play her third tournament was being discussed. Originally, she had been scheduled to play in Houston the last week in March, and then go to Europe the first week in May to get ready for the Italian Open. Gerry Smith had other ideas, though.

Smith had watched the scene in Boca Raton and realized that women's tennis had a genuine phenom on its hands, not just in terms of Capriati's playing ability but in her charisma. Capriati was *not* Chris Evert, in spite of all the advertising to that affect. Evert had never played the game with such unaffected joy, not at fifteen, not at thirty-four. Evert was all business on the court.

What's more, Evert's *game,* if truth be told, was a bore. Watching her stand at the baseline and grind opponents into the dust with one ground stroke after another was not exactly scintillating stuff. Evert needed the right opponent—someone who attacked, played differently than she did—to produce exciting tennis. Early in her career it had been Evonne Goolagong. Later, it was Navratilova. If Tracy Austin and Andrea Jaeger had not gotten hurt and had been Evert's primary rivals throughout the eighties, women's tennis might not have been around for the nineties. Austin and Jaeger were Evert clones. The only difference between Austin and Evert on court was that Evert grunted when she hit her shots; Austin squeaked.

Capriati was no Evert clone. She was already bigger and stronger than Evert, and she hit her first serve much harder than Chrissie ever did. She also liked to volley—not all the time, by any means, but often enough. Evert knew this better than anyone. She was quick to point out that Capriati was apt to hit more volleys in one match than she had hit during her entire career.

o

Gerry Smith didn't want Capriati to play in Houston. He wanted her to play in the Family Circle Cup on Hilton Head Island the following week. The reason was simple: TV.

The Family Circle Cup is the only women's tournament of the year that is broadcast on network TV. *Family Circle* magazine, which is owned by The New York Times Company, has sponsored the tournament for eighteen years and buys the TV time necessary to keep the tournament on NBC. For this one week Smith didn't have his Virginia Slims TV problem to worry about—and the women could showcase their game without having to share time with the men.

Getting Capriati to switch her schedule was more complicated than it sounded. No player on the women's tour could accept more than three wild cards into tournaments during a calendar year. Since she had no ranking yet, Capriati had used one at Boca Raton and one at Lipton. She was planning to use the third at Houston. After Houston, she would have played the three tournaments required to receive a ranking and would no doubt be ranked high enough to get into any tournament she wanted to for the rest of the year.

The problem, though, was timing. Entries for the Italian Open closed the week after Houston, which was why Capriati was playing there. With three tournaments and a ranking, Capriati would automatically be in the Italian Open. With only two tournaments and an approximate ranking (based unofficially on those two tournaments) she could be no higher than the first alternate.

It is very rare that the first alternate for a tournament does not get in. But the Capriatis could not afford to take a chance. To begin with, Capriati had a clause in her Diadora contract that required her to play in the Italian Open (Diadora being an Italian company) each year in order to collect her full guarantee. Stefano Capriati was Italian; the tournament was managed by IMG; IMG also managed Capriati. That all meant Capriati had to play in Rome.

Smith knew all this. He also knew he had to have Capriati at Hilton Head. So at the WITA's board meeting at the Lipton, he unveiled a plan. With the board's approval, Smith would go to the six-player ranking committee—which controlled matters like this—and receive permission for Jennifer to drop out of Houston at this late date and enter Hilton Head with her third wild card.

That done, Smith then approached Italian Open tournament director Franco Bartoni for a guarantee that Capriati had a spot in his tournament. Technically, she would remain the first alternate at the Italian, but

Bartoni guaranteed that if no one withdrew before the deadline, he would make another player withdraw and give that player Capriati's wild-card spot.

With the board, the ranking committee, and Bartoni lined up, Smith wrote a formal letter to Stefano Capriati and John Evert, asking them to change Jennifer's schedule under the conditions Smith had arranged. They were agreeable to the change. After all, Hilton Head had more prize money, more computer points, and more exposure. As long as Jennifer could get into the Italian, it was fine with them.

Smith had completely undermined the rules inherent to the smooth running of the tour. But he had no qualms about it. "For us to pretend that she's the same as all the other players is silly," he said. "We need Jennifer Capriati at Hilton Head. Now all we have to do is hope she makes it to the semifinals."

Smith knew this was a gamble. Capriati could easily run into another Nathalie Herreman by the time NBC's cameras were turned on. But he thought it was too good an opportunity to miss. While all of these negotiations were going on, the thirteen-year-old subject of them went to the Lipton player party the night of her loss and joined in a sing-along. The song Jennifer Capriati Inc. sang that night? "Girls Just Wanna Have Fun."

With Capriati gone, the women's field at Lipton lacked some sparkle. Evert was retired, Graf was still injured, and Navratilova wasn't dragging her thirty-three-year-old knees onto a hard court until it was time to prepare for the U.S. Open.

That left Gabriela Sabatini and Monica Seles as the only two name players in the field. Except that Sabatini didn't last much longer than Capriati. She was swept out of the quarterfinals by Conchita Martinez, an eighteen-year-old Spaniard who was still a virtual unknown even though she had finished 1989 ranked seventh in the world.

Sabatini and Martinez had a number of things in common. Both were, as Navratilova put it, "huge." Sabatini, who had first attracted attention as a petite, dark-haired fourteen-year-old, had grown like the man-eating plant in *Little Shop of Horrors.* She still had a stunning face, but she also had shoulders that would have made most football linebackers envious. She was five feet ten and weighed at least 145 (although the player guide listed her at 130).

Her walk, which reminded some people of that of Jim Brown, the great running back, was best described by Ted Tinling as "a provocative lurch. Seeing her approach," he added, "one might be well advised to feel a fair amount of apprehension."

Martinez was almost as big as Sabatini but with none of her beauty. Both were belters, backcourters who used their power to slug opponents into submission. Two months shy of twenty, Sabatini was already viewed by some as a has-been. Or never-was. She had never really lived up to the potential she had flashed in 1985, when she reached the French Open semifinals at age fifteen.

Her Latin beauty and a superb marketing job by ProServ had made her quite rich, but she had never won a Grand Slam title. Graf, her contemporary, had won nine—and had beaten her eighteen times in twenty-one matches. The word among the players was that Sabatini had the game to be a great player, but not the mind.

Sabatini was not very verbal. If she won a match she would invariably say, "I am feeling good mentally and physically. I was fighting to win. I was concentrated." If she lost, just as invariably the speech would go like this: "Physically I am okay, but mentally I am not. I was fighting, but I was not concentrated."

Her concentrated line came up so often that the question on the tour, when Sabatini played, became "Is Gaby orange juice [concentrated] today?"

Almost every player on tour speaks some English, but some are better than others. Becker is virtually fluent in English and Graf is almost as good. Every Swede since Borg has spoken good English. Sabatini had never been comfortable speaking English. But, according to Spanish-speaking players and journalists, she wasn't much more comfortable in Spanish. "Sometimes when I see her on TV, back home, I feel sorry for her," said Alberto Mancini, also Argentine. "She really doesn't have very much to say."

Against Martinez, Sabatini wasn't orange juice. She lost in straight sets. That left the tournament in Seles's hands.

Of course, it wasn't quite that simple. Seles came into the Lipton with a 1990 record of 2–3. The sophomore-slump whispers had already started.

What people didn't know was that Seles had been distracted by her mother's health. During the tournament in Boca, Esther Seles had undergone a hysterectomy. Monica had never had to deal with a serious illness in her family and, by her own admission, was a wreck. "I mean, I knew she would be okay and all, but it was major surgery and she was in the hospital," she said. "I really couldn't keep my mind on tennis." Seles lost to Laura Gildemeister at Boca but was able to slip away relatively unnoticed because of Capriati. Now, with her mother out of the hospital and back at courtside, Seles was starting to blast the ball again. At the Lipton, she whipped Judith Wiesner in the final.

"I'm just happy to feel comfortable on the court again," she said. "It doesn't matter who I beat. I'll have plenty of chances to play Steffi and Martina. I don't even know if I'm ready to beat them yet."

She would find out the answer to that question shortly.

As always, the Lipton was full of strange matches on the men's side. None was stranger than Ivan Lendl's three-set loss to Emilio Sanchez in the fourth round. Sanchez was a good player, solid on hard courts although more comfortable on clay, but he never seemed to beat the big names. This time he did—even after blowing four match points in the third set and letting Lendl break. Down 4–5, Lendl went up 30–0, serving to even the match. Then he collapsed, losing the last four points.

The wind swirled around the stadium throughout the match and Lendl clearly was unhappy with that. Lendl doesn't like anything that takes away from his precision. Gerry Armstrong, umpiring the match, knew Lendl was in trouble when he tossed the coin before the match began and the wind took it.

"Ivan had this look on his face," Armstrong said, "that said, 'I want out of here.' "

Lendl certainly didn't tank. He is beyond the stage in his career where he does that. But when the match was over he made no bones about the fact that he was delighted to get out of town.

"I've never liked playing in south Florida," he said. "The only reason I've always played here is because it was in my Adidas contract. I committed to play this year when I still thought I was going to be with Adidas. I'm not with them anymore, so I probably won't play here again in the future."

Lendl had split with Adidas at the end of 1989 and had signed a six-year contract, reportedly worth close to $20 million, with Mizuno, a Japanese company. The first time he had shown up wearing his new Mizuno clothing line in Sydney, Armstrong had said to him, "Are you really going to wear that stuff on court?"

"Why not?" Lendl asked.

"Because you'll take a lot of shit from me if you do," Armstrong answered.

Lendl grinned. "Gerry, you know who always has the last word when it comes to giving shit, don't you? Me."

The Mizuno clothes weren't nearly as ugly as some of the stuff other players were wearing. Of course, the deal did mean Lendl had to fly from Australia to Japan in January to make several appearances; he would have to play two tournaments in Japan each year. That was okay with Lendl, though. In 1990, he would receive about $250,000 up front for each Japanese tournament he played in.

Now he was gone from the Lipton and not at all sorry about it.

Boris Becker was gone too. He lost a round earlier than Lendl, in the third, to Jean Fleurian, 7–6, 6–1. Becker's mind just wasn't on tennis. He was in the process of breaking up with his girlfriend of the previous two years, Karen Schultz, and still not at all sure about what he wanted to do with his life. Play tennis? Party? Save the world? All of the above? None of the above?

Becker didn't leave Miami after his loss. He stuck around to play the doubles, reaching the final with partner Casio Motta, and to hang out with friends. After starting the year on the verge of wresting the No. 1 ranking from Lendl, Becker had now dropped behind Edberg into the No. 3 spot. If truth be told, he didn't much care.

Bob Brett knew all this. And he knew that at that moment there was nothing he could do as a coach to change it. He couldn't make Becker want to play tennis. Only Becker could do that.

After Lipton, Becker went home to Leimen to spend some time with his parents and sort out his thoughts. He was next scheduled to play—once he decided to be injured for Barcelona—in Monte Carlo. This was a tournament he couldn't pull out of. Like other players who maintained Monte Carlo as their official residence for tax purposes, Becker had to play in the tournament to keep the government happy. Monte Carlo signaled the beginning of the clay-court season for Becker, the toughest time of the year for him. Yet, since he'd never won the French Open, it was the time when he should have been most motivated.

"If things don't start to change on the clay," Brett said, "they may never change."

. . .

○

With Lendl and Becker gone, the Lipton became your basic Andre Agassi–fest. There was no doubt that Agassi was playing good tennis. He won three straight three-setters over Andres Gomez, Jim Courier, and Jay Berger (who reached the semis when Sampras had to default), and then beat Edberg in the final. Edberg was there only because a line judge had botched a call on match point in his quarterfinal against Jakob Hlasek. Hlasek had hit a half volley winner just inside the line while ahead 6–5 in the final set tiebreak. The line judge called it wide. Hlasek lost the next two points, and Edberg made the final even though he wasn't playing very good tennis.

Agassi rolled him in four sets, then acted as if he had won Wimbledon. "I guess people can't say I don't win the big ones anymore, can they?" he crowed afterward. Clearly, the kid had lost touch with reality. Even Butch Buchholz wouldn't claim the Lipton was a big one. Bigger than a bread box, perhaps, bigger than Memphis or Sydney or Bologna. But not quite up there with the Slams. After all, the Slams all knew where they were going to be held the following year. As the workers began tearing down the temporary stadium on Key Biscayne, Butch Buchholz had no idea where his tournament would be held in 1991.

10

CARILLO

Mary Carillo was walking. Fast. Always, Carillo walks fast. She has long, loping strides. Groucho Marx walked like Carillo walks but not as fast. "Lovely girl, but she walks like a bloody long*shore* man," Ted Tinling always said.

Carillo is always in a hurry to get somewhere. On this day, Brad Gilbert had just lost to Javier Sanchez in the third round at the Lipton. Sanchez blew seven match points in the second set before winning in three. Otherwise, it was a match that would be little noted and not long remembered.

But Carillo needed to know more. "I gotta find out how the Beej [Gilbert's self-declared nickname is Beej, as in B.G.] lost that one. Beej doesn't usually lose the ugly ones."

Notebook in her pocket, Carillo walked Groucho/longshoreman-style to the players' lounge, looking for quotes, information, gossip. A TV personality acting as a reporter. And loving it.

Carillo has always delighted in Tinling's description of her walk. She has no hang-ups about her femininity. She jokes about her tomboy youth. "If my brother got into a fight, I finished it," she says, laughing at the memory. "He won writing awards, I won athletic awards."

The tomboy grew into a stunning woman, tall and slender with big brown eyes. She also became a star. A real, live TV star. Her sister, Gina, remembers walking down the aisle at her wedding, basking in the glow of being a bride, and then, as she approached the altar, hearing the rabbi (the wedding was coofficiated) talking to the matron of honor.

"Hey, you're Mary Carillo," the rabbi said. "I see you on TV all the time!"

To understand Mary Carillo—the star—you have to understand her family. More than that, you have to understand her mother. Terry Sullivan Carillo grew up in a cold-water flat in what was then the Irish ghetto of Brooklyn. Terry's dad was a cop and an alcoholic who was never home.

Her mother worked as a waitress and spent Saturdays scrubbing tiles at a factory. She made one dollar for her day's work.

She was never completely healthy but always somehow made it to work. One Saturday, when her mother was too sick to go and collect her pay, Terry was sent to pick it up. She was embarrassed about going. "Don't worry," her mother said. "I earned it."

Terry Sullivan grew up loving school because it was a cheery, warm place. She loved the Catholic Church for similar reasons. When she was six, for Christmas she desperately wanted a red coat and a muff to stick her hands in. On Christmas Eve, two women from the church came by with the coat and the muff. "She was hooked after that," Mary says.

When Terry was seventeen, her mother died of cancer. Terry had to go to work full-time to support herself and her younger sister and to pay for her mother's funeral. She met Anthony Carillo while riding the subway to Manhattan, where she had a job as a secretary. Anthony Carillo was as quiet as Terry Sullivan was ebullient. According to his children, he enjoyed growing up during the Depression. "He loved the austerity of it," Mary says.

The oldest of five children, he had grown up a few miles from Terry in the blue-collar Italian section of Brooklyn. He had been winning awards as an artist since first grade and, after getting out of the army, had taken a job at an advertising agency. Every day, Anthony Carillo would sit quietly on the subway and watch Terry Sullivan laughing with her friends, full of joy and the thrill of being alive. One morning, she sat down next to him and started a conversation.

"You know, you really shouldn't be so loud and noisy and happy all the time," he said to her. "There are a lot of bad things going on in the world right now. You should think about that."

"You don't have to tell me that," Terry Sullivan said—and left, crushed.

A few minutes later a friend of hers who had heard the conversation sat down with Anthony and told him about how her friend had grown up and what her life had been like. Shortly after that, he and Terry began dating.

When he was twenty-eight, and she was twenty-three, they married. Time to start a family. But after six months, Terry Carillo wasn't pregnant. She went to the doctor, who told her there was a tumor on an ovary. He had to operate. "I want children," Terry Carillo told him firmly.

"I'll do what I can," the doctor said, without much hope.

He saved one half of one ovary. "Your chances of having a child are very slim," he explained.

"I'll be back," Terry Carillo promised.

She came back, pregnant with Charles. The doctor was thrilled. At least now she could have one child. But that was it—just one. After Charles was born, the doctor told her not to even think about another child. Terry Carillo went home and prayed to the Virgin Mary. "She's her favorite," her oldest daughter says, "but she's got the whole squad."

Fifteen months after Charles was born, a daughter came along, who was named—what else?—Mary. Four years later, just to prove the power of prayer one more time, Gina came along.

Mary was three days old when the family moved from Brooklyn to Douglaston, Queens. Mary got her first tennis racquet when she was nine—won it in a fishing contest at the Douglaston Pier. She picked the racquet, an old Alex Olmedo model, as her prize because she thought it would be ideal to use for crabbing off the docks. A year later, when she came down with swimmer's ear, she decided to give the prize a try as a tennis racquet, at the Douglaston Club. Once she got through picking the seaweed out of it, she found she could play pretty well.

She began spending hours hanging around the club, looking for people to play with. Most people used the club to swim or to bowl, but there were three clay and two hard tennis courts. She finally found a little runt two years younger than she was who was willing to play with her all day long. His name was John McEnroe.

They were both lefties and they both loved Rod Laver. "We played, like, fourteen sets a day, every day," Mary remembers. When Mary was twelve and John was ten, he began to grow a little and to catch up to her on the tennis court. One day he beat her 6–0, 6–0, hitting all these weird, wristy touch shots Mary had never seen anyone else hit.

After they were done, Mary looked at John and said, "You know something, someday you're going to be the best tennis player in the world."

"Shut up," John McEnroe said.

"My first foray into tennis commentary," Carillo says now. "And that was what my audience thought of me. I think I scared him. But he was operating in a place no one else was. Even then, he had this crazy touch game."

Mary and John both became top junior players. John began entering junior tournaments and urged Mary to do the same. He also encouraged her to start taking lessons at the Port Washington Tennis Academy, where Harry Hopman, the legendary Australian Davis Cup coach, was in charge. "John gets me addicted to the stupid game, convinces me to go to Port, gets me playing there every day of the week, and then shows up once a week," Carillo remembers.

That was okay, though, because she was hooked on tennis and on Hopman. "If he had been teaching badminton I would have wanted to play it every day."

McEnroe fought constantly with Hopman. One Friday night, McEnroe had everyone on his court playing all of his "touchy-feely" shots and Hopman blew up. "You want to play like a girl," he roared, "you go play on the girls' court!" Thirty minutes later, Hopman checked the girls' court and there was McEnroe, showing all the girls how to hit the same shots.

Her senior year of high school, Carillo was the No. 1 junior girl in the East and had a scholarship offer to play at Trinity University in Texas. She wasn't sure if she wanted to do that or take a crack at turning pro. When she went to Hopman for advice, he offered a compromise: to work for him in Florida where he was starting a tennis academy.

Mary went to Florida to work for Hopman for fifty dollars a week. She worked out and taught for several months. Just as she was getting bored and thinking about going to college, she went to the Bahamas for a tournament at a resort. It was a small, fun event, and Carillo made the semifinals. The next morning, when she went to check out of the hotel, she was told that she had run up a $200 bar bill during the week. Carillo didn't have $200. She walked over to the tournament office.

"What's the prize money for making the semifinals?" she asked.

"It's two hundred and fifty dollars."

"I'm turning pro," she announced. She took the prize money and paid her bar bill.

"The drinking man's pro, Mary Carillo," she says now, laughing. She didn't run back and report the news to her parents, however, knowing they still wanted her to go to college. Instead, several months later she said to them, "You know, I'm *thinking* about turning pro."

The following year—1977—the drinking man's pro played the European circuit. At the French Open, she and McEnroe entered the mixed doubles. McEnroe, still an amateur, had just graduated from high school. Glancing at the draw, McEnroe said to Carillo, "No reason why we shouldn't win this thing."

He was right. They won, the two kids from Douglaston. Carillo played superbly in the semifinals but couldn't deal with the center court pressure in the final. "I choked totally," she said. "I couldn't handle being on center court. John was right at home from the first point. Finally he said to me, 'Just get your serve in and let me do the rest.' He did."

One of Carillo's most treasured pictures is of McEnroe lifting her off the ground after match point, complete joy on his face and hers. "There was an innocence then," she said. "I'm not sure John ever felt quite that way again."

He didn't. Three weeks later at Wimbledon, McEnroe came through qualifying to reach the semifinals and announce his arrival as a star—and a controversial figure—on the tennis scene. In the quarterfinals, he faced Phil Dent, ranked eighth in the world, who had beaten him in five sets at the French Open. As he headed out to play him, McEnroe, the eighteen-year-old amateur, turned to Carillo and said, "If I lose to this guy again I might as well just bag this sport."

He didn't lose. It was in that match, though, that McEnroe's bad-boy reputation was born. In juniors, where players almost always call their own lines, McEnroe had a reputation for giving away points anytime a ball was close. He did that several times in the Dent match in Paris, often overruling line calls. After the match Dent said to him, "Sonny, in the pros you don't do that."

McEnroe listened. When close calls went against him at Wimbledon, he argued. And argued. And argued. He still hasn't stopped. In the semifinals, McEnroe lost to Jimmy Connors in four sets. "I didn't even think I belonged out there," he said years later. "I didn't think I was good enough to play a Wimbledon semifinal."

That same day, McEnroe and Carillo played their mixed-doubles quarterfinal against Dennis Ralston and Martina Navratilova. At 8–8 in the third set, Ralston hit Carillo with a shot. To this day, McEnroe thinks he did it on purpose. Ralston swears it was an accident. Accident or act of violence, McEnroe lost his cool.

"I really wanted to hit the guy," McEnroe said. "I really thought he did it on purpose and I was, like, that's just not the way you play the game. You don't go around trying to hit the girl. I was so angry I couldn't play after that."

Ralston and Navratilova won the match, and McEnroe played mixed doubles only a few more times in his life (when he was dating another player, Stacy Margolin). The joy and innocence of Paris was gone forever.

Carillo never reached that emotional high again as a player. She had undergone her first knee operation in 1976, and by the end of 1977 she needed surgery again. She knew her career wasn't going to last long, so she played whenever she could, wherever she could. In 1979 she reached the third round at Wimbledon and climbed to No. 34 in the world. A year later at Wimbledon she could feel things wandering around in her knee again. She played her first-round match late in the day on slippery grass in near darkness. She lost 6–1, 6–0 to Pam Teegarden and walked off the court, knowing her career was about over. She needed surgery again.

That was the year that McEnroe and Bjorn Borg played the extraordinary "tiebreak" final, won, of course, by Borg. Carillo was on the same flight as John and his dad that night and sneaked up to first class to say hello. "John was stretched out, sound asleep," she remembers. "But Mr. McEnroe was sitting there with all the London papers piled up. He had been reading them. When I tapped him on the shoulder, he turned around and he was crying because of all the things they had said about John. It broke my heart. I started to cry, too."

When the plane reached New York, McEnroe looked at his friend and said, "Jesus, what are you going to do now?" He knew she was through playing. Carillo shrugged. She had no idea. When she got home, though, part of the answer was waiting. Bill Bowden had called.

Carillo had first met Bill Bowden at Port Washington, although her memory of him there is vague. He was two years younger than she was, and she was a hotshot. "I remember him as someone to be ignored," she says now.

Bowden was smitten. Two years later he came down to work at Hopman's, and he and Carillo became friends, working in the pro shop together. "But then one night, after we had been hanging around for a couple of years," Carillo says, "I looked at him and said to myself, 'Hey, this guy is great looking, really sweet, and fun.' Boom, that was it."

By the time she was through playing tennis, Carillo had almost figured out that her future was with Bill Bowden. They were married, and moved to Naples, Florida.

Carillo wasn't looking to settle into the role of housewife, though. Before she and Bill got married she had returned to teaching at Hopman's. That fall, she was at the Avon Championships (now Virginia Slims) at Madison Square Garden, just hanging out. There was a delay one evening before the start of a match between Tracy Austin and Evonne Goolagong. Madison Square Garden Network, the cable group televising the tournament, was desperately looking for anything and anyone to fill time.

Peachy Kellmeyer of the Women's Tennis Association, running out of time fillers, sent Carillo up to the booth. She began talking. When the match finally started, Billy Talbert, who was doing color commentary, told the producer he wanted Carillo to stay. The producer said okay and Carillo did the entire match. When it was over, she thought it had been a lot of fun, didn't give it a second thought, and went home to Florida.

One person who heard her that night was Mark Stohlberger. Later in the year, the USA network hired Stohlberger to produce several women's tournaments it was televising. Stohlberger remembered Carillo and suggested she be hired as a color commentator.

"Mark came down to Hopman's and called me off the court to offer me the job," Carillo says. "I said, 'Are you kidding me?' "

He wasn't. At first Carillo was limited to women's matches. The thought of a woman doing commentary on men's matches was unheard of. But a year after she started at USA, she was hanging around the booth one night, watching Yannick Noah at the U.S. Open. Throughout the match she kept scribbling notes to play-by-play man Al Trautwig, giving him anecdotes and stories she had gleaned from other players.

Trautwig never used any of her material. Carillo was baffled. When the telecast was over, Trautwig took Carillo by the arm and said, "Come with me." He had the notes clutched in his hand.

"I thought he was really mad at me, that he thought I had stuck my nose where it didn't belong," Carillo said. "We went down to Gordon Beck [the producer], and Al showed him the notes. He said, 'She knows more about this stuff than any of us. She should be on the air doing it.' Gordon said he was right. From then on, I did men and women."

USA eventually led to ESPN and CBS, although it took CBS a lot longer than it should have to figure out it needed Carillo. In 1987, the network honchos finally hired her after she had been outreporting and outcommentating all their highly paid stars for years. Tennis producer Frank Chirkinian couldn't understand the move. "What do we need Carillo for?" Chirkinian asked. "She's strictly cable."

Carillo responded by taping the words *strictly cable* across her USA/CBS press badge (she worked for both that year at the Open). If Chirkinian noticed, he never said anything.

But it is ESPN, not CBS, that has made Carillo the most familiar voice in tennis today. ESPN does more tennis than everyone else combined, and Carillo is there, week after week. With NBC now doing only three tournaments a year—Hilton Head, the French Open, and Wimbledon—she has stepped into Bud Collins's shoes as the game's conscience.

Carillo knows the sport and knows the people. She is also a born reporter, someone who revels in finding and reporting things no one else knows. She does more work as a journalist than everyone else working on TV (Collins excluded) combined. She upsets players and officials with her honesty, her tough questions, and her willingness to take on issues. Often, she ends up fighting with her on-air partners, Cliff Drysdale and Fred Stolle (especially Drysdale), about what belongs on air and what doesn't.

When Andre Agassi backed out of playing Davis Cup in early March, ESPN asked Bill Shelton during the Lipton if Agassi would come on the air to tell his side of the saga. Shelton agreed, but only—*only*—if Drysdale did the interview. "Dr. No" would not allow Carillo to talk to his boy.

Drysdale threw Agassi one softball question after another and the two had an on-air love-fest. Three days later, after beating Berger in the semifinals, Agassi was trapped. Carillo was right there to do the on-court interview—live—and he had no choice but to talk to her.

He came out swinging, accusing Carillo of turning on him, of criticizing him unfairly on the Davis Cup issue. Carillo wasn't about to get into a shouting match on live TV. "Andre, I didn't turn on you," she said. "I expressed my opinion and I stand by that opinion. I think you should have played in the match [then a week away] against Czechoslovakia. If you find that unfair, I'm sorry. But that's the way I feel."

Carillo's tone of voice never changed. Agassi, whose voice gets shrill under pressure, squeaked back, "Well, let's talk about *this* match."

That was what Carillo had intended to do in the first place.

What makes Carillo unique in tennis TV is that she says what she thinks and doesn't worry about who will be upset with her. Like Drysdale, she is represented by Trans World International, a division of IMG, but that didn't prevent her from going after Agassi when she felt he deserved it. Drysdale wouldn't criticize Agassi even if he punched a spectator. The guy deserved it, Drysdale would probably say.

Carillo has even criticized her close friend McEnroe on the air. When she came down on him after the default in Australia, McEnroe was upset. He felt she had put her career ahead of their friendship.

"If I go on the air after something like that and defend him, what credibility do I have?" she said. "None. Then, when something happens where he really does deserve defending and I go on and defend him, everyone says, 'So what? Carillo defends everything McEnroe does.' "

○

Exactly. McEnroe, who has never been a grudge-holder anyway, forgave Carillo. Agassi has even forgiven her. Very few people can stay mad at Carillo. There is one person she worries about, though.

"When my mom finds out the real story about how I turned pro," she says, rolling her eyes, "she's gonna kill me."

PART THREE

THE CLAY

11

THE QUEEN, THE LEGE, AND THE KID

By the month of April, all the indoor tennis tournaments are over. The marking time after the Australian Open is finished. The game moves to the clay courts, and everyone begins looking ahead to the next Grand Slam, the French Open.

Clay has always been thought of as the surface of Europeans and South Americans. The red clay of Roland Garros, in Paris, and the Foro Italico, in Rome, are part of the sport's heritage, and players from the Continent and from South America do grow up on and, for the most part, do most of their playing on the stuff.

When you think of clay, you think of marathon matches on slow surfaces, players standing behind the baseline, trying to outlast their opponents in long, long rallies; players such as Guillermo Vilas and Manuel Orantes and Ivan Lendl and Mats Wilander and even a couple of Americans who made their mark in the seventies—Harold Solomon and Eddie Dibbs. Michael Chang ended a thirty-four-year drought for American men at Roland Garros in 1989. However, Bjorn Borg, playing a classic clay-court game, won Wimbledon five times. His fellow Swede and Wimbledon champ, Stefan Edberg, also has a classic serve-and-volley game rather than the more European style.

Clay is still the dominant surface on the men's circuit. There are more tournaments played on clay than on anything else. After the French Open is over, the clay-court circuit grinds on in Europe and South America throughout the summer. Many players never play on any surface but clay. Kent Carlsson, a Swede who may have been involved in more horrendously dull matches than any player in history, actually reached the Top Ten while almost never stepping off clay.

For the women it is different. So few of them serve-and-volley that clay is not very different from hard court or grass for them. That explains why Chris Evert, the prototype backcourt/clay-court player in the history of the women's game, could win Wimbledon three times and reach the final there ten times. It also explains why Martina Navratilova, the definitive serve-and-volleyer, could win the French twice and reach the final six times.

Evert learned the game on clay and throughout her career was almost unbeatable on it. She once won 125 straight matches on clay and won seven French Opens, including the last two of her eighteen Grand Slam titles in 1985 and 1986. Three of her six U.S. Open titles were won during the three years (1975–1977) that the tournament was played on clay. All told, ten of her Slams were won on clay.

Since the Open left Forest Hills for the hard courts of Flushing Meadow in 1978, there has been no great clay-court tournament in the United States. The U.S. Clay Court Championships, once played in Indianapolis, died there in the mid 1980s when the courts were paved (to induce the men to play there prior to the U.S. Open). The USTA still runs a U.S. Clay Court Championships in May, but very few players ranked in the top one hundred ever show up.

The women still have Hilton Head, though. For the past eighteen years, they have played the Family Circle Cup at the Sea Pines Plantation on Hilton Head Island, South Carolina. It represents the opening of the clay-court season for the women and has the feel of a big tournament, though it still retains the charm of a small one. The stadium at the Sea Pines Racquet Club seats about five thousand people. It is surrounded by soaring South Carolina pines which give the place a feeling of isolation. The real world seems much farther away than just across a bridge that leads to the honky-tonk towns and paper mills of the South Carolina and Georgia marsh country.

The field for this tournament is always strong. The prize money is as high as a non–Grand Slam women's tournament (other than the Lipton) can be: $500,000, meaning that, under Women's Tennis Association rules, at least one of the top two-, two of the top four-, and four of the top eight-ranked players must be entered. In 1990, Navratilova was there; Arantxa Sanchez was there; Zina Garrison was there, and so was Natalia Zvereva. But they were not the stars of this week.

Jennifer Capriati was at Hilton Head, courtesy of Gerry Smith's string-pulling. The only people pulling harder for her to make it to the weekend than Smith were the ones from NBC. For them a Navratilova–Capriati final would be straight out of *Fantasy Island.* Not only would they have a classic princess–grand dame matchup, they would have it with the grand dame's pal and the princess's hero/mentor—Christine Marie Evert herself—making her network debut in the commentary booth.

Evert and NBC had been a prearranged marriage for years. As early as 1985 the network had made it clear to her and to her agent, Bob Kain, that once Chris put down the racquet their microphone was her microphone.

Evert was extremely nervous about all this. She had seen other big stars fail miserably on television, and she wondered if she would be able to make the adjustment. When Mary Carillo kidded her at the U.S. Open about her impending TV career, Evert said to her, quite seriously, "Oh God, there's just *so* much pressure on me to do this well." There wasn't really that much more pressure on Evert to do this than there had been to do anything else well in her life. Evert is a perfectionist, though, someone who is used to succeeding at everything, someone who has been treated as royalty—first as the teenage Princess, then as the reigning Queen—since she was a girl.

The notion that TV critics might rip her made Evert nervous, so she asked Virginia Slims to send its media trainer to Florida to work with her for a couple of days, to make sure she would speak clearly, not lapse into clichés or *you knows* and *I means*.

In one sense, Evert was guaranteed to be a hit on TV. Much of America would think her wonderful no matter what she said or did. Bud Collins had nicknamed her "Chris America" years ago, and it fit. America had literally watched Chrissie grow up, going back to the 1971 U.S. Open when she came from a set and 5–1 down in the second set to beat Mary Ann Eisel on national television, reaching the semifinals before losing to Billie Jean King.

They had watched her go on from there to win Grand Slam titles; to date and almost marry Jimmy Connors; to go out with (among many others) Burt Reynolds and Jack Ford; to have a storybook romance and marriage to the dashing John Lloyd; to have that marriage fall apart, reconcile, and then fall apart again; and now, finally, to find true love with former Olympic skier Andy Mill, her second husband.

While her friends often giggled at her not-quite-accurate girl-next-door image, Evert was still the role model for every little girl in a tennis dress. It didn't matter that first Navratilova and then Graf had passed her on the tennis court. She was still The Queen, Chris America, and all the apple-pie stuff that came with it. Even David Letterman is almost reverent when she is a guest on his show.

All of which was exactly why NBC wanted her. She didn't have to be as good as Carillo to be a star. She was *already* a star. Realistically she *couldn't* be as good as Carillo. Evert would always be a tennis player in mind and spirit, if not in body. To start with, she was still the president of the Women's Tennis Association (president for life, it seemed), which made her a public relations arm of the tour. She was not about to go nosing around the locker room to find out what the gossip was in there.

She wasn't going to tackle any issue, much less a tough one, on the air. That was not in her nature in any case. These were, after all, her friends playing. Every time Evert referred to a player it was by first name. Graf would never play Seles or Navratilova with Evert in the booth, Steffi would play Monica or Martina. That was the way it was and always would be and that was fine with NBC.

And so it was that The Queen came to Hilton Head with the network hoping that The Kid would come through. She did—with flying colors. Still unseeded because she didn't yet have a ranking, Capriati had to play Sanchez in the third round. No problem: 6–1, 6–1. In the quarters, Capriati struggled a little against Helen Kelesi, but roared back to win. Now NBC and Gerry Smith had part of their wish—Capriati had made it to Saturday's telecast. She would play Zvereva in one semifinal. Navratilova would play a lanky young Czech named Regina Rajchrtova, a quarterfinal winner over Garrison.

Naturally, Capriati–Zvereva would be the Saturday TV match. To ensure that the court would be clear for The Princess when NBC came on the air at 2 P.M., the other semifinal was scheduled for 11:30. This did not exactly please Navratilova. She didn't relish the role of second fiddle, so she took her sweet time getting ready to go out and play. It was almost 11:50 before the match—which she won in a romp—actually began.

Navratilova may not have been thrilled with all the Capriati mania, but she understood it. "She's a fresh face, the new kid on the block, everybody loves her," she said. "I understand that. It's amazing how young she is, though. I had been on tour three years before she was born."

Navratilova was in the final. And after she destroyed Zvereva, so was Capriati, who by now was joyriding through the whole thing. She had a crew from HBO (which had reportedly paid the family well into six figures) dogging her for a documentary; she had a million questions on her friendship with Chris, and she had boys and men making eyes at her. When the HBO producer told her that a twenty-three-year-old had described her as "hot," Capriati rolled her eyes and said, "Oh God, don't tell my father." She also confided to friends that she had dreamed about TV star Johnny Depp and had a serious crush on Stefan Edberg. The Kid was growing up fast.

But she still sounded like a kid when she talked. When someone asked her about giving Zvereva a crucial point—overruling a call that had gone in her favor—she shrugged. "I just wanted to be fair. The ball was good. I should still have done the other points good."

As for playing Navratilova, well, that was really something. "I mean, it shows I'm up there with the great players, I guess," she said. "I mean, I always watched her play, and now I'll be out there on the court with her. To be out there with her will be great, you know, she's really a lege."

Lege was fourteen-year-old for "legend." Capriati was now reinventing the language. It was The Lege vs. The Kid. What more could anyone want? The Kid went off to the movies with her mother, Chris America and Andy America (Mill), and Anna Leaird, Chris's best friend who is also (surprise) the WITA's publicity director. They saw *Pretty Woman.* The next day Capriati reported, "It's a great movie, go see it." The Kid also did movie reviews.

Sunday was something straight out of a fairy tale: gorgeous and sunny, the little stadium sparkling, with the trees rustling in the spring breeze. Andy Mill admitted that the Capriati–Navratilova matchup made his wife a little nervous.

"I told Chrissie she shouldn't try to sugarcoat the situation," he said. "She and Martina are certainly friends, but she's closer to Jennifer. One is a friend, the other is a protégée."

Mill laughed. "Of course, if Martina loses I hope she sells her house in Aspen, because it's only a block from ours and I *know* we'll have to sell ours unless she sells hers."

Except for the fact that he is ludicrously handsome and could shoot seventy-nine at a very tough Harbour Town golf course, it is difficult not to like Andy Mill. He is friendly without being patronizing to everyone, whether they are important or unimportant, and he has no hang-ups about being identified as Chris Evert's husband.

He was a superb athlete himself, finishing sixth in the Olympic downhill in 1976, in spite of a badly sprained ankle. He and Evert met at a New Year's Eve party in Aspen in 1986, shortly after Evert's final split with John Lloyd. There had been some rocks along the way since then. The English tabloids had had a field day with the fact that Mill was still married (even though he was separated) when he and Evert began dating, and Evert's parents, good Catholics, had been less than thrilled with the divorce and the quick second marriage. Colette Evert still told people that John Lloyd would always be a son to her. Like everyone else, though, she couldn't help but like Andy, who married Chris nineteen months after meeting her. There was little doubt among her friends that Chris was happier than she had ever been. She had never been able to deal with the notion that Lloyd didn't have her steely-eyed desire to win. In 1986, she had been furious with him when, after blowing a two-set lead to Christo van Rensburg at Wimbledon, he had come into the interview room and announced his retirement. To Evert that was quitting. She couldn't stomach quitting.

That and the fact that they really had little in common had led first to a wandering eye, separation, a brief reconciliation, and then divorce. Lloyd was now happily remarried, as was Chris, and they were friends. Mill had been an Evert-type competitor. When Evert had come from 5–2 down in the third set in her last victory at Wimbledon in 1989, Mill had wept uncontrollably in the stands, because he wanted her to fight back and win so much.

Perhaps Evert should have walked away then, after losing to Graf in the semifinals. But she played through the U.S. Open, turning her retirement into a circus. Evert started it by selling her retirement story to *Sports Illustrated,* which, naturally, splashed the news all over its cover. Every Evert match at that Open became a melodrama. Poor Elise Burgin, who played her in the second round, was booed when she moon-balled her way to a 4–1 lead in the first set.

"That was the best way for me to play her," Burgin said later. "God, I couldn't believe the booing."

When Monica Seles played Evert on national TV in the round of 16 before a packed Sunday house, she froze completely. "I thought if I won I would never get out of there alive," she said, half kidding, later on. Evert played brilliantly that day. Two days later, though, Zina Garrison came from 5–2 down in the first set to beat her. Garrison refused to let the circumstances defeat her that day, but when she had shaken hands with her opponent and realized what she had just done, Garrison broke down completely. Evert, almost always gallant in defeat, hugged her as they walked off court, the loser smiling, the winner crying.

Garrison was the most ignored winner of a major tennis match in history. One TV interviewer broke down on the air while interviewing Evert. Even Carillo cried—though not on camera. One young reporter, David Aldridge of *The Washington Post,* viewing the mournful scene, couldn't help but feel a bit cynical. "Now I know what it was like the day Kennedy was shot," he cracked. It was an exaggeration—but not a major one.

Evert turned thirty-five in December—three months and eight days before Capriati hit fourteen. Now she sat in the TV booth with Dick Enberg as Capriati raced on court two steps ahead of Navratilova—"I wanted to get my lucky chair," she said—while Navratilova was nearly knocked over by the NBC cameraman pursuing the teenager. She was not amused.

That was Martina's last bad moment of the day, though. She was still The Lege and played near-perfect tennis to beat The Kid 6–2, 6–4 in seventy-five minutes. Capriati hardly seemed bothered by it all. During the awards ceremony she thanked just about everyone on the planet, and when Bud Collins, the master of ceremonies, started to pull the microphone back, thinking she was finished, Capriati grabbed it back. "Wait a minute," she said. "I'm not finished."

Collins, who knows a star when he sees one, dutifully handed the mike over. Navratilova was thrilled to win—"God, it was nerve-wracking!" she said—and Capriati was thrilled to be Capriati. NBC got the highest rating it had ever gotten on the Family Circle Cup, and a higher rating than it would get on the Wimbledon final. Evert's reviews weren't great, but they weren't bad. Gerry Smith couldn't stop grinning. And why not?

The Kid had come through like . . . well . . . like a Lege.

12

PARADISE

Gina Arias easily could have been one of the cognoscenti. On a perfect spring morning she sat high above the Mediterranean Sea, the water glistening in the sunshine, the coastline beyond it providing a spectacular backdrop to the whole scene.

Paradise.

At this moment, though, Gina Arias didn't even know the sea or the scenery existed. Her eyes and her mind were focused squarely on the red clay tennis court a few yards below her. On that court her husband, Jimmy, and Gary Muller, a tall South African with shoulder-length blond hair, were scrapping away in the red clay dust.

This was court 3 at the Country Club of Monte Carlo, far from the glamorous center court, far from the wide walkways where the rich and famous of the Riviera resort sipped wine and glanced down at the match below them. The only thing court 3 had in common with the center court was the background scenery. There, the beautiful people watched. Here, a couple of hundred tennis fans might stop for a few minutes before continuing their walk around the club's spacious grounds, all the while murmuring, pointing, or carrying on.

"Jimmy can't stand playing out here," Gina said quietly. "He's used to quiet, to closed-in places. This is distracting for him. He's spoiled."

One could hardly blame Jimmy Arias for being spoiled. In 1983, one month after turning nineteen, Arias was the fifth-ranked tennis player in the world. He was rich, he was famous, he had no reason to assume things would get anything but better.

"I grew up my whole life thinking that someday I would be the number one player in the world," he said. "When I got to number five, I wasn't satisfied, because I wasn't number one yet. Then I got mononucleosis, missed three months of tennis, and never got the drive back again. Never. Would I have stayed number five in the world if that hadn't happened? I don't know. But I don't think I would have dropped as far as I did."

In some ways, Jimmy Arias's story is a sad one. It is the story of a kid who since the age of eight lived his life to play tennis, who now, at twenty-six, must wonder what will come next—when it never really occurred to him that "next" would ever come. In another way, though, Arias's story is inspirational because it is the story of someone whose dreams were crushed but who still somehow emerged a better and stronger person, one with a far better understanding of the world.

"When I was coming up in the game and I was the young hotshot, there wasn't anything people couldn't do for me," he said, smiling at the memory. "I was everyone's best friend. For a while, when I started to drop, people were still my pals because they thought I would come back. Somewhere along the way people decided, 'This guy is done,' and since then, life has been a lot different.

"I'll never forget when I really understood that completely. It was two years ago, at Indian Wells [Palm Springs], when I asked the people at the transportation desk if I could borrow a car to go out and get something to eat. They said they were sorry, they didn't have any cars available. I walked across the lobby to call a taxi. As I was walking back, Ion Tiriac walked up and asked for a car. They said, 'Would you like to drive it yourself, Mr. Tiriac, or should we get you a driver?' That's when I knew it was time to start assuming no one was going to give me anything."

Arias is the second of Antonio and Francizka Arias's four children. Antonio Arias was born in Spain and left for Cuba with his parents during the Spanish Civil War. He grew up in Cuba and left there just before the revolution to attend college in the U.S. Jimmy's mother was the oldest of eleven children. She grew up in Germany and moved to Buffalo at age twenty-six, with money she had saved for years, to work as an au pair/housekeeper for a family. There, she met Antonio Arias, who had gotten a master's degree in electrical engineering and had moved to Buffalo to work for a local power company.

They met at a party, won a dance contest together, and ended up getting married, even though Francizka spoke no English when they first met.

Jimmy is the oldest of their three sons. At the age of three, his father, who had played on the Cuban National Team, began to teach him to play soccer. Two years later, Jimmy was playing on a 12-and-under soccer team. By then, his father had taken up tennis, and he took Jimmy along to pick up balls for him when he went to play. One day he put a racquet in Jimmy's hands—"a Dunlop Maxply with a four-and-five-eighths-inch grip," according to Jimmy, whose memory is photographic—and, as legend has it, the five-year-old hit ten straight balls back to his father.

Antonio Arias joined a tennis club shortly after that, and Jimmy was allowed to play for free in return for doing odd jobs. Eventually, he didn't have to do the odd jobs. He just played. His father taught him the game out of a book. By the time he was eight, Jimmy was playing all day during the summer and whenever he could get a court during the winter. "The summer I turned eight [1972] I decided I was going to be a professional tennis player," he said. "I never thought about doing anything else."

At ten, Arias reached the final of the 12-and-under nationals. That was when he first began to understand how demanding his father was going to be. He had beaten the second and third seeds to get to the final, but when he came home after losing to the No. 1 ranked player in the country, his father's only reaction was, "How could you lose so bad in the final?"

Jimmy laughs about that now, but he felt the pressure then. "My dad's philosophy was never tell you what you did right, tell you what you did wrong. I think that's what got me to number five in the world. I used to throw up before every match I played. I couldn't stand the thought of losing. When I lost that drive my dad gave me, I was never the same player.

"When I was twelve, Rod Laver came to Buffalo for an exhibition and I played him. He was past his prime but he was still Rod Laver. The first two games, he clowned around and I went up 2–0. After that he looked at me and said, 'Kid, you aren't getting another game.' He ended up beating me 7–5. It was another five years before I played at that level again. I was unbelievable that night. My father said to me, 'You played all right.' That was the closest he came to paying me a compliment."

At thirteen, Arias talked his parents into sending him to Florida to work with Nick Bollettieri. There was no sprawling academy then, just Bollettieri working out of the Colony Beach Hotel with a couple of teenagers. Arias roomed with Mike DePalmer and Chris Green, both three years older than he was. "They used to throw me out of the room every night when they wanted to talk," he said. "The first time I played DePalmer in a match, I won a tiebreak from him and he punched me in the stomach on the court change."

By his own admission, Arias was pretty full of himself in those days. "I remember Chris Green once saying to me, 'I'll quit tennis if I ever lose to you,' " he said. "I just said, 'Get ready to hang it up.' I thought I could beat anybody."

Most of the time Arias *did* beat anybody and everybody. When he was sixteen, he beat Eddie Dibbs, a top-twenty player, in an exhibition, and Bollettieri decided he should turn pro. His parents opposed the move; they wanted him to go to college. Back then, it was almost unheard of for a male player not to go to college for at least a year. Finally, Antonio Arias decided to relent *if* Bollettieri could get Jimmy a contract that would guarantee $100,000 to be put aside for his college education. No problem, said Bollettieri.

The agents were invited in to talk to the family. At the time, Bollettieri was represented by ProServ (he has since moved on to IMG), so Jimmy was informed that he would be signing with ProServ (even though he liked IMG's presentation better).

Arias's first year as a pro was miserable. He won matches and quickly moved into the top one hundred, but he was an outcast in the locker room. "The older guys didn't want me feeling comfortable, because I was a threat," he remembered. "I had a hell of a time finding anyone to practice with me. One day I was hitting with a guy named Ferdi Taygan, and this guy, Francisco Gonzales, just walked on court and said, 'Get out of here, kid, I'm taking the court.' Taygan didn't really want to hit with me anyway, so he didn't do anything. For two years my whole goal in life was to beat up Francisco Gonzales."

Arias never got to do that but he did begin regularly beating players on the tennis court. In 1982, just before he turned eighteen, he reached the finals of a tournament in Washington, beating Jose-Luis Clerc, a Top Ten player, in the semifinals. He called his father to tell him.

"Who do you play in the final?" his father asked.

"Lendl."

"Don't even call me if you don't beat him."

Arias didn't beat him. And didn't call.

Fourteen months later he lost to Lendl again—in the semifinals of the U.S. Open. By that point, he had won four tournaments that year, including the Italian Open and the U.S. Clay Courts, which was still an important title back then. He had also been accepted in the locker room, although weekends were still lonely. "My best friends were all the young guys who were leaving by the weekend to go to qualifying at the next tournament," he said. "I was still around for the semis and finals."

He lost to Lendl in a match he still insists he would have won if he hadn't gotten a bad call. "Lendl still choked in those days, and he was starting to choke then," Arias said. "If I win that set, he's going to choke and I'm going to play Connors in the final."

○

Instead Lendl played Connors—and choked—and Arias flew to Palermo to play in a meaningless tournament because he had a $20,000 guarantee. There, he came down with mononucleosis and a strep throat—yet won the tournament. On the way home, he missed his connecting flight in Rome and was so sick he just lay down in the middle of the terminal and tried to sleep. When he got home, he went straight from the airport to the hospital and was off the tour for three months. The guarantee still hasn't been paid.

"My whole career changed after that," he said. "I had never missed a day of tennis in my life. I used to practice on Christmas. Now, it didn't seem like a big deal if I missed a day. The next year I was still ranked fourteenth at the end of the year, but it was all a bluff. I couldn't play. Guys just hadn't figured it out yet."

In tennis, players eventually figure out all weaknesses. Arias was a typical Bollettieri player. He had one huge weapon—his forehand—some speed, and some smarts. Not much serve, not much backhand, no volley. That was going to catch up with him sooner or later. What's more, his success in 1983 had made Arias rich, well beyond the $100,000 his father had demanded. Almost every tournament he played in 1984 and 1985 was for a hefty guarantee, and his endorsement contracts had all been rewritten. He was long past getting sick before matches.

His ranking slipped gradually—from fourteen in 1984 to twenty-one in 1985 to forty-eight in 1986. The next year he made a minicomeback to No. 34, reaching the final in Monte Carlo and the fourth round at the French. That was the year he met Gina, at a tournament in Memphis. She was a senior at the University of Mississippi and had already been accepted to law school. She had gone to Memphis for the day with her mother and had been spotted in the stands by some of Arias's keen-eyed friends during Arias's singles match. That night, during his doubles match, Arias kept giving Gina the eye.

"All my mother's friends said, 'He's looking at you, Gina,' " she remembered. "I thought that was ridiculous. Professional tennis players don't give women the eye during matches. Anyway, I wasn't really interested."

Arias *was* interested. Big time. Much to his surprise, Gina Robinson was nowhere to be found when he came out of the locker room. "Usually, if you give someone the eye as blatantly as I had done with her, they show up outside the locker room," he said. "She didn't. So I went and sat in the stands near them. Then, as I got up to leave, I sort of tripped over the woman sitting next to her. It turned out to be her mom. I just introduced myself and said, 'Would you mind if I asked your daughter out?' "

Both Robinson women were charmed by that approach. Jimmy and Gina hit it off quickly, but when the week was over, that was that. Except that a week later, unable to get Gina off his mind, Jimmy called her. "I can't believe I'm calling you," he said.

"I knew you would," she replied. The relationship continued long distance. Then Jimmy convinced Gina to defer law school for a year to travel with him. In December 1989, they were married. Gina had already been on tour for over a year and had helped Jimmy through the trauma of his mother's death, in 1988.

Jimmy first found out that his mother had cancer at the end of 1987. The doctors thought they had caught it in time. But they hadn't. She got sicker and sicker during the next year. Jimmy would play one tournament, come home for a couple of weeks, and then go out and play again. He ended up playing only fourteen tournaments all year and lost in the first round in ten of them. His ranking dropped from 34 to 150. His mind was a million miles from tennis.

"I couldn't stop feeling guilty about having left home so early and never having been home for my mom," he said softly. "She never wanted me to go to Nick's. Every time I would come home, she would cry all the way home in the car because she was so happy I was there. She was one of these people who was always doing for everyone else in her family. I think the reason everyone in my family are such slobs is that mom always took care of everything.

"That whole year, she kept pushing me to go back and play. But when I did, I couldn't think about tennis at all. I never wanted to practice. Finally, on November fifth, she told me to go to this tournament I was supposed to play in. She wanted me to play. I went. She died the next day."

Arias wandered through 1989 not sure if he wanted to play tennis anymore. He had become the forgotten man of the tour. He had won so little in recent years that people thought he had been hurt or retired. "To this day people still come up to me and say, 'Great to see you back,' " he said, laughing. "I just say, 'Thanks, it's great to be back.' "

The person who kept him in tennis was Gina. Not because she loved the tour life—she didn't—but because she still believed her husband could be a very good player one more time. "Jimmy is too nice," she said. "I keep trying to get him to try to hit people at the net. I know that sounds awful, but sometimes you have to do it. Jimmy's too much of a sportsman.

Lendl would just as soon hit you as pass you. Jimmy needs to be more like that—at least some of the time. Sometimes when he gets tentative out there I just want to yell at him, 'Hit the ball!' One time I actually did that and he looked at me like I was crazy. Then he won the third set, 6–1."

The Ariases had started 1990 in Australia—Jimmy's first trip there—and he had started well, getting to the final in Adelaide and the quarterfinals in Auckland. But a quick loss to Jim Courier in the first round at the Australian Open set them back.

It was at that point that Gina decided to see a sports psychologist. She wanted help to figure out how to help Jimmy. "Be honest with him, but be positive, too," the psychologist told her. "Find something good in a match. When he says that he stunk, don't agree with him. Try to keep him up."

Gina was trying. But now, in Monte Carlo, the roles had been reversed. Jimmy was trying to keep Gina up. Her parents had split after thirty years of marriage. Gina felt betrayed by her father, hurt for her mother. Part of her wanted to be home with her mother, but she knew Jimmy needed her, too.

"It's been very rough," Jimmy said. "The fact is, I wouldn't be playing tennis right now if it weren't for Gina. She knows I need her. When I get in trouble in a match, I look at her. She keeps me fighting. I used to play for my dad; now I play for her.

"Since this thing with her folks, though, I've had to help her. Which is only fair. But keeping my mind focused on tennis through it all hasn't been easy."

Monte Carlo marked the beginning of the clay-court season, the time of year for Arias to shine. Because of his backcourt game, clay has always been his surface. On that sparkling morning, he was playing Muller, strictly a fast-surface player. "Jimmy can't let Gary play his slice games," Gina Arias said. "In Memphis, he was up a set and a break on him and lost." This was a long way from Memphis, though. Arias won 6–1, 6–3.

Arias ended the match with a good-old-days Arias forehand, and Gina smiled. At that moment, her husband was ranked sixty-fifth in the world. "You know, tennis isn't our whole life," she said as she stood up to go congratulate her husband. "I hope we'll never be that shallow. But right now, it's pretty damn important."

• • •

HARD COURTS

○

Boris Becker was about to go out and play his first match in Monte Carlo against French wild card Cedric Pioline. Becker was under contract to a German company to drink their Gatorade-type drink out of a bottle with the company's name on it during his matches. In tennis, drinks are divided into three categories: soda, water, and electrolytes (Gatorade-type liquid replenishers). At each tournament the promoter may sell the rights to advertise on court to one company in each category. If those rights are sold, a player may not use a different company's logo on the court, although he may drink another company's product. He just has to drink it in an unmarked bottle.

Coca-Cola was the official soda of the Monte Carlo Open. There was no on-court advertising, however, for an electrolyte or a bottled water. Thus, there seemed to be no reason for Becker not to take his electrolyte bottle on court.

Wrong, said Bernard Noat, tournament director, and his staff. They had sold the rights to all *three* drink categories to Coke. No drink logo of any kind could be taken on court except Coke. Becker didn't think that was right. Mark Miles—who had replaced Hamilton Jordan in March as CEO of the ATP—was brought in to mediate.

This was a delicate situation for him. The ATP Tour was advertised as a "partnership" between the tournaments and the players. Now, two of the partners were arguing over a bottle of liquid. Miles ruled for Becker.

"The way I see it, our rules say if there's no electrolyte that has bought the on-court rights, the player can do what he wants," he said. "Coke is no more an electrolyte than it is a coffee or a beer. The tournament didn't have the right to do what it did."

The tournament was furious. But this was tennis in the 1990s. "Unbelievable," said Stuart Wilson, who worked with Ion Tiriac handling matters like this for Becker. "The guy is supposed to be starting preparation for the French Open and we're sitting around arguing about a bottle of liquid."

Ivan Lendl wasn't playing any clay-court tournaments, preparing instead for the grass of Wimbledon. McEnroe, Agassi, and Wilander were all last-minute withdrawals. Monte Carlo still had Becker, now that he could drink from his own thermos, and it still had Stefan Edberg. It also had Alberto Mancini, who just happened to be the defending champion.

A year earlier, Mancini had been the talk of the tennis world. At nineteen, he was being billed as the new Vilas. He was a righty and Guillermo Vilas had been a lefty, but otherwise the similarities were striking. Both were dark, handsome Argentines who made many women crazy with passion. Both came across as quiet, brooding poets. Both were strong as bulls and could topspin you into the turf of any clay court in the world.

Mancini proved this definitively when he beat Wilander and Becker back to back to win Monte Carlo, then, three weeks later in Rome, came from a match point down to beat Agassi to win the Italian Open. He went on to the quarters of the French Open, and even after a five-set loss to Noah in the round of 16 at the U.S. Open, he finished the year ranked ninth in the world.

As a fifteen-year-old, Mancini had left home to move to an apartment in Buenos Aires so he could work with his coach full-time. He had been terribly lonely and homesick, but he had forced himself to keep going by dreaming of the riches and stardom tennis could bring him.

Now he was there. Everyone wanted a piece of Alberto Mancini. For 1990 he had guarantees almost every place he played. His contracts were huge. In Argentina he was as big a name as Gabriela Sabatini. And everywhere he went, women gathered to wait for him: outside locker rooms, in hotel lobbies, in front of restaurants. Anywhere he went.

"I have to be very careful," he said at the end of 1989. "It is very easy to get distracted."

Mancini had not been careful enough. By the time he got to Monte Carlo his ranking had dropped to seventeenth. The word on the tour was that no one was having a better time than Mancini. He had become the king of the weekly player parties, often staying up all night.

"Yes, I stay out," he said. "But it is only after I am out of the tournament."

Most weeks that was pretty early. He lost his first match in Rotterdam, his first match in Indian Wells, and his first match at Key Biscayne. But that was on hard courts. It would all change when he got to the clay. He had made his mark on the clay last year.

He finally won a match in Barcelona, beating Aki Rahunen, a young Finnish player with loads of potential. But he lost his next match to the immortal Diego Perez and then lost in the first round at Nice to the equally memorable Claudio Pistolesi. That brought him to Monte Carlo with a match record for the year of 1–5. His ranking had not yet dropped that far, but with two tournaments coming up in which he was defending champion, he stood to drop a long way if he didn't come around quickly.

In some ways, Mancini was going through the cycle that almost every good young player went through, and he was bright enough to understand that. "The first year you play on tour, everything is scary," he said. "It's exciting but you don't really feel like you belong. Then the second year you start to feel comfortable, to know people. But still there is no pressure. No one expects you to do anything. You just go out and hit the ball. The third year, after you do well in the second, you have all the pressure. Everyone is looking at you. And you have to defend all your points." The last may be the toughest. Players will tell you that the worst thing one can do on tour is worry about defending points. In layman's terms, defending points goes like this: Mancini wins Monte Carlo in 1989 and receives 300 computer points for the victory—250 for winning and 50 in bonuses for beating Wilander and Becker. His ranking shoots up. Three weeks later he does the same thing in Rome, and all of a sudden is ranked in the world top twenty.

Points stay on the computer for fifty-two weeks. Now, fifty-two weeks later, in Monte Carlo, the three hundred points Mancini won are about to come off. The very best he can do is equal those points by winning the tournament again. Anything less and his ranking will drop. A *lot* less, another early round loss, and his ranking will drop considerably. The same will be true in Rome.

When a player is doing well, he doesn't worry about defending points. If he loses points at one tournament, he knows he will make them up the next week or the week after. When he is playing poorly, he lies awake at night, thinking about the points he is about to lose, about how it will affect his ranking, how his corporate sponsors will react, and how it will affect his marketability in terms of guarantees and exhibitions. Mancini was caught smack in the middle of that syndrome. In 1989 he had played solid tennis on the hard courts, reaching the quarterfinals at Indian Wells and the fourth round at the Lipton. That had sent him to the clay full of confidence. This year, by the time he reached Monte Carlo, Mancini was full of self-doubts. He was fighting with his coach, his family, and his agent. He was uptight. He was hoping that returning to the site of his first big victory would get him going again.

The draw was kind to him in the first round. His opponent was Christo van Rensburg. On grass or on hard court, Van Rensburg would have been a very tough player for Mancini to beat. But on the red clay, Van Rensburg was almost helpless. He had neither the ground strokes nor the patience to beat *Henry* Mancini on clay, much less Alberto, who won easily, 6–2, 6–4. That night at dinner with friends and family, his old friend Prince Albert of Monaco stopped by the table.

A year ago the prince had presented Mancini with the winner's trophy during the awards ceremony. Now he sat down to renew acquaintances. He was fascinated by the fact that Mancini's agent was a woman—Micky den Tuinder of Advantage—and he lingered with the group for a while. Mancini felt good, back home again, confident.

But it didn't last. Mancini's second-round opponent was Henri Leconte, perhaps the most enigmatic player in the game. At his best, Leconte was D'Artagnan, a handsome, swashbuckling lefty who could hit any shot that existed and a few that didn't. On an off day, Leconte was another Van Rensburg on clay.

One year ago on this court, Leconte had hobbled away, his back killing him, in need of surgery for a second time. It had been a slow road back for him. He had appeared in Australia, looking a bit like a Macy's Thanksgiving Day parade balloon, and then in the U.S., had lost in the first round three straight times. He had played qualifying in Nice the week before Monte Carlo, come through it, and lost a tough match to top seed Jay Berger. Once ranked as high as No. 7 in the world, he was down to No. 161. But playing in front of a French crowd, with his confidence returning, Leconte was D'Artagnan again.

This was a match between two players headed in opposite directions. One could almost see Leconte's confidence rising, Mancini's fading. This was Wednesday, the annual kids' day at the tournament, and the place was loud, the court windy. Mancini was unnerved almost from the start and lost his serve quickly. "You could see he was nervous," Leconte said later. "I started to feel great out there."

He whipped through the first set, but Mancini, taking a deep breath, came back to go up 2–0 in the second. Up on the terrace, Mancini's buddy Prince Albert, and his sister Princess Stephanie, sipped wine and wondered if he could come back.

He couldn't. Leconte broke back to 2–2 and Mancini quickly unraveled. Down 2–3, 0–40, he pushed an easy backhand way wide. He slammed a ball, cursed loudly—drawing a warning for an audible obscenity—and a few minutes later was shaking hands, beaten 6–4, 6–4. Leconte, rejuvenated, blew kisses to the crowd. Mancini's ranking tumbled out of the top twenty for the first time in a year. His new ranking was No. 24. And that wasn't with a bullet.

The next night, shortly before 4 A.M. when the player party was wrapping up, Alberto Mancini was still on the dance floor. He did not appear too concerned about his ranking.

• • •

○

By Friday evening, Becker and Edberg were gone, too.

Both men had reason to want to do well on the clay this spring. Each believed that he had allowed the French Open to slip away the previous year. Becker had come from two sets down to go up a break in the fifth set against Edberg in the semifinals, but had run out of gas. That put Edberg in the final against Michael Chang. He went up two sets to one and had what seemed like a zillion break points in the fourth. But he never could convert, and Chang completed his miracle by winning in five.

Having come so close a year ago, each was pointing to Paris now. Lendl's absence from the clay-court circuit provided another bit of incentive. Both Edberg and Becker had a chance, if they played well, to take over the No. 1 ranking.

Edberg didn't look *close* to being ready. In his first match, he played Jimmy Arias. For six games, Arias looked liked his circa-1983 version, jerking Edberg all over the court. He got to 5–1, 40–15, but collapsed.

"I blew the two set points at 5–1, and the first thing that flashed through my mind was, Wouldn't it be something if I ended up blowing the set?" he said later. "Not a great way to think."

His premonition proved correct. Edberg won the set in a tiebreak and the second set 6–3. Arias knew he had let a major chance slip away. He also knew that Edberg was very vulnerable. "He plays someone who can return well, he's going to get beat," he said. "A good clay-courter will take him."

The next evening, Edberg came up against a good clay-courter. Juan Aguilera had been ranked seventh in the world late in 1984, at the age of twenty-two. But the next four years had been miserable for him. He had fallen out with his coach, Luis Bruguera, and his father had died of cancer. Also, assorted injuries had limited his court time.

But Aguilera, a quiet, sensitive man who played guitar and drums in a Spanish rock group, didn't give up. He won a small tournament in 1989, his first since the splurge of 1984, and moved back into the top one hundred. The week before Monte Carlo, he moved back into the top forty for the first time in five years, winning the tournament in Nice. In the second round of this tournament, he had won an emotional match from Sergi Bruguera—his old coach's son. That gave him a chance to prove Arias right. And he did just that, beating Edberg in two tiebreaks, 7–6, 7–6. Aguilera was too steady for Edberg, who looked impatient and nervous on the big points. It was almost nine o'clock by the time they finished but most of the crowd had stuck around. After all, the sun hadn't set yet and no one goes to dinner in Monte Carlo before ten o'clock anyway.

Edberg, who once shrugged off an early-round defeat at Wimbledon by saying, "There's always another tournament next week," hardly seemed disturbed by this loss. "I'm just not playing well at the moment," he said. "I missed too many easy shots, ones I would normally never miss. It's just a matter of time to get my movement right on clay. This isn't anything I'm going to worry about."

Ion Tiriac was worried, however, about Boris Becker.

In the quarterfinals, Becker looked to be on his way to an easy victory over Emilio Sanchez. He led 6–4, 5–3, and had a match point with Sanchez serving. He even got a second serve. Here, though, Becker's fast-court instincts took over. He went for too much on the return, pushing a forehand deep. Suddenly, Sanchez had life again. He proceeded to win seven of the next eight games—breaking Becker's serve three times in four tries. On clay, that can happen, even to Becker. To his credit, Becker didn't quit. He came back to force the final set into a tiebreak, but lost it 7–3.

Sitting in the stands watching, Tiriac was not happy. Becker was doing exactly what Tiriac had told him he could not do—playing clay-court tennis. The match had taken nearly three hours. To Tiriac's way of thinking, that was too long. Becker had to dictate the tone and style of the match, not be dictated to. Already, watching him practice, Tiriac had spoken to Bob Brett about his concern.

"I have told Bob that if Boris keeps playing this way, the entire clay-court season will be a disaster," Tiriac snorted. "Actually, worse than a disaster. Will Boris listen? Probably not."

Becker, Tiriac, and Brett had become the most interesting triangle in tennis. In 1987 Becker had split with his coach, Gunther Bosch, during the Australian Open, a divorce that had created huge headlines in the German tabloids when Bosch sold them his story. To this day Becker feels betrayed by Bosch, who now does German TV, writes a column, and coaches a few young players.

For the rest of that year, Tiriac served as Becker's coach, a role he enjoyed very much. "Being on the court is still what I enjoy the most in tennis," he said. "The deals make the money and I have to do it. But what I would really like to do is be on the court."

By the end of 1987, Becker's relationship with Tiriac was strained. There may be no two men in tennis with stronger wills. If Tiriac counseled Becker to serve-and-volley, Becker would insist he needed to stay back. If Tiriac thought a day off from practice was a good idea, Becker felt he needed a long workout. What keeps the relationship going is not—contrary to popular belief—money. Each man would continue to be quite wealthy without the other. What keeps them going is a deep-seated affection that dates back to 1984, when Becker was a gangly sixteen-year-old whom no one in tennis was overwhelmed by. "That year everyone was raving for [Mark] Kratzmann," Tiriac remembered. "I saw Boris lose to him and said this kid [Becker] is the one."

Tiriac is not above patting himself on the back. More often than not, though, the pat is deserved. But by the end of 1987, the redheaded kid was almost twenty, a two-time Wimbledon champion, extremely rich, and very unhappy with his tennis.

"I had money, but I had no freedom," he said. "I was doing what other people were telling me to do all the time. Every time I turned around I had to do something. All of it for money. I decided one way or the other, I wanted to do things my own way."

That was when he hired Brett and when he started keeping his journal. Tiriac told Becker privately and the world publicly that he didn't think Brett was the right coach for Becker. That got their working relationship off to a rocky start, although mutual respect made it workable on both sides. Becker struggled through 1988 but came roaring back in 1989, winning Wimbledon and the U.S. Open.

Then came six months of misery for all three men as Becker went through his I-don't-know-if-I-want-to-play period. During the first four months of 1990, Tiriac had been distracted by the revolution in Romania. Days after the Ceauşescu government was overthrown and the dictator executed, he began working with his friends in the German government to get supplies into Romania. He had even been presented with a petition urging him to run for president. "I would have been president ten days," he said. "Then they overthrow me."

Instead of becoming president, Tiriac became the country's link to the outside world. He told everyone that he was making these trips to Romania because, as a businessman, this was the opportunity of a lifetime. "We are talking about a brand-new country," he said. "Everything is there to be done."

There was no doubt that Tiriac intended to make money, lots of it, in Romania. There was also no doubt that he felt something inside that went well beyond pragmatism.

"Look, if you had told me on December twentieth that in my lifetime this would happen in Romania I would tell you that you are crazy," Tiriac said. "Romania is not like Czechoslovakia or Germany or Poland. There *was* no opposition. There was no Walesa in Romania. The Russians never had to roll into Bucharest the way they did Prague. So for me to sit there and watch this happen on television the last week in December, it was an absolute miracle. Nothing less.

"When French TV showed the Ceaușescu execution, a lot of people thought it was quite brutal. No doubt it was brutal. But if Ceaușescu had not been executed, many, many more people would have died. The people who killed him saved lives. Still, it is a difficult thing for people to understand. Ceaușescu was not necessarily completely evil, but he was crazy. There would be no compromising with him."

Distracted by Romanian politics, Tiriac left Becker and Brett pretty much on their own early in the year. For Becker, the turning point came in Key Biscayne, when he finally decided to break up with Karen Schultz. This was not an easy decision for him, not after two years. Becker is a one-woman type of man. But he had to make a choice.

"We were both a little bit unhappy with the other," he said. "She was older [twenty-seven], and that made us different. It was the best thing for both of us, but that doesn't mean it was easy. When you end a relationship like that, you feel very lonely and sad for a long time."

There was one place for Becker to turn, though: his tennis. He told Brett and Tiriac that he now knew he wanted to play again. The ruminating was over. When he arrived in Monte Carlo the second week in April to begin working with Brett, the coach saw that he had a new player, one who was eager and not distracted. This was a huge relief to Brett.

That didn't mean all was sanguine for Team Becker. Monte Carlo was home ground for all of them; each had an apartment overlooking the sea, in different buildings downtown. They were all together now and all had different ideas about the best way for Becker to win on clay. The Sanchez loss seemed to confirm Tiriac's speech to Brett. Yet Brett knew that trying to convince Becker of that right now would be impossible. He didn't want to push too hard, too soon. There were still four weeks left before Paris.

When the red clay dust had finally cleared on Friday night, the semifinal matchups were hardly as glamorous as might have been expected. Leconte, building on his victory over Mancini, had become the story of the tournament locally, by beating Andres Gomez and Horst Skoff. He would play Thomas Muster in one semifinal, Muster having beaten Aguilera. Often when a player pulls a huge upset, he has trouble coming back the next day. True to that form, Aguilera had been a shadow of himself after the Edberg victory.

The other semifinal matched Sanchez against Andrei Chesnokov, the talented Soviet with the great deadpan sense of humor. Chesnokov—Chezzy to everyone on tour—could easily have been a stand-up comic. His English was a good deal better than he liked to let on, although he would occasionally end long speeches in English by looking at his companion and saying, "You understand the language I am speaking?"

In any language, Chezzy was funny. But his postmatch interviews in English had become legendary. Chezzy understood English but was not fluent. When someone asked him a question in English he had to translate it to Russian in his head, grasp it, think of the answer in Russian, translate back to English in his head, and then answer. Often this brought on long pauses. He also had developed an instinctive habit of starting his answer to any question with the words "but no . . . yes." A typical Chezzy postmatch interview might go something like this:

Q: Andrei, was the key to the match the way you served?
A: But no . . . yes . . . I served very well today . . .
Q: So then you feel like . . .
A: But also I know if I get my first serve in I can win. His return is too good to serve second serves all day . . .
Q: So then you think . . .
A: But also I know in my next match I will have to serve even better because my second serve is still too weak to beat a good player with . . .
Q: Andrei, about your prize money . . .
A: But no . . . yes. [Chezzy rolls his eyes.] I keep my prize money.
Q: So then you . . .
A: But also I give some to charity. Lots of charities. Andrei charity, Chezzy charity, disco charity . . .

And so on. Actually, Chezzy did give a decent-sized chunk of his prize money to charity. A year ago, he had announced that he was tired of turning 90 percent of his money over to the Soviet Tennis Federation. By year's end, after some lengthy negotiations, Chesnokov had been given permission to keep his prize money, as long as he agreed to play Davis Cup and the Olympics for his country. It was similar to Natalia Zvereva's deal. That made him happy.

Chezzy was never very happy with his tennis, though. He was as fast as anyone in the game and, even though he rarely betrayed emotion on the court, an intense competitor. All week Chezzy had been playing down his chances. After he beat Jaime Yzaga in the third round, 6–2, 6–1, he said he was happy to be in the quarterfinals but didn't expect to go any farther. When he then whipped Marc Rosset, the six-foot-six-inch Swiss who could easily pass for Harpo Marx, he said he really wasn't playing well. Someone asked Chezzy how he would get ready for the semifinals.

"But no . . . yes. I go to disco," Chezzy answered. "Maybe I loosen up that way."

About the only thing Chezzy loved better than going to a disco was talking about it. If he spent as much time in discos as he claimed, he never would have beaten anyone. On Saturday he beat Sanchez in a strange three-setter. Sanchez dominated the first set, Chezzy the second. When Chezzy went up 5–3 in the third, he looked to be in control. But as he had done against Becker, Sanchez came back, winning three straight games to go up 6–5. Chezzy held serve to force a tiebreak, then surprised Sanchez by playing attacking tennis throughout the tiebreak. He won it 7–2. Chezzy, like most Soviets, is an excellent chess player. He had outthought Sanchez at the end.

Seen from the TV booths, this match provided a decent synopsis of the difference between American and British television. This was the epitome of European clay-court tennis: The balls were heavy and slow, the court red and slower, the rallies endless. If the net had been electrified neither player would have been in any danger.

One point summed it all up, a rally that lasted several minutes. In the British Satellite Broadcast booth, John Barrett reacted to the end of the point this way: "Aha! He's done it! Chesnokov has at last broken through the Spanish Armada, wearing down the will of the gallant Spaniard! Superbly played by the Soviet!"

Next door in the ESPN booth, Mary Carillo said this: "Jeez, that was a long point, wasn't it?"

Chezzy, of course, said he had no chance in the final. Muster had hammered Leconte; Chezzy didn't think he could beat him. "Thomas is playing very, very well," he said. "But also I think maybe I take him out tonight. Buy him a vodka at disco."

Chezzy was nowhere near a disco that night. But he played the next day as if he had taken some kind of elixir. Muster dominated the first set, grunting and pounding away on a hot, sunny day made for him. Down 5–3, Chezzy went to the afterburners. He won four straight games to take the set in seventy excruciating minutes, then was flawless the last two sets and won, 7–5, 6–3, 6–3. When the two-hour-and-forty-minute match ended, Chezzy threw his arms into the air, exhausted and thrilled.

The awards ceremony in Monte Carlo is second only to Wimbledon's in simplicity and dignity. A representative of the royal family, Prince Albert in recent years, comes on court to present the trophies. No speeches, no endless thanking of sponsors. When the trophy has been presented, the flag of the winner's country is raised above the scoreboard and his anthem is played. During the Soviet anthem, one of the loveliest in the world, Chezzy stood at attention, not rigid or melodramatic, just respectful. He was clearly moved by the moment. He was not alone.

13

ROME IS ROME

It was a gray, rainy Roman evening. The cobblestone walkways of the Foro Italico were crowded and slippery. It was eleven o'clock at night, there was no sign that play would resume anytime soon, and yet the place was packed.

"You have to understand," Cino Marchese was saying. "Rome is Rome. This is the cocktail hour. The discos don't even open until midnight."

It was day/night four of the Italian Open, and the packed house made Marchese a happy man. This was the women's week at the Italian and it had become the toughest ticket in town. Five years ago, if you had offered a Roman a free ticket to watch women play tennis, he would have offered you 50,000 lira—to go away and leave him alone.

"This is an amazing thing we have done," Marchese said. "I am proud to have been part of this. I think, if not for us, the Italian Open would have died. This would have been a tragedy for tennis."

Cino Marchese's pride in what the Italian Open has become was understandable. In the early 1980s, the tournament was rotting away, literally and figuratively. The Foro Italico, once one of the grand arenas in tennis, was a decaying pit. The men's field had been depleted by the flight of the top-name players to exhibitions and big-guarantee tournaments. The women's tournament had almost ceased to exist. It had even been moved out of Rome, in 1979. It was played one year in the town of Taranto and then moved to Perugia. One year there was no women's Italian Open at all. If not for the fact that Chris Evert's Ellesse contract called for her to play in Italy, it might have died completely.

That was where Marchese and his employer, IMG, came into the picture. To understand what the Italian Open means to Italians, one needs to understand Cino Marchese. If anyone has ever fit the stereotype of what Americans think an Italian mafioso looks and sounds like, it is Marchese. Tall and striking, Marchese has white hair as smooth as silk and a deep gravelly voice that can boom or whisper in equally intimidating fashion. His suits are elegant and impeccable and he speaks almost perfect, Italian-accented English, always lighting up one cigarette after another as he speaks.

He is a self-described member of the Italian bourgeoisie, the only son of a jeweler. He grew up in Varenza, a small town in northern Italy, destined, it seemed, to follow in his father and grandfather's footsteps in the jewelry business and as the local mayor.

But Marchese longed for more. He grew up loving sports, playing all of them at one time or another: soccer, basketball, and tennis. "I was very fond of tennis," he says, "but quite hopeless as a player."

He went to university, hoping to become an architect, but came home to help in the family business. He was restless, though, and when a friend with a small clothing business asked him to help out selling ski equipment, he agreed. When the company grew and his friend ventured into tennis, Marchese became his tennis marketing man. "All of a sudden I am being paid money to go to Wimbledon," he said. "To me, the possibilities of this were endless."

He made contacts in the tennis world. One was Mark McCormack, the head of IMG. Marchese helped McCormack stage some exhibitions in Italy in 1975. All the while he was working less and less for his father. "My parents could never figure out what it was I was doing," he says, laughing. "They would say to me, 'You are making money at *this*?' "

In 1979 McCormack offered to pay Marchese money on a full-time basis to run his Italian operation. Marchese accepted. Three years later, at Marchese's urging, IMG bought the Italian Open. There are many reasons why those who manage players should not be allowed to manage tennis tournaments. The conflicts of interest are obvious: As a tournament director, you control wild cards and, often as not, guarantees. IMG and ProServ often use wild cards as recruiting tools when they are after young players, and they hand them out to their own players—as you might expect—a lot quicker than to outsiders.

Wild-card abuses are as common as double faults. Check through any tournament run by a management company and you will find some strange wild cards. In Orlando, in 1990, for example, ProServ gave a wild card to John Ross, a twenty-six-year-old journeyman who was one of their clients. It refused a wild card to Tommy Ho, seventeen, the national junior champion two years earlier and a resident of Orlando. Ho, as it happens, is represented by Advantage. If he had been a ProServ client, you can bet he would have had a wild card in a second. Later in the summer Ross would get another wild card in the Washington tournament. Guess who ran it?

To pick on Ross and ProServ is unfair. IMG does the same thing, and Advantage, which is just now getting into the tournament business (almost exclusively on the women's side), will no doubt follow suit.

The fact is, though, conflicts of interest and all, the Italian Open might have died without IMG. As soon as the tournament was in his company's hands, Marchese went to the Italian Olympic Committee, which ran the Foro Italico complex including the adjacent Olympic stadium and the swimming complex. The tennis facility was falling down. Help was needed. The committee was willing to put money into the place if IMG did the same.

Agreed. Rebuilding was slow. In 1982 Marchese opened five corporate hospitality suites on the roof of the clubhouse. He sold two—to Sheraton Hotels and to Rene Lacoste, the clothing company. The next year he gave the entire roof to Sheraton, which, in return, agreed to give him carpeting and equipment to start a hospitality village at the far end of the grounds. By 1990 the village was filled for the two weeks. Marchese had at last followed in his family's footsteps. "I am mayor of the hospitality village," he said.

Getting the fans back was not as easy. In 1983, when Jimmy Arias beat Jose Higueras in the final, total attendance for the week was nineteen thousand—"And almost all of them got in free," Marchese said. The Italian fans were like the rest of the world: They wanted to see the game's stars. That was where IMG came in. Combining some serious guarantee money with the influence it had with its big-name clients, IMG began to rebuild the tournament field.

"We had to invest money in players to get them back," Marchese said. "Against the rules? Of course. But it was an open secret. You don't get players like Wilander, Noah, McEnroe, Lendl, for nothing."

With the men's tournament coming back to life, Marchese and IMG decided it was time to bring the women back to Rome. This wasn't easy, either. To begin with, the Italian Federation was afraid it would be a fiasco. What's more, the Women's Tennis Association was satisfied with the way things were going in Perugia. It was a nice little provincial tournament.

"The Italian Open could not be the Italian Open again without the women," Marchese said. "That is why I proposed making it a two-week event. Give the women their own week, but make it one event again."

This took some doing. IMG had to guarantee the federation that it would cover any losses. Then a sanction had to be found. The tournament in Perugia wasn't willing to give up its sanction. So IMG bought a tournament in Florida and moved it to Rome. The women's Italian Open today is actually descended from a now-forgotten Virginia Slims stop in Florida.

When the women came back to Rome in 1987, Marchese and tournament director Franco Bartoni forced box holders to buy a two-week package or nothing at all. They raised the ticket price by only 20 percent, though. They did the same with their corporate sponsors—for 20 percent more you got two weeks instead of one.

For five days the Foro Italico was virtually empty. People had bought tickets for the women so they could see the men. But then Steffi Graf, Martina Navratilova, and Gabriela Sabatini turned up in the semifinals. These were big names. People came, curious to see them. Sabatini and Navratilova staged a superb three-setter. The fans came back the next day, and by the next year they were hooked. A huge picture of that Navratilova–Sabatini match hangs in the interview room today, a reminder of the importance of the match to tennis in Italy.

Marchese had not been happy in 1989, when Evert, Seles, and Navratilova pulled out of the tournament late for various reasons. "I had strong words with WTA," he said. "They are usually very good about supporting their tournaments. I told them this could not happen again."

It had not. Graf had not come back to Italy since 1987 (she legitimately preferred playing the German Open, but another motivating factor was that some in the Italian media kept referring to her as "the ugly German girl").

Navratilova was here, though, and so were Sabatini and Seles. Most important, Jennifer Capriati Inc. was here. She was already the center of attention—having been introduced on the first day of the tournament as "the future of women's tennis"—and a good deal of controversy. After her second-round match, someone had asked Capriati during her press conference what had been the best thing and the worst thing about her two-month pro career.

"Well, the best thing has been getting to play all the pros and meeting so many people," she answered.

And the worst thing?

Capriati grinned. "You guys."

It was a joke, but in Europe, where the media hangs on to every phrase uttered by big-name athletes, it caused a stir. John Evert had to go into his Colonel Parker act (by now, even some of his IMG cronies had started calling Evert "The Colonel"). He got the family together and advised an immediate apology to the "offended" media.

The following day, having survived a tough three-setter with Italian Laura Golarsa in the first match of her life in which the crowd had been against her, Capriati came into the interview room and delivered a short speech.

"I just want to clarify what I said yesterday," she said. "I was joking when I said the toughest thing about being a pro has been the press. You guys have been great to me. Really."

Minicrisis averted. The Colonel breathed easier. Actually, Jennifer wasn't having nearly as much trouble dealing with the media as her father was. Being Italian-born, Stefano Capriati was the subject of a good deal of media attention in Rome. One magazine story described him as "awkward looking," pointed out that he had been unemployed when he married Denise, and that he had taken to wearing freebie Diadora clothes all the time. Worse than that, the story described him as "southern," an Italian euphemism used to put someone down as being uneducated or Mafia-connected.

Stefano Capriati was furious. He showed up the next day in unmarked clothing and called a meeting with the Colonel and Marchese. Both men listened. There was little they could do except let Capriati vent his spleen. He was a powerful man in their lives because he controlled Jennifer.

For John Evert, listening to Stefano Capriati rail had become part of his life, especially as the demands on Jennifer and her income potential had grown. Stefano wanted to cash in fast. The Colonel had negotiated a $50,000 deal with Gatorade for Jennifer to wear a Gatorade patch in Rome and Paris. This was a lot of money for a two-tournament patch deal, but Stefano wanted more. The Colonel was in the process of completing a huge deal with Oil of Olay, which would be announced at Wimbledon. But Stefano wanted everything done yesterday.

He was also upset—justifiably—with his daughter's scheduling here. Since there was only one singles match on the evening program each day, the tournament always tried to make it a glamour match. No one was more glamorous at the moment than Capriati. She had played singles Wednesday night, doubles Thursday night (with Navratilova), and was now scheduled to play singles *and* doubles on Friday night. Night matches are a nuisance anywhere, but in Rome they are worse; they don't begin until 8:45.

When the Colonel saw the Friday schedule he went right to Pam Whytcross, the WTA representative on the scheduling committee. "You have an obligation to protect your players," he said. "This schedule is ridiculous."

Whytcross didn't disagree that the schedule was tough, but she didn't buy Evert's argument that Capriati should be treated with kid gloves because she was fourteen.

"She's a big girl now," she told Evert. "She's a working pro like everyone else."

In truth, though, Capriati wasn't. Because she was fourteen, the number of tournaments she was allowed to play in was limited (although, as the Capriati demand kept increasing, that number kept changing). "If you're going to make rules for her because she's fourteen, you ought to protect her because she's fourteen," Evert said.

He wasn't wrong. But he wasn't going to get the schedule changed, either. As it turned out, Capriati didn't have to play her doubles match. When she saw the schedule, Navratilova, having won her singles quarterfinal in the afternoon, defaulted the doubles to rest for the semifinals. That *really* upset Stefano Capriati; Navratilova hadn't consulted Team Capriati before pulling out.

The Friday night quarterfinal between Capriati and Sabatini was easily the most anticipated match of the tournament. Sabatini, with her Italian heritage and dark Latin looks, was a darling here. So was Capriati. The Foro was filled as the two women walked on court, the chilly, damp night air filled with shouts of "*Dai,* Jenny" and "*Dai,* Gaby." *Dai* is Italian for "Come on!"

The Foro Italico at night, horrendous starting time or not, is one of the special places in tennis. The court, sunken below ground level, looks like a dusty red jewel, surrounded as it is by towering pine and cypress trees. Monto Mario sparkles with lights, directly behind the entrance to the grounds. The place is electric, the fans the most enthusiastic and verbal in the game. Their participation in the match triples when an Italian is involved—and these were two adopted Italians, no matter what their passports said. They were whooping and shouting on every point right from the beginning.

And then the lights went out.

It happened at 1–1 in the first set with Capriati down a break point. Just as Sabatini wound up to hit a backhand, everything went black. This had happened before in the Foro, three years earlier during a match involving John McEnroe. There had almost been a riot that night. Not this time, though. It took thirty minutes to get the lights back on. By the time they did, a light rain had started to fall. On clay, you can play in light rain because the court doesn't get too slippery. So they played.

Capriati looked out of sorts. Sabatini was slugging the ball with confidence and she won the first set easily. She was up 5–3 in the second when Capriati finally began to find the range. When she saved a match point with Sabatini serving for the match at 5–4 and then got to 5–5 with a crushed crosscourt forehand, the place went nuts. The night was young and the Romans wanted more tennis. Sabatini wouldn't allow it. She broke Capriati one more time and served the match out at love, punching the air in a rare outburst of emotion.

Capriati had nothing to be ashamed of. She had not played brilliantly but she had certainly held her own. The media kept asking her what had gone wrong, where she had lost the match, and she kept saying she didn't know. She really *didn't* know.

In the back of the room, Denise Capriati stood with her arms folded, watching her daughter struggle though the interview. It was so easy for outsiders to forget that this was a fourteen-year-old. Her mother never forgot, though. The next day, standing in the rain while Jennifer made an appearance for Diadora, Denise Capriati talked to Bud Collins—no cameras around—about her concerns for her family. For Jennifer and Stefano this was week two of a ten-week stay in Europe. She would go home the next week with her son, Stephen, so he could go to school and see his friends. Where was the normalcy in all this? Denise Capriati wondered.

It was only going to get worse. Stefano and the Colonel had made a deal with Arvida, the real estate developer, to move the family to a new Arvida resort that was opening in Boca Raton. She would be the "touring pro" for the new place. A house would be built for the family and Jennifer would be identified as coming from Broken Sound (the name of the resort), Florida.

Already the children were objecting to the move. Both liked living at Saddlebrook and neither wanted to leave their friends again. The family had moved before—and now they were moving again.

Earlier, Stefano had fired Tommy Thompson, Jennifer's coach at Saddlebrook, partly because he didn't like the Harry Hopman–like drills Thompson was using, partly because he felt Saddlebrook was capitalizing on his daughter's fame more than it ought to.

For the moment Jennifer was part of the U.S. Tennis Association's rookie pro program and was working with Tom Gullikson. That was all well and good. What was a joke, of course, was that the USTA and not the Capriatis was paying Gullikson. In a sport which desperately needs development programs for the underprivileged to expand its base, the USTA was paying for the coaching of a fourteen-year-old millionaire.

The Capriatis were very happy with Gullikson, one of the most likable people in the sport. He and his twin brother, Tim, had been an excellent doubles team during their playing careers and had been solid singles players. On the court it was easy to tell the Gulliksons apart: Tom was a lefty, Tim a righty. Off the court was another story. Those who knew them well said it was easy, especially since Tim had put on a few extra pounds since retiring. Those who didn't know them well took the simple way out and greeted any Gullikson who came into view with, "Hi, Gully."

Both were now in coaching—Tom in the USTA program, Tim, who had worked briefly with Martina Navratilova at one point, with Aaron Krickstein. Tom Gullikson was a good choice to coach Jennifer Capriati. The question was how long it would take him to earn Stefano's wrath.

When Jennifer finished her Diadora autograph-signing session, Jim Fuhse, a public relations liaison for Kraft General Foods, took her by the arm to get her through the crowd. Fuhse was built like a football linebacker and had become Capriati's unofficial bodyguard (he hated it when people called him that, but it didn't stop him from doing it).

That afternoon, the Capriatis went to the Vatican on a sight-seeing trip. A couple of Stefano's relatives, a bodyguard sent along by the tournament, Jim Sarni of the Fort Lauderdale *News-Sentinel,* and a photographer from an Italian magazine went along. Capriati's next stop would be in Marbella, Spain, for an exhibition. Then it would be on to Paris. As it turned out, the one bodyguard, one reporter, and one photographer would be the smallest entourage Capriati would have along on a sight-seeing trip for a long time. In Paris, between ESPN and NBC, Capriati would hardly make a move without a camera crew trailing her.

Normalcy would have to wait a while. A long while.

The weather turned wet and chilly on Saturday, forcing the four semifinalists to sit around and wait. If you ask tennis players what is toughest about their job, they will invariably mention two things: travel days and waiting.

Tennis is like no other sport in that most matches do not have a specific starting time. Unless they are competing in the first match of the day, most players will show up two matches before they are scheduled to play. They need to be sure to get in a warm-up and be ready to go in case of a short match or an injury that forces a default. It is not uncommon for them to wait four or five hours before they get on a court to compete.

In 1986 John McEnroe and Peter Fleming left McEnroe's Long Island home just as the match scheduled before theirs was beginning. Plenty of time. Only there was a default in that match, and they got stuck in traffic on the Long Island Expressway. By the time they reached the locker room it was too late, their match had been called, the clock had been started, and they had been defaulted.

That's why players take no chances. "The toughest thing is to think a match is about to end and then someone comes back and wins the set and you know you have to wait at least another hour," Navratilova said. "You go through a whole routine in terms of eating, warming up, stretching, so you'll be just right when you go on the court, and then it all changes."

Weather is a different kind of variable. Early in a tournament, when there are matches going on all over the grounds, it can play havoc with a schedule. Later, it takes an all-day rain to really create a problem.

This was almost an all-day rain. And for those running the tournament, it was a two-fisted headache, because while the women's semifinals were supposed to be taking place on center court, the qualifying for the men's tournament was supposed to start on the outside courts. Bad weather is almost never taken into account in a qualifying tournament. The schedule calls for three rounds to be played in two days. Rain makes that kind of schedule implausible.

It was six o'clock when the rain finally stopped. Amazingly, most of the crowd had stayed for a program scheduled to begin at 2:30. Monica Seles and Helen Kelesi got underway at 6:25—almost four hours late—and the stands were packed.

Seles and Kelesi didn't stay on the court for long. Kelesi had played well all week, especially in upsetting Arantxa Sanchez in the round of 16. The daughter of a Czechoslovakian defector, Kelesi was Canadian, a player who always seemed on the verge of cracking the Top Ten but never quite got there. She was working with a new coach now, who had encouraged her to lose weight so she could move better. The shots were there.

This was a problem not uncommon to women's tennis—lack of conditioning. Only when Chris Evert began to work out with weights did women tennis players become conditioning conscious. "Actually, Martina was the first one to do it," said Andre Leand, a Princeton graduate who had dropped off the tour to finish college and then came back. "But Chris is the role model. When she started doing it, other people started doing it."

Even so, conditioning was still a problem. John Lloyd, who had coached several female players since retiring, claimed that at least half the women on tour were overweight and out of shape. That comment caused a hue and cry from the women. Lloyd might have overstated the case, but if you walked around from court to court at a women's tournament, the number of players who would be well served by losing ten, fifteen, or twenty pounds was striking.

The WTA and the players were very self-conscious about this. In the 1990 WTA media guide, only 13 of the 201 players in the main section of the book were listed as weighing 150 pounds or more. That just wasn't accurate. Most of the women who did admit to weighing 150 plus were over six feet tall. Some of the listed weights were absolute jokes: Arantxa Sanchez was supposed to weigh 110 pounds, Andre Temesvari 135 pounds, and Helena Sukova 150. If any of them were within fifteen pounds of their listed weights, it was a miracle. And none of them were fat—just self-conscious.

There were also women who had gone to the other extreme and had been afflicted with anorexia, bulimia, or both. Carling Bassett-Seguso and Zina Garrison had talked publicly about fighting the two disorders. Several other players—all attractive, all North American—either had dealt with those eating disorders or were still fighting them.

"There's so much emphasis put on appearance," said Bassett-Seguso, a striking blonde who had starred at the age of fifteen in a movie financed by her father. "We all look in the mirror and think we're too heavy. When I first started talking about being an anorexic-bulimic, I actually had younger girls coming up to me and saying, 'Gee, what a great way to lose weight.' I looked at them and said, 'Are you crazy? Do you know how dangerous this is?' It wasn't until I got so sick that I landed in the hospital that I admitted to myself that I was sick and I had to do something."

Garrison finally faced up to her problem when she got so weak on court during a match that she almost couldn't finish. Still, others continued to pretend that Garrison and Bassett were flukes, exceptions. The fact remains that most women players feel tremendous pressure to look good.

The agents and corporate sponsors look for sex appeal as much as they look for a good forehand. Sabatini was rich as much because of her beauty as because of her tennis. Capriati's contracts were based on her appearance as much as on her potential. Evert *was* the role model—feminine, pretty, slender. That was part of the reason why Seles had started to doll herself up. Like any sixteen-year-old, she wanted to look more adult, wearing makeup and designer clothes, but there was more to it than that. Seles was in a competitive market, and IMG, which represented her and Capriati, wasn't going to discourage her from spicing up her image.

Seles certainly didn't need to spice up her tennis. Since her victory at the Lipton, she had been on a roll, winning two more tournaments before coming to Europe. She wasn't just beating people, she was killing them. In the quarterfinals she had lost two games to Manuela Maleeva-Fragniere, who was ranked ninth in the world. Kelesi did better than Maleeva—she won three games. The match took all of sixty-four minutes. The only person who didn't seem all that impressed was Seles.

"I think I played better two weeks ago in Tampa than I'm playing here," she said. "Today, I didn't even think we'd play. My dad and I played cards, so I stayed pretty relaxed. I really didn't think I played all that well today."

That certainly couldn't have been encouraging for Kelesi or anyone else on the tour. Seles had put most of her early-year troubles behind her. Clearly she had adjusted to her new height and to her new status as a star. Her mother was healthy. The only thing lingering was the controversy over her split with Nick Bollettieri.

No one questioned the Seleses' wisdom in leaving Bollettieri. He was so wrapped up with Andre Agassi that he had no time for anyone else, even a star like Seles. But in leaving, Seles had claimed that Bollettieri had never really coached her and that her father, Karolj, had always been her coach. Karolj Seles had started his daughter in tennis and had been involved with her game all along, but there was no questioning that Bollettieri had invested both time and money into Seles's game. To pretend that he had done nothing was silly.

If l'affaire Bollettieri was bothering Seles, it certainly didn't show in her play. She was as focused and enthusiastic as anyone in tennis. What people often missed, with all the grunting and giggling, was that this was a manic competitor, someone who brought to mind something that Don Candy, Pam Shriver's longtime coach, had once said about Evert.

"Christine Marie," Candy had said, calling Evert by her first and middle names, "only wants every single bloody point."

Monica was no different. Her opponent in the final turned out to be Navratilova, who won one of the best matches of the year in the second semifinal against Sabatini. On the kind of cold night that she really hated, Navratilova dug down to play one of the better clay-court matches of her life.

The funny thing about it was she had every reason not to come up with such a grand performance. She had a thigh injury that had been wrapped up all week, her battered old knees always bothered her in cold weather, and playing at night—it was eight o'clock when the players went on court—she often had trouble with her glasses fogging up.

Still, the competitor in Navratilova could not take the easy way out. Wimbledon was still *the* goal, but if she showed up to play somewhere, she gave everything she had to give. Watching her, one almost felt as if time had stopped. She still looked constantly over to her entourage—roommate Judy Nelson, coach Craig Kardon, and guru Billie Jean King—who shook their fists, clapped their hands, and yelled encouragement at her. Navratilova has always needed this, craved this, and her group is always there to give it to her.

She beat Sabatini 7–6, 7–5 in a two-hour match that had everything but a dramatic finish—Sabatini double-faulting on match point. The crowd was enthralled, screeching and screaming on every point. "I felt like I was at a soccer match or something," Navratilova said. "It's great to see the Italians get this excited about women's tennis. I can remember the old days, when no one in this country cared about us at all. I never would have predicted I would play in a match here with this kind of atmosphere."

Someone asked Navratilova if, given her clay-court play in a match like this one, she would reconsider her decision to pass up the French Open to get ready for Wimbledon.

"No way," she said. "Are you kidding? I certainly don't want to work *that* hard again any time soon."

If she had any doubts at all about that decision, they were wiped out the next afternoon. The rain and cold had cleared and the day dawned bright and hot. It had been ten o'clock by the time Navratilova got off the court the night before, and her thirty-three-year-old body just couldn't bounce back in sixteen hours. If she had been 100 percent fresh, the score of the final probably would not have been 6–1, 6–1, but she probably would have come up the loser in any case. Seles was rolling, hitting every shot with complete confidence, afraid of nothing.

Easy as it was, the match represented a breakthrough for Seles. It was her first victory ever over Navratilova and left Graf as the only top player she had not yet beaten. She had now won four straight tournaments.

From Rome she headed for Berlin and the tournament there. Navratilova went to Prague for a family reunion, her first trip home since the Communist government had been overthrown. For both, the next week would be an extraordinary one, although for entirely different reasons.

While the women had what amounted to a storybook week in Rome, the men had no such luck. Like Monte Carlo, the Italian did not have the field it thought it deserved—or expected.

Lendl, who had won the tournament in 1988, still wasn't playing any tournaments on the clay. Becker, having played the German Open the week before, was taking the week off. Edberg was doing the same. Agassi had played in Germany, lost listlessly in the third round to Magnus Gustafsson, and hopped a plane back to Las Vegas. He would not return to Europe until twenty-four hours before the French Open began. McEnroe had entered the Italian but, as with every other tournament he had entered since Philadelphia, had withdrawn.

That left the tournament with Brad Gilbert, Aaron Krickstein, Andres Gomez, Emilio Sanchez, Jay Berger, and Martin Jaite as the top six seeds. Tournament director Franco Bartoni was so desperate that on the Friday before the tournament he was trying to track down Jimmy Connors, who hadn't touched a racquet since February, to see if he would come over and play. Connors, no doubt, would have been paid quite well for his efforts—rules or no rules against guarantees in Championship Series events. As Marchese had put it, some things in tennis are an open secret.

It was no secret why McEnroe usually played in Rome. Money was one reason and the adoration of the Italian crowds was another. But the main reason was Sergio Palmieri—McEnroe's agent.

Palmieri is one of the better examples one can find of the incestuous nature of tennis. On the one hand, he was an independent operator, working for IMG as a tournament director at several tournaments in Italy. On the other hand, Palmieri worked for ProServ as an agent. When McEnroe had severed his relationship with Advantage, he had turned over that portion of his work to Palmieri, who for years had handled most of his business in Europe. Donald Dell wanted to put out a press release announcing that McEnroe had become a ProServ client. McEnroe, who detested Dell, wouldn't allow it. Sergio represented him, not ProServ, even though Sergio *worked* for ProServ.

Although IMG owned and managed the Italian Open, it was ProServ that sold the TV rights and produced the telecasts. For years Dell himself had done the color commentary on the USA Network cablecasts back to the U.S. That had created an interesting situation in 1988, when Lendl played Guillermo Perez-Roldan in the final. At that point, Lendl and ProServ/Dell were suing and countersuing each other. Much to his dismay, Dell was told by the USA producer that he would have to mention at the start of the telecast that this was going on.

Grudgingly, he did, saying to broadcast partner John Barrett, "I think everyone is aware, John, that we at ProServ are involved in some litigation with Ivan right now." Normally, the color commentator would do the postmatch interview. Not this time. When Barrett arrived, Lendl looked at him, smiled, and said, "I had a feeling it would be you."

Now, the question might be asked: Why would IMG allow hated rival ProServ to control TV at a tournament it ran? "It's simple," Marchese said. "We give ProServ something so we can get some of their players for the tournament. Tennis works this way. Everything is incest if you look at it closely."

One of Palmieri's assignments at the Italian was to deliver McEnroe. He had certainly tried. But McEnroe, who had just moved his family back to New York from Los Angeles, was in no mood to leave home. It had taken more than two years—and more than $5 million—to remodel his apartment on Central Park West, and he had no desire to leave his family or the apartment to play on European red clay.

"He's still trying to get to the point where he *wants* to be on the tour again," his brother Patrick said. "Right now, if you ask him where he's happiest, it's at home. There really isn't anything to get him back out here again."

Patrick McEnroe had spent a good deal of time with his brother in 1990, more time than in the past—something that made both of them quite happy. Their relationship had been strained at times even though each, in his own way, was the other's biggest supporter.

Patrick McEnroe's first memory of being labeled "John's little brother" dates back to when he was five. "There's a picture I still have of several of us at the Douglaston Club," he says. "I'm in it holding a racquet that's slightly bigger than I am. In the caption I'm identified as 'Patrick McEnroe, younger brother of top twelve-and-under John McEnroe.' "

For several years, that identification didn't bother Patrick. He was the younger brother of a good junior but was always a good junior player himself. It all changed in 1977, when John shocked the world with his charge to the Wimbledon semifinals and got himself labeled as the game's bad boy. Now Patrick was not only the younger brother of a star, he was also the younger brother of "The Brat." As John's game improved and his reputation worsened, Patrick's father warned him about what to expect.

"We talked about the fact that if I did anything at all wrong on the court, people were immediately going to start in with 'just like his brother' stuff," Patrick says now. "I think if not for John, I would probably have occasional outbursts on the court. Nothing like him, I just don't think I'm that way. But I wouldn't be as controlled as I am. I had to learn to keep things inside no matter what was happening."

People who have watched the two brothers play tennis talk about how different they are. John gets defaulted in Australia, Patrick wins sportsmanship awards. In truth, the similarities outweigh the differences.

Patrick is the third of the McEnroe sons. Mark, the middle brother, was good enough to play at Stanford but opted for law school and is now a lawyer in Manhattan. For years, John McEnroe—the father—often pointed out to people that only one of his three sons had ever been defaulted from a tennis match—Mark.

Patrick was always the calm one. Mary Carillo remembers him riding his tricycle down the street to the Douglaston Club when he was three. "He would walk around with this cut-off racquet, tugging at people's arms, saying, 'Wanna pway tennis?' " Carillo's younger sister Gina eventually became one of Patrick's playing partners, and the two would play until dark.

Like everyone else in the world, Patrick is not blessed with John's genius for the game. He is right-handed, uses a two-hand backhand, and his strength has always been his return, not his serve. He always had success as a junior, even with the "McEnroe's little brother" label dragging after him. When he was sixteen he learned how accurate his father's warning about his behavior had been, when he threw up his arms in disgust at a call during a tournament and opened the paper the next day to find his picture across four columns, with a caption reading, "Mac's little brother goes off."

"I knew then that I had no leeway," he said.

If you closed your eyes while talking to Patrick, you could easily think you were talking to John. Their voices are virtually identical, right down to inflection and terminology. One can pass for the other on the phone with little difficulty. Patrick is blonder than John, his hair straighter (and, at least for the moment, farther forward on his forehead), his build similar.

But where John, the natural, has always had things come to him easily, Patrick has always been the worker. He followed in both brothers' footsteps to Stanford, and had a successful career there as a player and as a student. He knew he wanted to give pro tennis a shot; he also knew that the specter of John would be waiting for him there. One of the people who pushed him to keep at his tennis was John.

"Pat can be a very good player," John said early in 1990. "I'd like to see him give himself a chance to do well for a couple of years. I think he needs to be more patient with himself. It isn't going to come to him overnight, but if he keeps at it, it *will* come."

John and Patrick were not close as kids because of the seven-year age gap. John went away to college and then the pros when Patrick was eleven. As they have gotten older, they have gotten closer—and more tempestuous. John, like any big brother, wants to see Patrick avoid some of the mistakes he's made.

"I never really enjoyed my success when I was young," he said. "I always made things tough on myself. I see Pat doing well in doubles, really improving, but I don't know if he's enjoying it. He's so serious about things. He should enjoy it more."

Patrick has no trouble listening to advice from John. The conflicts have come when he has tried to counsel John. Like everyone else who cares about John, Patrick sees him as not using his immense talent to best advantage. At times he has tried to talk to him about this, tried to get him to work more and party less. The result, in the past, has been shouting matches.

"It's hard for me to have him tell me what I should be doing with my tennis," John said. "I'm the one that has won seven Grand Slams. I'm the one who has been number one. I just don't think he's in a position to be telling me what to do."

Patrick understands that John has trouble listening to criticism from anybody, much less from his little brother. However, that hasn't stopped him from telling him what he thinks. At the start of 1990, things were tense between the two. John questioned Patrick's decision to become a member of the ATP Council and to play less doubles in pursuit of a singles ranking. Patrick wondered if John had really made the effort necessary to get back to the top of the game.

In Australia, John was confused about what to do next. "I look at my sons and I see Sean wanting to do everything that Kevin does," he said. "I guess I'd like Patrick to be more of a little brother that way." He smiled. "I'm certainly not saying he should do *everything* I do, but I guess I'd like to feel he looks up to me a little more. It's not like everything I've done has been bad, either. What I hope, really, is that maybe he calls me at some point and just comes out to L.A. and hangs out for a few days. I think that would be good for both of us."

That was exactly what happened. Patrick turned pro after graduating from Stanford in 1988, and did well playing doubles with Jim Grabb. There had been talk that the brothers would play doubles together when Patrick turned pro, but that idea went south quickly after they played together in Paris in the fall of 1988.

"My dad flew over for the match," John said. "It's always been a dream of his to see us play together. We were both awful. I couldn't believe that here I was, almost thirty years old, and I was still trying to please my father. It was just no good. Afterward I said to Patrick, 'The next time we play together it has to be somewhere that Dad can't find.' "

Having the partnership with John fall through was the best thing that could have happened to Patrick. If he had teamed with his brother, no amount of success would have brought him much credit. John has won eight Grand Slam doubles titles in his career and a lot of players will tell you he is the best doubles player of all time. It has often been said that the best doubles team in the world is "John McEnroe and anybody." If Patrick had won with John as his partner, he would have been just another anybody.

Because of that, his success with Grabb has been gratifying. The two were friends and teammates at Stanford and won a tournament (San Francisco) while Patrick was still in school. In 1989, Patrick's first full year on the tour, they became one of the best five teams in the world. They won the French Open and the Masters doubles and had people talking about them as a Davis Cup team in 1991, should Jim Pugh and Rick Leach falter.

But success in doubles was not enough for Patrick. At the end of 1989, he decided to concentrate on singles.

"I don't want to just be a doubles player," he said. "Winning the French and the Masters was great, and I think it helped me to establish my own identity on the tour. But if I'm going to do this professionally, I have to feel like I can succeed in singles. If I can't at least get into the top one hundred or one hundred fifty by the end of 1990, I think it might be time to get on with my life."

Part of the reason McEnroe felt this way was his girlfriend, Margaret Flanagan. The two had started dating at Stanford and she was working as an investment banker in New York. Patrick's travel schedule was tough on the relationship, and she wondered at times if he—and they—wouldn't be better off without tennis.

By the fall of 1989, Patrick's singles ranking had fallen to 450. He had gotten some wild cards during his first year on tour, because of his last name, but now he was back to square one. He played in a couple of Challenger events in Europe at the end of the year and moved up to 360. Still, there was a long climb ahead.

He skipped Australia to work out with his coach, Carlos Goffi, a longtime family friend, and started his year in San Francisco. He got through qualifying there but lost a three-set match in the first round to Tim Wilkison. Later that night, playing a doubles match in an empty, drafty arena, he felt something pull in his stomach while he was serving in the third set.

"I couldn't believe it," he said. "San Francisco was supposed to be a warm-up, because I was using one of my few wild cards the next week in Toronto. I took a few days off to rest it, but when I got into my match [against Paul Haarhuis] I knew I was in trouble. It killed me to have to default [down 6–4, 4–1] but I had no choice. I couldn't even serve."

He went back to New York to rest for a few days. By now, things had come to a head with Margaret. The two of them had a long talk and decided a break in the relationship would be best for both of them. "It wasn't like we were throwing things at each other or anything," Patrick said. "But we were making each other unhappy. I was feeling a lot of pressure to prove to her that my tennis was worthwhile. It just made things tough on both of us."

Patrick hung around New York, getting treatment for his stomach, resting for about ten days and climbing the walls. That was when he called John, who was delighted to have his brother visit him in L.A. They worked out together and talked, more as peers than ever before, about Patrick's career and about John's career. Patrick went off to play qualifying at Indian Wells (Palm Springs), feeling better physically and mentally.

He won his first qualifying match there and then had to play Brad Pearce in the second round. It was late in the day, and a desert windstorm made the conditions extremely difficult. McEnroe won the first set and was up 5–3 in the second. Pearce clawed back to a tiebreak. McEnroe went up 6–4—two match points—in the tiebreak. "By now my stomach was starting to get sore again," he said. "I wanted to get it over with."

He thought he had it over with on the second match point when he hit a good volley. But Pearce somehow got to the ball and chipped a passing shot just beyond his reach. McEnroe lost the tiebreak 8–6, had to play another set, lost it 6–3, and walked off the court with his stomach killing him.

"I was just so pissed off, I lost it completely," he said. "I walked into the parking lot and there was no one in sight. I took my racquet, threw it into a tree, then picked it up and started hacking at the branches. Between the close losses, the stomach, breaking up with Margaret, the whole thing, I just went nuts finally. I turned around and there were these two teenage girls staring at me like I was crazy. Which I was."

Things got better after that. He rested his stomach for three days, and he and Grabb made it to the doubles final. John then talked him into skipping qualifying at the Lipton to spend another week with him. Carlos Goffi came out and so did John's old doubles partner Peter Fleming. All three teamed up every day to drag John onto the practice court. Some days it even worked. Here, Patrick could see up close why it was so hard for John to leave home.

"I was walking out one day to practice," he said. "John was actually coming, too. Kevin grabbed me as I was going out and said, 'Hey, Uncle Pat, where are you going?' I told him to play tennis. He said, 'Is my daddy going with you?' I said I thought he was. And Kevin started shaking his head and saying, 'No, no. I don't want him to go. I want him to stay here with me.' Guess what? John didn't practice that day."

After leaving John's—much to John's horror: "You guys can't leave—who am I going to work out with?" he kept saying—Patrick began an odyssey that would have made Odysseus look like a troglodyte. He went to Florida for a week of practice, then to Chicago for an exhibition. He went back to Florida to play qualies in Orlando and lost another three-setter.

From there he went to San Francisco and spent a couple of days with Grabb. He saw a doctor who told him the only way to get completely healthy was to not play tennis for six months. Armed with that piece of good news, he flew to Tokyo to play qualifying there. "Usually, in Japan, you get at least one easy match in qualies because the Japanese players aren't very good," he said. "I drew some Swedish kid who was serving-and-volleying and killing me. I lost the first set and thought, This is unbelievable, I'm losing it completely out here."

There were no more than five people watching the match. One of them was Jeff Tarango, an old Stanford teammate. "Jeff, this is a disaster," McEnroe said on a changeover. "I can't do anything with this guy."

"Be more patient," Tarango said. "He won't keep this up forever."

McEnroe calmed down. Even so, serving at 5–6 in the second set, he faced match point. He came in behind a backhand, knowing the kid had been passing him most of the match. "I come in, hoping, hoping he won't pass me, and the guy just *shanks* the ball. I thought, My God, I just got lucky. I actually got lucky. It really turned me around." He won the set in a tiebreak, won the third, and breezed through qualifying. He then beat Nicholas Pereira in the first round, his first main-draw victory in a major tournament since August 1989. After that came another breakthrough match against Paul Chamberlin, a 1989 Wimbledon quarterfinalist. This time McEnroe came back from 4–1 down in the third set to win. The two victories put him in the top three hundred and not even a loss to Wally Masur the next day could dampen the achievement.

McEnroe went from Tokyo to Dallas for a big-money doubles exhibition and then, after a wild eighty-miles-per-hour ride back to the airport to catch a flight, flew to Singapore, where he reached the quarterfinals, then went to Hong Kong and made the quarters there. In both his quarterfinal losses, he had key calls go against him.

In Singapore, he had a match point and his opponent hit a ball that was called out. But the umpire overruled. In Hong Kong, after coming from 4–1, he had a point to go up 6–5—and was *again* victimized by an overrule. Somehow he kept his cool. Walking off court in Hong Kong, McEnroe looked over at the tournament supervisor and said, "Just remember, I'm keeping track of how much money you guys are costing me."

It wasn't the money that really concerned McEnroe; it was the computer points. If he had won his match in Hong Kong he would have received a special exemption into the U.S. Clay Courts the following week in Charleston. The field there wasn't very strong, and if he could win a couple of matches there, McEnroe would have been ranked high enough to get straight into Wimbledon without having to qualify. (Charleston was the last tournament before Wimbledon entries closed.)

"I might not have done that well in Charleston, anyway," he said. "When I finally got home to New York after Hong Kong I slept for a week. I think I had flown forty thousand miles in six weeks. I couldn't move."

He had come to Rome to play doubles to get ready for the European circuit. His ranking was now up to 145. He was tired, but for the first time, perhaps, feeling very comfortable as a pro.

"I know now I can play out here in singles," he said. "That's what I wanted to find out. I know it's hurt Jim and me in our doubles, but I think it was worth it. Against Dan Goldie, when I came back from four–one down to five-all in Hong Kong, the crowd was really going crazy. I can't ever remember feeling so pumped, so full of energy in my life. The *feeling* I had being on that court right at that moment was unbelievable. I want that feeling again. I know now that I want to keep at this for a while. I think I can still get better."

It seemed that ending the relationship with Margaret Flanagan had taken some pressure off him. There was also no doubt that mending fences with his brother had also done him a world of good.

"I hope John does come back for Wimbledon," he said one morning in Rome. "I think he will because he knows time is running out. He certainly doesn't want his career to end this way. I think he needs to come back. I also think tennis needs him to come back." He smiled. "I'd sure like him to come back. I think we're really starting to enjoy one another."

That statement alone was proof that 1990 hadn't been all bad for the brothers McEnroe.

The men's week in Rome was almost as gloomy as the women's week had been glorious.

With the tournament short of the ATP's commitment of six Top Ten–type players, the ATP Tour resorted at the last minute to the good old "extra designation" bonus, paying Carl Uwe-Steeb $25,000 to enter. This might have helped meet the player commitment but it certainly did nothing to sell tickets, which was supposed to be the point of the commitment rule.

By now, the "extra designation" fees had become public—Chesnokov and Berger had each gotten $25,000 for playing Barcelona—and rather than look at why people objected to them, ATP Tour officials decided to go on a witch hunt to find out who had leaked the news of their existence to the media.

The leaders of the hunt were Weller Evans and Vittorio Selmi, the two operations directors who had made the deals with the players to play in the tournaments. On the one hand both men defended the payments as necessary and right to meet the new tour's commitments. On the other hand they were furious that the payments had become public, and actually made threats against several people who they thought had talked to the press in a manner typical of the siege mentality surrounding the new tour. As a result, there was more and more talk that the ITF would announce its *own* tour for 1991, consisting of the four Grand Slams and eight selected tournaments.

The two remaining glamour names in the Italian field—Michael Chang and Yannick Noah—were gone quickly. Chang, still struggling five months after his hip injury, lost his third straight first-round match on clay, to Swedish journeyman Jan Gunnarsson, 6–3, 6–3. "I didn't feel like I was playing the French Open champion," Gunnarsson said. "I felt like I was playing a young player fighting an injury."

Noah wasn't injured and, in his three-set loss to Andres Gomez, he probably played his best tennis since Australia. Still, the result was the same—another loss. Since Australia, Noah had won one match. The loss to Gomez was his sixth straight first-rounder. The French Open was now one week away. No player in the world felt more pressure than Noah, in Paris, and he was in absolutely no shape to play there. Appropriately, he and Chang finished the week practicing together, each searching for an answer.

The Italian, with or without big names, remains one of Europe's grand traditions. The grounds of the Foro, remodeled now, are as scenic as any in tennis. There are only eight courts—two of them new in the last two years—and the stadium court has only recently been expanded to seat ten thousand. Once, fans sat on a grassy hillside to watch the matches, and sixteen Roman statues, all of them nudes, ringed the courts above the hillside. Now, fifteen of the statues stand with their faces pressed up against newly built stands. Only one can still be seen from the stadium. It stands in the farthest corner of the court, peeking over a scoreboard.

On one side of the grounds is Monto Mario, looking down majestically at the tennis. On the other side is the Olympic Stadium, which, in 1990, was the scene of feverish preparations for the World Cup soccer finals, which were to begin in Rome less than three weeks after the men's final.

In fact, all of Rome was torn up in preparation for the World Cup: streets, telephone lines, subways. Traffic, instead of being its usual complete mess, was an utter disaster. The key word at the Italian Open was *pazienza*—patience—a word foreign to most tennis people. But in Rome, they were forced to adjust.

For years the Italian was considered the most corrupt tournament in the game. Line judges routinely cheated foreigners who were facing

Italians. When Adriano Panatta won the tournament in 1976, almost every player he beat felt he had been cheated. One umpire quit in the middle of a match, when he was not allowed by the tournament referee to overrule several horrendous calls.

One story Italians tell holds that in the early 1980s, when Panatta, the god of Italian tennis, was beginning to slide, he would sit in on the draw—then done in private—to make sure he drew a first-round opponent he could beat. The story goes that one year, Panatta rejected three different names that were pulled out for him, the last being Ismael El-Shafei, an Egyptian who won a few matches on tour during his career. On the fourth try, El-Shafei's name came out again. Okay, Panatta said, I'll play El-Shafei. He did—and lost.

That is all different now. Officiating has been professionalized to the point where if a local line judge tried to cheat he would be removed quickly. The draw is also done in public.

When Saturday arrived, the four semifinalists were decidedly unglamorous names but very good clay-court tennis players. Chesnokov had once again had a remarkable week, coming from behind to beat Italian Paulo Cane in the second round in spite of the howls of the crowd; coming from behind in the third round to beat Jim Courier in the best match of the tournament; and then wearing Alberto Mancini down 7–6, 6–0 in the quarterfinals. His semifinal opponent was Emilio Sanchez, who was having his best and most consistent year in tennis.

The other semifinal was Thomas Muster against Andres Gomez. Muster was back to where he had been before his knee injury—perhaps even better. But it was Gomez who had the players whispering in the locker room because all of a sudden, at the age of thirty, he looked like a new man.

For twelve years Gomez had been a solid moneymaker, consistently ranked in the top twenty, and often in the Top Ten. He would win his share of tournaments—most on clay—occasionally beat a top player, and, generally speaking, make a very good living.

But there was no real fire in Gomez. He seemed content to make it to the quarterfinals at the Grand Slams, lose—usually to Ivan Lendl—and go home to Ecuador to drink beer and sit on the beach. He was always just a little out of shape, a step slow, a shot short. He had been to the round of 16 or better ten times in Grand Slams, but had never reached a semifinal.

In 1989 Gomez was ready to call it quits. His son was two years old, and leaving him at home was getting more and more difficult. His ranking had dropped all the way into the forties and he and his brothers had bought a shrimp farm outside of Guayaquil. When he lost in the second round of the French Open, he was asked if he wanted to do the commentary for Ecuadorian TV on the final. "No, I'd rather go home," he said. "But ask me again next year. I'll do it for sure."

Then, in the fall, a couple of things happened: His longtime coach, Colin Nuñez, left him, thinking it was time to start working with younger players. Gomez started working with Pato Rodriguez, and the change helped him. "It was something new and that was good for me," he said. "I had gotten a little stale, working with Colin."

Just as important was Lendl's announcement that he wasn't going to play the French in 1990. "The only player I really didn't think I could beat on clay was Ivan," Gomez said. "It always seemed like no matter how well I played, Ivan was always there in the quarterfinals and always beat me. When I heard he wasn't going to be there, I thought, 'This is my chance.' "

It was with that chance in mind that Gomez went to Australia, in January, for the first time in his life. He was out of shape at 210 pounds, just as he always was at the start of the year, but he reached the round of 16 there and surprised himself by getting to the Philadelphia final. Then he won two tournaments on clay in April. His ranking had come all the way back to No. 7, and he thought he might be in the best shape of his life. His weight was down to 184 pounds.

Against Muster, Gomez kept pounding away, feeding him the fastballs that he loves. At six feet five, Gomez is capable of plenty of power, and with his left-handed serve can be very effective coming in. He played pure power tennis—and almost won—losing 7–6 in the third after Muster saved three match points. When Muster finally closed the match out, he threw his racquet in the air, let out a scream, and fell to his knees.

Gomez was unmoved. Publicly, he credited Muster with playing well and said he was pleased with his own play, too. Privately, he said, "This is Rome, not Paris. You don't show a guy everything you have in Rome. We may meet again."

Chesnokov won the other semifinal, a three-hour-and-six-minute marathon. He was as exhausted and drained as Navratilova had been the week before. It was after midnight by the time he got out of the Foro.

He had played a total of 137 games to get to the final; Muster had played 103. He had also played at night four times; Muster once. With Muster at the top of his game, it was no surprise he won the final in a 6–1, 6–3, 6–1 rout. When Chesnokov was asked during the awards ceremony what he thought had gone wrong, he gave one of his trademark shrugs and said, "Just forget about it. He killed me."

For Muster, winning the Italian Open twelve months after he had watched the tournament on crutches was a great achievement. For Gomez and Chesnokov, though, the real goal was still ahead: Paris.

As for the Italians, they were still waiting for the next Panatta. In the meantime, they picked their heroes from among the foreigners, and when the tennis was over they lingered long into the night. Three hours after Muster had accepted the winner's trophy, several thousand of them were still in the restaurants and bars of the Foro, unbothered by the fact that the tennis had finished.

After all, Rome is Rome. And, with luck, always will be.

14

ROLAND GARROS

Behind Philippe Chatrier's desk in Stade Roland Garros there is a picture window. From that window, Chatrier can clearly see court 7. Its bleachers seat several hundred people—no more. Occasionally a match there will draw a crowd, but for the most part it is assigned decidedly unglamorous matches: mixed doubles, juniors, an occasional singles during the first few days.

Once, though, court 7 was a show court. That was before the ministadium that is now court 1 was built. That was before the new stands for court 11 went up, and the bleachers at court 9. Millions of dollars have been spent to turn this into one of the great athletic facilities in the world.

But every morning when he comes to his regal office, Chatrier can see court 7. In a sense, court 7 is what Chatrier is all about. He is tennis royalty—the president not only of the French Tennis Federation but of the ITF, the International Tennis Federation. He has all the arrogance one connects to the French, and his lofty position in the game pushes that arrogance even farther. But Chatrier is also the keeper of the game's flame. For all the arrogance and overdone pomp, he still believes that court 7—the past—should be important. To him, guarantees are a cancer eating away at the game; corporations, a necessary evil whose role *must* be kept under control; agents, a dangerous element that should be viewed with suspicion at all times.

"Money is killing our game," Chatrier says. "The motivation for true greatness is gone for most players by the time they are eighteen. They win a couple of matches as juniors and they are millionaires. Jimmy Connors says when he started playing you had to *win* to get rich. Now, you don't have to win, you just have to have an act."

Each year when the men's champion comes to the platform to accept his trophy, he is greeted by the three living members of France's famed Four Musketeers: Jean Borotra, Rene Lacoste, Henri Cochet. Roland Garros—named for a French World War I hero—was built for the Musketeers in 1928. They defended the Davis Cup here when it opened. It saddens Chatrier to know that many of today's players don't even know who the Musketeers were or what they meant—and still mean—to French tennis.

And yet, Chatrier can take pride in what French tennis has become in the last ten years. Like the Australian Open, the French went through very trying times in the 1970s. The balance of power in the game had swung to the U.S., and when Team Tennis sprang up in the early 1970s, it devastated the French; it conflicted with their Grand Slam tournament and offered the players far more money than the tournament could.

"Team Tennis offered them more money and they didn't have to come over here and play best-of-five on clay," Chatrier said. "It was a very tough thing for us to fight. If Team Tennis had succeeded, I don't know what would have become of us. Fortunately for us, it didn't."

Chatrier took a number of drastic steps to fight Team Tennis, including a ban on players who had signed with Team Tennis. In 1974, having played Team Tennis the previous year, Jimmy Connors was not allowed to enter the French. That was the year when he swept the other three Grand Slams. He was at the peak of his powers and might very well have won the tournament that year—and become only the third man to ever win the four Grand Slams in one year.

"It makes me sad when I think about that," Chatrier said. "I really believe that Jimmy would have won that year. He was so dominant. But hindsight is always perfect. Those were desperate times. We took desperate measures. Do I regret it now? Absolutely. But it changes nothing."

Those *were* desperate times for Chatrier and his tournament. Roland Garros had become outdated. It was too small, it was falling apart. There had been talk of buying up land outside of Paris and building a new facility there. Chatrier chose to stay, and hoped the city would meet his requests for more land.

"A tennis stadium needs ghosts," he said. "I didn't want to leave behind our ghosts.

"We did things in the seventies that I hated doing," he continued. "We had a title sponsor for two years. That killed me. We tried night matches to attract fans, but we found it got too cold at night in the Bois de Boulogne, no matter how hot it had been during the day. Our fields were not good."

The turnaround came in the late seventies. In 1977, the city of Paris finally came up with the land to allow for expansion. Then, in 1978, Chatrier convinced a friend of his at TF1—the French-government television network—to experiment with the notion of televising the tournament all day, every day, as the BBC had done with Wimbledon for years.

"I had an old friend from my days in journalism who was running TF1," Chatrier said, smiling at the memory. "I went to see him and he said, 'Philippe, anything I can do to help, just tell me.' "

When Chatrier told him what he wanted, "He looked at me and said, '*What!*' But he did it—against the wishes of his staff. That was the turning point for us. It made Roland Garros a national event. We were seen in every little village in France. The tournament became a matter of national pride."

By that time Bjorn Borg had become the dominant player in the world. He had won his first Roland Garros—no one in France calls the French anything but "Roland Garros"—in 1974. When he began winning Wimbledons in 1976, it helped give the French credibility again as a major championship. The facilities improved, the crowds began to come back, and so did the players.

"We have done two things that I think are very smart," Chatrier said. "We have put most of the money we have made back into facilities, and we have always opted for exposure over money. If we sold the TV rights to cable, we could make much more money, but then the tournament would not be a national event. Three years ago we gave Chinese TV the rights for free because we thought it would be good for us to have the tournament televised there. I think that now Roland Garros ranks only behind Wimbledon as a worldwide event."

Chatrier is right. While most Americans automatically think that the U.S. Open is second behind Wimbledon in prestige, to most of the tennis world the French has surpassed the U.S. Open. Chatrier and his people have done a superb job of building the tournament and making it into something that the tennis world looks forward to.

"We have the perfect dates for the tournament," Chatrier said. "Our weather is usually excellent. Now, everyone in France looks forward to the Roland Garros season."

No one was looking forward to this particular French season more than Michael Chang, who, on day one of the tournament, on court 1, at precisely 11:18 A.M., began defense of his title.

His victory the year before, less than four months after his seventeenth birthday, had made him quite rich. His corporate sponsors now included Reebok, Prince, Nissin Noodles, Panasonic, Longines Watches, and Cathay Pacific Airlines. In addition, his income in 1990 from guarantees and exhibitions would be well over $1 million.

But Chang had found out firsthand that money can't buy happiness.

After the French, he had lost the underdog status that he not only craved but fed off of. "I've always liked being the underdog," he said. "I think everyone does to some degree, but even when I was in juniors I always seemed to do better that way. Other guys would look at the draw and see that they had to play a seed and get all upset. I would get fired up because I always saw it as an opportunity. I never play a match thinking I don't have a chance."

After his debut at the U.S. Open in 1987, Chang had been considered a future star, although no one expected him to rise as quickly as he did. He was already in the top twenty *before* he won the French title; a player who relied on excellent speed, remarkable quickness, and a great mind to overcome his size—five feet seven and 140 pounds. Chang examined every question from every possible angle, whether on or off the tennis court, and usually came up with the right answer.

John McEnroe remembers the first time he ever played Chang. "We tossed the coin and he won, so it was his choice—serve or receive. He just stood there, thinking. I mean, the match was *indoors.* Finally, after thirty seconds I said, 'Is there a time limit on this or what?' "

Chang says he has always been this way: *very* careful. "I never like to make the same mistake twice," he said. "When I was in second grade I was in a spelling bee, and I had to spell the word *clothes.* For some reason, in my mind I was thinking about *close*—as in "close the door." So, I got it wrong. I went home that night and wrote down *clothes* two hundred times. I wanted to make sure I never got it wrong again."

Chang plays tennis exactly that way. He is less afraid to change tactics during a match than any player in the game. "He goes at it like a chess match," said Australian Mark Kratzmann. "If you have him in a losing position, he's going to change. A lot of players are scared to change; he's not. Then he almost forces you to decide whether to stay with your tactics or adjust to his. He makes you think, and a lot of guys can't handle that."

Chang's victory in Paris in 1989 is still one of the most remarkable achievements in tennis history. He came from two sets down, battling leg cramps in the fourth round, to beat Lendl. He won tough matches against Ronald Agenor and Chesnokov, and then a brutal five-setter from Edberg. After each and every victory, Chang thanked Jesus Christ and said he believed that his personal relationship with Christ was the reason he had won. A lot of people were offended by this, especially when Chang brought it up during the awards ceremony. He was whistled by many in the crowd.

Now, Chang rarely talks about his religion—unless you ask him. "I know it bothered a lot of people when I said all that, but if you really want to know what I'm about or what motivates me, you have to accept the fact that my Christianity is part of it," he said. "I really believe that I do have a better personal relationship with Jesus than other players do. That doesn't mean I always win, but I do feel that way. I know my saying that gets on some people's nerves. If you don't want to accept that, that's fine with me. But it is a very real part of me."

No one on the tour questioned Chang's sincerity on this subject. While everyone giggled whenever Agassi brought up his Christianity, seeing it as little more than just another public relations ploy, no one doubted Chang.

"We were on an airplane one time and Michael was sitting next to me reading the Bible," Pete Sampras said. "All of a sudden, he reaches over and wants me to read this passage with him. He said it was very important that I understand it. He was really determined to get me into it."

Chang grew up not caring very much about religion. Church was boring. "I hated sitting there every Sunday, listening to sermons I didn't understand," he said. "I really didn't want anything to do with it."

But one Sunday, Chang heard a sermon he *did* understand. It was about a group of people who missed a boat they thought they had to catch. They were angry, and wondered why God had let them miss the boat. Eventually they got on a second boat, one not nearly as comfortable as the first. But when they arrived at their destination, they learned that the first boat had been attacked and everyone on board had died. "The lesson was that God has a plan," Chang said. "Trust in God and things will work out for you, even if sometimes you can't see what He is doing."

Chang began reading the Bible after that sermon and was baptized late in 1988. Six months later, he won the French, and his life changed forever. "I never got that emotional when I won the tournament," he said. "I didn't have a chance to. I went straight from Paris to an exhibition and then to Wimbledon. When I finally got home I sat down by myself and watched the tapes of the Lendl match and the Edberg match.

"That's when I cried. That's when I realized that it really was some kind of miracle that I won. It *did* mean a lot to me."

Chang learned after his victory in Paris what all tennis players seem to learn when they have had success: achieving your dreams can be dangerous. You have worked all your life, pushed by parents, agents, coaches, to reach a pinnacle, and then you reach it—in Chang's case, at a remarkably young age. What next?

"For me, the year since I won the French has been the toughest of my life," Chang said. "I found out that winning in tennis doesn't bring joy, it brings *pressure.* Everywhere I've gone I've been the French Open champion. Since the injury, that's been really tough."

The injury happened in December, in Florida. Chang was working out with Brian Gottfried and tried to hit a two-handed backhand. Something popped inside his hip. At first it was thought to be a fracture. Then, it was thought not to be that serious. Whatever it was, it kept Chang off the tennis court for two months. And when he came back, he wasn't the same.

For Chang, a hip injury was more serious than for many other players. So much of his game comes from his quickness, his ability to change directions and chase down balls, that even if he was just a half step slower, it would be significant.

He struggled all spring, losing his first match at the three clay-court tournaments he entered to prepare for the French. There were even stories circulating that all was not well with Team Chang—father Joe, mother Betty, older brother Carl. At an exhibition in Marseille the week before his defense, Michael hurt his right wrist. He had become, by several accounts, hysterical; there had been a shouting match involving mother, father, and son.

By Sunday there were rumors that Chang might withdraw from the tournament entirely. But he showed up to play a one-set charity exhibition—an annual tradition at Roland Garros that most players take part in—with a bandage wrapped around his wrist. Wrapped around the bandage was his Longines watch. An endorsement is an endorsement, injury or no injury.

In the locker room, there wasn't a lot of sympathy for Chang. The ATP Tour staff always kept an unofficial list of the people they liked least on the tour. Michael's parents, Betty and Joe, were the 1990 leaders—by a substantial margin.

Even those who had known Chang a long time were baffled by him. Jim Courier, who had tagged him with the nickname "Grasshopper" when they played Junior Davis Cup together, had given up even trying to start conversations with Chang. "It seems as if he just doesn't want to talk to any of us anymore," Courier said.

David Wheaton, another of his Junior Davis Cup teammates and someone who shared Chang's deep religious beliefs, thought Chang had simply gone too far. "The stuff he says about having a better relationship with Jesus Christ, well, that's just offensive," Wheaton said. "He doesn't know that. He *can't* know that. None of us do. When I play Michael, if we're both Christians, does God choose one of us over the other? There's an arrogance to that kind of attitude that bothers me."

Wheaton also found that Chang never spoke to him anymore. "Heck, everybody talks about Andre [Agassi] being stuck-up," Wheaton said. "At least he talks to you. Michael doesn't talk to anybody."

One person who defended Chang was Boris Becker. "I'm one of the few people who can understand what he's gone through for the last year," Becker said. "I was seventeen when I won Wimbledon, the same age he was when he won Paris. Your life stops being your own. Everyone wants something from you. People don't understand, this guy is very special. He's going to come back and he's going to win a lot of tennis matches. I don't have any doubt of that. People are writing him off. That's crazy."

People *were* writing Chang off. Some thought he would never be the same because of the hip injury. Even Chatrier wondered if 1989 might have been a fluke. "I hope he wins a few matches here," Chatrier said. "This is a typical case of winning too early. The agents have played him and played him since he won, and his body has broken down. They don't understand what torture tennis can be on the body. I hope they haven't ruined his career."

That question hung in the air as Chang began his first-round match against Casio Motta, a thirty-year-old Brazilian clay-courter with thick legs and the kind of one-dimensional game that a healthy Chang would pick apart. But as Gunnarsson had pointed out in Rome, this wasn't the French Open champion, this was a kid coming back from an injury.

Joe Chang was nowhere in sight when the match began, adding to the speculation that the blowup at the exhibition had been serious. Chang started quickly, breaking Motta in the first game and rolling through the first set. The second set was tighter—Chang needed a tiebreak—but he won it and swept quickly through the third set. The losing streak was over. Betty Chang was on her feet clapping wildly. Chang even managed a smile.

"I don't know what it is about Paris," he said. "Maybe it's the bread." Still, a victory over Casio Motta hardly constituted a turnaround. Chang knew that. But he now had two days to rest and think about his second-round opponent—the towering and talented Swiss, Marc Rosset. Chang had forty-eight hours to figure out what to do. Which was just fine with him.

. . .

The first several days at a Grand Slam are normally manic but never get truly wild. At Roland Garros this year, things were hysterical almost from the start. Shortly after Chang battered Motta, Andre Agassi made his way out to court 2 to play his first-round match.

Agassi could hardly have asked for a better first-round draw. Martin Wostenholme, a twenty-seven-year-old Canadian ranked 122nd in the world, was a Yale graduate with a degree in economics who had never quite gotten around to seeing tennis as a life-and-death proposition. He had been on tour for six years and had cracked the top one hundred briefly in 1985, but not since then. The match should have been an easy stroll for Agassi.

Only, it wasn't. Agassi had not arrived in Paris until Sunday morning, and he was in a foul-tempered, jet-lagged mood. Since winning the Lipton in March, Agassi, who was rapidly replacing McEnroe as the game's most controversial player, had played in just one tournament—in Germany—although he had participated in a couple of exhibitions. He had gotten into a public war of words with U.S. Davis Cup captain Tom Gorman in March, after withdrawing from the American team that was going to Czechoslovakia. (He withdrew because Gorman had objected to Agassi's entourage; he found them distracting for the rest of the U.S. team.) Agassi immediately called for Gorman's replacement; he said Gorman was a follower, not a leader, and said the *players* should pick their captain.

Gorman, one of the gentle souls in tennis, had been wounded by these comments, especially since Agassi had made them during a tournament near Gorman's hometown of Palm Springs. Gorman selected Aaron Krickstein to replace Agassi for the match in Prague; Krickstein responded by winning two singles matches to lead the U.S. to a victory.

Naturally, Krickstein assumed he would be one of the singles players for the next match, against Austria, in September, in Vienna. However, David Markin, the USTA president, seemed to think he was on some kind of mission from God to return the Davis Cup to the U.S. He was in his second—and last—year as USTA president, and he wanted the Cup at all costs.

That was why Markin had called Gorman in early May and informed him he was to fly to Atlanta for a meeting with Agassi and his brother Phil. The meeting, Markin said, was to "clear the air."

When the air cleared, Markin had surrendered completely to the

Agassi brothers. Agassi would play in Vienna and he could bring any and all members of his entourage. He would also play in the final if the U.S. beat the Austrians.

Markin had taken control of the team away from Gorman. He had, in effect, made himself captain. Everyone in tennis knew this, although Markin, Gorman, and Team Agassi went along pretending no deals had been cut and that Gorman still had autonomy. It was silliness with a capital *S.*

So was Agassi's decision to show up in Paris twenty-four hours before his first match. No other player in the world would even think of such a move. Agassi was so arrogant—and so talented—that he not only *would* do it, he *could* do it.

It almost backfired on him. He quickly lost the first set and also earned a warning from umpire Sultan Gangji for racquet abuse (he threw his racquet and then stepped on it in a fit of pique over a call). It was a fortunate thing for Agassi that Gangji, a mild-mannered Englishman, was in the chair. If any of the top umpires had been there, Agassi would probably have been defaulted before the match was over.

During the second set he continued to have problems. He went down a break early and began arguing with Gangji again. At one point he called Gangji "a little shit," in a voice loud enough for everyone seated near the court to hear. Gangji claimed afterward he hadn't heard him. A little later, when a close Wostenholme shot was called good, Agassi walked to the baseline, pointed at Gangji, and said, "You get out of that damn chair right now and come check this mark!"

Gangji again ignored him. Wostenholme was trying hard not to let Agassi's antics get to him, but he was clearly upset when Agassi hit a ball right at him—and did not hold up a hand to indicate he was sorry or that it had been an accident.

"He was operating just below the boiling point," Wostenholme said immediately after the match. "He's very hyper and tense. Hitting the other guy is part of the game. It's legal. But it's a gray area of sportsmanship. If he was around I would say something to him about it. But I haven't seen him in the locker room."

There was a reason for that: Agassi wasn't *in* the locker room. He and his entourage had taken over an extra training room. They would spend the whole tournament there. Agassi *never* ventured inside the locker room. He even showered at the hotel.

The entourage was growing almost daily. On this trip, Agassi had with him his omnipresent brother Philip; his agent, Bill Shelton; his coach, Nick Bollettieri; his hitting partner, Raul; his Nike representative, Ian Hamilton; and the latest addition, strength coach/bodyguard, Gilbert Reyes.

Agassi had met Reyes during the winter and had hired him away from his job as strength coach at the University of Nevada–Las Vegas. Reyes was to work with him on conditioning and to shepherd him through crowds. Reyes liked to make himself look menacing by wearing sunglasses all the time. He had convinced Agassi that strength was the key to success in tennis and had him lifting weights constantly. Of course Agassi still ate fast food every day and constantly drank Coke and coffee. No one was sure exactly how that fit in with the new training regimen.

He *was* bigger and stronger, though. And lucky. He survived two set points in the second set and a tiebreak. Wostenholme collapsed, winning just one more game.

After the match, Agassi was fined $2,000 for his racquet throwing/stomping act, an indication that Ken Farrar, the supervisor, felt that Gangji hadn't been tough enough. The usual fine for racquet abuse is $500.

First Chang, now Agassi, had made it to the second round. Each was more relieved than happy. With good reason.

On court 7—the one that Chatrier could see from his office—David Wheaton was playing the towering Czechoslovakian Milan Srejber. Srejber, at six feet eight, was the tallest man on tour, a serve-and-volley specialist who had once reached the quarterfinals of the U.S. Open but then tanked so blatantly to Boris Becker that Becker had actually asked him during the match, "What the hell is going on here? This is a U.S. Open quarterfinal!"

Trying to figure out what was going on inside Srejber's head was nearly impossible. He was known as the unhappiest man in tennis; he was always muttering to himself on court, even after winning points.

Wheaton was also a serve-and-volley player, comfortable when he could use his own size (six feet four) to set up easy shots at the net. He was the better clay-court player of the two and was already looking ahead to a second-round match with Jim Courier, one of his closer friends on the tour.

It had not been an easy winter or spring for Wheaton. He had come back from Australia ranked twenty-eighth in the world and brimming with confidence. But his right foot was giving him trouble, especially when he landed on it after serving. He pulled out of San Francisco to rest it and hardly practiced at all before Toronto. "I tried to 'McEnroe it,' you know, practice just a little but be ready for the matches," he said.

It didn't work. He lost three-setters in Toronto and Philadelphia to Peter Lundgren and Glenn Layendecker. By the time he finished his doubles match in Philadelphia, the foot was so sore he could barely walk.

"I didn't lose to Lundgren or Layendecker because of the foot, though," he said. "I lost because I came back from Australia cocky. I had been in the quarters of a Grand Slam and really close, I thought, to beating Edberg. I thought I could just walk on the court against those guys even with my foot a little sore and win. I was wrong. You can't do that. At least I can't. So I learned a lesson. But by the time I got out of Philadelphia, I knew I had a problem."

Wheaton had first felt soreness in his leg and foot in the fall. A bone scan showed a small spot, but the doctor thought that it was merely inflammation of the covering of the bone. After Philadelphia, another bone scan showed a huge spot. He had a stress fracture. At a time when Wheaton thought he was ready to make a big move, he couldn't pick up a racquet for six weeks.

He went home to Minneapolis, bought himself a Jeep Wrangler, and "bombed around in it," seeing friends and family. He spent time with his grandparents, who are in their nineties. The Wheatons are an extremely close family and David didn't mind being at home one bit. "It was nice to be normal for a little while," he said. "I stayed in shape, swimming and lifting, and didn't really miss the tennis at all. We get so used to living this abnormal life that we forget how nice normalcy can be."

Eight weeks after the stress fracture was discovered, another bone scan showed no spot at all, so Wheaton began playing again. He played an exhibition in Atlanta and by the end of his second match, the foot felt almost as bad as it had in Philadelphia.

"Now I'm panicking," Wheaton said. "This thing was supposed to be better. What was going on? Was I ever going to be able to really play again?"

He and his brother John found another doctor in Atlanta. The doctor told the Wheaton brothers he thought the problem was "alignment." Wheaton's leg and foot weren't aligned quite right; each time he came down on the foot he was damaging it. The doctor inserted wedges into his shoes. That night Wheaton played Agassi—and lost—but did so without any pain. The next week he went to South Carolina for the U.S. Clay Courts, and even with only an hour of practice each day, won the tournament—his first pro title.

Most important, the foot didn't hurt. Wheaton flew to Rome and played his first-round match six hours after arriving. Predictably, he lost. But the memory of South Carolina buoyed him and he came to Paris thinking he had a real shot at making an impact in the tournament.

Srejber certainly didn't appear to be a problem. Wheaton whipped through the first two sets easily. He got careless in the third, giving Srejber a break, some confidence, and the set. Still, there were plenty of chances in the fourth—including two match points. Srejber saved both, though. Then, up 4–3 in the tiebreak, Wheaton double-faulted. By now he was talking to himself, complaining about calls and, in general, acting whiny and childish.

This was very out of character for Wheaton. Behind the court, in the now-packed little bleacher, John Wheaton stood with his hands on the fence, watching impassively. The fifth set went quickly. Again, Wheaton had chances that he couldn't convert. The only break came in the sixth game, when Wheaton missed a backhand sitter at deuce and then watched helplessly as Srejber hit a rare winner to break. In the last game, Srejber double-faulted twice to let Wheaton get up 0–40. Wheaton again couldn't take advantage, and it ended when he pushed one last forehand deep.

John Wheaton walked away from the court shaking with anger. David's brother is, under almost all circumstances, low-key and laid-back, a man blessed with both patience and good spirit. None of those qualities were in evidence now.

"If he's not sick, really sick, I'm leaving," he said. "I'm not going to stay over here and watch him pull this. I don't mind if he loses a match, but not that way. He just gave up. Things got a little tough and he threw in the towel. There's no excuse for that."

Was this an overreaction? In a sport in which players often tank when it suits their convenience, getting discouraged in a five-set match hardly seemed like a first-degree crime. Wheaton had not actually tanked—had not given up completely or tried to lose. But he had come close enough that his brother and Jose Higueras, his coach, were furious. This was not an exhibition in Atlanta or a 3 A.M. doubles match in Philadelphia. This was the French Open.

The Wheaton brothers had it out that night. At first, David did not understand why John was so upset. Slowly, though, the message got through.

"John was completely right," Wheaton said later. "I let everything get to me. First, I forgot that winning two sets doesn't mean the match is over. Second, when he came back a little I got frustrated and confused, and instead of digging in I started feeling sorry for myself. I forgot where I was, that this was a Grand Slam. You have to be willing to die out there to win a match at a Grand Slam. I told John he could be sure of one thing—it won't happen again."

John Wheaton had done something that very few people in tennis are willing to do: He had told his player off, no ifs, ands, or buts. Sure, the player happened to be his little brother. Andre Agassi had a big brother who traveled with him, too. You can be quite sure Philip Agassi will never tell Andre off that way, not in this lifetime. Which might explain why one little brother doesn't repeat his mistakes and the other one does—over and over again.

While there was certainly interest in Chang's debut and Agassi's travails, most of the French crowd on day one cared about one match and one match only: Yannick's.

At Roland Garros, Yannick Noah—Yannick to everyone in France—was God. His victory in 1983 had unleashed celebrations throughout France, and since then, whenever he walked on to center court there, the entire country stopped to watch.

"It's a great feeling and it's a bad feeling all at once," Noah said. "The mood of the crowd can turn quickly if I'm not winning. Actually, I prefer playing in New York. There, the crowd comes to see me *play.* In Paris, the crowd comes to see me *win.*"

Noah was as popular throughout the world as any player in the game. He had left his home in the Cameroons at the age of twelve, after Arthur Ashe had discovered him there during an exhibition tour. From that moment on he was the sport's Great Black Hope. Also France's hope. That combination put tremendous pressure on Noah, pressure he often found difficult to handle.

He grew to six feet four, possessing the kind of athletic grace and natural ability that made him into a romantic figure. He was strikingly handsome, with a sparkling smile and a whispered way of speaking that added to the mystique. If an official count had ever been done of groupies waiting outside the locker room on a per-player basis, Noah would have won year in and year out.

He was not a great player. His ground strokes were average. He had an excellent serve and his quickness made him tough to pass. In 1983, it had all come together in Paris. He had beaten Lendl in the quarterfinals, sending the crowd into ecstasy. Then came a bit of luck: Jimmy Connors was upset in the quarterfinals by another Frenchman, Christophe Roger-Vasselin. For Roger-Vasselin, the Connors match was his fifteen minutes of fame. He lost quickly to Noah in the semifinals. Noah then beat Mats Wilander, the defending champion, in straight sets in the final—the first victory for a Frenchman at Roland Garros since Marcel Bernard won in 1946.

Since then, Noah had never made it back to the semifinals. Now, with his year falling apart rapidly, he opened the tournament early on the first evening against a qualifier named Francisco Clavet.

There are few settings in tennis that can match Roland Garros in the early evening. There are no lights, so dusk is allowed to close in naturally and slowly—it is almost 10 P.M. before the sun sets—and with the stands filled it is a wonderful place to be.

Noah was struggling again, this time against a player ranked 180th in the world. A loss to a qualifier on *this* court might be the last straw for the French Hope.

It had already been a difficult five months. In Australia, the day before his semifinal against Lendl, he and his girlfriend of two years, Erica Moss, had gotten into a fight. That scene turned out to be the beginning of a protracted breakup, with contretemps followed by reconciliation followed by contretemps. The final breakup came in Monte Carlo, although Erica was still seen several times in the players' lounge in Paris.

Distracted by his personal life, Noah's tennis became progressively worse. He spent hours and hours on the practice court with his coach, Dennis Ralston, but that didn't seem to help. "Actually, the only good thing about all the practice was that it got me away from all my problems off the court," he said.

"It's a funny thing: Going into the [U.S.] Open in 1989, I thought it would be my last tournament. I had gotten to the point where I just felt like most of the things I wanted to do in my life were exactly the opposite of the things I needed to do to be a tennis player. I had to leave my family [Noah has two children who live in Paris with his ex-wife] all the time. I had to work harder than I wanted to. I had to give up my privacy.

"Then, at the Open, when I beat Mancini [in the round of 16], I felt like a tennis player again. It was a great match, the crowd was great, everything felt good again. That night I sat up late with Mancini. Think of that! That doesn't happen in tennis anymore, that kind of feeling between players.

"So, I kept playing, looking for that feeling again. And Australia was great right up until the night I had the fight with Erica. I played lousy against Lendl and I've played lousy ever since. Now I have to wonder again about looking for something else to do. I'm thirty. If it isn't time, it's very close."

The crowd didn't really care about Noah's troubles or his angst. It wanted to see the old Yannick, leaping through the air, diving in the dust for balls, making shots that couldn't be made. Instead, it saw a struggling, aging player hoping he could fake his way through a match against a player who should have been too scared to hit the ball, given the setting and the circumstances.

They split four sets. Dusk was closing in. They reached 5–4—Noah—and, since there is no tiebreak in the fifth set, it began to look as if the match might have to be finished on Tuesday. Noah had a match point. Clavet saved it. Then another. And another. He just couldn't finish him. Chair umpire Rich Kaufman made a key overrule in Noah's favor, and he had another match point. Five, six, seven, eight. Finally, on the ninth match point, when it seemed as if the stadium might explode if Noah couldn't finish the match off, Clavet missed a forehand pass.

The stadium didn't explode. But Noah did. He fell over flat on his back, his arms in the air, kicking his legs. "You would have thought I had won the entire Grand Slam," he said later. "The whole thing just hit me all at once.

"It was just so hard to win a match. It had been so long, like four months, and so much had happened. Then I blow eight match points. Eight! I felt like I had been in labor for fourteen hours or something. I mean, it was a really hard birth.

"So there I am, beating a guy who is one-eighty in the world, and I'm lying on my back going crazy. Everybody said, 'What's wrong with him?' Well, plenty. I wondered if I would ever win another tennis match."

In a sense, every tennis player goes through what Noah went through. Some wonder if they can make a living; others are expected to win Grand Slams and make millions of dollars. All acutely feel the expectations of others, because they are told so early in their lives that their one and only responsibility is to win tennis matches. It starts as a joyride when they're very young, because the ones who end up playing professionally, even briefly, are stars. The excuse parents give for pushing their teenage prodigies to practice for hours and hours and then play tournament after tournament is always the same: "They love the game." More often than not, what they love is the *winning.* But as those kids move up the competitive ladder, winning becomes tougher and, even if they continue to win, à la Becker or Graf or Capriati or Chang, the pressure increases. And it increases *tremendously.*

So many players feel trapped by the game they *thought* they loved as kids. It was the winning they loved—then the adulation, then the money that came with winning. A price was paid for all that: Senior proms and dances and social lives were sacrificed in the name of tennis. As they get older, they look around and realize they know nothing *but* tennis, the tour life, and all that comes with it.

"It's a totally unreal world we live in," Noah said. "It's very dangerous to know you can have anything you want. You don't really have a balance after a while. None of us choose tennis—tennis chooses us. One day you are the best player in your club, and the next thing you know, you're a tennis player. Tennis becomes your whole life.

"I'm thirty years old, and when I quit I will have to make my first real decisions as a man. Up until now, everything in my life has been taken care of for me. In one way, it's nice to be thirty and still be a kid. In another way, it's scary.

"I'm from the second generation of players who have made their living as pros since the Open era began twenty years ago. When I look at the first generation, I don't see too many role models. Most of them are still hanging around tennis in some way. It's like an addiction or something. Or maybe it's just too hard to jump out of this world because you're so used to going everywhere and being treated like a king or a queen. That's not reality, though. Sometime, I have to make myself step out of this world and into the real one. I know it won't be easy, but it's something I need to do."

Noah smiled. "You know, I've had a great love affair with my sport. But now, for me, it's like breaking up with someone after a long time. You feel alone. Your first instinct is to grab on to the first thing, the easiest thing, that comes along. I don't want to do that."

• • •

O

While Noah was hanging on for dear life to his love affair, two of the game's most romantic figures were slowly coming to grips with the realities of letting go.

Jimmy Connors and Chris Evert had once been tennis's most-talked-about couple. They had met as teenagers on tour, fallen in love, and gotten engaged in 1974. He was twenty-one, she was nineteen. That year they both won Wimbledon and danced the first dance at the Wimbledon ball. Storybook stuff. Only, the happy ending didn't happen. They broke their engagement that fall and went off in different directions.

Connors dated a Miss World and eventually married Patty McGuire, a onetime *Playboy* centerfold. There was turbulence in the marriage, a separation and reconciliation. Now there are two children, and people on tour will tell you that Patty Connors has done wonders in making Jimmy a more patient, forgiving person.

Evert's personal life has been even more turbulent. After Connors and her well-publicized relationships with such people as Burt Reynolds and former President Gerald Ford's son Jack, she married John Lloyd, then Britain's No. 1 tennis player. Lloyd was drop-dead good-looking, a charming, funny man, the perfect husband for Chris America. Their wedding ranked just behind Prince Charles and Princess Diana's when it came to publicity, glitz, and oohs, aahs, and sighs.

Evert finally had the storybook ending. Only this one fell through, too. She and Lloyd separated, reconciled, then separated again. She admitted to an affair with British rock star Adam Faith. Finally, in the fall of 1986, they separated for good and agreed to a divorce. At Martina Navratilova's urging, Evert went to Aspen for the holidays that year. There, she met Andy Mill.

For Evert, the whole experience of separation, divorce, and second marriage was traumatic. Her parents, strict Catholics, were horrified by her divorce and, at first, by the presence of Andy Mill in her life.

"My father didn't speak to me for months when John and I divorced," she said. "The whole thing was very tough on my whole family. Part of it was being Catholic, part of it was that they loved John. That's what made it so difficult for me. I agonized over the whole thing for two years. I still can't give you any one reason why John and I were divorced. It was just a lot of little things that both of us felt. Or maybe didn't feel. That rush you feel when the other person is in the room if you're in love just wasn't there anymore.

"My mother still thinks of John as a son and always will. Fortunately,

Andy won their hearts. Now my father loves everyone in his family, and they all get along really well. But when I first showed up with him, oh boy."

Here, Evert rolls her eyes at the memory of that week in March 1987, when she showed up to play the tournament in Boca Raton with Mill as her guest. She and Lloyd had agreed on the terms of their divorce at the end of 1986, but it wasn't yet final. "It took us about five minutes," Evert said. "We had a storybook divorce."

Evert had spent most of January and February with Mill, and called her parents to tell them she was bringing her new boyfriend to Boca Raton. "My dad hit the roof," she said. "He started screaming at me that the divorce wasn't final, that if I was seen in public with another man, John might ask for more money and all sorts of things like that. It was unbelievable. For one thing, John isn't that way. For another, he was *living* with someone. Finally I said to my father, 'Okay, Dad, I'll tell you what: I'm going to have John call you and tell you how ridiculous you're being.' That's what I did. John called my dad and said, 'There is absolutely nothing to worry about.' "

Of course, money was only one small factor in the whole equation. When Evert showed up at the tournament with Mill, everyone buzzed and buzzed. Ana Leaird, her best friend since childhood, drew the job of sitting with Mill and Colette Evert during Chris's first match of the tournament. "I needed a drink when it was over," Leaird said. "Actually, I needed it *before* it was over."

The trauma passed and Chris and Andy were married, although they are not married in the eyes of the Catholic Church. "I *do* have problems with that," she says. "I think of myself as a spiritual person. The idea that I'm not married in the eyes of the Church is something I've had trouble understanding. It just doesn't make sense to me."

Through it all, Evert's girl-next-door image has never changed. When she retired in 1989, three months shy of her thirty-fifth birthday, America wept. Its Chrissie was not only grown-up, but retired!

In truth, Evert's personal life has been no different than that of many American women. She had a great first love that fell apart. She rebelled in her early twenties against her strict upbringing by partying and dating a lot. She got married at twenty-four, divorced at thirty-two, and remarried at thirty-three. She grew up in a Catholic home but is pro choice. She likes to tell very dirty jokes, and she has smoked marijuana on more than one occasion—although she doesn't smoke it now and doesn't endorse kids trying it. "It's illegal and it's dangerous," she says.

"When I smoked it, it made me brain-dead. I was out of it completely." Evert's image has always been the subject of a good deal of discussion among tennis players. John McEnroe, knowing how her social life so differed from the public's perception of it, once told her she was "a fake, just like Jimmy [Connors] is." Evert responded by telling him there was a difference between being a fake and being diplomatic.

"First of all, I do feel I have an obligation because I know a lot of girls look at me as some kind of role model," she says. "I'm not going to lie about anything, but if I'm going to admit I smoked marijuana, I have to say that I really believe it is bad for you.

"I think my image has more to do with what the press and public *wanted* me to be more than anything else. I never claimed to be perfect or pure. If people ask me a question, I try to answer it honestly. I never wanted to say anything bad about another player in a postmatch interview. There, I was always diplomatic. But if people don't know how I feel about abortion, it's only because no one ever asked me.

"When I was younger, all anyone asked me was how I felt about my game, how I felt about Martina, and, when I was single, who I was dating, and, when I was married, when I was going to have kids. Now I get asked when I'm going to have kids and what do I think about Jennifer [Capriati]."

In Paris, Evert was being paid by NBC to tell people what she thought about Capriati and the rest of the women players. At the same time, Connors was being paid by NBC to share his views on the men. There was more than a little irony in the two of them beginning their TV careers together at the same network. Evert had been destined for NBC for years, but the Connors signing had been a surprise, especially since he was still hoping to play again.

Connors and Evert had, for the most part, stayed friends through the years once the initial hurt of their breakup had worn off. There had been one incident, in 1981, when Connors had played John Lloyd in the first round of the U.S. Open and, in Evert's view, tried to humiliate him. Two years after marrying Evert, Lloyd was struggling with his game, and Connors was up 6–0, 6–0, 2–0 before Lloyd finally won two games to save himself the embarrassment of a shutout. Connors had been as pumped during the match as he might be for a final. Afterward, he had claimed, "It was just another match." Evert knew that wasn't true and told Connors so.

That was all history now for the rookie TV commentators. Connors seemed to fit more easily into the role. Evert wasn't comfortable being critical or taking on controversial issues. Connors wasn't about to say *exactly* what he thought on the air—the FCC would have revoked NBC's license if he had—but he came a lot closer.

The big adjustment for both of them was *off* the air. Both were used to having people come to them for favors, to ask them for time. Now, that had changed. One evening after a futile day spent trying to set up interviews with a couple of players, Connors turned to some of his new NBC colleagues and said, "If I was this big an asshole when I was playing, shoot me right now."

Fortunately for him, none of them had a gun.

Evert figured out the problem fairly quickly. "I have never in my life had to ask people for favors," she said. "I'm used to people wanting to do things for me because I'm a tennis player. Now, I'm not."

She was still Chris Evert, still The Queen, but it *was* different. Evert felt the difference most acutely in her relationship with Capriati. "I can still remember her family when she was younger. I was still playing, they were watching me practice or coming to a tournament, and they just thought being around me was the greatest thing. Now, it's all different."

Some of this was inevitable. Capriati was getting older; she was a pro herself now. Evert's role with NBC had a lot to do with it, too. During Capriati's match with Navratilova at Hilton Head, Evert had made a couple of mild comments on the air about things Jennifer needed to improve in her game. Jennifer was upset. How could her friend/idol/mentor say those things about her? After Hilton Head, Evert had been asked by NBC to set up a pre–French Open interview with the Capriatis in Florida.

When she called to set up the interview, her brother told her Stefano Capriati didn't want to do it. Jennifer didn't have time. Evert was shocked and hurt. Eventually, the Colonel smoothed things over and Evert got the interview.

But the relationship had definitely changed. When Evert asked Capriati on the heels of her "lege" comment about Navratilova if she viewed Evert as a great player, too, Capriati shook her head. "It's different," she told Evert. "You're my friend. And you're a member of the press."

That one stung a little. Evert rolled with it, though. She knew that part of her new job was to use her access to Capriati and other players. In Paris, NBC wanted Evert and Capriati to go "shopping" for a feature it would use the day of the semifinals. Capriati did it, but Stefano complained later to the Colonel that his sister was taking advantage of her friendship with Jennifer too often. Evert, knowing her little brother was working with a difficult client, bit her tongue rather than respond to that one.

By the time day two was done at Roland Garros, the men's tournament was in complete disarray. On that second day, both Stefan Edberg and Boris Becker lost. Never in Grand Slam tennis history had the top two seeds lost in the first round.

Both losses were shockingly decisive. Edberg, playing at eleven in the morning, acted as if he were in a different time zone, winning a grand total of seven games against Sergi Bruguera, a Spanish teenager who had shown much promise in the past twelve months. Bruguera didn't even have to play very well to win this match, though. Edberg's performance was summed up perfectly by his coach, Tony Pickard: Asked what he thought had happened, Pickard shrugged and said, "There's not a word I can say about this match that's printable."

Becker didn't play nearly as poorly as Edberg, but he ran into a very hot, very talented player. Goran Ivanisevic was the same age as Bruguera—nineteen—but a completely different player. The Spaniard was a clay-courter all the way, a kid with solid ground strokes who would make a lot of money from the game without ever being great at it. Ivanisevic had greatness in him. He was from Split, Yugoslavia, a six-foot-five lefty with a serve that could be past you before you knew it was off the racquet. He could play superbly or horrendously no matter what the surface. He had been tossed out of the European Championships at the age of fourteen and, by his own admission, had a tendency to tank when things went wrong.

On this day, nothing went wrong. He beat Becker in four sets, playing, as Becker put it, "completely out of his mind."

Sadly, Becker was not in the best frame of mind for this match. After Monte Carlo, he had played well in the German Open, getting to the final, and had then gone to Düsseldorf the week before the French for World Team Cup.

This was an event Becker enjoyed. It was much more low-key than other events in Germany, and it gave him a chance to hang out with his Davis Cup teammates. This year, especially when he had opted not to play Davis Cup for the first time in his life, World Team Cup was something he had looked forward to.

Only, it hadn't turned out that way. The Germans had lost twice in round-robin play, first to the U.S. and then to Spain. During the match against Spain, the fans had booed them loudly and often, feeling they weren't giving 100 percent. Becker was hurt and angered.

"We've won two straight Davis Cups, we've won the Düsseldorf event twice, and now we lose once and they boo us?" he said. "I couldn't believe it. It really blew my mind that they could do this. I couldn't get a grip on it."

Becker and his teammates stayed up the whole night Friday consoling one another. It was 8 A.M. Saturday by the time Becker got to bed. Even then, he didn't sleep well.

For Becker, this was another in a series of events that he felt had estranged him from the German people. It all dated back to his Wimbledon victory in 1985, when he had been viewed as the country's hero and savior, a standard that was tough even for the brightest seventeen-year-old to deal with.

"When I won Wimbledon all you heard and read was 'what a great German day.' I was made into something much bigger than I should have been. I was a boy trying to survive in a man's world on the tennis tour. That wasn't always easy. I lost matches, I made mistakes, I got frustrated. Still, I won Wimbledon the next year, and I was very proud of that.

"But once the German people had built me up, there seemed to be this need to bring me back down. I had no privacy at all—okay, you have to accept that if you are a sportsman in a small country. But it was more than that. The first time I played Davis Cup, in 1985, I felt like the people understood me and knew how hard it was to go out and win for my country.

"By last year, though, it had all changed. Now, only the very rich people come to Davis Cup. They want to drink their champagne and watch us perform for them. I got to the point where I said, 'I don't want to perform for these jerks.' If I win, they say, 'Well, of course he wins, he should win, look at all the money he makes.' If I lose they say I am a piece of shit.

"I don't play tennis to entertain the rich. I play tennis for myself, for my friends and family, and maybe, I hope, so I can do some good off the court someday. Nothing I do seems good enough for the people in my country. After all we had won in the last few years, to be booed in Düsseldorf made me very, very angry. I couldn't get it out of my mind. I came to Paris on Saturday, but my mind was still in Düsseldorf."

At the highest level of any sport, the smallest thing can make the biggest difference. Becker always has trouble getting himself up emotionally during the first week of a Grand Slam. He knows from experience that he needs to be emotional to play his best tennis. But he cannot play a first-round match completely wound up and still have enough emotional energy left for the second week, when the matches are more difficult.

That approach, which is the only one Becker feels comfortable with, leaves a very small margin for error. Other top players are different. Lendl shows up in almost exactly the same frame of mind for every match he plays. That is why he loses early so rarely. McEnroe is almost always hyper no matter what the situation. When he isn't, he usually loses. Edberg, although he appears to be barely alive whether he is playing the first round in Indianapolis or the final at Wimbledon, is actually closer to Becker in this sense than any of the other top players. That is why he, too, can be vulnerable early.

If the draw had been different in Paris, Becker would have gotten away with not being quite there emotionally. If you had asked any seeded player to make a list of the three unseeded players they would least like to play in the first round, Ivanisevic would have been on every list, and at the top of most.

"If I had been one hundred percent that day, I would beat him," Becker said later. "But under the best of circumstances, I am not going to be one hundred percent in the first round. After Düsseldorf, there was no way."

Becker went home to Leimen after his loss and spent a few days writing feverishly in his journal. He was confused about his tennis, wondering if all the months of mental wandering had taken away the edge that had made him the best player in the world in 1989. He was lonely without Karen, whom he had seen during the tournament in Hamburg. "When you see someone in a situation like that, you tend only to remember the good times," he said. "It was very hard."

He remained baffled by his countrymen. Being German has been an issue for Becker ever since he emerged as a star at Wimbledon. Because he was big and aggressive, English writers could not resist bringing up the German invasion of their country in World War II when writing about Becker. It wasn't just the trashy tabloids, either. Rex Bellamy, one of the most respected English tennis writers, made reference to Becker's background in *The Times* of London the day after Becker's victory, leading his story this way: "On the same court that his countrymen bombed more than forty years ago, Boris Becker became a tennis champion on Sunday."

At seventeen, Becker was constantly asked if he felt an added responsibility as a spokesman for young Germans in the 1980s. Always, he said that he did, that he understood that the wounds of World War II had not yet healed completely. After a while, he came to resent the questions.

"I could just as easily be Italian or French or American," he said. "It's an accident of birth that I'm German. And yet, I have to answer these questions all the time. I was born more than twenty years after the war ended. It is part of history to me, just as it is to an American my age. Terrible, terrible things happened. But it doesn't seem fair to me that I am supposed to be responsible somehow, because I am a tennis player." It is not only hard to be Boris Becker, German tennis player, outside of Germany, it is also hard to be Boris Becker, German superstar, *in* Germany.

"I want to be seen as a good person, not just in my country, but everywhere. I am proud to be German, I love my country. But the people there have made it so I can't live there until after my tennis career is over—if then. That makes me very angry. I don't know why my country is so nationalistic. Everything in Germany is *big,* wins *or* losses. They seem to always want somebody to follow, to look up to, to be part of something. I see this in my father. In many ways, he is a typical German."

Becker believes his independence and stubbornness comes from his mother. Even now, when things go wrong, he escapes to his home, to his old room, to a place where his mother spoils him; does his laundry and shields him from the outside world. Paris was a jolt for Becker, a painful one that sent him home wondering when—and if—things would turn back around.

While the men were losing their two most glamorous names on the tournament's second day, the women were watching it all, feeling just a little bit envious. Upsets of the Becker–Edberg magnitude just didn't happen in the women's game. There simply wasn't enough depth for the top players to lose that early.

In the fifty-six Grand Slam tournaments of her career, Chris Evert had lost before the quarterfinals *twice*—in the third round at Wimbledon in 1983 and in the third round of her last French Open, in 1988. In the 1980s, Martina Navratilova *never* lost before the fourth round—and lost that early only three times in thirty-seven Slams. Steffi Graf had not lost before the quarterfinals of a Slam since 1985, when, as a fifteen-year-old, she had lost in the fourth round of the French to Evert.

Slowly, that was changing. Two of the top five seeds *did* lose in the first two rounds at Roland Garros, although it was clear that neither was playing close to the top of her game.

Zina Garrison, seeded fifth, lost in the first round to Wiltrud Probst, a gangly German who should not have been able to stay on the same court with her. Garrison was something of an emotional wreck. All year she had been blowing leads, and she did it again against Probst. After leading 5–2 in the third set, she lost the last five games of the match. She blew another match point—the fourth time in 1990 she had lost after holding a match point—and walked off the court near tears, an all too familiar scene.

"Same shot every time," she said afterward. "I've missed that forehand on match point every time. It's like a recurring nightmare I can't get away from."

That night, Garrison called her husband, Willard Jackson, at home in Houston and told him to please get to Europe as soon as possible. She now had almost four weeks to wait for Wimbledon to begin. Going home was pointless, but she didn't want to wait that long for Willard to come over. He understood. "I'll get there as soon as I can," he told her.

Garrison's defeat didn't shock many people. But when Arantxa Sanchez, the defending champion, lost to Mercedes Paz in the second round, it got people's attention.

Sanchez had been having an inconsistent year, and few people gave her much chance to defend her title. But even fewer people thought that Paz, her doubles partner, would be the person to knock her out of the tournament.

Paz was a month shy of twenty-four and had been on tour for six years. People said she could really be a factor if she ever got in shape, but at the end of 1989 she weighed 184 pounds. Even at five feet ten, that was a lot of weight to be carrying. She had finally gotten herself on a training regimen at the start of the year and had lost twenty-five pounds. She was still bulky and lacked quickness, but the difference in her game was evident.

Sanchez, meanwhile, was going through a difficult time. She had changed coaches earlier in the year, hiring Mike Estep to replace her longtime coach, Juan Nuñez. Estep had a simple philosophy when it came to coaching women: anybody can attack if they want to. He had made Martina Navratilova more aggressive when he began coaching her in 1983, getting her to come in behind her second serve, and he had preached the same kind of game to every player he had worked with since then.

At forty-one, Estep was thinking it might be time to get off the tennis merry-go-round. But IMG had called to say Sanchez was looking for a coach. They were willing to meet Estep's financial terms—which included first-class airfare for him and his wife, Barbara—and wanted him to meet with Sanchez. He did, liked her and her family, and took the job. Right now, though, Sanchez was caught in the middle. Part of her understood why Estep wanted her to be more aggressive, but a major part of her still felt more comfortable hugging the baseline. An indecisive player is almost always a losing player.

"What you can say?" Sanchez said in her fractured English after the match. "Last year I win here; this year, I don't. It happens."

She was exactly right. What Sanchez had done in 1989 was extraordinary. The problem was, in tennis, everyone demanded that the extraordinary be repeated over and over again.

No one knew that better than the two women everyone assumed would meet in the final—Steffi Graf and Monica Seles. For entirely different reasons, Seles and Graf were having a tough time of things in Paris.

Paris had never been kind to Graf. In 1986 she had gotten sick during the tournament and lost in the quarterfinals to Mandlikova. In 1989 she had been sick again and lost the final to Sanchez. Now, she arrived in an awful mood and promptly got sick again.

"I think," she said, "I'm allergic to Paris."

For an athlete in superb physical shape, Graf was downright sickly. Her immune system, for reasons doctors could not figure out, was amazingly vulnerable to any flu or virus that came anywhere close to her. By the fourth day of the tournament, Graf was so sick that it seemed possible she might have to default her third-round match.

Her physical ailments were, at this point, the least of Graf's worries. Two weeks earlier in Berlin, her father's personal life had exploded into tabloid headlines and into her own life. Peter Graf had warned Steffi as far back as Australia that there might be trouble ahead, but Graf, not knowing the full story, had never dreamed it could become as ugly as it now had. On the third day of the tournament, the tabloids screamed with stories alleging that Peter had fathered the child of nude model Nicole Meissner.

"A friend of mine told me what was going on," she remembered, months later. "I just couldn't believe it. I had a driver taking me around that week, so I told him just to drive far out from the city to find a quiet place somewhere. I went for a walk in a forest, trying to figure out what to do.

"What I really wanted to do was run away. Just disappear. I didn't want to face what I knew was coming. I thought, Why can't these people leave me alone? I was supposed to go to the theater with someone that night, but I canceled. I couldn't handle it. I was just so angry."

The next day, in Graf's postmatch press conference, a reporter quietly said, "Steffi, I hate to have to bring this up, but . . ."

"Then why bring it up?" Graf broke in.

"Because I have to," the reporter answered. He then asked about the story. Graf politely said that she really didn't want to talk about it or think about it. After that, reporters were informed that if questioning strayed from the subject of tennis, the interview would end immediately. This sort of censorship would later become a major issue at Wimbledon.

Graf made it to the final in Berlin, but was waxed by the now-rolling Seles. She was clearly distracted and unhappy. "I was hoping that, somehow, in the week before Paris it would all go away," she said, smiling sadly. "Of course, it didn't."

The story raged and Graf coughed, sniffled, and shivered. She was two weeks shy of twenty-one, as rich, as famous, and as talented as anyone could ever hope to be.

And as miserable as anyone could be.

Seles, in the meantime, was still joyriding—but also learning the realities of big-time stardom. With Graf so clearly not herself, Seles had become the cofavorite to win the tournament. The recent victories over Navratilova and Graf had focused people on just how hot she was—she had now won five straight tournaments and twenty-five straight matches—and the media was swarming everywhere Seles went.

To an outsider, Seles appeared to be dealing with all the pressures and demands with amazing grace and calm. But, ever so slowly, she was being forced to change her life-style. She had already told people that, next year, there was no way she could stay in the player hotel. Too crowded. Too many people who recognized her. Top players rarely stay at the designated tournament hotel at Grand Slams. Seles would now join those ranks.

The Friday before the tournament began, for the first time in her life, Seles told the hotel switchboard to block all her calls. "Actually, I was trying to watch the European gymnastics finals on television, and the phone just kept ringing and ringing," she said. "Finally I told them just to hold all my calls. I had never done that before, and I felt bad about it. But, actually, it gave me some privacy." She was also practicing at eight in the morning so she could get to and from the courts without attracting attention.

For the first time in her career, Seles at sixteen appeared a bit weary. She wasn't as sharp as usual in her early matches. She needed three tough sets to beat Kelesi—someone she had lost three games to in Rome—in the second round. Leila Meshki then took her to three sets, and Laura Gildemeister had her down 4–1 in the first set before she rebounded. Seles was winning on guile and guts and because her opponents didn't really think they could beat her. But she wasn't playing her best tennis.

"I do feel tired," she admitted. "I've been on the road a long time now, and I've played a lot of matches. Maybe next year I'll change my schedule."

That wasn't likely. The catch-22 of stardom in tennis is that the more you win, the more money you are offered to travel far and wide. Whether someone is sixteen or sixty, traveling across oceans and through time zones and checking in and out of hotels is exhausting. But most tennis parents seem to take the "get it while you can" approach. They keep telling their teenagers how much fun they are having. The teenagers nod their heads, hit the ball, still love the winning, and, by their mid-twenties, if not sooner, wonder why the hell they ever picked up a racquet.

It had been happening to Graf even before her father's troubles. It would happen just as surely to Seles and Capriati. All three had fathers controlling their careers. They were not alone in this or in their insatiable desire to cash in. At IMG, the agents had established their own version of the ATP rankings—Association of Tennis Parents. The more you were a pain in the butt, the higher you ranked. Peter Graf had been as dominant at the top of these rankings in recent years as his daughter had been dominant at the top of the women's rankings. But, in 1990, Stefano Capriati and Karolj Seles were starting to make inroads.

Tired as she was, Seles still made it through to the semifinals, matching up against Capriati. The other semifinal was Graf–Novotna.

The story of the semifinals was—surprise—Capriati. She had taken to the pressure of her first Grand Slam like a tennis parent took to cashing checks. She lost three games *total* in her first two matches and just kept going from there. In her fifth tournament she had become the youngest Grand Slam semifinalist in history.

"I mean, that's really neat," she said.

Capriati did it all in Paris. Every time she went sight-seeing it was with a camera crew. She and her ESPN crew went to Notre Dame one day, where, much to Capriati's dismay, there was no football field. Driving through town—with a crew, of course—Capriati's brother, Stephen, asked what Les Invalides was. Someone told him that Napoleon was buried there.

"Who is Napoleon?" Stephen asked.

"You know," Jennifer said, "he's the little dead dude."

When she wasn't winning her matches or looking for football fields and little dead dudes, Capriati did her share of shopping. She was in a shoe store one day, when a young Frenchman spotted her.

"*Jenneeefair,*" he cried. "Will you marry me?"

Capriati looked him over and then shook her head firmly. "No way," she answered.

Capriati's physical maturity was a great topic of discussion among the other players. Some wondered how much she would improve in the next few years, given that she was already as big and as strong as all but a few of the players on tour. Others made the argument that she still hadn't learned to use her strength, that when she added finesse to her game—she had absolutely no idea how to change-up, dink, or play a drop shot—she would be like a baseball pitcher who had a great fastball and a good curve too.

The other question was what would happen if she kept growing. Denise Capriati was a petite woman, but her daughter was already bigger than she was. Stefano, although not tall, was a stocky, broad-shouldered man. How big might Jennifer get?

Capriati was already drawing notice from boys—and male teenage players. Someone suggested to Aki Rahunen, the eighteen-year-old Finn, that he think about playing mixed doubles with Capriati as a way of overcoming his self-doubts as a doubles player.

"If you play with Capriati, it would be perfect for you. First of all, she's a pretty good doubles player. Second, she's a cute girl, and third, she's got big bucks."

Rahunen, who speaks English but hasn't quite mastered the slang, nodded eagerly. "I know she does," he said. "I saw them when she played on TV!"

For Jim Courier, there were no TV crews in Paris, no phones ringing off the hook, no entourages to feed and clothe.

Which was exactly how he wanted it.

Courier had built his year around this tournament. He honestly believed, even before Becker and Edberg made their premature exits, that he could win the French Open.

One year earlier, Courier had announced his arrival as someone to be reckoned with when he had beaten his old Bollettieri bunkmate Agassi in a major grudge match. He had improved steadily during the rest of 1989 and had played solidly during the first five months of 1990, moving into the top twenty, then into the top fifteen. But he had been frustrated all year by one close loss after another: Kratzmann in Philadelphia, Agassi in Key Biscayne, Chesnokov in Rome. The two that had really bothered him had both been to Jonas Svensson, in Australia, and then in Munich.

He was so upset after Munich that he left the locker room without showering and walked across the street to a park adjacent to the tennis center. "I put my head down and just walked," Courier said. "After a while, I had this feeling like people were looking at me. I looked up and noticed that everyone around me was *naked.* I had walked right into a nude park without even noticing. I turned around and walked out of there very fast."

In Paris, he had swept through his first three matches easily and, on the middle Sunday, who was waiting for him in the round of 16? Agassi.

Since his embarrassing first-round performance, Agassi had played much better tennis, although he had gotten himself into a verbal war with Philippe Chatrier. Chatrier had been quoted as saying he had serious problems with Agassi's multihued clothes. Agassi responded by saying that if Chatrier tried to ban his clothes, he would just skip the French the way he now skipped Wimbledon and the Australian. He then called Chatrier "a bozo."

That set up a wonderful off-court matchup: Bozo vs. The Clown.

Courier cared about none of this. He knew if he could repeat his 1989 victory over Agassi, he would have a legitimate shot at making it to the final. "I haven't had a really bad loss all year," he said before the match. "But I haven't had a really good win. This is the time to do it."

The middle Sunday of the tournament dawned cold and rainy. Killing time in the locker room, Courier was surprised when Chang walked over and sat down with him. "I couldn't remember the last time we had talked," he said. "We were both playing early [Courier–Agassi on center; Chang–Javier Sanchez on court 1], and I guess he was as keyed up and nervous as I was."

Courier couldn't resist asking Chang, who had bought a BMW

when he'd turned eighteen in February, if he had gotten his driver's license yet. Chang shook his head. "Haven't had time," he said.

It was still drizzling slightly when the match began. Agassi's entourage sat in the player's box, looking like a bunch of assistant football coaches who had been told to dress identically. All of them wore white Nike caps and sunglasses—even though it was almost too dark to play—except for Bill Shelton, whose suit was too expensive to be offset by a cap. They sat and yelled at Agassi about how strong he was, while Agassi kept up a running commentary with them every time he was on that side of the court.

"Guy's praying for rain . . . Did you see that shot? He never thought I'd get there. I'm there, baby . . . all mine now, isn't it? All mine."

On this day, Agassi backed up the talk. The first set was as good a set of tennis as anyone had seen all year. The two players stood at the baseline and slugged away at each other like a couple of boxers in the final round of a Rocky movie. Neither could knock the other down, though, and after an hour they went to a tiebreak. Agassi had three set points. Courier saved them all. Then, at 8–8, he cracked a backhand down the line to reach set point himself for the first time. Then he chipped a low forehand return, and when Agassi popped a backhand into the net, Courier had the first set after sixty-six draining minutes.

Pumped, he turned to *his* entourage—Coach Sergio Cruz—and pointed a finger. "That's one," he shouted. "That's one set!"

But it was the last one for Courier as Agassi took control of the match and didn't let go. Courier won only five more games. He had played one brilliant set; Agassi had played four. It was the first tangible sign that there was some substance behind all the blather about Agassi being stronger.

Agassi had now become the prohibitive favorite to win the tournament. Of course, he couldn't let a day go by, even one when he had played brilliant tennis, without stirring things up. When the Chatrier clothes controversy came up during his postmatch press conference, Agassi pounced.

"Listen to this, this is really good," he said, beaming. "I just thought about this. You know, when it comes to Chatrier's benefit, tradition goes right out the window. At Wimbledon there's only one sign on Centre Court, a little Rolex-watch sign. Here, there's not a space without an advertisement. So, when Chatrier can reap benefits, he doesn't care about tradition.

"Look at the fans out there, they love something different. I think if I walked out in white clothes, ninety-nine percent of them would be disappointed."

That last was certainly a stretch. Most fans didn't really care what Agassi wore—the pink and black he was favoring in France, or all-white. Still, it wasn't a bad little speech.

"Where did you come up with this, Andre?" someone asked, noticing the smirks and nods coming from the entourage, which had taken over a corner of the room (Gil still in sunglasses).

"I just thought of it now as I was coming off the court," Agassi said.

That was a good one. Agassi had been briefed at length the previous day by Ian Hamilton, the Nike representative whose clothes were benefiting greatly from all the publicity. For Hamilton, this scenario was a dream come true: The most visible player left playing in the French Open—an American, no less—was embroiled in a controversy with the most visible bureaucrat in the game of tennis and it was all because of his clothes. Nike clothes! He would have been foolish if he hadn't coached Agassi to keep the thing alive for a couple more days. Agassi had tried a little too hard, though. He was too eager and too ready when the question came up. His answer sounded rehearsed—because it was.

The entourage had now become omnipresent. Entourages are as much a part of tennis as the tiebreak, ranging in size from one (a coach, spouse, or parent) to seven or eight (family, coach, agent, stringer, masseur, psychologist, shoe rep, religious guru, strength coach, bodyguard). Capriati's entourage could match almost anyone's—mom, dad, brother, coach, hitting partner, agent, father's relatives, and all her various camera crews. The Chang Gang—mom, dad, brother, agent, hitting partner—was also competitive in any entourage battle.

The most confused man in Paris had to be John Evert. Was the Colonel part of Jennifer's entourage or his sister's? Or was Chris now part of Jennifer's entourage, too? And where did Andy Mill, who made the mistake of coming into the interview room with the Agassi boys one day, fit into all this? Only in tennis did the athletes meet with the press while surrounded by all their various minions. Since reporters couldn't get into the locker room, they often complained about the presence of families and agents in the interview room, which was usually the only place they could talk to a player. Agassi—among others—wouldn't even go to the interview room without his support crew.

The only one in the group who seemed at all aware of how silly it all was, was Shelton. There was no questioning Shelton's loyalty to Agassi.

He had become infamous in IMG staff meetings for defending even the most foolish things Agassi did. "Everything's the press with Bill," one IMG agent said. "Andre says something stupid, they quote him accurately, and it's their fault. He says he won't even read the papers anymore because the press is so mean to Andre. Unfortunately, part of his job is to read the papers whether he likes what he reads or not."

One afternoon later in the year, the entourage was walking down a hallway to watch The Lord and Master play. Phil led the way, followed by Gil, Bollettieri, Raul, and Shelton. Hamilton had the week off. As the group went by in careful single file, Benji Robins, one of the ATP Tour's marketing people, couldn't resist. "Bill," he said, "what are you, the caboose?"

Shelton blanched. Robins, a truly gentle soul, immediately felt guilty. "I shouldn't have said it," he said. "Poor Bill. He's the only one who even thinks about being embarrassed. But that *is* what it looked like."

NBC, which very much wanted to stay on Agassi's good side, since it was beginning to look as though he was going to win the tournament, passed out caps and jackets to the entourage. When Agassi played on NBC, the entourage duly wore the NBC stuff. Otherwise, it was strictly Nike.

After the Courier match, the tournament was Agassi's to win. He played Chang in the quarterfinals and won in four sets. For Chang, getting to the quarterfinals was an accomplishment and a relief. Losing to Agassi was nothing to be ashamed of, and he had proved that the year before had not been a fluke.

Agassi's semifinal opponent was Jonas Svensson, who had benefited not only from Bruguera's upset of Edberg (beating Bruguera in five) but even more, perhaps, from Henri Leconte's victory over Andrei Chesnokov in the fourth round.

This was the best match of the tournament. Chesnokov had come to Paris playing better clay-court tennis than anyone in the world. He honestly felt he could win the tournament, having been a quarterfinalist in 1987 and a semifinalist in 1989. At twenty-four, he was playing the best tennis of his life, and he knew there were no Lendls or Wilanders in his way.

Few people knew how much Andrei Chesnokov wanted to be a Grand Slam champion. His parents divorced when their only child was three, and Andrei grew up in a small Moscow apartment with his mother and grandmother. He began to play tennis at the age of eight, when he was chosen from a physical-education class by a coach named Tatiana Naoumko to come learn the game from her. Naoumko is still his coach—and best friend—today.

"Right away," she says, "I could see this was a special character."

Tennis was on a downhill curve in the Soviet Union in the 1970s. Although Olga Morozva had made the Wimbledon final in 1974 and Alex Metreveli had reached the final of a Wimbledon watered down by a player boycott the year before, the Soviets had pulled their players off the international circuit. Since tennis wasn't an Olympic sport, it didn't seem worth the risks involved in allowing athletes to travel.

Young Andrei hardly cared. "Tennis became a sickness for me," he said. "I used to always ask my coach, when practice was over, if I could please stay and play more. When she sent me home, I would hit balls all over our little apartment. My mother and grandmother always were angry with me. At night, when I went to sleep, I took tennis balls and my racquet to bed with me."

Like most Soviet youngsters, Chesnokov learned to play chess at a young age. He still plays but says he never became passionate about it. "Everyone in my country plays chess because there are two things we do not have there," he said. "One is money, the other is space. In chess you do not need either. So everyone plays. I could never sit still long enough to be very good, though. Always, I played tennis."

When Andrei was nine, Tatiana entered him in his first tournament, the Moscow 12-and-unders. Andrei was so hyper that he ran everywhere, even in between points. He remembers winning a game and running to the other side of the court, grabbing the balls, and getting ready to serve. "Then my coach [he always refers to Tatiana as "my coach"] calls me over and says, 'Andrei, match is over. You won.' I was so excited to play, I forgot what the score was."

By 1981, he was the No. 1 junior in the Soviet Union. Tennis had been voted back into the Olympics, and the Soviets were beginning to let players travel again. In 1984, Chesnokov began playing satellites. One year later, he qualified for the French Open and shocked eighth-seeded Eliot Teltscher in the second round. Few people were even aware of the fact that the Soviets were on tour again. Chesnokov's win caused a sensation. Even though he spoke little English, he was asked to meet with the press. Someone asked who his coach was; he answered that it was Tatiana.

That was the wrong answer. The Soviet Federation had sent another coach with him who was supposed to be given the credit for Chesnokov's play. Chesnokov was informed of his mistake.

After his next match he was asked again about his coaching. Was the gentlemen with him his coach? Some people were wondering by now if he was from the KGB.

"He is my coach," Chesnokov answered dutifully. But he couldn't leave it at that. "He is my coach on this trip. Coach who taught me to play is home in Moscow."

That last sentence earned Chesnokov an invitation to the Soviet embassy in Paris. He was supposed to play a mixed-doubles match that afternoon, but his plans were changed. At the embassy he was informed, in no uncertain terms, that when he was told who his coach was, he had better not say someone else was his coach.

"I knew then that if I am not careful, the road to the West can close anytime," Chesnokov says now.

That knowledge may explain his often unpredictable behavior during the next few years. As his English improved, Chesnokov became one of the most popular players on the tour. His play was brilliant at times—especially on clay—but rotten at others. The same was true with the media. Sometimes he was a delight; other times he was quiet and somber. He occasionally claimed—falsely—that he didn't speak enough English to be interviewed without an interpreter.

He cracked the top forty in 1986, slid back during one of his moody periods, but reached the top twenty in 1988. Early in 1989, encouraged by the reforms being made by the Gorbachev government, he signed a personal-services contract with ProServ. No Soviet player had ever taken this step before. ProServ had represented the Soviet Federation from 1986 through 1988, and Chesnokov had been pleased with what the company had done for him.

But in 1989, the federation signed a new deal with IMG. That was when Chesnokov took the step of signing his own deal with ProServ. Zvereva did the same thing several months later. Both then announced, within a couple of weeks of each other, that they were tired of turning their prize money over to the federation. For the rest of the year, both were hounded everywhere they went with questions about the money.

"I did not know what was going to happen," Chesnokov said. "Signing with ProServ was a very dangerous thing to do. The same was true for Zvereva. We both knew we could be cut off at any time. Things have changed at home, but they are still changing—every day. No one knows what will come next."

o

In October, just before he was to leave to play a tournament in Basle, Switzerland, Chesnokov was called to a meeting with the Soviet sports committee. The meeting was not in a downtown office where the newly free Soviet media might get wind of it. It was held in a small flat away from prying eyes. This sent a message to Chesnokov that the authorities meant business.

"They give me a paper saying I must turn fifty percent of what I win in Basle and for rest of year over to them," he said. "I didn't want to sign. They told me if I don't sign, I don't go to Basle. I signed."

Exactly what the federation was trying to prove, Chesnokov wasn't sure. In 1990, he was allowed to keep all his prize money, make his own schedule, and have Naoumko with him on the road. In return, he pays all his own expenses and plays Davis Cup and the Olympics.

"Right now, everything is okay," he said, twirling his watch, with the word *perestroika* written on it in English. "It can change anytime, though. Right now I think the government has more things to worry about than Andrei Chesnokov."

Chesnokov's concern in Paris was winning a tournament he believed he should win. But in the fourth round, he faced Henri Leconte. Playing Leconte in Paris is always an adventure, one way or the other. His relationship with the French crowd is like that of a longtime lover who has often been unfaithful. At his best, Leconte stirs the French like no one except Noah can. He is as dazzling as anyone in tennis, a natural showman who can light up a court. When he is injured—which has been often—or having personal problems—almost as often—Leconte can lose as quickly as anyone in the game.

At fifteen he was dumped by the French Federation because they thought he was too wild ever to be a good player. Tiriac signed him because "the guy has more talent than any of them. The French, they were crazy for [Thierry] Tulasne. I said, 'Fine, you take Tulasne.' "

Working with Tiriac, whose number one client then was still Guillermo Vilas, Leconte did have flashes of brilliance. But he was so immature that Tiriac nicknamed him "The Idiot." When he was twenty-one, Leconte left Tiriac, partly because Tiriac had signed Becker and partly because his new wife wanted to be more involved in his career. Tiriac was not a big fan of interference from family members. The split was amicable and the two are still friends.

In 1985, Leconte finally blossomed. He beat Noah in five sets at Roland Garros in one of the great matches ever seen in Paris. The two men hugged at the net when it was over, and France had a second hero.

Only, Leconte couldn't ever get to Noah's level. He reached the semifinals in both Paris and at Wimbledon in 1986, and then got to the final in Paris in 1988. That was when Wilander humiliated him and Leconte made his "now maybe you understand my game" speech to the fans.

"The minute I said it I knew I had made a mistake," Leconte says. "They didn't understand at all."

Crucified in the French press, he then went through a series of injuries, culminating with back surgery in the spring of 1989. At the same time, his marriage broke up. He played in Australia early in 1990, but was out of shape and not anywhere near the player he had been. In March, after a first-round loss at the Lipton, he asked Patrice Haguelauer to coach him again. Haguelauer had worked with Noah for years, but he was also the first person to ever give Leconte a lesson—when Leconte was seven.

They went back to square one. Haguelauer's advice to Leconte was simple: work hard and keep your mouth shut. Leconte listened. He made the semifinals in Monte Carlo and rekindled his relationship with the French fans. In Paris, he faced a potentially tough first-round opponent in Ronald Agenor, but won in straight sets. He raced through three rounds without losing a set and was brimming with confidence when he faced Chesnokov.

Chesnokov knew just how tough Leconte would be, and for two sets Leconte was untouchable. The place was electric, the cries of "*Allez Henri!*" echoing all around the sun-splashed stadium. But Chesnokov is as tough as any player in the world when down two sets. His opponents all know they had better get him out in three or he becomes dangerous. Chang is the same way.

Knowing this, Leconte tried too hard. He began going for too much with his shots. Chesnokov won the third set and the murmurs began. When he won the fourth set easily, the place was almost silent. Leconte was doing it again. The ultimate tease. At 2–2 in the fifth set, he dug himself a 0–30 hole. The murmurs were now grumbles. But somehow Leconte escaped. He hit a huge serve to reach 15–30 and then hit the shot of the day, a lunging forehand volley on what looked like a sure Chesnokov winner.

One shot *can* turn a tennis match around, especially a five-setter. Chesnokov thought he had hit a winner to make it 15–40. Instead, it was 30–all, and Leconte got one more push of adrenaline. The crowd reacted, too, knowing genius when it saw it. Leconte held to lead 3–2. Then, with Chesnokov serving at 3–4, Leconte came up with three straight winners, shots no one was going to touch. Magically, he was up 5–3 and serving for the match. And he served it out. Chesnokov was in shock. He thought he had the match won at two sets all, and then, without warning, Leconte had flicked his racquet a couple of times and Chesnokov's dream was gone.

Leconte was a hero again. All was forgiven. He blew kisses to every corner of the stadium as eighteen thousand people went mad. The relationship between a French player and a French crowd is more personal than any other in the world, even than that between the Italians. An Italian knows a home-country crowd will always be for him; a Frenchman has to earn its love.

"The guy plays unbelievable tennis all the time," Chesnokov said later. "Either unbelievably good or unbelievably bad. At the end, he was unbelievably good. The crowd kept him going when he was tired."

Leconte, exhausted, agreed. "The crowd won for me today," he said. "Without them, I could never have played the fifth set."

It had taken every ounce of energy for Leconte to beat Chesnokov, which became apparent in his match against Svensson, who, after dropping the first set, easily won the next three. That was a perfect setup for Agassi: no Chesnokov with his nerveless steadiness; no Leconte with his swashbuckling brilliance and the crowd cheering him on. Just solid, steady Jonas Svensson, who was delighted to be in the semifinals. Agassi won in four.

That put him in his first Grand Slam final. His opponent there would not be one of the game's great names; it would not even be one of the hot clay-court players of the spring—Muster, Chesnokov, or Sanchez. His opponent was Andres Gomez, the man who had been laughed at in Australia because he was so out of shape, the man who had told Ecuadorian TV a year ago that he would be glad to do the commentary on the 1990 French final for them. That was going to be difficult now—unless he was miked on court.

While Agassi had been making daily headlines, Gomez had moved quickly and quietly though the bottom half of the draw to reach the first Grand Slam semifinal of his career. The opponent was Muster, who had ended the brilliant run of Becker-beater Ivanisevic in the quarterfinals. In Rome, Gomez had shown Muster only one speed—fast—hitting everything as hard as he could. Now, he dug into his experience, dinking and slicing, feeding Muster low balls and high balls, never giving him any pace. Muster feeds off pace like lions feed off meat. Gomez made him look helpless: 7–5, 6–1, 7–5.

"I didn't come here to make the semifinals or the finals," Gomez said. "I came here to win. In Rome, I knew we might play here, so I didn't show Thomas everything I had. This is the time for that. Now, I have one match left to win."

The women's semifinals were as one-sided as the men's. No one expected Jana Novotna to give Graf any trouble, and she didn't, winning only three games. But Seles–Capriati was different. Seles had been in trouble in three matches, while Capriati had been brilliant the entire tournament, not losing a set. But Capriati never had a chance against Seles. A great player will often struggle in the early rounds of a tournament, but if they survive—watch out. Seles had saved her best tennis for the last weekend, and she blew Capriati off the court, 6–2, 6–2. The look on Capriati's face said it all—she was stunned. Seles, at sixteen, playing the role of veteran for the first time in her career, was steely-eyed from the first point to the last. "Now I know how Steffi felt playing me last year," she said when it was over. "I was really nervous going out there."

Capriati left Paris on the morning of the final. Yes, an NBC camera crew saw her off. Capriati waved good-bye. No doubt it was like leaving her family behind—but there would be others waiting in London.

The final was just what had been predicted: Graf–Seles. No one expected Graf to be in the same funk she had clearly been in during the Berlin final. But Graf was not the Graf of 1988 and 1989. She was distracted. "I remember losing concentration at times during the match," she said months later. "I was upset with myself because I had spent the week actually hating people for the first time in my life. I really hated the German media for what it was doing to me and my family. I had never thought of myself as someone who could hate, but I did. I couldn't get it out of my mind."

Even a distracted Graf was still about as good as any player in the world. She pushed Seles into a first-set tiebreak and quickly went up 6–2. Then, to the amazement of everyone in the stadium, including Seles, she fell apart, losing the next six points and the set. The most telling point came at 6–5. Graf double-faulted. No one could ever remember seeing Graf choke.

"Oh, yeah, I choked right there," she said. "I never felt like that on a tennis court in my life."

Seles was bright enough to understand this. The invincible Graf was gone. She blasted through the second set, and all of a sudden women's tennis had a star—the youngest French Open champion in history—who was pushing Graf for preeminence. On NBC, after the superb match, Karolj Seles grabbed the microphone from Bud Collins, yelling, "I am the only coach, I am the only coach."

Gerry Smith, who had spent most of the week fighting with the Grand Slam Committee over the issue of equal prize money here and at Wimbledon, walked around with a huge grin on his face. "I rest my case," he said quietly.

He could have used the men's final for further evidence. Agassi and Gomez were both in their first Grand Slam final, and it showed. Gomez hadn't slept all that well, not so much because of the match but because his brother was flying into Paris. "I never sleep well when my family is on a plane," he said.

He had breakfast with his brother, then went out to the courts with his longtime agent, Dick Dell. Gomez is one of the few older players in tennis who has never changed agencies. Dick Dell had been in the business eight years and had never had a Grand Slam champion. The first set was nothing but nerves. Gomez got the only break and won it 6–3, finishing with an ace. But Agassi turned it around in the second, breaking Gomez all four times he served, to win 6–2. The momentum was clearly with him. Gomez, even after just seventy-one minutes, looked winded. The entourage—in NBC gear today—was telling Agassi how strong he was.

Brawn doesn't always beat brains, though. Gomez broke early in the third, but Agassi broke back to 4–4. Gomez took a deep breath. "I knew I couldn't go five with him," he said. "I don't have the legs of a Wilander. I was lucky the first two sets were quick. But I figured I had to win it in four." Agassi went up 40–15 in the next game, but Gomez came back to deuce. The tennis still hadn't been great, but the tension of a Grand Slam final was in the air now. Someone was about to gain control of this match.

Gomez hit a brilliant backhand winner, and then, at break point, Agassi tried one of his silly drop shots. Gomez pounced on it, flicked a backhand winner, and was back in the lead at 5–4. He never looked back again. He served the set out and broke Agassi to lead 2–1 in the fourth. Now, Gomez was battling himself more than Agassi.

"When I held to 3–1, my mind started to wander," he said. "I began to think about holding the trophy and my speech. I knew I couldn't do that. If I gave him an opening now, he would take it because he was going for broke on every shot.

Gomez held at 30 for 4–2. At 4–3, Agassi had a break point. Gomez got off a huge serve to save it, then hit two winners for 5–3. For the first time in the match, he shook a fist. Agassi's entourage, for once, was quiet. Agassi held for 5–4.

Sitting in the chair during the changeover, Gomez fought himself one more time. "Right then I remembered practicing a couple of days before the tournament, when they rolled the trophy through the court," he said. "I had never even *seen* it before, and I thought to myself maybe it was an omen. That thought came into my head sitting there. Then, when I walked out to serve, my legs felt wobbly. My eyes were wet. I thought I was really losing it. Then I lost the first point, but that got my mind back into tennis."

Agassi got Gomez into a 15–30 hole with a gorgeous running backhand. He was swinging from the heels on every point now. Gomez attacked off a forehand and slammed an overhead. Two points away. Again, Gomez wound up his forehand—once, twice. Agassi lunged and couldn't get the second one.

Match point. Twelve years of work. One point from the dream. In London, in the players' lounge at Queen's Club, Boris Becker shouted at the TV, "Come on, Go-Go! Right now!"

Gomez took one more deep breath. His mind was clear now. He hit a big serve and Agassi's return floated back. He closed in on the ball, wound up for one more forehand, and hit it perfectly, right down the line. Agassi took one step to chase it, then stopped, turned, and jogged to the net, hand extended.

He had to wait there for a moment because Gomez had turned to the players' box to share the moment with his family, with Rodriguez, and with Dick Dell—who found himself fighting tears as soon as he saw the look on Gomez's face. Once he had shaken Agassi's hand, Gomez sprinted out of the stadium and ran around to the entrance to the players' box so he could hug his wife and hold his son.

When Jean Borotra handed him the trophy, there was no doubting what this meant to Gomez. In a voice that trembled slightly, he thanked all the right people and closed by saying quietly, "I want to dedicate this victory to the people of my country, Ecuador."

That was to be expected from Gomez. Nine years earlier at the U.S. Open, a chair umpire had made the mistake of introducing him as a Mexican. Gomez walked to the chair and said, "I'm not from Mexico, I'm from Ecuador."

"Oh," the umpire said, "sorry."

"Correct it," Gomez said firmly. Sheepishly, the umpire did.

"We're a very small country, only about ten million people," Gomez said. "It seems the only time we ever make a headline around the world is if there's an earthquake or something goes wrong with the government. It's nice to do something that will make people in my country feel proud."

Gomez couldn't know just how proud until he flew home from Paris two days later. A huge crowd greeted him at the airport. He and his family were put into a motorcade to ride into Guayaquil. As they reached downtown, Gomez looked up and saw thousands and thousands of people. Everywhere he looked were people: on the sidewalks, in the streets, hanging out windows, on top of buildings.

"I had never seen that many people anywhere in my life," he said.

The motorcade stopped at city hall, where Gomez was to address the crowd. "Give me a minute to go to the bathroom," he said.

He walked into a bathroom, locked the door, and cried. "I hadn't really cried in Paris," he said. "My eyes were wet at the end and I felt emotional. But when I saw all those people and saw what it meant to them and how good it made them feel, it all got to me. I cried and cried for about five minutes. Later, when we got home, I cried again. It really was my dream come true."

15

TIRIAC

Ion Tiriac moved through the lavishly furnished restaurant with the ease of a man who is accustomed to spending time with the rich and famous. To eat here, the box holders' restaurant at Roland Garros, you had to be one or the other—preferably both.

Tiriac sat in a chair held for him by a tuxedo-clad waiter, lit a cigarette, inhaled deeply, and blew the smoke out through his nostrils the way an angry bull might snort at the sight of a matador dressed in red. He waved at someone across the room and said something to him in German that got a laugh. He then turned to the waiter and ordered lunch in French.

He took another drag on the cigarette, shook his head, and, in English, said, "I'm not going to take the shit for this one. Bob can take it or Boris can take it because it's their decision. I think it is a big mistake and I told them that. But they don't want to hear it."

What Bob Brett and Boris Becker didn't want to hear was Tiriac's firm opinion that Becker should get himself on a plane that afternoon and fly from London to Paris for the International Tennis Federation's champions' dinner. It had been seven days since Becker's crushing first-round defeat in the French Open.

Each year, the ITF holds the champions' dinner on the second Tuesday of the French. "I told him that he may win this award again many times before he is through playing, or he might not, but one thing for sure is that he'll never win it for the first time again. Sportsmen never understand that respect is much more important than love. People love you today, hate you tomorrow, don't care about you day after tomorrow. But you can *make* them respect you *if* you respect them. I remember seven, eight years ago McEnroe flew in to accept the award. Probably took him six hours. He chartered a plane, shook a few hands, said thank you very much, and left. People still talk about that. Do they *love* McEnroe? No. But they respect him. Boris could charter a plane, he could charter the whole damn airline if he wants.

"But he won't. He says I don't understand him. Again. I understand Boris because I'm the same way. If someone tells me ten times not to do something I will always do it. That's Boris. Fine. But the sad thing is ninety percent of the athletes in the world have no life after sports. Boris will have one. But the one thing *all* athletes have is their memories."

The face that Ion Tiriac shows most of the world is a pragmatic one. He is a very shrewd, very wealthy businessman. At fifty-one he remains an intimidating physical presence with the wild curly hair, the huge mustache, and the mammoth hands that he often uses to clap people on the back so hard that if they are lucky they will begin breathing normally again a couple of hours later.

He is the ultimate deal-maker, a man who learned long ago how to play every angle available to him, whether on a tennis court, where his gamesmanship became legendary, or in a smoky room (most of the smoke created by Tiriac) cutting a deal.

Tiriac is, first and foremost, an agent. All agents begin stalking players routinely when they are in 12-and-unders (especially the girls), and often unofficial deals are in place with kids still playing junior tennis. The street goes both ways: Clever parents will often play agents off against one another, seeing what kind of guarantees they offer, what kind of deals they promise, how many wild cards they can produce. The agents don't even blink at this. It is all part of the business.

Tennis recruiting can be every bit as vicious as college-basketball recruiting is in the United States. There is one difference: In college basketball there are all sorts of rules that are always bent, frequently broken. In tennis, there are no rules. Anarchy reigns. That is why agents swarm junior tournaments, all of them carrying lists of names, buttonholing parents of players who may be as young as ten years old.

"If you sit back and think about the whole thing, it can make you kind of sick," said Bob Kain of IMG. "When I think of my son being recruited by an agent at the age of ten or eleven, I just think, 'That's impossible.' But it goes on all the time."

It is not easy to get Ion Tiriac—the tough-guy agent—to talk in sentimental terms. He has played this role for so many years—eating glass or swallowing cigarettes at parties, analyzing anything and everything coldly—that he is not comfortable talking about his boyhood in Romania, a country that was controlled once by fascists, later by communists.

His father died when he was ten. Tiriac remembers riding on the back of his father's bicycle as a little boy, remembers how much he enjoyed their brief time together. But the memory of his father that is most vivid dates back to World War II, when he was so tiny he really didn't understand exactly what was going on.

"We lived in a small apartment building with a number of different people in it. Downstairs, there was a Jewish couple. Next door, there was a German. A few others. One day, my father came up with the Jewish couple. He told me we were playing a game, that they were going to hide in the closet and if anyone came in, we weren't going to tell anyone they were in the closet. The Nazis came in, asked some questions, and left. Didn't even search the apartment. "Two years later, the Russians came through. They were looking for Germans. My father hid the German and told me again we were playing a game. Only when I was older did I really understand what he had done. He never saw anyone as a German or a Jew or as anything else. He saw *people,* in this case people who needed help. I never forgot that."

Tiriac became an athlete his father would have been proud of. He was an Olympian—in hockey—but soon figured out that hockey players almost never left Romania. Tennis players did. So he turned his attention to tennis when he was already in his early twenties.

Because he was not a great player himself, because he never got to hold a Wimbledon or French Open trophy, Tiriac wants the players he is associated with who have the ability to do those things to do them—over and over, if possible.

"When I stopped playing tennis, the transition for me was easy," he said. "I was always the one picking up the check, organizing things with the other players—[Ilie] Nastase, [Adriano] Panatta. Whomever I was with. For me to begin coaching players and then managing them was natural because I was doing it while I was still playing."

As his playing career was winding down, Tiriac began to work with Nastase. The two were complete opposites: Nastase had all the natural gifts and flair for the game that Tiriac never had. If he had had Tiriac's brain to go with it, he might never have lost a match. But no matter how hard Tiriac tried, he couldn't get Nastase to listen to him, to buckle down to the game long enough to dominate the sport. The memory of Nastase's wasted genius still haunts him and affects his relationship with Becker.

"People are always telling me I should lie back and enjoy what I have, that I have enough in my life," he said. "But I can never shake my memory of Nastase. Nothing has ever frustrated me more. With Nastase's talent he should simply have presented himself every Sunday to collect the winner's check. He won Roland Garros once and the U.S. Open once. Wimbledon, never. How can that be? How can Nastase have won less Grand Slams than Jan Kodes? This is impossible.

"But it happened that way. Boris has won Wimbledon three times, the U.S. Open one time. I say to him, 'So what?' You should win five, six, seven Wimbledons. He hasn't won Roland Garros or Australia. Why not? Three weeks before this tournament he arrives in the final of fucking Hamburg and loses to Juan Aguilera.

"Aguilera is a fine player, very fast. But my son, if he trains another three years, can beat Aguilera if he plays right. And Boris Becker? He *cannot lose* to Aguilera if he plays him right. Aguilera can't hurt him. But Boris is playing three yards behind the baseline, so he loses.

"I have said to him that the reason he wins on grass all the time is because he has no choice. He *has* to come in—that's the only way to play. Five years ago, everyone said he tried to hit the ball too hard all the time. Fine, so he changes. But you don't go all the way the other way. I cannot be right on this, though. He has to figure this out for himself. It can't come from me.

"If I thought about him all the time I would give myself an ulcer. People say now I don't care about him anymore because I'm not there with him in the locker room every match. He doesn't *need* that anymore. This is a different Boris than five years ago. I could make him five, six, seven times more money than he is making but he won't let me.

"Okay, fine. Money is like health. You only appreciate health when you are sick. You appreciate money when your kids are crying with hunger and you don't know if you are going to be able to feed them tonight or tomorrow. As a manager, I do what Boris wants me to do. As someone who cares about him as a tennis player, it is very hard for me to sit back and say nothing.

"Last fall, when he wanted to retire, I said to him, 'If you want to do this at twenty-two, that's fine. But you have a responsibility because of your talent. What can be more exciting than to be the best you can possibly be at something? What is more of a challenge in life than that?' "

Ultimately, that is what drives Ion Tiriac. He says when Becker quits—"I hope he lasts until thirty"—he will get out of tennis management.

Tiriac still wants to do things others haven't done. That is why he becomes animated when the subject of television comes up. "I will make a fortune in Romania, I'm convinced of that," he said. "But what would excite me is television. It is developing so fast. Nobody knows what Europe is going to be like in '92. Will Eurovision survive? Who knows. But something like that would interest me. Running it, owning it."

He smiled. "You see, I am a very rich man. I am rich because I can buy dinner at the most expensive restaurant in Paris and then buy a hundred more of them, no problem. I can charter a plane tonight if I need to. But I am also very poor. I cannot afford to buy Eurovision. I need someone else to say, 'This guy is not an idiot,' and let me run it. When I first came into Germany with my ideas, I was either going to get sent to jail, shot, or made minister of finance. The same thing would happen with TV. In Germany, it worked out. This time, who knows?"

Tiriac is a very smart man in a business where many people aren't terribly smart and few people are as smart as he is. He is multilingual—"I speak no language well but I know how to say, 'I am innocent,' in every language there is." Money may have driven Tiriac once; after all, he grew up without very much of it. He is still in business to make money—as much of it as he can.

Now, though, history drives him, wanting to be part of it through Romania, through television, through Becker. Becker remains a source of great pride and great frustration.

"I am strictly a manager now," he said. "But the thing I enjoy most is coaching. I think it is what I do best. I like to be with the player, to be involved with the player. In '87, when Boris split with [Gunther] Bosch, I coached him and I thought he played some of his best tennis early that year. But he wanted to work with Bob, and Bob is very, very good. We have separate departments now. Bob is on the court, I am off the court.

"If I had the choice, I would still be on the court. That's not the direction my life has gone in, though. Ten years ago [Mark] McCormack said to me that I was wrong, that I could not put so much feeling into a tennis player. I can't do it any other way, though. I put feeling into Nastase, into Vilas, into Leconte, into Boris."

He leaned forward, eyes blazing. "I was one of the best competitors *ever.* That's what I want Boris to be. He says it is hard for him to get up to play the first round of a Grand Slam. I understand that. But if you lose in the first round, then *it* is the final.

"When you are Boris Becker, you have to establish yourself in the first fifteen minutes of a match. These young dogs will rip your tail off if you don't chop their head off first. Simple as that. The loss here hurt him very much. That is why he doesn't want to come back for the award tonight. He says Paris is past, he wants to forget, that the dinner is about last year anyway.

"I can't be Boris. I can't sit in his chair and make him understand. I wish I could. I have to adjust my hopes to make them his hopes. Boris has thousands of friends now because he is on top. Someday, he may have only two or three. I tell him to look at his friend Bobo [Zivojinovic]. Four years ago he is Wimbledon semifinalist and everyone is his friend. Now, he can't find anyone who wants to practice with him.

"I want him to be happy. I want him to be a champion. I can't make him a champion. Only he can do that. You might say the guy is already a champion. He is. But is he? Can he do more? Of course he can, much more. That's what I want for him."

More. Always, Ion Tiriac wants more. Even now, when he has almost everything. For him, almost has never been good enough.

PART FOUR

THE GRASS

16

QUEEN'S

There is no sport in the world with a stranger schedule than tennis has. There are four months between the end of the first Grand Slam of the year (Australia) and the start of the second (France). Then there is a grand total of two weeks between the end of the French and the start of Wimbledon. In fact, since the U.S. Open begins only seven weeks after the conclusion of Wimbledon, the last three Grand Slams are played over a period of fifteen weeks.

There are no six weeks more frenetic or hectic in any major sport than those beginning on day one of the French and ending the last Sunday at Wimbledon.

In recent years, more and more players—almost all of them men—have started to skip one of the two tournaments. They claim it is just too tough to work for two months on clay, then switch to grass only two weeks before Wimbledon begins. Clay-court specialists use this as an excuse to skip Wimbledon all the time. Andre Agassi is the prime example, but he is not alone by any means. In 1990 no fewer than seven clay-courters ranked in the top twenty skipped Wimbledon.

Some go the other way, refusing to play in Paris. Brad Gilbert, who has been ranked in the top twenty for the past six years, last played the French in 1987. He has played there just four times, winning two matches—total. Tim Mayotte, a five-time Wimbledon quarterfinalist, also has two career victories in Paris. After skipping the tournament for three years, he started playing there again in 1988 "because I realized the Grand Slams, all of them, *are* tennis, no matter what the surface."

The truly great players understand this. It is why Becker and Edberg, both Wimbledon champions, want so much to win in Paris. It is why Pete Sampras, after reinjuring his hip flexor four weeks before the start of the French, wanted to go back and play there in spite of a doctor's advice to wait. "I know clay is my weakest surface," he said. "But how am I going to learn to play on it without going back and playing?"

Two players who had long ago proved themselves as champions

skipped the French in 1990: Ivan Lendl and Martina Navratilova. Each had won there—Lendl three times, Navratilova twice—and each desperately wanted this Wimbledon, although for entirely different reasons.

In 1987, Navratilova tied Helen Wills Moody's record of eight Wimbledon singles titles, but she lost the next two finals in a row to Steffi Graf. At thirty-three, she knew time was running out, and she wanted number nine more than she had ever wanted anything in tennis. Lendl had turned thirty in March, and he, too, was aware of time. His Wimbledon goal was far more modest than Navratilova's: He just wanted to win it once.

Lendl had once been as disdainful of Wimbledon as Agassi is. In 1981, clearly not interested in the match and just going through the motions, he lost in the first round to an Australian named Charlie Fancutt. A year later he skipped the tournament completely, claiming he was allergic to grass. Then he went off and played golf, which, as near as anyone could tell, was also played on grass. He has since lived to regret both the Fancutt match and the golf outing because those were years he should have been developing his grass-court skills. Now, having won the other three Grand Slam titles, Lendl freely admits to an obsession with winning Wimbledon.

Two things changed Lendl's approach to Wimbledon. One was his relationship with Tony Roche, the crusty Australian who has coached him since 1985. Roche was a French Open champion and a runner-up at both Wimbledon and the U.S. Open. Like most Australians, he has a great appreciation for the game's traditions, and he preached to Lendl the importance of Wimbledon.

"Ivan understands that as great a career as he's had, not winning Wimbledon would leave a void," Roche said. "He wants to be absolutely certain when he's fifty that he can look back, whether he wins Wimbledon or not, and know that he did everything he possibly could to try to win it."

Roche's influence was one factor in Lendl's changeover. The other was money. Lendl is candid about the fact that when he first left Czechoslovakia, he was obsessed with making money, with becoming the ultimate capitalist and acquiring material things in great quantity.

"When I was growing up, the thing that drove me in tennis was the idea that it could get me out of Czechoslovakia," he said. "That was my goal. Probably, it is the goal for most Eastern Europeans who play tennis. Or at least *was* the goal, until all the changes. But that was what motivated me. Then when I got out, for a while, I didn't really have any motivation. I had done what I wanted to do. Money became a motivation, but eventually you realize you need more than that, especially when you get older. Gradually, my focus changed to winning Grand Slams.

Lendl still makes plenty of money and is a rabid right-wing Reagan/ Bush Republican. When someone mentioned to Lendl, during a conversation about the 1988 presidential election, that he had voted for Michael Dukakis, Lendl grinned and said, "Oh, so you are Communist."

"No, I'm a Democrat."

"Same thing," Lendl answered, with a smile.

The Americanization of Ivan has been one of the more interesting stories in tennis during the past ten years. Once, Lendl used to come to postmatch press conferences only after Jerry Solomon promised to cut them off if the questions strayed at all from tennis. He was defensive and disdainful, never smiling, partly because he didn't find anything very funny, partly because he was embarrassed by the fact that his front teeth were crooked.

Eventually, he got the teeth fixed. His English improved steadily to the point where, except for the occasional dropped article (Lendl never says someone is *a* nice guy, he always says, "He is nice guy"), it is just about perfect. He's comfortable now with the press, often joking, even lingering after press conferences for a few minutes to chat with reporters he knows. When he showed up late for a Wimbledon press conference a year ago, he started by saying, "Sorry, guys [*guys* is Lendl's favorite word], I was in locker room trying to think up good quotes for you." He has become a big fan of the Hartford Whalers hockey team—he's now on their board of directors and does TV commercials for them—and a true golf junkie. Lendl is one of the few top players on tour who likes to play the first match of the day. That way, he can get in at least eighteen holes before dark.

"Few years ago, in Stratton Mountain, [tournament director] Jim Westhall called me one night and said, 'Ivan, I'm really sorry, but all top players requested late starts except you, so I stuck you with first match at ten A.M. I promise I will make it up to you.' I said, 'Fine, Jim, you owe me one.' Of course, I was thrilled because it meant I got to golf course by one o'clock."

During the U.S. Open, Lendl has his postmatch routine down to a science. As soon as his match is over, he walks into the catacombs beneath the stadium and goes directly to the private bathroom in the USTA office. There, he changes into clean clothes. He walks out of the office, meets Samantha, and goes to his interviews—TV and then print, or vice versa, depending on the time of day. Those finished, he goes out the back door of the interview room, turns left, then right, and walks about two hundred yards to his car. He is off the grounds no more than thirty minutes after his match ends, and can be on the first tee back home within ninety minutes of shaking hands.

Lendl is about an eight handicap, although friends point out that he plays with a lot more confidence at home than on the road. "Playing the same course every day, he'll shoot consistently in the seventies," said Christo van Rensburg, who frequently drives the fifty miles from his home in Great Neck to work out and play golf with Lendl. "Put him on another golf course, and he can shoot anything from seventy-five to ninety-five."

Lendl becomes far more animated when talking about golf than tennis. One is a job, the other a passion. On the golf course, Lendl bets on everything, the bets ranging from something as boring as one dollar to something as strange as twenty push-ups, depending on what kind of shape his opponent is in. He is the same way about Scrabble (he loves to discover a new word and throw it out during a press conference, hoping no one will know what it means), about the dogs he trains, about his involvement with the Whalers, about his art collection, and about the mansion he is building—and designing—in northwest Connecticut.

The plan is for the house to be 37,000 square feet—"only twenty-four thousand if you don't count gym and swimming pool," Lendl points out—and that is where he and his family will settle when he is finished playing tennis. "It will take about two more years to finish," he said. "By then, I should be near end of my career. I figure if you are building house you want to live in for the rest of your life, you should do it right."

That is the Lendl approach to everything. If you are going to do it, do it right—to the point of obsession, some would say—or don't bother at all. That is why he has become almost disdainful of almost any tournament in tennis that is not connected to one of the Grand Slams.

Now, his goals in tennis center on his role in the game's history He understands what Pete Sampras understood so clearly when he noted, much to Marilyn Fernberger's dismay, "No one remembers who wins in Philadelphia."

That is why he has built his schedule of the last five years around winning Grand Slams. He leaves for Australia a month early to get used to the heat and to train with Roche. He picks his tournaments less now on the basis of guarantees than on where they are scheduled in terms of the next Grand Slam.

The work has paid off in eight Grand Slams—three French, three U.S. Opens, and two Australians. The notion of skipping the French to prepare for Wimbledon first occurred to Lendl in 1988, after he lost at Wimbledon in a four-set semifinal to Becker. He had also lost the final there in 1986 and 1987 (to Becker and Pat Cash) and wondered if skipping the clay might make him that much sharper for the grass and get him over the last hurdle.

Interestingly, the first person to counsel against the notion was Roche. "I told him it was a hell of a gamble, that he would really be putting all his eggs in one basket," he said. "It could cost him the number one ranking, because of all the tournaments he missed, and it would certainly add pressure at Wimbledon. I didn't say, 'Don't do it.' I just said, 'Give it some more thought.'

Lendl did just that. There is almost nothing he does without a great deal of thought. Lendl has little use for spontaneity or improvisation. He is a creature of habit, someone who likes to do things the same way year after year. Stay at the same hotels or in the same flat. Eat at the same restaurants, train at the same courts. He is completely organized all the time. He can tell you almost to the minute exactly what he is going to do on a given day.

"I'm not saying my way is the right way for everyone," he said. "In fact, it's pretty obvious it is wrong way for a lot of guys. Some guys just couldn't do things the way I do them. It works both ways, of course. I can't be McEnroe or Becker, and they can't be me. But I have figured out that for me to be successful I need to do certain things certain way. So I do them exactly the way I am most comfortable."

Lendl decided to play in the French Open in 1989, after winning the Australian to start the year. In the back of his mind was the outside possibility of winning all four Grand Slams in one year. As it turned out, he lost in Paris—to Chang—and then lost what may be the most agonizing match of his career to Becker in the Wimbledon semis.

"Nothing is ever a sure thing, but if it doesn't rain, I think Ivan wins that match," Roche said. "You could see looking at Boris that he was down on himself, discouraged. The rain delay saved him."

That was the rain delay during which Bob Brett called Becker a loser and a quitter and stirred him into raising his game. Lendl is not a player who can adjust to his opponents' emotions. He plays the same way all the time. Becker turned the momentum around and won in five. Lendl was devastated.

"It was one of the few times after a loss I really needed some time alone," he said. "I just couldn't talk to anyone. I thought I was going to win the match and play Stefan in final."

The last time Lendl and Edberg met at Wimbledon was in the 1987 semifinals. Lendl won. Edberg had grown as a player since then, but so had Lendl. His chances would have been pretty good. Instead, Becker beat Edberg in straight sets. Lendl had already taken the Concorde home and was in his Greenwich, Connecticut, mansion by the time the final was played.

That match convinced him to skip the 1990 French. "If I could get that close playing Paris, I thought extra preparation might be the difference," he said. "I told Tony in August I was going to do it."

As always, Lendl had a carefully mapped plan. He had to play in Tokyo at Suntory the second week in April because of his Mizuno contract (and a $250,000 guarantee), but from there he planned to go to Australia to train on the grass for three weeks. Then he would return to Connecticut for the birth of his daughter.

This had been planned, too. Lendl's longtime girlfriend, Samantha Frankel, had gotten pregnant just before the U.S. Open, and the two of them had been married right after the Open. The only hitch in the plan was Samantha's morning sickness the day of the wedding. "I thought it was time to start a family," Lendl said. "After all, once you are past thirty, if you don't have children, it's pretty hopeless."

Samantha is only twenty-two, but that was Lendl's way. He was turning thirty in March, so it was time. Get married, have a baby, begin planning a 37,000-square-foot home to live in with wife and child.

And win Wimbledon.

Marike Lendl was born on May 4. Two weeks later, she and her parents flew to London and set up housekeeping in the three-story house in Wimbledon Village that would be their home, they hoped, for the next six weeks. The baby slept on the first floor, the father on the third, with the mother shuttling back and forth.

"I know this sounds terrible, but at least until Wimbledon is over, I have to get my sleep," the father said. "When we get home, I will help out more."

Lendl began practicing with Roche, playing some exhibitions and honing his grass-court game. By the time Gomez received the trophy in Paris, Lendl had already been in London for two weeks and had played in an exhibition tournament outside the city. Like the players who had huddled around the TV in the Queen's Club players' lounge to watch the final, Lendl was thrilled when Gomez won in Paris.

"He's one of the good guys in the game," he said. "He's worked long time. And the other guy [Agassi] is so bad for tennis. He's just a bad guy. I thought Muster was a jerk, but this guy is much worse."

Lendl may have been sensitive about Agassi because he could see a little of himself ten years earlier in him: the money chasing, the lack of respect for the game's traditions, the Wimbledon ducking. But Lendl's excesses were more understandable: He had grown up without material things. Agassi didn't grow up wealthy, but he did have a tennis court in his backyard. Lendl has outgrown a lot of his immaturity. Agassi is so surrounded by sycophants, a lot of people wonder if he ever will.

The first day at Queen's always provides stark contrasts to the last day in Paris. Almost invariably the weather is cold and rainy, as opposed to the warmth and sun of Roland Garros. This year was no exception. The day was bleak and windy, the temperature climbing no higher than fifty.

The Queen's Club (*not* Queens Club, but *The* Queen's Club, as in Buckingham Palace) has been at Baron's Court in west London for more than one hundred years. It is the very picture of a venerable English club, with its gabled, red-brick clubhouse sitting next to center court so that members can sit outside on the three balconies and watch the matches, or retreat inside to the bar if it gets either too boring or too brisk outside.

Most of the five thousand seats at center court are part of the temporary stands that are put up only during the tournament. Three outside courts are used, two of them with temporary bleachers, one with no bleachers but just some lawn chairs. Queen's has a feeling of intimacy that few of the world's tennis venues can match. Since there is almost no parking near it, most of the tournament's spectators come by underground, alighting at the Baron's Court stop, turning right at the station exit, and walking two blocks down to the main gate.

Once, Queen's was called the London Grasscourt Championships, and men and women played in the tournament. It has always been *the* men's warm-up for Wimbledon, but, like most tennis tournaments, it gave in to corporate sponsorships in the 1970s. Now, the tournament bears the name of a Belgian beer—the Stella Artois Grasscourt Championships.

o

Under any name, Queen's almost always draws an excellent field—it ends eight days before Wimbledon begins, the courts are generally considered the best grass courts in the world (yes, better than Wimbledon's), and its intimacy and location make it a tournament the players love.

This year, though, the field was even stronger than usual. Lendl had planned to play all along. So had Edberg. But Becker took a wild card after losing early in Paris. And John McEnroe, figuring it was now or never after four months off, was at Queen's for the first time since 1984. McEnroe had been involved in a run-in with the wife of one of the club's board members in 1985—she couldn't understand why the defending Wimbledon champion wouldn't get off *her* court and he couldn't understand why she was so offended when he called her a name women the world over find rather offensive. Five years later, all had been smoothed over, and McEnroe was coming back.

The most intriguing match of the blustery first day involved Pat Cash. Three years earlier, Cash had won Wimbledon with an extraordinary performance, dropping just one set in seven matches. He was only twenty-two, and it seemed likely that he, Becker, and Edberg would be the dominant names at Wimbledon for a long time to come.

But Cash, who had come back from a serious back injury to become Wimbledon champion, began having problems almost from the moment he bowed to the Duke and Duchess of Kent on center court. He had been labeled as the next great Australian hope as a junior, and had been in the limelight since 1984, when he reached both the Wimbledon and U.S. Open semifinals at age nineteen. But, somehow, winning Wimbledon was too much for him.

"I had always felt great pressure to win," he said. "That was nothing new to me. People forget what a small country Australia is. Everything I had done was news. I had a temper, and I became a bad boy. The journos [journalists] were all over that long before I won Wimbledon.

"But when I won, instead of sitting back and saying, 'My God, look what I've done,' I felt even more pressure. Most of it was self-inflicted. I felt like I had to win every match. Some people said I won only because Boris got upset in the second round. Frankly, I thought that was bullshit. I don't think anyone was going to beat me that year. But still, I responded to it. I got more and more uptight, and it certainly didn't help my tennis."

Cash was upset in the first round of the U.S. Open that year by a Swede named Peter Lundgren. He did manage to make the Australian final the following January but lost a superb five-setter to Mats Wilander. Personal problems, including a split with the mother of his two children, and various nagging injuries ruined the rest of 1988 for him, then, in April 1989, while playing in Japan, he went up for an overhead and felt his Achilles tendon snap. It was the second time he had been injured on that court, and it came in a tournament Cash would probably have liked to skip. But his racquet contract is with Yonex, a Japanese company, so Cash was in Tokyo—and in a hospital.

"I knew I wanted to come back," he said. "But I remembered how painful and difficult it had been to come back after my back injury. I'm not sure very many top athletes have come back from two major injuries like this. But I'm still young and I wanted to do it. I still don't think I've played my best tennis."

It took Cash almost nine months to get back on court. In Sydney, in January, he and Mark Kratzmann had won the doubles; he then played doubles with Edberg at the Australian. He started playing singles in March and, much to his surprise, won a tournament in Hong Kong in April. "That was much faster than I expected," he said. "But I have to remind myself, with an injury like this, it will probably take a year before I can seriously think about competing with the Top Ten again."

That fact was apparent at Queen's. Although he grew up playing often on clay, Cash has a game made for grass. He is as good getting to the net for his first volley as anyone in the game and seems never to miss a volley. His first-round opponent, though, was Paul Chamberlin, a solid grass-court player.

Chamberlin had, at the age of twenty-seven, been a quarterfinalist at Wimbledon in 1989, his first real breakthrough in the sport. That performance had put him comfortably into the top one hundred for the first time. But the aftermath of that performance had been disappointing.

Chamberlin had learned firsthand that when it came to commercial opportunities, a twenty-seven-year-old Wimbledon quarterfinalist and seventy-five cents would buy you a cup of coffee. Nothing more. The experience had left him with a sour taste in his mouth.

"The agents and the sponsors in this game are really only looking for the big hit," he said. "I guess I felt, coming out of Wimbledon, that there would be some opportunities for me. But there weren't. Everyone is looking to sign up sixteen-year-olds and hopes that one of them becomes Agassi or Chang. Guys like me are considered worthless."

While his Wimbledon performance didn't get Chamberlin any contracts, it did come at an opportune time, since he and his wife were expecting their first child in August. Chamberlin, who had never been ranked in the top one hundred, climbed as high as No. 49 after Wimbledon, finishing the year at No. 78. That meant, for the first time in his career, he could pick and choose his spots to play.

Chamberlin had never had it easy on the tennis tour. Although he came from an affluent background, his parents had told him he would have to make it on his own when he finished his eligibility at the University of Arizona and decided to turn pro. The twenty-two-year-old syndicated himself, raising $50,000 from businessmen he knew to pay expenses his first two years on the tour. In return, those in the syndicate got 15 percent of his gross prize money during his first *five* years on tour.

There were no wild cards waiting for Chamberlin, no agents at his door with contracts or guarantees. That may explain why he is so intense on court, the kind of in-your-face competitor that a lot of players don't like. Chamberlin says he had plenty of fun on tour his first couple of years, regardless of his financial struggles.

"I guess I fit the stereotype of the guy who did a lot of partying when he first came on the tour," he said. "The younger guys now are so serious, with all the money that's available and their entourages, that it isn't the same. But for me, it was just *there.* You'd walk out of any locker room anywhere in the world and the women were waiting. I had a lot of fun, although it probably didn't help my tennis."

He met his wife, Michelle, on an airplane—she was a flight attendant—late in 1986. They were married two months later. As his life-style quieted down, Chamberlin's tennis improved. With the baby due in 1989, he began playing better than he ever had. "I think that kind of pressure helped me," he said. "I like to set tangible goals for myself. If I make so much money, I can buy a car, things like that. We really wanted a new house last year, with the baby coming. After Wimbledon, we were able to do it."

A year later, Chamberlin was still ranked in the top one hundred, but with Wimbledon coming up, he knew he was going to be defending a lot of the points that had put him there. Drawing Cash in the first round at Queen's—with the winner to play Becker—was not exactly an ideal draw. He wanted badly to get at least one victory.

The crowd was clearly behind Cash. As a Wimbledon champion and a part-time resident of London—his flat is a fifteen-minute walk from Queen's—Cash has a following there. He lost the first set but came back to win the second, 6–1. It was almost six o'clock when the third set began, and the cold weather had turned even colder.

They were on serve, with Cash serving at 2–3, when Chamberlin got to break point. Cash served, and came in tentatively. Chamberlin's return almost went by him, but he lunged and hit a short backhand volley. Chamberlin closed and hit a forehand right at Cash. The ball glanced off his racquet—thrown up in self-protection—and Chamberlin had the break. Cash was furious, not with Chamberlin but with chair umpire Paulo Pereira.

"You didn't hear a let?!" he screamed, thinking his serve had been a let. Pereira had heard nothing. Chamberlin quickly held to 5–2 and served for the match at 5–3. Here, though, Cash dug in and hit three straight gorgeous winners to break back to 5–4. For a moment, he looked like a Wimbledon champion.

But only for a moment. Chamberlin immediately broke back to win the match, and Cash had a reminder of how long his road back was going to be.

Remarkably, the onetime Wimbledon champion was almost calm about his loss. "I didn't hit the ball badly today," he said. "I just can't put things together. I can hit one good shot or two, but I can't hit four. The fact that I can hit those two is a good sign, though. I just have to be patient."

This calm, philosophical approach was all part of the new Pat Cash. Every tennis player who starts out his career with a volatile reputation seems to reach a point down the road where he becomes a "new" person. Jimmy Connors's image was completely remade in his thirties. John McEnroe had been labeled "new" after he became a father. Someday, no doubt, there will be a "new" Andre Agassi.

All players certainly go through changes, but none are ever really "new." For all the marketing and packaging ProServ did with Connors, he remained as capable of turning obscene as any player in the game. McEnroe had shown in Australia just how mellow fatherhood had made him.

There was no doubting, however, that Cash had calmed down. A year earlier he had met Emily Bendit in a London nightclub. She was an American, as buoyant and happy as Cash was angry and depressed. A year later, they were living together (they were married in July 1989), and Cash had taken to wearing Greenpeace T-shirts. Where once he talked about how tough his life was and how much he hated all the attention, he now talked about how lucky he was to make so much money playing tennis.

"I've finally learned to enjoy life," he said. "I've met people outside tennis and had fun away from the game for the first time. I've realized there's a world out there that I can really enjoy. Em has changed my outlook on things completely."

So completely that not even a first-round loss at Queen's, in a match that ended on a double fault, could send Cash into a funk. "I've got two weeks to get ready for Wimbledon," he said. "I'll just see how it goes there."

One first-round loser who wasn't quite as sanguine as Cash was Paul Annacone. At twenty-seven, Annacone, unlike his contemporary Paul Chamberlin, *did* have shoe, clothing, and racquet contracts when he started on tour. But a few years later, when it was clear Annacone was not going to live up to his perceived potential, was certainly not going to become a "name" player, his first series of contracts ran out and weren't renewed. Annacone had signed agreements with Prince (racquets), Jantzen (clothes), and Nike (shoes) in 1984, at age twenty-one, after making it to the Wimbledon quarterfinals. He had just finished his junior year at the University of Tennessee and was viewed as a solid investment. Taken together, his contracts were worth about $100,000 annually.

For the next three years, Annacone was up and down the computer, getting as high as No. 13 in 1985. He was always in the top fifty and consistently in the Top Ten in doubles. But when his contracts were up in 1987, he found that no one really wanted to pay him anymore. "I was twenty-four and a half and they said I was too old," he said. "It wasn't like I was looking for six figures. But they were telling me I wasn't worth twenty thousand dollars a year. That really threw me for a loop. Now, I'm almost twenty-eight, and I feel lucky to have any contracts at all."

Annacone had made more than $1.3 million in prize money in his career. He and his wife, Tracy, whom he first met in the seventh grade, were building a dream house for themselves and their four-year-old son, Nicholas, back home in Easthampton, on the eastern end of Long Island.

But for the first time since he had turned pro, Annacone found himself worrying about how much longer he could continue to make a living on the circuit. He had missed two months in the spring because of a bad foot and had come to Queen's knowing his ranking was in jeopardy. He was already down to No. 65 and, having been a semifinalist at Queen's the year before, stood to take a real dive if he didn't have a good tournament.

He had drawn Marcus Zoecke in the first round. Other than having beaten Connors in Milan in the match in which Connors broke his wrist, Zoecke had done little to distinguish himself. But he was six feet five, with a huge serve. On grass, that is enough to be dangerous; on slick grass, even more so. Zoecke broke Annacone's serve once in the first set. Annacone broke Zoecke once in the second. Zoecke broke in the third. That was the match—three breaks, two of them for Zoecke.

And so, Annacone was faced with a huge drop in his ranking—he fell to No. 91—and questions about his future. "I'd like to play four or five more years," he said. "Let's face it, this is a great way to make a living. And I really haven't come up with anything else I want to do yet. I know I will, but I haven't yet."

To most people, Queen's would not really begin until Tuesday, when the big names would play for the first time. To Paul Chamberlin and Paul Annacone, that first cold, blustery Monday was extremely important. Their concern was not trying to win Wimbledon; it was trying to keep on making a living doing something they loved. In that sense, they were a lot more representative of what the sport is like than Lendl, Edberg, Becker, or McEnroe.

"One thing I really admire about those guys is that with all the money they've made, they still *really* want to play," Annacone said. "I'm not sure I would be that way if I had all they have. I might just want to go home and take it easy. But it's tough for me to even relate to the way they think. It's a whole different animal, a whole different life-style. It isn't anything the rest of us can understand, because we've never experienced it. It might as well be a different sport."

The question for John McEnroe when he arrived in London was whether he really did still want to play tennis. It had been almost four months since his loss to Reneberg in Philadelphia, and he had hardly played at all since then.

He had participated in a one-night charity exhibition with Agassi in Washington early in April, and had lost to him in three sets. Typical of an exhibition, the players had a tacit agreement to split the first two sets and then try in the third. McEnroe won the first set; then, after Agassi held serve to start the second, McEnroe walked to his chair and said, "I think the tide has turned in this one. Looks like it will go three."

Since the outcome meant nothing, the players looked at it as pure entertainment. There were 10,637 people in the Capital Centre outside Washington that night, some paying as much as $250 a ticket. They loved the whole Agassi–McEnroe show and didn't much care how hard the players were trying. It *looked* as if they were trying (and in the third set, they were), and they could all tell their friends they had seen Agassi–McEnroe.

Tanking and splitting sets were common at "special events" (promoters have done away with the dirty word *exhibition*). Players often scheduled their lives in such a way that making it to the final of a special event was a *bad* thing; it often ruined their tournament schedule. One top young player, who was willing to tell this story only if his name wasn't used, had played in a special event during the spring that had a Sunday final. The player had scheduled a flight to Europe for Saturday night; he was playing in a tournament there the following week. That meant he *had* to lose his semifinal on Saturday. He won the first set easily. Then he lost the next two sets, the third in a tiebreak. The crowd thought it was a great match, his opponent thought he had made a remarkable comeback, and the player caught his plane to Europe.

After the exhibition with Agassi, McEnroe and his family moved from Los Angeles to New York City. Each week when he was scheduled to play a tournament, McEnroe pulled out, citing a groin injury and a shoulder injury. Everyone working for the ATP Tour knew McEnroe *could* play, but no one ever questioned him.

"It's easier for them *not* to ask questions," he said. "They don't want to know what I'm really thinking. At my age, if you don't play with some nagging injuries, you don't play at all. I just didn't want to be on the tour, it was as simple as that. I've gotten to the point in my career where I feel like if I'm going to keep playing, I have to be like Connors—worry only about me. I don't necessarily like that, but it's pretty apparent no one *else* is going to worry about me. So I have to do it.

"The tour should be willing to let me play where I want, when I want. Does that sound selfish and self-serving? You bet. But are they better off with me playing when I want to or without me at all?"

At Queen's, the magic of the McEnroe name was still apparent. On the day he played his first match, against Ramesh Krishnan, the attendance was 6,877, a tournament record.

This was a match McEnroe was perfectly capable of losing. Krishnan's nickname among the players is "The Surgeon"—he can carve you up so delicately you don't even know that you're bleeding. At twenty-nine, he had twice been a U.S. Open quarterfinalist, and once a Wimbledon quarterfinalist. His father, Ramanathan, was a Wimbledon semifinalist in 1960 and 1961. Like McEnroe, Krishnan's game is all finesse and touch. Power means little.

"The two of us are like a couple of relics the way we play," McEnroe joked.

For a long time, it looked as if the Surgeon was going to make McEnroe's return to Queen's a brief one. He led 6–4, 4–1 before the older man found a rhythm and won eleven of the last twelve games to escape. "The best thing is, I didn't just bag it when I got behind," McEnroe said. "The last few years, when I get behind, I tend to start thinking, What the hell am I doing out here? instead of figuring out a way to come back and win. One of the things I want to do now is try to stay in every match, even if I lose. Just keep on trying until the end."

McEnroe had given some long, hard thought to quitting before he got on the plane to come to Europe. He had wondered if he actually wouldn't be happier without tennis than with it. He had finally decided to come back one more time—but only after giving himself a stern lecture about commitment.

"You know, last year when I was ranked fourth, people kept coming up to me and saying, 'Great comeback.' I thought to myself, What comeback? All I really did was keep it together enough that I played in a lot of tournaments. When I played, I almost couldn't help but win some matches. I never beat Lendl, Becker, or Edberg when it mattered. I got to the semifinals at Wimbledon, but I won my first match 8–6 in the fifth. I could have been gone in the first round. I got a little bit lucky.

"In some ways, I went backward. For the first time in my life I really didn't want to play Davis Cup. I didn't go and play the match in Germany because I had hurt my shoulder at Wimbledon and it was still a little sore. I could have played—but I didn't. I feel bad about that. But I wasn't sure if I even wanted to be part of the team anymore. The guys playing now are doing it for the money and because it's good publicity.

"I know that. They can talk until they're blue in the face and I'll know that's the truth about them. Brad Gilbert doesn't do anything unless it's for money. I know it, he knows it, everyone knows it.

"I think Tom Gorman is a nice guy, but he's not a fighter. When Arthur [Ashe] was captain, he and I weren't even speaking at times, but we respected each other because we both wanted to win, no matter what. Gorman always goes by the chalk, the easy way. He won't take a chance with a Courier or a Sampras. He'll let Markin push him around and make him play Agassi. If they win, Gorman ought to quit, tell them to take the job and shove it, but he won't.

"When I was away, I thought about how I used to love Davis Cup and now I don't. I thought about the tour and all the things I don't like about it. I thought about the default in Australia and all the people who were going around saying 'They got McEnroe' like it was some great victory. Did I want to come back to all that? No.

"But I also didn't want to go out like *this.* I feel like the last four years, I haven't really made a commitment to work at my game. I wasn't willing to give up enough socially, physically, mentally. If I want to play a couple more years, I have to do that. I have to slog through all those tournaments I don't want to play. Do my homework. I haven't done my homework for four years, and I've paid for it. I'm just not ready to be a former athlete yet. I like being an athlete. I like being part of the present. That's why I'm here. I'm not convinced this is the right thing to do, but it seemed like the best play for right now. So, I'm here."

After surviving the Surgeon, McEnroe won two more difficult three-setters, first from Veli Paloheimo, then from Richard Fromberg, a twenty-year-old six-foot-five-inch Australian with size fifteen feet. Fromberg had beaten Pete Sampras 10–8 in the final set the previous day to deny Sampras his first crack at McEnroe.

McEnroe's victory over Fromberg set up the dream semifinals everyone had hoped for. Lendl had ripped through his three matches without even losing serve once. Edberg had won his matches almost as easily. Becker, after beating Chamberlin in a tempestuous two-set match (Chamberlin had accused him of wearing illegal shoes at the start of the match), had barely survived Alex Antonitsch, coming from a set and a break down to win 9–7 in the third. Then he beat David Wheaton in the quarterfinals.

For Becker, coming to Queen's was like a homecoming. His first tournament victory had been here—in 1985. In the final, he had beaten Johan Kriek, then a Top Ten player. After the match, Kriek had said, "If he plays like that at Wimbledon, he can win the tournament." No one had paid much attention to the comment until three weeks later, when the Duke of Kent handed the Wimbledon trophy to Becker.

Being back at Queen's had slowly brought Becker out of his post-Paris funk. He had arrived in London still depressed, and the first few days had done absolutely nothing to change his mood. The weather, predictably, was lousy. His play was spotty and he was having technical problems with his serve. And with Wimbledon. The day after he arrived, he and Brett were driving past the front gate of the All England Club en route to a private court they were renting. Becker suddenly had an idea.

"Let's practice here," he said to his coach. "If I can't feel like I want to play tennis here, I won't feel it anywhere."

Brett thought the idea sensible, so they pulled onto the grounds and found an empty court. As a Wimbledon champion, Becker is an honorary member of the club. Only once had a Wimbledon champion not been offered membership after winning the title—McEnroe, in 1981. That rift had been sorted out after twelve months of negotiating. Becker had no such problems. But as he and Brett began to warm up, a member of the club's staff came on court. Brett was not a member of the club and the rules stated that members could not bring guests with them on weekends.

Becker and Brett were annoyed, embarrassed, angry. There was no arguing with the staff—there never is at Wimbledon—so the two men left. When John Curry, the new chairman of the club, heard what had happened, he was mortified.

"One thing we have to start doing more often is using common sense in enforcement of our rules," he said. "The rule is there so that amateur members don't overrun the courts with guests on the weekends. If every court had been packed, the situation would have been different. But they weren't. When they were through playing, someone should have had a word with Boris and asked him in future to ring up first before coming to play. But that's all that should have been done. Nothing more."

Later, Becker could laugh about it. "What is it about me that always finds trouble?" he said. At that moment, though, it hardly seemed funny.

Then came the row with Tiriac over the champions' dinner. "I was just starting to feel comfortable again in London, and he wanted me to come to Paris," Becker said. "He wanted me to come and smile and be a phony and act like I was happy to be there. I just couldn't do that."

When Queen's finally started, Becker wasn't comfortable with his game, but he felt pointed in the right direction. He was eager to play Edberg in the semifinals to see exactly where his game was. When he beat him, 6–4, 6–4, it was the most satisfying win he had had since the long-ago five-set victory over Mecir in Australia.

The story of this weekend, though, was Lendl. All the careful, painstaking preparation seemed to be paying off. For years, Lendl always struggled on grass, no matter who he played. Every match seemed fraught with potential disaster, even in the years when he made it to the Wimbledon final. "I think I would go five sets if I played my mother," he had once said after surviving a five-setter.

None of that was happening at Queen's. He dropped six games to Simon Youl, then three to Scott Davis and six more to David Pate. None were stars but all were competent grass-court players.

Next came McEnroe. It had been seven years since he had played McEnroe on grass—in the 1983 Wimbledon semifinals—but that had been a different McEnroe and a different Lendl. This year, McEnroe did no better than Youl and Pate, winning only six games.

"I never was able to shake his confidence," McEnroe said. "That's what you have to do with him. Once you do that, he's very fragile. But he's more confident now than he's ever been on grass. It will be interesting to see how he does against Becker."

The day of the final dawned hot and sunny. Queen's was a little bit like Noah's ark must have been when the rain finally stopped. People kept blinking their eyes as if they had never seen blue skies before. The umpires' green windbreakers and rain jackets were replaced by bright red blazers; the atmosphere was a bit like that of the opening day of a state fair.

For Lendl, the whole day was a party. He had to save four break points in the second game of the match, but once he did, he never looked back. He broke Becker in the next game and raced through the first set in thirty-five minutes. He broke at the start of the second and again to end the match. The score was 6–3, 6–2. It took all of seventy-three minutes. Lendl had broken four times; Becker, not at all. No one could remember seeing Becker dominated in this manner on grass—*ever.*

Becker realized early in the match that to make it close, he was going to have to give everything he had. He wasn't ready for that, mentally or physically. "It was too early to play at that level," he said later. "The Wimbledon final was three weeks away. I couldn't make myself do it. He played perfect tennis, but the conditions were very different than at Wimbledon."

Very different. For one thing, the grass at Queen's is so well conditioned that the courts play almost like hard courts. The ball bounces higher and truer—perfect for Lendl, who gets more chances to take a full swing at his ground strokes. At Wimbledon, the bounce would be lower and less consistent.

What's more, Lendl was not likely to play any better at Wimbledon than he had at Queen's. He had not lost his serve once in five matches, an extraordinary feat. "Everything has gone as well as it possibly could have," said Roche. "My only fear with this plan was that if Ivan lost early in the warm-up tournaments, he might not be match-tough going into Wimbledon. That won't be the case now. He will never be more ready to win Wimbledon than he is right now."

Lendl knew that. So did Becker and Edberg. Wimbledon was eight days away. Lendl was ready *now.* Becker and Edberg were just as glad to wait. And McEnroe? He still wasn't sure whether he belonged in England—or in tennis.

17

THE UMPIRES

Standing on the second-floor balcony of the clubhouse at Queen's Club, Gayle Bradshaw had an excellent view of center court. On that court, John McEnroe and Ivan Lendl were going at each other, the kind of matchup most tennis fans covet. Gayle Bradshaw likes tennis as much as anyone. But to him, McEnroe–Lendl was nothing more than a potential nightmare.

And that nightmare was becoming quite real. Midway through the third game of the match, McEnroe had gotten upset at one of the line judges about a call. Already, he had complained about three calls, all of them by the same man. Now, as the players changed sides, with Lendl having just broken serve to go up 2–1, McEnroe was angrily telling chair umpire Paulo Pereira that he wanted the line judge removed.

Bradshaw watched Pereira intently, hoping he wouldn't look up toward him. No such luck. As McEnroe walked away, Periera glanced toward the balcony and, ever so slightly, nodded his head. That was a signal to Bradshaw that he was needed on court.

Bradshaw was now in the same shoes that Ken Farrar had been in when he had been called on court in Australia. This was an ATP Tour event, not a Grand Slam, and Bradshaw, an ATP Tour supervisor, was in charge of the umpires and line judges. Tall and lean, a chain-smoking Oklahoman, Bradshaw had been the tournament referee at the U.S. Open for seven years until offered the chance to travel the world for the ATP. He liked his job and the people he worked with. But he dreaded days like this.

"All week, I had been hoping to avoid a confrontation with John," he said later. "I knew he was bound to come in uptight because he hadn't played for so long. I only had two pros working, which left me short-handed."

"Pros," in the vernacular of tennis officials, are full-time chair umpires, men and women who are paid full-time salaries to be umpires. It is a surprisingly young profession. The first two pros were hired by the

Men's Tennis Council in 1985. Prior to that, the only full-time officials had been supervisors. The women's game still didn't have any full-time pros, although Lee Jackson, the WTA supervisor of officials, had worked full-time as a supervisor and as a chair umpire for almost twenty years. The ITF also had pros working for it now, supervised by Ken Farrar.

The only pros working for Bradshaw at Queen's were Pereira and Gerry Armstrong. Bradshaw wasn't about to put a part-time umpire, even an experienced one, on a McEnroe match. Not this week, at least. That meant Armstrong and Pereira would have to take turns. The last time Armstrong had chaired a McEnroe match had been on January 21, in Melbourne. The entire tennis world remembered what had happened that day. Nonetheless, when McEnroe walked on court for his first match at Queen's, Armstrong was in the chair.

"Not exactly ideal," Bradshaw said later, shaking his head. "But I had to make a decision: Do I throw Gerry out there and get it over with for both of them, or do I take a chance on having Gerry work a semifinal between McEnroe and Lendl? I had to plan ahead. I finally decided that trouble was less likely during McEnroe–Krishnan than during McEnroe–Lendl, especially given the history between McEnroe and Lendl. I didn't want Gerry in the chair if trouble started between those two."

Bradshaw's plan worked. McEnroe was clearly less than pleased to see Armstrong in the chair for his first match and refused to acknowledge him at all—handshake, head nod, wave—afterward. That was okay, though. There were no problems. After his second match, to prove he was an equal-opportunity player, McEnroe also ignored Pereira. And when he got to the semifinals, Bradshaw had Pereira in the chair.

So far, so good.

But when he arrived for work on the morning of the semifinals, Bradshaw found out he might be in for a long day. McEnroe had gone out to warm up with Vitas Gerulaitis a couple of hours before the match. While the two of them were hitting, Scott Davis had launched a water balloon from the locker room that had landed right at Gerulaitis's feet. Under any circumstances, a water balloon exploding at one's feet on a tennis court is going to be a shock. In London, in a climate where underground stations were routinely evacuated at the first sight of an empty package, Gerulaitis jumped about five feet into the air.

That was the intended affect. Davis had been lugging the water-balloon launcher around the world with him the entire year. A number of players had become involved in launching the balloons at unsuspecting people; in New Zealand, doubles partners Luke Jensen and Charlie Beckman had almost been arrested after several passersby complained below their hotel window.

Davis was delighted with his direct hit on Gerulaitis. McEnroe wasn't. He screamed at Davis from the court and continued to scream at him when he got back to the locker room. He was shaking with anger before he was through.

Hearing all this, Bradshaw sighed and hoped—against hope—the match would be without incident. Now, it had taken all of three games for Pereira to signal for him from the balcony. Bradshaw ran down the steps and, as casually as was possible, wedged his way close to the court.

"He wants a switch," Pereira said quietly.

Bradshaw nodded. He had figured as much. Players often ask for line judges to be changed. Sometimes they are ignored. Sometimes the umpire will quietly switch two of the judges on court, perhaps taking someone off the service line and moving him to a baseline. Occasionally, if both players agree that someone is doing poorly and the umpire does, too, a line judge will be removed. Usually, though, to mask the removal from the crowd, a supervisor will send out an entirely new crew—line judges are usually rotated after one hour of play—so that the person being removed isn't singled out.

Once Pereira had told Bradshaw what McEnroe wanted, Bradshaw had a decision to make. McEnroe was clearly uptight, perhaps close to an explosion. If he gave him his change, it might calm him down. What's more, Bradshaw knew that there had been trouble between McEnroe and this line judge before. The scheduler he worked with at Queen's Club—each tour stop has a local referee who works with the pro supervisor—should not have put him on the match to begin with. Bradshaw decided to make a change.

He went back upstairs and began looking for a full set of line judges so he could make the change as quietly as possible. But this was the weekend. Most of the judges had either gone home or to the next tournament, so Bradshaw could find only three people before the next changeover. When the new line judges walked on court, the fans knew exactly what was going on. They hooted loudly. The bigger problem for Bradshaw was Lendl.

"That's big mistake," Lendl said to him. "If I want someone changed you better change him real quick. You guys always do things for him. Never for me."

Bradshaw knew Lendl felt this way. The funny thing was, he had never done anything for McEnroe before, not in all the years at the Open, not on tour. *He* had been the one who had defaulted McEnroe and Fleming at the Open in 1986. As the departing line judges passed McEnroe, he couldn't resist a dig. The line judge in question turned and took a step back toward McEnroe. Fortunately, his two colleagues interceded before anything could happen. Bradshaw walked off the court feeling miserable.

"I made a mistake," he said the next day. "Lendl was right. I should have just let it ride. But I was trying to calm things down. I should have at least waited until I could round up a full crew so it wouldn't be so obvious. I was really afraid Lendl was going to do something today [during the final], demand a change or something. If he had, I was just going to go out there and say, 'Ivan, you've made your point.' "

Bradshaw lit another cigarette. "Oh, well," he said. "On this job you live and learn."

The phrase the umpires use is "welcome to the job." Anyone who decides to make his living forty weeks a year as a tennis umpire or supervisor knows there is going to come a match, a day, or perhaps an entire week so miserable he will wish he had never heard of the sport of tennis.

"It happens to everyone," Richard Kaufman said. "The only question is *when,* not *if.*"

To many of the pros, Rich Kaufman is a role model. He was one of the first two pros hired by the Men's Tennis Council, along with an Englishman named Jeremy Shales. Kaufman made the program work just by being so damn good at the job that doubters were quickly silenced.

Kaufman was born November 22, 1950, and can still remember sitting in a music class, planning his thirteenth birthday party, when his teacher announced that President John F. Kennedy had been shot. He was the son of two teachers—his father was an economics professor at Penn State and his mother taught reading in the State College (Pennsylvania) school system.

Kaufman played tennis and basketball growing up but really wanted to be a baseball player. He ended up playing tennis at Hiram College, a small, twelve-hundred-student school in Ohio best known for its music program. After graduation, Kaufman went to the West Coast to work as a musician, doing a lot of studio-session backup work on keyboards. In 1976, he decided to enroll in a University of Southern California extension program in London to pursue a master's degree in international relations.

One morning the following summer, he drove north of London to Cumberland, hoping to get into the qualifying draw of a small tournament there. He couldn't and was about to leave for an afternoon seminar in Windsor when a man named Peter Quinn walked up and introduced himself. Quinn told Kaufman that the tournament was short of line judges for the day. Would he like to work? Kaufman was unsure. Quinn persisted. Kaufman finally agreed. He enjoyed the work and was good enough that Quinn arranged for him to work in the qualifying tournament at Queen's the next week. He arrived to learn that the qualifying had been moved indoors because of rain and that a flu bug had put most of the umpires in bed. "I worked ten chairs that weekend on the boards [wood courts], with no line judges," he said. "The courts were like lightning. It was two years' worth of training in two days."

Kaufman came out of the qualifying with a splitting headache and an offer to work the main draw at Queen's. An umpire had been born. For the next seven years, Kaufman took summers off from his job as a researcher at the University of Washington to work as an umpire. He worked his first Wimbledon in 1978 and by 1983 was good enough to chair the U.S. Open final. That match—between Ivan Lendl and Jimmy Connors—stands out in his mind because it is a shining example of how unprofessional umpiring in tennis was at the time.

"Connors got $175,000 for winning that day," Kaufman said. "I got $50 for working the match. It wasn't the money that bothered me, it was the notion that so much was at stake for the players, and they were working with what were essentially amateur officials."

Ever so slowly, the MTC was changing that. The first full-time supervisors had been hired in 1980; in 1985 Kaufman and Shales were hired as the first full-time umpires. From the very beginning, the program was second-guessed. Long entrenched part-time umpires resented the implication that officiating needed to be improved in the sport. Tennis is nothing if not glacial when it comes to moving forward, and it was no different within the officiating community.

Kaufman and Shales had a difficult time that first year. Some of their colleagues shunned them, at least in part out of jealousy. Why them and not me? went the thinking in many places.

"There were plenty of times that first year when the easiest thing to do would have been to just go home," Kaufman said. "But I would have felt like I was letting down a lot of people who had put their faith in me. The players wanted professional officiating. There was no doubt about that. But they didn't like the idea of seeing the same authority figures week in and week out. They tested me and they tested Jeremy quite a bit."

Kaufman thought the toughest part of the job often came on weekends, when he might have a tough semifinal with a player and have to umpire the final—with that same player—the next day. "One thing we've found now is that there's strength in numbers in this job," he said. "If you have a tough match with a player, regardless of why, it's good for both of you if you don't have to see him again the next day."

By the end of 1985, the MTC was looking to hire more officials. All over the world, experienced umpires lined up, hoping that Farrar and David Cooper, the program's administrator, would hire them. When the name of the new umpire was announced, the reaction was universal: *Who?*

The new hire was Richard Ings, who had just celebrated his twenty-first birthday. Like almost everyone in tennis officiating, Ings had started his career as the result of a fluke. As a teenager he played soccer, never quite reaching a strong enough level to make the Australian national team. He also refereed soccer matches on the side. One January morning, he happened to see an ad in the newspaper seeking volunteer line judges for the New South Wales Open at White City. Ings had played some tennis and thought it might be fun. So he applied.

After one day's training he was put to work. Within a year he was chairing doubles matches. In 1984, at nineteen, he worked his first Australian Open. By the following year he was working a men's semifinal there between Lendl and Edberg. That was when the MTC first noticed him and the first time Ings met Kaufman.

"I'd become fascinated by umpiring by then," he said. "There were so many different things that were involved in a match. I had watched just about everyone in Australia work and I honestly thought I was as good as any of them. But when I saw Rich work, I knew he was on a different level. He had such a calm, controlled manner.

"No one ever questioned him. What I found out from Rich is the thing that's key to all umpiring: It isn't the call that matters as much as your ability to sell the call. Most people can make the right call most of the time, but it's the tough calls at the tough moments that matter. And that's all salesmanship. If the players think you're *sure,* they aren't likely to question you."

Cooper and Farrar hired Ings in spite of his age and his lack of international experience. They liked his potential, but they also saw the hire as an easy compromise. They no longer had to choose among all the veterans scrambling for the job. Ings came on tour in the spring of 1986, looking even younger than he really was. "One of my first matches on the job, I had Yannick Noah in a match," he said. "I missed a call and Yannick shouted, 'Why do they send me a boy to do a man's job?' "

That entire year proved a major test for Ings and the entire program. The Grand Slams didn't want the MTC telling them who should umpire the big matches, and the USTA in particular was resentful of something—anything—new. As a result, Kaufman and Ings found themselves working as line judges on junior matches at times during the U.S. Open.

Kaufman was confident enough in his own skills that the USTA attitude didn't really bother him. Ings was not. This was his first long trip abroad; he was homesick and had been through a spate of "welcome to the job" matches. The topper came at the Open, when he finally got a chair. The match was between Emilio Sanchez and Thierry Champion. It was a long five-setter. At one point, Sanchez, unhappy with a call, playfully took his racquet and tipped a female line judge's hat off her head. Ings saw the act as playful and took no action.

"When you warn somebody, you get a feeling in your gut that tells you to do it," he said. "I didn't have that feeling."

The match ended on a Sanchez drop shot that Champion, or so Ings thought, raced in and got to, tapping it back. Unfortunately, Ings was the only person in the state of New York who thought Champion had reached the ball on one bounce. Sanchez simply caught the ball, thinking he had won the point. Ings called game, set, and match for Champion. Sanchez looked at him in disbelief. "You thought he got to that?" he asked.

Ings nodded. Sanchez looked at Champion. "Oh, no," Champion said. "I'm not giving you the point. I just got screwed on another call down at this end."

It ended that way. Ings walked off court miserable, certain he had blown the call. That proved to be the least of his worries. When he got back to the umpire's lounge, he learned that the female line judge had filed a complaint against him with the supervisor, saying he had failed to back her up when Sanchez tipped her cap off her head. Ings was sternly lectured and had to be talked off several ledges by Kaufman.

But he survived. And so did the program. Gerry Armstrong was hired the next year and the fraternity continued to grow. Ironically, one year after he had been a goat at the Open, Ings became a hero. Working a match on the stadium court between McEnroe and Slobodan Zivojinovic, he became embroiled in one of McEnroe's more infamous scenes, when McEnroe went crazy at the end of the second set, spewing profanities in every direction.

Ings calmly gave him a warning, a point penalty, and a game penalty. As McEnroe raged on, Ings, in a voice filled with ice, said quietly, "All right, John, I think I've had enough of this conversation." The boy of twenty-one who had blown the Sanchez–Champion match had become a man of twenty-two, able to stand up to John McEnroe, who calmed down and managed to win the match in five sets. When Ings came off court, Kaufman and Armstrong were waiting for him. This was well beyond "welcome to the job." Ings had gone toe to toe with McEnroe on TV, in front of millions of people around the world. His name and picture would be in every newspaper the next morning. He was completely drained. Armstrong and Kaufman took him in hand that evening to make sure he knew he had done a good job.

When Ings looked at the tape with Farrar, he knew he had done well. The next morning, when he walked into the morning meeting of the umpires, he received a standing ovation. Just as Armstrong would feel uncomfortable two and a half years later, when people began congratulating him for defaulting McEnroe, Ings felt uncomfortable with the applause. He had done his job and had gotten through a tough match without a default. But he didn't feel like any sort of hero. Ings was supposed to go home that day, having put in one week at the tournament. He was exhausted. But Farrar felt he should stay and work one more match, to "show the flag." He was assigned a match the next day between Anders Jarryd and Lendl. His request that the umpire not be introduced was denied by the USTA.

"The guy said my name and twenty thousand people booed," he said. "I looked over and Lendl was cracking up. He loved it." By 1989, the umpires had become a genuine on-tour fraternity. Farrar had strict no-fraternization rules, requiring that they not stay in the same hotel with the players or even dine in the same restaurants. Those rules made the group even more close-knit than it might otherwise have been. Nicknames abounded: Armstrong nailed Ings with "Skippy" shortly after the movie *"Crocodile" Dundee* came out; it has stuck like glue. Dana Loconto, with his drawling Alabama accent, is "Bubba," and Kaufman is always "Coffers."

Armstrong is the funniest member of the group. He is the only one with genuine lineage in officiating: His father, George Armstrong, was a

Wimbledon umpire for years. He worked both the men's and women's finals and got Gerry started working lines in 1973.

In 1988, one year after joining the MTC, Armstrong worked the Wimbledon final. That made him half of the first father-son combination to have worked Wimbledon finals. It also marked a rite of passage. "Until then I was always 'George's boy' at Wimbledon," Armstrong said. "Now he's retired, and when he comes back there, he's 'Gerry's dad.' "

That Wimbledon final, between Becker and Edberg, was rained out Sunday at 4–4 in the first set. On Monday, after a long delay, the players got in a set and two more games before it rained again. When they came out to warm up a second time, Armstrong instructed the ball boys to use the balls that had been in play for the warm-up and then put new balls into play—it was two games until a ball change would be made, and a warm-up is considered to be two games long. The match began again and Armstrong happened to look down at the foot of the chair. There sat the new balls.

"I panicked completely," he said. "My first thought was that everyone in the stadium and everyone watching on TV knew I hadn't double-checked to make sure the new balls had been put in play. I was really miserable. First Wimbledon final, and I had messed it up. Then I realized that no one knew. The players didn't know and neither did anyone else. So, I just waited two games and called for new balls. It wasn't a problem. But it scared me half to death. I could see the headlines in the tabloids right before my eyes."

There are now ten full-time umpires on the ATP Tour and five full-time supervisors. Not everyone who is hired succeeds at the job. At the start of 1990, Chris O'Brien, a twenty-year-old Australian, was hired. David Cooper introduced him to his new colleagues as "the next Richard Ings."

It didn't work out that way. At his very first tournament, in Adelaide, O'Brien worked a difficult semifinal between Thomas Muster and Sergi Bruguera. Bruguera's father, Luis, is one of many coaches who gives his player instructions from the stands. Watching him closely during the final-set tiebreak, O'Brien saw him signaling to his son.

O'Brien had a choice here. Coaching goes on at almost every match on the tennis tour. Umpires rarely penalize a player for being coached unless it is blatant. This was blatant. It was also in the middle of a deciding tiebreak. O'Brien called it. That was a warning. Bruguera then argued at length. When he kept on arguing, O'Brien gave him a point penalty.

"So far," Ings said later, "he's doing well. You can go either way on the coaching, but if it was blatant, fine, call it."

But in the confusion, O'Brien somehow lost track of the score. When Muster hit a winner to make the tiebreak score 6–1, O'Brien thought it was 7–1. He called, "Game, set, match, Muster." It got embarrassing after that. Muster told him he had the score wrong. The supervisor had to come out and straighten things out. Muster won the match for *real* two points later, but the damage had been done.

Ings and Armstrong were waiting for O'Brien when he came off court. "Welcome to the job," they said and carted him off for several beers and a review of events.

That was all fine. Baptism by fire and all that. Except things didn't get better for Chris O'Brien. He was a bright, funny guy who everyone liked. But when the older umpires tried to counsel him after he made mistakes, he had answers, explanations.

"There's never been an umpire born that's perfect," Kaufman said. "We all tend to be suspicious of those who think they are."

At the Lipton, Kaufman attempted to talk to O'Brien about how he had adjudicated a couple of situations and found him unwilling to listen. "When Rich Kaufman tells you something and you think you know the job better than he does, you've got a problem," Ings said later. By April, O'Brien had quietly been sent to work the Challenger circuit. At the end of the year, he was dropped. To the credit of the tour, umpires aren't like judges: They don't serve for life, regardless of competence. "The lesson we learned," Dana Loconto said at the U.S. Open, "is that there's only one Richard Ings."

Loconto was also a new hire in 1990, and he was as much a success as O'Brien was a failure. This was no surprise, though. As a "part-time" umpire in 1989, Loconto had worked forty weeks, including the U.S. Open final. A successful businessman who had owned six different companies in Alabama, Loconto sold four of them to become an umpire.

"I love tennis and I love traveling," he said. "It's a perfect combination. I worked forty weeks last year because I wanted to get good at this."

He had gotten plenty good, so good that McEnroe himself had gone out of his way to compliment his work after a match. The ATP Tour was quite happy when Loconto signed on.

In 1989, the fraternity was heavily damaged by the ATP/ITF split. Cooper, the administrator, went with the ATP and quickly signed up most of the top umpires. Farrar, who had traveled the world with the umpires as their supervisor, went with the ITF. There were hurt feelings on both sides.

"I know the guys feel like I let them down," Farrar said. "But I had problems with the ATP approach and thought the ITF opportunity was too good to turn down."

Farrar won't talk specifically about his problems with the ATP, but they boil down to one thing: lack of autonomy. As part of the ATP Tour, the umpires now work *for* the players. Everyone involved with the ATP Tour denies that this causes problems, and no one would question the integrity of the umpires even for a second.

But it is true that after the McEnroe incident in Australia, the ATP umpires were warned by their supervisors to be more careful in dispensing code violations, since there were now only three steps to default rather than four. They also agreed that in the future, an umpire would have the discretion to *not* give a player an automatic code violation if his racquet cracked the way McEnroe's did in the Pernfors match. It became a judgment call.

One month after the McEnroe default, Ings had a tough match with Becker in Stuttgart. Becker is rarely a problem on court, but when he gets upset he can be stubborn—as Tiriac and Brett can attest. Becker had hit a ball bounced to him by a ball boy into the stands, and Ings had given him a warning. Becker had argued that he had not meant to hit the ball that hard, that it was an accident. Ings let him argue for a while and then tried to get him to play. Becker kept arguing. Ings gave him a point penalty.

Just like that, Becker was one step from default. He demanded to see the supervisor. The supervisor, Ed Hardisty, backed Ings up and eventually told him to put the clock on Becker, who continued to argue. "Boris," Ings finally said, "you're five seconds from default."

Becker played. But later in the match, he threw his racquet down—much the same way McEnroe had in Australia. The racquet didn't crack, but it was thrown pretty hard. "I thought about it for a second," Ings said. "And then I decided I wasn't going to default Boris Becker for slamming a racquet. I felt like I had gone a little too fast under the new system in giving him the point penalty, and I should give him the benefit of the doubt."

Common sense, or so it would seem. The ITF took a different view: The three-step rule had been created by the ATP—and adopted later by the ITF—as a way of tightening the code and improving behavior. Now it seemed, at least on the ATP Tour, that it had taken some authority from the umpires.

There was also a good deal more fraternization on the ATP Tour than there had been in the MTC days. Often, the umpires stayed at the same hotels as the players and they frequently bumped into one another. As the year wore on, players and umpires occasionally played golf together. This was clearly dangerous. Imagine one player knowing that his opponent had played golf with the chair umpire the previous day.

The two groups work together at all four Grand Slams but remain rivals. Farrar, under the aegis of the ITF, has started a massive, worldwide training program. The best thing about it all is that, more and more, tennis officiating is being professionalized. That can only be good. Because if the two groups have nothing else in common, they *do* all love the game and want to see officiating get better.

"It's amazing how slowly officiating has grown compared to the game itself," Farrar says, "Maybe now we're starting to catch up—slowly—but at least we're going in the right direction."

Even John McEnroe would probably agree.

18

EASTBOURNE

Martina Navratilova was nervous. She fidgeted in her seat and glanced at her watch for the fourth time in an hour. "I definitely have a case of stage fright," she said. "I slept all afternoon so that I would be ready for this."

Three days before the start of Wimbledon, one could understand why Navratilova would have a case of nerves. She had been preparing for Wimbledon, in her words, "since the moment the final ended last year." Now those preparations were all but finished.

Only, her nerves on this night had nothing to do with tennis. Navratilova *literally* had a case of stage fright. She was about to make her debut as a performer in the annual players' talent show that had become a tradition at Eastbourne. "This is the only player party I go to every year," she said. "People actually look forward to this."

The women have played a Wimbledon warm-up tournament at Eastbourne since the nineteenth century, after all these years still playing at the same site, Devonshire Park.

Eastbourne is two hours southeast of London, an easy train ride or a harrowing drive along narrow country roads. It sits on the English Channel and is the English version of St. Petersburg, a small resort town where a substantial part of the population is over the age of seventy.

Devonshire Park is a two-hundred-yard walk from the beach, a veritable melting pot of the tennis world. The old is very much in evidence: the north stand, which was built in 1881, is often filled with septuagenarians who have been coming here for as long as anyone can remember. Towering oak trees rise up behind the north stand and sea gulls often swoop by noisily, distracting the players.

Two things make Eastbourne different than other tournaments. First, it is a six-day tournament, ending Saturday. That is one reason why Navratilova and other top women players have consistently played here through the years: With a Saturday final, they are guaranteed at least two days off before playing a Tuesday first-round match at Wimbledon.

The second thing that makes Eastbourne unique is the player party. Every tennis tournament in the world has a player party. On the women's tour, WTA public relations and marketing people as well as their counterparts at Kraft and Virginia Slims usually spend the first few days at each tournament trying to round up players to come to the party. For the players, one more party with one more group of sponsors telling them how wonderful they are is boring, a time-waster. They understand they have to do their share to keep these people happy, but they don't enjoy it very much.

Eastbourne is different because of the talent show. The players—even Navratilova—show up because they expect the show to be funny. The person most responsible for making it funny every year is Elise Burgin, director, writer, and star.

"I actually feel as much pressure to come up with a funny show every year as I feel going out to play a match," she said. "Which tells you a lot about my priorities, I guess."

This year's show was built around a mock game show. Burgin was the host. Four players would be the panelists: Jennifer Capriati, played by Australian Louise Field; Martina Navratilova, played by Robin White; Mary Pierce, a teenager who had grown up in Florida who was now playing as a French citizen (her mother is French), played by doubles specialist Sandy Collins; and Monica Seles, played by Natalia Zvereva—who did the Seles grunt better than anyone on tour.

The stars of the show, though, were their cheering sections. This was where Navratilova came in. Burgin had asked her to play Judy Nelson, her roommate. Once upon a time, Navratilova would have felt uncomfortable with such a role. But she and Nelson had lived together for seven years and Navratilova had publicly acknowledged her homosexuality four years earlier, in her autobiography. There are few secrets on the women's tour; Navratilova and Nelson were simply accepted as part of the scene.

The other cheerleaders were French player Sophie Amiach as Stefano Capriati; Brenda Schultz, a Dutch player who looked a foot taller than her listed height of six feet one, as Navratilova guru Billie Jean King; and Roslyn Fairbank as Jim Pierce, Mary's manic father, waving—what else?—a French flag.

Most of this was very *inside* humor. If you weren't a part of the women's tour in some way, the jokes meant little. Amiach cracked the crowd up with her Stefano Capriati imitation: "I deserve the credit," she said. "I produce the child. I teach the child. I coach the child. I am the star." To his credit, Stefano Capriati laughed as hard as anyone.

Schultz, as King, kept jumping out of her chair every time White, as Navratilova, successfully answered a question. "Go for it, Martina!" Schultz/King would shout. "You're the best! No one can beat you!" This was an on-the-money imitation.

Navratilova did a good job as Nelson, wearing one of her trademark hats and explaining to the audience that she knew more about tennis than any of Martina's various coaches and gurus. Each time White, as Navratilova, answered a question, Navratilova, as Nelson, would rush onstage, fix her makeup, and comb her hair. It was perfect.

It was also a strong indication of just how comfortable Navratilova felt going into Wimbledon. In the right mood, there is no one more charming or funny than Martina. In the wrong mood, there are few people more difficult. This hardly makes her unique in tennis. Star tantrums are commonplace. Some are legendary. Once, having been beaten in an exhibition tournament by Betsy Nagelsen, Chris Evert went into a complete tizzy. She couldn't believe that no one had told Nagelsen that it was okay to give her a *close* match but certainly not okay to *beat* her. She was furious with Nagelsen and with IMG—which was running the event—for *allowing* Nagelsen to beat her. Evert had forgotten one thing: As important a client as she may be, *no one* at IMG was about to tell Nagelsen to lose a match—she's married to Mark McCormack, IMG's founder and chairman.

Stars in a snit are a part of life on the women's tour. "That's the way it is with stars," Ted Tinling once said. "I've never met a great champion who couldn't be an absolute bitch."

The bitchiness usually came out when a star, no matter who it was, knew he or she wasn't really ready to play. At Eastbourne, Navratilova knew she was ready for Wimbledon.

"My preparation has been letter-perfect," she said. "Last year, I really only had six weeks to get ready, and I played as well as I could in the final. Steffi was just too good. This year, I feel like I've had a year to get ready. I've done everything I can possibly do to prepare. If somebody beats me, then they beat me. But it won't happen because I'm not ready."

Such an admission from an athlete was rare. No excuses, no poor-mouthing. In fourteen months, Navratilova, with ample help from King, had turned herself around. In April 1989, after a semifinal loss to Natalia Zvereva at Hilton Head, she seriously thought about retiring. She had not won a Grand Slam since the 1987 U.S. Open. Graf was dominating the game completely. What's more, Navratilova wasn't even making finals anymore. She had lost in the fourth round at the 1988 French to Zvereva;

in the U.S. Open quarterfinals, to Zina Garrison; in the Virginia Slims quarterfinals, to Gabriela Sabatini.

The ninth Wimbledon title, which she coveted, seemed out of reach. "I was completely burnt out," she said. "Physically, I was tired, but most of it was mental. I had put so much effort into trying to keep up with Steffi that I wasn't even giving myself a chance to do the things I was still capable of. I was obsessed with her, so much so that I kept losing before I got to play her in tournaments because my mind was so focused on playing her."

Since she had split with Mike Estep at the start of 1987, Navratilova had gone through several coaches. None seemed to hit the right notes. "I needed someone who I thought knew more tennis than I did," she said. "I asked Rod Laver, but he was too busy. So I went to Billie Jean, who I *knew* was too busy. But I had to have her help and she knew it."

King and Navratilova had been friends since Navratilova's early days on tour. They had also been doubles partners. King agreed to help. The first thing she did was tell Navratilova to forget about being No. 1 again. "Focus on something that isn't so far away," she told her. "That's Wimbledon." The second thing she told her was to stop feeling old. "If I had your body I would still be playing—and winning," she said.

Navratilova has always been an excellent pupil. Estep remembers how willing she was to take instruction from him from day one. "Her attitude was, I'm paying you to make me better, so I'm going to listen to you. But you better be right," he said. "That puts pressure on you. But it also means you don't have to fight your pupil every day."

King had encouraged Navratilova to start keeping a journal to record her progress on-court, her feelings about her game, what she had done right and wrong in matches. It became a reference book, something Navratilova went back to when she was unsure of something: how to play an opponent, what shots were working well, what her state of mind had been at a given time.

King's pupil progressed well in 1989. She played nicely at Wimbledon, losing in three sets to Graf in the final. At the Open, she was up a set and 4–2 on Graf and should have won the match. For months after that loss, King made Navratilova look at the tape. The message was clear: You can beat Graf if you don't get ahead of yourself. King focused on one moment in that match: Navratilova turning to her entourage after going up 4–2 in the second set and holding up two fingers to indicate she needed two more games.

"I was thinking in the future, not the present," Navratilova said.

"Instead of just turning around and trying to win the next point, I was thinking ahead to winning the whole match. That was where I lost it."

Navratilova began 1990 by skipping the Australian; she also skipped the French again. Once, passing up Grand Slams was unthinkable. Now, the only question was "Can it help win Wimbledon?" If the answer was no, she didn't go.

After losing the Italian final to Seles, Navratilova had gone home to Czechoslovakia. It was her second trip there since her defection in 1975. This was much different than 1986, when she had gone back as part of the U.S. Federation Cup team and had been part of a media circus. Now, the government that had expunged her name from all the Czech history books had been overthrown. Vaclav Havel, the revolutionary playwright, was the new president. The country was free.

For Navratilova, the trip was thrilling and devastating. Old, buried emotions surfaced. She visited the grave of her father (she had grown up with her mother and stepfather), who she had hardly known, and the grave of her grandmother, to whom she had been very close. There was great catharsis and great pain. She found herself an emotional wreck.

"Fortunately, I knew what was happening," she said. "At first, I thought maybe I was just getting uptight about Wimbledon. Then I realized that wasn't it at all. I had never dealt with the pain of my grandmother's death, and when I did, it was as if she had just died. I cried and cried. But now, for the first time, I can actually talk about it."

She had straightened out her thoughts about the homecoming just before it was time to leave for England. Now, in Eastbourne, she, King, Nelson, and her coach, Craig Kardon, felt as if everything was in place.

"I know Steffi has a chink in her armor," she said. "That helps. But, really, I'm not even thinking in those terms. Who knows? I might not even play her. The difference for me now is simple: Two years ago, every time I fell behind 3–2 in the first set of a match, I started thinking, Should I be out here? Am I too old to play? Now, no matter what, I feel *lucky* to be out here playing. I want to win this Wimbledon very, very much. But if I don't, I still feel I have a chance next year. I'm ready for a fight, no matter who I play.

"I'm looking forward to my retirement, but now I'm not even thinking about when it will come. Until I win that ninth Wimbledon, I'm not finished."

She smiled and turned into the Texan she had become during her ten years of living in Fort Worth. She made a baseball analogy: "My inspiration right now is Nolan Ryan. He's ten years older than I am and he just pitched his sixth no-hitter. He's a good ole Texas boy. So why can't a good ole Texas girl win Wimbledon one more time?"

While Navratilova was sailing through Eastbourne week, worried more about her acting than anything else, things were not quite as smooth for Jennifer Capriati.

All spring, John Evert had been concerned about what would happen when the Capriati teen-tour hit England. Stefano Capriati had proved himself very sensitive to any criticism from the media—and he hadn't seen *anything* that could begin to approach what the English tabloids could do with a new phenom like his daughter.

For the English tabloids, particularly during the four-week English grass-court season, everyone and anyone is fodder. Almost nothing is secret. Airports and hotels are staked out. If a tennis player goes to dinner, to the movies, or to the bathroom it is probably going to show up in a tabloid the next day.

The players themselves are at least partly at fault. While they complain bitterly when the tabloids write untruths about them—or truths they don't want to see in print—virtually all of them are willing to take money from them when it is offered. Players "writing" columns for the tabloids had become such an epidemic several years earlier that Wimbledon had passed a rule saying no one entered in the tournament could work for a media outlet during the two weeks of the tournament. The rules didn't cover the reams of *pre-*Wimbledon coverage, though.

Among those who had taken tabloid money over the years were McEnroe, Connors, Lendl, and Evert. This year, since she was no longer playing, Evert was doing a diary for the *Daily Express* throughout the tournament. Her fee: $45,000.

Capriati's debut in England was, of course, big news. When she went to the movies one night with some friends who had come over from Florida, the tabloids had stories about her "boyfriend" taking her out. Another rag featured a huge spread about the touring-pro deal her father had made in Florida. It included pictures of the "mansion" the Capriatis were going to live in. The deal *had* been made and the Capriatis *were* planning to move to Broken Sound in the fall—but the house they were going to live in hadn't been built yet. Oh, well, the tabloids can't get *everything* right.

Capriati's real problem came at Eastbourne on Tuesday. As well as she had played in her first five tournaments as a pro—she was already ranked thirteenth on the computer—this was her first pro tournament on grass. As dominant as she had been as a junior on clay and on hard courts, she had actually lost in the quarterfinals in the Wimbledon juniors; this was one surface where she was vulnerable.

When the rain cleared off on Tuesday morning, Capriati played her opening match and won easily. Naturally, the English media wanted to talk to her. The WTA's postmatch interview policy gives a player who has to play another match that day—which, because of the rain, Capriati did—the right to defer her interview until after that match. Usually, this provision crops up when a player has to play doubles shortly after singles or when a player has lost a tough match.

The English media did not want to wait for Capriati to play her second singles match to talk to her. It might not end until eight or nine o'clock, and all of them had early deadlines. They didn't really care about her tennis; all they wanted were a couple of quotes about England, the weather, the grass, and Wimbledon—the usual—to make their Capriati-starved editors happy. A deal was struck: Capriati would come in after her first match but not after her second-round match later that day against Gretchen Magers. "Fine, fine," most of the reporters said, "just bring her in as soon as possible."

Capriati came in. She did her "everything is wonderful" routine and everyone was happy. There was just one problem: Gretchen Magers.

Like Elise Burgin, Gretchen Magers had become accustomed to being the warm-up act for the game's stars. She admits there are times when she chafes because of it, but she accepts it.

"Sometimes I feel like some sort of sideshow; I think we all do," she said. "But the fact is, that without the stars, the rest of us don't make the money we're making. So it's kind of tough to complain."

Magers was acutely conscious of money in 1990. She and her husband, Stephen, had bought a house at the start of the year for $325,000. That was a major step up from the houseboat they had been living on in San Diego Harbor since their marriage in 1986. "We still haven't sold the houseboat," Magers said. "If we could get forty thousand dollars for it, that would be very nice."

The Magerses had felt they were ready to buy a house at the end of 1989. Gretchen had just had her best year as a pro, winning more than $184,000. She had even qualified for the Virginia Slims Championships, earning the sixteenth and final spot at the last tournament of the year, in Chicago. For a tennis player to have the best year of her life at age twenty-five is very unusual, but that's what Gretchen Magers had done.

She had beaten Pam Shriver 12–10 in the third set at Wimbledon, reached the quarterfinals there, and used it as a springboard for the rest of the year.

"I was never any kind of star in juniors," she said. "You don't see a lot of tennis phenoms coming out of Pittsburgh."

Magers had twice been a Grand Slam quarterfinalist during college (U.S. Open, 1982; French Open, 1983), but her first couple of years on tour were a struggle. "I honestly thought, coming out of college, that I could be a Top Ten player," she said. "This life is full of disappointments. It's very hard to be in a job where every single week there is a major letdown, two, actually, if you count doubles, because just about every week you lose. Every week when I lose, I'm ready to go home.

"But the fact is, I can't afford to quit now. Stephen is finishing his master's thesis and we've got a mortgage to pay. There's nothing I can do at twenty-six where the money is going to be comparable. So when I lose, I just have to take a deep breath and say, 'next week.' This game is a constant cycle of hope and disappointment. You lose in Paris on the clay, you tell yourself, 'It will be better on the grass.' "

Now, on the grass, with dusk closing in, Magers quickly fell behind Capriati 6–2, 4–1. Capriati was cruising. Magers was angry with herself. In 1989 she had won her tough matches. This year, she seemed to be losing them. She didn't want to be embarrassed by Capriati. So she dug in and picked up her game at a time when it would have been easy to say, "next week."

Capriati was caught completely off guard. Watching her, Tom Gullikson could see that she was surprised. "In juniors, whenever she was up 6–2, 4–1, the other girl was thrilled to have won three games," he said. "This was different. This was a solid pro who didn't think the match was over until they shook hands. Jennifer had never really dealt with that before."

Magers came back to win eleven of the last thirteen games—and the match. By the end, with the sun almost gone, Capriati looked like a fourteen-year-old, not the world's No. 13 player. When she left the court, her entourage quickly closed ranks around her to escort her off the grounds. However, the media didn't want to let her do that. The loss had made her earlier quotes meaningless. They wanted to talk to her again.

That wasn't going to happen. Capriati had done her interview and no one from the WTA or Kraft/Virginia Slims was about to tell Stefano Capriati that his daughter's loss rendered the earlier deal moot. Security hustled the Capriatis away. The newspapers in London the next day reported that she had fled the grounds in tears. Hype—yes; completely inaccurate—no. It wasn't until Friday—three days later—that she came back to talk to the media. By then, she had received her first roasting—albeit a mild one by British standards—from the media.

Even in victory, Gretchen Magers was still the sideshow. She handled it graciously, but it brought back memories for her of a match she had watched several years earlier between Chris Evert and Barbara Potter. Potter had won the first set and led in the second. Watching, Magers noticed the stands filling up with tournament officials, sponsors, tour staff, media. "The word got out that Chris was in trouble and everyone showed up," Magers said. "A couple of calls went against Barbara, she got flustered, Chris started playing better, and it all turned around. I looked up and everyone had left. They were all relieved. Chris was okay so they could go back to work. Barbara was just an afterthought."

This time though, Magers was not an afterthought. On Friday, she won two more matches and made it to the fourth final of her career. Waiting for her there was Navratilova. Martina won the match 6–2, 6–0, and Gretchen Magers had to deal with that weekly letdown. This week, though, it wasn't quite so bad. It had come late and it had come after some very satisfying moments.

As for Navratilova, she had gotten exactly what she wanted out of Eastbourne: a victory, another shot of confidence, and a big round of applause for her Nelson imitation. The preliminaries were over now. It was time for Wimbledon.

19

WIMBLEDON

Nothing in tennis can match the tension of day one at Wimbledon.

Everyone is tight, nervous, ready to explode with pent-up energy. The other Grand Slams are very important; Wimbledon is *history.* Only at Wimbledon do first-time players venture immediately out to Centre Court just to *look.* Only at Wimbledon does the mere thought of playing on Centre Court make players tremble. Only at Wimbledon does *Centre Court* stay empty from the day of the final until the Saturday before the tournament begins the next year.

Only at Wimbledon do you walk underneath the huge sign over the door leading to Centre Court, which quotes Rudyard Kipling: "If you can meet with triumph and disaster and treat those two imposters the same."

Any player who tells you that another tournament means more to them than Wimbledon is lying, stupid, or both.

There are also practical reasons why Wimbledon crackles with tension at the start. Because it begins only two weeks after the French has ended, most of the players have not been home in between. Most go straight from Paris to the grass to begin preparing.

The weather in England is almost always rotten. Rain cuts practice time, as does a lack of practice courts. At Wimbledon, practice time on the sixteen outside courts is limited to thirty minutes at a time—unless two seeded players are practicing together. Then, they can get an hour. The adjacent practice courts at Aorangi Park (so named because the land was once owned by the government of New Zealand) are not as tight, but still tough to come by. By the time the tournament begins, people are a little tired, a little homesick, frequently frustrated, and very, very nervous.

For some, just getting to play inside the main gate is an achievement. Wimbledon's qualifying tournament is not played at Wimbledon; it is played at the Bank of England tennis club, at Roehampton, about eight miles from the All England Club.

Everyone who has played there—and almost everyone *has* at some point—will tell you that the toughest tennis tournament in the world is the one at Roehampton. "There is nothing in the world farther from Wimbledon than Roehampton," John McEnroe once said. "You survive there, you're a hell of a tennis player."

McEnroe had come out of Roehampton in 1977 to make it to the semifinals. Often, qualifiers, while not matching McEnroe, have done quite well in the main draw at Wimbledon. After three matches at Roehampton, almost anything they face in the main draw seems simple by comparison.

There are sixteen courts at Roehampton. Unlike the pampered, protected courts at Wimbledon, they are in constant use—and it shows. There are brown patches everywhere—or, to be accurate, green patches on the brown—and, after it rains, players would be well advised to show up wearing cleats rather than sneakers.

Most players come to the courts dressed to play; they shower after returning to their hotel. Not that there aren't locker-room facilities at Roehampton: A sign scrawled on a blackboard outside the swimming pool locker room says "Wimbledon changing rooms." If you don't mind sharing space with the swimmers, you can grab a locker.

When the players arrive at Roehampton, they report to the referee's tent to sign in; then they await court assignments. Waiting for their matches to be called, most kill the time sitting on a large, grassy knoll that serves as both the players' and the umpires' lounge. The P.A. system is the focal point of all life at Roehampton. Announcements calling players and umpires to their courts, paging people to the telephone, seeking drivers to take players back to hotels, or updating schedules can be heard around the grounds all day long.

The P.A. is just one of a number of distractions players must deal with while they are playing. Admission to Roehampton is free; there are no ushers and no security. In this sense, it is a wonderful throwback. There isn't a corporate banner anywhere in sight, and no one has to make any rulings on what players can or cannot drink on court.

But the atmosphere is not the kind tennis players are accustomed to—people talking and laughing while strolling past the courts, kids running in all directions, balls constantly bouncing from one court to another because the courts are so close together. If one wants to qualify for Wimbledon, one has to earn it.

Roehampton is both a launching pad and a graveyard. Young players come here wide-eyed at the thought of getting into Wimbledon. Older ones come here hoping to hang on one more year. It takes three victories to get into Wimbledon, with the last men's match a best-of-five. Qualifying begins the Monday before Wimbledon starts and is supposed to end on Thursday. Most of the time, however, it is Saturday by the time the last doubles match is over.

The first day of qualifying, June 18, was Luke Jensen's twenty-fourth birthday. He did not get the present he wanted most. Jensen showed up Monday morning for sign-in and found out that the ranking cutoff to play qualifying was No. 440. He was ranked 450th. Happy birthday, Luke.

"I made a decision at the beginning of the year to play in the biggest tournaments I could find," Jensen said. "It's worked out well for me in doubles, but obviously it has hurt my singles."

Jensen was one of a new group of doubles-playing road warriors created by the ATP Tour. Under the rules of the new tour, every tournament was required to supply all players in the main draw of either the singles or doubles with "hospitality," the tennis euphemism for a free hotel room, free transportation, and free breakfast each morning. Hospitality lasts the entire week, regardless of whether you are still in the tournament. In prior years, hospitality had been optional and most tournaments had opted to cut it off when a player was eliminated or, in some cases, give it to only the top players—the ones who needed it least.

Mandatory hospitality was a great incentive for players like Jensen to play in the top tournaments. Jensen had qualified for the main draw in singles twice in 1990—at Rotterdam and Rome—and had earned $8,097 in those two tournaments. But he and Charles Beckman, his doubles partner, were ranked fifty-first and forty-ninth respectively in doubles, which meant they were placed straight into the doubles draw everywhere they went and were thus entitled to hospitality.

With free lodging everywhere they went, lower-ranked players saw no reason to take time off. Jensen and Beckman had played in nineteen tournaments during the first twenty-five weeks of 1990. "We're going for Tomas Smid's record," Jensen said, referring to the veteran Czechoslovakian who had played so often during his career that he had become legendary. Why turn down $1,200 (first-round prize money in doubles most places), a free room in a five-star hotel, *and* the chance to travel the world?

"I think it's a great life. Charles and I have been in Europe so much this year, guys think we've bought a house here. My plane ticket from

Nice [in mid-April] through Stuttgart [mid-July] cost twenty-seven hundred dollars. I made that the first two weeks."

Jensen grew up in Michigan, dreaming of being a football player at Notre Dame. He was so eager to play football that he talked his parents into sending him to a different school to repeat eighth grade because he was the youngest kid in his class. "It was a red-shirt [repeat] year in junior high school," he said. "Everything I did was pegged to football."

While spending that year in Grand Rapids, Jensen began playing a lot of tennis. By the time he was ready to play football, as a sophomore, he was convinced his best route to a college scholarship was tennis. Good decision. Jensen ended up the No. 1 junior in the country at eighteen and, after considering turning pro, enrolled at Southern California. He stayed two years.

There was good reason to believe Jensen would be a star on the circuit. His game was unique because he was completely ambidextrous, often switching his racquet from one hand to the other in midpoint. "I do it without even thinking," he says. "It's whatever feels right. I just go on instinct, because that's the way I've always played."

Labeled Two-Hand Luke, Jensen signed with IMG out of college. But injuries slowed him and he never cracked the top 150 in singles. His IMG contract had lapsed quietly and, going into Wimbledon, he seemed almost resigned to life as a doubles specialist.

Jensen had made $45,000 for the year as Wimbledon started. Respectable, but a far cry from what could be made if one had success in singles. "That's where the decision comes in," he said. "I know, realistically, if I want to make it in singles, I have to go back and play satellites and Challengers. But that's tough to do. I feel like I'm in The Show right now, and going back to the minors wouldn't be a lot of fun."

Patrick McEnroe, who had been Jensen's doubles partner when the two were juniors, had taken that step backward at the start of the year. He had taken a chance on hurting his doubles play to play smaller tournaments in singles.

As far as McEnroe was concerned, the gamble was paying off. The week before Wimbledon qualifying, he had reached the semifinals of a grass-court warm-up tournament in Holland—his best week ever in singles—and had won just under $40,000 for the year as a singles player. More important, he was now ranked 136th and felt he had an excellent chance of qualifying for Wimbledon.

Things rarely go as they are supposed to at Roehampton—as evidenced by the fact that only one of the sixteen seeds in the qualifying ended up earning a spot in the main draw. McEnroe's first match was with Francisco Maciel, a Mexican who played little on grass. The match started in a drizzle, and McEnroe quickly learned that the slippery, chewed-up courts of Roehampton were a lot different than the dry, well-conditioned courts he had been playing on in Holland.

"I was afraid to move," he said. "I really thought I could get hurt. Of course, it was the same for both of us."

The match took two days because of rain delays. When it was over, Maciel had broken serve twice. That was enough to win 6–4, 6–4. McEnroe had pointed to Wimbledon all spring. Now, he was once again a doubles specialist. He went back to the house his brother was renting, fully prepared to spend the afternoon sulking. John promptly talked him into going to Wimbledon (the club, not the village) to practice. "I hit the ball better than I had hit it in weeks," Patrick said. "I couldn't miss a shot. I wanted to kill myself."

It was 1:59 P.M. when Boris Becker and Luis Herrera walked on Centre Court to play the traditional opening match of the 1990 Championships. On the grounds of the All England Club, Wimbledon is never called Wimbledon. It is called, simply, The Championships.

The traditions associated with The Championships have changed over the years. Once upon a time, play began each day at 2 P.M.—precisely. Now, play on sixteen of the eighteen courts begins each day at twelve-thirty; the extra ninety minutes of play is necessary to finish the tournament on time. Only on Centre Court and court 1 does play begin at two, and even that can vary. The players are held in the Centre Court waiting room until the Duke and Duchess of Kent—or any other royalty in attendance that day—is seated. That can be a couple of minutes before two or a couple of minutes after. The term *precisely* has become an anachronism.

Wimbledon had a different look in 1990. New laws, passed after the soccer disaster in Liverpool, had forced the club to remove the standing-room area that had been so much a part of its tradition. For years, people had lined up to pay three pounds to stand. Now, that area had seats—expensive ones—and something had definitely been lost.

Yet, the air was still electric when Becker and Herrera, an eighteen-year-old Mexican qualifier, walked out, stopped at the service line, turned, and bowed to the Royal Box.

The Royal Box, which seats seventy-six people, had a different look in 1990, too. Seated between the duke and duchess, in the cushioned seat (only the front-row seats are cushioned) reserved for the chairman of the All England Club, was John Curry, a fifty-one-year-old businessman who had been named chairman the previous December.

The man Curry had succeeded was R.E.H. Hadingham. No one called Hadingham R.E.H. or even Reginald Edward Hawk. He was known to one and all as Buzzer. "A lot of people think it's because I'm always buzzing around," he said. "Actually, it's because my older brother couldn't say *brother* when we were little. He always introduced me to people as 'my little buzzer.' It stuck." Growing up, the little Buzzer was a respectable tennis player. He went to work for his father's company, Slazenger, at age seventeen and there moved up the ladder rapidly. His career was interrupted by World War II; Hadingham spent three years as an antitank commander. He came back from the war and became general manager of Slazenger. In 1947, Herman David, a member of the All England Club's management committee, asked him if he wanted to apply for membership to the club.

"My dad had been a member since 1920," Hadingham said. "And since I also knew Herman I got in very quickly—in ten years."

Ten years *is* a short time to spend on the club's waiting list. There are three hundred male members at Wimbledon and seventy-five women. The only time a new member is admitted is if someone dies or resigns. The waiting list usually consists of about eight hundred applicants, who must have a proposer, a seconder, and two supporters. That's *just* to get on the list. In 1989, five spots opened up. Dues are next to nothing—approximately thirty pounds a year—largely because the club makes so much money on the tournament.

"I had two cousins who were down [on the waiting list] for more than fifty years and never got in," Hadingham said. "I was very lucky."

He became a member of the All England Club's committee in 1972. The committee consists of twelve members elected to three-year terms by the membership. Along with seven members of the British Lawn Tennis Association, they form the Wimbledon Committee of Management. In 1983, after eleven years on the committee, Hadingham was elected to succeed Sir Brian Burnett as chairman. He had just turned sixty-eight when he was elected, but was so full of energy few people would never have guessed that.

Without saying it, Hadingham set one goal for himself: move Wimbledon into the twentieth century. Burnett had taken a couple of baby steps in that direction, actually becoming the first chairman to ever speak *directly* to the players. Hadingham not only attended the players' pretournament meetings, he told the players jokes.

"I thought it was important to change the players' perception that the committee looked down on the players, and I worked like hell on that," he said. "I told the other members of the committee that I wanted the players to feel as if the bow tie [which committee members wear on the lapel of their jackets] meant they could find help. I like to think that we broke a few barriers down."

Hadingham was the first chairman who made himself accessible to the media. He helped convince club members to elect a woman—Virginia Wade—to the committee for the first time. He allowed IMG to aggressively market the tournament, increasing the club's revenue tremendously. He started The Final Eight Club for all players who had made the quarterfinals in singles or the semifinals in doubles.

"I got that idea when I ran into a man named Jozsef Asboth on the grounds during the tournament one day," he said. "Asboth was a semifinalist in 1948 and the French champion. He was Hungarian. Lovely ground strokes. I asked him what he was doing and he said, 'Just wandering around.' He had a grounds pass, nothing more. I thought that was wrong. This man had been *part* of Wimbledon. So, when I had the chance, I created a place where all these people could still *feel* a part of Wimbledon."

Hadingham's strength was in his ability to relate to people. If Buzzer wanted something, he usually got it. He sounded like an aristocrat but behaved like a regular guy. He had a daughter who lived in Florida, and during a stay with her one year he became a baseball fan—specifically, a New York Mets fan. "Dammit, I never did get to see the Mets all those years going to New York for the Open," he complained. "I can't tell you how many times we'd go by Shea Stadium on the way to Flushing Meadow and I would find myself wishing I could go in and see the baseball game."

Clearly, this was a different Wimbledon chairman. He developed relationships that had never existed before with the top players. In 1989, when Boris Becker and Steffi Graf won the singles titles, Hadingham sought out Becker after the on-court awards ceremony.

"The previous year, when Steffi had won for the first time, she arrived at the champions' dinner and told me she could only stay forty-five minutes," he said. "I had to stand up after the soup and make my toast to her so she could give her speech and leave.

"I thought it was quite awkward for everybody, and I really thought Steffi was missing out on something by leaving. To be toasted as the champion of Wimbledon is no small thing. It's something you should enjoy. I told Boris how I felt and he agreed. He had a chat with Steffi and she stayed the whole dinner. I was very glad she did."

As chairman, Hadingham had started to do something that no one had done at Wimbledon before—separate tradition from silly rules. "I believe in tradition as much as anyone," he said. "Tradition is one of the most important things about Wimbledon. But whenever a question came up in terms of changing something, I tried to decide what was *fairest* for the people involved and be flexible."

Technically, the club chairman is elected each December by the committee. In December 1988, Hadingham told the committee he would serve as chairman one more year and then step down. "I'll be seventy-five in December 1990," he said. "I thought one more year was about right. I would rather leave a little soon than linger a little too long."

Wimbledon is like anyplace else when a coveted job is at stake. There was all sorts of back-room maneuverings during 1989, and when it was all over, Curry had emerged as the chairman. Hadingham stepped down with one genuine regret: "I would like to see our [Great Britain's] men do better," he said. "I think we will have a top male player again soon, I really do. We're pouring all sorts of money into junior programs, so it's bound to happen.

"Now, every time one of our players wins a match, the press goes absolutely mad. The players overreact and become conceited. They can make a very good living here just by being fair players. They don't seem to have the drive to be champions. I think it may be the English mentality. If we're driven right into a corner—like at Dunkirk in 1940—we'll do something, but not until then."

Curry, Hadingham's successor, is the youngest chairman the club has ever had and one of the first to hold a full-time job when elected chairman. His father was a very successful builder in the Far East; Curry was born in Burma in 1938. He, his mother, and two brothers got the last plane out of Rangoon at the outbreak of World War II.

Curry was a good junior player, good enough to play in the Wimbledon junior tournament at sixteen. In those days, the tournament was held in September, apart from the regular tournament. "A friend and I were in the locker room, waiting to play a match, and we decided we wanted to see Centre Court," he said. "We grabbed four tennis balls, ran out there, and hit them to one another. There was no net, no lines, but we did it. It was fun. Still, if I had been caught, I never would have become a member, much less chairman."

Curry became a temporary member while he was a student at Oxford. As captain of the Oxford tennis team, he was assigned to escort the Harvard and Yale players when they came to England to play in the traditional matches against Oxford and Cambridge. The captain of the Cambridge team was Barry Wetherill, one of the men whom Curry would beat out for the chairman's job more than thirty years later. In order to escort the Yale and Harvard players around Wimbledon, Curry was made a temporary member. He managed to hang on to that status for eight years. By then, he had made enough friends to gain full membership.

After Oxford, Curry married and went to business school at Harvard. "My wife got her PHT at Harvard," he said, " 'Putting Hubby Through.' She even got a scroll for it." At twenty-eight, Curry returned to England and started a business with his brother. At thirty he became a member of Wimbledon, and in 1980 was elected to the committee.

Curry's first six months on the job had not been easy. Before a ball had been hit during his chairmanship, he had undergone back surgery to repair damaged discs.

Still sore from the surgery, Curry had to oversee the hasty redesign of Centre Court, brought on by the new post–Liverpool soccer disaster laws, and come up with new crowd-control rules for the grounds. In the midst of all that, he also had to deal with the game's never-ending political controversies. He found the stubbornness and egomania on both sides aggravating. "There's no reason for things to have gone this far," he said. "The Grand Slam Cup can't possibly be good for tennis. But the ATP didn't talk to the ITF for six months last year, just ignored them. So the ITF created the Cup. Now, it's going to be around for a few years. I see the need for it—but I wish that need wasn't there."

Like Hadingham, Curry thought communication with the players was critical for a Wimbledon chairman. "I tried to tell Boris the other day how sorry I was about the incident on the practice court two weeks ago," he said. "It was craziness, and I told him that. He just shrugged and said, 'These things always happen to me.' To tell the truth, I don't think he had any idea who the hell I was. I hope to change that." Curry had even attempted to set up a meeting with the world's best-known Wimbledon basher, Andre Agassi. Wimbledon certainly didn't need Agassi but Curry thought it was a shame that one of the world's top-ranked and best-known players skipped the tournament. He had flown to Paris during the first week of the French Open and asked Bob Kain of IMG to arrange a session.

"I just wanted him to know that we would do whatever we could to make him comfortable," Curry said. "The more comfortable players feel when they get here, the better off we all are."

Curry never got the chance to communicate that to Agassi. Kain came back to him with word that Agassi didn't want to meet with him. The mountain had gone to Muhammad and Muhammad had told the mountain to take a hike. Curry shrugged off Agassi's rudeness.

"It's sad for *him,*" he said. "He'll never know how he can do here if he doesn't try. All the people around him are terrified of him, aren't they? No one stands up and tells him when he's wrong. That's really too bad."

Curry had better luck with the rest of the men. When he spoke to them on the Saturday before the tournament, he decided to risk a risqué joke: "What are the three words a man wants to hear *least* when he's making love?" he asked. Answer: "Honey, I'm home."

The room broke up. Curry had communicated. He had even convinced a few people that a Wimbledon chairman could be mischievous.

Wimbledon went on without Agassi. At 2:08 P.M. precisely, Becker twisted in a serve and Herrera, clearly not intimidated by the circumstances, blasted a perfect return at his feet. The duke and duchess clapped. John Curry smiled. "Once they hit the first ball, the job is fun," he said. "It's those other fifty weeks that can get tough."

The first prominent name to lose in London was the only man who had not lost in Paris—Andres Gomez. He was knocked out by twenty-six-year-old Jim Grabb, a good grass-court player and Patrick McEnroe's doubles partner. Few people found the loss surprising. Gomez was at Wimbledon only because he felt the French Open champion should be there. "If I had really wanted to do something, I would have had to come straight here from Paris," he said. "Once I went home, I had no chance."

Gomez had not picked up a racquet during his ten days in Guayaquil. Even after he arrived in London, preparing for the grass was difficult. He was overwhelmed and amazed by the outpouring of congratulations he received from other players. He knew that part of their happiness was that he'd beaten Agassi, the most unpopular player on tour, in the final. Agassi's refusal to even enter the locker room in Paris had been the subject of much joking. But Gomez also knew that most of what was said to him was heartfelt and had to do with the kind of person he had been for twelve years. He had proven that being thirty didn't make you too old to win the big ones.

"Some of the things guys said really shocked me," he said. "They were very emotional about it. A couple of times I sort of stopped and said, 'Are you talking to me?' Tennis players aren't that way. They think about themselves and that's it.

"The only problem is, right now, I feel empty. I worked so hard and so long to win in Paris, it's going to be tough for me to get really psyched to play. I hope that feeling doesn't last long. There are still things I want to do in my career. I've done okay at Wimbledon [one quarterfinal] and I know I can play well at the Open. That's still there for me. But right now, the feeling just isn't there."

Gomez didn't take the loss too hard. He dropped out of the doubles and was on a plane home by noon the next day.

So was John McEnroe.

Two hours after Grabb had finished off Gomez, McEnroe walked onto Centre Court with Derrick Rostagno. McEnroe had not caught any breaks in drawing Rostagno, a player everyone in the locker room knew was capable of beating anyone, especially if his opponent was unprepared.

Nine months earlier, in New York, it was Rostagno who had come within a net cord of knocking Becker out of the U.S. Open in the second round. That match haunted him, the memory of Becker's forehand hitting the net and hopping over his racquet as he was poised to put away the winning volley still vivid.

"I still dream about that shot," he said. "I can still see myself standing there. I was on the shot, I had it. Who knows what a win like that would have meant to me? It was against Boris Becker, it was in my home country, it was in a tournament where I knew I could play well, because I had been to the quarterfinals the year before.

"That was a career-changing moment, there's no question in my mind about that. Essentially, that match was what I had been working for all these years and it was right there. But, hey, you have to keep things in perspective. I've been very lucky in life. One bad break on a tennis court doesn't change that."

Rostagno's view of the world was considerably different than that of most of his fellow pros. He had lived in Germany, Argentina, and Los Angeles growing up and, unlike most of the Americans on tour, spoke a second language—Spanish—fluently. He had gone to Stanford for two years before deciding to try the tour at the end of 1985.

Shortly after turning pro, he won a Challenger event in San Luis Potosi, Mexico. That put him into the top two hundred for the first time in his life. Satisfied with that performance and ready to go home, he decided to skip the satellite that was scheduled to start in Mexico City the next day. He called his parents, told them he was going to come home, and booked a flight to Los Angeles.

But when he got on the flight the next morning, he learned that it stopped over in Mexico City. When the plane landed there, Rostagno looked at his watch: It was a little after eight o'clock in the morning. Sign-in for the satellite was at 9 A.M. "I figured, What the heck, maybe I'm meant to play in this thing anyway. I got off the plane, went straight to the courts, signed in, and had to play two matches that day because I didn't get a wild card into the main draw.

"I didn't get to the hotel to check in until about eight that night. I was exhausted. As I was checking in I looked over and saw a newspaper. There had been a plane crash. I recognized the flight number—it was my flight. It had crashed just after leaving Mexico City. The story said there were no survivors."

Before he even had a chance to think about how close he had come to death, Rostagno thought about his parents. He had never had time to call them to say he wasn't coming home. He raced to a phone.

"When they heard my voice they both started sobbing on the phone," he said. "They thought I was dead. My aunt had heard a report on the radio, and she had called and asked them if I was flying on Mexicana from Mexico City that morning. They said they thought I was. She said, 'I don't want to tell you this but . . .' They went through agony that whole day."

It wasn't until days later that Rostagno—who went on to win the satellite—really had a chance to sit down and think about what had happened. "It was as if someone had said, 'Here's a gift,' " he said. "I didn't go through a life change or anything dramatic like that, but it did make me think about a lot of things. It also helped put a lot of things, like tennis, into perspective."

It was not coincidence that a whim—deciding to get off a plane at the last second and play a tournament—had saved Rostagno's life. That is the way he is. Once, at a tournament in Florence, he took a job during the week as a motorcycle mechanic, just for fun. When a train strike in

Austria left him stranded, he spent a couple of days hitchhiking and taking pictures rather than just renting a car or finding a plane flight. He often travels the tour in a motor home.

At twenty-four, Rostagno is about as close to being a flake as you are likely to find in the regimented, everything-must-be-planned world of tennis. He is at the opposite end of the spectrum from Ivan Lendl. He is also one of the more thoughtful people in the game.

"I look at a lot of these guys who have made the huge money, and I don't see a lot of happiness," he said. "When we're kids and we start playing this sport, we see this ideal out there, the illusion of life as a pro.

"None of us sees the reality of it. We're all working toward *something,* but we aren't sure what. Every one of us is a fanatic. I like to think I have other things in my life, but let's face it: In a nutshell, this is what I've devoted my life to—at least up until now. A lot of guys keep working and working and then they achieve something really big, like winning a Grand Slam. Or maybe it's just being in the top one hundred or the top fifty. Whatever it is, was it worth giving up my childhood for?

"I remember the first time I won a [professional] tournament, I went back to my hotel room and was completely depressed. There was this great high at the moment I won and then that was it. All my friends had left town to go to the next tournament. I felt all alone, and I realized getting that high I had felt on the court back would be very, very hard, even if I won another tournament.

"You keep working, though, you keep looking. That's why the Becker match hurt so much. I had put in the work. I was ready to win the match." He smiled. "Just once, I want to walk off after one of those the winner, not the noble loser."

Rostagno knew he had a superb opportunity to do that against McEnroe. After Queen's, McEnroe had spent a restless week playing in a disastrous exhibition outside London. On the first day of the exhibition, McEnroe and Jonas Svensson had endured three rain delays—without finishing the first set—when everyone decided to call it quits and come back at noon the next day.

McEnroe, who had his brother-in-law Patrick O'Neal traveling with him, got into his car to head back to the house he was renting in Wimbledon. Five minutes later, the sun came out. McEnroe exploded.

"Can you believe this shit?" he said, gesturing toward the sky. "If we had waited five minutes, we could have finished that match. Jeez, I can't believe we didn't wait. I'm supposed to practice with Edberg tomorrow; now I have to call it off. I feel like a complete dork."

He sat back on the seat cushion for a minute in silence. Then he started up again. "See, this is the kind of thing I can't let ruin my day. But I'm capable of it. I'm angry right now, really frustrated. I need to do everything right to get ready for Wimbledon, and I just screwed up big time. Goddammit, I'm just so mad at myself."

He smiled, picturing how people would react to his outburst. "If I told somebody I was upset because I have to go forty minutes back to Wentworth tomorrow, do you think they would care? Do you think they would understand why it pisses me off? I doubt it. Maybe I shouldn't be pissed off."

He sat back for another moment. "*God,* this pisses me off!" he said as the car pulled up to the house.

When he walked into the house, his brother and Vitas Gerulaitis, who had come to England as a practice partner for McEnroe, were waiting. McEnroe went through the whole story, getting angry all over again as he did. The phone rang. It was Tatum. McEnroe disappeared into the bedroom for a few minutes. When he returned, he was smiling.

"I'm okay now," he said. "Sean [his younger son] is upset because he doesn't have a blanket exactly like Kevin's. That puts it all back into perspective for me. I miss my family, but knowing that they're back there helps me keep myself together."

He was clearly on a tight string, though. Two days before the tournament started he decided to try a wide-body racquet, hoping it would give him some of the power he felt his game had been lacking the last couple of years. The fact that he was willing to experiment with a new racquet two days before Wimbledon was a clear sign of how unsure of himself McEnroe was.

The new racquet didn't help. McEnroe was never really in the match. He did manage to break back when Rostagno served for the first set, to get to 5–5. But Rostagno promptly broke at love and served out the set.

Once, McEnroe had been Wimbledon's bad boy. Now he was the prodigal son and the crowd, usually semicomatose, tried desperately to wake him up. McEnroe wanted to respond. He argued a couple of line calls in the second set—even winning one of the arguments, which so upset Rostagno that *he* received a code of conduct warning. That victory proved pyrrhic, however. It seemed to spur Rostagno to play even better. He broke in the next game to lead 4–2, and eighty-nine minutes into the match was up two sets.

By now, the screams from the stands had turned to pleas. Rostagno had blown a two-set lead against Becker in New York; maybe McEnroe could match that comeback. Maybe he would get a lucky net cord. No such luck. It was Rostagno who got the net cord. Serving for the match at 5–4, he slipped coming in, reached out, and tapped a half volley that clipped the net and dropped over. That put Rostagno at match point.

Rostagno walked back to the baseline, a sheepish grin on his face. "You bet I was thinking about New York," he said later. "I guess this one was meant to be."

It came to be a moment later. After Rostagno double-faulted on the first match point—"nice choke there," he said—he nailed a clean service winner and it was over. Quick, clean, and complete. The only thing McEnroe did right the whole afternoon was grabbing Rostagno by the arm when he was about to walk off without bowing to the Royal Box.

Mary Carillo had watched Lendl thrash McEnroe at Queen's. Now this. Sitting at home, for the first time she found herself thinking, "I wish he would quit."

Others who cared about McEnroe had similar thoughts. Even his brother wondered if maybe it was too late for that last comeback he wanted so much. The house in Wimbledon was very quiet that night. Peter Fleming, McEnroe's old doubles partner and longtime friend, came over. Patrick McEnroe was happy to see him because he felt John needed someone to talk reality to him—someone who wasn't his little brother.

Fleming and Patrick McEnroe were blunt in their assessment of the situation. "We told him that he had been saying for four years now that he was going to work hard and the bottom line was, he hadn't," Patrick said. "If he wasn't so talented, it would have caught up with him sooner. Peter said to him, 'If you really don't want to work, that's fine, pack it in.' "

John McEnroe didn't want to pack it in. He didn't want to go out as a loser. "I can't go out this way," he kept saying. And, for the first time, Patrick McEnroe heard his brother say he felt he had let people down—not just himself, but others. "I've let down the people who have cared about me and stuck with me," John McEnroe said. "I've let the power game beat me, I've let Lendl beat me. I've let people think his way is the right way. When I played him at Queen's, he pissed on my second serve every time. How can I let that asshole do that?"

As always, John McEnroe rambled. But every time he started to back off from making a full commitment, his brother and his friend wouldn't let him. "At one point," Patrick remembered, "he said he was just going to kick back in London for a week, take it easy. Peter and I both said, 'No, no, you can't do that. You've got to stop this six-months talk. You've got to start making every day matter. You haven't got any time left.' "

For once, John McEnroe listened. He knew that Fleming and his brother were saying these things only because they wanted a happy ending as much as he did. "I think he understood that he had really sunk to a new low," Patrick McEnroe said. "No knock on Rostagno, but John was never in the match. I could tell that morning he wasn't ready to play, because he had started an argument with me about the whole ATP Tour thing. That just wasn't John. Usually on the day of a match, he's so focused you can't talk to him about anything."

McEnroe had been jolted. He flew home to New York the next day and called his boyhood coach, Antonio Palafox. He had been kicking the idea around in his head for a while. Now, he stopped thinking and picked up the phone. His message was simple: I need help. Tony Palafox already knew that. When McEnroe went to see him, he asked him what he really thought about his game.

"John," Palafox said, "you're missing shots you made look easy when you were twelve years old."

John McEnroe didn't argue. The two old friends went to work. The U.S. Open was eight weeks away.

The country of Great Britain lasted twenty-four hours and one round longer than McEnroe at Wimbledon.

This was nothing new, of course. Virginia Wade had managed to win Wimbledon in 1977, but no English male had won the tournament since Fred Perry won the last of his three titles in 1936. There was a statue of Perry just inside the main gate, and one of the running jokes was that the statue might still be the best player in the country. There were lots of jokes about British tennis. The country had one man—Jeremy Bates—and one woman—Sarah Loosemore—ranked in the top one hundred, Bates at No. 87, Loosemore at No. 89.

Bates was twenty-eight, a sullen, whiny man who always seemed to be complaining about something, win or lose. In a sport known for players who acted spoiled, Bates was ranked near the top of most people's lists when it came to ill-mannered behavior. He spoke to almost no one in the English media because he felt they had crucified him unfairly over the years. Few of those he didn't speak to felt they were missing very much. Nonetheless, any Bates victory—because it was a British victory—was big news.

Loosemore, on the other hand, had star quality. She had just turned nineteen and had moved up more than two hundred spots in the rankings since the start of the year. She was a striking woman: five feet nine, with long blond hair and a very English, regal way of carrying herself. She had solid ground strokes and pretty good power, and when she beat Barbara Paulus, the sixteenth seed, on opening day, the tabloids went wild. That result, combined with Sara Gomer's upset of eighth seed Manuela Maleeva and Bates's five-set win over Peter Lundgren, was enough to send the English media into paroxysms of joy.

The joy didn't last, of course. Gomer lost her second-round match, Loosemore lost in the second round, and Bates also lost—to Rostagno, in four sets. Hadingham's Dunkirk had not yet arrived for English tennis

While the men were losing McEnroe, Gomez, the still-struggling Tim Mayotte, Jim Courier, and, sadly, the ever-inconsistent Henri Leconte during the first week, the women were proceeding with few surprises. Six of the top eight seeds reached the quarterfinals and the two who didn't, Manuela Maleeva and Arantxa Sanchez, both lost in the first round, proving again that grass was not their surface.

The focus for the women as week two began was on the old and the new—Steffi Graf (the old, at twenty-one) and, of course, Jennifer Capriati. The luck of the draw had placed them against each other in the fourth round, although Capriati had to survive a huge scare from Robin White in the third.

Even though the White match had been difficult, Capriati's first week had been a breeze compared to Graf's. Graf had hoped that her health problems would be left behind in France, although she knew her father's troubles would certainly make the trip across the English Channel.

Peter Graf's personal life was very much a concern of the Wimbledon Committee. The English tabloids were carrying interviews with Michelle Meissner, alleging that Peter Graf had fathered her child. Graf had been asked the questions before and had handled them, but the committee didn't want her to have to do that here. The Hadingham/Curry "make the players comfortable" creed was now being carried over to press conferences. And so, each time Graf came to the interview room, her committee escort, Bernard Neal, would read what he described as a "health warning."

"The committee does not wish the lady champion to be upset," Neal read. "And so, if at any time the questions put to her deviate from the subject of tennis, the conference will be ended immediately."

Most of the media assumed that Graf had asked the committee to take this step. She hadn't, although she certainly didn't object. When several members of the American media pointed out to committee members that this sort of censorship was silly, that Graf was capable of simply saying "no comment" if she chose to, Neal said that while that might very well be true, "the very act of having the question asked might upset Steffi."

This was silliness in the first degree. Being asked about a choked forehand or a critical double fault was also upsetting to a player. Where was the line to be drawn? If Graf didn't want to be asked about her father's troubles, what prevented McEnroe from being asked about his lousy tennis? What would prevent Agassi, in some future year, from saying it would be upsetting to be asked why he hadn't played here in the past? The precedent being set was dangerous—and unnecessary.

The "health warning" was mercifully abandoned after the quarterfinals, and Graf was asked about how her father's problems had affected her tennis. She answered the question with little trouble—saying that while she didn't enjoy what was going on, it didn't affect her tennis. That wasn't true, but that wasn't the point. She was asked the question, answered it, and no walls tumbled down.

Nothing the committee did could protect Graf from her continuing health problems, though. Her sinus misery continued unabated. By the end of the first week, after three easy victories, she was having trouble breathing. Her doctor told her that a hospital back home in Germany had special equipment that could give her some temporary relief. Could the equipment be flown to London? No, Graf had to go to Germany.

After winning her third-round match from Claudia Kohde-Kilsch on Friday (losing just two games), Graf chartered a plane to Germany. The treatment seemed to help, but on the trip back to England, Graf came down with a middle-ear infection.

"It was one o'clock in the morning; I felt sick and terrible and awful," she said. "I said, 'What in the world am I doing here?' But at the time it seemed like the right thing to do."

Somehow, Graf managed to play her best match of the summer against Capriati. She never let her get into the match, winning 6–2, 6–4 in fifty-nine minutes. Capriati had nothing to be ashamed of. She had played some brilliant points and held her own against the best player in the world. Naturally, the teenager was completely undaunted by the loss.

"Well, now I know why they call it The Forehand," she said. "I mean, I really had fun out there. Look at all the people who came. Even Princess Fergie went there."

Sarah Ferguson, the Duchess of York, had indeed been there and she had picked a good day to show up. The men and women were both playing their fourth rounds and every court was packed. One of the most surprising things about Wimbledon is how small it is. Centre Court itself is tiny compared to the one at Roland Garros, Flinders Park, or the U.S. Tennis Center. It is a cathedral in green with no upper deck. There are bad seats—pillars cause many obstructed views—but no one is very far from the court. The outside courts are intimate, too. Court 1 is one of the best places in the world to watch tennis; the seats are almost on top of the court.

The bleachers on the outside show courts are similar. "Out back," away from the glamour courts, people sit or stand on benches to watch, the spire of St. Mary's looming in the background. Half those courts have no bleachers, just benches. When a match gets close at one of those courts, or if a popular player happens to be assigned there, people practically stand on top of one another to get a view. Empty, the entire club can be walked from one end to the other in seven or eight minutes. Packed, it can take an hour to fight through the crowds—although the new laws had created a bit more breathing room.

On the second Monday, the toughest decision to make was where to turn next. Everyone—Fergie included—had raced to Centre Court for the first two matches of the day there—Becker–Cash and Graf–Capriati.

Becker–Cash was a matchup one would normally expect to see in the semifinals or final. Cash had won the tournament in 1987; Becker had won it in 1985, 1986, and 1989. Now, though, Cash had needed a wild card to get into the tournament; he still hadn't made it back into the top one hundred. He had survived a difficult first-round match against a Soviet qualifier, Dmitri Poliakov, coming from two sets to one down to win, and then won two easy matches after that to reach the round of 16.

Becker, after surviving a brief scare against Herrera, had a genuine scare against Wally Masur in the second round. A tough match with Masur was no surprise to Becker. Masur had beaten him in the Australian in 1987 and had beaten McEnroe at Wimbledon in 1988. He was a typical Aussie: competitive, tough-minded, never one to back down. He had been born in England (his parents were on vacation), and the English media always referred to him as "Southampton-born Wally Masur."

Bob Brett believed that the Masur match was the key to Becker's Wimbledon. "If he can win this match," he had said beforehand, "he can have a very good tournament. But there's going to come a time when he's going to be in trouble against Wally, and then we'll find out how tough-minded he is right now."

The moment came early. Masur won the first set in a tiebreak. Becker broke to go up 2–1 in the second, but Masur quickly had him down 0–40, trying to break back. This was the moment Brett had talked about. If Masur broke right back, the match might very well be a long, difficult one. Becker responded. He came up with five straight big serves to pull out the game. Masur got the message. Becker won easily in four.

"That match told me I had finally put Paris behind me," Becker said. "I knew my next two matches wouldn't be easy, but that didn't bother me. I knew I was ready to play now."

Becker beat Dan Goldie, a solid grass-court player who had been a quarterfinalist in 1989, in the third round, and that brought him to Cash. He had a brief scare in the first set, when Cash twice had set points, but he hung in, won the set in a tiebreak, and cruised from there.

The match of the day was the last of the day. All eight women's matches had been decided in straight sets and there had not been a five-setter on the men's side. Brad Gilbert and David Wheaton changed that. Playing in the twilight on court 1, the two Americans went at it for more than four hours.

This was a grudge match between two players who could not have been more different. Wheaton had just turned twenty-one and was only beginning to understand his potential. Gilbert was twenty-nine, the game's ultimate scuffler. He had been ranked as high as No. 4 in the world, though no one could figure out how. Gilbert would play anywhere, anytime, and made no bones about the fact that he played the game for money.

Jerry Solomon, who had at times advised him at ProServ, had often argued with him about his schedule over the years, pointing out to him that he never gave himself enough rest or preparation time before the Grand Slams. Gilbert shrugged him off. "His attitude was that he probably wasn't going to win a Grand Slam anyway, so why not go play where he could make the most money," Solomon said. "I didn't necessarily agree with that approach, but that's what he's been comfortable with."

Gilbert's approach to the Grand Slams was reflected in his record in them: In twenty-two tournaments, he had reached one quarterfinal. In 1989, his best year as a pro, he had not won a single match in Grand Slam play.

He had come to Wimbledon with a slightly different plan than in the past. "I just decided I'm going to the net, no matter who I play," he said. "That's the way I have to play on grass, and if someone beats me playing that way, fine. But that's the way it's going to be."

Gilbert had played solidly to get this far, but Wheaton felt confident he could win. He admitted that he badly wanted Becker in the quarterfinals, to see if he could play him a little tougher than he had at Queen's. He had already proved to himself and to his brother that he had learned from the Srejber loss in Paris. He had won tough five-setters in the second and third rounds, beating Paul Annacone after trailing 3–0 in the fifth set and then coming from two sets down to beat Jonas Svensson.

Both were matches in which he could have gotten discouraged. Being down a service break in the last set to a grass-court player of Annacone's caliber was no small thing. The Svensson match was even more encouraging. It was Svensson who had beaten him in three straight tiebreaks at Wimbledon in 1989. That ghost had now been purged.

Gilbert was another ghost. Wheaton had been up a set and a break on Gilbert in the semifinals at Stratton Mountain the previous summer. But he had let Gilbert back into the match and ended up losing. This time, he led again, winning the first set in a superb tiebreak and the second easily. Becker loomed. Wheaton again let his mind wander. Before he knew it, Gilbert had blown through the third and fourth sets. Wheaton dug in again. He broke Gilbert and served for the match at 5–3.

This is where Gilbert is at his best. He can talk himself back into a match better than any player in the world. Twice, Wheaton had match point. On the first, he hit a forehand that looked like a winner. "I was on my way in to shake hands," Gilbert admitted. The ball landed two inches wide. On the second, with what looked like an easy forehand volley, Wheaton tried to play a drop shot instead of punching a winner. "I can't even tell you why I played it that way," he said. "I don't think in that situation; I just react."

Which is exactly why Wheaton will be a fine grass-court player someday. But on this day, his instinct was the wrong one. Gilbert got to the ball and pushed a clean winner past Wheaton. A moment later he broke, and when he held, it was 5–5. John Wheaton wondered if his little brother would hang in or get down on himself. He hung in. Both men did. It was 11–11 and near dusk before Gilbert came up with two brilliant returns to break.

He held to win 13–11 and let out a shriek of joy. Walking off the court, John Wheaton had a far different look on his face than he had in Paris. "I'd like to have a couple of points back," he said. "But I couldn't be prouder of David. Gilbert's a winner. He proved that for sure. But David never let up, even after he blew the match points. That's all I can possibly ask of him."

David Wheaton wasn't quite as philosophical. When he got to the locker room at 9 P.M. it was virtually empty. He did his very best to destroy it. "I just went crazy for a minute," he said. "It really, really hurt to lose that match. Fortunately, when I almost caved in the rafters swinging my racquet against them, I calmed down because I was afraid I was going to get in trouble. The locker kids helped me clean up."

When Wheaton got finished cleaning up, he came to meet the media. Someone asked what he thought of Gilbert's chances against Becker. "He doesn't have a chance," Wheaton answered, always honest. "I think I would have had a chance, not a great one, but I don't think Brad has the shots to beat Becker. He'll lose in three."

Predictably, Gilbert took the comments personally. "That's why he's ranked thirty spots below me and keeps blowing leads against me," he said. "I think I have a good chance to win if I play well."

Wheaton had lost the match but he knew his tennis: Gilbert won nine games against Becker. That hardly comforted Wheaton, who spent most of the summer trying to put the Gilbert match out of his mind.

"I kept watching the tape over and over," he said. "I must have watched it twenty times. I was certain if I watched it enough times, I'd make that volley on match point one time."

He shook his head. "It hasn't happened yet."

The men's quarterfinal matchups, in addition to Becker–Gilbert, were Goran Ivanisevic (who had beaten Rostagno)–Kevin Curren; Christian Bergstrom (who had beaten Grabb)–Stefan Edberg, and Ivan Lendl–Brad Pearce.

Pearce was the biggest surprise in the group. Every year at Wimbledon someone seems to come out of nowhere to make a mark. Some have been major stars announcing their arrival—McEnroe in 1977; Pat Cash in 1984; Becker in 1985. Others were merely having a brief stab at glory: Pat DuPre was a semifinalist in 1979; Rod Frawley, a semifinalist in 1981; Chris Lewis, a finalist in 1983.

"I know a lot of people think I just fell out of a cloud to get here," Pearce said after he had beaten Mark Woodforde in the fourth round. "But an awful lot of work went into this."

There was little doubt about that. Pearce was twenty-four, the great-

great-grandson of John David Lafayette Pearce, a general in the Mormon battalion that had fought the Indians in the St. George area of Utah. His father, Wayne, had given up his dream of becoming a pro while in college and had gone on to get his MBA. But after graduation he was offered the job as tennis coach at Brigham Young. He accepted, thinking he would do it for a year—and stayed twenty.

Wayne Pearce met Carol Douglas while both were undergraduates at the University of Utah. They were married after graduation and had five children. Brad was number three. Wayne Pearce taught all his children to play tennis.

"It became our family thing," Brad remembered. "In a Mormon family, time together is very important, and tennis became the thing we all did together."

All the Pearces were good players, but Brad was the best. He can remember first wanting to be a pro at the age of six and was extremely disappointed when he was the only member of the family not blessed with great height. "My dad is six feet, both my brothers got to be over six feet, my older sister is five feet nine, and my youngest sister is already five feet seven, at fourteen," he said. "I never got past five feet nine. They got the size, but I seemed to get the hand-eye coordination."

Pearce played in his first nationals at age twelve and won the doubles title. But later that summer, the family was struck by tragedy. His oldest brother, Evan, who was eighteen, drowned in a swimming accident. Twelve years later, Pearce still feels the loss.

"I wasn't that close to him because of the age difference," he said softly. "But I remember how crushed my family was, especially my dad. For the next year, he was like a shadow. Then, the pain I felt was mostly for him and for my mom. Now I feel it more myself. There's no relationship like brother and brother. I wish Evan and I had had more time together."

As a teenager, Pearce went through one stage in which he wanted to quit tennis, then another in which he wanted to devote his life to it. The second stage was the one that stuck, and Pearce asked his parents to let him move to Los Angeles to live with a friend during his junior year of high school so he could focus on his tennis. They were reluctant because of the cost and the sacrifices they knew Brad would have to make in his personal life, but finally agreed.

"It was the decision that made me a tennis player," Pearce said. "But it was a tough time for me. I had no social life. At home, I was pretty popular and had a lot of friends. In Los Angeles, I knew no one except the family I lived with. I didn't have a date my last two years in high school."

He was the No. 2 junior in the country his senior year and decided to go to UCLA. He planned to stay one year but stayed two. "The summer after my freshman year I played the tour and did horribly," he said. "I was really discouraged. I went back to school and worked harder than I ever had in my life. I went to class, studied, went to the weight room, and played tennis. That was it. Everyone started calling me The Hermit.

"At the end of the second quarter, I cracked," he said, laughing. "I was sitting in a history class one day when all of a sudden I said, 'I have to get out of here.' I jumped out of my seat and started climbing over people to get out of the room. I'm sure a lot of people thought I was crazy."

Pearce dropped out of school at the end of the quarter and turned pro. He had immediate success, winning a couple of Challengers to get into the top one hundred. But because of his lack of size, he felt he had to find more power; he began fiddling with his serve. It caused him nothing but trouble. "My dad begged me not to mess with my serve but I didn't listen," he said. "It took me two years to figure out that he was right."

Pearce married Cindi Abbott in April 1987. The two had grown up on the same street but never dated until college. Even then it was sporadic. Brad was at UCLA; Cindi, at Brigham Young. After his first year on tour, Brad came home at Christmas and, pretty much out of the blue, proposed.

"We had more or less broken up when I went on tour," Pearce said. "She was dating someone else. But I had really missed her while I was traveling, and I just made up my mind I was going to ask her to marry me.

"The funny thing is, when I asked her, she misunderstood me. She thought I was speaking in the hypothetical. She said, 'Yes, I think I would marry you.' She thought I meant in the future. When I took out the ring, she flipped out."

She still said yes. A long engagement was planned, but Pearce couldn't handle it. "With Mormon values, traveling together was out of the question," Pearce said. "We were young, we both had a lot of hormones going."

Their decision to marry that April proved to be a good one because it gave Carol Pearce the chance to see her son get married. She had been fighting cancer of the colon for several years. Being on the road, Brad didn't understand just how sick she was. When he came back from his honeymoon, she had faded to almost nothing. Two weeks later, she died.

The next year was difficult; his tennis wasn't very good. Brad was concerned about his father. He and Cindi were not only adjusting to marriage but to traveling together on very little money. "There were times when we wrote a check somewhere for twenty dollars and then had to scramble to get money into the bank in time to cover it," he said. "I was very, very uptight about everything. I had always been calm, cool, and collected on a tennis court. I lost that. I became really quick-tempered. Anytime something went wrong, I just lost it. I tanked a lot of matches just because I got frustrated.

"I felt torn in a lot of directions. I believe in eternal life and I believe I'll see my mother and brother again. But the loss was still there. There were times when I'd just burst into tears because something would make me think about them. It even happened on the court a few times."

By the end of 1988, Pearce was on the verge of giving up tennis. He had gone from a high of ninetieth on the computer down to No. 302. He was just about out of money. He decided to give himself a few more months and try to change his attitude. "I had been trying to win tournaments and get in the Top Ten," he said. "It was as if I felt if I couldn't do that, nothing else was worth doing. I decided to just try to play hard every single match and see what happened."

Slowly, he began to turn his game around. He began to calm down on the court, to hang in matches. He had his ranking up to 161 by the end of 1989. He made just under $50,000 for the year, and that was enough to convince him it was worth trying for another year.

"I set a simple goal for myself at the start of the year," he said, "to get into Wimbledon without playing qualifying. I had lost three straight years in qualifying."

He had to play in a lot of qualies to get into enough main draws and thus have a shot at getting straight into Wimbledon. "I became known as Mr. Qualifier," he said. At Indian Wells, after saving match points against Patrick McEnroe, he upset Andrei Chesnokov in the first round. He beat Amos Mansdorf to make the quarterfinals in Hong Kong. That got him into the U.S. Clay Courts, the last tournament before Wimbledon entries closed. "I figured out I had to win one match to get in," he said. "The field isn't that strong, so I thought I had a pretty good shot."

It wasn't an easy shot. Pearce drew Jim Grabb, the second seed. "I played the best match of my life," Pearce said. "It proved to me once and for all that I could play well in a pressure situation."

He won, 6–1, 6–4, and that got him into Wimbledon. Now he had taken full advantage of the opportunity. In the fourth round, he easily beat Woodforde, who had upset Jim Courier in the third round. Best of all, his father had flown in that day to watch.

Two days later, Brad Pearce walked onto *the* Centre Court for the first time in his life. His opponent was Lendl. "I was worried that I wouldn't be able to hit a shot, wouldn't be able to even bend my elbow," Pearce said. "Just walking out there is like nothing else in tennis. I wanted to prove that I belonged."

He did just that. Lendl won the match in four tough sets, one break deciding each one. Pearce heard the crowd calling his name, heard the cheers as he walked off, and couldn't help but tingle. "The top guys take all of that for granted, I understand that," he said. "But for me, whatever else happens, I'll never forget the feeling of playing on that court—and playing well."

There were also pragmatic reasons to feel good. His performance at Wimbledon was worth $47,588. He and Cindi had a daughter now, and they had moved out of their apartment in Provo in January, unsure of where they would live next. "Now we can think about a house," Pearce said. "We don't have to be vagabonds anymore."

Pearce's ranking shot up to No. 80 after Wimbledon. He would now go straight into any tournament he wanted to play. No more Mr. Qualifier. His days as a vagabond tennis player were, at long last, over.

Once Graf had beaten Capriati, the women's match that everyone was looking forward to was a rematch of the French final: Graf–Seles in one of the semifinals.

Zina Garrison knew that almost everyone in tennis was counting on a Graf–Seles rematch. She had other ideas, though. Very quietly she had worked her way to the quarterfinals. Perhaps never in Wimbledon history had a fifth seed been so universally ignored as she progressed through the draw. Garrison dropped just three games in each of her first three matches and then surprised even herself with an easy 6–3, 6–3 victory over Helena Sukova in the round of 16. Sukova is an excellent grass-court player, a six-foot-three-inch Amazon whose huge serve makes her extremely tough on grass.

○

Garrison handled her on court 3, the sixth of Wimbledon's six show courts. It was the closest Garrison had gotten to the spotlight. She had not been requested in the interview room once. "I'm used to it," she said with a shrug. Then she smiled. "I did notice that Jennifer [Capriati] was on Centre twice and court one once. It might have been nice if they'd have gotten me in there once."

Being ignored, overlooked, left alone, was nothing new to Garrison. Long ago, she accepted the fact that being black in tennis made life tougher, that the same people who threw millions of dollars at Jennifer Capriati and Andre Agassi wanted little to do with a black player, that many fans looked at you as an oddity. Long ago, she accepted the fact that almost nothing would come easy.

It didn't bother her because nothing in her life had ever come easy. She grew up in Houston, the youngest—by ten years—of seven children. Her father was a postman who worked long hours to support his children. He died when his youngest daughter was five, and she can still remember the story in the newspaper in which the family's neighbors talked about what a good, honest man her father was.

It was her brother, Rodney, twelve years older than Zina, who introduced her to John Wilkerson and asked him to teach his sister, then ten, to play tennis. Wilkerson, who ran a public-parks tennis program for kids, taught her far more than tennis. Zina took to the game quickly and within two years had a national ranking. She was paired with another remarkable talent, Lori McNeil, who was thirty-two days younger than she was. They traveled the country together throughout juniors, played doubles together, forged a relationship that would survive numerous tremors through the years.

When they traveled in the south, John Wilkerson made it clear to Garrison, McNeil, and his other young players that they were to stay with the group at all times. "He didn't want us wandering into situations that were going to cause problems," Garrison remembered. "We knew at most tournaments that we were the only blacks there and that some people didn't want us there. John never tried to pretend that we weren't different, but he also never let it affect where we went or how we played."

Tennis has produced about one great black player per decade. Althea Gibson broke down the first barriers in the 1950s, when she won Wimbledon and the U.S. Championships. Arthur Ashe won the U.S. Open in 1968 and Wimbledon in 1975, and Yannick Noah won the French Open in 1983. In 1990 Garrison was the best of six black women playing the tour regularly. Two young black Americans, Malivai Washington and

Bryan Shelton, had popped into the top one hundred on the men's side.

Washington, having grown up in Michigan, had few memories of any blatant racism. Shelton, from Huntsville, Alabama, had a very different experience. "There were tournaments at certain clubs that I didn't try to enter as a kid because my family knew that blacks weren't welcome there," he said. "I suppose we could have made an issue out of it, but we didn't. I remember one tournament I played in when I was thirteen, in Birmingham, and I won it. The next year I wasn't invited back. The message was pretty clear."

All the black players agreed that, for blacks, tennis was a catch-22 situation: it was still a game in which a considerable amount of money was required to make a prospect into a player. Black youngsters rarely have the money needed to become top players. They have also had very few role models. Ashe was Garrison's role model.

"I remember sitting in a room with about thirty people, watching the Wimbledon final in 1975," she said. "When he won, we were all unbelievably excited. We all ran outside and started screaming, 'I'm going to be like Arthur, I can hit the ball just like Arthur.' But he was the only tennis player any of us could relate to. I mean, what did I have in common with Jimmy Connors or Bjorn Borg or Chris Evert?"

Very little. And that, says Ashe, is a large part of the problem. "In the United States, black kids, especially the boys, grow up wanting to be basketball players. They all want to be Michael Jordan or Magic Johnson.

"But that's just a small part of it. If you look at most of the young white kids coming along in tennis, they're the product of family projects. Mommy, Daddy, or both have put a lot of time and effort into making them tennis players. In the cities, that just isn't going to happen in black families. Many of them are one-parent homes, and even for those that aren't, where is the time to get in a car and cart them around to lessons or tournaments? How many of them have cars?"

Ashe has put together several tennis programs for young blacks, most notably in Newark, New Jersey. Late in 1989, he held a clinic/fund-raiser and convinced Boris Becker to come out and hit with some of the kids in the program. One of them, an eleven-year-old named Kishmar Cliney, hit the ball so well that Becker dropped his racquet to applaud him, then shook his hand when they were through. Ashe watched the scene with a small smile on his face.

"That's a kid whom we can really help," he said. "We're looking for a few gems here. Six months ago, this kid was flunking his classes in school. Now he's getting A's. But it's still going to be uphill. Look at him, he's a natural for the game. But will he stick with it? Or will the tyranny of the streets get to him? We'll have to keep right on top of him for him to have any chance at all."

Ashe believes that most black kids need an outsider—such as himself—to offer that extra financial or emotional push, if they are going to make it in tennis. "It takes a John Wilkerson or someone like Dr. [Ronald] Johnson, who helped me, for a black kid to make it," he said. "The USTA is part of the problem. It doesn't have a policy of discrimination except in the de facto sense. A lot of people in the hinterlands are scared that if you give the blacks an inch, they'll dominate the whole damn sport. Who knows if that's true? But the fact is, this is still a country-club sport and when a black kid shows up at a country club, the *best* he can hope for is to be patronized. Remember one thing about Zina Garrison: The toughest thing she's had to overcome in tennis is culture shock. The world she's lived in the past five years is completely different from what she grew up in."

Garrison doesn't disagree. She was the top junior in the country as a senior in high school and wanted to turn pro after she won both the Wimbledon and U.S. Open junior titles. Her mother objected. She wanted her daughter to go to college, which she had the opportunity to do on a full scholarship. They argued at length. Zina finally convinced her mother to allow her to try the pro tour and she had success almost immediately, reaching the quarterfinals at the French Open in 1982 and finishing the year ranked sixteenth in the world. She was lonely, though, because Lori had gone to college. She was pretty much alone on tour.

In 1983, things got better. Lori turned pro and Wilkerson began to travel with his two protégées. Then, at the end of the summer came tragedy: Garrison's mother died suddenly. Zina remembers waking up in the middle of the night on the road, thinking something awful had happened to her mother. When she called home, she found out her premonition had been horribly correct.

For the next year she felt constant guilt about her mother. She had let her down by not going to college, by not being home more often. Often she found herself picking up the phone to call her. Sometimes she would even begin to dial before she remembered that her mother was gone.

Although her ranking didn't go down in 1984, she began to have trouble dealing with pressure situations on the court. She failed to reach the quarterfinals in any of the Grand Slams and lost in the second round at Wimbledon to an over-the-hill, almost-forty-year-old Virginia Wade.

"People still use that match as an example of collapsing under pressure," Garrison can say with a smile now. "I remember I was crying on the court."

She remained a consistent Top Ten player the next five years, but never could get past the toughest pressure situations. In 1987 she and McNeil met in the fourth round of the U.S. Open. The USTA, in a prime example of the kind of de facto racism Ashe talks about, put the match—between two Americans ranked in the Top Ten—not on the stadium court, not on the grandstand court, not on court 16 (the primary outside court) but on court 3, the fourth of the four show courts at the National Tennis Center.

McNeil and Garrison played a superb match, one of the best of the year. Garrison had a match point in the final set tiebreak and thought she had won the match when McNeil's return cracked the net tape. Somehow, though, it crawled over the net and dropped. Buoyed by that break, McNeil came back to win.

Tears again for Garrison. "She's the luckiest player in tennis," she said then, unable to hide her bitterness. "Things like that happen to Lori all the time."

They never seemed to happen to Garrison. The next year, she finally had a breakthrough in a big match, beating Martina Navratilova in the Open quarterfinals. Even though she lost to Gabriela Sabatini in the semifinals, she felt she had taken a giant stride forward. A year later she beat Evert at the Open, in the match that ended The Queen's career, and Zina cried again.

"It was a strange moment for me," she said. "I wanted to win the match very badly, but still I had so much respect for Chris and the kind of person she is that I felt badly. That's what's so weird about that picture of us walking off the court. She's smiling and I'm crying. Chris has always been like that when she loses, very gracious. I've always been like that, win or lose, very emotional."

Garrison has a copy of that picture in her house. "I kept it to remind myself that I didn't want to be remembered *only* as the person who ended Chris Evert's career," she said. "I'm still only twenty-six. I like to think I have my best tennis ahead of me."

The victory over Evert at the Open came at the end of Garrison's best year—as a player and a person. She finished it ranked fourth in the world, and, two weeks after the Open, she married Willard Jackson. A mutual friend had introduced them the previous year, and a whirlwind romance had ensued. For almost the first time since her mother's death, she began to feel her self-confidence returning. In a story in *Sports Illustrated* she admitted that she had been bulimic and had sought help only after almost passing out on court during a match in Kansas City.

She left for Australia with high hopes for 1990. With Navratilova and Seles not in Australia and with Sabatini out of the tournament early, she knew she had a golden chance to reach her first Grand Slam final. But she lost her quarterfinal to Mary Joe Fernandez after twice serving for the match.

That loss sent her into an emotional tailspin that continued to affect her all winter and spring. At the Lipton, she was up 4–0 on Julie Halard in the third set and lost. In Houston she had two match points on Arantxa Sanchez and lost. She had a match point on Natalia Zvereva at Amelia Island and lost again.

"I had gotten to the point where I knew I could get ahead, but I didn't think I could win," she said. "Every time I would get close to winning, I would start to think, Is it going to happen again? Of course, as soon as I thought about it, it was a sure thing that it would happen."

After the loss to Sanchez in Houston—in front of friends and family—Garrison decided she needed help. She had been down on herself since Australia. This was supposed to be *her* year but it sure wasn't turning out that way. Houston convinced her she had to make changes. The first was to see a psychiatrist. She asked Moses Venson, who had been her trainer for seven years, if he knew anyone among the people who worked out at his gym who she might see. He did.

"I went three times over a period of a few weeks," Garrison said. "The key was that I had to find a way to make myself relax on the court, to not want it so much. On big points I was gripping the racquet so tightly, I could barely hit the ball. I realized, thinking back, that on all the match points I had blown I had missed the same shot—an easy forehand."

The psychiatrist gave Garrison some breathing exercises to do when she felt herself tightening up. He told her to try to keep her mind clear while she was playing, to not think about the consequences of a defeat or the rewards of a victory.

There was more. Garrison had stopped working with John Wilkerson on a regular basis at the end of 1987. They were still friends, but he no longer traveled. She had traveled with different hitting partners since then, but never with a full-time coach. She decided it was time for a coach, and asked Sherwood Stewart to take the job. Stewart was also a Texan, one of the great doubles players in the game's history, someone

Garrison felt comfortable with, having played mixed doubles with him. They had won the U.S. Open together in 1987, and Garrison felt Stewart understood her game.

She also decided to change agents. This may have been the most difficult decision of all. Garrison had been friends with Sara Fornaciari since her days as a junior and felt close to her personally. But she was no longer comfortable being represented by ProServ. The lack of a clothing contract bothered her, and so did the fact that no one at ProServ—other than Sara—seemed to think that was a problem.

"All the time I was represented by ProServ, I think I met Donald Dell twice," she said. "What does that tell you about how important he considered me? I had been offered a couple of clothing contracts, but to tell the truth, they were really insulting. I know how the business works, I know I'm not going to get paid as much as some of the more glamorous players, but I wasn't going to accept something just to say I had a contract.

"I had heard from people that a lot of ProServ thought I was wrong for not accepting any contract I was offered. When I heard that, I knew it was time to get out. Sara will always be my friend, but maybe that was part of the problem too. Because she was my friend, she didn't see me as a client she had to do a job for."

Fornaciari had always been honest with Garrison about her marketability. "When someone from one of these companies goes out to watch Zina play, or Lori, they look around and they see several dozen black faces," Fornaciari said. "And that's it. There just aren't that many blacks interested in tennis because there aren't that many players. None of it is fair, but that's the way the business is."

Early in April, Garrison signed with Advantage, specifically with Phil dePicciotto, who represented Graf. She left for Paris in late May with a new on-court approach, a new coach, and a new agent. She also brought Moses Venson with her. Venson knew Garrison as well as anyone, having worked with her since she was nineteen and Rodney had taken her to Venson's gym and said, "This is my sister; she's fat. Help her get in shape."

All the changes produced the same depressing result in Paris. Garrison led Wiltrud Probst 5–2 in her first-round match and had a match point. She blew it—again. She missed a forehand—again. She lost the match—again. She walked off the court in tears—again.

"As down as I felt, Sherwood and Moses wouldn't let me stay down," she said. "They said, 'Okay, now we head for the grass; you're a good grass-court player.' I kind of wanted to go home, to tell the truth. But I called Willard and asked him to come over early. Once he came over, things started to get better."

She won the grass-court warm-up in Birmingham, but then lost early at Eastbourne. Sometimes the breathing exercises worked, sometimes they didn't. She worked hard preparing for Wimbledon and hoped to get a fast start there. "I didn't want to just win my first match; I wanted to win it easily," she said. "I wanted to prove something to myself."

She did just that, whipping Samantha Smith of Great Britain 6–2, 6–1. She then beat Cecilia Dahlman by the same score and Andrea Leand 6–0, 6–3. That brought her to Sukova. When she won that match easily, she was convinced she could beat Seles.

The day of the women's quarterfinals was the first to produce true London weather—cool and cloudy with the sun occasionally poking through the clouds. The schedulers put Garrison–Seles on court 1—not on Centre—because it wasn't expected to be a memorable match. That was a mistake.

Seles, still flying after Paris, her winning streak at thirty-six straight matches, came out blasting. Winner after winner came off her racquet. "She may have played the best set anyone has ever played against me," Garrison said. "The first couple of matches of the tournament I had been hyper and nervous. Moses and Sherwood kept telling me to calm down. After Sukova, I knew I was playing well, so I stayed calm. I felt if I stayed close, I had a chance because she still didn't really understand how to play on grass." The old Garrison might have become tentative in the face of Seles's brilliance. This Garrison kept attacking. Seles finally began to miss and Garrison took the second set. Then, as always, Garrison bolted in front in the third set. Seles dug in. Whenever she had fallen behind during the streak, she had been able to turn her game up another notch. She did it again, unleashing a flurry of grunting, screeching winners. Suddenly, Garrison found herself serving, down 4–5.

Déjà vu? "I still felt calm," she said. "The breathing exercises were working—finally. I just kept my mind on what I had to do."

She held to 5–5. Court 1 was jammed. The match was now at the stage where every point seemed vital. There is no tiebreak in the final set at Wimbledon so, at 6–all, they battled on. Seles held to go up 7–6. Garrison was playing from behind. The pressure kept building. Up 15–0, she double-faulted. A deep breath and a backhand winner—up 30–15. Another deep breath. But chasing a Seles forehand, she slipped and fell.

o

It was 30–all. Garrison got up slowly. The umpire asked if she wanted an injury time-out. Garrison shook her head.

"I was thinking that whenever I fell, I always came up with a good shot afterward, for some reason," she said. "I didn't want to stop."

That decision looked shaky when she missed a forehand on the next point. It was 30–40; match point for Seles. The silence was deafening. Garrison served, Seles returned. The ball went back and forth twice. A Seles forehand floated a bit and Garrison closed on the ball. It was a forehand—that same forehand. "I just said to myself, 'This time, go for it; walk off knowing you went for it, even if you lose,' " she said.

The ball whizzed by Seles and landed in the corner—good by two inches, a perfect shot. "Best shot I've ever hit in my life," Garrison said. "After that, I just knew I was going to win."

Seles won one more point. Garrison, the nonfinisher, finished by winning eleven of the last twelve points. When Seles's last backhand landed long, Garrison was leaping into the air; so was the entire crowd. It was the match of the tournament and the match of Garrison's life.

But it was not enough. "In 1988, I beat Martina in the quarters at the Open and lost to Sabatini; in 1989, after I beat Chris, I lost to Martina. I didn't want to lose in the semis again." Changing that pattern wasn't going to be easy. The opponent was Graf, who had followed her victory over Capriati with a straight-set win over Jana Novotna. Just as people had assumed Graf would meet Seles in the semifinals, they now assumed that Navratilova would meet Graf in the final.

Navratilova kept up her end of the bargain, beating Sabatini easily. But Graf found herself playing a Zina Garrison she didn't recognize. Garrison, attacking on every point, won the first set. Graf knew she had to change tactics. She began coming in herself, knocking off volleys, not giving Garrison a chance to get to the net. She won the second set easily. Everyone sat back. Garrison had given it a terrific shot, but it would not be enough.

Only, Garrison thought differently. "Steffi wasn't playing *her* game," she said. "She's not an attacker. Sooner or later, that had to affect her."

Sure enough, it did. At 1–1, Garrison surprised Graf with a perfect lob to get to break point. Then she drilled a backhand return. She was ahead 2–1. But could she stay there? Graf had a break point in the next game but missed a backhand. Garrison drilled a backhand pass—with Graf looking uncomfortable at the net—and was up 3–1. They went on serve to 5–4. Garrison walked out to serve for the match exactly two hours after they had started.

Centre Court—Garrison had finally arrived there for the semifinals—was electric. Could Garrison pull this off? In the friends' box, Peter Graf looked on, impassive. Willard Jackson shook a fist at his wife. Moses Venson kept his arms folded, frozen by nerves. Sherwood Stewart pulled his cap a little tighter. Garrison breathed and relaxed. Graf ripped a forehand winner. It was 0–15. More deep breaths. A perfect backhand volley—15–all. Three points to go. Graf missed a forehand. Two points left. Garrison spun a serve to the backhand. Graf lunged and netted a backhand. *One* point left.

"Serve wide," Garrison told herself. "Get her off the court and set up a volley." She walked to the service line and tossed the ball. As she let go of it, she changed her mind. Something told her to go down the middle. She did, landing the ball almost right on the line. Graf never moved. She had been leaning wide, looking for the serve Garrison had planned. It was a clean ace. For a split second no one moved. Then, the cathedral exploded as it rarely does. It was one of the great upsets in Wimbledon history.

Graf was gracious in defeat. She credited Garrison with playing superbly and refused to use her father as an excuse. "She just didn't make the mistakes she usually makes," Graf said. "Usually, under pressure, she makes errors. Today, she didn't."

Garrison was in her first Grand Slam final.

She was now facing a woman on a mission. Navratilova had played almost perfect tennis for two weeks. She had lost just twenty-four games in six matches and hadn't come close to losing a set. Off the court, she had been hyper almost the entire two weeks, but whenever she stepped on court, she was ready. Now, with one match to go, the nearness of it all hit her. On Friday night she sat down with Billie Jean King and Craig Kardon at her kitchen table to talk about their game plan for the final. This had become a ritual. Now, King changed the ritual.

"You make the game plan," she said. "Get out your journal and tell me what you need to do."

Navratilova pulled out her journal and began going through it frantically. She finally boiled it down to four pages of notes.

"Not good enough," King said. "I want one page. I want your mind clear." Navratilova was becoming hysterical. She looked at King and

Kardon. "This is the most important match I've ever played in my life," she said. "I don't know if I'll ever be this close again. Do you think I'll be able to play? Will I be able to hit the ball at all?"

King nodded. "You'll play well," she said. "You've never been better prepared in your life."

Navratilova calmed down. She got her notes down to one page: "Stay in the present," she wrote.

"I had to keep my mind off winning," she said. "Winning was the future. I had to be in the present. Think about that point and that point only."

She also knew she had to attack, especially off Garrison's weak second serve. Get on top of her, don't give her the chance to come in. All tournament, she had intentionally *not* thought about playing Graf in the final, in case that very thing happened. Now, she was thinking only about Garrison. Navratilova was 27–1 against Garrison, lifetime. She knew she was ready to play. That night, for the first time in two weeks, she slept soundly.

Things were not as calm at Garrison's house. As soon as Garrison's ace had whizzed past Seles, dePicciotto and his Advantage operatives had swung into action. This was their chance. Garrison would be watched on Saturday by more people than had ever watched her play in her life.

Phone calls were made, meetings were set up, deals were made. Zina mania reigned. One company was willing to pay $5,000 if Stewart would wear their cap for the TV cameras. Another would pay $5,000 for Venson to wear *their* cap. A third offered $10,000 for Willard to wear *their* cap. That one was turned down; Willard thought it undignified. Two patch deals were made, one for each shoulder.

Most important was the clothing deal: Reebok wanted Garrison to wear their clothes for the final. DePicciotto said it couldn't be a one-time deal. Reebok agreed: Garrison would get a long-term deal that would be finalized after the tournament.

There was one hitch in the Reebok deal. Since February, Garrison had been wearing the Martina Navratilova clothing line. The clothes were designed by Judy Nelson; she and Navratilova were going to market them nationally beginning in the fall. Garrison wasn't being paid to wear the clothes yet, but they had talked about a contract later in the year. Now Reebok was offering a five-year deal—worth $500,000 for clothes and shoes. DePicciotto knew Navratilova couldn't match that. The deal was now or never—Reebok wanted that worldwide exposure on Saturday. So he accepted.

He then called Nelson with the news. She was not thrilled. She felt betrayed and told dePicciotto so—loudly. "We didn't blame Zina," Navratilova said later. "The opportunity was there and she had to take it."

That was what dePicciotto was thinking. He had a lot to do. He had to get the new clothes, the patches, and the caps to Garrison on Saturday morning. The companies had put them on different airplanes Friday night. Patrick McGee of Advantage woke up at 5 A.M. and got in a minicab (cheaper than a regular cab). First he went to Gatwick Airport, then to Heathrow Airport, covering more than one hundred miles. Cost of the cab: seventy pounds. He got the clothes, the shoes, and the caps—and so did Garrison.

At 2 P.M. precisely, Garrison and Navratilova walked on court for the final. Navratilova had walked on to Centre Court for the Wimbledon final eleven times; now she was trying to walk off it with a major piece of history. Garrison had no thoughts of history or, for that matter, of the match as she walked out. She thought, instead, of her mother. "My mother never would have believed it," she said later. "She just wouldn't have believed it was me going out there to play the Wimbledon final. She would have been impossible to talk to."

Thinking about her mother, Garrison could feel tears welling up but forced herself to focus on tennis. She started well, holding serve, then having break points in the second game. But Navratilova held and, following her game plan perfectly, moved into a zone that was untouchable. She was on top of the net all day, never missing a volley. Her serve was almost flawless, her returns low and at Garrison's feet. In many ways it was a repeat of all their matches of the past. The styles were similar. One player just played it better.

It ended on one last Navratilova backhand. Overwhelmed, drained and exhausted, Navratilova fell to her knees. She raced up through the stands to her entourage, kissing Kardon, hugging King, and hugging Nelson. Once she would have been afraid to hug Nelson in public; now, she did it without hesitation.

Nine times she had been handed the plate by the Duchess of Kent, but this time the duchess gave her a kiss before handing it over. Navratilova cried as she held it above her head.

The biggest cheer was reserved for Garrison. Navratilova had won; Garrison had inspired. She had overcome so much to get there that losing the final couldn't diminish what she had achieved.

That night, both women celebrated. Garrison, her entourage, and about twenty friends went to a London restaurant and toasted what they had accomplished. Navratilova threw a party at her house and got drunk. "Two whiskey sours did it," she said. "I hadn't had a drink other than a glass of wine with dinner or a sip of beer for years. I just sat in the corner and laughed."

The joy at the two parties was genuine. Both women deserved to eat, to drink, to be merry. To laugh. And to cry.

The men's semifinals did not produce the kind of drama that the women's had, but they did produce a brilliant tennis match.

The opener was Lendl–Edberg. This was the beginning of what Lendl hoped would be a two-part final exam after his six-week sojourn in England. He had known that in the end, all the work would boil down to one simple question: Could he beat Edberg and Becker, the two best grass-court players in the world, when it mattered the most?

There had been hints throughout the tournament that Lendl was not going to dominate here the way he had at Queen's. In his very first match, against Christian Miniussi, he dropped the opening set. In five matches, he won only one in straight sets. He knew he had to pick his level up for Edberg.

But Lendl is not that kind of player. His level never goes very far up or down. By contrast, Edberg, who could be way off on any given day, had built to the final weekend. He had faced one real scare when Amos Mansdorf had him down two sets to one in the third round, but he rallied to win 9–7 in the fifth set. He blasted Michael Chang in the fourth round and beat Christian Bergstrom in the quarters. That put him exactly where he wanted to be—in the semis, with all eyes on the other player. Edberg was the most intensely private of all the top players in the game. Occasionally, a dry sense of humor would creep into his conversation, but most of the time he seemed to go out of his way to be dull.

"I don't mind talking about my tennis, but I don't like to talk about my private life," he said. "I think that should be private. I understand that I have to talk to the press. The people I have contracts with expect me to do that. But if I never did another interview the rest of my life, it wouldn't bother me at all."

This was not atypical of the European attitude toward the media. The press was an evil—not necessarily even a necessary one—to most athletes from Europe. Graf certainly felt that way, even before her father's troubles. Becker was an exception to this rule. Lendl had changed after moving to the United States.

○

Edberg, by his own admission, had never felt comfortable in the U.S., even though he spoke English fluently.

"There are places there I like," he said. "But I could never live there. Ideally, I'd still live at home. But I need a tax haven. For me, that means Monte Carlo or London."

He was one of the few players who opted for London. The weather wasn't as good and the life not nearly as glamorous. Edberg was willing to put up with the weather in return for the fact that few people in London recognized him. He lived in a penthouse apartment near Hyde Park with his longtime girlfriend, Annette Olsen (a Mats Wilander ex), and worked out with his coach, Tony Pickard, an Englishman.

Edberg was the classic small-town kid thrust into the very-big-town world of tennis. He grew up in Vastervik, a town of 22,000 in southeast Sweden, and started taking tennis lessons at age seven when his parents saw an ad in the newspaper for a "tennis day" at the local tennis club. He didn't own a tennis racquet, so the trainer at the club loaned him one. When he showed talent his parents bought him his own racquet for fifty Swedish crowns—about $4.

At thirteen he began traveling to Stockholm two days a week because he had outgrown the program in Vastervik. By the time he was fifteen he was one of the best juniors in Sweden. This was in the post–Bjorn Borg era and tennis had exploded in the country.

Edberg played a decidedly un-Borglike game, serving-and-volleying all the time. He was sixteen when Wilander won the French Open. "I didn't think Mats was that much better than I was," he said. "When he won the French, I decided to see how I could do as a pro."

With his parents' blessing, Edberg dropped out of school. Unlike a lot of tennis parents, Bengt and Barbro Edberg had no desire to travel the world, basking in their child's reflected glow. Bengt Edberg was—and is—a cop. When Stefan wanted to take a shot at a career in tennis, Bengt took out a mortgage on his home to raise the money needed to pay his expenses.

It didn't take Stefan long to pay his father back. In 1983 he won all four junior Grand Slams and soon after signed a number of lucrative contracts. He was labeled the next great Swedish player, exactly the kind of label he would have liked to avoid.

"I've heard since I was seventeen I should be number one," he said. "I've accomplished a lot in tennis, but I haven't been number one, so I feel like I haven't achieved what I'm supposed to yet. Sometimes it's frustrating that people always seem to want more from me, but at the end of the day I have to think I've been very lucky."

Edberg won his first Grand Slam title in Australia in 1985, beating Lendl and Wilander. He won again in Australia in 1987, beating Cash in a five-set final. Eighteen months later, he won his first Wimbledon, beating Becker in a final that ended on Monday because of rain. That victory put him very close to No. 1. Two months later, when Lendl lost an early-round match at Stratton Mountain, the ATP put out a release saying that Edberg would move to No. 1 on the computer the next week. The next day they recanted. They had made a mistake.

The two years since Edberg's Wimbledon victory had not been easy for him, although he had become extremely wealthy. In 1989 he received more than $1 million in guarantees and made another $1.6 million in prize money. His contract with Adidas was worth about $2 million a year, and he had a number of other endorsements, especially in Japan, where his blond hair and blue eyes made him an idol, a fact that both amused and bemused him.

But money had not bought happiness. Edberg left Advantage early in 1989 in a dispute over their handling of his taxes. That had meant breaking with Tom Ross, his agent since he had first signed with ProServ (before the Advantage split) at the age of sixteen. Edberg didn't hold Ross responsible for the tax problems but did feel he had to have more control of his money.

"Tom is still my friend," he said. "But the fact is, most agents shouldn't be trusted. When I signed, I was sixteen, my mother spoke very little English, and my father spoke none. We barely knew what we were signing. The agents do that all the time. They sign everybody up and then worry only about the ones that do well. I'm lucky I did well, but now *I* make the decisions, not my agent."

In 1989, Edberg seemed star-crossed. He had to default in Australia with a back injury; he lost the French final to Chang and the Wimbledon final to Becker. He then lost to Jimmy Connors in the fourth round of the Open, a match in which he looked incapable of winning even if Connors had played right-handed.

Edberg never made excuses for any of his losses. "Bad day at the office" was what he said most of the time. It was more than that, though. His parents had split up; he was distracted and upset the entire summer. In the incestuous world of tennis, there are very few secrets, but Edberg is so private that this *stayed* a secret.

His luck didn't get any better in 1990. He had to default during the final in Australia—a pulled stomach muscle—in a match he almost surely would have won. With a chance to take over No. 1, he had gone into Paris and played horribly, losing in the first round. But Edberg had come to Wimbledon feeling very good about his chances.

"Everyone is talking about Becker and Lendl," he said two days before the tournament started. "That's just the way I like it."

The Lendl match was also very much to his liking. From the beginning, he had Lendl backpedaling. Only the second set was close. It went to a tiebreak. At 1–1 in the tiebreak, Edberg served an ace and then crushed two forehand returns. Lendl closed to 4–2 with a backhand return of his own. Edberg responded with another service winner and then two perfect returns—a backhand, a forehand. Seven points; six untouchable winners. Lendl had a look on his face that said twelve months of work was going down the drain.

All the work disappeared completely thirty minutes later. Edberg broke to go up 4–2 and served the match out. It had taken less than two hours. Lendl, usually the stoic in defeat, looked as though he was fighting tears when he came into the interview room.

"Actually, last year was more disappointing, because I had a chance," he said. "Today, Stefan completely outplayed me." That fact, after all the preparation, clearly devastated Lendl.

The Becker–Ivanisevic match was as memorable as the Edberg–Lendl was one-sided. Ivanisevic began by hitting four straight winners to break Becker's serve. Becker caught himself grinning.

"I thought to myself, So this is what it felt like five years ago when I was seventeen. The guy comes out in his first semifinal and just starts hitting winners."

Ivanisevic didn't stop. He won the first set and broke to go up 6–5 in the second. Becker sat down on his chair and had one of his little chats with himself. "I thought, Okay, this is it. You break here or you lose this match. Everything you've done to get here is for nothing."

Becker got the break to get to 6–6, then won the tiebreak. Ivanisevic suddenly stopped flying. Becker won the next set in nineteen minutes—6–0. Ivanisevic won only seven points. It was not, however, one of his tank jobs. It was simply the best tennis Becker had played all year. He hit every line that could be found. To his credit, Ivanisevic came back in the fourth set. He raised his level to Becker's and the two men played as good a set of tennis as one could hope to see on grass. They went to another tiebreak. Ivanisevic went up 5–4. Becker hit two unreturnable serves to go up 6–5.

Match point. Ivanisevic unleashed one more huge serve. Becker chipped a forehand and Ivanisevic, lunging, popped the ball into the net.

Becker put an arm around Ivanisevic as they shook hands. "You played a hell of a match," he said.

Walking off the court, Becker felt a surge of pride. He had been forced to the wall and he had responded. He was overjoyed in a way he had not been since winning the Open.

"It all came back to me after that match," he said. "It was like a revelation of some kind. I understood again why I was a tennis player. The feeling of satisfaction I had after that match, I can't get from anything else in my life. I just felt so *good.*

"The next afternoon, after I practiced, I just sat in the garden in the backyard of my house [in Wimbledon] and said, 'Shit, you did it again. Unbelievable. After all the troubles, you are in the final again.' It was one of the nicest days of my life."

There was one problem, though: The tournament wasn't over. Becker still had to play Edberg. He woke up Sunday morning feeling tired and sluggish. "When you play a Grand Slam you almost have to put yourself in a cage for two weeks," he said. "You can't let anything out. After Friday, I let too much out. I called my parents and some friends. I felt satisfied with myself. It was too soon to feel satisfied. I made a mistake."

When Becker walked on court for the final, on a glistening, postcard-perfect day, there was another problem. Katarina Witt, the glamorous German ice skater, had come to town earlier in the week. She was in the process of making a deal with Tiriac, and he had invited her to Wimbledon. Becker, single again, had spent some time with her.

It didn't take long for the London tabloids to get cranked up. Now, as Becker walked on court, he looked up toward the friends' box, expecting to see Brett and Tiriac's assistant, Heather McLachlan, sitting there. That had been the drill the entire tournament. But now, in addition to Brett and McLachlan, Becker's sister was there. That was fine. So was Katarina Witt. That wasn't fine.

From his seat, Brett saw a look pass over Becker's face. "It was a shock," Becker said later. "I never expected to see her there. Heather had just given her the ticket to sit there without thinking about what it would mean. She told me later she was sorry, that she made a mistake."

What it meant was tabloid mania. Front-page pictures galore, rumors about a Becker–Witt romance everywhere. It wasn't what Becker needed starting a Wimbledon final.

○

Those thoughts, his feeling of satisfaction after the semifinal, and Edberg's brilliance made Becker look helpless the first two sets.

"I just didn't feel like I was in a Wimbledon final," he said. "I didn't even feel nervous going on court. Then I got a little distracted at the start [by Witt], and the next thing I know it's 6–2, 6–2. Then, my only thought was to not make a complete fool of myself."

Edberg was almost as shocked as Becker. How could it be this easy? He had lost three Grand Slam finals in eighteen months. Maybe it was his turn at last.

Or maybe not. Edberg had a break point in the first game of the third set. It was, for all intents and purposes, a match point as far as Becker was concerned. He came in and Edberg teed up another backhand. He ripped it crosscourt. Not this time: Becker read it perfectly and knocked off a sharp backhand volley. From there, he held. Given a glimmer of life, he broke Edberg for the first time in the next game. Maybe, he thought, I can win a set.

He won it. Then he won another. They had played for two hours and fifteen minutes. Now they would play the first fifth set in a Wimbledon final since McEnroe–Connors, in 1982. Becker was wound up, stoking. Edberg was reeling. "I was all the way to fifth gear," Becker said. "He wasn't there yet. I needed to take him out before he got there."

He had his chance. Serving at 1–2, Edberg served two double faults, the second one an ugly balloon that almost went over the baseline. Becker was up 3–1. The match was on his racquet.

"But somehow I couldn't keep my mind right there on the match," he said. "I started to think about holding the trophy again. I knew that if I served the match out, I would be on the same side of the net where I had been the other three times I had won. Those were the *wrong* thoughts at that time. If I win the game at 3–1, he's finished. But I couldn't keep my concentration."

Becker needed to, as Navratilova would put it, stay in the present. Instead, he had let his mind wander into the future. At 30–all, Edberg chipped a backhand and Becker didn't get down far enough for the volley. He netted it. Break point. Becker came in behind a serve and had an easy forehand volley. He pushed it wide.

Edberg pumped a fist. Becker had let him get into fifth gear. "He was in fifth and I was out of gas," he said later. With Becker serving at 4–4, Edberg came up with the shot of the match, a perfect backhand topspin lob that landed on the line, to get one last service break. He skipped to his chair while Becker slumped. Becker tried to talk himself back into it one more time but it was too late. Edberg served it out, finishing with a perfect kick serve that Becker just got to but pushed wide.

As the ball landed, Edberg hurled the ball he had in his hand toward the sky as Pickard leapt from his seat, screaming. Becker, never classier, climbed over the net and hugged Edberg. His eyes were glassy.

"I really couldn't believe I had lost after coming so far back," he said. "I went home the next day and wrote for hours and thought and tried to figure it out. In the end, I thought maybe it was *his* time. He had lost three straight finals. He had been hurt in one that he probably would have won. We've played so many times [Wimbledon was their twenty-fourth match] that we both deserve some good things. He's a good guy. He's different than me, he doesn't show emotion, but he is a great player.

"I decided he deserved this Wimbledon. There is a reason for everything. I got something out of it, too, though—my love for tennis. I came out of the tournament knowing I wanted to be a tennis player, to really work at my tennis for a long time. That made it all worth it."

The only one who felt a little bit sick about it all was Brett. His last words to Becker going on court had been direct: "If you get ahead, don't coast." Becker had not gotten ahead until 3–1 in the fifth. Then he had coasted for a single moment. That had cost him the match. Brett blamed himself. "It's up to me to figure out what went wrong," he said. "That's what I'm paid to do."

Brett had earned his money. He had done everything he could do. So had Becker. And so had Edberg. That was the way a Wimbledon final should be. Two great players who respected one another going all the way to fifth gear—and beyond.

For Edberg, this second Wimbledon was even better than the first because of the travails of the past two years. He even got to go to the champions' dinner. In 1988, with the final postponed until Monday, he hadn't been able to go. This time, he got to go. When he arrived at the dinner, he raced up to Navratilova, panicked.

"What kind of dance do we have to do?" he asked her.

Navratilova laughed. Once, it had been part of Wimbledon tradition for the two champions to dance the first dance together. But in 1978, the dinner had been moved to the Savoy Hotel. There was no room in the ballroom for a dance floor and no more first dance.

Edberg was relieved. The thought of dancing in front of a thousand people was far more terrifying than the thought of being down 3–1 in the fifth. He had survived that and he didn't have to dance. A perfect day.

Edberg and Navratilova sat at the head table and got to hear the toast that climaxes every Wimbledon. Shortly before midnight, John Curry stood up and raised his glass.

"To the Queen," he said.

Everyone in the room stood. "The Queen," they chorused back. The Championships of 1990 were over.

PART FIVE

THE YANKS COME HOME

20

NEWPORT

For most of the tennis world, the end of Wimbledon meant taking a quick, deep breath before diving into the hard-court season that led to the U.S. Open. Seven weeks separated the end of Wimbledon from the beginning of the Open. There was the rare opportunity for a short rest, a respite after the six intense weeks that encompassed the French, the grass-court warm-ups, and Wimbledon.

Some players barely paused for breath, however. The day after the tournament ended, Stefan Edberg got on a plane and flew to Japan to play in an exhibition tournament. He would make almost $300,000 for the week but—after hurting a knee in the semifinals—would come away knowing he had almost made a crucial error in chasing the money. The injury turned out not to be serious—but Edberg knew he had been lucky. Zina Garrison and Monica Seles went straight from London to Yugoslavia to play exhibitions against each other. Jennifer Capriati, who had been in Europe for ten weeks, barely had time to unpack before heading off to an exhibition in New Hampshire.

Boris Becker went home to Germany to contemplate what had happened at Wimbledon, and Ivan Lendl returned to Connecticut to recover from his trouncing by Edberg. He had been designated by the ATP Tour to play the following week in Stuttgart. There was no way he was going to play there—he had made that clear to tour officials—but as it turned out, the knee injury he used as his official excuse for withdrawal was real. He missed a tournament in Toronto the next week—one he always played in—and would not come back to the tour until just two weeks before the U.S. Open.

Martina Navratilova went home to Aspen and collapsed. She was used to having emotional letdowns after winning Wimbledon, but this one was the most severe of all. She felt empty. A life's goal had been achieved and now she had to convince herself that there were other goals worth chasing.

"You almost have to pretend," she said. "There's no way anything is going to top a ninth Wimbledon, but you have to tell yourself that winning the Open again or getting a tenth Wimbledon can be really big. You know they can't be *as* big, but they can still excite you. At least, I hope they can."

Steffi Graf went directly from her loss to Garrison to the hospital to have her sinuses operated on. The doctors told her she could wait until the end of the year for the operation but would be in considerable pain if she did. She decided to get it over with.

"Actually, being in the hospital turned out to be a relief," she said. "It was so restful after what I had just gone through. The only people there were my family, and I just escaped from the world for a few days. The doctors told me I would need at least a month off, but I decided I wanted to play in the Canadian Open, which was three weeks away. It gave me something to work toward."

While Graf was in the hospital, she got a call from a friend—Becker. Her father had called Becker's father, ostensibly just to chat, and had mentioned to him that Steffi was having the operation. The two stars talked several times while Graf was in the hospital, with Becker playing the role of the older brother.

"I told her that what happened to her with the media was inevitable," he said. "Sooner or later, they get you. She had to understand that, in Germany, this was part of being a star. I told her the only way to handle the whole thing is to try to ignore it. That's almost impossible, but the more you are able to do it, the better off you'll be."

Graf and Becker have known each other since childhood. She thinks Becker is a trifle melodramatic when he goes on about the vagaries of life and talks about reading Goethe, but she genuinely likes and respects him. Their talks helped cheer her up, and prepared her to get on with her life.

The sport itself never rested. Less than twenty-four hours after Edberg and Becker embraced at the net, five tennis tournaments began: four on European clay—two men's events, two women's events—and one in the United States—on grass, at Newport, Rhode Island.

Newport is the last vestige of the old U.S. grass-court circuit, one that used to roll through the East Coast in the summer months and led up to the U.S. Championships, held in those days on the grass at Forest Hills. Merion, South Orange, Southampton, and Longwood were all stops on the summer tour, quaint private clubs with handsome hedges, manicured grass, and polite, small crowds that came out to watch the "amateurs" prepare for Forest Hills.

Forest Hills switched to clay in 1975, and the USTA switched from

Forest Hills to Flushing Meadow and hard courts in 1978. New tournaments sprang up, most of them in stadiums far better equipped to handle the booming interest in the sport than the country clubs were. By the mid-1980s, most of the pre–U.S. Open tournaments were being played on hard courts for big money, with corporate sponsors behind them.

Newport survived—barely. As the site of the International Tennis Hall of Fame, it had enough tradition to stay on the calendar as a sort of post-Wimbledon ode to grass. Newport's prize money wasn't very big and it didn't pay guarantees to the men, so its field was usually weak. Occasionally, an older player would enter just to say he or she had played there, but for the most part, the highlight of the two weeks was the annual Hall of Fame induction ceremony.

If the people who came to see the tournament cared that the big names passed up their tournament, they hardly showed it. Newport is all ambience, a trip into the past.

The Newport Casino is located at 149 Bellevue Avenue, directly across the street from the Bellevue Shopping Center and a few steps from the A&P and Fotomat. From Bellevue Avenue or even from the A&P parking lot, the casino looks like little more than just another canopy on a busy street.

Walk inside the front door, however, and you have walked through the looking glass and returned to the nineteenth century. The Horseshoe Piazza is twenty-five yards and one hundred years away from Bellevue Avenue. In the middle of the piazza is the Hall of Fame court, the grass a lush green. The court is surrounded by the canopied Hall of Fame restaurant, museum, and administrative offices. If someone sends you a postcard from Newport, it will almost surely be of the piazza.

Beyond the piazza, on the other side of the restaurant, are the outside courts, the clubhouse, and the stadium court. A bleacher was added to the stadium ten years ago, so it now seats 4,100. The outside court closest to the clubhouse is known as the Sears Court, named in honor of Richard Dudley Sears, who won the first U.S. Championship on that court in 1881, one year after the casino was opened.

The casino is not a casino at all, in the American sense. There is no gambling there and never was. *Casino* is Italian for "place of pleasure"—a euphemism for brothel—and that is what the place was before newspaper publisher James Gordon Bennett bought the land and built a private club, complete with tennis courts, after he had been thrown out of an exclusive Newport men's club for convincing a friend to ride through the bar on a horse.

Only seven of the top one hundred ranked men in the world opted to come to Newport in 1990. There was no more perfect example of how guarantees had hurt tennis than a week like this one.

David Wheaton, who had talked all through England about how comfortable he felt and how much he enjoyed playing on grass, had gone to Gstaad to play on clay rather than play at Newport. The Gstaad tournament paid him a guarantee of $30,000. Every tennis player had his price, that was the message, whether it was Wheaton's $30,000 or Edberg's $300,000. Certainly, neither of those amounts were chump change—but just as certainly, neither player was going to go hungry if they played without a guarantee. Wheaton would have enjoyed Newport, perhaps learned from the experience.

Nine of the thirty-two men in the Newport field were South Africans. Most South Africans are fast-court players. Johannesburg is six thousand feet above sea level; players grow up charging the net to avoid energy-sapping rallies. The typical South African player is a serve-and-volleyer who plays very good doubles and has a game suited to grass.

The men's tour has always been dotted with South African players (there are a few, but not nearly as many, on the women's tour), although very few have been consistent Top Ten players. Cliff Drysdale was a consistent Top-Tenner and a finalist at Forest Hills in 1965. Kevin Curren and Johan Kriek both had moments in the Top Ten; Curren was a Wimbledon finalist in 1985, and Kriek won two weak-field Australian Opens in the early eighties.

All three were now American citizens. Drysdale lived in Wilmington, North Carolina, and had become a very successful tennis commentator for ESPN and ABC. Kriek lived in Florida, and Curren in Texas.

The latter two readily admit that their change in citizenship was done strictly for the purpose of convenience. South Africans cannot play in Sweden, Japan, and Canada—all three countries have antiapartheid policies—and traveling on a South African passport is difficult. That would begin to change in 1991. When the subject of apartheid comes up, both Curren and Kriek have always said that apartheid is wrong. However, they always add quickly, "But you can't understand what goes on in South Africa if you aren't from there."

Tennis officials wish the topic of South Africa and South Africans would somehow go away. For years, the Men's Tennis Council sanctioned a tournament in South Africa. Every year, players who went there would later be subjected to questions from the media and, sometimes, irate demonstrations from fans around the world.

Players kept going because the guarantees were extremely high. Some agents advised their clients not to play in South Africa; others told them what they had been offered—Pat Cash reportedly got $500,000 to go in 1987—and what the potential consequences of playing there were.

John McEnroe had always refused to play in South Africa—once turning down a $1 million offer to play an exhibition against Bjorn Borg—but most players were willing to go for the right price. When he was sixteen, Becker played there, but has stayed away since. Most of the Swedes won't play the tournament because of their government's stance on apartheid.

When the ATP Tour displaced the MTC, it announced it would sanction not one but *two* tournaments in South Africa. The chairman of the MTC at the time was Ray Moore, a South African who lived in California. His influence in this decision was apparent. The tour was promptly buried in a barrage of criticism and eventually relented. Both South African tournaments were dropped.

The most amusing part of the whole chain of events was then ATP CEO Hamilton Jordan defending the decision to place two tournaments there, saying that "politics and sports don't mix." As Jimmy Carter's chief of staff, Jordan had been the point man for Carter's boycott of the 1980 Olympics.

"Different circumstances, different times," Jordan said, looking back a year later. "Sometimes sports and politics have to mix. In the case of South Africa, I didn't think they had to. We weren't doing anything different from the MTC by sanctioning a tournament there, so why did we get buried for it?"

The answer was simple: The ATP Tour had promised it would be different from the MTC. It had picked the wrong spot to maintain—or double—the status quo.

With the tournaments off the calendar, the issue became the players themselves. South Africa produced a steady stream of top one hundred singles players and many excellent doubles players, including Pieter Aldrich and Danie Visser, who came to Newport as the No. 2 team in the world. The players didn't like to talk about politics. In fact, most of them asked to be introduced as being from whatever city in the U.S. in which they had a residence. Roslyn Fairbank, the top female player from South Africa, had gotten the WTA to list her as an American citizen—even though she wasn't. Christo van Rensburg, the highest-ranked South African male, was usually listed as being from Great Neck, N.Y.

Van Rensburg was the most outspoken of the South Africans on political issues. Most of them shrugged their shoulders when politics came up and said they were interested only in tennis. Wayne Ferreira, a talented eighteen-year-old, said he didn't even read the newspapers to find out what was happening back home.

"I'm not interested," he said. "It doesn't affect me and I can't do anything about it. I'm just a tennis player."

Van Rensburg was twenty-seven and had been on tour for eight years. He was extremely sensitive to the apartheid issue and had even gone so far as to write a story in *The Australian,* that country's national newspaper, during the 1990 Australian Open, trying to explain his position. This came after antiapartheid demonstrations were held during the tournament.

"Apartheid is wrong," Van Rensburg said. "I think it's something that is going to be gone fairly soon. Not soon enough, I agree, but we are making progress. I've been able to do clinics in black areas the last couple of years, and we're starting to see some very good young black players. I did a clinic with both blacks and whites in my hometown, and it was terrific. I drove by two hours later and they were all playing together. Five years ago, two years ago, even, that would have been impossible. Our top twelve-and-unders—both boys and girls—right now are black. I think in the next few years, there will be South African blacks on the tennis tour."

Van Rensburg knows his time is dwindling. He would like to play Davis Cup and the Olympics for his country, although South Africa has been banned from both events. He is hoping the International Olympic Committee will negotiate a return for South Africa in 1992.

"I would love for that to happen," Van Rensburg said. "My country is flawed, but I still love it and I would love to play *for* South Africa. What bothers me is that people around the world judge me not for who I am but for where I'm from. I don't think that's fair."

For the most part, the South African players kept to themselves on tour, socializing together, almost always playing doubles together. Van Rensburg, who had played doubles for years with Paul Annacone, was an exception to this rule. So was Gary Muller, a flamboyant, long-haired blond who lived in Los Angeles, dated an actress, and usually flounced around the court with his sleeves pushed up to his shoulders so all the world could see his biceps.

Muller was pure power on the court, the kind of player with a game made for grass, and at Newport, he reached the semifinals, playing against Aldrich, another South African. The other semifinalists were Darren

Cahill, the Australian nicknamed Killer because he was so quiet, and Eric Jelen, who had been Becker's Davis Cup sidekick for several years.

The semifinals were scheduled for Saturday on the stadium court; the women's qualifying matches began at the same time. But the main focus of attention was on the Horseshoe Piazza, where the Hall of Fame induction ceremony was being held.

The 1990 inductees were Jan Kodes, the Czechoslovakian who had won two French Opens, a Wimbledon title, and had played in two U.S. Open finals; and Joseph F. Cullman III. Joe Cullman was seventy-eight. He had been the chairman of Philip-Morris, and it was Cullman who had made the decision in the early 1970s to put a huge chunk of the corporation's money into women's tennis. Some wondered whether spending a corporation's money should make one a Hall of Famer—but there was never much doubt Cullman would be elected. In addition to all his connections, he was the executive director of the Hall of Fame.

The induction ceremony was short, sweet, and simple. The inductees were introduced and escorted on court, where they gave brief speeches. Everyone stood in a circle around the piazza and watched. On a gorgeous summer day, it was a lovely place to be.

On the piazza stood Kodes, the champion of the 1970s, being inducted into the Hall of Fame by, among others, Bill Talbert, a champion of the thirties and forties, and Pam Shriver, a champion of the eighties. Shriver and Talbert were Hall of Fame board members. Alongside them stood Cullman and another symbol of the game's dependence on corporate and television money, Donald Dell, the chairman of ProServ. Dell was also the Hall of Fame's president. Next to them was Gene Scott, the head of the nominating committee. Scott was a member of the media, the editor and publisher of *Tennis Week* magazine, and a tournament director—he had formerly run the Masters for the MTC; now he ran the Moscow event for the ATP.

Fame, power, money, and history were present in every corner of the piazza. Several yards away, on the other side of the restaurant, Lise Gregory, ranked 222nd in the world, and Belinda Borneo, ranked 318th, struggled away in the sun in a women's qualifying match, each searching for a tiny sliver of that glamour—tangible and intangible.

Forty yards farther away, Muller and Aldrich went at it in a virtually empty stadium, ignored in a way that the game's powers wished they could ignore all of South Africa. Aldrich won the match and went on to win the tournament the next afternoon, beating Cahill in the final. A week later, Arantxa Sanchez, the only female Top Ten player in the Newport tournament, beat Jo Durie in the women's final.

As 1990 ended, Virginia Slims and Hall of Famer Joe Cullman had sold the Newport women's tournament to IMG for a reported $1.7 million, and IMG moved the event to Europe. Cullman, ever the sentimental historian, insisted before the Hall of Fame induction ceremony that there would be a Virginia Slims of Newport in 1991. His idea was a junior/senior doubles tournament, matching women over thirty-five with girls under sixteen. That idea, mercifully, fell through.

The men's sponsor took a different route. Instead of selling the sanction, Volvo Tennis simply dropped out of the tournament. They claimed that a downturn in auto sales forced them to cut back on its tennis involvement. Of course, the company then went out and spent close to $1 million for the right to put up banners at the ATP Championships in Germany—unlike at the quaint Newport, those banners would be seen on worldwide TV. As the new year began, Newport had a spot on the men's calendar but no sponsor. Finally, in March, a beer company picked up the sponsorship.

The rich and powerful had gone and sold Newport down the river—or across the ocean. But best of all, they could all come back next July to toast themselves again and tell one another stories about how wonderful they had made the game.

○

21

SUMMER HEAT

Most players play only three or four tournaments between Wimbledon and the U.S. Open. Some stay in Europe on the clay until the last possible moment, others fight the heat of the North American summer to play the hard-court warm-ups. Once Newport is over, the men's circuit runs from the choking heat of Washington to Toronto, Los Angeles, Cincinnati, Indianapolis, New Haven, Schenectady, and Long Island.

The women have a more abbreviated schedule. They take one week for Federation Cup, their version of the Davis Cup. It is played over one week, each match consisting of a best-of-three—two singles and a doubles. The U.S. hosted it in 1990, beating the Soviet Union in the final, in the brutal heat of Atlanta.

The tournament, run by the ITF, lost about $500,000. The tournament director hired by the ITF was Karen Scott Happer, wife of Marshall Happer, executive director of the USTA—a key member of the ITF. Karen Scott had run tournaments for ProServ before she married Happer (ProServ was now negotiating a new U.S. Open contract for the USTA), so no one questioned her competence. Still, the coincidence did not go unnoticed.

After the Fed Cup—or, as Mary Carillo, doing the matches for ESPN, called it, "The Fed-Up Cup"—the women moved on to Montreal, San Diego, Los Angeles, Albuquerque, and Schenectady.

When the 1990 schedule was made there was also a tournament scheduled in Mahwah, New Jersey, the week before the Open. But politics and money intervened again. The tournament promoter, John Korff, had sold his sanction; the Mahwah tournament would now be played in Leipzig, East Germany.

Korff and Advantage International, which had brokered the deal for him, came up with an idea so season box holders wouldn't have to trade in their tickets for cash. They decided to hold an exhibition and, as all promoters do, pretend it was a full-fledged tournament. Advantage provided Graf—who had always played Mahwah—Zina Garrison, and every Maleeva it could round up. Jennifer Capriati was paid a few dollars, perhaps fifty thousand of them, to come and play. Korff got to sell his sanction for almost $2 million while retaining ownership of a lucrative event. A contrived draw, in which some players had to win three matches to reach the semifinals, while Graf, Capriati, and Garrison had to play only one, was put together and everyone was happy. Graf ended up playing Capriati in the final, and The Kid took her to three sets. She was thrilled. Graf was not. "It's an exhibition," she said, using the forbidden word. "I was trying things I would never try in a tournament."

Capriati didn't know from exhibitions. She just played wherever and whenever—and that was pretty often—she was told. She had played as hard as she could and had assumed that Graf had, too. Ten days later they would meet again at the Open, and Capriati would learn the difference between an exhibition and a Grand Slam.

Andre Agassi had been missing in action from the tour for five weeks, ever since his loss to Gomez in Paris. He had skipped Wimbledon for a third straight year and gone back to Las Vegas to continue his quest to become Mr. Olympia. "I need to get stronger," he kept saying, almost as if it were a mantra.

He returned to the tour in Washington, on July 17. ProServ and Donald Dell had run the Washington tournament since 1969. For years, Washington had been the poor stepchild on the summer tour. No one wanted to play there in July, when the temperature was somewhere around a million degrees and the facilities were, at best, fifth rate.

But Dell had convinced some of his corporate pals to build him a stadium and finally he had respectable facilities. The weather was still horrible, but with Agassi needing to play and McEnroe wanting to play wherever he could after his late-night post-Wimbledon session, Dell and his cronies suddenly had a dream tournament.

Unfortunately for them, McEnroe didn't last very long. He beat Paul Chamberlin in his first match but then lost *again* to Rostagno. The day before the match, McEnroe, honest as ever, had commented that "if I play like I can, I should kick his ass." Naturally, this was repeated to Rostagno, who played one of the better matches of his life and won, going away in the final set, 6–1.

Agassi had some trouble in his first match with Brad Pearce, who was still playing with great confidence after Wimbledon. Pearce was up a break in the first set but began to have trouble breathing in the stifling humidity. He had played three long sets in the midday heat in the first round while Agassi had a bye. Agassi broke back, won a tiebreak, and cruised. He played solid tennis the rest of the week to win the tournament, beating Jim Grabb in the final.

When the final was over, the tournament promoters put on a twenty-four-minute awards ceremony. That was four minutes longer than Agassi and Grabb's first set had taken, but they had to fill the TV time. Who was doing the TV? Why, it was Donald Dell, whose company just happened to run the tournament *and* produce the tournament's TV package *and* provide the TV commentators.

The summer did not go quite as smoothly for Agassi after Washington. He lost to Chang in the quarterfinals in Toronto, to Richard Fromberg in the third round in Cincinnati, and to Peter Lundgren in the quarters in Indianapolis, where he produced one of his no-effort 0–6 second-set specials. Any rumors that Agassi had quit tanking were clearly exaggerated.

His behavior became more and more curious. Arriving in Cincinnati, Agassi was met at the gate by Lynn Gottschalk, a volunteer driver sent by the tournament to transport him thirty-five miles from the airport to the tournament hotel.

When Gottschalk introduced herself to Agassi, his first words to her were "Look, you're going to have to get some security to escort me out of here. Otherwise, I'll be mobbed."

Gottschalk looked around the empty airport and then at Agassi. "Andre," she said, "it's eleven-thirty at night. We're in Kentucky. Unless you've appeared on *Hee Haw* lately, no one here is going to mob you."

Agassi's preoccupation with security continued that entire week. The night after his loss to Fromberg, his entourage appeared en masse in tournament director Paul Flory's office. Agassi wanted to go to a baseball game in Cincinnati. That was no problem. As always, the tournament had arranged for tickets for any players who wanted to go. The entourage wanted more.

"They said, 'We need two of your marshalls for security for Andre,' " Flory said. "I said, 'Why? How many people will recognize him at a baseball game, especially if he wears a cap?' "

That wasn't good enough. Whether he needed it or not, Agassi wanted security. Perhaps someone should have purchased him a blanket.

The entourage had, by now, become part of the entertainment on the men's circuit. The fact that the names Gil (Reyes), Phil (Agassi), and

Bill (Shelton) could be rhymed was irresistible. They were the three stooges. Nick (Bollettieri) didn't rhyme, but nonetheless he was right there, along with his assistant, Raul, Agassi's hitting partner.

The security hang-up was nothing new for Andre. When he had hired Reyes to be his trainer, Reyes had also become his bodyguard. Everywhere Agassi went, Reyes led the way, often putting an arm out to keep people away—even when there weren't any people around. Phil was usually a step behind.

Those who knew Agassi were quick to tell you that he wasn't a bad kid; he simply wasn't very bright and had been thrown into an extraordinary situation. Rarely did Agassi seem malicious; he just had no guidance.

The person who was with Agassi the most and had the most influence with him was his older brother. One often wondered exactly what Philip Agassi would be doing with his life if his brother could not hit a tennis ball. He had been a decent junior tennis player but had never been blessed with the kind of talent accorded Andre. He was twenty-nine, bald—until he started wearing a toupee—and walked around with a perpetual sneer on his face.

Unlike Andre, Phil *was* meanspirited. He seemed to revel in being a tough guy. The previous year at the Open, a gushy fan had rushed up to him with a picture he had taken of Andre and Phil in Philadelphia. He wanted Phil to have a copy of it. Instead of taking the picture and saying thank you, Phil shoved it back toward the man and sneered, "We don't like Philadelphia very much, you know."

On another occasion at the Open, Ed Dubrow, a longtime broadcaster for Mutual Radio, rushed up to Agassi as he was being escorted from court to interview room after a match.

"Andre, when you're finished, if you could do just thirty seconds for Mutual I would really be appreciative," Dubrow said.

Agassi turned to his older brother. "At the end of the press conference, this guy gets thirty seconds," he said.

"Make it twenty," Phil snarled back.

That was typical. The way to explain the relationship between the brothers was this: If the two of them happened to be walking down the street one day, and Andre tripped over a sleeping homeless person, he would probably turn around and say, "Oh, sorry, I didn't see you." Before the sentence was out, though, Phil would have kicked the homeless person in the head and said, "Hey, what do you mean, getting in Andre's way?" When Phil finished, Andre would then say, "Yeah, that's right. Don't do it again!"

Privately, almost everyone at IMG agreed that Agassi would be much easier to handle if Philip wasn't around. But few people are going to fire their own brother.

Second in the line of influence was Reyes. Agassi was a typical kid in one way: he was into fads. Reyes and weight-training were definitely in during 1990, much the way Fritz and Christianity had been in during 1988. Conveniently, Reyes was a born-again Christian, too; at times he insisted that Agassi pray for forgiveness after on-court transgressions. In spite of his sinister appearance, Reyes was friendly and outgoing to those who were deemed okay by the entourage. After Bud Collins interviewed him during the French Open, Reyes became his new best friend. This was no doubt comforting to Collins, since one doesn't want Reyes as a new best enemy. Buildings had been known to cringe when Reyes looked at them the wrong way.

After Reyes came Bollettieri and Shelton. This was where the direction should have been coming from. Both were veteran tennis men who knew both the business and the people in the business. Shelton had been extremely well liked throughout his career, first as Bollettieri camp rep, then as a representative for Prince racquets and then at ProServ/Advantage. But the "Andre experience," as it was called, had changed him. He had become defensive, paranoid, and often hostile. In IMG staff meetings, when an Agassi screwup was mentioned, Shelton would often get angry at his colleagues for being critical of his/their client. He was long past the time he could or would tell the Agassi brothers what to do.

So was Bollettieri. This was his chance to *finally* have a champion. Bollettieri had coached such players as Jimmy Arias and Aaron Krickstein into the Top Ten, but neither had ever made it to the zenith of the sport. The day of the French Open final, Bollettieri shook his head and said, "I've waited thirty years for this, thirty years. I wondered if the day would ever come."

Agassi had given Bollettieri a car as a token of his gratitude, and he paid Bollettieri quite well to travel with him. Cars were an Agassi hobby. He carried pictures of some of his cars with him; later in the year, when he decided to sell a few of them, they were advertised in the tennis magazines as "Andre Agassi–owned cars."

In both Cincinnati and Indianapolis, Agassi's behavior was strange—even for him. In addition to his security obsession (Agassi claimed he was "mobbed" when he went to Kings Island one day), he wasn't playing very good tennis.

When he lost to Fromberg, he came in after the match and said,

"I played like a plumber." Then he launched into a tirade, saying it was impossible to get up to play "guys like this every week" (this particular "guy" was ranked thirty-second in the world). He also said that the ATP Tour was asking too much of stars such as himself. "We have to play too much," Agassi said. "The problem is, the tour is trying to support too many players. I don't see why a guy should get five thousand dollars for losing in the first round."

That comment didn't go over too well in the locker room, especially among those who were playing thirty-five to forty weeks a year in order to make a living. Cincinnati was Agassi's eighth tournament of the year; he had played ten weeks (the French and Lipton being two-week tournaments) out of thirty-two. He had *chosen* to play in exhibitions several other times but was still playing less than 50 percent of the time.

The following week, in Indianapolis, after his tank job against Lundgren, Agassi said he was just uptight and not in a good mood. When a reporter asked rather innocently what was bothering him, Agassi said, "What did you pay in taxes last year? That's right, it's none of your damn business." There was little doubt that Agassi *was* uptight. His on-court behavior, once exemplary, had gone rapidly downhill from his 1988 dream year. In Cincinnati, Gayle Bradshaw fined him $1,850 for twice using the word *fuck* during the Fromberg match. That marked the second week in a row that Agassi had been fined for saying "fuck" on the court. For the year, he'd been fined four different times at ATP tournaments, and once—for his racquet-bashing—at the French Open, running up a total penalty of $5,650.

The money itself was meaningless to Agassi, but the fact that he had been fined in four of the eight tournaments he had played in indicated a pattern. During the tournament in Indianapolis, Bradshaw tried to talk to Agassi about the problem but—surprise—couldn't get past the entourage. Andre understood, they said, and would not get into any further trouble. That was a vow that would hold until the U.S. Open.

The Cincinnati/Indianapolis swing was, for many players, the highlight of the summer. These two tournaments had become the model on how to spoil tennis players that the players hoped others would copy. "We wanted to make them feel wanted" was the way Mark Miles, the tournament director in Indianapolis, before becoming the ATP Tour's CEO, explained his approach to player relations.

Cincinnati had been a favored stop on the tour ever since 1979, when it had become the ATP Tournament. For years, it was the only tour stop that contributed funds to the players' pension funds. It was also a prime example of how a tournament could grow by promoting itself as an *event* rather than by just showcasing name players.

Paul Flory, the tournament director, was a minister's son who had grown up in Dayton and worked most of his adult life for Proctor & Gamble. He had been tournament director since 1975, when the Cincinnati tournament was still the Western Open and was played on clay in a small club down by the Mississippi River.

The tournament had moved to Kings Island in 1979, when the ATP offered itself to Flory if he could find a site with hard courts. Flory moved the tournament and had built the stadium slowly, adding stages each year as the tournament became a summer staple in the Cincinnati area. The stadium now seated ten thousand. Flory's tournament was less dependent on corporate sponsorship than most: Only 30 percent of his revenue came from sponsors. He got 30 percent from box holders, 20 percent from ticket sales, 15 percent from concessions, and 5 percent from the new luxury boxes, which went for $15,000 to $25,000, depending on the size of the box.

"I've always believed that if you want to be in this for the long term, you have to sell people on coming to the event itself," Flory said. "A lot of tournaments over the years would go out and buy a big name—a Borg or a McEnroe or a Connors—and act like they were the whole tournament. Once you do that, people get spoiled. They won't come unless it's to see someone like that play. I see tournament directors whose lives are built around getting McEnroe or Agassi in their tournaments.

"We've been lucky because, being the ATP's tournament, we're always going to get a decent field. But our fans don't come just to see the names; they come for the tournament."

There was evidence of that. Cincinnati was one of the few tournaments in the world that drew several thousand people for *qualifying.* And when the anticipated Friday night quarterfinal of McEnroe–Agassi became Scott Davis–Fromberg instead, there were almost no no-shows. Going to the tournament had become a habit for people—no matter who was playing.

The tournament benefited the Cincinnati Children's Hospital, and a number of players visited during the week. Some took this responsibility quite seriously. Jim Courier went back three times. Miguel Nido, a qualifier, went around the players' lounge one day trying to round up players. Benji Robins, the tour's marketing-services coordinator, worked all week trying to encourage players to go to the hospital.

It wasn't easy. A couple of players actually asked tournament officials if they could get *paid* to visit the hospital. On Friday, eight players were scheduled to go. One—Nido—showed up.

That afternoon, the tournament got a bit of an unexpected bonus, when Edberg beat Chang in a superb three-set quarterfinal and officially moved past Lendl to become the No. 1 player in the world. Being No. 1 was no small thing. Edberg was only the eighth man to be No. 1 since the start of computer rankings, in 1973. The women's No. 1 club was even more exclusive—it had only six members.

Edberg actually appeared excited about becoming No. 1. Remembering his twenty-four hours as No. 1 in 1988, after the ATP staff's error, he smiled and said, "I hope this time they got it right. It's nice that I can say I was number one in the world, even if I don't keep it for long. Not many guys get there. For years, people told me I could be number one or I should be number one. I'm glad I made it."

Tennis is a game that takes players to all corners of the earth. It was therefore fitting that on the night he became the No. 1 player on the planet, Edberg, a Swede who lived in London, slept in room 536 at the Embassy Suites Hotel in Blue Ash, Ohio.

Regardless of where he was, Edberg was playing brilliant tennis. The Wimbledon victory had clearly given him renewed confidence. He won in Los Angeles in his first tournament since Wimbledon, and he won rather easily in Cincinnati. The Chang match was his most difficult. He beat Gomez and Gilbert in the semifinals and final respectively, without losing serve once. The score in the final was 6–1, 6–1. It was over in fifty-nine minutes. When someone asked Gilbert if anyone could have beaten Edberg, he shrugged. "All I know is there's no way *I* could have beaten him, that's for sure."

Edberg was feeling so good about things, he even made a joke in his postmatch press conference. When someone jokingly asked if President Bush had called to congratulate him on becoming No. 1, Edberg shook his head. "No, he didn't," he said, deadpan. "But he did call and ask me about that Iraq thing."

The headline the next day should have read: EDBERG BECOMES NO. 1; TELLS JOKE!

Edberg's ascendancy did cause another silly ATP Tour moment. Before the semifinals, a major debate took place about how he should be introduced. Technically, he was still No. 2 on the computer, but on Monday he would be No. 1. The easiest answer was to say he had begun the week ranked No. 2 in the world but would move to No. 1 in the next week's rankings.

J. Wayne Richmond, the ATP's commissioner of North America (nice title), didn't like that. He opted instead for "unofficially ranked number one and currently ranked number two . . ." which confused the crowd completely.

Richmond is a friendly, very sincere person who tends to be overly serious about things, particularly if those things relate to North American tennis. Three weeks earlier, in Washington, he had somberly approached Charlie Brotman to speak to him about his public-address announcements.

Brotman, who had been the Washington tournament's public relations director and PA announcer for twenty-two years, had made his PA announcements a tournament tradition. He would ask the crowd to participate in quizzes or to stand up and stretch or would make jokes about cars that needed to be moved or had their lights on.

"Charlie, I'm sorry, but you have to tone down your PA announcements," Richmond said. "They're distracting the players."

This was part of a pattern with the ATP Tour. Everything was very serious. Miles *did* have a sense of humor but was a no-nonsense guy. He insisted that ties be worn in the office, and when it came time to make travel schedules for 1991, he insisted on knowing *exactly* why anyone was going *anywhere.*

"Keeping a closer eye on the budget is a good idea," one staff member said. "But we've gotten to the point where no one seems to want to have any fun. It's like, this can't be fun; this is tennis."

The most fun part of the Edberg–Gilbert final was the awards ceremony: It took exactly seven minutes.

From Cincinnati, most of the players headed to Indianapolis, only a two-hour drive away. The Indianapolis tournament officials sent transportation for the players. Some went by car, some by bus. Agassi insisted on a tour bus solely for his group. Naturally, he got it.

Most of the players had left for Indianapolis by Saturday night because the official players' golf tournament was Sunday. The winner got a Rolex watch. No one had any trouble getting the players to show up for *that* commitment.

• • •

○

Boris Becker had wanted to play in Cincinnati. But he had committed himself the previous fall to play in a clay-court tournament held in Kitzbühel, Austria, the week before Cincinnati. Ion Tiriac had a financial interest in the tournament and had repeatedly asked him to play. Finally, Becker had relented and agreed—for a $300,000 guarantee.

"I never should have said yes to Ion," he said. "I played there in 1985, the week after a Davis Cup match. We won the match on Sunday; I played in Kitzbühel on Tuesday. I tried, but I was tired and I lost. When I did, the fans threw *chairs* at me. I should never have agreed to go back."

But he had. After Wimbledon he went home to rest, then went to Monte Carlo to play again and have some fun. He was romantically unattached for the first time in four years, and, as he said with a smile, "There are a lot of nice people in the world." He was enjoying himself immensely with some of those nice people when he realized he had to leave for Kitzbühel in another week.

He didn't want to go. The money meant nothing, he was having a good time, he certainly didn't need to play on clay three weeks before the U.S. Open, and his knee *was* a little sore. He decided it was sore enough that he should withdraw from Kitzbühel.

The tournament people weren't buying that excuse. They had built new bleachers in anticipation of Becker's appearance and had built their entire advertising campaign around him. Their message to him was simple: If you don't come, we'll sue you for the cost of the new bleachers—3 million Deutsche marks (approximately $1.8 million).

Becker did have a contract and he really wasn't hurt enough not to play. Regardless of the outcome, a lawsuit would be embarrassing and ugly. So, he played Kitzbühel. He didn't tank, either, winning two matches before losing in the quarterfinals to Karel Novacek, a very solid clay-court player. He also played doubles, just so there wasn't any doubt about fulfilling his commitment.

The person who benefited the most from Becker's threatened pull-out was Brad Gilbert. When the tournament thought Becker wasn't going to play, it panicked, thinking it had to have another name player in addition to Thomas Muster and Emilio Sanchez. Gilbert was the only Top Ten player even willing to think about coming. The offer was $100,000. Gilbert—surprise—said yes.

He flew to Kitzbühel on Sunday night, lost to Horacio De La Pena 6–2, 6–4 on Tuesday, and was back in Cincinnati, to get ready to play there, by Friday. Talk about found money! Exactly why the tournament would pay Gilbert this kind of money was mystifying. Not only was he virtually certain to lose quickly on clay, but the number of people in Kitzbühel who would buy a ticket to see him play would easily fit in a phone booth.

Becker would have been justified if he had asked Gilbert for a cut of his guarantee. Instead, he took a week off after Kitzbühel, then came to Indianapolis. He was in good spirits, able to joke about the Kitzbühel experience: "I always seem to bring out the best in people," he said, laughing.

He opened the tournament with an easy victory over Brian Garrow. Since he had never played Garrow before, Becker had done a little research on him before the match. He had caught himself giggling when he read a line that described Garrow as "a promising young player." Garrow *was* a promising young player. He was twenty-two, nine months younger than Becker.

"Sometimes I'm amazed how long I've been around," he said. "I'm one of the older players now, in terms of time on the tour. But I'm still only twenty-two. Sometimes it confuses me. I'm young, but I feel old. And yet I make the mistakes of a young person all the time."

On the night he beat Garrow, Becker had dinner with another person who was trying to figure out whether he was young or old: John McEnroe. It had been a long, tough summer for McEnroe. He had kept to his pledge to work hard and play in all the tournaments he entered. It had been painful. After losing to Rostagno in Washington, he lost to Pete Sampras in the quarterfinals in Toronto, and to Scott Davis in the third round in Cincinnati. Before the week was over, Kelly Evernden, a workmanlike player from New Zealand who had once owned a bar in Fayetteville, Arkansas, would be added to the list of McEnroe beaters.

McEnroe was frustrated by his tennis, by the tour, by being thirty-one. He and Becker had gotten off to a rocky start in their relationship, but in the last year had become friends. They shared the pressures that came with stardom and with being brutally honest people in a business in which being boring or being a fake seemed to be encouraged. Becker had planned to go to a concert that night, but when McEnroe asked him to have dinner, he canceled. McEnroe needed a pep talk. Becker's message was similar to the one Fleming and Patrick McEnroe had delivered in London: Don't stay in the game unless you are prepared to really work at it.

"He can't do it fifty percent or seventy percent or eighty percent,"

Becker said. "He's got to do it one hundred percent or not do it at all. Watching him play this way is painful. It's bullshit. It isn't even John McEnroe out there."

Becker felt that the game needed McEnroe, his flair, his personality, his honesty. He could also relate to McEnroe's confusion, even though he was nine years younger. "Sometimes when we talk, I feel like I'm the older one," he said. "John says sometimes he feels like the younger one."

The week turned out far better for Becker than for McEnroe, who lost badly to Evernden—6–2, 6–4—and went home wondering if he would snap out of his malaise in time for the Open. He had pointed to it all summer, saying after each loss that he didn't mind losing if the work he was doing got him ready for that Grand Slam. It was looking more and more as if that might be his last stand.

Becker looked ready to defend his Open title. Like most of the players, he enjoyed the week in Indianapolis. The tournament had nearly died in the early 1980s, when it was still the U.S. Clay Court Championships and no one had wanted to play on clay so soon before the hard courts of the U.S. Open. But the courts had been converted four years ago, GTE had taken over the sponsorship, and the tournament was flourishing. It had a remodeled thirteen-thousand-seat stadium and the world's largest players' lounge, complete with Ping-Pong tables, a pop-a-shot basketball game, dart boards, and model Indy cars to drive. A week-long contest was held among the players in each "sport," with the overall winner receiving a Jet Ski. When Gary Muller won the previous year, he decided he didn't need the Jet Ski. He could have given it to charity but this was tennis in the 1990s—he sold it to Derrick Rostagno.

When ATP supervisor Gayle Bradshaw saw the players' lounge, he shook his head. "I hope we don't have a rain delay," he said. "We'll never get the players out of there. It looks like *Romper Room.*"

Becker won in Indianapolis, losing only one set along the way—to Jim Courier, who then had to retire in the third set with heat cramps.

"I'm excited about the Open," Becker said. "I'm actually looking forward to it. It's been a long time since I felt that way about a tennis tournament. I feel like I've gotten something back that I had lost."

Bob Brett wasn't quite sure his player was all the way back yet. "The first six months of the year were lost," he said. "I think he's still recovering from that. We're going in the right direction now—finally—but it may take him six more months to get back. We'll see."

• • •

o

While the men were in Indianapolis, the women were a few miles outside of Los Angeles, in Manhattan Beach, at the stylish Manhattan Country Club.

Two weeks earlier, in Montreal, Graf had come back to the tour as she had promised. She won there, then won in San Diego. She was taking this week off, but the rest of the women's top five—Navratilova, Seles, Garrison, and Sabatini—were in Manhattan Beach.

The story of the tournament proved to be a name from the past, if one could consider a twenty-year-old as someone from the past. Stephanie Rehe had been the youngest player to ever receive a computer ranking—at thirteen years and two months old—and had been another of the teen phenoms of the eighties. She had turned pro at the U.S. Open in 1985 because there was nothing left to do as a junior.

She had been a glamour recruit for the agents, a tall (five feet eleven), attractive girl who could play. During her first summer in Europe, IMG had gotten her three wild cards as part of its recruiting effort. She had signed initially with ProServ but later switched to IMG. She won her second tournament as a pro, signed a big contract with Reebok, and soared to No. 13 on the computer by the following May. She was still only sixteen.

But then the injuries started, as they so often do when young players are asked to push bodies that look more mature than they really are. She played the French Open in 1987 with a throbbing pain in her stomach, one that she had felt before. When she got home after the tournament, she had a sonogram done. It turned out that she had been playing with a torn muscle.

"I figured it would be a couple of weeks," she said. "I couldn't pick up a racquet for *three months.*"

Her right side was so weak that she had to learn to eat left-handed—which she still does. She finally came back late in 1987 and promptly pulled a groin muscle. After that, she decided to get into a regular conditioning program. She started slowly in 1988, but began to turn things around at the Lipton, where she made the semifinals. For the rest of the year, she played superbly, moving back into the top twenty. She was back at No. 13 and had secured a spot in the Virginia Slims Finals when she went to Chicago for the last regular-season tournament of the year.

She won her opening match against Larissa Savchenko, got a massage, and got into a tournament car to go back to the hotel. She was in the backseat with her coach when the accident happened. Rehe won't talk about exactly what happened or exactly what she felt at the time, because she still has a lawsuit pending against the tournament. All she will say is that she was sore enough to spend six hours in the hospital that night.

She did play her doubles match the next night, though, but tripped on the edge of the court (it was set up on a hockey rink), sprained an ankle, and had to default. She also had to pull out of the Slims Finals. Back home, she began to feel regular back pains. She saw a specialist, Arthur White, the same man who had operated on football quarterback Joe Montana's back. He didn't want to operate unless he had to. As time passed, the pain would subside a bit and Rehe would try to play. Then the pain would come back. When it spread to her legs, White had to operate, removing two herniated discs. The surgery was done in July 1989.

"They told me that, at best, I had an eighty percent chance to play tennis again, and that my chances to play top tennis again were almost zero," she said. "I was scared. Tennis is something I've always done, something I loved.

"The thought of not playing again frightened me. I didn't pick up a racquet again until three months after the surgery. I was really scared because I didn't know what it would feel like. Somebody just dropped a few balls and I hit them very carefully. I didn't want to go too fast."

It was late February before Rehe could start practicing. Sometimes the pain would come back and she would have to stop. At times the pain was bad enough that she wondered if she could ever make it back. She considered applying to college.

But in the spring, the pain began to ebb. It never went away completely, but she began to be able to move around on the court relatively pain free. She played doubles in a couple of tournaments in July, then entered San Diego, an event she had won in 1988.

Who did she draw in the first round? Steffi Graf. Welcome back to the tour, kid.

"Actually, I was thrilled," she said. "To be able to test myself against the number one player in the world was great. Just walking on the court, I had chills."

It had been twenty-one months since the accident. The first set went quickly: 6–0 to Graf. But in the second, Rehe began to find a rhythm, began to feel like a player again. She had a point to reach 4–4, lost it, and lost the set 6–3. Still, she felt good. She had been able to compete. Graf congratulated her on the effort.

A week later, in Los Angeles, her draw was a little better—Betsy Nagelsen. Ranked sixtieth, at thirty-three Nagelsen was no slouch—but also no Graf. Rehe beat her. The following day she played Gigi Fernandez, ranked twenty-seventh in the world. Rehe won again. That put her in the third round against Sabatini, someone she had grown up with in the game.

It was a hot, breezy afternoon in Los Angeles, perfect tennis weather. Manhattan Country Club was just about sold out. The first set was good power tennis, both women bombing from the baseline. Sabatini pulled it out, 7–5. When she went up 4–1 in the second, it looked as if Rehe would walk away feeling good about her effort but a little shy of a victory.

Then, Sabatini took a tumble and came up holding her ankle. She was okay and kept on playing, but the momentum had changed. Rehe ripped off the next five games to take the set. Sabatini was moving fine, but now Rehe was really into the match—as was the crowd.

They went on serve to 3–all in the last set. Rehe ripped two returns and a forehand pass to break. The crowd, sensing a remarkable upset, was involved, trying to push her to the finish line.

Rehe served for the match at 5–4. She got to match point with a lunging backhand, shaking a fist when the ball dropped in. Sabatini saved it, though, with a textbook backhand topspin lob. *"Yes!"* she screamed. A moment later, she pushed a backhand wide. Match point two. Rehe attacked off a forehand. Sabatini lined up a forehand pass. As it floated by her, Rehe screamed, *"Get out!"* The ball listened. It landed wide. Rehe shrieked, threw her arms into the air, and tossed her head back in disbelief.

"It was my best moment in tennis," she said later. "I had gone through so much. There were times I really felt sorry for myself. I kept thinking, Why me? I thought I might not make it back and that devastated me. Tennis is the only thing I've ever really thought of, the only thing I've ever wanted to do.

"When I got behind Gaby, I realized that I wasn't being aggressive on the big points. The great players are aggressive. They make something happen. I think in the third set I did that."

Twenty-four hours later, drained by the Sabatini match, Rehe lost her quarterfinal to Mary Joe Fernandez. But that didn't really matter. The Sabatini match was hers to treasure for a long time.

"So many people have been coming up and congratulating me," she said. "I think I'm probably a different person now than I was before I got hurt. I think I may be a little easier-going, a little *nicer.* I appreciate what I've got now because I came so close to losing it.

"On the women's tour you get used to the idea of people not really being warm. I hear that on the men's tour, guys will go out and have a beer together. That doesn't happen with the women. I'm not sure why, but we tend to stick to ourselves a lot more. People are friendly, but they aren't really friends. Still, these last couple of weeks people couldn't have been nicer." She smiled. "You know, playing on the tour isn't easy. You're alone a lot, even if you travel with someone. But I think I'll handle it better now than I used to. I'll certainly never, ever take it for granted again."

Rehe wasn't the only onetime whiz kid having a big week in Los Angeles. On the same day that she beat Sabatini, Kathy Rinaldi beat Jana Novotna on an outside court. Almost no one noticed Rinaldi's victory; she had been back on tour for almost two years since she'd returned from her injury.

Rinaldi had been almost as close to losing her career as Rehe. At fourteen, she had been the youngest French Open quarterfinalist in history, the Jennifer Capriati of her time. She was pretty enough that glamour magazines put her on their covers, and a good enough player that she was ranked No. 7 in the world by the time she was eighteen.

Some had expected more, but she was still doing quite well until she slipped while walking up steps one day in Monte Carlo, put her hand down to catch herself, and watched, horrified, as her hand began to swell like a balloon.

"The first thing I did was run to my room to see if I could grip a racquet," she said. "I just knew my thumb was broken."

She was supposed to be out for eight to ten weeks. It turned out to be a year. The bone didn't set right, and every time she tried to play, it ballooned again. Even after she came back to the tour, a year later, in the summer of 1988, the thumb continued to bother her. She hardly ever practiced. She started losing to players she had beaten easily before the injury. That continued all through 1989 and into 1990. She came to Los Angeles ranked sixty-ninth. As satisfying as the victory over Novotna was, it was followed by a 6–1, 6–0 loss to Navratilova the next night. Yet, Kathy Rinaldi was undaunted.

"I'm twenty-three going on thirteen," she said. "I've been doing this so long, I can't imagine *not* doing it. I can't imagine not living out of a suitcase. I still believe in my talent. I still believe I can get it going. I like being onstage, performing for people. Sure, it's a roller coaster, but I love it.

"I probably should have waited six more months to come back, but I couldn't stand the waiting. I would go to tournaments to see people and would feel totally out of it. It was as if I was a ghost or something. I'd ask for a player badge and people would say, 'Player badge? You aren't playing.' That hurt.

"Now, I *am* playing. I don't like to lose, but I'm playing. That's what matters. When I get down now, I just think back to when I was thirteen. I was playing in a tournament with Zina Garrison. One night we were talking, and she just looked at me and said, 'Kathy, wouldn't it be great to get *paid* to play tennis someday?' "

Kathy Rinaldi smiled. "I've seen both sides," she said. "Getting paid is nice. Getting to play is *great.*"

One person who was not thrilled by Stephanie Rehe's victory over Sabatini was Dick Dell.

Dell had been Sabatini's agent since 1984, when she'd first signed with ProServ as a promising fourteen-year-old. He had watched her blossom into a top-five player, one of the game's most glamorous and wealthy names. But after reaching the French Open semifinals, at the age of fifteen, Sabatini had never taken that next step. First, Graf had zoomed by her; now others were starting to do the same.

When Andres Gomez won the French Open, he commented to friends, "I know Dick always thought he would represent a Grand Slam champion, but I'm sure he didn't think it would be me."

Everyone had thought it would be Sabatini. Now many people wondered if that would ever happen. "There's no doubt, the talent is there," Dell said, sitting on the balcony of the Manhattan Country Club. "But she's got to make changes in the way she plays. She knows that. The question now is getting her to do it."

Sabatini's stagnation frustrated Dell, not because it cost him—or ProServ—any money as her agent—Sabatini was worth more than $20 million—but because he still felt deeply about the game and wanted to see his players live up to their potential.

Dell had played professionally in the early seventies, reaching No. 55 on the computer. But to everyone in tennis he was—and always would be—Donald Dell's younger brother. At forty-three, he was nine years younger than his brother, and looking at him, there was no mistaking the fact that he was Donald's brother.

That was where the resemblance stopped, though. Donald Dell was loud, aggressive, arrogant, pushy, and maniacally driven. And that was the way his *friends* described him. Dick Dell was soft-spoken, laid-back, calm, and still lived in a bachelor's apartment in Arlington, Virginia. His brother owned forty acres of land in upper-crust Potomac, Maryland.

Dick Dell never planned to be an agent. He had gone to law school for one year before being drafted, in 1970. After the army, he had played for a while and then moved to Hawaii to teach tennis. He came back to the University of Virginia in 1981, and picked up where he had left off at law school eleven years earlier.

He worked at ProServ in the summer of 1982, then spent a good portion of his final year at UVA trying to recruit the seven-foot-four-inch UVA basketball star, Ralph Sampson. "I really didn't know if I was going to work in tennis or not," he said. "I was ready to try ProServ for a while, but the tennis division was full."

That was before the split that created Advantage. Suddenly, ProServ needed people in the tennis division. Dell was put in charge of recruiting. One of his first recruits was Sabatini. He was also assigned Gomez and, later, signed Aaron Krickstein.

"When I first came into the business, I think I was very idealistic," he said. "I was going to be the agent who really had a positive affect on people's lives, who did more than just make them money. After a while I found out that a lot of it is just bullshit. You make deals for guys, you take a hard line as a negotiator, and that's it. That's all they want.

"Andres winning the French was special because I felt I *did* play a part in that. He really wasn't sure if he wanted to keep playing or if he was good enough to win a Grand Slam. I think I helped convince him he was.

"I'd like to be able to do the same thing with Gaby. I was the one who encouraged her to bring in [new coach] Carlos [Kirmayr] and try to change her game. She's got the size to attack; she has to start using it more. She's the most predictable top player in the world. I said to her today on the practice court, 'You know, just once while I represent you I would love to see you hit a drop shot down the line. If I know it's going crosscourt every time, don't you think the other players do, too?'

"She can do it if she wants to. She's still only twenty years old. I know people wonder if she's got the mind to win a Grand Slam. She does. She may not be a genius, but she understands the game well enough to win. It's a matter now of her believing that she can do it."

It was late at night now, and the Manhattan Country Club was emptying. Dick Dell looked out toward the mountains and smiled. "This has been a very strange year. I've had one player everyone thought was finished win the French Open. I've got another one who should be reaching her peak who people are ready to write off.

"Who knows in this sport? No one in the world thought Andres would win in Paris. I remember, during the last set I kept thinking, Don't even *think* this can happen. But it happened."

He laughed. "Let's see what happens at the Open. Maybe something crazy will happen there, too."

22

CRAZINESS RULES

For a tennis player, the only thing worse than playing in the U.S. Open is *not* playing in the U.S. Open.

This is the Grand Slam everyone loves to hate. The traffic is horrendous, the schedule is awful, the locker rooms are tiny, and there aren't nearly enough practice courts. The weather can be brutal. But everyone plays.

They play because the court surface is the most neutral in the sport. A grass-courter can win on a hard court; so can a clay-courter. A serve-and-volleyer can win, as can a baseliner. They also play because the Open is the end of the year, the climax of the summer. The two tours slog on into November, with lots of money to be made and points to be acquired, but the fall tournaments—most of them indoors—lack electricity. There is no Grand Slam event just ahead.

In 1990, the first week of the Open had just about everything *but* electricity. The National Tennis Center was a giant sauna for five days; the heat and humidity made everyone miserable. Tempers were short; twenty players were fined for on-court behavior during the first four days, when the heat was at its most vicious. During the three previous Grand Slams in 1990, twenty-eight players had received fines—*total*—during six weeks of play.

There was one piece of good news for the players, though: The airplanes were gone. For twelve years, since the first day the tournament had been played on this site, airplanes taking off next door at LaGuardia Airport had roared directly over the stadium. Some days it wasn't bad; others, it was constant. It all depended on the wind.

Now, though, with talk in the air that the USTA might move the Open out of New York in response to the players' complaints, newly elected Mayor David Dinkins had stepped in. Dinkins, an avid tennis player and fan, had worked out a plan so that runway 13 at LaGuardia, the one that sent the planes over the stadium, would not be used during the two weeks of the tournament. This was good news. It also raised an obvious question: If there was no danger in not using the runway, as Dinkins and his people claimed, why had it taken thirteen years to do something about it?

Nobody much cared about the answer, though, and Dinkins, with New York in the midst of a never-ending budget crisis and an awful wave of violent crime, was at the Open almost every day, sitting in a box marked in huge letters that read: THE HON. DAVID N. DINKINS, MAYOR OF NEW YORK.

The players were very happy that the planes were gone, and they were encouraged by USTA promises to finally spend some of their TV megabucks on improving the facilities. The traffic, they knew, would always be a mess. That was part of the deal in New York.

What made everyone crazy—and angry—was the schedule. Both the Australian and U.S. Opens have night matches. But in Australia only one court is used, which means no more than four players have to play nighttime singles, and after the first two rounds, only one singles match is scheduled for under the lights.

At the Open, two courts are used at night and play is scheduled to start at seven-thirty—but, thanks to the vagaries of television, they never start before seven-forty-five. Day schedules also run late a couple of times each year, which delays things even further. If there are any weather problems, the schedule is a disaster.

The other scheduling fiasco, the one that angers the top players, concerns the final weekend. The other three Grand Slams follow the same formula for the last four days: women's semifinals on Thursday; men's semifinals on Friday; women's final on Saturday; men's final on Sunday. This means that the finalists have a day off after their semifinals so that both will be rested and the final will be as fair a test as possible.

The Open holds the women's semifinals on Friday and the men's on Saturday—with the women's final in between the two men's matches on Saturday (the men's doubles final is played in between the two women's semis). The men's final is then played Sunday. This means no day of rest for the finalists. It also means that the player who wins the second semifinal will have considerably less rest than the player who wins the earlier one. Worst of all, it means that the two women playing the final wake up on Saturday having no idea what time they are going to play—it all depends on how long the first men's semifinal lasts.

The reason for all of this silliness is, of course, television. The U.S. Open is run by CBS. The USA Network, which does the weekday cablecasts, has some say, but CBS is clearly in charge. CBS is *so* much in charge that agents will call the network to find out what court their clients are being assigned and even to lobby just a bit for a spot on a show court.

Example: Dan Goldie went into the Open in 1990 with his endorsement contracts about to expire. His agent, Tom Ross, was in the process of negotiating extensions—not easy, since Goldie had not had a very good year. When Ross saw that Goldie was playing Pete Sampras, the twelfth seed, he called a friend at CBS to find out what court Sampras and Goldie would be on. He was told court 1—at night. That was perfect for Ross: a show court on television. The fact that Goldie got the assignment because he was playing Sampras didn't matter. He was there. And that's what counts to Nike, et al. Ross was prepared to lobby with CBS for a show court, but he didn't have to.

Goldie was there because CBS wanted him there and put him there. Everyone knew that. Yet, David Markin, the USTA president, kept trying to dispute that. As the Open began, the USTA was in the process of renegotiating its contracts with CBS and USA. There had been an option in the previous contract for CBS to extend the contract, for $19 million a year, if the USTA re-signed without putting the tournament up for bid.

IMG, which had negotiated the USTA's TV deals for twenty years, recommended that they take the $19 million and run. Ratings for tennis in general (and the Open specifically) had dropped steadily for several years.

Markin didn't like that idea. He told CBS he wanted $50 million a year, which so infuriated CBS Sports president Neil Pilson that he announced his opening bid in an auction would be $12 million. Markin was unswayed. He dropped IMG, shopped around, and hired ProServ to negotiate the contract. This did not thrill his new executive director, Marshall Happer.

During his years as administrator of the MTC, Happer had tried to pass rules to lessen the power of the management groups. Clearly, having a management group negotiate for the Open (as one did for each of the Slams) was a conflict of interest. If ProServ brought in a good contract, the USTA would be beholden to them. That might help a ProServ player in need of a wild card. It could also affect scheduling: A ProServ player might get on a show court or get to play an early match when he/she wanted to do so. Maybe the USTA might push a young player working with its "rookie pro" program toward ProServ. On the other hand, if ProServ didn't produce a good deal, maybe its players would find things a little rougher in dealing with the USTA.

Naturally, all parties involved would deny that any such thing could take place. Clearly, though, it could. "I am against conflicts of interest," Marshall Happer said when asked about ProServ's relationship with the USTA.

Wasn't this a clear conflict of interest?

"I am against conflicts of interest," Happer said. "Have you got another question?"

It was difficult not to like Marshall Happer. He was a fifty-two-year-old real estate lawyer who had gotten involved in tennis while building a racquet club in Raleigh, North Carolina. He was a big man with longish gray hair, the sad eyes of a basset hound, and the drawl of a Southern sherriff.

Happer had run the MTC for nine years. During that time he had taken several stabs at cleaning up the game, policing some of the more blatant conflicts and occasionally trying to curb the runaway guarantees. In return, the game had, for all intents and purposes, kicked him out. The MTC had deteriorated into complete chaos. No one listened during meetings; members often took out newspapers and began reading in mid-meeting. A consensus could never be reached on anything.

When Hamilton Jordan first became a member of the MTC, in his position as ATP executive director, he was amazed by the anarchy. "The one guy I really respected in the whole group was Marshall Happer," Jordan said. "I think he wanted to do the right things. But the way the system was set up made it impossible for him."

When the MTC died, Happer was hired by the USTA as executive director. He came in with an unwritten agreement that, for the first time, the president was going to let the executive director run things. It hadn't turned out that way. Each USTA president serves for two years. Before they get to be president, they spend years working their way through the USTA bureaucracy. Once they are in office, most want to make a mark, somehow make certain they will be remembered. Ego becomes a very big factor in their decision-making.

Markin, whose huge, bushy eyebrows made him look very much like the TV character Eddie Munster, was the very picture of an ego-crazed USTA president. He had been a boss all his life: Born into wealth, he had taken over a company started by his father and made it bigger and better. He was the kind of person who believed that his power was so absolute he could say anything and no one would question him. This was never more apparent than in the two player meetings the night before the Open began. In the men's meeting, Markin was asked why the men and women received equal prize money at the Open. This irked many of the men, since they played best-of-five sets and the women played best-of-three.

"I understand why you feel you deserve more money for playing more," Markin said. "But in this country, we're bound by equal-opportunity laws. We have no choice but to pay the women what we pay the men."

An hour later, in the women's meeting, Markin was asked if the USTA would continue to hold off the men's demands that they be paid more than the women.

"As long as I am *alive,* women will get equal prize money at the Open," Markin said. "I promise you that."

When those two quotes appeared back-to-back in *The National,* Markin was outraged. During a meeting that afternoon with WTA executive director Gerry Smith, he said, "I was completely misquoted, Gerry. That's not what I said to the men at all."

Smith found that interesting, since he had met with Mark Miles of the ATP Tour that morning, and Miles had told him that the quote in the paper was *exactly* correct.

That was Markin's way, though. He said whatever he felt like saying and then got angry with those who called him on it. Throughout the tournament, Markin and the USTA kept jumping through hoops to keep both CBS and USA happy.

When reporters accused Markin of letting TV run the tournament from stem to stern because of the ongoing negotiations, he angrily denied that was true. "I'm telling you categorically that TV does not dictate to us," Markin said. "All we allow them to do is advise. We make our own decisions."

As he spoke, Markin was standing a few feet away from the player entrance to the stadium court. At the very instant that he finished his sentence, Jennifer Capriati and Anke Huber walked up, ready to go on court for their first-round match. They were stopped abruptly by Keith Johnson, the tournament referee.

"I'm sorry, ladies, you'll have to wait here for a couple of minutes," Johnson said. "TV is in commercial and they want you to stay in the tunnel until they come back."

The first day of the tournament was so humid that just sitting in the sun to watch a match was painful. Aki Rahunen, the talented young

Finn, had to quit in the fourth set against Thomas Muster after heat cramps had worn him down completely. Tim Mayotte didn't quit against Thierry Champion, but he was completely lackluster, losing to him in four sets.

That match was the climax of a perfectly awful year for Mayotte. He hadn't won a single match in a Grand Slam tournament, never recovering, it seemed, from his two losses to Pete Sampras in Australia.

Mayotte had decided after Australia to split with his longtime coach, Bill Drake, and then, after back-to-back first-round losses to Jim Pugh at Indian Wells, and Alexander Volkov at Lipton, had taken a long break to decide exactly where he was going in the sport. His girlfriend, Cathy Barnett, wanted him to seriously think about quitting. He would be thirty in August, and he had made a lot of money; maybe it was time to get off the road and get on with his life.

This is easier said than done for an athlete, even a bright one like Mayotte, who has had success and has never stopped believing he can't have more. He hooked himself up with a new two-man coaching team and came to Queen's, saying he still thought his best tennis was ahead of him. His tournament at Queen's had lasted five games before a pulled muscle in his back forced him to default. Wimbledon wasn't much better—a first-round loss to Gary Muller—and the summer had been more of the same: a loss to Robbie Weiss at Newport, a loss to Todd Witsken in Washington, a respectable quarterfinal loss to Jay Berger in Toronto, and a first-round loss to Darren Cahill in Cincinnati.

He came to New York with his ranking down to twenty-sixth and dropping. Against Champion, in the heat, he never could get going. By the end of the tournament, he and his brother John were negotiating with Billie Jean King to see if she would be interested in coaching him.

Shortly after Mayotte's defeat, a violent electrical storm hit, stopping play for three hours and severely curtailing the first day's play. It didn't prevent Dan Goldie from getting his shot on the show court, though. He and Sampras went out to play shortly after eight o'clock, in front of a grandstand crowd of no more than one thousand people. The rain had sent most fans home.

Which was probably a good thing for Goldie and his endorsements. Sampras waxed him in straight sets. For Sampras, the victory was a relief. Still, in the back of his mind was his first-round loss at Wimbledon to Christo van Rensburg.

"That match really bothered me," he said. "Not that Christo isn't a good grass-courter; he is. But I had just won Manchester the week before, I had my injuries behind me, and I thought I was ready to do some damage in that tournament. Then, when it got tight, I started to play a little scared. I stopped hitting the ball, and the next thing I knew, I was out.

"I went home and really moped around for a few days. I turned on Wimbledon one day, and Kevin Curren was playing. That was *my* spot in the draw, where *I* should have been. That killed me."

After Philadelphia, Sampras had become the fresh young American everyone was pointing to. Agassi and Chang were still young, but hardly fresh. Their acts, as different as they were, had already started to wear on people. Sampras had a way about him, an innocence, that was appealing. When no less a figure than Fred Perry picked him to win Wimbledon, his response was "That's really nice to have someone say, but come on, Fred, get a grip!"

Sampras was as close to normal as a successful, wealthy eighteen-year-old who had dropped out of high school to play tennis could possibly be. "I think I'm a normal person doing very abnormal things," he said, a reasonable assessment.

He had played solidly through the summer, beating McEnroe in Toronto before losing a tough three-set semifinal to Chang. He lost 7–6 in the third to Edberg in the semis in Los Angeles, and then lost another close match to Chang, in Cincinnati. The only loss that had bothered him was another 7–6 in the third, this one to Richey Reneberg, in Indianapolis.

"I didn't play a really bad match all summer," he said. "I lost some matches that I could have won, but I realized as I went along that these were just tour stops, just places to work to get yourself ready for the Open. The day after I lost I would always end up on the golf course, and before I knew it, I would be looking ahead, not back. The only match that did bother me a little was Reneberg, but then I thought to myself, The guy is thirty in the world and you're pissed because you lost to him. That shows how far you've come.' "

He had come a long way since his victory over Wilander a year earlier at the Open. Some people saw him as a legitimate dark horse when the tournament started. Sampras didn't buy that: "I'm a couple of years away. I'm really happy with the way I've improved this year, but I'm not ready to win a Grand Slam. Someday, I hope, but not quite yet. Not this soon."

. . .

The person many people were picking to win was the new No. 1—Edberg. He was, without question, the hottest player in the world. In fact, he had not lost a match since the Bruguera debacle in Paris—a streak of twenty-one matches and four tournaments. He had won all three events he had entered after Wimbledon: Los Angeles, Cincinnati, and the Hamlet Cup, on Long Island, the week prior to the Open.

In the past, Edberg had played two weeks before the Open and then taken off the week before it began. He had changed that this year because of a new touring-pro deal (read guarantee) he had signed with the Hamlet, a golf/tennis resort that had once employed Jimmy Arias as its touring pro. Part of the deal—which was worth about $2 million for four years—was that the touring pro played in the Hamlet tournament. Edberg not only played, he won it, playing three matches the last two days because of rain delays.

That may have had absolutely nothing to do with what happened to him on the second morning of the tournament. After all, his pre-Open preparations in the past had not produced sterling results, so a change might not have been a bad idea. Or maybe it was.

In any event, Edberg showed up for his match with Alexander Volkov with the hangdog look he had worn in Paris. He didn't play quite as poorly as he had against Bruguera, but he came close. Once again he was bounced from the first round of a Grand Slam and once again it was in straight sets.

"I just never felt comfortable," Edberg said. "I can't tell you why. I thought I would do well here. But it's all over now."

Volkov had been so certain he would lose that he had committed to play in German League matches that weekend. "I was supposed to fly out of here tomorrow," he said. "I was surprised Stefan played so poorly."

Volkov made it to his German League commitment. The day after beating Edberg, he lost to Todd Witsken in straight sets—winning only seven games.

Almost everyone had expected an Edberg–Lendl semifinal in the top half of the draw. Now that was out of the question. But the craziness was just beginning.

Almost without fail, the shocking upsets during the first week of a Grand Slam take place on the men's side. The top women are just too strong to lose an early round match. The Open began exactly that way: Monica Seles, playing the first match of the tournament, started with a

6–0, 6–0 victory over Elena Pampoulova (spell that three times fast). Steffi Graf dropped two games in her first match; Martina Navratilova dropped four; Zina Garrison, four; and Gabriela Sabatini, two. By the end of the first week, though, the women had the kind of delightful chaos on their hands that's usually reserved for the men. The first to fall, in what may have been the single most stunning upset of the year in the women's game, was Seles.

There had been some hints that Seles might be vulnerable. She had shown up in Los Angeles wielding a new Yonex racquet, part of a huge multiyear, multimillion-dollar deal she had signed with the company after Wimbledon. This was all well and good, but Yonex had insisted, as part of the deal, that Seles use the racquet at the Open.

Seles had been playing with a Prince—with pretty fair results—and to ask her to change racquets two weeks before a Grand Slam was a mistake. But Yonex wanted to make a splashy pre-Open announcement, and IMG and Seles's army of advisers didn't want to chance losing the deal.

So, they chanced losing the Open. Seles had won Los Angeles, beating Navratilova in a wonderful final. But it had been clear there that she wasn't hitting the ball with the same authority as in Europe. She was still plenty good and would no doubt get better as she grew accustomed to the racquet, but a lot of people wondered if it would affect her at the Open.

It did. Seles lost in the third round to Linda Ferrando, a twenty-four-year-old Italian ranked eighty-second in the world—seven spots below Elena Pampoulova. Seles had practiced with Ferrando earlier in the year, in Chicago, but had completely forgotten the session. She expected her to stay back. Ferrando, after dropping the first set 6–1, began attacking on almost every point. She won the second set 6–1 and led throughout the third. She even had three match points but couldn't convert them, making choky errors on each one. It looked as if Sales would escape when they went to a tiebreak in the final set.

Only, she didn't. Ferrando jumped ahead in the tiebreak, and when she got to match point again, she made sure she didn't choke. She charged in behind a backhand return, and Seles, trying to hit a perfect shot, smacked a backhand into the net tape. She let out a tiny shriek of surprise and anguish, then dealt with the defeat graciously. "I never thought she would come back after I won the first set 6–1," she said. "I think I just got nervous at the end."

Ferrando was still in a little bit of shock. "I can't tell you why I won," she said. "Maybe I can tell you tomorrow."

In tennis, you have to come up with the answer today because, by tomorrow, you may be forgotten. Ferrando was a case in point: Two days after beating Seles, she lost in straight sets to Leila Meshki.

Seles' loss appeared to be a huge break for Navratilova, who was supposed to have met her in the semifinals. Martina didn't feel much like celebrating, though. She had won easily to reach the fourth round, but she knew her game was a long way from where she wanted it to be. The emotion she knew she needed to feel starting the second week of a Grand Slam just wasn't there.

"I kept hoping it would show up, but it doesn't work that way," she said. "I came to the tournament feeling like I needed another week to be ready. I don't know if that would have made a difference or not. But I just never felt good the whole week."

It had not been an easy summer for Navratilova. The post-Wimbledon letdown had been expected, but along with it had come cruel comments made by Margaret Court. The week after Martina's victory, Court had said that she felt Navratilova was a very poor role model for young tennis players and for young people because of her homosexuality.

This stung Navratilova. She had come a long way in recent years in dealing with her sexuality and the inevitable reaction some people had to it. But to be publicly bashed by another tennis player, and another great champion at that, really hurt.

"It took me a long time to realize that there's no way I can change people who are going to put labels on me because of my personal life," she said. "If someone wants to be a homophobe, that's their right. I can't change them. I feel sorry for people like that, because what scares them is the unknown.

"It's no different than racism. Most people who hate blacks don't know any blacks. They can't relate to them, because they've probably never spoken two words to a black person in their life. It's no different with homosexuality. A lot of people out there think that every gay man in the world is ready to jump on any man that comes near him because he's so sex crazy. I've always tried to educate people by example, by being a good person. That's all I can do.

"I've always been opinionated and outspoken on a lot of things. I know I'm too liberal for a lot of people, but that's fine. Judy has helped me with this a lot. She says to me, 'Do you want people to love you for something that you're *not*?' The answer is no. I didn't understand that in the past.

"Anybody who tells you that they don't want to be loved is either lying or not a nice person. Everyone wants people to know that they're wonderful. But I would rather have a smaller group of people really respect me than have everyone falling all over themselves because they think I'm something that I'm not."

Even so, having come to grips with the notion that some people will never understand or accept her, Navratilova admitted it is difficult sometimes to see the adulation—and the money—that others on the tour receive.

"Seles is making more money from Yonex than I am," she said. "If I said that doesn't bother me, I'd be lying. Capriati is probably making more than Graf *right now.* I sit back and look at my record, and, sure, I'm a little bit jealous. It isn't a matter of needing the money; it's other people putting some kind of value on you. I hope Jennifer becomes a great champion; I think she will. But, gee, so much, so soon. It's scary."

There is one other person Navratilova is a little bit jealous of: Evert. Long ago she made peace with the fact that Chris America would always be the darling wherever they went, but a little bit of resentment, part of it a natural outgrowth of their rivalry, simmers—on both sides.

Like a lot of others, Navratilova thinks Evert has cultivated the girl-next-door image well beyond reality. Evert, on the other hand, thinks that Navratilova can be too quick to pick on her, to look for flaws.

During the Open, Evert was featured in a USTA commercial encouraging people to play tennis. Her line at the end of the commercial was "Pick up a racquet and play." The racquet she picked up was a Wilson Profile, a new model that the company was promoting. Navratilova told a number of people that this was an example of the commercial side of Chris, which no one ever noticed. Evert didn't play with a Profile, but implied that she did by holding the racquet during the commercial.

When Evert heard through the grapevine what Navratilova was saying, she was annoyed, partly because she was experimenting with the Profile in her exhibitions that fall, partly because she saw it as an example of Navratilova's nit-picking. When the two women played each other in their series of exhibitions later that fall, Navratilova was surprised to see Evert using a Profile.

"So you *are* using that racquet," she commented.

"That's right, I am," Evert answered. "I wasn't just holding it up because Wilson wanted me to."

Message delivered.

Still, both players agree that their friendship is remarkable, given the intensity and length of their rivalry—eighty matches over seventeen years, with Navratilova holding a 43–37 edge. There have been angry moments, especially after their 1988 semifinal at Wimbledon. Navratilova won that match 7–5 in the third set, when an Evert crosscourt forehand on match point was first called good, then ruled out after Navratilova turned and glared at the line judge.

"I thought she intimidated him into making an out call," Evert said. "I just didn't think that was the right thing to do. When I talked to her about it a month later, she said, 'Well, I watched the tape and the ball was out.' I said, 'You know, I watched the tape, too, and I saw the ball in.' The point was, she shouldn't have been trying to sway the call and she did."

That kind of tension is bound to exist between two intense competitors who are such different people. For every memory like that one, there are ten that are warm: Navratilova walking around the net to hug Evert after losing perhaps their greatest match ever, the 1985 French final; Evert, playing on a sore knee at the end of a week in Prague in 1986, which she hated, dedicating the U.S. Federation Cup victory to Navratilova; Navratilova's warm toast to Evert in Paris, in 1987, at a party commemorating her seven French titles.

Both women can be difficult—stories about their demanding ways are legion on the women's tour—but both have also given back to their game in spades over the years. They have taken time to befriend younger players, to try to be examples, to be there when the WTA and Virginia Slims have needed them. In a sport where selfishness is almost a necessity, both have pushed aside selfish instincts on more than one occasion.

Navratilova had often worried how she would react when Evert retired, if losing their rivalry would take away too much of her competitive fire. The emergence of Graf and the drive to win the ninth Wimbledon had taken care of that problem. Now, though, as she prepared for a fourth-round match against Manuela Maleeva, she knew she needed another battery recharge.

"I knew I was in trouble because I was having to concentrate so hard on concentrating," she said. "That's never a good sign."

At twenty-two, Manuela was the oldest of the Maleevas, a consistent Top Ten player since 1984. But she had never been in a Grand Slam semifinal, and she had never beaten Navratilova. She came to the Open—having lost to her in the quarterfinals there in 1989, 6–0, 6–0—obsessed with beating Navratilova. That she was ready to play was evident from day one of the tournament, when she beat Amy Frazier, the highest-ranked nonseed in the field, 6–1, 6–3. She dropped only three games in her next two matches, to set up the meeting with Navratilova.

From the start, Maleeva was on, blasting passing shots past a surprised Navratilova. She won the first set, got a little nervous when Navratilova began to attack more consistently, and dropped the second. The consensus was that Navratilova was okay now, that Maleeva had shot her bolt, and that the third set would be a cruise.

"I was still worried," Navratilova said later. "I could see how into it she was. I was trying to be into it, but I wasn't. I was faking it, and this time it didn't work. Normally, I win the match, but this wasn't normal. She played the match of her life."

She played the *set* of her life in the third, winning it 6–3, then racing to the box seats and tearfully throwing herself into the arms of her husband. She readily admitted it was the greatest moment of her tennis career, something she had always dreamed about doing. "When I saw those quotes in the paper," Navratilova said, "I knew she wouldn't win another match. She had done what she wanted. She was finished."

That premonition proved correct: Maleeva lost her quarterfinal to Mary Joe Fernandez. That didn't soothe Navratilova, though. Her first instinct—to retire—disappeared overnight, but the second week of the tournament (she and Gigi Fernandez won the doubles title) was difficult. She knew an opportunity had gone and that there weren't too many left.

"I'd like to play another two years, through the Olympics in 1992," she said. "I need goals. I think as I get closer to another Wimbledon, a shot at the tenth one, I'll get more excited. It's really a question of whether the old body can hold up a while longer."

On November 13, four weeks after the old body turned thirty-four, Navratilova underwent knee surgery. The doctor told her the surgery should give her at least three more years of play without pain. She came out of the surgery with 223 days left to get ready for Wimbledon.

The Open is a climax—an ending and a beginning for tennis players. At the conclusion of the Open, players ranked in the top fifty are required to submit their schedules for the following year to their respective governing bodies so decisions can be made on designations, and fields can be balanced to meet the commitments the WTA and the ATP have made to their tournaments.

For the top players, especially on the men's side, this means nailing down guarantee deals with tournament directors. Traditionally, guarantee negotiations heat up at Wimbledon. Walk into the Wimbledon tearoom at any given moment and you will find agents and tournament directors seated in booths—usually the ones near the back, away from the traffic flow—their heads close together, talking in low tones.

At the Open, the deal-making is less obvious. The players' lounge, a couple of converted indoor tennis courts, is huge, so the agents and tournament directors can spread out. Sometimes they will go down the hall to Slew's Place, the restaurant named after W. E. (Slew) Hester, the former USTA chairman who boldly moved the tournament from the West Side Tennis Club, in Forest Hills, to Flushing. The agents and TDs can also be found in sponsor tents or in Racquets, the amazingly expensive restaurant ($28.00 for a steak—à la carte) that has glass windows with a view of the grandstand court.

While the agents and TDs hammer out guarantees—some within the rules, others totally outside of them—a lot of players are making their schedules without anyone offering them any money. For some, that means answering a basic question: Do I want to keep doing this next year? The answer to that question is almost always yes, but that raises a more difficult question: *Can* I keep doing this next year?

Elise Burgin and Glenn Layendecker each faced that question at the Open. Burgin would turn twenty-nine in March 1991; Layendecker would be thirty in May. Both were college graduates, Burgin from Stanford, Layendecker from Yale. Both had experienced enough problems during 1990 to wonder what 1991 would bring.

Both dropped off the tour for a while, though for entirely different reasons. Burgin had taken her sabbatical after the Lipton. She still needed to recuperate from the traumas stemming from the death of her mother. She came back in Europe and had played reasonably well there. Still, questions lingered in her mind. She could look around the locker room and see the players who were still hanging on, scratching out a career in doubles or lingering around the fringes of the tour, hoping to find work coaching, or with the WTA or Virginia Slims. She knew she didn't want to fall into that trap. And yet, it was not an unattractive trap.

"I've always said, when I'm thirty, I'll be out of tennis," she said. "By then, it will be time to go on to my adult life. This certainly isn't adult life. But now, thirty starts to get closer, and even though I still say I'll quit by then, it's kind of scary.

"There's no question I have a niche here; I have a place in this world and it is very comfortable. I could hang on and make a pretty good living just playing doubles until I'm thirty-five. I know I don't want to do that, but I can see myself rationalizing things and still being out here.

"When I leave, it will be very hard. I will miss this life and the people in it. I'll be starting something new at thirty, and that won't be easy. This year I've played places I've never played before because the thought has crossed my mind that this could be it. I don't think it will, I'd like to play another year, but who knows?"

At the Open, Burgin lost her first-round match to Csilla Bartos, a twenty-four-year-old Swiss who had jumped from 194th on the computer at the end of 1989 to 87th. Burgin came into the Open ranked eighty-ninth. After the loss to Bartos, she dropped out of the top one hundred for the first time since her knee surgery, in 1988. It wasn't going to get any easier as 1991 got closer.

The same was true for Layendecker, although he had started the year playing the best tennis of his life. Unlike Burgin, who had been a star junior by the time she was ten years old, Layendecker was a classic late bloomer. He had been a good junior player, growing up in California, but had never become a tennis junkie. "My mother was the person who always pushed me," he said. "When I was a teenager, she wanted me to be a great player more than I really wanted to be one. That caused a lot of tension between us. There were a lot of times when I really wanted to quit."

None of the big-name tennis schools recruited Layendecker, and he went to Yale (which doesn't give tennis scholarships) not even sure if he wanted to play varsity tennis. "At Yale, tennis is fun," he said. "The team is pretty good, but it isn't an obsession for people. It isn't just a training ground for guys before they turn pro, like a lot of places are."

It was at Yale, with his mother three thousand miles away, that Layendecker became enamored of the sport. Still, he spent most of his college career playing behind Martin Wostenholme and, until his senior year, really didn't think of himself as someone with a professional future.

"At the end of first semester, I had to put together a résumé, either for grad school or to get a job," he said. "I really didn't want to write that résumé. So, I decided I'd try the tour when I graduated."

Layendecker still hadn't written that résumé—although he'd continued to think about it. He made his way through satellites and Challengers and pieced together a solid career. The only real problem was a recurring one: his knees.

The first injury occurred in Hong Kong in 1986, jumping for an overhead. The pain came and went for the rest of the year, although Layendecker continued to play pretty well. He cracked the top one hundred in singles for the first time, finishing at No. 73, and moved up to No. 36 in doubles. But by early 1987, his doctor told him he needed surgery.

The surgery wiped out a good portion of 1987—he dropped almost three hundred spots in the rankings—and then he needed surgery on the other knee early in 1988. He came back wearing the largest, ugliest-looking knee brace in the history of tennis, but slowly worked his way back into the top one hundred. By the end of 1989, he was back up to eighty-fifth, but both knees were giving him trouble again. The doctors told him he needed more surgery.

So Layendecker put together a plan. He would play the first three months of 1990 and then have the surgery in early April. He was getting married on April 28 and had told his fiancée, Kathy Zaninovich, that he would take the month of May off to honeymoon and spend time with her. Clay was his weakest surface, anyway, so Layendecker figured that coming back for the grass-court season would work out fine. "That would give me ten weeks to rehab after the surgery," he said. "I wouldn't have played that much during that time, anyway, so I just decided to play all I could until then."

The plan worked almost perfectly. Layendecker did well in Australia and then had his best indoor season ever. He beat David Wheaton in the second round at Philadelphia before losing 7–6 in the third to his close friend Tim Mayotte. In Memphis, a tournament he had thought about skipping because he was a little bit tired, he upset Michael Chang in the second round and reached the semifinals. That moved him to forty-eighth on the computer, the highest ranking of his life.

He was fifty-first a month later when he played his last presurgery tournament, in Orlando. In three months, he had made just under $60,000, which wasn't a bad prenuptial nest egg. The surgery—on both knees—was successful, and Layendecker came back, as planned, to play on the grass. To his surprise, he reached the quarterfinals of his first tournament back, in Rosmalen, the grass-court warm-up tournament in Holland, but came away with the knees feeling sore.

He then lost an aggravating first-round match to Karel Novacek at Wimbledon, losing the fifth set 6–0 after being up two sets to one and having break points in the fourth. By the end of that match, his left knee was hurting badly. He had to pull out of all the tournaments he normally played in July, and went to see a specialist in Boston. The doctor told him there was a good deal of scar tissue on the knee, nothing that rest couldn't take care of.

Layendecker rested until Cincinnati. He lost in the first round there to Reneberg, his doubles partner, and then lost in the first round at New Haven to Dan Goldie. The knee was sore again. He went back to the doctor, who gave him the same message: It isn't that serious, but rest is what you need.

Layendecker had decided to play the Open, because who knew where he would be in a year. He got lucky with his draw, playing a qualifier named Dick Bosse in the first round. He won that match in four sets before losing a good four-setter to Franco Davin. The knee still hurt.

"I'm supposed to play Brisbane, Sydney, Tokyo, but right now I just don't know," Layendecker said. "In some ways, this has been a frustrating year; in other ways, it hasn't been. I played well early, which was very satisfying. It's been tough to see my ranking drop [it was now 98th] because I've been hurt, but I've also gotten to spend a lot of time with Kathy.

"I've made very good money even with the time off, because the new tour is paying us so well. I'd like to play another year, because of the money and because I felt I was competing better than I ever had before the surgery. I just don't know if the knee is going to allow that, though.

"Time seems to go very fast when you're an athlete. Last week I was talking to my mom, and she mentioned that she had just made the last payment on her car. When she said that, I remembered that she had bought that car just before my dad died. He had cancer, and it was a very, very rough time for all of us. It suddenly occurred to me that it was five years since my dad died. I can't believe that much time has passed. One minute, you're just starting your career as an athlete; the next, you're figuring out what do next."

Burgin and Layendecker were both hoping they could put off those decisions for at least another year.

Two men took center stage during the first week of the Open. Andre Agassi was expected to win his matches and move on to the second week, and he did—but not without a fire storm of controversy. No one knew what to expect from John McEnroe—controversial or otherwise—and what he *did* produce was entirely unexpected.

But not quite as unexpected as the performance Agassi put on during his second-round match, against Petr Korda. Agassi had gone home after

Indianapolis to rest (and get stronger) prior to the Open, and he showed up for his first-round match, against Grant Connell, in a new outfit that looked like something designed to glow in the dark. It was some sort of lime-green, black-and-white concoction, with a shirt that hung down long in the back but was cut short in the front. Agassi had insisted that it be designed this way so that his stomach would be revealed for all to see every time he hit a forehand.

His entire first-round postmatch press conference was devoted to questions about the outfit and what Wimbledon might think about it. "Oh, I'll have come up with two or three new ones by then," Agassi said proudly. He was hinting strongly that he would play Wimbledon in 1991; there was little doubt that the Nike people were thinking up some kind of outfit that would conform to Wimbledon's rules and get the company more attention at the same time.

Basking in the attention given his new clothes, Agassi seemed to be well past the funk he had been in during August. But Korda was not the easiest of second-round matches. No one on the tour could figure him out. He was Czech, left-handed, and, according to everyone, nuts. He could be brilliant, as against Brad Gilbert in Davis Cup when he had wiped him out in three sets, or awful, depending on his mood. He had gotten as high as twenty-second on the computer but had slipped back to thirty-third after a mediocre summer.

The match was at night—the USTA making sure TV got its Agassi fix—and was taut and tense for two sets. Agassi won the first, but late in the second he exploded in a manner that brought back memories of McEnroe at his worst.

The trouble began when chair umpire Wayne McKewen, a young Australian who had come up through the same White City program in Sydney that had produced Richard Ings, overruled an out call on a shot hit by Korda. Agassi argued at length, didn't get what he wanted, and charged the chair using his favorite word—*fuck.* McKewen immediately tagged Agassi with a code of conduct warning for an audible obscenity.

Agassi continued to rail. As he finally turned to walk away, he could be clearly heard on the television microphones, saying, "You sonofabitch, you." Fortunately for Agassi, McKewen didn't hear that comment. If he had, that would have been a point penalty and would have put him one step away from being defaulted.

Korda went on to win the game to go up 6–5. As Agassi walked to his chair for the changeover, he turned his head toward McKewen as he went by him and spit. The saliva landed on McKewen's leg and foot. He wasn't even certain what had happened, because Agassi kept on walking. By now, Ken Farrar was standing in the tunnel, with referee Keith Johnson. McKewen, looking down at his leg and foot, signaled them to come on court.

Farrar had been sitting in his office, making out the schedule for the next day, when Agassi had had his first outburst. This would turn out to be a break for Agassi.

"I got caught," Farrar said. "There's nothing worse than going on court and not being clear on what has happened. I made a mistake not being out there, because when I went out, the situation was very serious and I was flying a little bit blind."

McKewen explained that he had already given Agassi a warning and believed that Agassi had just spit on him. When Agassi heard McKewen tell Farrar that he thought he had been spit on, he panicked, knowing that it could be judged gross misconduct and he could be defaulted on the spot.

"Spit on you, no, no, did you think I did that?" Agassi said in his best little-boy-lost voice. "It was an accident, *really.* Here, do you need a towel?" At that point, Agassi took his towel and started to wipe McKewen's foot. McKewen—who, it should be remembered, had missed the second audible obscenity—told Farrar he wanted to give Agassi a point penalty for spitting.

Agassi repeated his vow that it had been an accident. Farrar then did something he would later regret. "I gave the player the benefit of the doubt because I hadn't seen what happened," he said. "When I saw the tape, I realized I shouldn't have done that."

McKewen initially misunderstood Farrar's instruction not to penalize Agassi and announced the point penalty. Agassi charged after Farrar, who came out and told McKewen there was to be no point penalty. In his effort to be fair to Agassi, Farrar had undermined his chair umpire and made him look bad in the eyes of the crowd, which was hooting and whistling loudly by now. Worse, Farrar had sent a message to players and umpires that some sort of double standard was in affect; that Agassi, American star, was getting a break on his home turf.

McKewen, who signed a contract later in the year to work for the ITF in 1991, has categorically refused to discuss the incident for the record ever since it happened. But the other umpires were unanimous in their response: Farrar had messed up.

Farrar does not dispute that. Agassi went on to win the match in four sets without further incident. Whatever fire had been in Korda disappeared after the incident, and his play dropped off considerably in the last two sets. Agassi then came into his postmatch interview and again denied having spit—even though on TV replays it was crystal clear that he had.

The next morning Farrar went straight to the USA Network trucks to look at the entire tape of the incident. He was shocked. He hadn't realized that McKewen had missed the second profanity, and, looking at the tape, he knew that Agassi had lied about the spitting.

"It's clear from the tape that he spit in McKewen's direction," he said. "I wouldn't say he spit *on* him, but he definitely spit *at* him. There's a difference, but it isn't a big difference. If he spit on him, you would default him immediately. For spitting *at* him, he should definitely have been given a point penalty."

Should McKewen have penalized Agassi for calling him a sonofabitch?

"If he had heard it, absolutely."

That would have been step two. The spitting would have been step three. That meant if the code had been applied properly, Agassi would have been defaulted.

"*You* said that," Farrar said.

Was the statement wrong?

"No," Farrar said softly. "No. It's not wrong."

After looking at the tape, Farrar decided to fine Agassi $3,000—$500 for the audible obscenity and $2,500 for the spitting. Considering that a default fine was $5,000, Farrar obviously considered the spitting incident quite serious. He called Agassi at his hotel, told him what he had seen on the tape and how much the incident concerned and upset him.

"Andre, this could have been a lot worse than it is, I want you to know that," Farrar said. "I expect you to behave impeccably the rest of this tournament."

"You won't have any more trouble from me," Farrar quoted Agassi as saying, "I'm sorry it happened."

Farrar hung up, hoping that was the case. "I think he's genuinely sorry," he said.

Once again, Farrar was a bit naive. After his next match, a straight-setter over Franco Davin, Agassi was asked about the fine. "The whole thing wouldn't have happened if the umpire had been doing his job," Agassi said. "The guy was looking for trouble. He was looking to start something with me. He had something against me from the start."

When Farrar heard these comments, he was furious. Twice, he had believed Agassi—on the court and then on the phone—and twice Agassi had been proved deceitful.

Farrar wasn't the only one getting tired of Agassi's act. The spitting incident, his constantly changing, always convoluted explanations of his bizarre actions, and the sense that almost everything he did was contrived had clearly affected the public's view of him. When he walked on court to play Davin, Agassi heard boos. The New York crowd had loved him in 1988, still liked him in 1989, now wasn't so sure about him. The teenyboppers still shrieked and lined up for autographs and locks of hair, but there was a growing sense that Andre mania was waning.

"It's just the media," Ian Hamilton of Nike insisted. "The media has turned on Andre, the public hasn't." But it could not have comforted Hamilton to hear the boos for his big-ticket item.

The media doesn't boo. The public—the clothes-buying public—does.

While Agassi was fighting with umpires, supervisors, and the media, a new hero had emerged in New York: John Patrick McEnroe, Jr.

For years McEnroe's relationship with his fellow New Yorkers had blown hot and cold. When he first came on the scene, he was the perfect foil for Jimmy Connors. Suddenly, Connors wasn't the bad boy anymore, McEnroe was. Connors became the grand old man, Old Blood-and-Guts himself, the crowd's darling. In both 1980 and 1981, when he beat Borg in the final, McEnroe had done so with the crowd pulling for the Swede. In 1984 and 1985, when he played Lendl in the final, McEnroe had the crowd with him, but that was as much a reaction to Lendl as anything else.

"Maybe when I'm old and vulnerable they'll be for me," he said back then. "When you're young and you're winning, people don't pull for you. They pull for the underdog. Someday, when I'm the underdog, maybe the people will be for me."

He was the underdog now. He was thirty-one, he had gone through a miserable summer, and a lot of people thought this might be his last Open. For the first time since 1977, McEnroe came into the Open unseeded. Since Queen's, where he had squeaked through to the semifinals, McEnroe had a match record of 8–6 and his ranking had dropped to twentieth. The seeding committee had the right to move players up or down if it wanted, but McEnroe had done nothing to justify being seeded.

Connors had always told people, "You'll appreciate me when I'm gone," and now, it seemed, the fans knew McEnroe might be gone soon. They didn't like that idea. They knew they would miss him, so they urged him on.

It started in his first-round match, with Javier Sanchez. This was no cakewalk. Sanchez was one of the most improved players in the world and had been in the top thirty earlier in the year. The first set was a marathon. No service breaks, just taut tennis in searing heat. If the match dragged on too long, the heat would surely wear McEnroe down.

Sanchez had a set point in the first-set tiebreak. He chipped a good, low return as McEnroe came in. Bouncing up and down on his toes, McEnroe moved into the half volley as if trying to smack it into a corner, and then suddenly pulled his racquet off the ball, landing a perfect drop shot just over the net.

For a split second, as Sanchez lunged for the ball, nobody breathed. He couldn't get it. The place exploded. The shot was pure McEnroe, circa 1984—dangerous, nearly impossible, and yet it had looked easy. He went on to win the tiebreak and Sanchez sagged. It was over after that, the crowd growing louder and louder. By the end, they were standing and cheering and he was saluting them, shaking his fists, waving as he went off.

"After all these years," he said, "it's nice to feel like I'm playing on my home court."

It built from there. McEnroe easily beat David Engel in the second round. This was a special afternoon for the McEnroe family. Early in the day, Patrick McEnroe, playing his first Grand Slam singles match ever, had won an extraordinary five-setter from his old college friend Jeff Tarango. Patrick won the first two sets, lost the next two, then came from a service break down twice in the fifth set to finally win 7–5, after more than four and a half hours. He was so exhausted afterward that he had to have an IV to restore fluids, and he spent most of the night at home, getting sick. No doubt, though, it was worth it.

"He's just worked so hard for this," his father said. "I'm not sure anyone knows just how hard Patrick has had to work to get to this point."

John's victory later that afternoon put him into the third round, against Andrei Chesnokov. Chezzy was the tenth seed, and the USTA, *not* because of television, of course, scheduled the match as the late show on Friday night. That ensured a wild, pro-McEnroe crowd, which was fine with McEnroe. He respected Chesnokov, liked him, knew he was a very tough competitor, and hoped to beat the hell out of him.

Which is exactly what he did.

Chesnokov was impressed, but not overwhelmed. "He played good tennis on the big points," he said. "I still think he is a long way from winning the tournament. He will have to play much better to win his next match."

McEnroe didn't disagree. "It's getting better," he said. "Each match, I feel a little better. But I still feel like this is a long-term project—a year, maybe eighteen months. Anything I do here is gravy."

McEnroe kept saying that, but he didn't say it with a lot of conviction. Deep down, he knew he wasn't that far away from being ready to win a big match. And he knew that with the adrenaline the crowd pumped into him at key moments, he was capable of doing something special—not twelve or eighteen months down the road, but right *now.*

On Sunday afternoon, in the round of 16, he did something that went beyond special. His opponent was Emilio Sanchez, Javier's older and higher-ranked brother. Emilio Sanchez was having his best year in tennis, having cracked the Top Ten for the first time. He had not, however, played well in the Grand Slams, a pattern that had existed throughout his career. He had come to the Open prepared, though, and, with Edberg out of the top half of the draw, felt he had a good chance to make a serious run.

The day was warm and humid again, but there was a hint of cloud cover, just enough to make it bearable on the stadium court. The level of tennis was high from the start. The stadium was completely packed, unusual for the first week of the tournament, since other matches were going on all over the grounds. The outside courts looked like a ghost town. On court 1, David Wheaton and Kevin Curren played with no more than 150 people watching.

"It was really eerie," Wheaton said after winning the match in four sets. "There you are, playing a round of sixteen match for a spot in a Grand Slam quarterfinal, and there's absolutely no one watching. Every once in a while you would hear this roar from the stadium, and you knew Mac had done something. I had to keep my mind on the match. If I'd started thinking about what was going on over there, I would have wanted to go over and watch."

Everyone else was watching. With Sanchez up two sets to one, the fourth set was a melodrama. McEnroe broke to 2–0; Sanchez broke back to 2–2. The rallies were long, the time between points longer as McEnroe tried to conserve energy. Sanchez kept hitting winners. McEnroe was diving and lunging and grunting at the net, hanging on. They had been playing for more than three and a half hours when McEnroe served at 4–4.

"I knew I was going to need a second wind or a last wind or something to have a chance," he said. "I kept trying to hold on until he might start missing a little."

Sanchez knew he didn't want a fifth set no matter how tired McEnroe looked. The crowd would carry him if it went that far. He had to get him out as quickly as possible. At 30–all, he cracked a backhand return that flew past McEnroe for a clean winner. McEnroe's shoulders sagged visibly. As he walked to the baseline, the crowd started clapping, slowly at first, then louder. By the time he turned around to serve, almost twenty thousand people were standing and clapping and shouting, trying to will him through the game.

McEnroe responded with a clean service winner. It was deuce. Sanchez dug in again, and this time he ripped a forehand down the line. Another winner. Another break point. Another point to serve for the match. Again, McEnroe walked back slowly. Again, the crowd began clapping. Again, a standing ovation.

This time, he missed his first serve. The groan was audible.

Throughout the match, McEnroe had been serving Sanchez wide in the ad court on his second serve. Sanchez had long ago figured that out and was jumping to his left, running around the backhand and bombing his forehand. McEnroe guessed Sanchez would do that again.

"If I go down the middle and he's not trying to run around and hit a forehand, I'm in trouble," he said. "But I figured if he hit any kind of forehand, I was in trouble. So, I gambled."

Sanchez leaned left, McEnroe served right. The ball went straight down the middle, untouched. *Ace!*

The place was crazed. McEnroe didn't look tired anymore. He served out the game and walked to his chair, pumping and stoking. One more standing ovation greeted him. "When they gave me those two big hands on the break points, it was nice," he said. "But it crossed my mind that it might be a farewell hand."

It wasn't. Sanchez had let his last, best chance escape. McEnroe was all over him now, taking the ball early and charging in no matter where Sanchez placed his shots. A backhand volley put him at set point. An overhead gave him the set. It was two sets all, but it was over.

McEnroe had his arms in the air. In their box, the McEnroe family was more intense than it had ever been at a Grand Slam final. There was a feeling in the air that this was a moment that might not come again.

Patrick McEnroe, who had lost in the second round of the singles, was sweating more than he could ever remember sweating.

"At 4–4, in the fourth, someone from CBS [Lesley Visser] came over and asked if I could come on and talk at the next break," he remembered. "I said that would be fine. But at the end of that game, when John had saved the break points, I was just too wound up. I couldn't talk. I asked her if we could do it a little later. She came back at 1–0, in the fifth. By then I was okay."

So was his brother. He broke Sanchez at 2–all and served it out, losing just three points on serve in the final set. Match point came on a vintage McEnroe serve and a wristy volley that looked simple. It had taken four hours and twenty minutes, but he had done it. Sanchez wasn't Lendl or Becker or Edberg, and McEnroe knew it. But he *was* a very good player playing very good tennis. More than that, however, was McEnroe himself, digging down for something he thought might be gone forever and finding it was still there. At a time in his life when many thought he was washed up, he had played in the match of the year—and won it.

Jim Grabb, Patrick McEnroe's doubles partner, once said that there are only two things in tennis that will make the players stop what they are doing in the locker room to watch a match: a big upset in the making or John McEnroe walking on court. "He has an aura that no one else has," Grabb said.

There was no mistaking that on this Sunday afternoon. McEnroe had grabbed the Open by the throat and made it his, electrifying the entire sport. He tried not to get carried away with the whole thing because, after all, a champion wasn't supposed to be all that excited about making the quarterfinals of a tournament. But his mood, the look on his face, the bounce in his step, gave him away. He felt young again and the sport felt young with him.

"Do you think," Boris Becker asked the next day, "that anyone else in tennis could get a crowd that excited?" Only McEnroe. Only McEnroe could, in one year, completely transcend two Grand Slam tournaments—both times on the middle Sunday afternoon—with performances completely at odds with each other: one ugly and boorish, the other brilliant and ingenious. And yet, both performances were pure McEnroe from start to finish. One way or the other, good or bad, his personality dominated tennis.

• • •

Pete Sampras watched McEnroe–Sanchez from his hotel room. He was scheduled to play the night match, against Thomas Muster, but as the drama wore on, it became apparent that it would be well after eight o'clock before he would get on court.

He went out and got himself some take-out pasta, then returned to his room to watch the end of the match. "I knew John was going to win," he said. "You could just see the adrenaline the crowd was feeding him. Sometimes, even when the other guy is playing really well, you know someone's going to win a match. This was one of those times."

Sampras had a knack for staying calm before a big match that was admirable. Playing Muster, the No. 7 player in the world, for a spot in his first Grand Slam quarterfinal was no small thing. But Sampras was happy with the way he had played in his first three matches and convinced that, if he served well, he could win.

He calmly ate his pasta and then left for the courts. By the time he got to the locker room, he wasn't as calm. "Something was wrong with the pasta," he said. "I started feeling sick to my stomach. I remembered pulling my groin before I played Noah in the fourth round in Australia, and I thought, No, not again."

For most of two sets it looked like "yes, again." The first set went to a tiebreak, and Sampras had three set points. He blew them, lost the last five points in a row, and was down a set. In the second, he went up 5–1 and promptly blew *that* lead, forcing another tiebreak. His stomach was really bothering him and his head wasn't too hot, either.

"I had to give myself a pep talk," he said. "I said, 'Come on, Pete, this isn't another tour stop, this is the U.S. Open. Do you want to be watching the whole second week? Do you want to be playing golf? No.' I really had to make myself focus for that tiebreak. If I lose it, I'm probably gone."

He won it, 7–3. The match turned. Sampras began to find the range with his serve and Muster began to fade. Sampras's stomach was still sore, but he put it out of his mind and won in four sets, getting stronger as the night wore on.

On the heels of McEnroe–Sanchez and Maleeva–Navratilova, his victory hardly caused a ripple. It was a minor upset. Everyone knew Sampras was capable of beating Muster and he had done it. For Sampras, though, the victory meant a lot, not only because he was in the Open quarterfinals but because now he would have a chance to play Ivan Lendl.

"I remember watching Lendl in all those Open finals," he said. "I was eleven when he played his first one, and everyone was against him. So I rooted for him."

Six years later, when Lendl was No. 1 in the world and Sampras was a brand-new seventeen-year-old pro, Lendl invited him to Greenwich, to work out with him during the week of the Masters. Lendl likes to have young players work with him. They are eager, attentive, and challenging. Sampras didn't disappoint Lendl and Lendl didn't disappoint Sampras.

"He taught me what it means to really be a pro," he said. "There were times I hated him because he made me ride the bike or run until I was about to drop, but I learned from him. He also told me over and over to worry about one thing in tennis: the Grand Slams. He said he wished he had learned that when he was younger."

As much as he respected Lendl, Sampras had a quiet belief that he could beat him. Everyone in tennis knew that the Wimbledon loss had damaged Lendl's psyche. The hunger to win every single match and every single tournament wasn't there anymore. He had played in only one tournament prior to the Open and had lost his first match—to Malivai Washington—in New Haven.

Sampras had watched him play Michael Stich in the second round. Stich was a tall, twenty-one-year-old German who was quietly moving up the computer. But he certainly wasn't a match for Lendl on a hard court. And yet, Stich kept Lendl on court for four difficult sets. "It wasn't like the difference was huge," Sampras said. "The guy was still great. But he wasn't quite at the same level as I remembered in the past."

Sampras was hyper the day of the match, wandering from the locker room to the players' lounge to the training room and back to the players' lounge. Lendl sat quietly in the locker room with Tony Roche, waiting to play. Remarkably, he had been to eight straight Open finals. This was nothing new to him.

The hot item in the lounge that afternoon, as it had been all week, were the pink Ray-Ban caps all the coaches and entourage members were wearing. The new rage? Well, sort of. The Ray-Ban people, knowing TV's penchant for constant shots of coaches/family/friends watching from the stands, were paying anyone in a player's entourage who was likely to show up on camera $500 a match to wear their caps. TV viewers were probably amazed at how popular the caps had become. Why, people were even wearing them at night!

Sampras had the smallest entourage of anyone in the game. As he walked on court to play Lendl, his coach, Joe Brandi, and his agent, Ivan Blumberg, were in his box. Neither wore a cap. Sampras felt nervous, but better than he had against Muster. The Italian take-out place he had gone to on Sunday had lost a customer for good. He had eaten chicken the night before.

The match was a roller coaster ride. Sampras, coming up with huge serves at all the key moments, won the first two sets. But Lendl didn't roll over at this stage of his career, not in a Grand Slam. He came back to win the next two sets. Sampras felt tired, frustrated. Lendl seemed to be getting stronger. But, down 4–0 in the fourth, Sampras found a second wind. He came all the way back to trail 5–4 and even had two break points to get to 5–5. Lendl saved those and served out the set, but Sampras felt as if he was in the match again.

"Coming back in the fourth really helped me psychologically," he said later. "If Ivan had rolled me in the fourth, he might have just kept on going in the fifth. As it was, I started the fifth feeling pretty good, thinking I had a good chance."

Lendl, having come back to even the match, felt pretty good about his chances, too. But, serving at 1–2, he got into trouble—with his thirteenth double fault. Sampras had returned so well that Lendl felt he had to make his second serves almost perfect and, as a result, had missed a few. Lendl saved that break point and had two game points of his own. Sampras kept coming, though. He got to break point again and bombed a crosscourt forehand that Lendl couldn't touch. Lendl swiped his racquet angrily at the ground. He was down 3–1 and knew that breaking Sampras again would be difficult.

Sampras was trying hard to stay in the present. "I just had this feeling I was going to win the match, that it was meant to be," he said. "I really felt that way. But I didn't want to think about any of that before it was over."

He had one scary moment, when Lendl had a break point with Sampras up 4–2. Sampras took a deep breath and served a clean winner. He followed that with an ace—his twenty-third of the match—and closed the game with another service winner. With a chance to get back into the match, Lendl hadn't put a ball in play for three straight points. The look on his face told the story. Six points later, it was over. Sampras hit one more solid backhand. Lendl chased it down and threw up a weak lob. As Sampras watched it float toward him, he felt chills run through his body. "Just hit the ball," he told himself. He did, cleanly, and his arms were in the air in triumph.

It was another four-hour marathon (four hours and five minutes, actually) and another stunning upset. Sampras was the young American most fans hadn't heard of, but they knew who he was now. When he walked into the interview room, Sampras looked at the writers, photographers, and TV types jammed into every corner of the room and said softly, "Are there enough people in here?"

Like it or not, Sampras's life had just changed forever. He was no longer a prospect or a rising young American. He was now a star, a just-turned-nineteen U.S. Open semifinalist—one who had beaten Ivan Lendl to get there.

Lendl was calm in defeat. He understood that the sacrifices he had made to prepare for Wimbledon had not only cost him the French but had also severely damaged his chances at the Open. "I knew that chance was there," he said. "But if I had it to do over again, I would do the same thing."

As for a Sampras–McEnroe semifinal, assuming McEnroe went on to beat David Wheaton that evening? "If Sampras goes out as if he's going against Player X or Player Y, I think he will win," he said. "If he goes out as if he's playing McEnroe, he'll lose."

He paused. "To tell the truth, I fancy Sampras," he said. "I think he can handle the pressure."

This was all new to Sampras. He went to dinner with Brandi, Blumberg, and Blumberg's wife, and found, for the first time, that people were coming up to him, asking for autographs or just congratulating him. When he got back to his room, he was exhausted.

"But I didn't sleep a wink," he said. "I sat there in bed and thought to myself, You just beat the best player in the world on his favorite court. I couldn't believe all this was happening so fast."

Fortunately, courtesy of the screwy Open scheduling, Sampras had two days off after the Lendl match. McEnroe had beaten Wheaton, in three quick sets, to keep his roll going. Wheaton had been playing good tennis coming into the match, but he wasn't prepared for McEnroe, who was still flying high from the Sanchez match and still had the crowd with him.

"I thought if I played well, I had a chance," Wheaton said. "But he never gave me a chance to play well. He just did everything right from the start."

Wheaton certainly had nothing to be ashamed of. He had started the year in qualifying at Sydney and would end it ranked in the top thirty in the world. McEnroe thought Wheaton was a fine young player, but when he looked to the semifinals, he expected an entirely different match.

"Sampras is far more advanced than Wheaton," he said. "He just has a lot more game right now."

New York had gone Mac Mad. So had the rest of the country. No place else in the world would a semifinal between Andre Agassi and Boris Becker be the "second" match, but that was the way it would be on Saturday. Agassi and Becker would have to start at 11 A.M. because CBS wanted The Old Man and The Kid for prime time. For once, you couldn't blame them.

With Navratilova and Seles out of the tournament by the end of the first week, the consensus was that Graf was a lock to win the women's title.

She certainly did nothing to discourage that thinking when she opened the second week of the tournament by bombing Capriati 6–1, 6–2. This was the day when the weather finally broke, the humidity giving way to comfortable, breezy conditions. It was Labor Day, and a huge crowd had come out to see Jen-Jen–Steffi II. They had all read about Capriati taking Graf to three sets in Mahwah, and most thought Graf's talk about it just being an exhibition was rationalization.

What they didn't understand was that Graf didn't do that. She was extremely self-critical, honest about her game and that of her opponents almost to a fault. If Capriati had taken her to 6–4 in the third on a day when she was giving everything she had, she would have given Capriati credit.

When Graf looked across the net at Capriati, she could not help but think back eight years—"Can it really be eight years?" she said—and think about the joy she had taken from the game when she first turned pro. "When I did it," she reminisced about turning pro, "it was for one year. We decided to see how I liked it and then decide if I would go back to school or keep playing."

After that first year, Graf still wasn't certain if this was what she wanted to do. Her father convinced her to try it for one more year. "The second year was when I became addicted to the sport," she said. "I was winning, and that was nice, but what I loved was *competing.* When I got to number one, people asked me how long I had dreamed about being number one. I never really thought about it until I got to number two. Before that, for me, what I liked was competing with the best players, with Chris and Martina and Pam and Hana."

She competed with them and, eventually, began beating them. By 1986 she was No. 3 in the world and had two match points against Navratilova in a third-set tiebreak in the U.S. Open semis. A forehand return on the second one cracked the net tape. Two inches higher and the match would have been over.

"No one could talk to me after that match, I was so angry," she said, laughing at the memory. "I was so mad I got halfway to the airport and realized I had left without my coach. I had to go back and get him."

The next time she played Navratilova in a Grand Slam was in the French final in 1987. She won that one, after trailing 5–3 in the third, for her first Grand Slam title. The next year, she won all four of them. That was when the joy began to fade.

"Everything was really fine until I won Wimbledon," she said. "I remember when I won that match [beating Navratilova in three], it was the best feeling I had ever had in tennis. It was Wimbledon, it was Martina, and I had been behind 7–5, 2–0 and played my best tennis to come back and win. But from that moment on, everywhere I went all I heard was 'Are you going to win the Grand Slam?'

"When I won it, I didn't feel any joy. All I felt was relief that it was over. That was an awful day for me. I felt terrible, I acted terrible. I had a huge fight with my father. I didn't even get to stay in New York and celebrate. I had to get on a plane and go right home. That made me very angry." She smiled as she thought back to the early days when she was an eager kid with an amazing forehand. "Back then, there was no pressure," she said. "I just played the tennis. I still love the tennis. I'm still addicted to it. I love going on the court and hitting the ball. If I didn't love that, I would quit. Because I hate the attention. Even before this year, I hated it. I've just never felt comfortable standing up in front of a group of people. I really don't think I'm very good at it."

Shy as she is, Graf had actually become quite good at talking to people. In Paris, at the champions' dinner, she had saved the evening, in Becker's absence, with a short, poignant speech about Ted Tinling. "I miss him," she had said softly. "I will always remember what he used to tell me: 'Enjoy your tennis and enjoy your life. Appreciate how lucky you are.' Sometimes I forget that. Ted always reminded me."

She was not in a poignant mood against Capriati, though. She had come to the Open feeling better than she had all year; she was fitter and more confident than she had been at any time since her father's personal life had first crashed down on her.

Capriati had been having her usual Wonderful Life at the Open, sitting in the stands with Wilt Chamberlain during one match, meeting Tom Cruise during another, getting to talk to her dream man Stefan Edberg in an elevator, and getting to go to two innings of a Mets game the day before the match. Her father had cut her off after two innings, though. "Time to practice," he told his daughter. She campaigned for one more inning. The answer was no. After all, Graf certainly wasn't watching a baseball game.

As it turned out, the Capriatis might as well have stayed all nine innings. Graf was rampaging. She needed all of fifty-three minutes to wrap the match up.

Capriati walked away a bit shell-shocked. She said "you know" twenty-three times in her postmatch press conference, largely because there wasn't much else to say. Everyone *did* know. But her first three Grand Slams had produced a semifinal loss to Seles in Paris and fourth-round losses to Graf at Wimbledon and the Open. Not a bad beginning.

"I still haven't beaten the really top players," Capriati said correctly. "That's where I want to get to next."

Next for Graf was Jana Novotna, who seemed to show up on her side of the draw everywhere. The result—at least in 1990—was always the same: Graf, easy. That put her into the semifinals, not against Zina Garrison as she had hoped, but against Arantxa Sanchez. Garrison had sprained an ankle during her first-round match, and it had worsened as the tournament wore on. By the time she played Sanchez in the quarterfinals, she could hardly move at all, and Sanchez won easily.

Sanchez was finally beginning to feel comfortable with Mike Estep's attacking game and had taken giant steps since her disappointing play in Europe, but Graf blew her away, too. The other semifinal was a lot tighter. Mary Joe Fernandez, as predicted by Navratilova, had beaten Maleeva. That meant she was one round farther than Wheaton, who she had been dating, so he had to behave himself and come watch her play. Unfortunately, Wheaton was on court just before Fernandez played her semifinal, losing the doubles final along with Paul Annacone to the South African duo of Pieter Aldrich and Danie Visser.

Fernandez's semifinal opponent was that twenty-year-old has-been Gabriela Sabatini. Almost no one had picked Sabatini to be a factor in this Open. Nothing she had done prior to the tournament indicated that she could turn her year around in New York.

Elise Burgin, who had played her at Wimbledon, was one person who still thought Sabatini could be a champion. "It's really all up to her now," Burgin said. "There's no doubt about the talent. The only question is, with all the money she's made, does she really want it that badly?"

Sabatini always insisted she did. Her match against Fernandez was the best women's match of the tournament. Sabatini was now committed totally to Carlos Kirmayr's and Dick Dell's plan that she attack all the time. Once she got to the net she had a huge wingspan and was tough to pass. Fernandez, a baseliner all the way, stood back and blasted. Sabatini kept coming in—until she won a dramatic and gutsy three-set victory.

But it hardly seemed to matter. Graf was playing like the Graf of old and Sabatini's 3–20 lifetime record against her was hardly encouraging. Especially since all three victories had been on clay. So it was no surprise when the first set of the women's final was a 6–2 romp. Except for one thing: It was 6–2 *Sabatini.*

Graf was spraying passing shots all over, mishitting forehands that would have endangered the planes if they'd still been flying overhead. Sabatini, feeling more and more confident at the net, was in at every opportunity.

"I knew she was going to play that way, that was no surprise," Graf said. "The way I played was a shock, though. I felt good, ready to go. Then I went out and was terrible."

Terrible for Graf is still not bad. Also, she had lost the opening set to Sabatini in the past. In fact, Sabatini had won the first set when they played in the Open semifinals in 1989.

However, this was a different Sabatini, one who wouldn't allow Graf to get a rhythm from the baseline. She kept pounding away and served for the match at 5–4 in the second. Here, for the first time, she got nervous. Graf, sensing vulnerability, broke and quickly held to lead 6–5. She had two set points in the next game. The first one she botched with another errant forehand.

On the second one, she hit a good crosscourt backhand, only to watch helplessly as Sabatini cut it off with a superb touch volley, the kind of shot she would not have even thought to play a few months earlier.

They went to the tiebreak. Sabatini could sense now that this wasn't Graf's day. She kept coming, Graf kept missing. On match point, Graf clipped the top of the net with her return. Sabatini closed in on it and hit a forehand right down the line. Graf stared, as if hoping a mark might appear that would indicate the ball had gone wide.

None did. It was a clean winner. Sabatini was jumping up and down and Graf, who had won eight of nine Grand Slams coming out of Australia, had lost three in a row.

Dick Dell's whimsical prediction of three weeks earlier had come true: Something crazy *had* happened at the Open. Sabatini had combined a little bit of luck, a lot of heart, and her new style, one in which she used her size and strength to best effect, to win a championship that almost no one thought she could win.

"She's playing the right way now," Navratilova said after watching the match. "She's so big, you can't pass her. I didn't think she could win, because her second serve is so weak. But no one seemed to take advantage of it." Why Graf had played so poorly was a mystery. As she came off the court, her father made a point of giving her a warm hug. Prior to the match, he had gotten into a scuffle with a photographer. Had his daughter known? Had that upset her?

The Nicole Meissner story had not gone away by any means. Before the year was over, Peter Graf would be ordered by a court to undergo a blood test to determine whether he might be the father of Meissner's child. The test showed he was *not* the child's father. By that time, Steffi Graf was hoping she could start anew, that her troubles would all go away, and that she could somehow again feel the joy she had once felt as a tennis player.

As always, the men's semifinals sandwiched the women's final, so Becker and Agassi had to be on court at eleven o'clock in the morning. Only at the U.S. Open could a semifinal match start with the stadium half empty.

Those who came late missed a wonderful seventy-one-minute first set. Becker saved four set points and Agassi three. Becker finally won in a 12–10 tiebreak.

Sitting in the stands, neither Brett nor Tiriac felt overjoyed at the end of it. Relieved, yes. Perhaps, they thought, Boris would escape on his will and his guile, because, once again, he was not playing the kind of tennis either man wanted to see him play. Point after point, he stood behind the baseline exchanging ground strokes with Agassi. Only when he had to, it seemed, did he come in.

Brett and Becker had sat and talked at length after Becker's quarterfinal victory over Aaron Krickstein. Becker had been down a set and a break in that match before he had snapped out of his lethargy to win the match in four sets. "He knows very well," Brett said afterward, "that he can't even *think* about playing that way on Saturday if he wants to win."

And yet, here it was, Saturday, and Becker was back behind the baseline against a man he had to attack to beat. Maybe the conditions—cold and windy, a complete switch from earlier in the tournament—threw Becker off. Whatever it was, he could not keep up the clay-court style of game he was playing. Agassi's shots began finding their mark regularly. Becker wasn't even making him sweat to hold serve. At one point, he won six points in eight games that Agassi served. When Becker didn't get his first serve in, Agassi controlled the points.

Agassi broke Becker nine times in thirteen service games during the last three sets. No doubt, he had returned extremely well. But Becker doesn't get broken nine times when he is coming in. It can happen only if he plays behind the baseline.

Agassi won in four sets. He ended it with a service winner and promptly knelt in a prayerful pose somewhat akin to *The Thinker*—remarkable behavior from someone who, a week earlier, on this same court, had spewed profanities and spit on an umpire. Becker said nothing, but he noticed.

Considering the fact that a young American had just beaten the defending champion, the crowd was surprisingly quiet. The applause was a little more than polite, but not much. Becker tried too hard to be gracious in his press conference. He claimed that he had played better tennis against Agassi than he had in 1989, in the final against Lendl. "Andre was just too good," he said.

Later that night, Becker admitted he had gone too far in praising Agassi. "I didn't want to sound like a bad loser," he said. "He *did* play well, but I probably went too far, saying what I did. I didn't want to be one of those guys who just says, 'I was bad,' as an excuse for losing."

Becker had dinner with Brett and some friends in Manhattan that night. He knew that he and Brett were going to have a long talk about the tactics he had used. That would come later. Shortly after 1 A.M. Becker knocked on the door of Peter Bodo, a senior writer for *Tennis* magazine. He and Bodo had become good friends over the years, to the point where Bodo had more or less excused himself from writing about Becker.

Becker and Bodo sat up in Bodo's East Side apartment until 5 A.M., talking about tennis and life and winning and losing and Andre Agassi. Becker still seemed eager about the game, although he clearly wasn't happy with what had happened on Saturday afternoon.

It was just before sunrise when Bodo walked Becker down to his car, which was parked on Eighty-first Street. As they said their good-byes, an impish grin came across Becker's face. Suddenly, he kneeled on the sidewalk and went into the Agassi/*Thinker* pose.

Bodo grinned. He knew what Becker was telling him. He who kneels last, kneels best.

This was a great day for American tennis. In 1986, one American man, Tim Wilkison, had reached the Open quarterfinals. Four years later, there had been five American quarterfinalists. No American had been in an Open final since McEnroe, in 1985. Now, with Agassi having beaten Becker, the U.S. was assured of having the men's champion for the first time since 1984. The USTA was taking all sorts of bows for this renaissance, but it had almost nothing to do with it. None of the top young Americans were products of any of the USTA's programs. One, Michael Chang, had benefited from some clay-court coaching from José Higueras, but that was it. The rest were products of their families, private coaches, and their own desires.

The crowd didn't care about any of that. It just knew McEnroe was on court. Sampras, who had been the hero Wednesday, against Lendl, was now cast in the role of villain. He was ready for it.

"I know they're all going to be for John," he had said on Friday morning. "If I was sitting in the stands, I would be for John. I understand it, but I just have to shut it out. I think the match will be decided by who can come closest to keeping his level where it was Wednesday. One of us is bound to have a letdown. I hope it isn't me."

In truth, it figured to be Sampras. He had played the match of his life on Wednesday to beat Lendl. On Thursday morning, over breakfast at Wolf's Delicatessen, Blumberg told him that he had concluded a lengthy renegotiation of Sampras's contract with Sergio Tacchini. The new contract was for five years and would guarantee Sampras at least $4 million, although it could go considerably higher if Sampras continued to improve.

"Normally, Ivan and I don't talk any business during a tournament," Sampras said. "But he wanted to tell me about this, as a kind of bonus after the Lendl match."

Having beaten Lendl, having become extremely rich, Sampras would have been excused if he had a letdown against McEnroe. It never happened, though. He came out bombing untouchable serves, and before McEnroe knew it, the first set was gone, 6–2. In the second set, McEnroe began to creep into the match. Down a break, he broke back to 4–all with a miraculous scoop half volley. For the first time all day, the crowd was into the match.

If it bothered Sampras, it didn't show. He hit two perfect returns at McEnroe's feet to set up a break point. McEnroe, trying to avoid another return like that, went for too much on a second serve and double-faulted. Sampras calmly served out the set.

What was happening here? How could McEnroe, who had played so superbly in his last two matches, be getting manhandled like this? In a sense, McEnroe was looking across the net and seeing himself, circa 1979: young and brash, supremely confident, and equipped with one weapon—the serve—that could keep any opponent off balance.

The difference, of course, was in Sampras's demeanor. He wasn't bratty at all. He played one point, then another. No flash, no dash, no whining or crying. "I wasn't always that way," he said. "When I was fourteen and I was still playing from the baseline with a two-handed backhand, I was a real little whiner. But then I saw some tapes of Rod Laver, and I said, 'That's the way I want to be.' I've tried to act that way ever since."

He was succeeding. Much as the crowd wanted to see McEnroe complete his miracle, it couldn't help but marvel at Sampras. McEnroe did come back and win the third set, but even with the crowd now manic, Sampras didn't wilt. He started the fourth set with his sixteenth ace of the day, broke McEnroe to go up 4–2, and served the match out, ending it with—what else?—an ace.

McEnroe walked off to one last huge ovation. He was disappointed but not devastated. "I don't think I played badly," he said philosophically. "His power really put me off. He served well when he had to. I think he's really in a groove right now, and that's a good thing. I think the guy is really good for the game."

He smiled. "Hope springs eternal. Rosewall played in two Grand Slam finals when he was thirty-nine. I'll be thirty-two next year. The next time I play Sampras or Agassi, they'll be favored. The pressure will be on them."

Lendl had said that the key for Sampras was to forget he was playing John McEnroe. He had been able to do just that, largely, he felt, because he had played McEnroe earlier in the summer, in Toronto. Then, it had taken him a set and a half to forget who his opponent was and just play. This time, he had come out firing. He had beaten Muster, Lendl, McEnroe. The question now was, could he do it one more time?

An hour before the final, Helen Zimman, whose husband, Harold, had produced the programs at the Open for more than forty years, bumped into Nick Bollettieri coming out of a USTA official's office where Agassi and entourage were encamped—again avoiding the locker room.

"Helen!" Bollettieri said, grabbing her by the shoulders. "Do you realize what today is? Do you understand what this is about? Forget all those other tournaments. Forget Wimbledon, the French. This is what it's all about. Andre's going to win the U.S. Open right here in his own country. *That's* what it's all about, Helen!"

Helen Zimman hadn't known that. Apparently, Agassi didn't know it either. Because, as he put it so eloquently later, he went out in quest of the U.S. Open title and came back 102 minutes later, after "getting my ass kicked."

Without kneeling or wearing any glow-in-the-dark clothes or carting a half-dozen people around, Sampras played one of the most memorable matches seen in a long time. He never lost his serve—not once. Agassi, who had broken Boris Becker's serve ten times the previous day, had three break points in the entire match. The score was 6–4, 6–3, 6–2, but it wasn't even that close. Agassi won eight points on Sampras's serve in the first two sets—in nine games. Sampras sensed from the start that Agassi was nervous, and he jumped all over him.

"The first point of the match, he spun the ball in rather than going for a first serve," he said. "I thought, Wow, he's really tentative. I could feel it. Against McEnroe, I was a little nervous at times. Not against Agassi. I just had a great time out there from start to finish."

Agassi's one chance to climb into the match came in the first two games Sampras served in the third set when he had the break points—two in the first game of the set, one in the third. Sampras saved them all. On the first point of the fifth game, he served a let. As he did, Bud Collins sat back in his seat. "He's got the serving motion back," he said. "This match is over."

Collins knows his tennis. Agassi didn't win another game. When Agassi netted a forehand on match point, Sampras turned, arms in the air, toward Brandi and Blumberg. That morning, Blumberg and his wife had gone out and bought Sampras a new sweater that he could wear on the morning news shows just in case he won. "He was only getting it if he won," Blumberg said.

Sampras would get his sweater and a whole lot more.

The only people not overwhelmed by Sampras's performance were

o

Soterios and Georgia Sampras. While their son was winning the U.S. Open, they were wandering through a shopping mall, killing time.

"My dad can't watch," Pete said, smiling. "During the Muster match, he ran five and a half miles to kill the time. He gets so nervous when I play, he has to go out and do something. Usually, he runs. He's lost twenty-five pounds this year, running during my matches."

The Samprases didn't have to kill much time on this Sunday. Shortly after three o'clock Pacific time, Soterios and Georgia wandered by an electronics store. A TV was on and Georgia Sampras thought she saw an awards ceremony. She couldn't resist. She walked up to a man watching and asked, incredulously, "Is the match over?" It had started less than two hours ago.

"Yeah," the man said. "The Sampras kid killed Agassi."

"Are you sure?" Georgia Sampras asked.

"Yes, I'm sure."

"Oh my God," Georgia Sampras said. "That's my son! My son just won the U.S. Open!"

He certainly had. Agassi did his best to be gracious, telling the crowd, "The better man won today." He said later that he wanted to take Sampras back to Las Vegas with him. "Anything he touched turned to gold," he said. "I'd like to turn him loose in the casinos."

But when the question was raised about just how good Sampras might be, Agassi couldn't take it anymore. "Hey, let's not get carried away here," he said. "The guy's still got a lot of tennis to play before we start assuming too much about him. He still has a lot to prove."

Sampras had beaten Muster, Lendl, McEnroe, and Agassi in eight days. He was the U.S. Open champion, the youngest in history. That certainly proved something. "You know what matters to me," he said. "No matter what else happens to me in my tennis career, I'll always be a U.S. Open champion. That's what matters."

That was exactly right.

23

DAVIS CUP

Two weeks after the conclusion of the Open, the semifinals of the Davis Cup were held in Sydney, Australia, and Vienna, Austria. One match was a foregone conclusion: Argentina, playing on the grass courts of White City, had no shot against Australia. The score was predictable: 5–0.

The other match was far more intriguing: the United States, seeking to win the Cup for the twenty-ninth time, against Austria, which was seeking to win it for the first time. Austria, in fact, had never reached a semifinal before. This time, however, with the match to be held on the red clay that Thomas Muster and Horst Skoff, the team's two singles players, had grown up on, the Austrians felt they had a great shot at beating the Americans.

And why not? As Tom Gorman, the American captain, pointed out, in the eight years since it had last won a Davis Cup, the U.S. had made a lot of players heroes in countries around the world. Argentina, West Germany, Sweden, Australia, and Paraguay (yes, Paraguay) had all beaten the Americans since 1982. That year, Arthur Ashe was captain and John McEnroe was the world's dominant player. When the U.S. defeated France to win the final that year, it was the fourth time in five years that a McEnroe-led team had won the Cup.

McEnroe always played Davis Cup in those days. He started playing in 1978 and continued to play every time he was asked—which was always. Davis Cup almost died in the seventies because the top players were too busy playing big-money exhibitions to waste their time with it. Davis Cup offered very little money, only bone-wearying best-of-five-set matches with no tiebreak sets.

Almost single-handedly, McEnroe brought Davis Cup back to prominence. When he began playing, other top players took note. They saw what it did for his public image and for his endorsements. They saw the pleasure he clearly derived from his success. So they began to play again. The resurgence of interest in Davis Cup led to a big-money corporate contract with NEC, the Japanese computer company, and that ensured the viability of Davis Cup for the future.

McEnroe played Davis Cup so often and with so much intensity that one of the jokes in tennis was that if the authorities really wanted to punish him for his on-court transgressions, they should take away his USA warm-up jacket.

When people asked McEnroe why he played Davis Cup, he had a number of answers: He enjoyed being part of a team, something a tennis player rarely got to do; he wanted to do something for his country; he thought Davis Cup was good for tennis. There was validity in all these answers. But it took a little digging to get McEnroe to give you the real reason why he played.

"When I started playing tennis, I promised my mother two things," he said. "One was that I would graduate from college. The other was that I would play Davis Cup. When I dropped out of college, I figured I damn well better play Davis Cup."

The case can be made, then, that the Davis Cup exists today as a major event because of Kay McEnroe.

Sadly, though, McEnroe no longer played Davis Cup whenever asked. His romance with the event started to go sour when the ever-righteous USTA decided to ask all American Davis Cup players to sign what amounted to a loyalty oath, promising not to misbehave during Davis Cup matches.

This came about after the 1984 final in Sweden. The U.S. lost that match, with McEnroe and Jimmy Connors playing singles. Connors had avoided Davis Cup in the seventies, but he had agreed to play after his agent, Donald Dell, told his mother that if she wanted Jimmy to exit tennis as a truly beloved player, he had to play for his country. Kicking and screaming, Connors went to Sweden. The fact that his wife was about to give birth to their second child the week of the match did nothing to improve his mood.

Connors and McEnroe both played poorly in Sweden. Connors behaved abominably; McEnroe's behavior was far better than Connors's: He whined about some calls, nothing more. Connors ranted, raved, and screamed obscenities. Naturally, the two were lumped together when people started complaining about the Americans' behavior.

"John's tennis over there was lousy," said Ashe, who was still the U.S. captain. "But his behavior was fine. Jimmy was the one who caused the problems."

Louisiana-Pacific, the USTA's corporate sponsor for Davis Cup, didn't care about details. It cared only about making a grandstand play. And so, it wrote to the USTA threatening to withdraw financial support if something wasn't done about the behavior of the boys. Naturally, the USTA panicked at the thought of losing corporate dollars. Against Ashe's wishes, it came up with the loyalty oath.

McEnroe was outraged. "For seven years I've been there every time they've asked me, and now this?" he said. "How can they do that to me? I know my behavior hasn't been perfect, but I wasn't the problem in Sweden."

That didn't matter. There were corporate dollars at stake. McEnroe didn't play in 1985, and the U.S. lost to West Germany. Ashe resigned as captain—which didn't really bother the USTA. After all, he hadn't won in three years. The new captain was Tom Gorman, one of the best-liked people in the game. Soft-spoken and mild-mannered, Gorman, now forty-five, had grown up in Seattle and had played tennis at Seattle University. He pieced together a solid pro career that included appearances in the semifinals of both Wimbledon and the U.S. Open. After retiring, he had settled in Palm Springs, as the head pro at a resort.

Gorman wanted the captaincy. He wanted to get back into the tennis mainstream for commercial and personal reasons. But he never could have dreamed of the turmoil the job would bring. In his first year, Gorman was told by then–USTA president Randy Gregson that he could not name McEnroe to the team. The loyalty oath had been dropped after being publicly bashed by almost everyone, but Gregson still didn't want McEnroe.

Gorman thought briefly about resigning, but pragmatism prevailed. He took Gregson's orders, and McEnroe, struggling through his first tennis sabbatical but still eager to play Davis Cup, was left off the team. That produced a rift between McEnroe and Gorman that has never been entirely repaired.

That first year was a joyride, though, compared to 1987. That year, the U.S. lost in the opening round to Paraguay, one of the most embarrassing upsets the country had ever suffered. That loss put it into a "relegation round" match against West Germany. The relegation round—which has since been revamped—involved the eight first-round losers each year. The four teams that lost relegation matches dropped out of the sixteen-team World Group the following year—they could not compete for the Davis Cup. They had to play their way back in through zone competition.

The U.S. lost the relegation match to the West Germans even though McEnroe returned to Cup competition (Gregson's tenure as president had been mercifully concluded) and played one of the great Davis Cup matches ever, losing in five sets and almost seven hours to Boris Becker. That loss meant the U.S. had to play in zone competition in 1988. With McEnroe and the new American star Andre Agassi on the team, it easily got back into the World Group for 1989.

Two easy victories put the U.S. into the semifinals in West Germany. The team was supposed to be McEnroe and Agassi, with Ken Flach and Robert Seguso playing doubles, as they had done for five years. But McEnroe suffered a minor shoulder injury at Wimbledon. He still wasn't thrilled with playing for Gorman and wasn't all that happy with Agassi as his teammate. So he copped out, said he was hurt, and decided not to go.

"I still feel badly about that," he said, a year later. "I just didn't want to be part of that team. Feeling that way depresses me, but that was the way I felt. Once, I would have played Davis Cup with a broken arm. Not anymore. I felt some pain, so I decided the heck with it. I'm not proud of that, but that was just the way I felt."

Gorman asked Michael Chang to replace McEnroe. Chang said he was too tired after his extraordinary summer in Europe. So Gorman called Brad Gilbert, who got on a plane, flew to Germany, and won the first singles match—the match many people thought would be the key to the weekend—against Carl Uwe-Steeb. Agassi then lost to Becker in a brilliant match that had to be finished on Saturday morning. Agassi won the first two sets and served for the match at 5–4 in the third before Becker made a miraculous comeback to win 7–5 in the fifth. Still, if the U.S. could win the doubles, it would lead 2–1, with Agassi then playing Steeb.

Only, the U.S. didn't win the doubles. Flach and Seguso lost their first Davis Cup match ever, and now Agassi had to beat Steeb to give Gilbert a shot at Becker. That might seem like a long shot, but Gilbert had won four of five matches from Becker in the previous three years. No one ever found out if he could have won again, though—because Agassi lost to Steeb.

He fell behind two sets to one and then tanked—blatantly and completely. Gorman spent the entire fourth set begging his star to try, but Agassi kept shaking his head and saying, "It's just too tough."

Agassi had gotten into the habit of giving up and quitting when he was behind during 1989, but no one ever dreamed he would tank a Davis Cup match, if only because of what it would do to his image. He did tank it, though, and Gorman walked away, wondering if he could ever bring himself to use Agassi again.

"It shook me up, no doubt about it," he said later that year. "I just couldn't figure out a way to get through to Andre. If he's going to play for me again, he and I are going to have to communicate a lot better. I don't think I could go through a match like the Steeb match again."

Other players figured that Agassi was definitely out of the Davis Cup picture for 1990. "I never thought Tom would pick Andre again after what happened in Germany," Aaron Krickstein said. "I guess he's a very forgiving guy."

Forgiving, and a bit desperate. By now, David Markin was president of the USTA, and he had made it clear to Gorman that the only way he could possibly save his job for another year was by winning the Cup in 1990. Markin didn't care who played or why, just so long as the U.S. won.

Gorman knew he had a lot of talent to choose from in 1990. Seven Americans had been in the Top Ten during 1989. That was a luxury *and* a headache. "The good news is, you know whomever you put in there, you're going to have a strong team," he said. "The bad news is, every time you call two guys and tell them yes, you have to call five others and tell them no."

Make that four guys. After several long talks with Gorman, McEnroe was fairly certain he didn't want to play. Then came the meeting at the Masters in November 1989, in New York. With most of the potential singles players in town, Gorman asked to hold a meeting. He had asked the USTA to name a ten-man Davis Cup "team" for 1990, to make everyone feel like a part of what was going on—even if they weren't selected to play a specific match.

The meeting was a disaster. Michael Chang, whom Gorman was planning to have play in the opening round against Mexico, never showed up. Markin and McEnroe did show—and got into a shouting match. McEnroe ended up storming out of the meeting.

The opening match with Mexico would be in the U.S. the week after the Australian Open. Gorman wanted to play Chang and Krickstein in the singles and Rick Leach and Jim Pugh in the doubles. Ironically, it was the doubles selection that caused the most controversy.

Leach and Pugh had been the most successful doubles team in the world for two years. But Flach and Seguso, with only one loss, in Germany, in five years of Davis Cup play, didn't think they deserved to be dropped. They said so—publicly—ripping Leach and Pugh, especially after they were upset in the Australian semifinals. Flach and Seguso said the loss was proof that Leach–Pugh couldn't handle pressure.

Gorman stayed with his selection. But the singles players would not be Chang and Krickstein, as he had planned. The day after the team had been announced, in December, Chang was practicing in Florida when he felt something pop in his hip. He was out for ten weeks. Gorman named Gilbert to replace him. The *real* trouble then began when Krickstein pulled a groin muscle during the Australian Open, just six days before the team was to assemble in La Costa, California.

"As soon as I heard that Aaron was hurt, I called up Andre and Jay [Berger] and told them what had happened," Gorman said. "I told them I wouldn't know Aaron's status for a few days, but I wanted them to know I might need them at the last minute."

Four days later, Gorman found out Krickstein's status: out. He called Agassi, who had not played in Australia and was rested. Gorman thought that this match, which figured to be fairly easy, might be the way to reopen communication with Agassi.

Agassi agreed to play. Gorman then told him that for this match, he wanted the players to bring only one guest with them for the four days of prematch practice. The rest of Agassi's entourage was welcome once the match began, but he wanted to create a team atmosphere, at least for a few days beforehand.

"I had given this a lot of thought," Gorman said. "A lot of it had to do with Leach and Pugh. This was their first time on the team, they were flying right in from Australia, they were bound to be under some pressure, and I wanted as few outsiders around as possible. I wanted them to feel comfortable and part of something before we started.

"The other part of it was Andre. I felt I needed some time to try to connect with him. After what had happened in Germany, I had given a lot of thought to what I could do to be a better captain and coach in terms of getting the players to respond to me. I wanted him to build some confidence in me, and I wanted to build confidence in him."

Two hours after agreeing to play, Agassi called Gorman back. He had changed his mind. He said he strongly objected to Gorman's no-entourage policy. Gorman reiterated that he wanted to try it this way for at least one match. The two argued for about ninety minutes. They never connected. "We left it that we agreed to disagree," Gorman said.

As soon as he hung up with Agassi, Gorman called Berger in Florida. It was well after midnight. All Berger said was, "When do you want me there?"

The U.S. easily beat Mexico. Berger and Gilbert won easily, and Leach and Pugh, after a shaky start, won their doubles match in four sets.

That put the Americans into a quarterfinal match against Czechoslovakia—in Prague, the last weekend in March.

For the next three weeks, Gorman was out of touch with the tennis world. On Valentine's Day, his second child, Kelly Ann, was born. Because he was busy with the baby, it was March 1 before Gorman began contacting players about the quarterfinals.

"Too late," Gorman said. "I know the guys like to get their schedules set up farther in advance than that, but with the baby, I was distracted."

Gorman had kept up with how everyone was playing during February, and he was convinced that Agassi and Gilbert were the best singles players available to him. Gilbert was ready to go. Agassi wasn't. He told Gorman his schedule was heavy in March, and he thought he would be too tired to give his best effort in Prague. Gorman disagreed. Agassi was playing two tournaments. He had not yet had to travel overseas in 1990. Agassi told Gorman he thought Krickstein should play. Gorman said no, I want you.

Finally, after several phone calls back and forth, Agassi agreed to play on one condition—he wanted Gorman to hold a team meeting the next week in Indian Wells to discuss the entourage question. Gorman said that was fine. The next Monday—at Indian Wells—the team was announced. Two hours later, Agassi quit—again.

Stunned, Gorman tried once more to convince him to play. Agassi was adamant. He was insulted that he had only been fourth in line for Mexico and he was concerned about being told whom he could and could not have with him. The next morning, Gorman found Krickstein and asked him to replace Agassi. He agreed.

When the switch was announced, both Gorman and Agassi were asked by the media what had happened. Agassi talked about his schedule and the whole entourage scenario. "I don't understand," he said, "how it's going to help my tennis if I eat dinner with Rick Leach and Jim Pugh."

That, of course, wasn't Gorman's point, although Agassi, in fact, might have learned a *lot* by eating with Leach and Pugh. When Gorman was asked if he questioned Agassi's commitment to Davis Cup, he played the diplomat—as always—saying, no, he didn't question Agassi's commitment, but he was concerned about Agassi reversing himself. The media read between the lines—accurately—and reported that Gorman wondered about Agassi's commitment to the team.

Agassi read that and proceeded to blast Gorman, saying he wasn't a leader, shouldn't be Davis Cup captain, and that the players should be consulted before a captain was chosen. Gorman picked up the Palm Desert *Sun* the next day, and on the front page was the headline AGASSI BLASTS DAVIS CUP CAPTAIN.

"Remember, that's my hometown newspaper," he said. "That's where I live. It was all very upsetting. It was the first time I'd really been involved in something like that. For the next couple of weeks my stomach was as tight as a closed fist."

The only distraction came when the team went to Prague. With Gorman's job very clearly on the line, Krickstein, Leach, and Pugh came through with superb tennis. Krickstein won both his singles matches, and Leach and Pugh won the doubles after the opening day's singles had been split. Their victory gave the U.S. a 2–1 lead, and Krickstein clinched the victory by winning the first match on Sunday.

That set up the semifinal, in Vienna. Leach and Pugh had now proved their mettle in Davis Cup. They would play doubles. Krickstein, having played the role of the cavalry, would certainly be one of the singles players. The other would be decided during the summer. The only person who wasn't a candidate was Agassi.

Only, David Markin had other ideas. It was now apparent that if the U.S. could beat Austria, it would win the Cup. The final with Australia would be at home, and the Australians simply didn't have the players to beat the U.S. in a match unless it was in Australia, on grass. Markin knew that Agassi was the best clay-court player the U.S. had. The fact that he had tanked in Germany, had twice quit the team after committing to it, and then publicly blasted the captain didn't matter to Markin.

He felt he needed Agassi to win. So he made his deal with the devil. Gorman first learned something was going on when he got a call from Markin in late April. A meeting had been arranged with the Agassi brothers in Atlanta (the "exhausted" Agassi was playing an exhibition there), and Gorman was to fly in for the meeting. The knot in his stomach growing, Gorman went.

The meeting was in Agassi's hotel suite. Gorman was informed that he and Agassi would make up. They needed to communicate better, that was all. "We agreed that the problem was we hadn't talked to each other before we had talked to the press," Gorman said later. That wasn't the problem. They *had* talked to each. But they had disagreed—*that* was the problem. Markin changed all that. He surrendered unconditionally to Agassi. The entourage could come to Vienna whenever it wanted. Not only that, but if the Americans won in Vienna, Agassi was guaranteed a spot on the team for the final—regardless of how he played in the semis.

Once again, just as in 1986, with McEnroe, Tom Gorman had a choice: stand up to a USTA president and risk his job or shut up and do as he was told. He shut up.

A month later, in Paris, some of the frustration was still apparent. "Even if we win, I might just walk away from it," he said. "I might just say, 'Five years is plenty, it's been fun, so long.' I don't know if I really want to do this anymore."

As he spoke, Herb Krickstein, Aaron's father, walked up. "You know, the sooner you can tell us about Vienna, the better for us," he said. "I hope you'll remember that Aaron has always answered the call. Andre hasn't. In fact, the last time around, he wasn't very damn nice about it at all."

Gorman just nodded. There wasn't much he could say. Herb Krickstein didn't know that David Markin had already decided that Agassi would be on the team. A month later, when Gorman selected Chang over Krickstein for the second spot, Krickstein was hurt and angry. And he told Gorman so on the phone.

"I really got upset," Krickstein said. "I know I've been hurt this summer, and I wouldn't play if I was hurt. But I think I'll be ready to go by the end of September. I don't think Gor would still be captain if I hadn't won those two matches in Prague. I told him I think loyalty should count for something."

Loyalty counted for very little on this Davis Cup team. Gorman had no choice in the matter of Agassi, but he could have chosen Krickstein for the second spot. He thought Chang was playing better tennis, though. Even so, when he called Chang to offer him the spot, Chang wasn't sure he wanted to play. It had been a long summer, and he had a lot of traveling to do in the fall. Gorman kept calling and Chang finally agreed to play. And so, Gorman and the U.S. went to Vienna with the two singles players who had less feeling for Davis Cup than anyone else who could have been selected.

Nonetheless, they combined with the Austrians to produce a dramatic match. To Austria, this was a huge event. Thomas Muster's manager, Ron Leitgeb, who liked to call himself the Tiriac of the Danube, was running the match. He had set everything up Tiriac-style. It would be held in one corner of a soccer stadium; there would be about seventeen thousand seats, most of them close to the court.

Muster had never lost a Davis Cup match on clay. The other Austrian singles player, Horst Skoff, was one of the tour's genuine flakes. Two weeks earlier, in Geneva, Skoff had been backed into by a car as he was getting his racquets out of a trunk. He wasn't hurt seriously, but throughout the ensuing match he kept consulting with a lawyer he knew who was sitting in the front row. ATP officials finally stopped him, thus inventing a new tour rule: no lawsuit-planning while a match is in progress.

Muster and Skoff made the Americans look like a close-knit unit. They never even spoke to each other. "This isn't soccer," Muster said. "We all have a job to do. We don't have to like each other to do it."

Muster certainly did his job. On a cold, dreary afternoon, with his countrymen singing and chanting to back him up, he whipped Chang in four sets. Agassi came back in match two to beat Skoff. The match was tied at 1–1.

During that second match, Gorman kept getting out of his courtside chair and walking over to where the U.S. delegation was sitting. Every so often, someone from the Agassi entourage would hand him a note. Casually, Gorman would take the note, walk back to his chair, read it, fold it up, then talk intently to Agassi at the next changeover.

Sitting a few feet away, ESPN's on-court reporter, Mary Carillo, quickly figured out what was going on: Gorman was playing middleman for messages from the entourage. If this was not a technical violation of the Davis Cup rule against communication during a match by anyone but the captain, it was certainly a violation of the spirit of the rule. Markin, who would talk before the weekend was over about the wonderful spirit of the competition, sat a few feet away, watched, and said nothing. Gorman also said nothing. It was clear who was running this team.

With the score tied 1–1, Leach and Pugh came through in the doubles again. On another cold, windy, rainy day, they survived the grit of Muster and Alex Antonitsch to win in four sets. Pugh played solid tennis, but Leach was the star, playing the match of his life. After all the talk about whether they deserved to play, they had become Gorman's rocks. They showed up, they practiced, they played. They even ate with Agassi.

Not that night, though. The Austrians threw a lavish dinner for the two teams in the ceremonial room of the Hoffberg Palace. It was an evening filled with warmth and charm, and the toasts were full of the old Davis Cup spirit. Muster and Skoff, although they had to play singles the next day, were there. "This is part of Davis Cup," the Austrian captain, Filip Krajcik, said. "They will still be in bed early. We are the hosts. We should be gracious."

Their guests were not nearly as gracious. Neither Chang nor Agassi even made an appearance at the dinner.

Agassi might as well have shown up and danced all night, because Muster killed him the next day. All the notes in the world couldn't help Agassi. Carillo even got a cameraman to tape the note-passing, just in case anyone from the USTA wanted to deny that it had happened.

That left it all up to Chang. Certainly, under this kind of pressure, with seventeen thousand people cheering feverishly against him, Chang was the person Gorman would most want playing. Even so, he dropped the first two sets as Skoff, feeding off the emotion of the Muster match, blasted one huge forehand after another. Slowly, though, Chang came back. He won the third set just before darkness set in, meaning everyone would have to come back Monday for the finish. Chang was trying to do what no American had done since Don Budge in 1938—come from two sets down in the deciding match of a Davis Cup. Budge had done it to Germany's Gottfried von Cramm in a match played at Wimbledon (Davis Cup matches were occasionally played at neutral sites in those days).

Ted Tinling, who had been in charge of escorting the players to and from the locker room, remembered that day vividly.

"A few minutes before the match was to start, the phone rang," Tinling remembered fifty years later. "In a distinctly German accent, someone asked to speak to Von Cramm. I told him that was quite impossible, he was about to go on court."

"This is Adolf Hitler," the man said to Tinling.

Tinling didn't know if it was someone playing a joke or not. He went and found Von Cramm. "He said to me, 'It probably *is* him,' " Tinling said. "He came back from the phone and said that Hitler had called to give him a pep talk."

The pep talk almost worked—but not quite. Chang tried a similar strategy. He went home Sunday evening and called his brother, Carl, in California. Carl, after watching the match on tape (ESPN did not show it live) had a simple piece of advice for his brother: Hit to the guy's backhand every single time, no matter what.

Gorman called home, too. "Your daughter stood up in her crib for the first time today," his wife told him.

Gorman smiled. That put the Davis Cup into a little bit of perspective. He had been in Vienna a week and had not seen anything other than the tennis court and the hotel. He found Dick Leach (Rick's father), and the two men went for a late-night walk around the city. They bumped into a group of reporters who were doing essentially the same thing. It had been raining the entire week and it was raining now.

Gorman was serene. Standing on a street corner, he shook his head and said, "I just think Michael's got this guy figured out. I really believe he's going to win."

Gorman was right. With Carl's help, Chang had figured Skoff out. He kept pushing him over and over into the backhand corner the next day and won the last two sets. For the first time in four days, Prater Stadium was silent. "I never won a match that important in my life and heard absolutely no noise," Chang said. "It was weird."

Also gratifying. After being kicked around for months by Markin and by Agassi, after wondering if he really wanted the job anymore, Gorman couldn't conceal his emotions after the match. He choked up during the on-camera interview with Carillo. For her part, Carillo had mixed emotions. She was glad for Gorman, someone she liked, but felt bad having seen him reduced to the role of messenger for Agassi.

Beating the Austrians virtually clinched the Cup for the U.S. The final against Australia was a dreary, one-sided mess held in the Suncoast Dome, an awful indoor baseball/football arena with all the atmosphere of a mausoleum, in St. Petersburg, Florida. To make sure Australia would have no chance, and to justify choosing Agassi and Chang for singles—ignoring Pete Sampras, the U.S. Open champion—the USTA played the match on red clay.

The Australians howled about the fact that no tennis in the U.S. is played on red clay (Davis Cup rules called for the match to be played on a surface used in that country). It didn't matter. Neither did the ludicrous 5 P.M. starting time the USTA cooked up to make sure neither of the Australian singles players could come back to play in the 1 P.M. doubles on Saturday.

The U.S. could have stayed within the rules, not played all its silly games, and still won easily. It could also have played somewhere with a real Davis Cup atmosphere, but that would have meant less money for the USTA. The match was full of bad feelings on both sides, not at all like what the U.S.–Australia rivalry had been in the past. This was the greatest rivalry in tennis—the U.S. had won twenty-eight Davis Cups; Australia, twenty-six. It had always been full of intensity and good feeling. But not in the Markin/Agassi era.

"The U.S. and Australia has always been what Davis Cup was all about," said Bud Collins. "Going at it as hard as you can, trying like hell to win, then being able to drink a few beers together. The problem is, David Markin thinks the Davis Cup is only about winning at all costs."

The USTA tried to pretend all weekend that the Australians didn't exist. Even the T-shirts for sale just said, "US Davis Cup Team." Traditionally, Davis Cup T-shirts have the names and the flags of the two competing countries on them. Not this time.

The whole match was a dud. Leach and Pugh wrapped up the Cup by coming from behind in the fourth set to win. Agassi and Chang had won their singles—Chang blasting Darren Cahill, Agassi barely surviving a five-setter against young Tasmanian Richard Fromberg.

Fromberg had beaten Agassi in Cincinnati during the summer, on the day Agassi had given his "I can't get psyched up for guys like this" speech. This time, after managing to win, Agassi gave a speech about how deathly ill he had been all week, so sick he couldn't even roll over in bed.

"I just won it on sheer guts," he kept saying over and over.

Fromberg just shook his head when he heard this and said, "What a lot of rubbish."

The match ended on an appropriate note. The two singles on Sunday were meaningless. But after losing the first set to Cahill and then winning the second, Agassi defaulted. He had pulled a stomach muscle, he said, and couldn't continue. He walked off to a mixture of boos and cheers. Two hours later, after Fromberg had beaten Chang, the U.S. formally received the Davis Cup for the first time since 1982.

Agassi wasn't around. He was about to become embroiled in one more controversy. This one cropped up when, late that night, he and his brother were overheard by a reporter in a pancake house, ripping Gorman and saying they had to find a doctor who would certify that Agassi was too hurt to play in the Grand Slam Cup, which was ten days away. Agassi had entered, dropped out, and reentered—only after the ITF had threatened to suspend him from the French Open if he didn't play. Now, he was dropping out again.

When the reporter, Barry Lorge, wrote a paragraph about the accidentally heard conversation in his column, Agassi's honesty was again in question. Three doctors later swore that he was hurt, and Agassi claimed that Lorge had misunderstood what he and Philip had been discussing. He also tried to deny that they had been ripping Gorman. Lorge vs. Agassi on a question of integrity was as much of a mismatch as Lorge vs. Agassi on the tennis court.

Fittingly, the Davis Cup ended not with a celebration, not with memories of Chang's guts in Vienna or the consistently excellent play of

Leach and Pugh all year, but with people wondering what the hell Andre Agassi was up to now.

Markin had his Holy Grail. Gorman had his job for at least another year. But Davis Cup 1990 was summed up best by none other than Brad Gilbert.

Gilbert was in St. Petersburg, working as a commentator for ESPN, another Markin innovation. Since the USTA had final approval on all announcers, he insisted on having Gilbert work as an apologist for himself and for Agassi during the final weekend.

Gilbert was on the court along with the other members of the team after Leach and Pugh had clinched the Cup with their doubles victory. As he high-fived with the other players, Brad Gilbert kept repeating one word over and over again in a happy singsong voice:

"*Bonusezzzz,*" he said, grinning happily. "*Bonusezzzz.*"

Yes, the players would get their performance bonuses. That, it seemed, was what the Davis Cup was all about. Making money. Winning at all costs. The United States won.

Hurray.

o

EPILOGUE

After the U.S. Open, the tennis tours slog on—and on and on and on. Indoor tournaments abound for both men and women. There is plenty of money to be made, from Sydney to Tokyo to Stockholm and back to Brisbane—if one desires.

The people who manage the sport work extremely hard to keep interest alive. There are constant updates on the "race to the championships"—the Virginia Slims Finals in New York for the women, the ATP Finals in Frankfurt for the men. The latter made its debut in 1990, replacing the Masters, which had been the men's season-ender for twenty years until the death of the Men's Tennis Council.

Tennis people kept close track of all these races, and there was no doubt that many of the indoor tournaments drew excellent fields. The Paris Indoor event, at the end of October, offered almost $2 million in prize money and may have had the strongest field of any tournament in the world, with thirty-seven of the top thirty-eight men entered.

But the moment the U.S. Open champion holds the trophy over his head, the game's electricity is gone until January. The titles that matter have all been won. The only thing at issue during the last ten weeks is money, and in the 1990s, money is no longer a motivator for top tennis players. It might as well be Monopoly money to them. At year's end, the ATP Tour fined Ivan Lendl, Stefan Edberg, and Andre Agassi severely for failing to meet their tournament commitments for the year—more than $100,000 for Lendl and Agassi and about $85,000 for Edberg. The response from the players was a collective yawn. Any of them can make twice that from a guarantee in one week. Lendl and Edberg probably made $500,000 apiece in guarantees during the fall. Agassi made less only because he played less. His need for money was put into focus when he fought like a cat to avoid playing in the ITF's Grand Slam Cup, in which the top prize was $2 million. Show up, you get $100,000. Win a match, you get $300,000. Two matches, $450,000. Three matches, $1 million. Sorry, Agassi said, not interested.

EPILOGUE

○

The year-ending championships *can* provide intrigue. In 1990, the Virginia Slims championships were full of excellent matches and a fair amount of drama, topped off by a superb five-set final won by Monica Seles over Gabriela Sabatini. The men went to Frankfurt, with Boris Becker still having an outside shot to catch Stefan Edberg for the No. 1 ranking on the computer (which he finally did in 1991, by winning the Australian Open). Edberg clinched No. 1 in 1990, but lost the final to Agassi.

All worthy of note. But only—*only*—if they provided clues as to who would succeed in next year's Grand Slams. Because no matter how much tennis people want to think otherwise, only the Grand Slams keep the game legitimate. With all the under-the-table money, the over-the-table money, and the sponsor deals, the only thing motivating the great players to stay at the top of their game is the Grand Slams.

Ion Tiriac put it best: "Do you think people someday will write about Nastase that he won the Masters four times? Of course not. They will write that he won Roland Garros and the U.S. Open. And they will say, How could he not win Wimbledon even one time?"

The bottom line is that the Masters or the ATP Championships or the Virginia Slims Finals are all just extensions of Philadelphia, Barcelona, Tokyo, and Sydney. And, as Pete Sampras put it so eloquently after winning Philadelphia, "No one remembers who wins Philadelphia."

The autumn in tennis, then, is a long, lucrative march through Philadelphia. The sport's upper class is thinking only about next year. The middle and lower classes continue to scuffle for ranking and money. To them, the fall tournaments represent an extra opportunity; the top players are more vulnerable in the fall, the matches that really matter being behind them.

Even as the money accumulates, almost everyone is thinking about the long plane flight to Australia in January, a trip from the ice of winter to the hot sun Down Under. It is the tennis version of baseball's spring training. A new beginning, when everyone thinks this will be *his* year.

It is difficult to say exactly how 1990 will be remembered in tennis. Certainly, it will be remembered as a year of monumental change: Chris Evert left; Jennifer Capriati arrived. Ivan Lendl gave up No. 1; Pete Sampras made a giant move toward that spot. There were eight different Grand Slam champions—Steffi Graf, Monica Seles, Martina Navratilova, and Gabriela Sabatini for the women; Ivan Lendl, Andres Gomez, Stefan Edberg, and Pete Sampras for the men.

The politics of the game remained as turbulent and full of anarchy as ever. The MTC died. The ATP and ITF started out squabbling and finished squabbling. The names changed, but the issues stayed the same, as murky and confusing as ever. The ITF began 1991 knowing that the WTA was becoming restless with its role in the game; the WTA continued to wonder how to increase exposure for the women when its chief sponsor was legally unable to sponsor the sport on American television.

The three most recognizable men in the game—John McEnroe, Boris Becker, and Andre Agassi—did not win a Grand Slam title. Each had, in very different ways, a wild trip through 1990. Becker began the year not sure if he wanted to be a tennis player, and ended it more eager than he had ever been. McEnroe began and ended the year with high hopes, but almost quit in between. Agassi started 1990 in search of a new body and ended it in search of a new image.

The never-ending confusion in the game may have been best defined by what became of the four men most intimately involved in the McEnroe default in Australia.

Mikael Pernfors, the winner of that match, was injured shortly after the Australian Open and played only sporadically the rest of 1990. After making $26,000 for reaching the quarterfinals in Australia, he earned only $16,285 the rest of the year and dropped to 174th on the computer. As 1991 began, his tennis career appeared to be in serious jeopardy.

Gerry Armstrong, who faced a death threat after declaring the default, went through a nightmarish summer, which began when he was arrested and charged with shoplifting near his home in England. Armstrong had picked up a large plant and walked to his car, when he was stopped by security people and accused of stealing the plant. He explained that he had planned to put the plant in his trunk and then go back in to pay, because he had been too loaded down by the plant to stand in line with it. The authorities chose not to accept that explanation and charged him with shoplifting.

Naturally, the English tabloids got hold of the story, and when it appeared during the first week of Wimbledon, Armstrong was, in effect, banned from the tournament. Wimbledon officials said they sent him home so he would not be embarrassed by questions about the incident—but it was apparent their concern was more for the tournament's image than Armstrong's. After working two consecutive finals at Wimbledon, Armstrong was dismissed—perhaps never to return.

The charges against him were later reduced to unlawful removal and he paid a fine. He continued to work for the ATP Tour—and was promoted to supervisor—and was in Australia when the New Year began. Whether he would work in an ITF tournament again was doubtful.

Ken Farrar did not get injured or sent home from a tournament. But the Agassi incident at the U.S. Open, in which he failed to stand behind his umpire, was damaging. Many umpires wondered if, subconsciously at least, Farrar had been affected by the circumstances: Australian umpire vs. American superstar in New York, in front of a rowdy night crowd.

"None of that ever crossed my mind," Farrar said.

No doubt it hadn't. But Farrar knew he had let Agassi put one over on him, and he knew he had let chair umpire Wayne McKewen down. Being as fair-minded as he is, Farrar could not help but be bothered by what had happened.

And then there was McEnroe. His heroic performance in New York ranked just behind Sampras's flawless performance there in terms of drama. He proved that he wasn't washed up, that there was still magic left in his wand.

When he came from two sets down later in September to beat Goran Ivanisevic in the final in Basle, it really looked as if he were on his way back to the top five. But he couldn't sustain the momentum. Early-round losses in Stockholm and Paris kept him from qualifying for the ATP Championships. He then stuck to his vow—along with Becker and Mats Wilander—not to play in the Grand Slam Cup, and began preparing for Australia.

But before he could get there, havoc reentered his life. Just before Christmas, on a stopover in San Francisco while en route to Hawaii with his family, McEnroe got into a shoving match with a female airline official after missing his connection. The woman ended up with a dislocated finger, although no charges were ever brought against McEnroe. Instead, there was just the usual spate of newspaper headlines and embarrassing questions.

Whether the airport incident convinced him he was too uptight to return to Australia or he didn't want to be away from Tatum, who was pregnant again, McEnroe announced a week later that he was withdrawing from the tournament. His given reason was the old shoulder injury—the reason that always popped up when he didn't want to play somewhere.

EPILOGUE

On February 16, he turned thirty-two—the same day that his old pal David Markin turned sixty—and celebrated by losing a semifinal in Philadelphia to Pete Sampras. He did have one week that he truly enjoyed. It was in Chicago, when he and Patrick both reached the final. It was truly a heartwarming scene: the two brothers playing; the proud father seated courtside, watching. Kay McEnroe didn't come. She was too nervous to watch.

For both brothers, it was a strange situation. "During the match I kept thinking how disappointed I was going to be if I lost," Patrick said later. "But then I thought, 'If I lose, it will be bad, but if John loses it will be much, much worse.' "

John didn't lose, although it took him three sets to win. After Chicago, though, John's struggles continued. When he lost a first-round match to Todd Witsken in Hong Kong in April and came close to being defaulted, he openly wondered if the time for him to quit wasn't very near.

"If I keep playing like this, I'll have to retire," he said. "If I keep behaving like this, they'll retire me anyway."

With the baby due in May—a girl named Emily—it was likely that he would once more skip the French. That meant he would come to Wimbledon questioning his future as a tennis player.

Again.

For Patrick McEnroe, the story was very different. He played extremely well throughout the fall and finished the year ranked 114th in singles, close to his goal of cracking the top 100. He and Jim Grabb got back together and won the last tournament of the year in London.

His singles ranking meant that in Australia, for the first time in his life, Patrick went straight into a Grand Slam draw without qualifying or needing a wild card. He more than made the most of that opportunity. Two sets down in his first-round match against Thomas Hogstedt, he came back to win in five. In the third round he upset twelfth-seeded Jay Berger. In the fourth, he routed Mark Woodforde, silencing a partisan Aussie crowd in the process. Then, in the quarterfinals, he won another five-setter, beating Cristiano Caratti, a rising young Italian, in spite of a pulled stomach muscle.

Amazingly, he was in the semifinals—matching his brother's best performance in the Australian. He had quickly become a favorite of the media with his easy manner and self-deprecating sense of humor. After beating Caratti, he came into the interview room, shrugged, and said, "Isn't this what everyone expected—a semifinal with Lendl, Edberg, Becker, and McEnroe?"

The fantasy ended in the semifinals against Becker, but not before McEnroe won the first set and scared the hell out of Boris. Since Grabb was not in Australia, McEnroe played doubles with David Wheaton, and they reached the final. That made Patrick only the third player in the Open era to reach the semifinals of a Grand Slam in both singles and doubles. The other two? Stefan Edberg and that other McEnroe.

The Australian shot Patrick's ranking to No. 55 and made him an instant celebrity at home. Exhibition offers began coming in from all over and he became "Mr. Media" at every tournament he played in. The hype grew even more after Chicago and reached a crescendo when he beat Becker in the third round at the Lipton. By then, Patrick had played so much tennis that his shoulder was throbbing. He lost to Marc Rosset the next day and decided to skip the tournaments he was planning to play in the Far East in April.

He had come a long way in a year, from the qualifying match in Tokyo, where Jeff Tarango had to talk him into not losing his cool completely, to a singles ranking of thirty-eight and all sorts of endorsement offers. Nike was thinking about a commercial with the McEnroe brothers, and agents were lined up wanting to work with him.

The best news, though, was on the home front. After the U.S. Open, Patrick and Margaret Flanagan had decided to try to make a go of their relationship again. She could now see why he had wanted so much to find out what he could do in tennis, and he felt much more secure and confident about what he was doing with his life. The relationship continued to have ups and downs—but it did continue.

"Things are really good right now," he said at the Lipton. "I need a rest because I've played more tennis than I ever dreamed about playing the last few months. But I'm really excited about everything that's happened in the last year."

Life was good for Patrick McEnroe. Of course, he will always be John's little brother. That's just fine with him.

As 1990 ended, for the first time in years, there was no clear-cut No. 1 player for either the men or the women. The computer said Stefan Edberg and Steffi Graf were No. 1, but there was ample evidence to dispute that.

Edberg had lost in the first round of two Grand Slams, which made it difficult to think of him as the best player in the world. The ITF took that view when it selected Lendl as the 1990 men's world champion.

Graf's position was a little clearer. She was by far the most consistent player in the world, even with all her troubles during the year. She had been in three of four Grand Slam finals, and had won the most tournaments, the most matches, and the most money. But she was 0–2 against Monica Seles and had lost in the Virginia Slims semifinals to Sabatini, who then lost the final to Seles.

Seles continued to be a wonder. She turned seventeen in December and was closing rapidly on Graf. Still, her father kept pushing her to play in too many exhibitions—she was in Buenos Aires five days after the Slims final playing Sabatini, then played in Europe, then went to Australia to play in the hokey Hopman Cup. She then pulled out of the Sydney warm-up for the Australian and talked about going home because she was so tired.

Fortunately, she stayed. Graf's troubles continued in Melbourne: She was shocked in the quarterfinals by Jana Novotna, and Seles ended up winning the tournament, saving a match point against Mary Joe Fernandez in the semis, then beating Novotna in the final. A month later, she officially became No. 1 on the computer, and when she defended her title at Lipton, beating Capriati (in a superb match), Fernandez, and Sabatini, it was apparent that she would not be easy to unseat at the top.

Graf's problems on the court continued. The Slims loss to Sabatini was the first of four straight losses to her old doubles partner—someone she had once had a 20-3 record against. When she lost to her at the Lipton after winning the first set 6–0, it was apparent the tables had turned completely. Sabatini, now a Navratilova-type serve-and-volleyer, clearly had control of the rivalry, and one wondered if perhaps she—and not Graf—would emerge as the top challenger to Seles.

In spite of those losses, Graf was feeling better about life than she had in 1990. The turning point may have come in Leipzig in late September. She was both the star and the villain of the first tournament held in East Germany.

Throughout the week she was pilloried by the East German media for not doing more to promote the tournament. "They said I hadn't done press conferences or held clinics or gone to hospitals," she said. "Everything was my fault. The crowds were small, and that was my fault too."

Feeling sorry for herself, one afternoon Graf asked her driver for the tournament to drive her to Berlin. "I wanted to drive through the Brandenburg Gate once, while it was still there," she said.

Her driver was a tournament volunteer, a man who worked for Opel. From the moment they drove through the gate into the West, Graf could see his eyes go wide. "He had only been in the West for one hour in his life," she said. "He couldn't believe what he was seeing.

"The whole thing hit me right there. I had spent so much time feeling sorry for myself during the year because of everything that had gone on, and here was this man who couldn't even begin to imagine the way we live. You can read and read about what life is like behind the Iron Curtain, but there is no way to really understand it without living it. I knew that right at that moment. Just watching him, I realized I had taken everything in my life for granted."

On the day of the final, Graf decided she would donate her check for the week to the East German Tennis Federation to use for youth tennis. She wiped out Arantxa Sanchez in the final, playing as well as she had played all year. During the awards ceremony, she broke down two sentences into her speech. She finally managed to get out her plan to give away the prize money and then, for the first time all week, she was heartily cheered. Graf cried.

"Afterward, when I was alone, I cried again," she said. "I think I cried the whole day. It was as if the whole year just kicked in all at once that week. Everything that my life was and wasn't, I thought about. But when it was over, I felt better."

Graf even managed to find a reminder in the U.S. that being Steffi Graf isn't all bad. Driving through Connecticut to a tournament in Worcester, Massachusetts, she told her coach, Pavel Slozil, that they had to stop and find a drugstore that would give her a prescription. She had been struck by yet another viral infection. "I knew just what I needed, but I also knew you couldn't get it without a prescription," she said. "I walked into this drugstore and explained to the druggist that I was sick, I needed a prescription, and my doctor was in Germany. He was very nice, but he said he just couldn't do it.

"I understood. We were about to leave when this other druggist came out from the back and said, 'Steffi, Steffi Graf! Wow, what are you doing here?' I told him the problem. He said, 'We'll take care of you.' He called a doctor he knew and got the prescription from him."

She smiled. "I guess being Steffi Graf has its advantages, too."

Being Jennifer Capriati had advantages, also—many of them financial. By year's end, Capriati had signed yet another lucrative deal, this one with Oil of Olay. Many people wondered if Capriati's *mother* was old enough to use Oil of Olay. "It's never too soon to think about skin care," Jennifer said, right on cue.

The Capriati family moved to Broken Sound but left after one day because neither Jennifer or Stephen were happy there. Yet, Capriati continued to play and play. When a tiny bit of doubt crept up about her qualifying for the Virginia Slims finals, the Women's Professional Tennis Council, which had already amended rules three times in less than a year because of her, amended one more rule so that she could play an eleventh tournament—and ensure that she would qualify. By that point, Roman numerals were being used to keep track of all the Capriati rules. Capriati IV got her into a tournament in Puerto Rico.

She went to San Juan, won the tournament, missed some more school, and qualified. A traveling tutor had been hired briefly for a trip to a September tournament in Tokyo—with a four-hour-plane-ride side trip thrown in for an exhibition with Seles in Singapore—but that idea was soon abandoned. By year's end, Jim Fuhse, the Kraft General Foods public relations man, had added Jennifer-tutoring to his bodyguard duties.

Two weeks after the Virginia Slims final, Capriati went to Europe to play more exhibitions. The USTA, always looking to help struggling young players, announced that it would continue to pay for Capriati's coaching in 1991. Her relationship with Chris Evert continued to evolve. In a year-end interview with *Tennis* magazine, Capriati said that Evert was *not* her idol anymore. "I'm my own idol," she said.

Evert rolled her eyes when she heard that and wondered what it would be like when NBC sent her to interview Capriati next. Would Capriati's agent, Evert's brother—the Colonel—make his client available? More important, would the Colonel be able to convince Stefano to make his daughter available?

And would Jennifer continue to improve in 1991? She finished 1990 ranked thirteenth in the world and came back to the tour for the Chicago tournament in February. She was bigger and heavier than she had been, and her entourage quickly decided she needed to lose weight. By Lipton she had lost ten pounds, and she played wonderfully against Seles, winning the first set, before losing 6–4 in the third.

By the end of that match, she was so drained her legs appeared wobbly. And yet, barely more than an hour later, she was back out in the Florida heat playing doubles with her new partner, Sabatini. As she walked to the court at three in the afternoon, Capriati was yawning—still exhausted.

EPILOGUE

o

On March 29, Capriati turned fifteen. A week later, at Hilton Head, she was upset in the third round by Leila Meshki. There would be no Lege vs. Kid rematch for NBC. Capriati had now been on tour for a little more than a year and her future still looked very bright. One had to wonder, though, why a just-turned-fifteen-year-old had to work so very, very hard at her job. For that matter, one wondered why it had to be a job.

Clearly, though, that is exactly what tennis had become for Jennifer Capriati: her job.

At IMG, the year-end Association of Tennis Parents rankings were closer than ever before. Peter Graf continued at No. 1, but Stefano Capriati and Karolj Seles had moved to No. 2 and No. 3 respectively. Jim Pierce, the oft-profane father of fifteen-year-old Mary Pierce, was a star in the making.

But the biggest shock at IMG came from none of those people; Mary Joe Fernandez and family announced in November that they were leaving to be represented by Tiriac.

This was seen as a small measure of revenge by Tiriac for losing Seles to IMG. The Fernandez family told IMG that Mary Joe was ranked fourth in the world but almost no one knew who she was. That was not inaccurate. Whether that would change with Tiriac was something that would bear watching.

ProServ ended the year with the game's fastest rising star, Pete Sampras, under contract for three more years. That was the good news. The bad news was that Sampras's feet could not handle wearing the Sergio Tacchini shoes he was being paid a lot of money to wear.

Sampras first had problems during the U.S. Open. He came out of the Lendl match with sore feet, but shrugged it off and went on to win the tournament. However, his problems continued throughout the fall: Shin splints and blisters limited his play and hobbled him when he did play. Even during the week of the Grand Slam Cup, which he won to take home $2 million, he continued to have foot problems.

"This can't go on," he sighed. "I'm nineteen years old. I have to be healthy."

Tacchini went so far as to have him come to their factory to test all different makes of their shoes to find one that was comfortable. It didn't work. Sampras offered to wear another shoe and paint the Tacchini logo on it. Players often do this with racquets when they aren't comfortable with what their sponsoring company is making them use. Tacchini said no. They wanted Sampras in their shoes.

It wasn't going to do them much good to have Sampras wear their shoes if he couldn't play. The company continued to look for an answer while Sampras headed for Australia. He wasn't there long. He withdrew from the Rio Challenge exhibition after one match, then pulled out of the Australian and flew home, frustrated and worried.

After more experimentation, Tacchini finally came up with a shoe that Sampras felt comfortable wearing. He returned to the scene of his first victory—Philadelphia—and lost a superb five-set final to Lendl after beating McEnroe in the semis. It looked like he was back on track. But then came a groin pull that forced him to pull out of Indian Wells and an embarrassing second-round loss at the Lipton.

Still, Sampras managed not to get too down. He had split with his coach, Joe Brandi, briefly at the end of 1990 in a dispute over money, but after Australia things had been patched up. He also had his first serious girlfriend, an "older woman" (twenty-five), introduced to him, ironically, by his ex-agent Gavin Forbes. If he could just keep his body from falling apart (and if he would play a few less exhibitions), there was every reason to believe that Sampras could contend seriously at Wimbledon and the U.S. Open before 1991 was over.

Sampras's pal Jim Courier had become the early story of 1991 on the heels of a disappointing performance in 1990. After getting as high as fourteenth on the computer, he had slid to twenty-fifth at the end of the year. He also split with his coach, Sergio Cruz, not over money but performance. Tennis coaches are like coaches in every sport: they, not the player, get fired when a player does poorly.

Courier hooked up with José Higueras, who had been the magician behind the Chang miracle in Paris in 1989, and immediately began to make the progress he had been hoping for. He lost a good five-setter to Edberg in the fourth round in Australia and then really opened eyes when he won Indian Wells and the Lipton back to back. Those two victories jumped him to No. 9 on the computer and helped get him named to the Davis Cup team for the first-round match against Mexico.

Even two nervous losses there couldn't prevent Courier from feeling strongly that this could be his spring in Europe. He had been close the year before. Now, a year older and wiser, his time on the clay might be right now.

Courier's victim in the Lipton final was David Wheaton. Losing the match was a disappointment for Wheaton, but the tournament itself was a huge relief since he hadn't won a single match in 1991 until he got to Key Biscayne.

He had done well enough in the big tournaments in 1990—two Grand Slam quarterfinals and the Grand Slam Cup semifinals (beating Lendl)—that he had made himself quite rich. The Grand Slam Cup alone was worth $450,000—minus the $5,000 he was fined for engaging in a shoving match with his old nemesis Brad Gilbert during a semifinal loss.

Playing in the Grand Slam Cup was lucrative, but when Wheaton agreed to step in and replace Sampras in the Hopman Cup, it meant his offseason lasted exactly ten days. His play in Australia reflected that: first-round loss in Sydney, first-round loss—to Gilbert *again*—in Melbourne.

By the time he reached the Lipton, Wheaton's ranking had dropped to forty-sixth and his match record for the year was 0-4. But he *had* finally gone home and gotten some rest. He blew Agassi off the court in the round of 16, beat Edberg in the semifinals, and ran out of gas against Courier in the final. Still, his ranking popped back up to twenty-three, and he headed toward the spring and summer feeling excited about his chances.

Sampras, Courier, and Wheaton were all worth watching closely. Wheaton, the oldest of the three, would turn twenty-two in June.

The two Americans who had made most of the headlines before Sampras emerged, Andre Agassi and Michael Chang, both skipped Australia again. Too far to go so early in the year, they said, even though both had hopscotched all over the globe in 1990 in pursuit of guarantees and exhibition dollars.

Chang's year had been saved by his Davis Cup performance in Vienna. After dropping from sixth on the computer at the start of the year to as low as twenty-fifth, he did climb back to fifteenth. His results continued to be spotty. The hip injury had clearly thrown him off and, with his nineteenth birthday in February, he was hardly over the hill.

His ProServ contract would be up in the fall of 1991. Already, Advantage International, which had suffered through a difficult year on the men's side, was hoping to re-sign him. Whether ProServ, with Edberg and Sampras in the fold, would be that crushed by such a move was another question. Advantage did continue to do well in the women's game, adding Zina Garrison to its large stable of Europeans led, of course, by Graf, and did sign two top young teenage men, providing some hope for the future.

Agassi finished the year nicely, winning the ATP Championships and helping the U.S. win the Davis Cup. But off court he continued to get himself into trouble. During the last week in October, he signed up to play in the inaugural Grand Slam Cup; then, two weeks later during the ATP Championships, he announced that he was pulling out. He said he felt the Grand Slam Cup detracted from the ATP Championships.

Agassi could have easily *not* signed up in the first place, the way McEnroe, Becker, and Wilander had. Instead, he tried to pull out of a written commitment.

The night before he made his announcement, Agassi sat up in a hotel room with his brother, Bill Shelton, Bob Kain, and Mark Miles. He asked both Kain and Miles what they thought of the notion of him pulling out. Miles never told him he should pull out, but he didn't tell him not to, either. For his part, Kain told Agassi that if he withdrew he would surely be fined, but not suspended.

Both Kain and Miles messed up. Miles should have said: "Andre, if you hadn't signed the commitment form, I would have applauded you. But you did sign. There is no way I would condone any tennis player backing out of a commitment for *any* tennis tournament."

Kain, who had pressured Agassi all year to meet his commitments more often, should have said: "Andre, you signed up. Go play. No ifs, ands, or buts."

Agassi withdrew and all hell broke loose. The ITF was about to announce that Agassi would be suspended for the French Open in 1991—which would have made his sponsors extremely unhappy—when Agassi relented and said he would play. Then came the mysterious injury during the Davis Cup final, another withdrawal, and the ITF investigation, which ended in January, with Agassi fined a meaningless $25,000 and avoiding suspension because three doctors swore he was genuinely injured.

Bill Babcock, the Grand Slam Committee administrator who conducted the investigation, made it clear in his report that he found Agassi's behavior shameful. Even when he said he would play, Agassi continued to rip the tournament. Babcock hardly found that a good-faith reentry.

This episode, combined with all that had gone on during the year, sent Agassi's image plunging. By the time New Year's arrived, Kain had taken more control of Agassi than ever before, and a careful image-enhancing campaign was under way. Agassi hadn't done a one-on-one interview with a print journalist for almost two years. Suddenly, Bill

Shelton—Dr. No—became Dr. Yes-Yes-a-Thousand-Times-Yes. Reporters all around the country began getting phone calls from Shelton. Did they want to spend some time with Andre? An hour, five hours, ten hours—you name it. Andre will pick you up at the airport.

Almost everyone took the bait: *The New York Times,* the *Los Angeles Times, USA Today*—even *The National.* Roy Firestone, who had been trying to get Agassi on his ESPN show for a year, suddenly got a call from Dr. Yes saying Andre would sit for not just one but two interviews. "I've always dreamed of meeting you," Agassi told Firestone.

This was all New Nixon stuff. Everyone wrote stories saying Andre wasn't such a bad guy; Andre was misunderstood; Andre had learned from his mistakes. If there is one thing IMG can do, it is run a PR campaign. The New Andre campaign was as good as it gets.

There was just one small problem: The New Andre wasn't playing tennis nearly as well as the Old Andre. In his never-ending quest to get stronger, Agassi could now lift Gil Reyes, but he might not be able to beat him in tennis.

He started his year by losing to Brad Gilbert in San Francisco, and then dropped his first-round match in Brussels to Christian Saceanu, who had finished 1990 ranked 154th in the world. Agassi won five games. This one had all the earmarks of an Old Andre tank job. He had to play Brussels because the tournament was sponsored by Donnay, one of his sponsors. Then again, he didn't have to play for long.

Agassi then lost to Courier at Indian Wells and to Wheaton at the Lipton after barely surviving a couple of three-setters there in his first two matches. By now, the whispers were around the locker room: Andre was *too* strong. Watching him, his fellow players thought he looked slower. All that bulk was tough to move around the court. The big question was this: Would Agassi enter Wimbledon or the Mr. Olympia contest?

Boris Becker's image didn't need any improving at the end of 1990. His tennis did.

He began 1991 before 1990 was over, flying to Australia on December 19 to get the early start on preparing for the Australian that he had promised during the summer. He also began seeing Karen Schwartz again.

Australia—as always—was a struggle for him and for Bob Brett. Becker lost his first-round match in Sydney and came perilously close to another early exit in Melbourne. He had to play a tournament-record five hours and eleven minutes in the third round to beat Omar Camporese—

he blew a two-set lead and ended up winning 14–12 in the fifth—but once past that match, he played brilliantly.

In the final, he dropped the first set to Lendl but came back and played almost perfect tennis the next three sets to win the match. The victory finally put him at No. 1, and both Becker and Brett were completely overcome. After shaking hands with Lendl, Becker raced to a nearby park to have a few moments alone while Brett wept in the stands. Becker had won on his coach's home turf and become No. 1 at the same time. It was an extraordinary moment for both men.

"It was also the moment when we should have said to each other, 'Enough,' " Brett said later. "Really, that was the time to end it. We had done everything we set out to do together. We both knew it was time to go in different directions. He's past needing—or wanting—someone who will be on him thirty-five or forty weeks a year."

Brett and Becker hung on until Brussels, a tournament Becker entered only because he was hoping to keep the No. 1 ranking he had worked so hard to achieve. He lost it anyway when he pulled a groin muscle during the semifinals and had to default.

By then, both men knew it was time. Brett was being recruited by IMG to coach Goran Ivanisevic. They talked about a twelve-weeks-a-year arrangement, à la Roche and Lendl, but finally decided the break should be clean. Becker signed German Davis Cup captain Nikki Pilic to work with him during Grand Slams, then split with him in May. Brett, still only thirty-seven in spite of one hundred years as a coach, headed for a new challenge with the flaky Ivanisevic.

Becker's victory over Lendl in the Australian final upped his record in Grand Slam finals to 5–2, including 3–0 against Lendl. The loss was tough to take for Lendl. As usual, he had spent a month in Australia getting ready for the tournament. He had survived two match points in the semifinals against Edberg, and when he won the first set looked ready to win a third straight title.

He didn't, though, and whether he could regain the No. 1 spot was a major question mark as 1991 unfolded. Once again, Lendl planned to skip the French to get ready for Wimbledon, although he would play a couple of clay-court tournaments to keep his ground strokes in some sort of shape. He turned thirty-one in March. He needed wrist surgery in May. Time was growing short.

• • •

EPILOGUE

Andrei Chesnokov, after his brilliant spring on clay, never completely recovered from his loss to Henri Leconte in Paris. He still finished the year ranked twelfth in the world. He skipped the inaugural Kremlin Cup, held in Moscow in November, because, he said, there was too much pressure on him to perform at home. Tennis clearly *had* arrived in the Soviet Union. . . .

Yannick Noah, after losing to Boris Becker in the second round at the Open, was named captain of the French Davis Cup team. He said he planned to continue playing for at least another year. . . .

His countryman, Henri Leconte, continued to be dogged by injuries. He missed almost two months in the fall due to shoulder problems and, although he was still only twenty-seven and ranked thirtieth in the world, it was questionable whether he would ever again achieve the brilliance he had shown in Paris. . . .

Richey Reneberg had a solid summer and an excellent fall, reaching three semifinals. He finished 1990 ranked higher than he had ever been ranked in his life—twenty-third—and for the first time in his career found that not one but *two* management groups—IMG and Advantage—wanted to handle his finances for him. He re-signed with IMG and reached the semis at the Lipton before losing to Courier.

Derrick Rostagno, McEnroe's summer tormentor, used his two victories over McEnroe as a springboard. He won his first Championship Series tournament in August, in New Haven, and finished the year ranked forty-eighth in spite of another heartbreaking U.S. Open loss, this one 7–6 in the fifth set (with an 11–9 tiebreak) to Cristiano Caratti. By May he had risen even further—to No. 25. . . .

Jimmy Arias played steady, unspectacular tennis throughout 1990. His ranking jumped from eighty-eighth at the start of the year to a high of forty-eighth before he finished the year ranked sixtieth. At the U.S. Open, he upset Guy Forget in the opening round, then lost a tough match to Chang in the second round. "I feel like I've got my forehand back for the first time in years," he said. "I really feel like I can play the game again." The new year started well, and Arias headed for the clay just outside the top fifty—at No. 52.

His wife, Gina, reconciled with her father and began dealing with the idea of her parents as separate entities. Her father spent time with her during the Open, and Jimmy even began doing some business with him. In the meantime, Gina formed an ATP Tour wives group, partly to combat the boredom of the tour, partly to feel as if she was doing something positive. The idea was to get the wives together at

Grand Slams and to try to do some kind of charity work at as many tour spots as possible.

Brad Pearce finished the year ranked seventy-seventh in the world and earned just under $180,000 in prize money, giving him and his family some financial security for the first time. After considering moving to Ponte Vedra to be closer to more practice partners, the Pearces decided to stay near their families in Provo and bought a five-bedroom house. Vagabonds no more. . . .

Alberto Mancini had the most disastrous year anyone could remember in years. He began the year ranked ninth in the world and finished No. 127. During the fall, he lost in the qualies of several tournaments. He was still only twenty-one years old, but clearly he was going to have to change his life-style and his work habits if he was going to make a comeback in 1991. He began the year on the Challenger circuit—an amazing comedown. . . .

The British finished the year without a player ranked in the top one hundred. Jeremy Bates, who had been in the top one hundred the first six months of the year, dropped to No. 128. Andrew Castle, the once Great Hope, was No. 253. And Danny Sapsford, who had won two matches at Queen's and climbed into the top 175, was back down to No. 264 as the year closed. When the British Davis Cup team lost its qualifying match to France in September, relegating it from the World Group for a fourth straight year, Davis Cup coach Warren Jacques said, "We're ten years away from being competitive in Davis Cup." That problem was no longer Jacques's to worry about, though: He was fired and replaced by Edberg's coach, Tony Pickard. . . .

Glenn Layendecker, his knees still tender, dropped to No. 134 on the computer at the end of 1990. That put him five spots out of a straight-in slot at the Australian Open, but he made the trip there anyway, hoping to qualify. He didn't, but got in as a Lucky Loser and won two matches. A good start. Still, by May, his ranking was down to 150. He turned thirty on May 9. He ended up making almost $104,000 in 1990, which wasn't bad for somebody who had never written a résumé. . . .

Paul Chamberlin and Paul Annacone both suffered through difficult years, dropping to Nos. 146 and 165 respectively on the computer. Chamberlin would be twenty-nine in March; Annacone, twenty-eight. Annacone had found a new doubles partner in David Wheaton. The pair won Toronto and reached the U.S. Open final and planned to play together as often as possible in 1991. . . .

Luke Jensen finished the year ranked No. 413 in singles, but continued to make a living playing doubles, in which he was ranked No. 66 and won $81,000 in prize money. He also ranked in the Top Ten—at least—when it came to having a good time. . . .

Although some of the men skipped Australia, most of the women—Navratilova being the notable exception—made the long trip.

Elise Burgin seriously thought about not going. Her ranking continued to plummet—she was 149th in singles when the year ended—but, as she had predicted, she was still making a good living in doubles and earned $92,111 in 1990. She started 1991 thinking it was probably her last year as a player. By April she was 199th in singles and 32nd in doubles. "Time to look for a job," she said—again.

Shaun Stafford, who had started the year ranked fifty-first, ended it at No. 150. She had made some serious changes in her life. Most notably, she broke up with her boyfriend in the spring and began to work out in a gym on a regular basis. She reached the third round of the U.S. Open and won two matches in the opening tournament of 1991, in Brisbane. She had just turned twenty-two and still hoped that the best of her tennis was yet to come. . . .

Stephanie Rehe had even more reason to be optimistic. She played only six tournaments in 1990 but still finished the year ranked fifty-eighth on the computer. Amazingly, after all of her injuries and lost time, she had just turned twenty-one in November. She was up to fiftieth in April. . . .

Pam Shriver *had* been around forever. It had been more than twelve years since her stunning debut at the U.S. Open in 1978. She missed the last seven months of 1990 after shoulder surgery and spent most of that time working on her television career. She started 1991 by losing her first match, in Brisbane, but said, "This is a twelve- to eighteen-month process; I'm not discouraged."

The next week in Sydney, she won her first match since breaking her foot in Boca Raton. "I still think I can be a force in tennis," she said. She would be twenty-nine on the Fourth of July. . . .

Carrie Cunningham, who played so well against Steffi Graf in Australia, graduated from high school in the spring. She even went to her senior prom and her graduation—extremely unusual for a tennis player. "I was determined not to miss them," she said.

She was less certain about what direction to go with her life. She was accepted at Stanford and thought about going there to play tennis and pursue a degree in architecture. But she also wanted to try the tour full-time to see just how good she might become. She settled on a compromise: defer her acceptance to Stanford for a year and play the tour as an amateur. This would be a hardship financially, but it meant she could test tour life and still have the option of going back to Stanford on a full scholarship if she didn't enjoy trekking around the world with a tennis racquet. By March, she was thirty-eighth on the computer. Her decision was made: she turned pro at the Lipton. Stanford would have to wait. . . .

At almost the same time that Carrie Cunningham decided to be a tennis player, Angelica Gavaldon decided not to be. After her fast start in 1990, Gavaldon—Ted Tinling's Lolita—had turned pro. She got as high as thirty-eighth on the computer and seemed headed for big money on and off the court. But she faded during the second half of the year and by early 1991, she was sick of tennis.

So she quit. She pronounced herself sick of travel, sick of hotels, and sick of tennis, and decided—at seventeen—to go back to school. One wondered what Ted would have said. . . .

Natalia Zvereva got to keep almost all of the $462,770 she earned for the year. She also got the car she had always wanted—a BMW—and finished the year ranked twelfth in the world. Most important, for the first time in a long time she said she was happy with her life.

"I have a relationship now," she said, smiling. "I am having much more fun."

There was, of course, one problem. Her father didn't approve. "My boyfriend is a student," she said. "My father doesn't understand why he isn't working. We argue about him a lot."

At last, some normalcy! What could be more normal than a father fighting with his daughter over a boyfriend? . . .

Zina Garrison finished 1990 ranked tenth on the women's computer—six spots lower than she had been at the end of 1989. She did make a lot of off-court money in 1990. Her Wimbledon performance not only got her a clothing contract, it helped get a new racquet contract from Yonex, worth more than $500,000 over the next five years.

She was disappointed by her injury at the U.S. Open and not happy with her tired, listless performance in a first-round loss to Conchita Martinez, in the Virginia Slims finals.

"Other than Wimbledon I really didn't have a very good year," she said. Perhaps so. But somehow that didn't really matter. Garrison didn't just beat Monica Seles and Steffi Graf; she beat her own self-doubts. She proved once and for all that she could compete with anyone in a sport that makes it almost impossible for someone from her background to succeed.

Over the years, tennis has been a sport for the white and the wealthy and for the immensely talented. It has been a sport in which ruthlessness is considered an asset and being a phony seems to make you rich. Zina Garrison came to tennis with none of those qualities. She grew up without a lot of money; she grew up black; she grew up talented—but not talented like Graf or Navratilova or Seles. She certainly isn't ruthless, and there isn't a phony bone in her body.

"Andres Gomez was thirty when he won the French this year," she said. "I'll be twenty-seven next year. I hope I'll get a Grand Slam before I'm thirty. I'm certainly not going to give up. I hope I have at least one more great tournament in me."

Gomez never could find the fire again after his great French Open. By April, he was talking again about retirement after a series of early-round losses in 1991. It seemed possible—though not likely—that he might not even defend his title in Paris. Regardless, it was almost a certainty that if Ecuadorian TV wanted him to do the final this year he would be available. . . .

Always in tennis there is change and upheaval—especially off the court. Chris Evert got pregnant right around her thirty-sixth birthday, meaning she would at last be able to stop answering questions about when she would have a child.

"All my life, I've been asked the same two questions," she said. "When I was single, it was always, 'Who are you dating?' When I'm married, it's always, 'When are you going to have a baby?' "

So, Chris, when are you going to have another baby?

Mary Carillo was also pregnant, due in September, two weeks after the U.S. Open. She insisted to everyone that she would work at the Open for CBS when eight and a half months pregnant. Few people were betting against her. . . .

The shocker, though, was Martina Navratilova's breakup with Judy Nelson after more than seven years together. Rumors that they were going to split first began making the rounds at the end of the year, but they seemed impossible to believe. By January, though, the word was out and Nelson was sending out postcards with her new address and phone number.

o

Peter Johnson of IMG was put in charge of damage control, trying to work things out so there would be no lawsuits and no ugly court proceedings. In the meantime, the tabloids ran wild with the story. Navratilova's Wimbledon defense would almost undoubtedly be tougher off the court than on it.

What next for tennis? The ATP Tour and the ITF will continue to snipe at each other. Led by Gerry Smith, the WTA will go through radical changes in the next few years.

Early in 1991, Smith unveiled a plan to make over the women's tour, creating a series of elite, big-money tournaments that would—if the concept worked—put the top players together more often and increase prize money considerably. Sponsors reacted with horror but Smith pushed forward.

He also kept pushing the ITF to create a Grand Slam Cup for women and to make prize money equal for men and women at Wimbledon and the French Open. He and Philippe Chatrier were on an almost certain collision path, but Smith felt he had to keep pushing for more exposure every chance he got.

"The thing we have to understand is that 1990 was a dream year for women's tennis," he said. "Capriati exploded onto the scene, we had four different Grand Slam winners, Zina Garrison was a wonderful story at Wimbledon. Everything broke right.

"We have to understand that, next year, things probably won't be as wonderful. It would be nice if they were, but how often are you going to get The Kid against The Lege? We have to be very aggressive about getting more exposure on television, at the Grand Slams, everywhere."

One thing Smith had accomplished was getting the Virginia Slims finals on live national television for 1991. To do so, he had to get Virginia Slims to agree that the tournament would be referred to during the telecast as "the WTA Championships." The finals were tied to a TV package in the United States that Smith was piecing together.

Smith and Mark Miles were actually working together, the first time in known history that the leaders of the men's and women's player groups had been in regular contact with each other. For the first time, the ATP and the WTA would have the same drug-testing policy and, they hoped, the same on-court conduct rules.

Drug testing has long been a murky issue in tennis, with different countries having different laws and different enforcement. It has only been five years since drug testing on any level began, and the number of positive tests have been few and far between, most of those for marijuana.

That is not to say that there are not tennis players who have tried cocaine. Many have. In fact, it has ruined the career of at least one Top Ten player. Noah has admitted to drug use in the past and openly says he still regularly smokes marijuana. "When my kids are old enough, they'll smoke for the first time with me," he said. "That way they'll understand what it's about, what is dangerous and what isn't. I want them to come to me to talk about drugs, not learn about it on the streets."

Other players are scared to death about going public with admissions of drug use, because it would hurt their commercial images. Over all, though, drug use in tennis is relatively minor. The sport is too individual for a regular user to survive very long.

"When I first came up in the game, guys played with hangovers all the time," said Leif Shiras, who came out of Princeton and has played the tour for ten years. "The typical night was go to dinner, have a few beers, and go to a club. That's all changed now. The younger guys all have their entourages and the money is so big, no one really wants to go out anymore. The locker room is such a dead place that a guy got mad at me a few weeks ago for telling a dirty joke."

The women's tour has always been like that. Parents began traveling with their daughters in the 1970s, when players began turning pro in their teens, partly because the girls needed an adult along, partly because of the stories about some of the older homosexual players recruiting teenagers. There was a grain of truth to those stories—but also a lot of exaggeration.

Nowadays the women's tour is far more heterosexual than the general public thinks, although there are still a number of homosexual relationships among players. Navratilova and Judy Nelson were quite open about their relationship, but for the most part, although everyone on tour knows who the female couples are, the relationships are just whispered about. There are also homosexuals on the men's tour, though not as many as on the women's. All the current stars in the men's game are heterosexual. "It seems like most of the men on tour are dating or are married to a former Miss World," Chris Evert joked. Among the four most significant women of the Open era—Evert, Graf, Navratilova, and Billie Jean King—the latter two have admitted to homosexuality.

That certainly doesn't represent a trend, but sports tend to be labeled based on the behavior of their stars. The men's game has carried a reputation for being filled with whining, spoiled, profane people ever since Jimmy Connors and John McEnroe became stars.

o

"I don't think there's any doubt that one of the reasons I became the girl-next-door to the public was my sexuality," said Evert. "People could relate to the fact that I was always dating men."

Even with the sport's image problems, even with the economic recession, which has forced corporations to cut back on their involvement in sports, the money in tennis continues to be astronomical.

For a chosen few. In 1990, there were 2,042 tennis players who had earned at least one point on either the men's or women's computer. Among those, perhaps two hundred were making a good living. Of those two hundred, about fifty—maybe—are extremely comfortable. About fifteen are filthy rich. The 2,042 with a computer point represent the elite among hundreds of thousands who dream about striking it rich in the sport. Thousands of parents think their daughters are the next Evert, Graf, Navratilova, Seles, or Capriati. Thousands more look at their sons and see Lendl, McEnroe, Becker, Edberg, Agassi, or Sampras.

They are the ones who are the symbols of the sport. They make the most money, receive the most attention and adulation. TV ratings depend on them; so do sponsorships. The stars give the sport glamour and glitz—all very necessary to its success. They are not the ones, however, who give the sport its texture, who bring life to the two tours as they wend their way on their never-ending trip around the world.

The depth and personality of the sport come from people like Jim Courier, who had time every day in Cincinnati to stop at the Children's Hospital. It comes from Elise Burgin, who willingly spends an entire week writing and producing the talent show in Eastbourne because she knows how much everyone on the tour enjoys it. It comes from the legacy of Ted Tinling, who told all his stories enough times to enough people that he—and they—will never be forgotten.

It comes, most of all, from the people who truly *care* about the sport, regardless of its flaws. Dick Enberg, who has worked with Bud Collins at NBC for the past nine years, once looked at Collins and asked, "How can you care so much about a sport with so many bad people in it?"

Collins just smiled. His friends often say he would have found some good even in Hitler. "Not Hitler, no," he says. "Mussolini, maybe."

And somehow, he always finds good in the sport he loves. As a year on the tour comes to a close, the stories and the days and the nights and the airplanes tend to run together. For some reason, one memory sticks out.

It was a hot, sticky day in Paris, at Roland Garros, and Collins had talked a friend past the often-vicious French ushers to the NBC compound. The purpose was to grab a quick sandwich and a quiet moment. Collins sprawled on the grass next to one of the trucks, eating a sandwich while his friend rested against a fence. On the other side of the fence was court 6, one of the out-of-the-way side courts.

"Who's playing out there?" Collins asked casually.

"Roberto Azar and Lawson Duncan."

Collins sat up straight as if a lightning bolt had landed at his feet.

"Lawson Duncan? *Lawson Duncan?*" He scrambled to his feet, dropping the sandwich. "I've never seen Lawson Duncan play!"

Lawson Duncan, it should be remembered, was once ranked forty-seventh in the world. Collins raced to the fence, bent down, and peeked through a hole in the green backdrop. He was silent for a few moments. He stood up when his back began to ache.

"You finished eating?" he asked. "Let's go watch these guys for a while."

Why not, thought his friend. He *had* seen Lawson Duncan. But he had never seen Roberto Azar.

o

ABOUT THE AUTHOR

Hard Courts is JOHN FEINSTEIN's fourth book. His first three, all on college basketball, were *A Season on the Brink,* the best-selling sports book of all time; *A Season Inside,* also a national best-seller; and *Forever's Team,* the critically acclaimed story of the 1977–78 Duke University basketball team.

Mr. Feinstein, himself a 1977 Duke graduate, spent eleven years at *The Washington Post* and has worked as a special contributor to *Sports Illustrated.* His stories have also appeared in *Sport, Inside Sports, The Sporting News, The National,* and *TV Guide.* He has won sixteen U.S. Basketball Writer's awards and three National Sportswriter's and Sportscaster's awards as Washington writer of the year. In addition, his work has appeared in *Best Sports Stories* seven times.

Currently, he is a contributing editor to *World Tennis and Basketball Times,* a commentator for National Public Radio, and a regular on ESPN's *The Sports Reporters.*

Mr. Feinstein lives in Bethesda, Maryland, and Shelter Island, New York, with his wife, Mary.